A History
of Keyboard
Literature

A History of Keyboard Literature

Music for the Piano and Its Forerunners

STEWART GORDON

SCHIRMER BOOKS
An Imprint of Simon & Schuster Macmillan
New York

Prentice Hall International
London   Mexico City   New Delhi   Singapore   Sydney   Toronto

ML 700
G65 199€

Schirmer Books
An Imprint of Simon & Schuster Macmillan
1633 Broadway
New York, NY 10019

Library of Congress Catalog Card Number: 95-31762

Printed in the United States of America

printing number
1 2 3 4 5 6 7 8 9 10

Library of Congress Cataloging-in-Publication Data

Gordon, Stewart, 1930-

  A history of keyboard literature: music for the piano and its forerunners / Stewart
Gordon
    p. cm.
  Includes bibliographical references and index
  ISBN 0-02-870965-9 (hardcover: alk. paper)
  1. Keyboard instrument music--History and criticism. 2.
Piano music--History and criticism. I. Title.
  ML700.G65 1996
  786--dc20   95-31762
                                                                                    CIP
                                                                                    MN

This paper meets the requirements of ANSI/NISO Z39.48-1992 (Permanence of Paper).

Contents

Preface

Pianists are unusually blessed with an abundance of keyboard literature. For almost two and a half centuries, masterworks have been written specifically for the fortepiano or the piano. Moreover, pianists have often chosen to include music written for other stringed instruments, primarily the harpsichord or the clavichord, in their active repertoire. The positive aspect of this abundance is that there is a vast amount of exciting, wonderful music that invites exploration and performance. The problematic aspect is, of course, that trying to form an overview, even a limited one, of this musical treasure tends to be daunting.

This volume is an attempt to provide a reference text that will assist the pianist in gaining a comprehensive grasp of that portion of the literature that is studied and played by pianists. In conceiving the scope of the volume, I have tried to touch upon most of the works of master composers, undertaking to mention features of every one of the sonatas of Haydn, Mozart, Beethoven, and Schubert, as well as all of the major sets of smaller works of the master composers of the late eighteenth, nineteenth, and early twentieth centuries. Earlier music, works by composers of lesser fame, and music written in the last half of the twentieth century are presented in less detail. On the other hand, a special attempt has been made at least to indicate the vast amount of music written for the piano in the early decades of the twentieth century which has, by and large, yet to be explored and assimilated by pianists.

As a professional pianist of more than forty years, I found it impossible to write about piano music without reflecting my own ardor for many of these works and, at times, lesser degrees of enthusiasm for other works. I would be the first to acknowledge that my personal reactions are not necessarily shared by other professional musicians. Different viewpoints, indeed, provide a fountainhead of continuing study of and fascination for the music itself. I can only hope that my prevailing philosophy shines through. That philosophy regards all of these pieces like God's children—they are all loved, notwithstanding their strengths and weaknesses. Furthermore, I firmly believe that as pianists we must take the time and summon the energy to explore the literature broadly, seeking instances of beauty rather than perfection.

Bibliographical information of secondary literature appears at the end of the volume and has been organized by chapter. This arrangement has been adopted in order to make digging more deeply into a given area, subject, or composer somewhat easier. Listing of the music itself has been confined to providing information regarding complete editions, when they have been compiled, and some of the more famous anthologies. Unpublished doctoral dissertations, of which there are many in all areas, have not been listed. The reader should seek this information in the bibliographies attending appropriate entries in standard reference works, such as *The New Grove Dictionary of Music and Musicians*.

Appreciation is due to many more individuals than I can possibly mention. I must acknowledge a few, however. My first mention should be of Verne Waldo Thompson, Professor of Keyboard Literature at the Eastman School of Music in Rochester, New York, during the years of my own doctoral study. It was Verne Waldo Thompson who opened my eyes to the vastness and importance of keyboard literature and who, through his own copious notes, engendered in me the concept of this volume. My piano colleagues at the University of Maryland, College Park and currently at the University of Southern California, Los Angeles, have all contributed both directly and indirectly to this work over the years through their own exploration and playing of the literature. My many students have not only joined me in exploring both well-known and little-known literature but also provided an ongoing learning process for me as they master these works. Finally, on a more personal level, I am keenly aware of the fact that the love of processing detail meticulously was given to me by my father, Lynell Frank Gordon, and whatever talent I have as a writer by my mother, poet Guanetta Gordon, and the encouragement to see this project to its conclusion by my closest friend, Jonathan Christopher Reynolds, III.

A History
of Keyboard
Literature

CHAPTER ONE

Stringed Keyboard Instruments

The earliest stringed keyboard instruments are generally known as *chordophones*, from the Greek words for string (*chorde*) and sound (*phone*). Chordophones have strings stretched between two ends of a board or stick. Of these zither-type instruments, several are significant in that they were forerunners of instruments with keyboards.

The **monochord** consisted of a single string stretched between two fixed bridges. It was said to have been invented by Pythagoras (sixth century B.C.), who first used it for acoustical measurements. A moveable bridge provided the means with which to alter the pitch. Drawings from the twelfth century show the addition of a resonating box under two or three strings. The theorist Jehan des Murs (ca. 1300–ca. 1350) in his treatise *Musica speculativa secundum Boetium* described an instrument of nineteen strings. He also described moveable tangents instead of bridges and suggested the possibility of adding a key mechanism. The single-stringed monochord was used as an instrument to study acoustical properties of sound and to assist in the construction of organ pipes and bells until around 1700. Early clavichords also used moveable bridges, and the points at which the bridges were placed in order to define given pitches were often determined by the monochord. As a result, early clavichords are often referred to as *monochordia* by sixteenth- and seventeenth-century writers.

The **psaltery** was an ancient and medieval instrument that consisted of a number of strings stretched over a flat soundboard, usually in a triangular or rectangular frame. Single or double rows of strings were plucked with the fingers, a plectrum, or a combination of both. The psaltery was placed on a table and played from a sitting position or strapped around the neck to be played while standing. By the eighteenth century its use had waned considerably, as it was replaced by the dulcimer, clavichord, or harpsichord.

The **dulcimer** was similar to the psaltery but was built in such a way that the strings could be struck with hammers. Its history can be traced from about the fifteenth century, and it is associated particularly with folk music around the world. Its type is represented by the well-known Hungarian **cimbalom**.

The exact form of the instrument known as the **chekker** (exaquier) is unknown. The earliest reference to it is as a gift given by Edward III of England to John II of France (1360). Later references appear in a poem by Machaut (ca. 1369) and in letters written by Philip the Bold of Burgundy (1387 and 1388). The instrument was described as similar to an organ but with strings. Its name may be derived from the fact that the keyboard's appearance resembled that of the counting board of the Middle Ages, which was often a shallow, long tray with horizontal lines. By the sixteenth century, with the advent of the clavichord and harpsichord, references to the chekker became increasingly rare.

Of the early instruments that had keyboards, the organ was the most prominent. Among the earliest was the **hydraulis,** a water organ that was an ancestor of the pipe organ. The earliest reference to the hydraulis comes from the third century B.C. in Philo's *Pneumatica*. Its invention is attributed to Ctesibius, a famous Alexandrian engineer also of the third century B.C. Two writers described the instrument in the first century A.D., Vitruvius (in his *De Architectura*) and Hero of Alexandria. The instrument used the tendency of water to seek the lowest level as the source of power with which to drive the air flow.

More detailed knowledge of the operation of the hydraulis has been reconstructed from a clay model found in 1885 in the ruins of Carthage and from parts of an actual instrument discovered in 1931 in an old Roman fortress near Budapest. The instrument had eighteen keys, each 8 inches long and 2 inches wide. When the keys were depressed, they pushed against metal slides that were held in position by springs and pierced with holes. Thus, wind provided by the air pump was admitted to three ranks of pipes (eighteen pipes in each).

Construction details of other organs from early times varied. Oftentimes the size of the organ and the resulting loudness were the factors with which writers delineated various types. Documentation of the development tends to be sporadic until about the eleventh century, from which point onward the evolution is more easily traced. Early descriptions of the keys themselves are sometimes astounding, for they are described as from 3 to 5 inches wide, 2 inches thick, from a foot to a yard in length, and with a fall as much as a foot deep! Fists and elbows were needed to play such monsters when wood swelled in damp weather.

About 1200 A.D. many keyboards had a compass from G to e″, nearly three octaves, spanning the seven hexachords expounded in the theoretical works of Guido d'Arezzo (ca. 991–after 1033). Keyboards continued to expand, and chromatic keys were added. By the thirteenth century, the organ keyboard compass was three octaves with a number of semitones in the middle range. Further expansion is reflected in keyboard music of the fourteenth century, for all the chromatic tones were employed in at least one octave.

The first role of keyboard instruments was that of accompanying singing. After 1400, they gradually became independent, their emancipation being fully achieved in the Renaissance. As late as the seventeenth century, however, collections of music were still designated "to be played or sung." The fact that polyphonic music was easily adapted to the keyboard helped create an independent literature for keyboard instruments.

The Clavichord

The earliest mention of the clavichord occurred in "Minne regal" (Rules of the Minnesingers; 1404), a poem by Eberhard Cersne von Minden. Early representations of the instrument have been found in a carved altarpiece dating from 1425 from Minden in northwest Germany and in a *Wunderbuch* (ca. 1440) from Weimar. Early descriptions of the construction of the instrument were included in a manuscript treatise (ca. 1440) by Henri Arnaut de Zwolle and in Sebastian Virdung's famous work *Musica getutscht* (1511), the earliest printed book on instruments. Early clavichord performers of note were Pierre Beurse (late fifteenth century) and Henri Bredemers (ca. 1472–1522), a Flemish keyboard player and teacher. Among the oldest existing tangent clavichords is one dated 1537 in the Metropolitan Museum of New York City and another built by Domenico da Pesaro around 1543 in the Musikinstrumenten Museum of the Karl Marx University in Leipzig.

The sixteenth-century clavichord was framed in an oblong wooden box of about 2 by 5 feet. Instruments often had no legs and had to be placed on tables in order to be played. The sound was produced by small brass wedges called *tangents* contacting the strings. The tangents were inserted into the key levers at the lower end, and the top end was flattened for contact with the strings. As the tangent made contact, the string was divided into two segments. The segment between the tangent and the hitch pin was set into vibration, producing a small but intense sound, which was enhanced by the soundboard. The other segment was interwoven with a strip of cloth that acted as a damping device.

The range of the sixteenth-century clavichord was about three-and-a-half octaves. Early instruments were built around C, using all white keys. The first black key to appear was B-flat; later F-sharp was added. Repeated pressing of the key resulted in slight pitch variations caused by the tangent's pushing harder against the string, increasing string tension slightly. This technique was called *Bebung,* and it was indicated in the score by a series of dots under a curved line, (⌒). It was considered a highly expressive device, and its use was often left to the taste of the performer.

Until the eighteenth century, all clavichords were fretted (in German, *gebunden*). In these instruments, one string was used for several keys, sometimes up to four, and the tangents struck the strings at various points. As a result, chords that contained more than one tone produced on a single string would sound incomplete. The invention of a fretless clavichord (in German, *bundfrei*) around 1720 is ascribed to one Daniel Faber. The fretless clavichord had one string for each key, so the bundfrei clavichord became highly desirable. Fretted clavichords, persisted, however, because of their convenient size, ease in tuning, and lower price.

Eighteenth-century clavichords usually had five octaves. The keyboard was set back into the case, and the cases were often richly decorated. Keys were veneered with ivory. Strings for each pitch were often doubled, sometimes even trebled. An exceptional instrument was built by Gottfried Silbermann (1683–1753) in 1721. It was called a *cembal d'amour*, and its strings were of double length and were struck in the middle. Thus, each segment vibrated, yielding increased tonal volume. Although none of these instruments has survived, they were celebrated in their time, being mentioned in important treatises of the period: *Critica musica* (1722–25) by Johann Mattheson (1681–1764) and *Musica mechanica organoedi* (published posthumously in 1768) by Jacob Adlung (1699–1762).

The clavichord was played most often in the home, where its small voice and intimate nature were appropriate. A distinct literature emerged for the instrument, one that was often written in only two parts and underscored sweet, delicate sentiments. Types of compositions included song transcriptions, little dances, pastorales, rondos, and *Handstücke* (exercises or etudes). Although the harpsichord began to become the more popular instrument in the sixteenth century, the clavichord retained many adherents who loved its "beseelter Ton" (soulful tone).

During the second half of the eighteenth century, renewed interest in the clavichord was generated, chiefly due to the efforts of Carl Philipp Emanuel Bach (1714–1788), who paid eloquent tribute to the instrument in his famous treatise *Versuch über die wahre Art das Clavier zu spielen* (Essay on the True Art of Playing Keyboard Instruments). In C. P. E. Bach's work, the technique of playing the clavichord was recommended as the means for attaining a sensitive touch. The author further states that Bebung is to be used for "long and affectionate notes," the expressive result having great advantage over tone generated by either the harpsichord or the pianoforte. The compositions C. P. E. Bach wrote to illustrate the *Versuch*, called *Probestücke*, are good examples of idiomatic writing for the clavichord, and they are among the few pieces that clearly indicate the exact use of Bebung.

The Harpsichord

The earliest reference to the harpsichord dates from 1397. It comes from Padua and claims that one Hermann Poll had invented a *clavicembalum*. An early representation of the instrument appeared on the previously mentioned altarpiece dating about 1425 in Minden in northwest Germany. The harpsichord existed not only in the usual trapezoidal, horizontal arrangement but also in an upright version, called a *clavicytherium* (Italian, *cembalo verticale*). A third, smaller version was the virginal or spinet. Earlier models of the spinet were oblong or pentagonal in shape, and eighteenth-century examples were formed as a short triangle with strings running diagonal to the keyboard.

Many names were given to the various types of harpsichords, including the Italian terms *clavicembalo* and *gravicembalo,* the German *Klavicembal* and *Kielflügel,* and the French *clavecin.* Some of the terms used were of obscure origin, and several of them were frequently interchanged. The smaller tabletop instruments were most frequently referred to, however, as spinets or virginals. The term *virginal* most likely derives from the Latin word *virginalis* and came about because young ladies often played the instrument, or perhaps because the instrument was thought to have a sweet, pristine tone. Other theories of how the term originated are based on association with the title of a frequently encountered hymn, "Angelus ad Virginem," or the Latin word *virga,* meaning rod or jack, a reference to part of the instrument's mechanism.

In fifteenth- and sixteenth-century England, all varieties of instruments with plucked strings were called virginals, and those who played or composed for them were referred to as virginalists. In the seventeenth century, the use of the term *virginal* became more limited and referred to smaller instruments, most frequently of rectangular shape. The term *pair of virginals* was often used to refer to a single instrument. The origin of the term remains obscure. An old meaning of "pair" was a matching set of any number, as in "a pair of stairs." Thus, it is believed the term *pair of organs* was suggested by the matching pipes. Perhaps the appearance of the keyboard suggested matching keys in the case of the virginal. The terms *single* and *double* referred to the range of the instrument, notes below G being the "double" notes.

The earliest written references to the harpsichord occur in "Minne regal"; a manuscript known as *Pauli Paulirini de Praga, Tractatus de musica* (ca. 1460) now in Cracow University; and *Musica getutscht* (1511) by Sebastian Virdung. An amusing couplet was inscribed as part of a proverb on a wall of the English manor house at Leckingfield, probably dating from the late fifteenth century: "A slac strynge in a virginall soundeth not aright. It doth abide now wrestinge it is so loose and light. . . ."

Early harpsichords were usually small enough to be placed on a table, and they existed in a variety of shapes. When legs began to be added, the case assumed a wing shape. The instrument remained fairly light in weight, for no metal was employed in the case. Harpsichords were often built with two manuals, sometimes even three. Most instruments had several stops by which various combinations of jacks and strings were brought into use. The manuals and the stops combined to achieve a modest degree of registration, bringing a means of changing tone color or dynamics.

The strings in the harpsichord were activated by *plectra,* which were quills originally made of crow, eagle, raven, or ostrich feathers soaked in olive oil to harden. Later plectra were made of leather. A pin hinged each plectrum to a *jack,* a small shaft of flat wood standing free on the rear of the prolonged key lever and held upright by a type of rack inserted into the soundboard. As the key was pressed, the jacks jumped up, causing the quill to pluck the string. When the key was released, the jack fell back, a spring-hinge device allowing it to return without replucking the string. A *damper* made of felt was fixed to the upper part of the jack so that as the jack fell back the damper came into contact with the string, stopping vibration. A wooden bar above the row of jacks prevented them from jumping out of their holes when the keys were struck forcibly.

At first there was only one string to a note. Later, however, several strings for each key produced higher or lower octaves (4, 8, or 16 foot). From the early seventeenth century, treble and middle-range strings were made of steel and bass strings of brass. Marin Mersenne (1588–1648) mentioned strings of silver, gold, and even silk in his book on instruments, *Harmonie universelle* (1636–37). It should be noted that the plucking of the harpsichord string creates a loop, setting the entire string into vibration. By contrast, the tangent of the clavichord creates a node, resulting in the vibration of only a segment of the string.

The range of harpsichords varied considerably. Earlier ones were often four octaves (C to c'''). Seventeenth-century harpsichords made by Ruckers, the noted Flemish family whose harpsichords were preeminent in Europe from the sixteenth to the eighteenth centuries, varied from forty-five notes (E to c''') to sixty-three notes (F_1 to g'''). Johann Sebastian Bach wrote for a keyboard of four octaves, although three low notes outside the range (down to A_1) were sometimes required. After Bach, the usual compass of the harpsichord was five octaves.

In sixteenth- and seventeenth-century harpsichords, lateral stops often pierced the right wall of the case, being prolongations of bars that controlled the jacks. These were often almost beyond the reach of the player. Thus, there was no possibility of changing stops in the middle of a piece. In the eighteenth century, frontal stops were used, but the hands still had to be taken off the keys in order to manipulate the stops. Pedal stops were invented in the seventeenth century, but it took almost another hundred years for their use to become widespread. Pedals acted as couplers between octaves and keyboards.

The tone of the harpsichord, although more delicate than that of the piano, was nevertheless powerful enough to be effective with orchestras of the period. Neither intensity nor quality of tone could be modified by playing the keys, so careful phrasing and the use of nonlegato touch became very important for the projection of melodic lines and phrase shapes. Ornaments were used for stressing important notes, and dynamic contrast was achieved by shifting from one manual to another or by changing stops. As a result, the use of dynamic contrasts that coincided with structural sections of a composition, called *terraced dynamics*, became characteristic.

Various arrangements of the keys in the lower register of the keyboard were usual. Some English harpsichords of the seventeenth and early eighteenth centuries, for example, divided the lowest black keys (F-sharp and G-sharp) transversely into two parts, each capable of activating a string. The front portion of the keys sounded D and E, and the back portion F-sharp and G-sharp. Another arrangement, the so-called short octave, could be found on all types of keyboard instruments. It, too, was an alteration of the pattern of keys at the lowest end of the keyboard. Because the lowest chromatic tones—C-sharp, D-sharp, F-sharp, and G-sharp—were not frequently played, and, moreover, because before equal temperament these tones were not used as tonal centers, it was practical to omit them in the construction of keyboard instruments.

Two arrangements for the keys in the lowest octave were commonly found:

	C	D	B-flat				D	E	B-flat		
E	F	G	A	B		C	F	G	A	B	

These arrangements made the playing of widely spaced chords quite easy. The final chord in Peter Philips's "Cosi morirò" in the *Fitzwilliam Virginal Book* (no. 72) is an example of a chord that would require stretching or breaking for most players on modern instruments but could be managed quite easily when played on a keyboard with a short octave. Occasionally, an additional key was added below the lowest C of the keyboard, tuned to G_1.

The virginal or spinet was usually constructed in the shape of an oblong box, to be placed on a table or held in the player's lap. The instrument was small enough to be carried by many of the ladies who performed on it. The earliest instruments were often limited in range to two octaves. Sixteenth-century Italian spinets, divided into F and C instruments, were, however, nearly always four octaves and a semitone, the semitone being either the lowest E or B. By the seventeenth century, the compass of most virginals or spinets was four octaves. The instruments were also improved and enlarged by additional strings and jacks, increased keyboard range, modifications of construction design, the addition of stops to produce "lute" or "bassoon" effects, and the use of a double keyboard.

During the seventeenth century, the harpsichord gradually eclipsed the clavichord in all countries except Germany. The harpsichord was especially popular in England, France, and Italy. Composers such as Domenico Scarlatti, Handel, Chambonnières, Couperin, and Rameau wrote specifically for it. The harpsichord was used not only as a solo instrument but also for accompanying, to provide the continuo part in ensemble performances, and to support the *recitativo secco* in opera and oratorio.

The best harpsichords were made in Italy during the sixteenth century. In the seventeenth century, however, the Italians lost supremacy in this field. Possibly the finest instruments were made by the Ruckers family in Antwerp. Hans (senior) was the first to use the octave stop on the harpsichord. He was also responsible for the double keyboard and the change from the short-octave keyboard to one that was completely chromatic. The Ruckers instruments were often decorated with paintings, usually on the underside of the lid, by such famous masters as Brueghel, Rubens, Van Dyck, Teniers, Salvator Rosa, and Boucher. The last member of the Ruckers family group was Andries (junior, 1607–67). In the eighteenth century, Tschudi and Kirchmann (anglicized Shudi and Kirckman) became famous as harpsichord manufacturers in London.

After a century of relative neglect, the harpsichord has enjoyed a notable revival in the twentieth century, being used for both solo and ensemble performances. A vital interest in the music written during those periods in which the harpsichord was the predominant keyboard instrument has been mostly responsible for such a revival, but a desire to re-create accurately the performance practices of those eras has played a role as well. Various individuals and groups have devoted themselves to the restoration of old instruments, the building of new ones, and the study of the instrument's literature. This activity has, in turn, stimulated many twentieth-century composers to write new music for the harpsichord. The clavichord has also received renewed attention in the twentieth century, but to a much smaller extent.

The Piano

History credits the invention of the piano to **Bartolomeo Cristofori** (1651–1731), who was in the service of the Florentine court of Ferdinando de' Medici as the tuner of harpsichords and the keeper of instruments. The date for the completion of the first *gravicembalo col piano e forte*, as it was called, has been established as 1700 from an inventory of Medici instruments. A description of the Cristofori piano was written by Scipioni Maffei and published in the *Giornale dei Letterati d'Italia* in 1711. It stated that in 1709 Cristofori had built three wing-shaped instruments and one of less elaborate construction.

The idea of using hammers in conjunction with a stringed keyboard instrument was not entirely new, for a four-octave keyboard instrument shaped like a dulcimer, with hammers and no dampers, dates from 1610. Furthermore, there is reference to an instrument called *piano eforte* in two letters sent by Paliarino to Alfonso II, Duke of Modena, in 1598. Unfortunately, however, there is no description of the instrument. These earlier moves in the direction of the piano, coupled with the fact that there were at least two other "inventors" of the instrument hard on Cristofori's heels, seem to suggest that the time was ripe for the emergence of this new keyboard instrument.

Several problems had to be solved before the principle of the piano could be made to work successfully, and it is to Cristofori's credit that he addressed and solved with a reasonable degree of success the basic difficulties that had been major stumbling blocks. Possibly the most important problem that faced Cristofori was the matter of escapement. When the hammer is forced against the string, it must have a way of rebounding away from the string instantly in order to prevent it from damping the sound it has produced. The hammer must fall back away from the string even though the key remains depressed. If the key is to be repeated, then it is necessary for the hammer to fall back into position, ready to be activated for the next action.

The first Cristofori action consisted of an arrangement wherein the far end of the key, rigged with a leather pad attached by a brass wire, contacted the hammer, flinging it against the string. This action was extremely unreliable. Unless the key was struck with considerable force, the hammer would not quite be propelled to the string, with the result that there would be no sound at all. On the other hand, too much force would cause the key to lock against the hammer, forcing it to remain against the string so that the string was prevented from vibrating. This malfunction was known as "blocking." This simple single-lever action continued to be used by some piano manufacturers until almost 1800, in spite of the fact that Cristofori replaced it with a more complex, more efficient arrangement as early as 1726. The complete solution to this problem did not, however, belong to Cristofori but rather to a piano manufacturer of the nineteenth century, Sébastien Érard.

Still another important device that was employed on Cristofori's later pianos was the use of dampers. Cristofori's damper was a wooden lever lying horizontally over the strings with a piece of cloth attached to the free end. At the extreme end of the key a stick raised the damper off the string at the same instant the hammer was impelled toward the string. The device was crude but effective, employing the same principle still in use today. Another improvement on Cristofori's later pianos was the addition of a back check, a device for each hammer that prevented rebounding and hitting the string a second time.

The strings in Cristofori's piano were above the soundboard, two strings for each note. In his last model, he incorporated an *una corda* device. Worked by stops under the keyboard, the mechanism slid the keyboard and action laterally so that the hammers struck only one of each of the pairs of strings. The ranges of the Cristofori pianos were four octaves, C to c''', or four-and-a-half octaves, C to f '''.

By and large, Cristofori's work was overlooked by the generations that followed him. Other "inventors" of the piano brought out their models, some of them less advanced than Cristofori's, and the important centers of piano manufacturing shifted northward to Austria, Germany, France, and England. Three of Cristofori's pianos still exist. One in Leipzig in the Karl Marx University collection is dated 1726; another, dated 1720, is in the MetropolitanMuseum of Art in New York City; and the third, the least known (dating from 1722), was formerly in Padua but is now housed in Rome.

For about a century after the piano came into being, there was a good deal of dispute over who actually did make the first instrument. Claimants to the title of the "inventor" of the piano included a Frenchman, **Jean Marius** (dates unknown, living 1700–16), and **Christoph Gottlieb Schröter** (1699–1782). A Marius piano was presented as a *clavecin à maillets* to the Académie des Sciences in Paris in 1716. It was a relatively simple instrument that made no use of either escapement or damping. Schröter claimed to have invented the piano in Germany. He was inspired by the performances of the dulcimer virtuoso Pantaleon Hebenstreit (1669–1750). Schröter presented his models to the elector of Saxony in Dresden in 1717, hoping for financial aid. When Schröter was turned down, he exhibited the instruments publicly. Schröter's models were copied by Gottfried Silbermann. As late as 1738 Schröter claimed that both Silbermann and Cristofori had stolen his invention. Schröter's instruments experimented with both down-striking and up-striking actions. The down-striking one was named Pantaleon in honor of Hebenstreit. The dampers fell on the string immediately, before the key was released, so that sustained sound was not possible.

Gottfried Silbermann (1683–1753) became the leading piano manufacturer of Germany, and his influence was felt in England through one of his workmen, Johannes Zumpe, who moved to London in 1756. It is reported that Frederick the Great bought fifteen of Silbermann's pianos, although by the end of the nineteenth century only three could be found. It is in connection with Silbermann's instruments that Johann Sebastian Bach's acquaintance with the piano took place. Silbermann was reported to have sought an endorsement for the new instruments from Bach. According to the story, Bach admired the tone of the instrument but criticized the action as being too hard to play and the upper register as being too feeble. When Bach visited Frederick the Great in 1747, Bach is said to have examined an improved model of the Silbermann piano and given it complete approval. The fact remains, however, that the elder Bach did not pay much attention to the piano, the new instrument playing a greater role in the careers of his sons than in his.

The Silbermann piano had a double-lever action that later came to be known as the English action. It was harder than the so-called Viennese action represented by the Stein piano. Silbermann's dampers were made of fringed wool and placed on the ends of sticks, their effectiveness being regulated by stops. An experimental Silbermann model used a keyboard that was moveable in order to effect transposition.

Johann Andreas Stein (1723–92) started his career as a workman in Silbermann's shop, but in 1751 Stein settled in Augsburg, where he built his own reputation as an organ builder and piano maker. Wolfgang Amadeus Mozart, in a letter to his father dated October 17–18, 1777, gave his impressions of Stein's pianos in some detail:

> This time I shall begin at once with Stein's pianofortes. Before I had seen any of his make, Späth's claviers had always been my favorites. But now I much prefer Stein's, for they damp ever so much better than the Regensburg instruments. When I strike hard, I can keep my finger on the note or raise it, but the sound ceases the moment I have produced it. In whatever way I touch the keys, the tone is always even. It never jars, it is never stronger or weaker or entirely absent: in a word, it is always even. It is true that he does not sell a pianoforte of this kind for less than three hundred gulden, but the trouble and the labor that Stein puts into the making of it cannot be paid for. His instruments have this splendid advantage over others, that they are made with escape action. Only one maker in a hundred bothers about this. But without an escapement it is impossible to avoid jangling and vibration after the note is struck. When you touch the keys, the hammers fall back again the moment after they have struck the strings, whether you hold down the keys or release them.

Stein's piano represented Viennese action. It was of the single-lever variety, with the hammer actually attached to the end of a key. Escapement was effected by means of a moveable bar at the back end of the hammer. The hammerheads were light, sometimes hollow, and covered with buckskin leather. The dampers were weighted wedges. There were two strings per note, except for a few notes in the upper register. The touch was light, but key repetition was considered excellent. There was a knee pedal for sustaining effects.

Stein's business was carried on by his son, Andreas, and his son-in-law **Johann Andreas Streicher** (1761–1833), the latter moving the operation to Vienna in 1802. Streicher experimented with yet another version of a down-striking piano but abandoned it after several years.

In England, **Johann Christoph Zumpe** (exact dates unknown, but was living between 1735 and 1783) had managed to popularize the square piano, in spite of the fact that the action he used was a relatively crude one with but a single lever and no escapement. A Swiss harpsichord maker named **Burkat Shudi,** or Tschudi (1702–73), began to manufacture pianos with his son-in-law, a Scottish cabinetmaker named **John Broadwood** (1732–1812). From 1773 to 1780, the Shudi-Broadwood pianos were copies of Zumpe's instruments, but from 1780 on Broadwood began to produce his own pianos, over the years effecting many improvements.

Around 1780, Broadwood initiated the use of foot pedals for sustaining and una corda. About 1788, with the assistance of personnel from the British Museum, he worked out the proper strike points for the strings and determined optimum tension. The soundboard bridge, which up to that time had been continuous, was divided. By 1794, the range of the instruments was extended to six octaves. The action on the pianos, known as English, was of the double-lever type. It was reliable, but heavier, and repetition was slower than that of the Viennese action. This action combined with a heavier case to produce a more powerful, resonant tone.

As the piano entered the nineteenth century, its place on the musical scene seemed assured. Although many refinements and improvements had yet to take place, the instrument had attracted enough attention to ensure that finding solutions to its remaining structural problems was uppermost in the minds of manufacturers. Among the most difficult problems that still remained was the sluggishness of the action, resulting from the fact that both the hammer and the key had to return all the way to starting positions before they could be reactivated. The solution to this problem was embodied in the "double escapement" concept, which was patented by **Sébastien Érard** (1752–1831) in 1821.

Érard was a cabinetmaker by trade, but early in life he went to Paris to become an apprentice in harpsichord making. In 1777, he constructed his first pianoforte for the duchess of Villeroy, an instrument that was modeled from those of Zumpe. Érard continued as an instrument maker in Paris, except for a period in London (1786–96), where he became completely acquainted with the English action, which he adopted. Érard's greatest achievement was the addition of double escapement to the English action, adding the last essential to complete the action used on today's grand pianos.

Double escapement simply meant that a second escapement mechanism was added to the action so that the hammer, after striking the string, would fall back only part of the way as long as the key was held down. The hammer was held in this new position by the second escapement mechanism, while the first one was free to return to its original position. Thus, the key could act a second time on the hammer, which was not required to return to its starting position. As a result, speed of repetition was greatly increased.

The aesthetic demands of the times were such that composers and performers were asking for a greater volume of sound and more resonance from the piano. About 1810, steel wire of a high tensile strength began to be manufactured in the United States. The use of this metal for piano strings, instead of previously used brass, permitted higher tensions, resulting in a greatly improved tone. Such tension, however, also demanded a stronger frame. Érard had used metal to brace the piano frame in the first piano he built in 1777, and several experiments by various piano manufacturers had been undertaken since that time to strengthen the frame by using metal at various points. Notable was Broadwood's "iron piano" of about 1820. The most important achievement in this area, however, was made by Alpheus Babcock (1785–1842) of Boston, who in 1825 designed and cast the first successful iron frame.

Other significant contributions came in rapid succession. In 1827, James Stewart invented the method used today of stringing around the hitch pin without a loop. In 1828, Henri Pape, formerly of the firm of Érard, patented the method of cross-stringing, or over-stringing, whereby long bass strings cross over those of the treble, making possible the use of longer, more powerful bass strings. Experimental use of felt in the piano started as early as 1780, but Babcock in 1833 and Pape in 1835 took out the first patents on felted hammers. In 1843, Robert Wornum perfected the action of the upright piano in England virtually to the level in use today.

The finest instruments of the 1850s were thus essentially the piano of today. There have been small additional improvements and refinements added in later years, but the basic structural concept has undergone no radical change since that time. The two most significant refinements have been the addition of a third pedal between the damper pedal and the una corda pedal, known as the *sostenuto* pedal, and the so-called *accelerated action*. The sostenuto pedal, invented by Claude Montal in Paris in 1862, makes it possible to hold a given sonority after the keys have been released without holding any of the subsequently played notes. Accelerated action has been featured on twentieth-century Steinways in the United States. It was an invention of Frederick A. Vietor in the 1930s and employs a rounded, instead of square, fulcrum below the key. This rounding, along with lead weights inside the key, results in an increased responsiveness.

The grand piano of today is a precision instrument, embodying a complex system of levers. There are approximately 100 working parts for each of the 88 keys. All of the parts are precision-made, correct to within 1/1000 of an inch. There are about 230 steel wires, each exerting somewhere in the neighborhood of 170 pounds of tension.

An overview of the history of the piano's development gives the appearance of continuity and logical progression, concealing much of the experimentation and many of the failures connected with the instrument's evolution. An interesting, thought-provoking aside is provided by mentioning a few of the many versions of the piano that have fallen by the wayside. In 1843, Louis Schoene of London built the most famous models of the pedal piano. Schumann received an upright and Mendelssohn a grand, both having pedal boards of 29 keys. In 1845, Schumann wrote Opp. 56 and 58 for pedal piano, and Alkan wrote his Opp. 64, 65, 69, and 72 for the instrument.

Mageot's double keyboard (1878) was set up so that the lower keyboard, intended for the right hand, had the usual arrangement, but the upper keyboard, intended for the left hand, reversed that arrangement, so that the higher notes were on the left and the lower ones on the right. This made possible identical fingering patterns for scales, claimed to be an advantage. Janko's keyboard (1882) presented six short rows of keys, like a typewriter. The Clutsam keyboard (1909) was arranged in a slightly curved line, an arrangement said to facilitate the arm motions of the player. Around 1920, Emanuel Moór, a Hungarian pianist, invented a double keyboard with a coupler between the two. The upper keyboard, placed slightly behind and higher, sounded an octave higher, giving the player a two-octave range in each hand. By using the coupling pedal, the upper and lower keyboards were joined so that octaves could be played with one finger or chords of twenty of more notes could be managed.

Quarter-tone keyboards were the focus of attention for a brief period during the early twentieth century. Alois Hába (1893–1973) composed in all media for quarter tones around 1917, inventing a new system of notation in the process. Hans Barth (1897–1956) perfected a quarter-tone portable grand piano, which he played at Carnegie Hall in 1930. The Baldwin Piano and Organ Company built a quarter-tone piano for the United States composer John Becker (1886–1961), who, in turn, wrote a concerto for the instrument (1930).

Various marriages with electronics in the later twentieth century have resulted in a variety of instruments. Some of them preserve the basic concept behind the piano's production of sound (that of sounding a string by striking it with a hammer), simply enhancing or altering the resulting sonority through electronics. Other instruments are further removed from the concept of the piano, for they use alternate means to generate the sound, but borrow devices associated with the piano, such as keyboard or pedal arrangements.

Amid all of these experiments, the piano has remained remarkably stable, and musicians dedicated to the performance of its literature have been staunchly loyal to the instrument that evolved from the mid-nineteenth century. The piano's popularity as a center of musical-social activity has, however, seen a gradual decline in the twentieth century. Audiences for piano recitals have grown small, and the piano's role as the ever-present utilitarian instrument in schools, churches, theaters, and commercial centers is being eroded by synthesizers controlled by MIDI (Musical Instrument Digital Interface) keyboards. The demand for pianos has sharply decreased, and manufacturers of pianos have had to branch out, often into the production of electronic instruments, in order to survive. The place of the piano in our culture is thus undergoing profound change, notwithstanding a small group of devoted and ardent fans, both performers and listeners, who hold out for continued preeminence of the instrument.

CHAPTER TWO

Keyboard Music to the End of the Renaissance

The earliest examples of Renaissance keyboard music date from the second half of the fourteenth century. Most of these early pieces are transcriptions of polyphonic vocal music and dance-types of the period, adapted to the keyboard. By the fifteenth century a style of music that could be considered indigenous to keyboard instruments began to develop. Even then, keyboard instruments were considered interchangeable for the most part, for more emphasis was placed on the functional and structural values of the music than on the timbre peculiar to any given instrument. Not only were keyboard instruments employed with voices and in ensemble combinations but also as solo instruments. Solo instrumental performance began to assume a position of importance, and some of the solo music demanded considerable skill for its performance.

Renaissance literary sources contain many references to the clavichord and the harpsichord, as well as to builders and performers of these instruments. This fact seems to indicate that, in addition to the organ, keyboard stringed instruments were much used in the fifteenth and sixteenth centuries. Even so, the amount of music written specifically for the clavichord or harpsichord is not great. Those examples that are available show a similarity of style to music written for the lute. Dance forms especially, much used in lute music, were firmly established in this literature well before the end of the sixteenth century. Much of the music shows a strong feeling for harmonic structure and a fairly complete list of nonharmonic devices such as passing tones, neighboring tones, suspensions, and appoggiaturas.

Italy

The fertility of the Italian Renaissance quite naturally made Italy an important leader in the area of keyboard music. The construction of fine keyboard instruments was far advanced there, and as early as the fourteenth century instrumental music was receiving special attention.

An important manuscript of instrumental music of the late fourteenth century was the Faenza Codex (ca. 1400; Biblioteca Communale, 117). Over half of the works in this collection are for keyboard instrument. These are transcriptions of polyphonic ensemble works by French and Italian composers, presented in mensural notation on two six-lined staves with bar lines. Included are three works by **Francisco Landini** (1325–97), a noted blind musician who became the organist at the Church of San Lorenzo in Florence.

There are no extant sources for Italian keyboard music of the fifteenth century. It may be assumed, however, that the role of keyboard instruments in general (and particularly that of stringed keyboard instruments) was increasing in importance. In the fifteenth century, the frottola, a light, polyphonic vocal piece popular in Italy, was often accompanied by stringed keyboard instruments. With the onset of the sixteenth century, however, there is evidence of a great deal of activity centered on keyboard playing.

The *Frottole intabulate da sonare per organi* was published by **Andrea Antico** in Rome in 1517. It contained twenty-six pieces transcribed for organ, printed in Italian keyboard tablature. The pieces are light, moderately polyphonic, sectional, and show the beginnings of an instrumental style. A set of pieces called *Ricercari, motetti, canzoni* (1523) were written by **Marco Antonio Cavazzoni** (ca. 1490–ca. 1570) under the name of Marco Antonio da Bologna. The two ricercari contained in the work are not highly polyphonic pieces but rather exhibit a free, improvisational style with many contrasting sections. There are also two transcriptions of motets and four transcriptions of French chansons.

As the sixteenth century progressed, a number of important instrumental forms began to emerge. Although the names attached to a given style of writing are not always consistent, it is possible to discern characteristic stylistic types. Even so, lines of differentiation are often not clear between types, and a given name may very well be linked with an entirely different style of music in a later period.

As noted, the ricercare was used by Marco Antonio Cavazzoni as a title for a rather free, improvisational composition of many sections. In 1542, **Girolamo Cavazzoni** (ca.1520–60), Marco Antonio's son, employed the term for a polyphonic composition of several sections. Polyphonic writing continued to be associated with the term, and eventually the ricercare became known as a prefugal form of several sections, sometimes introduced and concluded with passages in a homophonic style.

The fantasia began to appear first in Italian lute tablature. The term was later applied to keyboard music by the German composer **Hans Kotter** (ca. 1485–1541). Early fantasias were moderately polyphonic, similar in style to the later ricercare. The fantasia did not become associated with a free, rhapsodic style of writing until the seventeenth century.

The canzona developed from the Franco-Flemish chanson and was yet another piece written in imitative counterpoint. It is generally less serious than the ricercare.

The toccata was an extended composition usually of several contrasting sections, sometimes chordal, and at other times imitative. The toccata typically contained improvisatory passages of running figurations, designed to display keyboard technique.

The prelude was a free piece, often containing passagework and chords intermingled. When the prelude was used as an introductory piece to a polyphonic work in a church service, the name *intonazione* was frequently employed. Various dances also appeared as keyboard music. Typical were dances grouped in pairs, such as the slow pavane (in duple or triple time) and the faster galliard (in triple time), or later the moderate passamezzo (duple) and the faster saltarello (triple). Sometimes the paired dances even shared the same melodic motive.

In turning to composers of this period, several should be mentioned whose work was not focused directly on keyboard music but who nevertheless influenced later composers and developments. The first of these is **Adrian Willaert** (ca. 1485–1562). Although Willaert was born in Flanders, he spent most of his career serving as maestro di cappella at the Cathedral of San Marco in Venice. Willaert is credited for having brought the intensely contrapuntal Flemish style to Italy. Not only did he have a number of famous pupils, but he also became the first of a long line of famous musicians in and around the Cathedral of San Marco. He is thus regarded as the founder of a great Venetian school of composition. Three composers of this group are prominent in the area of keyboard music: Andrea Gabrieli, who actually studied with Willaert; Claudio Merulo; and Giovanni Gabrieli. Willaert was, furthermore, one of the first musicians to give attention to the instrumental ricercare, his compositions in this form having been transcribed for keyboard at various times and having been influential in establishing the importance of the ricercare. In this context, two famous Flemish musicians who wrote significant instrumental ricercares should be mentioned: **Jacques Buus** (ca. 1505–65), who possibly studied with Willaert and who was appointed assistant organist at San Marco in 1541; and **Cipriano de Rore** (1516–65), a pupil of Willaert who later became maestro di cappella at San Marco.

The group of composers who addressed themselves directly to writing keyboard music left a legacy in that medium that is considered the most important Italian keyboard music of the period. Leading that group is **Andrea Gabrieli** (ca. 1510–86), who studied with Willaert and enjoyed fame as an organist, becoming second organist of San Marco in 1566. Among his students were his nephew, Giovanni Gabrieli, and Hans Leo Hassler. Andrea Gabrieli wrote over thirty ricercares, several sets being published with the designation "for all kinds of keyboard instruments." His ricercares are highly skilled, imitative, and somewhat austere. He also wrote intonations, toccatas, and canzonas. All of these compositions foreshadow the expansion and richness of Merulo and Giovanni Gabrieli. They are freer than ricercares, showing many passages of idiomatic keyboard writing.

In 1542 and 1543, Girolamo Cavazzoni published two volumes entitled *Intavolatura cioe ricercare canzoni himni magnificati*. The ricercares in these sets are the first to be written in imitative counterpoint, thus establishing the style that is generally associated with the ricercare. His canzonas mark the beginning of an independent keyboard literature in this form. Cavazzoni's style exhibits frequent use of close counterpoint. Free passagework is used sparingly.

Claudio Merulo (1533–1604) was born in Correggio and is sometimes referred to as Claudio da Correggio. One of the most extraordinary keyboard players of his age, he was appointed second organist of San Marco at the age of twenty-three. He became principal organist ten years later. His keyboard works were published as *Canzoni d'intavolature d'organo* (1592), *Toccate d'intavolatura d'organo* (1604), and *Ricercare d'intavolatura d'organo* (1605). Merulo was known for his toccatas, pieces that combined free, virtuosic writing with the imitative style of the ricercare. The toccatas usually presented between three and five sections, with display sections being separated by imitative ones. Merulo commanded an unusually imaginative use of keyboard figuration. His concept of the toccata was later adopted by Frescobaldi, Buxtehude, and Johann Sebastian Bach.

Giovanni Gabrieli (1557–1612) was the nephew and pupil of Andrea Gabrieli. He lived in Munich between 1575 and 1579 but moved to Venice in 1585 to become the principal organist at San Marco, succeeding Merulo and occupying that position until his death. He was a very influential teacher, counting among his students the German composer Heinrich Schütz. Giovanni Gabrieli published twelve intonations in 1593 with those of his uncle, Andrea. In 1595, a similar volume appeared containing ricercares of Andrea and Giovanni, but only two pieces were by Giovanni. Two other compositions, a toccata and a canzona, were published as examples in one of the several editions of Diruta's *Il transilvano*. Giovanni Gabrieli brought sixteenth-century Italian keyboard music to its peak, particularly through his ricercares and canzonas. He was unusually adept at writing principal themes in contrapuntal textures. He showed keen awareness of developmental sections, exhibiting his most skilled work in the highly polyphonic style that characterize much of his music.

Girolamo Diruta (b. ca. 1560) was a pupil of Merulo, Andrea Gabrieli, Zarlino, and others. He worked in Venice around 1582 to 1583. Diruta is remembered for his treatise on playing keyboard instruments,

Il transilvano. The work was published in Venice, appearing in two parts, the first entitled *Dialogo sopra il vero modo di sonar organi i istromenti da penna*(1593) and the second as *Dialogo diviso in quattro libri sopra il vero e la vera regola d'intavolare ciascun canto* (1609). Imaginary dialogues with the prince of Transylvania lead to elucidation of hand positions and fingering; discussions of differences between organ and harpsichord playing; and rules for notating melodies, writing counterpoint, improvising, transposing modes, and accompanying a chorale harmonically. Musical examples were provided through pieces (mostly toccatas) of Diruta, Giovanni Gabrieli, and Merulo.

Germany

The use of keyboard stringed instruments in Germany is established by pictures and writings as early as 1250. There are, however, no notable sources of German keyboard music until the fifteenth century. At this point in history no other country provides us with as many manuscripts.

Keyboard music was written in one of two types of tablature. "Old" German keyboard tablature was used before 1550. It employed a staff with notes for the upper voice (or part) and letters for the lower voices. Time values were shown by stems with or without flags, and chromatic inflections were indicated by the use of a diagonal dash at the stem of the note or, when inflecting the letters, by a loop. "New" German tablature, used after 1550, employed only letters.

Several types of compositions appeared frequently in the German keyboard literature of this period. Intavolature were arrangements of vocal music, usually ballades, motets, rondeaus, or virelais. The cantus firmus piece offered music built on melodies from either sacred or secular sources. The cantus was most often set with two voices moving more rapidly above it or sometimes with one voice above and one below it. Confusingly, these settings are also often called intavolature. The prelude was first written in a style similar to that of a cantus firmus setting, a polyphonic texture often alternating with sections that featured chordal writing or keyboard figuration. Preludes were often improvised in church services before a more complex polyphonic composition.

Various types of dances continued to be important in instrumental music. Dances began to be paired in the fifteenth century, frequently encountered pairs being the *basse dance* and *nachtanz*, the French pavane and galliard, the Italian passamezzo and saltarello. The basse dance was one of the most important dances of the fifteenth century, its name coming from the low, gliding step used in its execution. The music oftentimes employed standard bass patterns over which were placed various melodies, exemplifying a technique not far removed from that of the cantus firmus. The *nachtanz* ("after-dance," or dance that follows) was usually a fast dance in triple time.

There exist but a few manuscripts to serve as examples of the keyboard music of the first half of the fifteenth century. These may be found in the libraries of various German cities: Berlin, Munich, Hamburg, Breslau, and Erlangen. Many of them are actually treatises on other subjects or sermons, the musical examples having been included for illustrative purposes. The more famous of these manuscripts are the three to be found in Breslau (Staatsbibliotek, Ms. I Qu 42; I Qu 438, known as the Sagan manuscript; and I F 687) and one in Berlin (Staatsbibliotek, theol. Quart. 290, known as the tablature of Ludolf Wilkin of Windersheim).

The pieces represented in these manuscripts are usually keyboard settings of a portion of the Mass. They often exhibit the long notes of a cantus firmus in the bass, above which is a more rapidly flowing descant. The music is simple and typically somewhat austere.

The middle and last decades of the fifteenth century provide three significant sources of keyboard music. One of these is primarily a method of composition, using musical examples as illustrations of principles, but the other two are genuine collections of keyboard pieces.

The *Tablature of 1448* was the work of **Adam Ileborgh**. The introduction to the work states the following: "Here begin preludes in various keys written in the modern style skillfully and diligently collected with various mensurae appended by brother Adam Ileborgh, in the year of our Lord 1448, during the time of his rectorate in Stendal." The tablature contains five short *preambulae* (preludes) and three longer *mensurae*. The preludes represent one of the first attempts to write absolute keyboard music inasmuch as the long bass notes do not apparently come from any other source. Thus, although the style is similar to that used in cantus firmus writing for keyboard, there is apparently no actual cantus. The preludes are rhythmically free. The mensurae are compositions in which the cantus firmus is drawn from songs. Here the rhythm is measured. The manuscript of the tablature is in the library of the Curtis Institute in Philadelphia.

Conrad Paumann (1410–73) was born blind in Nuremberg. He became famous as a great organist and was highly skilled on several other instruments. His career centered in Munich after 1467. His most celebrated work, *Fundamentum organisandi* (1452), was written to teach the principles of organ composition. Illustrative compositions were mostly by Paumann, but two other composers, Paumgarten and Legrant, were represented. The work contains three preludes, counterpoint exercises over rising and falling bass patterns, cadence designs, and song transcriptions.

The Buxheim Organ Book (ca. 1460) was discovered about 1900 in a monastery in Buxheim, near Munich. The manuscript is now in the Munich Staatsbibliotek (Cim.352b). The book is a collection of about 250 keyboard pieces. Over 200 are transcriptions (intavolature) of vocal music: motets, rondos, virelais, and ballades of composers such as Dunstable, Binchois, Dufay, and lesser-known musicians. Of more significance are the 30 preludes attributed to Paumann and others. Stylistically these consist of improvisatory passagework alternating with chords. Also to be found here is a keyboard adaptation of *fauxbourdon*, the technique associated with the Burgundian school of composers of using parallel chords built on intervals of thirds and sixths.

In the sixteenth century, Germany continued to provide important examples of keyboard music. Other countries as well, however, began to present a reasonably complete picture of the extent and style of keyboard compositions, so that Germany was no longer the only source, as had been the case for much of the fifteenth century. Nevertheless, several sixteenth-century German musicians should be noted.

Arnolt Schlick (1460–ca. 1517) was yet another blind organist. He served the Count Palatine at Heidelberg. Schlick was famous for a treatise on organ building, *Spiegel der Orgelmacher und Organisten* (Mirror of Organ Builders and Organists; 1511). His keyboard compositions were published in 1512 under the title *Tabulaturen etlicher Lobgesang und Liedlein uff die Orgal und Lauten zu spielen* (Tablatures of Various Hymns of Praise and Small Songs to Play on the Organ and Lutes). This volume, the first to have been printed, contains fourteen organ pieces, twelve lute songs, and three lute pieces. These compositions are written in a cantus firmus style, using three or four voices. The cantus was taken mostly from Gregorian melodies with an occasional song melody being used. In the latter category is the well-known "Maria zart."

Paul Hofhaimer (1459–1537) was a highly celebrated organist and composer who served various courts, including that of Emperor Maximilian I. Hofhaimer was ennobled by the emperor in 1515 and also made a Knight of the Golden Spur by King Ladislas of Hungary. Hofhaimer was influential as a teacher, having fathered a "school" of composition through his students: Hans Buchner, Hans Kotter, and Leonhard Kleber. Only a few of Hofhaimer's compositions, however, are extant, and most of those have been found in the tablature books of his students and others. Hofhaimer's style has been deemed "warmer" and more refined than that of Schlick and other composers of the time. Hofhaimer used careful spacing of voices for richness and included the interval of a third in most of his chords, thereby eschewing the austere quality of the open fifth.

Hans Buchner (1483–1538) was famous for a *Fundamentbuch* (1551), a volume in three parts, the first containing instruction on notation and performance, the second consisting of cantus firmus compositions, and the third of compositions in free counterpoint.

Hans Kotter (ca. 1485–1541) produced a tablature (1513) that contained cantus firmus settings, song arrangements, preludes, and seven

early German dances. His style of writing, particularly in the dances, suggests that these pieces were intended for clavichord rather than organ.

Leonhard Kleber (ca. 1490–1556) compiled a tablature (1524) that
contained over a hundred pieces. Several composers are represented in
the collection: Hofhaimer, Josquin, Obrecht, and others. Kleber wrote
preludes, fantasias, and pieces entitled *finales,* using both sacred and secular themes. His compositions abound in trills and turns, thus causing
him to be called the first of the "colorist" school.

The group of composers during the last half of the sixteenth century known as the colorist school made use of a large number of embellishments in their keyboard compositions. Emphasis shifted away from
the serious cantus firmus compositions based on plainsong to highly
embellished compositions based on Protestant chorale melodies. Dance
types also became much more important. The colorist school did much
to further the development of keyboard technique, concerning itself
with fingering and standardizing the execution of ornamentation.
Representative composers of the group are Elias Nikolaus Ammerbach
(ca. 1530–97), Bernard Schmid (the elder; ca. 1520–90), Jacob Paix
(1556–1616), and August Nörmiger (ca. 1560–1613).

Spain

The sixteenth century was a golden age in Spanish music, producing composers and performers of the highest rank. These musicians
excelled in polyphonic compositions, music for the lute (*vihuela*), harp
(*arpa*), and keyboard. The term *tecla* was used to represent the entire
group of keyboard instruments: the organ, the clavichord, and the
harpsichord. Although specific indication for the use of the two stringed
keyboard instruments is often not found, their use may be assumed, for
there is considerable evidence that these instruments were part of the
culture and that many Spanish musicians were expert performers on
them.

The types of compositions were, for the most part, not vastly different from those used in other countries, although they often went
under the guise of another name. Thus the ricercare-type was known as
the tiento, liturgical cantus firmus settings were called hijanos or salmos,
and transcriptions of secular songs appeared as romances, villancicos, or
canciones.

In the development of the variation form, however, Spanish composers, along with those in England, forged far ahead of others. Not
only were there variations on a theme in which the harmony was
changed (differencias), but also there emerged striking examples in
which long notes of a theme were changed into rhythmic patterns to the
extent that a virtual rewriting of the material took place (glosas).

Leading the list of composers of the time is **Antonio de Cabezón** (1510–66). Blind from birth, Cabezón was the organist to the court of Emperor Charles V and later to that of his son, Philip II. Cabezón accompanied the Spanish court to Italy, Flanders, and England (1548–54). His influence was thus felt by composers on the Continent and especially by English virginalist composers. Cabezón's instrumental works were collected and published by his son, Hernando, under the title *Obras de musica para tecla, arpa y vihuela* (1578). This collection contains two- and three-part exercises, four-part tientos, arrangements of hymn tunes and motets by Josquin and other Netherlanders, and variations on well-known melodies. The music is oriented toward polyphony, harmonically full of invention verging on chromaticism, and expressively full of variety and imagination. Cabezón has been called the Spanish Bach, a title justly deserved in light of his stylistic refinement and expressive beauty.

Luis Venegas de Henestrosa (ca. 1510–ca. 1557) was the organist and composer in the service of Cardinal Juan Travera in Toledo. Venegas de Henestrosa edited the oldest known collection of Spanish keyboard music, *Libro de cifra nueva para tecla, arpa y vihuela* (1557). The collection contains 138 pieces by Venegas and others, some anonymous. It also contains solo songs with instrumental accompaniment and transcriptions of sacred works written in Spanish keyboard tablature.

Fray Tomás de Santa Maria (ca. 1510–70) was a Dominican monk and a student of Cabezón. His *Libro llamado Arte de tañer assi para tecla* (1565) was published as a treatise devoted to instrumental technique and interpretation with special emphasis on the clavichord. The work included rules for improvisation and performances of fantasias; recommendations for hand positions, touch, fingering, and ornaments; and illustrative material that included pieces by Santa Maria. It is interesting to note that all five fingers are employed with alternate fingerings for different tempi.

In Portugal, **Padre Manuel Rodriquez Coelho** (ca. 1583–ca. 1523), who was the clavierist at the Royal Chapel in Lisbon in 1620, published the earliest printed music in Portugal: *Flores de musica o instrumento de tecla & harpa* (1620). The volume contained tientos (preludes and ricercari).

France

The development of keyboard music in France and Belgium during this period produced less significant examples overall than are provided by other countries. Organ and stringed instruments shared the same style. That stringed keyboard instruments were important is established by written records that provide the names of famous clavecinists and by the flourishing of the trade of instrument making. Examples of keyboard music of the period are represented in collections produced by well-known publishers.

Pierre Attaignant (ca. 1494–ca. 1552) was the most famous printer of music in Paris in the first half of the sixteenth century and probably the first in France to use moveable type. He issued seven books of keyboard music between 1529 and 1531, each containing music for "Orgues, Espinettes, et Manicordions" (organs, spinets, and clavichords). Three of these volumes contain sacred music: cantus firmus settings as well as some preludes and arrangements of motets. Four books contain secular music, mostly dances: basse dances, branles (a popular, energetic group dance), pavanes, and galliards. Stylistically there is very little that is strikingly different from characteristics already noted in the music of other countries. It might be noted that the inclusion of so many keyboard dances marks the beginning of an association between keyboard music and dance forms, one that was to grow in importance.

Another significant keyboard collection was published in Lyons by Simon Gorlier. The title of the collection, *Premier livre de tablature d'espinette, chanson, madrigals, et galliards* (1560), suggests the rising importance of the clavecin, for no reference is made to either the organ or the lute.

Netherlands

Jan Pieterszoon Sweelinck (1562–1621) is the dominant figure of the period in northern Europe. He was the organist at the Old Church in Amsterdam for most of his life. He was a close friend of the English virginal composer John Bull, and his influence as a teacher spawned an entire generation of organists from northern Germany, including Samuel Scheidt, Heinrich Scheidemann, and Jakob Praetorius. Sweelinck was said to have studied with Zarlino in Venice as a youth, but there is considerable doubt as to the truth of this assertion. Sweelinck did, however, carry Venetian ideas and techniques into northern Europe, combining them with influences from the English virginal school. Sweelinck wrote about seventy keyboard works, most for organ. These include contrapuntal fantasias, toccatas patterned after those of Merulo, and variations that use both sacred and secular melodies.

England

Several early sources should be noted. The *Robertsbridge Codex* (British Museum Ms. Add. 28550) is the earliest documented keyboard music anywhere, dating from about 1350. It contains three estampies and three arrangements, two of motets and an incomplete one of a hymn. The next group of manuscripts, also in the British Museum, dates from the early sixteenth century. The most famous of these is the one bearing the designation Roy. App. 58. Dating from about 1525, it contains two famous pieces very likely intended for the virginal, Hugh Aston's "Hornpype" and "My Lady Carey's Dompe."

The *Mulliner Book* (ca. 1550; British Museum Ms. Add. 30513) was copied by Thomas Mulliner, Master of Choristers at St. Paul's Cathedral. The collection contains 117 compositions, the majority of which are sacred vocal compositions arranged for organ. There are a few pieces for unspecified keyboard instrument. The number of lines used in the staves varies, twelve, eight, seven, and six lines being used. Clefs frequently change within the same staff. Representative compositions are airs, galliards, voluntaries, fantasias, and In nomines. The composers are often anonymous, but some are specified, such as John Redford, Thomas Tallis, John Blitheman, and John Taverner.

From the beginning of the sixteenth century, virginal playing spread rapidly throughout England, flourishing particularly during the first thirty years of the seventeenth century. The virginal was not only an instrument used by the aristocracy but was considered a "popular" instrument as well. At one point, it was even provided for the entertainment of waiting patrons in barber shops! Samuel Pepys reported in his diary (Sept. 2, 1666) that, during the great fire of London, every third boat loaded with personal possessions in the Thames River carried a pair of virginals.

In outward appearance, sixteenth-century manuscripts show no difference between organ music and virginal music, two staves being used in all cases. An idiomatic keyboard style associated with the virginal began to develop during the sixteenth century and reached its height in the early seventeenth century. Rapid scales, repeated notes and chords, broken chord and octave figures, use of parallel thirds and sixths—all of these devices were features of the new style.

The music of the virginalists most often exhibits a consonant triadic basis. Elements of melody and counterpoint were combined, the contrapuntal invention usually existing as an accompaniment to a more prominent melodic line. In general, the music contained fewer accidentals than lute music, notwithstanding some passages of striking chromaticism. There is much use of drone-like accompaniment. Patterns of accent depend upon agogic inflection. Often the music is characterized by mixing and juxtaposing major and minor thirds and sixths. Notation was usually on six-lined staves, c′ being represented by both the lowest line in the treble and the highest in the bass. The only key signatures are those of one or two flats, in most cases indicating transposed modes.

Of the forms encountered, dances and variation forms appear most frequently. Dances were often presented in pairs, a slow dance in duple time being followed by a more rapid one in triple time. The second dance was sometimes a variation of the first. The most frequent coupling was that of the pavane and galliard. Also used were the alman (allemande), coranto (courante), gigge (gigue), branle (brawl), and the dompe, the latter being a piece composed in memory of some important person who was recently deceased.

Variations developed from the Spanish keyboard variation, but English variations tended to be less introspective, more brilliant, and often reached virtuoso levels. The theme upon which the variation was based was generally well known. Thus, the first section of the composition was often called the first variation, since modification of the melody began at once. Bisectional tunes were often given varied repeats. This procedure was sometimes referred to as "double" variation. Fixed cadences were often omitted, although double bars indicated sections that suggest cadential treatment. Frequently the melody was presented in full harmony at the end of a composition as a kind of summing up.

The fantasia (fancy) was similar to the early Italian fantasia, a contrapuntal piece, possibly less strict than the imitative ricercare. The fantasia was described in detail by Thomas Morley in his famous treatise *A Plaine and Easie Introduction to Practicall Musicke* (1597). The In nomine was a cantus firmus composition based on a melody that appeared in the Benedictus of the Mass *Gloria tibi Trinitas* by John Taverner (ca. 1495–1545). The piece of melody that was borrowed for the cantus firmus is that which sets the words "in nomine Domini" (Example 2.1).

Other cantus firmus compositions, such as the *Felix namque*, were based on plainsong melodies. Even the medieval theory of Guido d'Arezzo served as the basis for cantus firmus pieces, for several were derived from his six diatonic tones known as the hexachord. Such pieces were usually given the title *Ut, re, mi, fa, sol, la* (Example 2.2) In addition

Example 2.1 John Bull: *In nomine (FVB* 37) mm. 1–5

Example 2.2 William Byrd: *Ut, mi, re (FVB* 102) mm. 1–4

there were a number of pieces in free form that are called preludes and a great number of descriptive compositions, these sometimes being cast in one of the well-known dance forms.

Music of virginalist composers was assembled into collections, and these volumes constitute the sources for the music itself. *My Ladye Nevells Booke* (1591) contains forty-two compositions by William Byrd, composed and copied by John Baldwine. *Parthenia* (1611) was the first printed collection of virginal music. It contained twenty-one pieces by three composers: William Byrd, John Bull, and Orlando Gibbons. Its title page pictured a young lady playing the virginal. The volume was widely used, for it was reprinted in 1613 and 1635.

The most important and extensive collection of the period was the *Fitzwilliam Virginal Book* (ca. 1620). Its name was derived from the fact that the manuscript of the work belonged to Lord Fitzwilliam at the end of the eighteenth century and is now housed in the Fitzwilliam Museum (founded in 1816) at Cambridge University. The book contains 297 compositions by many composers, including 72 by William Byrd, 53 by Giles Farnaby, 44 by John Bull, 19 by Peter Philips, 9 by Thomas Morley, 5 by John Munday, 5 by Thomas Tomkins, 2 by Orlando Gibbons, and 2 by Thomas Tallis. The music was written over a period of time from about 1550 to 1620. Although a variety of styles is presented, the volume contains an overall representation of the resources of the period. There are over 130 dances, 17 organ pieces, 47 arrangements of popular songs, 9 madrigals, 22 fantasies, 19 preludes, and 6 pieces based on the hexachord. There is frequent use of modality, represented by Dorian, Mixolydian, Aeolian, and Ionian modes with their plagal counterparts. One flat usually signifies transposition of a mode up the interval of a fourth; two flats, up two fourths ("double transposition").

Other significant virginal collections should be noted. *Benjamin Cosyn's Virginal Book* (ca. 1620) contains 98 pieces by various composers, including John Bull, Orlando Gibbons, and Benjamin Cosyn. Will Forster's Virginal Book (1624) contains 78 pieces, almost half by William Byrd. Other composers represented are Thomas Morley, John Ward, and John Bull. *Elizabeth Rogers hir Virginall Booke* (1656) assembled 79 compositions, most of which have no indication as to composer. There are numerous virginal arrangements of songs and dances as well as one identified work by William Byrd, an early programmatic suite entitled *The Battell*. *The Dublin Virginal Book* (1583) contains 30 pieces, most of them anonymous.

It now remains to consider individual composers and representative works. **Hugh Aston** (ca. 1480–1522) is possibly the earliest well-known virginal composer, although his compositions are by no means confined to keyboard works. He received his music baccalaureate degree from Oxford (1510) and then took up a study of canon law. In 1509, he became a prebend of St. Stephen's, Westminster, and in 1510 archdeacon of York. His most famous keyboard piece is one called "Hornpype," one of the earliest known virginal pieces. The piece is 118 measures long and presents a set of variations over a drone bass, which alternates basically between harmonies built around C and F. Melodic patterns are imaginative, using leaps, scale passagework, and cross-rhythms.

William Byrd (1543–1623) was probably the greatest English composer of his age, excelling in all types of composition. There are about 125 pieces for organ or virginal that have been preserved. It is believed that he received his training from Thomas Tallis. In 1563, he was appointed organist of Lincoln Cathedral. In 1570, he was elected a member of the Chapel Royal and in 1575, together with Tallis, was the organist of the Chapel Royal.

Byrd's keyboard works fall into four groups: fantasias, dances, variations (sometimes over repeated bass patterns called grounds), and those in free form. He is particularly successful in the variation form, where he employs all of the expected devices: rapid scales, ornaments, leaps, and cross-rhythms. The right hand generally sustains the melody, but often one finds the melody in the alto register in the penultimate or final variation.

Perhaps Byrd's most celebrated song variation, "As I Went to Walsingham," appears in the *Fitzwilliam Virginal Book* (no. 68). Walsingham Priory is in Norfolk and in the thirteenth century was referred to as the "English Holy Land." The tune itself dates from an earlier period. A dialogue is suggested in the opening statement, the melody often appearing in the middle or lower parts (Example 2.3). The twenty-one variations that follow include triplets and sextuplets against longer note values (variations nos. 16 and 17), the tune presented in various parts (nos. 2, 3, 4, and others), contrasted upper and lower voices (no. 13), and motivic derivations (nos. 7 and 11). Ornamentation is used throughout the set. There is a short coda that is unrelated to earlier material.

Example 2.3 William Byrd: "Walsingham" (*FVB* 68) mm. 1–4

Example 2.4   William Byrd: Fantasia (*FVB* 8) mm. 1–4

The Fantasia that appears in the *Fitzwilliam Virginal Book* (no. 8) is in Mixolydian mode with seven segments that present thematic fragments in a series of imitative entrances (Example 2.4). The counterpoint becomes less strict as the piece progresses, finally yielding to brilliant scale passages and a closing homophonic dance. "Mr. Birds Battell," which can be found in *Elizabeth Rogers hir Virginall Booke*, is in twelve sections: the "Souldiers' Summons" suggests great confusion amid bugle calls, "Marche of the Footmen," "Marche of the Horsemen," "The Trumpetts," "The Irish Marche," "The Bagpipe and the Drone," "The Flute and the Droome," "The Marche to the Fighte," which uses a long crescendo in the key of C with heavy chords, "The Retreat," "The Burying of the Dead," "The Morris," and "Ye Souldiers Dance."

John Bull (1563–1628) was born twenty years after Byrd and represents an emphasis on virtuoso writing. Bull studied with John Blitheman, succeeding his master as organist of the Chapel Royal in 1591. The next year Bull received his doctor of music degree from Oxford, and four years later he was appointed professor of music at Gresham College on Queen Elizabeth's recommendation. In 1613, Bull left England to become organist for the archduke at Brussels, and later still he was appointed organist of Notre Dame in Antwerp. He was acquainted with Sweelinck and was a significant influence on the development of keyboard styles in northern Europe. Over 200 compositions are attributed to him.

Bull's greatest virginal work is a set of variations on the same tune Byrd used, "Walsingham" (*Fitzwilliam Virginal Book* no. 1). Bull's variations are less contrapuntal than Byrd's, but Bull exploits many devices that later became important in keyboard technique, such as arpeggios, leaps, and brilliant runs. In Bull's "Walsingham" the tune is always in the uppermost part, either in a simple or embellished version (Example 2.5). The thirty variations that follow lead to a strong climax. They feature repeated notes (no. 8), continuous eighth-note patterns divided between the hands (no. 10), alternating arpeggios in contrary motion (no. 12), use of triplets (nos. 20 and 21), use of sextuplets (nos. 22, 23, and 24), cross-accents (no. 22), left-hand passagework (no. 23), crossing

Example 2.5 John Bull: "Walsingham" (*FVB* 1) mm. 1–4

of hands (no. 28), and a finale in which the tune is presented in solid five-part harmony (no. 30).

The *Ut-re-mi-fa-sol-la* (*FVB* no. 51) is a fantasia based on the hexachord with a scheme of modulation that may be derived from the circle of fifths. The hexachord is used in both ascending and descending forms successively in the following keys: G, A, B, D-flat, E-flat, F, A-flat, B-flat, C, D, E, F-sharp, and G. The work closes with a short coda that features syncopation.

Giles Farnaby (1560–1600) was of Cornish descent, but little is known of his early life. In 1592, he received his doctor of music degree from Oxford. He lived in London during his last years. His music shows a fine sense of musicianship and a sensitivity for the musical phrase. His melodies are distinguished by a rustic sweetness. Folk-song variations show him at his best. Although none of his music was published during his life, he had over fifty compositions published in the *Fitzwilliam Virginal Book* shortly after his death. "Wooddy-Cock" (*FVB* no. 141) presents six variations that feature broken octaves and repeated notes. Variation no. 5 employs an unusual running accompaniment, and the final cadence embellishes the leading tone. The "Ground" (*FVB* no. 260) consists of fourteen variations on a theme of ten whole notes. The upper contrapuntal part is successively built in half notes, quarter notes, eighth notes, and sixteenth notes.

Orlando Gibbons (1583–1625) was born forty years after Byrd and represents an art two generations away from that of the earlier composer. Gibbons was appointed organist of the Chapel Royal in 1604. Later he was appointed chamber musician to the king, and in 1623 he became organist at Westminster Abbey. His fame rests primarily on his church music, but his contributions to the virginal literature are significant. He brings to his music a sensitivity and refinement that are unique. His style exhibits the use of simple melodies, an almost Baroque-like counterpoint, experiments in homophonic writing, and rhythmic freedom. An example of his work is the pavane that appears in part as no. 292 of the *Fitzwilliam Virginal Book*. Representative of Gibbons's style in a more extended, imitative work is the fantasia that appears in the *Parthenia*.

Several other composers may be noted in passing. **Thomas Morley** (1557–1603) was a pupil of Byrd, graduated from Oxford with a doctor of music degree (1588), and was made a gentleman of the Chapel Royal (1592). He is represented in the *Fitzwillian Virginal Book* by nine pieces. His book *A Plaine and Easie Introduction to Practicall Musicke* (1597) is a valuable source dealing with Elizabethan musical life.

Peter Philips (ca. 1560–1633) spent most of his life on the Continent, where he held several important posts. He is reported to have met with Sweelinck, and Philips's music often contains counterpoint reminiscent of the Flemish master. Nineteen examples of Philips' music are in the *Fitzwilliam Virginal Book.*

Thomas Tomkins (1573–1656) came from a family of musicians, was a student of Byrd, received his doctor of music degree from Oxford (1607), and became organist of Worcester Cathedral, holding the position for about fifty years. Five examples of his music are in the *Fitzwilliam Virginal Book.*

John Munday (ca. 1555–1630) was a student of his father, William, received his doctor of music degree from Oxford (1624), and was organist of both Eaton College (ca. 1585) and St. George's Chapel. Four of his pieces appear in the *Fitzwilliam Virginal Book.* Curiously, a set of folksong variations entitled *Goe from my Window* are attributed to both Munday and Morley.

Benjamin Cosyn (ca. 1570–1652) was the organist at Dulwich College (1622–24) and the first organist of the Charterhouse (1628). Cosyn's music appears mostly in his own virginal books. It exhibits highly ornamented lines, elaborate virtuoso techniques, and is considered quite difficult to play.

CHAPTER THREE

Baroque Keyboard Music in Italy, France, England, and Germany

The term *baroque* is said to be derived from the Portuguese word *barroc-co*, which means a pearl of irregular shape. In its artistic connotation, the term was meant to imply stylistic fantasy and grotesqueness, resulting in extravagance and lack of proportion. Recent assessment of the Baroque, however, has led to a concept that differs considerably from that originally implied by the term. The Baroque is now seen as a period of considerable experiment, growth, and change but one that produced significant artistic contributions and culminated with the magnificent achievements of men such as Johann Sebastian Bach and George Frideric Handel.

In keyboard music, evidences of the Baroque can be observed as early as the second half of the sixteenth century, particularly in Italy, where the Baroque began. Characteristics to be noted are an increased use of chromaticism, the employment of dissonance to achieve dramatic and expressive effects, and initially a reaction against polyphonic complexity. Gradually, the system of modality was replaced by that of tonality, with new importance being given to harmonic progression.

Thoroughbass, or figured bass (*basso continuo* in Italian, *basse chiffre* in French, and *Generalbass or Bezifferterbass* in German), was developed and universally used in the Baroque. Thoroughbass resulted from the increasing awareness of chordal functions and harmonic progression. It is a kind of musical shorthand in which accompaniment is indicated by writing only a line of single notes in the bass. Underneath those notes are a set of numbers that indicate the intervals above the bass notes that are components of that particular chord. Oftentimes a low string instrument, perhaps a viola da gamba or a violoncello, acted as the medium for emphasizing the bass line, in which case only the one bass note was heard. Very often, however, the harpsichord acted as the medium through which the figured bass was "realized." In such cases the player improvised the entire series of chords as directed by the figures and the bass notes. Sometimes the low string instrument and the harpsichord were both used, the former reinforcing the bass line and the latter realizing the chord progression.

Outside the area of keyboard music, the Renaissance contrapuntal forms were seriously challenged at the onset of the Baroque. Keyboard forms from the Renaissance continued to appear, however, in the Baroque and continued to incorporate much of the polyphonic technique that had developed with the form itself. Thus, the initial rejection of counterpoint that ushered in many of the new vocal forms of the Baroque is not as apparent in much of the keyboard music. Dances and variations, to be sure, are often still relatively homophonic, but in addition to these is a host of larger types that lie in a direct line with their predecessors. In all forms, both the contrapuntal and the more homophonic, there is an ever-increasing orientation toward tonality and harmonic awareness, the polyphony, when used, being regulated by chordal sequence.

The toccata continued to be an idiomatic keyboard composition with contrasting sections of chords, imitation, and brilliant passagework. In the hands of composers such as Frescobaldi, the toccata was patterned after the concept of alternating fugal and free sections, a concept initiated by Merulo. The ricercare continued to stress imitation and to be scholarly and dignified in character. The contrapuntal writing could either be polythematic, as in the style of a motet, with short overlapping points of imitation, or present a single idea in consecutive, varied expositions. The fantasia continued to be imitative but was generally freer than the ricercare. The canzona was also imitative but stressed lively rhythms, lightness, and short note values. Musical ideas in the opening of the canzona often used the pattern of a half note followed by two quarters. The canzona also frequently exhibited formal clarity and balance, such as an ABA pattern. It might also present structural contrast, the imitative texture giving away to a homophonic style, or a free dialogue-like texture. The chaconne and passacaglia were terms used interchangeably for continuous variations over a repeated bass pattern.

Other forms tended to break away from contrapuntal textures. The capriccio was a form in which great variety was to be found. It might be imitative but less strict than the ricercare. Often it could be descriptive and even use the principle of thematic variation. The partita was a series of variations in the early Baroque. Later the term was associated with the dance suite. The sonata first simply meant a piece to be played rather than sung. As a result, early "sonatas" might be patterned after any other existing form.

In the context of the short dance-types one can see the emergence of binary structure. This two-part form was usually divided by a double bar with indications that each of the two parts be repeated. Growth toward a second musical idea in the first section, usually in the dominant before the double bar, may be observed. Evidences of key changes, fore-shadowing developmental techniques, can sometimes be seen following the double bar.

Italy

A group of composers working in Naples is given credit for writing music with characteristics that usher in the Italian Baroque. Three fig-ures among this group may be noted. **Giovanni Maria Trabaci** (ca. 1580–1647) published two collections of keyboard works during his lifetime. They consisted of ricercares, canzonas, capriccios, partitas, and galliards. The partitas and galliards were very likely for harpsichord. **Antonio Valente** (ca.1520–ca. 1580) also produced two collections, the first (1575) containing ricercares, fantasies, and canzones written in Spanish keyboard tablature; the second (1580) presented an early type of partita. **Ercole Pasquini** (ca. 1580–1614) was born in Ferrara and achieved fame as an organist, being appointed organist to the Cappella Giulia of St. Peter's (1597–1608). Only about thirty keyboard composi-tions have been discovered, but they establish Pasquini as an important predecessor to Frescobaldi. Pasquini's works include toccatas and the earliest examples of the variation canzone.

Girolamo Frescobaldi (1583–1643) was the towering figure of the period. He was born in Ferrara, where he studied with Luzzasco Luzzaschi. Frescobaldi lived in Brussels in 1607 but returned to Rome in 1608 to succeed Pasquini as organist at St. Peter's, a post he held until his death with the exception of a short period spent in Florence as court organist for Ferdinando II de' Medici (1628–33). Froberger studied with Frescobaldi for four years (1637–41).

Frescobaldi's music is marked by effective use of chromaticism, striking tonal colorations, and modulations that forecast the future importance of tonality. His counterpoint is often severe, and there is a quality of nervousness in much of his music as a result of using short, jerky themes, syncopation, and cross-rhythms. He often incorporated a broad use of the suspension figure, and he recommended the use of rubato in performance.

Although much of Frescobaldi's music is titled "di cembalo et organo," it may be considered the cornerstone of the seventeenth-cen-tury harpsichord school. His cembalo compositions include several types already noted. Dances generally sustain strong harmonic pro-gressions under delicate counterpoint. Dance-types encountered are the corrente, galliardo, balletto, and passacaglia. Frescobaldi's toccatas are structured like those of Merulo but are more chromatic, using stronger contrasts between sections. The imitative sections are often very short with fragmatic themes. There is a liberal use of virtuoso devices in the free sections. Partitas are true variations, showing cleverly contrasted polyphonic textures and rhythms. Themes are often taken from well-known songs such as the "Bergamasca" or "La follia." Fugal pieces use imitative counterpoint with a fixed number of voices to present several motivic ideas.

Frescobaldi's published works that designate the cembalo as the instrument of performance are *Toccate e partite d'intavolature di cembalo* (1615) and *Il 2⁰ libro di toccate, canzoni, versi d'inni, magnificat, gagliardi, correnti, et altre partite d'intavolature de cembalo et organo* (1616). From these, several specific works may serve as examples of his writing. The First Partita presents four correntes in binary form, all only about thirty-two measures long, using homophony with many figurations in thirds for the right hand. The Second Partita consists mostly of ballettos followed by correntes. The movements are all related by some means, either bass movement, harmonic progressions, or melodic features. *La Frescobalda* is a celebrated set of variations (Example 3.1). An expressive aria in the manner of early Italian opera is followed by four variations. The third variation is in the style of a galliard, and the last is a lively corrente.

Frescobaldi's influence may be traced through his student Johann Froberger all the way to the culmination of the late Baroque in Germany. Recent Frescobaldi research has suggested that he is now being regarded with increasing importance and that his role in the overall history of keyboard music is assuming ever greater significance.

Although other keyboard composers of seventeenth-century Italy do not reach Frescobaldi's stature, several of them contributed significantly enough to warrant being noted as follows. **Michelangelo Rossi** (1600–74) was a pupil of Frescobaldi who imitated his teacher mostly in toccatas. **Alessandro Poglietti** (d. 1683) was an Italian musician who became the court organist in Vienna (1661–83). In addition to the usual types, he wrote an extended suite dedicated to his patroness, the Empress Eleonora Magdalena Theresia. This work, entitled *Rossignolo,* presents a set of programmatic variations, such as "Bohemian Dudelsack" (no. 8), "Old Hag's Procession" (no. 13), "French Kiss-the-hand" (no. 15), and "Polish Swordplay" (no. 17). The final two movements imitate the song

Example 3.1 Girolamo Frescobaldi: *Aria detta la Frescobalda* mm.1–3

of the nightingale. **Bernardo Pasquini** (1637–1710) wrote virtuoso toccatas in a terse, vigorous style. He was one of the first musicians to write for two harpsichords. His pieces were published in Paris in a collection entitled *Toccates et suites pour le clavecin de MM. Pasquini, Poglietti et Gaspard Kerle* (1704). **Alessandro Scarlatti** (1660–1725) was born in Palermo, Sicily, but moved to Rome in 1672, spending most of his career in ecclesiastical appointments in Rome and Naples. He is especially important for his operas, cantatas, and oratorios, being considered the father of a "Neapolitan" school of opera composers. His style shows thematic development, balance of melodic phrase, and chromatic harmony—all woven into a smooth and supple texture that foreshadows the music of Mozart and other Viennese classical composers. **Azzolino Bernadino Della Ciaja** (1671–1755) was one of the first Italian composers to focus on the sonata. His pieces are highly ornamented and incorporate many technical devices later used by Domenico Scarlatti.

France

After the collections of keyboard music printed by Attaignant, only a small amount of clavecin music appeared in France before Chambonnières, who is usually regarded as the first significant clavecin composer. Beginning with Chambonnières' time, clavecin music developed rapidly, an idiomatic style emerging almost immediately. That style was influenced partly by the English virginalists but also by a large body of literature for the lute. Added to these influences was the French predilection for imaginative pictorial devices and for profuse ornamentation of the melodic line. Although textures sometimes suggested lines at different levels, the counterpoint was of a very free type, imitation often being only momentary.

Other influential factors were the emergence of social status for the performer and the growth of a music-consumer public drawn from royal and aristocratic segments of society. French musical activities were centered in Paris and Versailles, where positions in wealthy homes and court appointments furnished avenues to fame for clavecinists. Moreover, teaching music to the children of well-to-do bourgeois families offered an extra source of income. Not surprisingly, the result was a focus on music designed to please, to entertain, and to reflect elegant life-styles.

Dance-types gained increased popularity, almost all of these using binary form. The concept of grouping dances in pairs, prevalent in the Renaissance, was now expanded so that several dances were played together. Thus, the concept of the dance suite came into being. The suite was not, however, the cohesive work later represented by the suites of Johann Sebastian Bach. The allemande, courante, and the sarabande were often present, even sometimes in that order, but there were likely to be several examples of each type of dance. The implication seemed to be that the performer was free to choose dances of each type from the groups. After the sarabande came all manner and variety of dance forms, some being derived from the theatrical ballets of Cambert and Lully, many having descriptive titles, and a few, such as the rondeau and the chaconne (or passacaglia), cast in some nonbinary form. The gigue, although frequently encountered, had not yet been accepted as the finale of the suite. There is a definite leaning toward grouping dances written in the same key together, but there is only a moderate degree of consistency in the practice. In addition to the dance-types, the variation form was extremely popular.

Jacques Champion de Chambonnières (ca. 1602–72) is considered the founder of the seventeenth-century clavecin school. He achieved in his works a true clavecin style that can be easily distinguished from the organ counterpart of the time. As a performer and composer Chambonnières concentrated on the clavecin and did not concern himself with other members of the keyboard family.

Chambonnières served at Versailles as the court musician to Louis XIV. Among his students were Louis Couperin, Jean-Henri d'Anglebert, and Nicolas Le Bègue. His influence was felt even in Germany, through Froberger and others. Chambonnières was highly praised by Mersenne, the French theorist, for beautiful melodies and for a unique harmonic and rhythmic charm. Chambonnières focused on dance-types rather than contrapuntal or church music. His style is dignified and refined, containing such features as irregular phrases, changing meters, unexpected modulations at cadence points, numerous ornaments, and, whenever contrapuntal levels can be discerned, a tendency to write in three voices (Example 3.2).

Thirty suites in two volumes were published in Paris in 1670, although they were written for the most part around 1640. They include allemandes, courantes, sarabandes, gigues, pavanes, and other dances. A table of ornaments offered help to the performer and established a practice that was followed by many composers after Chambonnières. A suite in *g* (no. 44 in the complete works) is representative. It presents an allemande in four voices structured in three sections. The first gigue is in quarter-note movement in three-four time, using mostly a three-voiced texture. The courante uses dotted rhythms and shifts between three-two and six-four time. A final gigue is in three voices, the upper two in canon.

Example 3.2 Jacques Chambonnières: Allemande from *Pièces de clavecin* (1670) mm. 1–2

"La Verdinquette" is a piece that relies heavily on the key of *C* until after its double bar and builds variations over a harmonic pattern that returns rondo-style after contrasting sections. *Pezzi per clavicembalo* is composed of six groups of dances, each group adhering to a single key. The first set is in *d* and contains an allemande, three courantes, a sarabande, a piece entitled "Les Barricades," and two gigues.

Louis Couperin (ca. 1626–61) was the first noted composer of the Couperin family, establishing a line that lasted until 1860. His nephew was François Couperin (often referred to as François le Grand). A sensitive and original composer, Louis Couperin was a pupil of Chambonnières, with whom he went to Paris. There, Louis Couperin became the organist at St. Gervais and played violin and viola in the court orchestra.

Louis Couperin wrote comparatively few suites, but in these he employed various contrapuntal devices. Of particular interest are his preludes, for these are typically in three sections, a fugato being presented between two unbarred, toccata-like segments. He used all the keys possible in meantone temperament. Typical is a Passacaille in *g* (no. 99 in the complete works). It is written over a dignified ground four measures long. Four notes descend from tonic to dominant. Each variation is repeated with alterations. The piece contains much lyrical writing with some use of chromaticism.

Jean-Henri d'Anglebert (1635–91) was another distinguished pupil of Chambonnières, carrying his teacher's formal and stylistic characteristics toward an even higher degree of refinement. D'Anglebert succeeded Chambonnières as the court clavecinist to Louis XIV. D'Anglebert used the full resources of the clavecin, his music being characterized by loftiness and grandeur. He wrote unbarred preludes, rondeaux, chaconnes, variations, and miscellaneous dance pieces (Example 3.3). D'Anglebert's style was often florid and heavily ornamented, and some of his preludes

Example 3.3 Jean-Henri d'Anglebert: Sarabande from *Pièces de clavecin* (1689) mm. 1–4

and suites show cyclicism. Among d'Anglebert's pieces are twenty-two variations on the famous melody known as "La follia," or sometimes "Folies d'Espagne," a tune used by many other composers, including Farinelli, Pasquini, Alessandro Scarlatti, Corelli, Liszt in his *Rhapsodie Espagnole,* and Rachmaninoff in the *Variations on a Theme of Corelli.*

Nicolas-Antoine Le Bègue (1670–1702) was yet another student of Chambonnières. Le Bègue's clavecin suites were distinguished by the use of more than one key, the avoidance of descriptive titles, and more chromaticism than exhibited in styles of other composers of the French school. His two books of clavecin pieces (1677) contain suites made up of allemandes, courantes, sarabandes, gigues, gavottes, minuets, and canaries.

Jean-Baptiste Lully (1652–87) and **Michel-Richard de Lalande** (1657–1726) achieved fame in other genres, the former in opera and the latter in church music. Neither devoted much creative effort to writing clavecin music, but both produced a few clavecin pieces based largely on dance forms.

England

It has been noted that English harpsichord music attained an extremely high level in the Renaissance and was of great influence on Continental composers. In the seventeenth century, however, harpsichord music in England was not able to sustain its elevated position, for English composers lost their strong initiative for the most part and fell under influences from both France and Italy. Dance movements were arranged into "suites of lessons" or "setts of lessons." Compositions based on repeated bass patterns, called *grounds,* were frequently written as well as arrangements of chamber music and songs. In the later Baroque, composing toccatas and sonatas in the Italian style became fashionable.

Music publishing flourished in the hands of the Playfords, father and son: John (1623–86) and Henry (1657–ca. 1710). In 1663, a volume appeared entitled *Musick's Hand-maid, New Lessons and Instructions for the Virginal or Harpsichord.* It was a small oblong book that contained undistinguished pieces for the most part. That it enjoyed popularity, however, is evident, for it was reprinted both in 1678 and 1689. The 1689 publication was edited by Henry Purcell, and he included in it some examples of his own music.

Matthew Locke (ca. 1630–77) was a chorister in Exeter Cathedral and composer for Charles II at the time of the Restoration (1661). Later he was appointed the organist to Queen Catherine (1672). He wrote an instructional work entitled *Melothesia, or Certain Rules for Playing upon a Continued Bass* (1673). It was perhaps the earliest English work on figured bass and contained seven organ pieces. His dances appeared in *Choice Collection of Lessons for the Harpsichord or Organ of all sorts,* along with works by Gregory, Banister, and others.

John Blow (1649–1708) was a chorister in the Chapel Royal at the Restoration. He was appointed organist of Westminster Abbey (1668), the king's "musician for the virginals" (1669), and a gentleman of the Chapel Royal, as well as a master of the children of the Chapel Royal (1674). His memorial tablet in Westminster Abbey states that he was "master to the famous Mr. H. Purcell." In fact Blow influenced an entire generation of choristers at the Chapel Royal, such as William Croft, Jeremiah Clarke, Daniel Roseingrave, and Daniel Purcell. Blow composed a large amount of church and secular choral music. For the keyboard, he wrote suites, numerous single dance movements, and short pieces such as preludes and grounds. Gravity, nobleness, and strength are combined with a delicate, personal expression in his harpsichord music. A certain harmonic daring, even awkwardness, may be found on occasion. His music is often good-natured, unsophisticated, and even somewhat boisterous.

A volume entitled *A Choice Collection of Ayres for the Harpsichord* (1700) contained music of Blow, Pigott, Clarke, and Barrett. A collection of four "setts" by Blow waspublished without a date by Walsh, possibly in 1704. A second undated volume was called *Psalms Set Full for the Organ or Harpsichord*.

Henry Purcell (1659–95) was not only the greatest composer of this period in England but also one of the greatest in the entire history of English music. He alone makes the English Baroque worthy of close study in all genres. Purcell was probably born in the city of Westminster and became an orphan at an early age. As a practicing musician, Purcell led a very busy life, gathering to himself several important "offices" of employment under the crown and holding those offices simultaneously during his career, an achievement that attests to the regard in which he was held. As a singer in the Chapel Royal, he studied under Cooke, Humfrey, and Blow. After his voice broke, he was the first assistant "keeper of instruments" (1675), then "composer in ordinary for the violins" (1677), succeeding Matthew Locke in the latter position. In 1679 Purcell succeeded John Blow in the post of organist at Westminster Abbey. Purcell became one of three organists of the Chapel Royal (1682), and a year later he was appointed "keeper of the King's wind instruments." He was buried at Westminster Abbey.

Both French and Italian influences are strong in Purcell's music, but he achieved a style of his own, bringing together the diverse trends within the English Baroque and summing up the best of what had gone before. Church music, odes and welcome songs, chamber music, music for the stage, and a small amount of harpsichord music compose the treasure he left. With sensitive imagination and complete mastery of form, Purcell wrote clear, direct melodies, to which he added with striking effect daring harmonies, bold dissonances, impressive counterpoint, and expressive musical devices.

Example 3.4 Henry Purcell: A Ground in Gamut mm. 1–6

Purcell's music for the harpsichord was cast mostly in small forms, utilizing a two- or three-voice texture (Example 3.4). Many of the single dance tunes were arranged from theater pieces and songs. Purcell's suites were written as didactic material and, as a result, usually contain a fewer number of movements than might be ordinarily expected. Apparently the only example of virtuoso writing for the keyboard is a toccata in *A,* a piece attributed in error to both Michelangelo Rossi and Johann Sebastian Bach.

A Choice Collection of Lessons for the Harpsichord or Spinet was published in 1696 by Purcell's widow. It contains suites and miscellaneous pieces, mostly dances in binary form with highly ornamented melodic lines. Instructions for fingering, incidentally, used numbering from the left, so that the little finger of the left hand was designated as number one. *Musick's Handmaid, Part II,* published by Playford (1689), contained a variety of small pieces, including marches, minuets, grounds, a Scotch tune in G, a popular Irish tune known as "Lilliburlero," and a farewell tribute to a famous male soprano known as Siface. Purcell's complete works began to be published by the Purcell Society of London in 1878. The sixth volume of the complete works contains the harpsichord music.

Although neither the composers contemporary with Purcell's generation nor those that followed achieved the level of Purcell's work, several wrote worthy harpsichord music and should be noted.

John Eccles (ca. 1650–1735) centered his career on writing theater music. He was made a member of the king's band (1694) and later a master of the same group (1700). He was a popular composer, writing numerous birthday and new-year odes, some forty-six theater works, and over one hundred songs. *A Collection of Lessons and Airs for the Harpsichord or Spinnett by J. Eccles, D. Purcell, and others* was published in London in 1702.

Jeremiah Clarke (ca. 1673–1707) began his career as a chorister in the Chapel Royal under John Blow with Purcell as a fellow student. He held organ posts at Winchester College (1692) and St. Paul's (1695). Clarke, along with William Croft, was made a gentleman extraordinary of the Chapel Royal (1700), and later the two men became joint organists of the chapel (1704). Clarke wrote music for church and theater. Six of his harpsichord pieces appeared in *A Choice Collection of Ayres for the Harpsichord* (1700), and a volume of pieces was published posthumously (1711) under the title *Choice Lessons for the Harpsichord or Spinett being the Works of the late Famous Mr. Jeremiah Clarke.*

John Barrett (ca. 1674–1735) studied with Blow and became master of music at Christ's Hospital in London (ca. 1707) as well as organist at the church of St. Mary-at-Hill (ca. 1710). A "set of ayres" appeared in *A Choice Collection of Ayres for the Harpsichord* (1700), consisting of three pieces entitled Almand, Corant, and Sarabrand (!). Other pieces entitled "St. Catherine (Rigaudon)" and Minuet were not with the set but may have been meant to be a part of it.

William Croft(s) (1678–1727) was one of the greatest of Purcell's contemporaries. He was a chorister in the Chapel Royal under Blow, was made a gentleman of the Chapel Royal (1700), shared the appointment of organist to the chapel with Clarke, and was made sole organist after Clarke's death. Croft was made organist of Westminster Abbey, succeeding Blow in that position. He is buried in Westminster Abbey. He was important as a composer of anthems, overtures, theater music, and sonatas for violin and flute. He wrote twelve suites for harpsichord, mostly three-movement works, of which eight are in minor keys, unusual for the time.

Thomas Roseingrave (1690–1766) was an Irishman who won the position of organist at the fashionable church, St. George's in Hanover Square. He was a teacher to London's elite society and a personal friend of Domenico Scarlatti. Roseingrave returned to Dublin (ca. 1749), where he gave concerts and composed. He edited "forty-two suites" of Scarlatti's keyboard music for the English public, introducing each with music of his own. Two other volumes of Roseingrave's harpsichord music were also published, *Eight Suites of Lessons for Harpsichord or Spinet: Voluntarys and Fugues, Made on Purpose for the Organ or Harpsichord* (1730) and *Six Double Fugues for Organ or Harpsichord* (1750).

Thomas Augustine Arne (1710–78) was the son of an upholsterer and coffinmaker in the Covent Garden district of London. Arne was sent to Eton to study law, but he finally overcame his father's misgivings about music as a profession. He earned a doctor of music degree from Oxford (1759). Among his students was the writer Charles Burney. Arne composed many refined, elegant dramatic works, masques, and theater pieces popular in his day. A volume entitled *VIII Sonatas or Lessons for Harpsichord* appeared in 1756.

Germany

The religious conflicts that took place in Germany in the seventeenth century and the fact that the country was politically decentralized gave rise to an artistic climate that nurtured a divergency of musical styles. As in England, both Italian and French influences were strong. German composers, however, added a measure of their own initiative and imagination to an extent far exceeding that of English composers. The resulting style was the fertile ground out of which grew the culmination of Baroque keyboard music—the compositions of Johann Sebastian Bach.

Italian influences were felt most strongly by those composers who worked in Austria and southern Germany. There was a continued use of many of the forms originating in Italy, exemplified by the toccata, the ricercare, and the canzone. Keyboard idioms associated with Italian music were also influential, particularly those characteristic of the music of Merulo and Frescobaldi.

French influences were felt not only by that group of composers in Austria and southern Germany but also by a group that centered in Nuremberg, Stuttgart, Halle, and the smaller cities of central Germany. From France came the concept of the dance suite as a unified art form and the character of each of the various movements. Other stylistic elements from Lully and the clavecinists can be observed, such as the occasional use of florid ornamentation, the use of programmatic concepts, and a leaning toward clarity and refinement.

A third important influence should also be mentioned. It came from northern Europe and centered on Sweelinck and his students, particularly Samuel Scheidt. This influence combined the warmth and directness of the Italian school with the inventiveness and variation mastery of the English virginal composers. These characteristics emerged in seventeenth-century Germany as the expressive styles and techniques employed in the chorale variation, the toccata, and the fugue. This Flemish-English influence made its way particularly into the writing of composers in central and northern Germany, where it was expanded into a style that was unique, one that exhibited both originality and imagination and that was eventually a strong influence on Johann Sebastian Bach through Dieterich Buxtehude and Johann Pachelbel.

Although some of the music of this period is obviously intended for organ, there is a great body of music that is intended for any keyboard instrument, as had been the case with much music written in other countries. In Germany the term *clavier* was used to designate music for any keyboard instrument. As the term continued to evolve, however, it became more frequently associated with music for either the harpsichord or the clavichord.

The emergence of the forms of the German Baroque presents an unusually complex picture. Often several names were used to designate compositions that are basically of the same type. Moreover, several names that had come to be associated with one type of composition now begin to refer to music with altogether different characteristics. New designations begin to appear frequently (as in the case of the sonata), and old types, slightly altered, take on new names (as in the case of the fugue).

The toccata continued to be a work of from three to five sections, having descended from those of Merulo and Frescobaldi. In northern Germany composers such as Buxtehude began to develop an expanded concept of the toccata, using longer sections, imaginative figuration, colorful harmonic shifts, and devices calculated to produce dramatic effects. The fantasia is now no longer a composition in a rather strict imitative style but rather becomes almost indistinguishable from the toccata. The prelude and fugue was related to the concept that guided the alternating sections of the toccata in that a highly imitative composition was preceded by one of relative freedom.

Variations, existing in several types, continue to play an important role. To be found were variations on a simple melody, a popular air, or one of the standard melodies, such as the *romanesca, ruggiero,* or *passamezzo moderne.* Such variations were often called a *partita.* Another type of variation was constructed over a recurring bass pattern and was designated by any one of three names: chaconne, passacaglia, or ground bass. Chorale variations are typical of the organ music of the period but are also occasionally found in the harpsichord and clavichord literature, most often appearing in those keyboard works that cannot be restricted to any one keyboard instrument, such as the chorale variations that are presented in Scheidt's *Tabulatura nova.*

The concept of the dance suite was borrowed from France, but the stabilization of the format took place in Germany. The sequence that is now associated with the Baroque dance suite is one that is exemplified most clearly in the works of Johann Sebastian Bach. It is as follows:

allemande	(A)	
courante	(C)	
sarabande	(S)	
optional	(O)	added movements such as the minuet, bourrée, gavotte, polonaise, passapied, aire, etc.
gigue	(G)	

Before Bach, arrangements of movements varied. For example, Johann Erasmus Kindermann used ACS only, and Matthias Weckmann AGCS. Johann Jacob Froberger was the most important figure before Bach in the development of the dance suite in Germany.

The sonata took its point of departure from the Italian *sonata di chiesa.* The first use of the term *sonata* is attributed to Adriano Banchieri (1567–1634) as a title for musical examples found in a treatise he wrote on organ playing, *L'organo suonarino* (1605). Other early examples of the sonata are works by Gioanpietro De Buono (1641), pieces that are cantus firmus settings of a vesper hymn, and Giorgio Strozzi (1687), whose works are in three or four contrasting movements but use an imitative style much like that of the canzona. The first German composer to use the term (as a movement of a suite) was Johann Heinrich Schmelzer (ca. 1623–80). Johann Kuhnau (1660–1722) called fourteen of his works sonatas, adding to his late works in this form elaborate programs and descriptive elements. Early sonatas contained from three to six contrasting movements, often arranged in a sequence that alternated slow and fast tempi. The style could be either songlike or contrapuntal, the bass often functioning as a continuo for two upper parts.

Samuel Scheidt (1587–1654) was one of the important links between the Franco-English style of northern Europe and Germany, having studied with Sweelinck in Amsterdam. Scheidt spent most of his life in Halle, a city in central Germany, in the post of Kapellmeister to Margrave Christian Wilhelm of Brandenburg. Although most of Scheidt's keyboard works are associated with the organ, the *Tabulatura nova,* his most important collection, was written for keyboard instruments in general. Scheidt is considered one of the first important composers in the development of the organ chorale.

The *Tabulatura nova* (1624) was originally published in three volumes, the first example in Germany of keyboard literature written in notation as we know it today rather than in tablature. The volume presents pieces in both homophonic and polyphonic textures and contains chorales, toccatas, fantasias, passamezzi, psalms, hymns, Magnificats, and a Mass. A second important work of Scheidt was the *Goerlitz Tablatur* (1650), which comprised one hundred well-known chorale melodies in four-part harmony.

Johann Jacob Froberger (1616–67) began his career as a choirboy and organist in Vienna. After his voice changed, he received a stipend from Emperor Ferdinand II to study with Frescobaldi in Rome (1637). After three-and-a-half years in Rome, Froberger returned to Vienna until 1657. At that point in his career, he embarked on a series of concert tours that took him to Paris and London. He finally settled near Héricourt in the service of the Duchess Sybille of Württemberg.

Froberger was a key figure in the development of the dance suite. His style is unusually personal and sensitive. He indicated no ornamentation in his music but rather left this important matter entirely up to the performer. Froberger's keyboard catalogue includes twenty-five toccatas, eight fantasias, six canzonas, eighteen capriccios, fifteen ricercares, and thirty suites. Ten of the suites appeared in a volume entitled simply *Suites de clavecin* (1693). The original order of the movements was ACGS or AGCS, but the publisher put the works in a "better order" after the composer's death, establishing the sequence associated with the suite, ACSG (Example 3.5).

Johann Casper Kerll (1627–93) studied in Rome with Carissimi. Kerll held the post of court Kapellmeister at Munich (1656–74), became the organist of St. Stephen's in Vienna (1674–84), and finally returned to Munich. His most important keyboard work is for organ, *Modulatio organica super Magnificat octo tonis* (1686). Other keyboard works include

Example 3.5 Johann Jacob Froberger: Allemande from Suite in *b* mm. 1–3

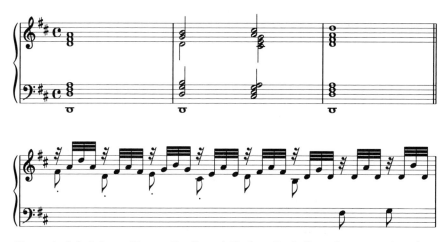

Example 3.6 Johann Kasper Ferdinand Fischer: Präludium from *Les Pièces de clavecin* (1696) mm. 1–4

canzones, capriccios, and toccatas.   Kerll is fond of using descriptive devices in his keyboard works.

Dieterich Buxtehude (1637–1707) was the organist at Marien-kirche in Lübeck from 1668. His reputation became widespread, and he was influential on both Handel and Johann Sebastian Bach. Although most of Buxtehude's keyboard works were for organ, a small body of harpsichord works was recently discovered (1942). It consists of nine-teen suites (ACSG), six sets of variations, and three other smaller pieces of questionable authenticity. These pieces are believed to have been products of Buxtehude's youth. They exhibit a direct, relatively uncom-plicated style, fused with considerable warmth and imagination.

Johann Kaspar Ferdinand Fischer (ca. 1650–1746) was born in Bohemia but spent most of his career in Germany, serving as the court conductor to the margrave of Baden. His keyboard works show a strong French influence. Some of his earliest suites include a prelude as an opening piece before the dance movements. The order of dances in his suites varies and is often not ACSOG. The movements are often quite short, but they show skill and imagination (Example 3.6).

Les Pièces de clavecin (1696) contains eight suites, each one opening with a prelude before the dance movements. The order of the dance movements is ASCG plus optional movements such as the gavotte, minuet, ballet, rondeau, canaries, passepied, bourrée, branle, plainte, and chaconne. The work was republished in 1698 under the new title of *Musicalisches Blumenbüschlein* (Small Musical Flowering Bushes). Somewhat confusing is the fact that a later volume used the same title but was a collection of twenty-four pieces drawn from the original volume and from two other sets, *Blumenstrauss* and *Musicalischer Parnassus*.

Of perhaps greater significance was the *Ariadne musica* (1702). Twenty preludes and fugues were presented as a demonstration of equal temperament, along with five ricercares. The pieces rarely exceed twenty measures in length, and only nineteen keys are actually used, *C-sharp* and *F-sharp, g-sharp, e-flat,* and *b-flat* being omitted. The *Ariadne musica* was, however, an important forerunner of the *Well-Tempered Clavier* of Johann Sebastian Bach and was probably influential on Bach. A second work by Fischer that combined the prelude and fugue was the *Blumenstrauss* (1732). In this volume, eight preludes are followed by six very short fugues, varying from between six and forty measures in length. A short finale is included. The use of pedals suggests that the work was probably meant for organ. In *Musicalischer Parnassus* (1738), the composer presents a set of nine suites, each one named for one of the Muses of antiquity.

Johann Krieger (1652–1735) studied with his older brother, Johann Philipp Krieger (1649–1725), and succeeded him as court organist and conductor at Bayreuth (1672). Johann Krieger later held posts at Greiz (1678–1681) and Zittau. Krieger's two principal keyboard works are *Musicalische Partien* (1697), a set of six suites in which the order is ACSG, the gigue often being followed by optional movements, and *Anmutige Clavier-Übung* (1699), one of the first works to couple the prelude and fugue (or ricercare) in the same key.

Georg Muffat (1653–1704) began his career as the organist to the Molsheim Cathedral (1671). He then migrated to Austria (1678), where he was in the service of the archbishop of Salzburg. Muffat moved on to Italy (1681), where he studied with Corelli and Pasquini. From there he traveled to Paris to study Lully's style. Finally, he returned to Passau (1687), where he was appointed organist to the bishop of Passau and later Kapellmeister. His most important keyboard work, *Apparatus musico-organisticus* (1690), was written for organ. Central to this collection are twelve large-scale toccatas, which show influences of both Corelli and Lully. There are a few harpsichord pieces, but their authenticity has been questioned.

Johann Pachelbel (1653–1706) began his career by serving as the organist at St. Stephen's cathedral in Vienna (1674). He went on to hold a series of court and church positions in Eisenach (1677), Erfurt (1678),

Stuttgart (1690), and Gotha (1692). He finally settled in the city of his birth, Nuremberg, accepting the position as the organist of St. Sebald's (1695). Pachelbel wrote extensively for all the keyboard instruments of his day in all of the accepted forms. His organ works are considered especially important in that they foreshadow those of Johann Sebastian Bach. An interesting sidelight is that Pachelbel's son, Carl Theodore, went to the United States in 1730 and was an active musical force in the cities of Boston, Newport, New York, and Charleston.

Pachelbel's *Musicalische Sterbensgedanken* (Musical Memorials; 1683) was written as a work for keyboard instruments in general. It contains three sets of variations on chorale melodies. Another work appeared in the same year (1683), a set of seventeen suites ordered ACOSG. *Hexachordum Apollinis* (1699) consists of six arias, each followed by from five to eight variations. The *94 Fugues on the Magnificat* (ca. 1702) was probably intended for organ, for the fugues were likely used in the church service to introduce congregational singing of alternate verses of the Magnificat. Although the fugues are fairly short and monothematic, the set is considered one of the most important examples of fugue writing before Johann Sebastian Bach.

Johann Kuhnau (1660–1722) received his early training in Dresden and then attended the University at Leipzig (1682–84). He organized a collegium musicum there while studying law, and he eventually became the music director of the University of Leipzig (1700). A year later he was appointed cantor at the Thomaskirche, thus becoming Johann Sebastian Bach's immediate predecessor in that position. Kuhnau devoted a good deal of his creative effort to writing keyboard music and was one of the more prominent figures in the development of the early keyboard sonata.

Neuer Clavier Übung appeared in two parts in 1689 and 1692. Each part contained seven partitas (suites) ordered ACSOG. The second part also contained Kuhnau's earliest sonata, one in *B-flat* in four short sections, the sequence of tempi being slow-fast-slow-fast. *Frische Clavierfrüchte (Fresh Keyboard Fruit;* 1696) contains seven sonatas, each of from three to six movements, usually alternating fast and slow tempi. The movements include various types of pieces such as the chaconne, fugue, or aria. The composer provides quite detailed dynamic and tempo markings. *Musicalische Vorstellung einiger biblischer Historien in 6 Sonaten* (1700) is Kuhnau's most celebrated set of sonatas. Each sonata is based on a biblical narrative. The music is quite sectional, each section bearing a heading that states what the following music is to depict. The first sonata, for example, tells the story of the battle between David and Goliath. The plight of the Israelites before the battle is represented by the choral melody "Aus tiefer Not." The opposing forces then gather to march-like sections. Other segments depict David's innocence, Goliath's might, the moment when the rock from David's slingshot hits Goliath,

Example 3.7 Johann Kuhnau: *The Mortally Ill and then Restored Hezekiah* from *Biblical Sonatas* mm. 1–4

the giant falling, Goliath's death throes, the flight of the Philistines, and the triumph of the Israelites. This descriptive music is somewhat naive but cleverly crafted in its effects and entertaining. The subjects of the remaining five sonatas are *Saul's Melancholy Cured by David's Music; The Marriage of Jacob; The Mortally Ill and then Restored Hezekiah; Gideon, Saviour of Israel;* and *Jacob's Death and Burial* (Example 3.7).

Georg Böhm (1661–1733) studied at the University of Vienna. He later became organist at the Johanneskirche in Lüneburg (1698), when Johann Sebastian Bach was the organist at the Michaelkirche in the same city. That Böhm was a possible influence on Bach is evidenced by the fact that one of Böhm's minuets was found in the *Clavierbüchlein* of Anna Magdalena Bach. Böhm's harpsichord works consist mainly of eleven suites, most of them ordered ACSG. The second one is an exception to this pattern, containing an overture, air, rigaudon, rondeau, minuet, and chaconne.

CHAPTER FOUR

George Frideric Handel and Johann Sebastian Bach

Born **Georg Friedrich Händel** (b. Halle, Germany, Feb. 23, 1685; d. London, Apr. 14, 1759), the composer anglicized his name late in his career. He was the second son of a late marriage his father contracted at the age of sixty. At the age of seven, Handel went with his father to visit an older stepbrother who was in the service of the duke of Saxe-Weissenfels. While at the court, Handel gained access to a chapel organ. The duke, noting the boy's interest and musical talent, persuaded Handel's father to provide for lessons. These were undertaken with the organist at the Halle cathedral, Wilhelm Zachau. In 1697, Handel's father died, and, out of respect for his father's hopes, Handel went to the University of Halle as a student of law. After a year of study, however, he began to pursue his musical career.

Handel's first position was that of a violinist at the German Opera in Hamburg. Two early operas, *Almira* and *Nero,* were produced there (1705). With money earned from music lessons, Handel journeyed to Italy, visiting Florence, Venice, Naples, and Rome (1706–10), composing works and securing performances for them in each city. He returned to Hanover (1710) to assume the position of Kapellmeister to the elector of Hanover. Handel began to make trips to England at this point, his theater or dramatic works being produced there during each visit with considerable success (1711, 1712, and 1713). Upon Queen Anne's death, the elector of Hanover became King George I of England, and Handel decided to reside permanently in England with his patron, in 1727 becoming a British subject.

Handel's career in England was often stormy, as productions of theater works, confrontations with rivals, or financial troubles came and went. In general, however, his successes outweighed his failures, and the years brought many achievements and honors. He was appointed the director of the Royal Academy of Music (1720), an institution devoted essentially to the production of Italian opera. Oxford University offered

him an honorary doctor of music degree (1733). His work was generally celebrated, and he was accorded the honor of being buried in
Westminster Abbey, where a magnificent monument by Roubiliac marks
his interment.

Handel was a man of the theater, having written forty-six operas in
addition to the many oratorios for which he is so well known. He was
also a master of the instrumental style of the period, as is evidenced in
his output of concerti grossi, sonatas, organ concertos, and incidental
music. Having traveled widely, he came under the influence of various
forms and styles: French, German, Italian, and even English by way of
Purcell. Realizing performances of many of Handel's instrumental compositions frequently calls for a considerable amount of improvisation on
the part of the performer.

Handel's music shows not only influences of the musical styles that
had preceded him but also a foreshadowing of many ideas that were to
develop after him. He often borrowed from the music of other composers, a practice not uncommon in Handel's time, and he often reused
his own music. Musical ideas that he thought might be useful later were
jotted down in notebooks he kept.

Handel's keyboard music is relatively unimportant when compared
to his overall output, but it is, nevertheless, a significant contribution to
the literature of the period. In general, his keyboard pieces are rather
short compositions that are grateful to play but are not marked by great
profundity or seriousness of purpose. His style is often broad and stately with a continuous flow of controlled energy.

Handel's compositions for keyboard include sixteen suites in three
books, six fugues or voluntaries, many minuets, the *Forest Musick,* a
march, and some other short pieces. His harpsichord music is of uneven
quality, the first set of suites being possibly the strongest. Many pieces
were composed for young performers, junior members of royal or aristocratic households. The pieces in variation form, including passacaglias
and chaconnes, offer perhaps the best teaching material. Many of the
courantes and gigues are also attractive.

Several projects to assemble Handel's works have been undertak-
en. In 1786 a thirty-six volume edition of Handel's works was published
by command of George III. The contents of this set, however, were
incomplete and often incorrect. The Händel-Gesellschaft edition under
the editorship of Friedrich Chrysander was produced by the German
Handel Society between 1858 and 1894. To complete this edition, J. M.
Coopersmith added an additional ten volumes and issued a thematic
index. A more recent project was instituted by the city of Halle in 1955
and edited by M. Schneider, R. Steglich, and others. It is still in
progress.

Handel's first published instrumental music (1720) was a set of eight
harpsichord "lessons" or suites. These suites vary with regard to arrange-

ment of movements and the types of dances used. Suites 1, 2, 5, and 6 contain four movements each; nos. 4 and 8, five movements; and nos. 3 and 7, six movements. Suites 1, 5, 6, and 8 open with preludes. Opening movements also include an adagio movement (no. 2), a presto (no. 3), and a French overture (no. 7). Nos. 3 and 5 contain airs with variations, the latter bearing the nickname *Harmonious Blacksmith*, probably written on a tune popular at the time. Five suites include fugal allegros (nos. 2, 3, 4, 6, and 8) and one (no. 2) presents an Italian sonata da chiesa with a slow-fast-slow-fast sequence of tempi. Final movements of the suites exhibit variety and include gigues (nos. 1, 4, 6, and 8), a fugal allegro (no. 2), a presto (no. 3), an air with variations (no. 5), and a passacaglia (no. 7). Movements of the suites all adhere to the key of the group with the exception of no. 2, where the relative minor is employed for one movement. The finale of no. 3 appears as the second movement of the oboe concerto Op. 3, no. 6, as well as in the fourth organ concerto.

A second set of nine suites was published without Handel's consent (1733). Nos. 1, 5, and 6 contain three movements; nos. 4 and 7, four movements; no. 3 has five movements; and no. 8 has seven movements. Two chaconnes appear in the set: the grave with twenty-one variations in no. 2 and an andante with sixty-two variations in no. 9. The first suite contains the air (with variations) that Brahms later used in his *Variations and Fugue on a Theme of Handel,* Op. 24.

The third set of pieces was published (1793) after Handel's death. The first two works are suites of four movements. The pieces that follow include two capriccios, a fantasia, a sonatina, two sonatas, a chaconne, and other miscellaneous pieces. A set of six fugues or voluntaries was published by Walsh for organ or harpsichord (1735). These are short improvisational works probably written fifteen years earlier. All are written on two staves, since English organs of the day often did not have pedals. Two of the fugues were later used in the oratorio *Israel in Egypt*, no. 1 as "He smote all the first-born" and no. 5 as "They loathed to drink of the waters." Handel had also used the fourth fugue previously in the overture to the *Brockes Passion*.

Several other keyboard works should be noted. The *Klavierbuch aus der Jugendzeit* is a collection of early versions of pieces that later appeared in the suites (particularly the 1720 set). *Forest Musick* (1742) is a small work written in Dublin for an Irish amateur and containing references to Irish melodies. A volume of *Stücke für Clavicembalo*, containing seventy-six small pieces, was sold at an auction of the library of the Earl of Aylesford in 1918. This volume is one of probably very early works and contains a sonata, a sonatina, various airs, fugues, minuets, and variations. A collection entitled *Zwölf Fantasien und vier Stücke für Cembalo* appeared in the estate of the Zurich music publisher Hans Georg Nägel. With the exception of the first piece, a Fantasie, none of the pieces appears in the Händel-Gesellschaft. The pieces probably come from

Handel's youth. The volume includes fantasies, an allemande, a sonata, a carillon, and other miscellaneous pieces.

Johann Sebastian Bach

The family of Johann Sebastian Bach (b. Eisenach, Mar. 21, 1685; d. Leipzig, Jul. 28, 1750) can be traced from the sixteenth century to the early nineteenth century. It produced a variety of musicians of every kind who lived and worked in central Germany, particularly in the principality of Thuringia. The lineage of which Johann Sebastian was the culmination extended through eight generations over three centuries. This remarkable concentration of musical talent within a single family has been a constant source of fascination for those who research the relationship between genealogy, aptitude, and, of course, genius.

Johann Sebastian was the last of eight children (of whom but four survived infancy) born to Johann Ambrosius and Maria Elisabeth (née Lämmerhirt) Bach. Johann Ambrosius was the director of town music of Eisenach and a court trumpeter. Johann Sebastian began his education in the humanities and theology in the Lateinschule in Eisenach. In 1694, his mother died, and the following year so did his father. Thus, at the age of ten, Johann Sebastian was sent to live with his older brother Johann Christoph, who was an organist in the town of Ohrdruf. Johann Sebastian attended the lyceum there until the age of fifteen. It is believed that, although Johann Christoph instructed his younger brother in keyboard playing, Johann Sebastian was essentially self-taught as a composer through copying the works of others.

In 1700, Johann Sebastian continued his education at the school run by the Michaelkirche in the town of Lüneburg, where he was able to secure a paid scholarship for singing in the choir and accompanying. It is believed that influences on Bach during this period were Georg Böhm (1661–1733), who was organist at the nearby Johanneskirche, and Jan Adams Reincken (1623–1722), the organist at the Catharinenkirche in Hamburg, about 50 kilometers from Lüneburg.

In 1702, Bach was unsuccessful in his quest for a position as the organist of Jakobkirche in the town of Sangerhausen, but he was able to find work a year later as an understudy musician in the court of Duke Johann Ernst at Weimar (younger brother of Duke Wilhelm Ernst, whom Bach later served). In 1704, Bach secured his first professional position as the organist of Arnstadt's Bonifaciuskirche (known also as the Neukirche, having been rebuilt after a fire). Although Bach's weekly schedule was such that he had time for composition, he was at odds with the church administration for most of his stay there, partly due to the intermittent and incompetent participation of the groups of students who were hired as performers and partly because of Bach's own truancy. Having been granted a month's leave of absence to journey to

Lübeck to hear Buxtehude, Bach left in mid-October 1705, and did not return to his duties until early February 1706. There followed months of considerable acrimony between Bach and the consistory of the Neukirche. Bach continued to hold the post at Arnstadt, however, until the summer of 1707, when he was given an appointment by the city council of Mühlhausen as the town composer and organist at the church of St. Blasius.

Although Bach was successful in the Mühlhausen position, he resigned it a year later to accept the more important appointment as court organist to the Duke Wilhelm Ernst of Weimar. By 1714, Bach became the Konzertmeister of the court as well. Although Bach's relationship to his employer remained formally cordial, fallout from disputes within the court family and the fact that the duke was seeking to fill the post of Kapellmeister without consulting Bach led to a gradual deterioration in their relationship. Bach was offered the position of Kapellmeister by Prince Leopold of Cöthen in August 1717, but Duke Wilhelm refused to release Bach. By late autumn Bach persisted in his demand to be released to the point that the duke had Bach imprisoned for about a month, finally releasing him in disgrace in December.

Prince Leopold was in his early twenties, a young man who, according to Bach himself, loved and understood music. Bach served him at Cöthen in a relationship that was generally amicable and productive until 1721, when the prince's marriage to his cousin Friderica, princess of Anhalt-Bernburg, resulted in a diminishing interest in the arts in the court. It was not surprising, therefore, that Bach became one of several candidates for the position of Kantor at the Thomasschule in Leipzig. The position itself was not ideal, for it required the teaching of Latin in addition to service as the civic director of music. Bach himself looked upon it as a step downward in his career, notwithstanding the fact that it was deemed one of the most prestigious positions in Germany for a musician. Two other candidates were preferred over Bach: Telemann, who had to refuse the appointment because he could not obtain a release from his post in Hamburg; and Graupner, who withdrew at the last minute because he found a higher-paying position at Darmstadt. The selection council finally agreed on Bach in late April 1722, one of the councilmen commenting that since the best men could not be obtained they would have to be content with the mediocre, another hoping that Bach's music would not be too theatrical.

Bach's duties at Leipzig were centered on training students at the school, being involved in the music programs of four churches, the Thomaskirche, the Nicolaskirche, the Matthaeikirche, and the Petrikirche, and arranging for music at all other civic events of the town. Although Bach brought a high level of energy to the position, the attitudes surrounding his appointment had set the stage for wrangling. Thus, arguments ensued over the degree of Bach's responsibility for music at services held at the university, the selection of songs to be sung before and after sermons, and other matters. Bach's struggle to maintain his artistic independence in the face of bureaucratic pressure resulted in continuing disputes over trivial details, most of them documented in the public archives of the town. In an attempt to affirm his independence and to be more involved in secular music, Bach insisted in 1729 on taking over the directorship of the collegium musicum, a volunteer organization of professional musicians and students who gave weekly public concerts.

By 1749, Bach was suffering from eye trouble, specifically cataracts, and the town council began to search for a new Kantor. Two unsuccessful eye operations weakened Bach's stamina, and the composer passed away on July 28, 1750, after suffering a stroke.

Bach's enormous catalogue of works reflects his official duties in the various posts he held. Most of Bach's organ music, for example, was written at Arnstadt, where his primary responsibilities were those of an organist. Similarly, most of his chamber music was written at Cöthen, where he was a court musician, and the main vocal works were written at Leipzig, where he was a Kantor. It is thus not surprising that the study of Bach's music has been traditionally divided into the periods named after the towns in which Bach worked.

Bach's output encompassed every musical genre of his day except opera. His music combined harmonic and contrapuntal considerations in near perfect balance. Although Bach never left Germany, his style is regarded as an amazing combination of German, French, and Italian characteristics, the composer having drawn the best from the styles of his contemporaries. Cited as influences are many famous German keyboard composers of the day, such as Froberger, Fischer, Pachelbel, and Buxtehude, as well as the French clavecinists and Italians, such as Frescobaldi and Vivaldi. Bach was, moreover, equally gifted in vocal and instrumental styles, often combining the two with amazing versatility. Bach's individuality in an era where copying was accepted and encouraged is noteworthy. His works show striking originality, abundant fertility in thematic invention, and consummate mastery of all materials.

Much of the keyboard music written by Bach is obviously for organ since it makes use of the pedals, often as a distinct voice level in counterpoint to those parts played by the hands. The body of music that pianists play was designated by Bach as being for the *clavier,* a generic term that included any keyboard instrument. The stringed keyboard instruments available to Bach were the clavichord, the harpsichord, and the early piano. Although Bach is said to have preferred the clavichord, he probably used the harpsichord for concerted music. The early piano was an instrument Bach encountered rather late in life. The piano builder Gottfried Silbermann claimed to have offered an instrument to Bach sometime after 1730, but Bach criticized it as having a weak upper register and action that was too heavy. According to Silbermann, an improved instrument met with Bach's complete approval when the composer inspected those owned by Frederick the Great on the occasion of a visit to Carl Philipp Emanuel, who was serving as a clavecinist to Frederick at Potsdam.

Only a few of Bach's keyboard works were published during his lifetime. The six partitas appeared intermittently in very limited editions, no. 1 in 1726, nos. 2 and 3 in 1727, no. 4 in 1728, and nos. 5 and 6 in 1730. In 1731, the plates of the partitas were reprinted together as the *Clavierübung I. Clavierübung II* was issued in 1735 and contained the *Concerto nach italiänischen Gusto* (Italian Concerto) and the *Ouvertüre nach französischer Art* (Overture in the French Manner, often referred to as the Partita in *b*). *Clavierübung III* (1739) was devoted to the Catechism Chorale Preludes for organ, and *Clavierübung IV* (1742) was the *Aria mit verschiedenen Veränderungen* (Goldberg Variations). It might be mentioned in passing that two of Bach's late masterworks, the *Musical Offering* (1747) and the *Art of Fugue* (1750), were also published quite early. The *Art of Fugue* was published posthumously and, it might be added, somewhat carelessly by Bach's sons. It was reissued by Carl Philipp in 1752, but shortly thereafter the plates were disposed of for their value as metal inasmuch as only thirty copies of the work had been sold!

In 1850, the Bach-Gesellschaft (BG) was founded in Leipzig to issue a complete critical edition of Bach's works. The project was well intentioned, and the handsomely bound volumes looked impressive. A high degree of inaccuracy throughout the undertaking, however, resulted in considerable criticism from Bach scholars. The society was dissolved in 1900 after the last of the forty-six volumes was published, but the organization was immediately reconstituted as the Neue Bach-Gesellschaft, its purpose being to popularize Bach's music and promote continuing research. An important catalogue of Bach's works was published by Wolfgang Schmieder (b. 1901) in 1950 as the *Bach-Werke-Verzeichnis*. Programs that document performances of Bach's works often use the numbering from this catalogue, designating the entry with either S. (Schmieder) or BWV (*Bach-Werke-Verzeichnis*).

Bach's keyboard works exhibit a large variety of types, encompassing most of the styles of his day. Many works were written as teaching pieces for members of his family or students. Some compositions are of interest primarily because they foreshadow later, more important works and serve as examples of Bach's development. Bach was an inveterate transcriber of the works of others, as well as his own. Some compositions posthumously ascribed to Bach were later discovered to have been written by predecessors or contemporaries. Moreover, exact ordering of Bach's keyboard works is often difficult to determine, especially among those pieces thought to be written during the early part of his career. (In the following discussion, both the location of the music in the Bach-Gesellschaft edition—by volume and page number—and the Schmieder thematic index number are noted in parentheses.)

The most frequently encountered work from the Arnstadt and Mühlhausen years (1703–8) is the *Capriccio on the Departure of His Beloved Brother* (BG 36, 155; S. 992). A programmatic work in six short sections, it describes the departure of Bach's brother, Johann Jacob, to join the Swedish army of Charles II as an oboist. The descriptive titles are: (1) "Friendly Attempts at Dissuasion"; (2) "Dangers" (represented by much ornamentation); (3) "Lamentation" (chaconne bass); (4) "Leave-taking"; (5) "Postilion's Horn Call"; and (6) "Fugue" (a short fugue with a subject based on the postilion's horn call). The work is slight but charming, somewhat reminiscent of the *Biblical Sonatas* of Kuhnau.

During Bach's second period in Weimar (1708–17), the composer produced several significant keyboard works. The *Aria variata alla maniera Italiana* (BG 36, 203; S. 989) presents a slow, two-part theme, followed by ten figural variations, ending with a lyrical variation in four voices. Also, five of the seven clavier toccatas were written during this period. The Toccata in *D* (BG 36, 26; S. 912) opens with a free, fantasy-like section. Following are a jaunty section in concerto grosso style, an adagio, a free-style transition, and a final fugue. The Toccata in *d* (BG 36, 36; S. 913) is in four sections, the second and fourth being long fugues. The fugue of the second section uses a figure that may have been borrowed from the *Capriccio on the Departure of His Beloved Brother.* The Toccata in *e* (BG 36, 47; S.914) is one of the more popular of the toccatas. It opens with a contemplative, improvisatory section. There follow a ricercare-like fugue, a recitative-like interlude, and a final fugue of three voices in perpetual motion that builds to an effective, climactic closing. The Toccata in *g* (BG 36, 54; S. 915) opens with a figural flourish and an adagio. The following sections consist of a fugal allegro in *B-flat* that suggests the style of Handel, a second adagio, and a long, closing fugue that features a gigue-like subject. The Toccata in *G* (BG 36, 63; S. 916) contains but three sections: a cheerful, opening allegro; an expressive, imitative adagio; and a final fugue.

The final two toccatas come from the Cöthen period (1717–23). It was in Cöthen and Leipzig that Bach produced the greatest number of masterworks for clavier, ranging from relatively easy teaching pieces to works that require mature technical control and expressive flexibility. The Toccata in *f-sharp* (BG 3, 311; S. 910) opens with a bravura introduction (Example 4.1) It is followed by an expressive adagio; a section in a rapid, imitative toccata style; and a final ricercare-like fugue. The Toccata in *c* (BG 3, 322; S. 911) contains three basic sections: an improvisatory opening, an expressive adagio, and a long, double fugue in three voices. The work ends with elaborate flourish, incorporating both a short adagio section and a final rapid, descending run.

Example 4.1 Johann Sebastian Bach: Toccata in *f-sharp*, S. 910, mm. 1–2

Written at Cöthen were the sets of pieces known as the "English" Suites (BG 13[2], 3; S. 806–11) in *A, a, g, F, e,* and *d* and the "French" Suites (BG 12[2], 89; 45[1], 89; fragment in 36, 229; S. 812–17) in *d, c, b, E-flat, G,* and *E.* The first five "French" Suites appear as teaching material in the 1722 version of Anna Magdalena's *Clavierbüchlein.* The designations of "English" and "French" were not given by Bach and are somewhat misleading. The suites contain the types of pieces associated with French clavecin composers with even the use of the French names allemande, courante, sarabande, gigue, and so forth. The conceptual unity of the suites, however, follows the thinking of Froberger, and the ordering of the movements elaborates on the pattern used by Froberger's publisher and other German composers (ACSOG). The dates of composition of the suites have not been determined, but it is generally believed that the "English" Suites were written before the "French" Suites.

All of the "English" Suites present a prelude before the allemande. The preludes of nos. 2–6 are lengthy pieces that contain both imitative sections and figural sequences reminiscent of Italian-style orchestral writing of the period. The prelude of the first "English" suite is more modest and is along the lines of those found in the *Well-Tempered Clavier.* It uses, incidentally, a gigue-like theme that some scholars believe to have been borrowed, the material showing similarity to gigues of both Charles Dieupart (b. after 1667–ca. 1740) and Gaspard Le Roux (b. after 1650–ca. 1705).

The dance movements are almost always cast in two-part form, each part sharing the same thematic materials and each marked to be repeated. Modulation to the dominant typically occurs somewhere near the end of the first part. The second part returns to the tonic, usually closing with material heard near the end of the first part.

The allemande comes first in the sequence of dances, the name itself derived from a French designation for Germany. Bach's allemandes exhibit typical characteristics of the dance as it evolved from the seventeenth century: figural writing in broken counterpoint, the use of duple meter to be played at a moderate tempo, each section opening with an upbeat.

The courante or corrente is a more rapid dance that usually comes after the allemande, its name coming from the French verb meaning "to run." Two styles of this dance, French and Italian, have been identified. The French courante is used in all of the "English" Suites and two of the "French" Suites (*d* and *b*). This style typically makes use of a compound meter and a broken contrapuntal texture. Bach consistently employed a time signature of three-two with the exception of the courante in the *b* "French" Suite, where six-four is used. These signatures offer opportunities for shifting groups of beats in hemiola-like patterns. Bach adhered to subdividing each measure into three parts most of the time, with strong beats on the counts of one, three, and five. At cadence points, however, he consistently shifts the emphasis to subdivisions of two, with strong beats on one and four. By contrast, the Italian corrente uses a simple triple meter, Bach employing three-four in the four examples in the "French" Suites. The texture of the corrente is much less complex, usually featuring rapid, running figurations in two-part counterpoint. Although the two words *courante* and *corrente* are sometimes used to designate the two styles, observation of the different spelling cannot be depended upon as a reliable guide to the style of the music, for publications have often used the terms interchangeably without regard for the music itself. The "English" Suite in *A* includes two variants of its courante; these variants are more highly ornamented versions of the same piece and are designated *doubles* by Bach.

The sarabande served as the slow movement of the suite. Originally from Persia via Spain, the dance was condemned by several writers of the early sixteenth century, including Cervantes, because of its suggestive nature. Its character changed about 1600 to that of a slower, more dignified dance. Typically it is in triple time and uses long notes on the second or third beats of the measure, giving a graceful but halting effect. The slow, expressive nature of the sarabande invites ornamentation, and Bach provided written-out ornamented versions in the "English" suites, in *a* and *g* as well as in *d,* where the ornamented version is called a double.

For the so-called optional dances that are presented between the sarabande and the final gigue, Bach frequently turned to the bourrée, in quick duple meter with probable origins in the French province of

Auvergne; the gavotte, in duple meter and popularized in France in the mid-seventeenth century by Lully; the minuet, in moderate three-four meter and fashionable in the court of Louis XIV; and the passepied, a fast dance in three-eight or six-eight meter, said to have come from the Bretagne province of France. Less frequently used are the anglaise, usually in quick duple time; aire, its title suggesting a songlike rather than dance-like character; loure, in a moderate six-four meter with dotted rhythms; and the polonaise, the early version of the Polish court dance in three-four meter that later became a heroic symbol of Polish nationalism in the hands of Chopin and Liszt.

The gigue, like the courante or corrente, has been identified as having a French and an Italian type. The French type is the one usually associated with the final movement of the suite. It typically uses meters that accommodate triplet-like figuration, such as three-eight, six-eight, twelve-eight, or twelve-sixteen. Only twice, in the "French" Suite in *d* and the later Partita in *B-flat*, does Bach use duple meter, and in both cases alternate notation is devised to maintain triplet-like movement in the music. Imitative fugue-like entrances at the opening of the first section make the gigue easy to distinguish. Often the inversion of the subject-like figure serves to open the second section. The Italian type, sometimes called giga, is much less contrapuntal in concept, featuring triplet figuration in continuous motion with some kind of simple accompanying part. Only two examples can be cited in Bach's keyboard works, the gigues of the "English" Suite in *a* and the Partita in *B-flat*.

From the Cöthen period comes also the first version of the *Chromatic Fantasia and Fugue* in *d* (ca. 1720), later revised in Leipzig (ca. 1730; BG 36, 71 and 219; S. 903). The opening section of the fantasia presents an array of dramatic, improvisatory figurations that build to a sonorous cadence on the dominant about halfway through the piece. Thereafter is a series of recitative-like fragments that employ daring harmonic shifts. A moving codetta features a series of descending diminished-seventh harmonies over a pedal point on D. The fugue that follows is built on a subject that contains a motive of four rising, chromatic notes (Example 4.2). The fugue continues in three voices and builds to a powerful, concluding climax.

Finally from the Cöthen period comes much of the easier but well-known didactic material. Anna Magdalena's *Clavierbüchlein* (1722 version) contains the first five "French" Suites and several other pieces,

Example 4.2 Johann Sebastian Bach: *Chromatic Fantasia and Fugue*, S. 910 mm. 1–7 of fugue

including an organ fantasia in *C* (BG 38, 209; S. 573) and an air with variations (BG 43, 2 and 4; S. 991). Of considerable interest is Wilhelm Friedemann's *Clavierbüchlein* (BG 36, 118; 1720–21). Written as study material for Bach's oldest son when the boy was ten, the volume explains ornaments, these examples being the only preserved record of Bach's realization as well as the only extant example of Bach's fingering. The pieces that followed were arranged in order of difficulty. The volume contains the fifteen two-part inventions (called *Preambulae*), fourteen of the three-part inventions (called *Fantasias*), seventeen preludes, of which eleven were later used in the first volume of the *Well-Tempered Clavier,* and miscellaneous pieces, some by other composers. The manuscript of Wilhelm Friedemann's *Clavierbüchlein* was purchased by the Yale School of Music in 1939.

The fifteen two-part and fifteen three-part inventions (BG 3, 1; S. 772–86 and 787–801; 1720–23) bear the following inscription: "Upright Instruction wherein the lovers of the clavier, and especially those desirous of learning are shown a clear way not alone (1) to learn to play clearly in two voices, but also after further progress, (2) to deal correctly and well with three *obbligato* parts; furthermore, at the same time not alone to have good *inventions* [ideas], but to develop the same well, and above all to arrive at a singing style in playing and at the same time to acquire a strong foretaste of composition. Provided by Joh. Seb. Bach, Capellmeister to his Serene Highness the Prince of Anhalt-Cöthen. Anno Christi 1723."

The term *invention* was likely borrowed from Francesco Antonio Bonporti (1672–1749), whose Op. 10 consisted of ten inventions for various stringed instruments and continuo. Four of Bonporti's inventions, for violin and continuo, were mistakenly attributed to Bach and included in the complete works (BG 45[1], 172).

The order of each set of Bach's inventions follows the ascending scale from C to B, alternating parallel major and minor, with keys that use more than four flats or sharps being omitted, as is *f-sharp*. A single motivic idea introduces each piece and serves as the basis for the imitation and transposition that follow. Overall, Bach exhibits a wide variety of styles and techniques in these miniature teaching pieces. Canonic passages are featured in the two-part inventions in *c* and *B-flat*. Syncopation between the two voices is the hallmark of the two-part Invention in *E*. Chromaticism is highly evident in the three-part Invention in *f*. Giguelike figurations form the basis of the two-part Invention in *G* and the three-part Invention in *E*. The three-part Invention in *E-flat* lays down a framework for elaborate, ornamental decoration. Several inventions seem essentially lyrical in nature, such as the two-part in *E* or the three-part in *e*, *g*, and *B-flat*. It is often possible to trace a similarity in mood between the two-part and three-part inventions in the same key, such as the jocular, concerto grosso energy of both pieces in *F*.

The first volume of the *Well-Tempered Clavier* (BG 14, 1 and 45[1], 216; S. 846–69; 1722) also comes from the Cöthen period. Its title page contains the following inscription: "The Well-Tempered Clavier of Preludes and Fugues through all the tones and semitones both as regards the *tertia major* or *Ut Re Mi* and as concerns the *tertia minor* or *Re Mi Fa*. For the Use and Profit of the Musical Youth Desirous of Learning as well as for the Pastime of those Already Skilled in this Study drawn up and written by Johann Sebastian Bach, Capellmeister to His Serene Highness the Prince of Anhalt-Cöthen, etc., and Director of His Chamber Music, Anno 1722."

The title and contents of the work show Bach's endorsement of the twelve-tone chromatic system and "equal temperament," a compromise tuning in which intervals were not "pure" or acoustically correct, as were those found in Pythagorean tuning and just intonation. There were several systems of "unequal" temperament already in use, such as the mean-tone tunings defined by Schlick in 1511 and Salinas in 1577. These made it possible to play in most keys, but keys that were furthest removed from the key around which the tuning was constructed were apt to sound badly out of tune. The theory behind equal temperament was one that sought to spread the out-of-tune properties of remote keys throughout the system of keys by dividing the octave into twelve equal parts. By using this device, it became possible to play in all keys, albeit all were out of tune to the same small degree. Proposals for equal temperament are traceable to the work of Grammateus (1518), Tsai-ye (1596), and Mersenne (1635).

It is probable that Bach used Johann Kasper Ferdinand Fischer's *Ariadne musica* (1702) as a model for the first volume of the *Well-Tempered Clavier*, for there is a high degree of similarity in the two works between the style and mood of the pieces in a given key. Fischer used only nineteen keys, and his pieces were considerably smaller and less developed, often being extended only a few measures past the presentation of an opening motive. Bach, on the other hand, wrote structured pieces of significant length and used all twenty-four keys, arranging them in ascending chromatic order from *C* to *B*, placing parallel major and minor keys side by side.

Typically the preludes are built on a single idea, presented in the tonic key at the onset of the piece and then developed, using modulations to several closely related keys. There is always a return to the home key near the end of the piece, but Bach usually does not restate the opening material in such a way that it suggests a recapitulation or rounded structure. Several preludes present distinct sections. For example, no. 2 includes a more rapid presto section followed by a free, cadential recitative near its end. Number 10 begins as a songlike arioso but then presents the same material in a presto section. The toccata-like drive of the opening of no. 21 shifts midway through the piece to dramatic, recitative-like cadenzas. Only one prelude in the first volume is in two-part form, with the sections marked to be repeated (no. 24). Textures range from the use of simple chordal figuration, such as the famous opening prelude in *C*, to the use of broken-style counterpoint (nos. 4, 7, 12, 16, 18, 19, and 23). Often only two parts are used, similar to the texture of the two-part inventions (nos. 3, 11, 13, 15, 20).

The preludes offer a wide variety of styles, many of which have characteristics associated with other types of compositions. Several preludes suggest etudes, presenting toccata-like technical display (nos. 2, 3, 5, 6, 11, and 21). Others are more lyrical (nos. 4, 9, 12, 13, 16, 18, 19, and 24). At least two of the slower pieces suggest an emotional intensity reminiscent of Bach's religious works (nos. 8 and 22). A gigue-like character is suggested by the triplet figures of no. 15, and the vigor of no. 17 can be likened to that found in allegro movements of the concerto grosso.

Attempts to establish motivic connection between the preludes and fugues have been made, but if such a relationship exists it is not an obvious one. The fugues are usually monothematic, one subject serving most of the time to give unity to the piece. Fugues typically present a clearly defined exposition in which a subject with easily recognizable characteristics is stated in each voice. Expositions are followed by episodes based on fragments of the subject, countersubject, or other contrapuntal figuration that has been introduced in the exposition. Subject restatements appear periodically in one or another of the voices, often in closely related keys. Near the end of the fugue the tonic key is reestablished, sometimes emphasized with strong dominant pedal points or the appearance of the subject in stretto. Throughout the composition the observance of contrapuntal voice levels is usually fairly strict in that Bach almost never allows the texture to revert to a "broken" contrapuntal style or homophonic writing. Underlying harmonic patterns are clearly defined, the progressions being imaginative and often chromatic. Number 5 uses figuration and dotted rhythms suggesting a French overture. Although Bach does not indicate tempo markings, several fugues, all of them in minor keys, seem to be slow, serious pieces (nos. 4, 8, 12, 14, 18, and 22).

Only one fugue in the two volumes of the *Well-Tempered Clavier* is in two voices (1, no. 8), and two are in five voices (1, nos. 4 and 22). The other fugues use either three or four voices in almost equal division. In the first volume, there are nine "real" answers in the exposition (note-for-note entry of the subject in ensuing voices) and fifteen "tonal" answers (entries of ensuing voices with invervallic alteration). Mirror occurs in no. 6; augmentation in no. 8; stretti in nos. 1, 4, 6, and 8; melodic inversion in nos. 6, 14, 20, and 22; pedal point in nos. 1, 2, 4, and 20; the use of double counterpoint in nos. 7 and 10; and the use of triple counterpoint in nos. 3 and 21. Elaborate modulation occurs in no.

Example 4.3 Johann Sebastian Bach: *Well-Tempered Clavier I*, S. 869 mm. 1–3 of fugue

Example 4.4 Johann Sebastian Bach: *Well-Tempered Clavier II*, S. 872, mm. 1–2 of fugue

24. The subject of no. 12 uses nine of the twelve chromatic tones, the answer using the remaining pitches. The subject of no. 24 uses all twelve tones (Example 4.3).

The second volume of the *Well-Tempered Clavier* (BG 14, 91; S. 870–93; 1738–42) was completed almost twenty years later in Leipzig, but the concept and ordering of the pieces follow the same pattern used in the first volume. The preludes exhibit much the same stylistic quali-ties as those in the first volume but tend to be somewhat more extended with a more frequent use of a broken-contrapuntal style (nos. 1, 4, 5, 7, 9, 11, 14, 16, 19, 21, 22, and 23). Preludes nos. 8, 10, 13, 15, 20, and 24 are written in a two-voiced texture. Ten of the preludes are written in two-part structure, each part marked to be repeated (nos. 2, 5, 8, 9, 10, 12, 15, 18, 20, and 21). Prelude no. 3 is in two parts with the second part being a fughetta. Prelude no. 16 uses dotted rhythm that is reminiscent of French overture style. The chromaticism of no. 20 is worthy of note. Fugues, too, are similar to those of the first volume, fifteen in three voic-es and nine in four voices. Expositions use both "real" and "tonal" answers, twelve in each category. Examples of stretto occur in nos. 4, 5, 8, and 22; of inversion in nos. 2, 3, 4, 6, and 22; of diminution in nos. 3 and 9; augmentation in no. 2; and a case is sometimes made for a single example of retrograde in no. 3, where the brevity of the subject invites figural treatment (Example 4.4). A few fugues in the second volume introduce new motivic material somewhere well within the body of the piece, each voice taking up the new motive as if another exposition were being presented. The new material is at some later point combined with the original subject of the fugue. These so-called double fugues (or triple fugues, when the later exposition occurs twice) are represented by nos. 14, 18, and 23.

The second version of a *Clavierbüchlein* for Anna Magdalena was written at Leipzig (BG 43[2], 6; S. 933–43; 1725). It contained early versions of two of the partitas (nos. 2 and 6) as well as other teaching material, including the first prelude from the first volume of the *Well-Tempered Clavier,* chorales, arias, and pieces by Böhm and Couperin.

The six partitas (BG 3, 46; S. 825–30; 1731) were published during Bach's Leipzig period as *Clavierübung I.* Bach uses a format similar to that used by Kuhnau in the *Clavier Übungen* of 1689 and 1692. Based on the concept of the dance suite, Bach's six sets of pieces are in *B-flat, c, a, D, G,* and *e.* Each opens with an introductory movement: in order, praeludium, sinfonia, fantasia, ouverture, praeambulum, and toccata. The ouverture and sinfonia feature stately dotted rhythms typical of the French overture. The partitas each include an allemande, a courante, and a sarabande. All of them end with a gigue except no. 2, which concludes with a highly contrapuntal capriccio. The gigue of no. 1 is of the "Italian" type, featuring a figural pattern that requires constant crossing and uncrossing of the hands. Unusual optional movements also occur: a rondeau and caprice in no. 2 and a burlesca and scherzo in no. 3.

A partita in *b* was published as part of *Clavierübung II* (BG 3, 154; S. 831; 1735). Known as the *French Overture,* its full title is *Ouvertüre nach französischer Art.* The pattern of its movements is even more free than those of the partitas. It opens with the overture from which it gets its title, a majestic dotted-rhythm adagio being followed by a fugal allegro. There follow a courante, two gavottes, two passepieds, a sarabande, two bourrées, a gigue, and an echo, a movement that exploits dynamic contrast to achieve its effect.

Published with the French Overture as part of *Clavierübung II* was the *Concerto nach italiänischen Gusto,* known by keyboard players simply as the *Italian Concerto* (BG 3, 139; S. 971; 1735). A keyboard adaptation of the orchestral concerto grosso, the work makes use of contrasting sections that are easily imagined as those of full orchestra (tutti) and solo instruments. The opening allegro presents a first theme adapted from a movement of a symphony in Georg Muffat's *Florilegium primum* (1695; Example 4.5). The second movement presents an extraordinary, longlined arioso melody over a continuo, ostinato-style bass figure. The final movement features an exuberant ascending scale in its opening theme. Probably intended for a two-manual harpsichord, the *Italian Concerto* is filled with vigor and tuneful melodies. It has become a staple in the piano recital repertoire.

The *Clavierübung III* (1739) contains organ works, but four pieces in two-part called *Duets* (BG 3, 242; S. 802–5) work well on the piano and have thus found their way into the pianist's repertoire. Written in *e, F,*

Example 4.5 Johann Sebastian Bach: *Italian Concerto*, S. 971, mm. 1–4

Example 4.6 Johann Sebastian Bach: *Goldberg Variations*, S. 988, Aria mm. 1–4
Reprinted by permission of G. Schirmer, Inc.

G, and *a,* they are not unlike the two-part inventions in concept but present more elaborate contrapuntal complexities.

The so-called *Goldberg Variations* were published under the title *Aria mit verschiedenen Veränderungen* as *Clavierübung IV* (BG 3, 263; S. 988; 1742). The story of how the work came to be written is related by Bach's early biographer Forkel, and although its authenticity has been doubted, it has become well known. Johann Gottlieb Goldberg was a pupil of Bach and in the service of Count Kaiserling, a former Russian ambassador to the electoral court of Saxony. Kaiserling was ill and often sleepless, so he prevailed upon his harpsichordist, Goldberg, to play for him during his nights of insomnia. Kaiserling mentioned to Bach that he would like to have some soothing music for Goldberg to play during these times. Bach felt he could best fulfill this request with a set of variations. The count was so pleased that he rewarded Bach with a golden goblet filled with one hundred gold coins (*louis d'or*), and the count referred thereafter to the music as "his" variations.

The theme of the variations was written on a chaconne bass taken from a sarabande in Anna Magdalena's *Clavierbüchlein*. It presents a lyrical melody in two-part form, each marked to be repeated (Example 4.6). The variations that follow are set up in a recurring pattern: two free variations are followed by one constructed in canon. The free-style variations

Example 4.7 Johann Sebastian Bach: *Goldberg Variations*, S. 988, Var. 30, Quodlibet mm. 1–3
Reprinted by permission of G. Schirmer, Inc.

include a fughetta (no. 10), a French overture (no. 16), a lengthy adagio (no. 25), and a sarabande (no. 26). The nine canons that appear at every third variation (nos. 3, 6, 9, 12, 15, 18, 21, 24, and 27) are at intervals successively from the unison to the ninth. Thus, no. 3 is at the unison, no. 6 at the second, no. 9 at the third, and so on. The variations at the fourth and fifth feature contrary motion. The final variation is a quodlibet that combines two popular melodies with the chaconne theme (Example 4.7). Ten of the variations are written to be played on two manuals. The use of the second manual is optional in three more variations. For fifteen variations, a single keyboard is prescribed. Two variations lack specific directions.

There is a large body of miscellaneous pieces by Bach, the composition of which encompasses his entire career. Included are dance suites and movements of suites, written mostly in Cöthen and Weimar (S. 818–23, 832–33, 841–43); preludes and fugues (Cöthen and Weimar; S. 894–96, 900, 901–2); two fantasies and fugues in *a* and *c* (Leipzig; S. 904, 906); two very early fugues in *a* and *C* (S. 944 and 946); two fugues on themes by Albinoni in *A* and *b* (Weimar; S. 950–51); and two fugues, both in *a* (Weimar; S. 958–59). Pieces called sonatas (S. 963, 965–67) are often arrangements or adaptations of movements from the works of other composers, particularly those of Reinken. There are numerous preludes, fughettas, and short dance movements that appeared in the *Clavierbüchlein* written either for Anna Magdalena or Wilhelm Friedemann. Finally, there are over forty small keyboard pieces that bear Schmieder catalogue numbers but are of doubtful authenticity or have been deemed spurious.

CHAPTER FIVE

The Galant *Style*

The stature of Johann Sebastian Bach at the end of the Baroque tends to obscure changes that had been working their way into musical thought since the beginning of the eighteenth century. Bach pulled together and synthesized several diverse trends that had preceded him. Yet by the end of his life, he wrote in a style that was no longer in vogue, with the result that his work was minimized in the eyes of those composers who had kept pace with the times, including his own sons. The fact that there are only four decades between the death of Bach and the death of Mozart, when viewed with regard to the completely different styles their works represent, is somewhat inexplicable until it is supplemented with the understanding that many of the changes that eventually emerged as the Classic style had already begun during Bach's lifetime.

Even so, the changes in style appear to have been effected rather swiftly, and they present as complex and confused a pattern as might be found anywhere in the history of Western music. Different trends are evidenced in different countries, some of them growing gradually out of elements of the Baroque style, while others seemingly spring up in opposition to the old style, these usually being presented with appropriate aesthetic rationale. The period is populated with many composers whose actual musical significance may be assessed as relatively modest but whose historical contribution is important enough to warrant mention. There are other composers whose music is exceptional but who do not directly represent the mainstream of historical development. Finally, an overall picture of the period is somewhat clouded, because research, although blessed with an impressive beginning, is not yet complete. A more definitive evaluation of the relative importance of the diverse elements of the time is still in progress and ultimately may yield a more clearly defined picture.

Aesthetically, music joined hands with the philosophical trends of the day. The Muse was released completely from the necessity of performing religious, spiritual, or even serious duties. First priority was now given to providing entertainment and pleasure, a goal that had previously often been peripheral. Such music found its audience not only among the elegant court life but also gradually in a bourgeois public that patronized concerts. Opera had already attracted such an audience, but now that public became interested in instrumental music as well.

Composers rejected the learned counterpoint of the Baroque in favor of a much more homophonic style. An aesthetic code that called for a "return to nature" also demanded simple melodies. Although these were often profusely decorated with ornamentation, they were placed in the uppermost part of the texture, where they could be easily heard. Contrast was achieved through dynamic change.   Mood changes occurred more frequently, often within the framework of a single movement, a practice that differed from the Baroque preference of having but one "affection" in each movement.   Structurally, the sonata form emerged after much experimentation, sweeping the scene as the most important form not only for keyboard music but also for chamber and orchestral music.

The term *rococo* is often applied to this period, the word coming from the French *rocaille* and referring to shell work or in general to decorative, superficial elegance. The term *galant* was also used to describe the new style, especially the music of the French harpsichord composers, whose music will claim our attention first in the examination of changing trends.

France

François Couperin (1668–1733), sometimes referred to as *le Grand*, stands as a direct descendent of the clavecin school represented by Chambonnières and Louis Couperin. Born in Paris, François Couperin inherited the post of organist of St. Gervais from his father, Charles, while still in his teens. François held the post all of his life. His first musical studies were with his father, and later he studied with Jacques-Denis Thomelin, whom he succeeded as organist of the Chapelle Royale in 1693. François's career at the court of Louis XIV continued to flourish through the years, and periodically he received various titles and honors that proclaimed such lofty sentiments as being the king's keyboardist or the master of the clavecin for the children of the court.

Couperin is almost a generation earlier than Johann Sebastian Bach, but his music stands somewhere between the serious purposes of the German Baroque and the frivolity that has come to be associated with the rococo. His compositions are based on the principle of continued bass and frequently project a considerable degree of contrapuntal complexity. Voices are often handled quite freely, and the melody usually remains clearly in the uppermost line. Also present are much ornamentation and a fondness for descriptive titles aimed at being charming, witty, or fashionable.

Music for harpsichord is important in Couperin's overall output. His keyboard writing is imaginative and idiomatic, and in many of his pieces he uses a single motivic figure to establish a momentum that pervades an entire work. The range of moods presented is large, extending from simple homophonic dances to melancholy, cantabile songs, encompassing sophisticated wit and idyllic pastoral scenes.

The harpsichord works are arranged in twenty-seven suites, called *ordres* by Couperin. These were published originally in four volumes, each titled *Pièces de clavecin:* ordres 1–5 in 1713, 6–12 in 1717, 13–19 in 1722, and 20–27 in 1730. In 1733 a complete edition of the works of Couperin was published in Paris, edited by Maurice Cauchie and others. In this edition the harpsichord works appear in volumes 2–5. Each of the ordres contains from between four to twenty-three pieces, most of them in the same key, sometimes in closely related keys. Most pieces are in binary form, each part marked to be repeated.

Early ordres contain those dance-types usually associated with the suite: allemandes, courantes, sarabandes, and gigues interspersed with movements such as gavottes or rondeaus. Some of the pieces have descriptive titles. Later ordres phase out the use of familiar dance titles, substituting descriptive ones. Included are portraits of people, such as "La Princesse Marie" or "La Manon"; nature studies, represented by "Les Papillons" (Butterflies) or "Les Moucherons" (The Flies); and animated objects, such as "Le Bavolet flottant" (The Floating Bonnet; Example 5.1) or "Les Petits Moulins à vent" (The Little Windmills). Social commentary is behind the title "Les Fastes de la grande et ancienne Mxnxtrxndxsx." The last word should properly have been *menestrandes,* its corruption being an attempt to satirize a group of minstrels who were trying to force clavecin teachers to join their guild. Even abstract concepts are represented by "L'Ardeur" (Ardor) and "L'Esperance" (Hope).

One of Couperin's most important contributions is the influential treatise on harpsichord playing, *L'Art de toucher le clavecin* (The Art of Playing the Harpsichord; 1717). The volume contains directions for the execution of ornaments, a system of fingering, and eight preludes.

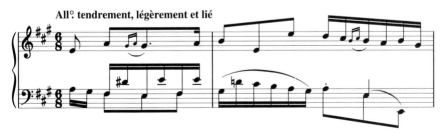

Example 5.1 François Couperin: "Le Bavolet flottant" mm. 1–2

Performance directions for the preludes state that, although measured, they are to be interpreted freely, as in the tradition of lute playing.

Jean-Philippe Rameau (1683–1764) had an unusual career in many ways. Born at Dijon, he received his early training there. As a youth he traveled to Italy and toured as a violinist. He held church organ posts at Avignon, Dijon, Lyons, and Clermont-Ferrand before finally settling in Paris in 1723. By this time, he had written his *Traité de l'harmonie* (1722), the work for which he is possibly most famous. As a theorist, Rameau is given credit for codifying the system of harmony that was to remain virtually unchallenged until the twentieth century, setting forth the concepts of building chords by using intervals of thirds, classifying chords and inversions, and clarifying root movement in harmonic progressions.

Rameau enjoyed a reputation of being the leading French organist of his day. After the age of forty, he began to compose opera, embarking on a career that gained him even greater fame in the eyes of his contemporaries. Rameau's contribution as a composer of harpsichord music is quite significant, notwithstanding the fact that he is remembered primarily as a theorist and as a composer of opera.

Rameau's harpsichord style is more intense, more virtuosic, of more serious purpose, and of heavier texture than that of François Couperin. Rameau is thus often deemed to be less galant than Couperin. Rameau's textures are more sonorous, foreshadowing idioms to be associated later with the piano. Most of Rameau's pieces follow the format of the dance suite, but he uses descriptive titles more sparingly than Couperin, never abandoning completely the inclusion of expected dance-types such as the allemande, courante, sarabande, an so forth. Most of Rameau's harpsichord music was published during his lifetime in three volumes. A complete edition of his works was edited by Camille Saint-Saëns, Charles Malherbe, and others (1895–1924, revised in 1968).

The first volume, *Livre de pièces de clavecin* (1706), contains only ten pieces: a prelude, two allemandes, courante, gigue, two sarabandes, "Venitienne," gavotte, and minuet. All are in the key of *a* except for the second sarabande, which is in *A*. A two-part texture is used for the pieces with the exception of the prelude, which is free and has an opening section without bar lines.

Pièces de clavecin avec une méthode pour la mécanique des doigts (Pieces for Harpsichord with a Method for Finger Technique; 1724, with reprints in 1731 and 1736) contains two sets of pieces, ten in *e* or *E*, eleven in *d* or *D*. The first set contains several dance-types and two descriptive pieces: "Le Rappel des oiseaux" (The Call of the Birds; Example 5.2) and "La Villageoise" (The Village Maid), the latter being designated a rondeau. The second set has five rondeaus, one minuet, and pieces with descriptive titles such as "Les Soupirs" (Sighs), "L'Entretien des muses" (The Discourse of the Muses), and "Les Cyclopes" (The Cyclopes).

Example 5.2 Jean-Philippe Rameau: "Le Rappel des oiseaux" mm. 1–3

The final volume, *Nouvelles suites de pièces pour clavecin avec des remarques sur les différents genres de musique* (New Pieces for Harpsichord with Remarks about the Different Styles of Music; 1731), contains two suites consisting of seven pieces in *a* or *A,* along with nine in *g* or *G.* These pieces represent the high point of Rameau's harpsichord music, for they are more extended and virtuosic than the previous sets. The first suite contains an allemande, a courante, and a sarabande, followed by descriptive pieces, and concluding with a gavotte and six variations. One of the descriptive pieces is "Les Trois Mains" (The Three Hands), in which virtuosic crossing of the two hands presumably gives the effect of having three. The second suite contains two minuets and descriptive pieces such as "La Poule" (The Hen) and "Les Sauvages" (The Savages), the latter having been used in his opera *Les Indes galantes* (The Galant Indians). The pedagogical material mentioned in the titles of the 1724 and 1731 sets of pieces presents short discussions of the use of fingers, wrists, and elbows as well as some general advice on matters of tempi and other points of interpretation.

A single piece, "La Dauphine" (1747), was published in honor of the bride of the Dauphin on the occasion of his second marriage. It is purported to be the only extant manuscript of a harpsichord piece by Rameau. In addition, five short pieces were transcribed from a suite for harpsichord, violin (or flute), and viol (or another violin). *Cinq pièces en concert reduites pour clavesin seul par l'auteur* (1741) is composed of rondeaus with descriptive titles such as "L'Agaçante" (The Provoking Girl), "La Timide" (The Timid Girl), and so forth.

Contemporary with Couperin and Rameau is a sizeable group of French composers whose harpsichord music follows along the same general lines. Many of this group lean even more toward frivolity, sometimes to the extent of producing music sometimes deemed insignificant. Such works are, however, representative of the period, and they occasionally appear on programs either as curiosities or to serve as light-hearted contrast to more serious offerings.

Perhaps the most interesting of this group was **Gaspard Le Roux** (d. after 1705). Although little is known of his life, he was apparently a celebrated musician in Paris during his time, functioning as an organist, clavecinist, and teacher. His harpsichord style is forward looking both harmonically and stylistically. Of interest is **Jean François Dandrieu** (1682–1738), who was born into a musical family and succeeded his uncle, Pierre Dandrieu, as organist of St. Barthélémy. His keyboard style is more accessible than that of Couperin or Rameau, but even so, he is able to retain much of their grace and elegance. **Louis-Claude Daquin** (1694–1772) is remembered especially for a piece entitled "Le Coucou" (The Cuckoo), one from a set of pieces published in 1735.

Other composers of this group may be mentioned in passing: **Louis Marchand** (1669–1732); **Louis-Nicolas Clérambault** (1676–1749); **Jean-Baptiste Loeillet** (1680–1730); **François Dagincourt** (1684–1758); **Louis-Antoine Dornel** (ca. 1685–1765), who is also remembered for having been selected over Rameau for the post of organist at Sainte-Madeleine en la Cité; **Joseph de Boismortier** (1691–1755), who published over a hundred opus numbers; **Charles Dieupart** (d. ca. 1740); and **Jacques Duphly** (1715–89).

Italy

A discussion of the keyboard music of Italy at this point in history needs to begin by dealing with the development of a new formal structure, the *sonata*. Not only was this form to become the most important in keyboard literature for the next period of music (as well as one of the most important right down to the present day), but also it ushered in new stylistic concepts. How pleasant it would be if so significant a form could emerge with clarity and tidiness. Unfortunately, such is not the case.

It has already been pointed out that the term *sonata* is related to that of *sonata da chiesa*. This relationship is exemplified by the use of four or more movements in a sequence of alternating slow and fast tempi. It was this multisectional concept that formed the point of departure for Kuhnau and other composers who first applied the term *sonata* to keyboard compositions.

There are, however, other connections. The sonata of the galant period often employed movements that have an internal form much like the binary form encountered in the Baroque dance suite: two parts, each marked to be repeated. This pattern eventually evolved into the first-movement form of the sonata, with sections labeled much later as exposition, development, and recapitulation. It is by means of this internal two-part structure that the sonata of the galant period is linked with another type of Baroque sonata, the *sonata da camera,* a type that was little more than a dance suite under a different name. The sonata da camera type in keyboard literature was usually called a suite or a partita by composers, but in chamber and solo string literature it frequently turns up as a sonata.

Still another ancestor of the sonata is the Italian operatic overture, associated with Alessandro Scarlatti and Neapolitan opera. This type of overture, which often went under the name *sinfonia,* consisted of three sections: fast, slow, fast; the last section was not a recapitulation of the first. This format was expanded into a pattern on which the sequence of movements in the sonata was based. These, in turn, influenced the development of the three-movement pattern of the Classical sonata.

Given these forerunners and a measure of imagination, it is not hard to believe that a form such as the sonata might very well have emerged. Tracing such an evolution, however, has been very difficult, for the lineage is one of great complexity, containing many experiments, deviations, and offshoots. Furthermore, even after a great deal of careful research, the main line of the sonata's development remains confused, and continuing research seems to add only new layers of detail on a picture that is already laden with diversity and inconsistency. Deeper understanding of this research problem thus remains a fascinating challenge.

(Giuseppe) Domenico Scarlatti (1685–1757) stands alone in this period as the outstanding Italian keyboard composer. Born in Naples, he received his early training from his famous father, Alessandro. By the time Domenico was sixteen, he was holding important organ posts in Naples. He was sent to Venice to study with Gasparini, and in 1709 he was in Rome, where he met Handel. The years until 1720 were spent in that city as maestro di cappella to Queen Maria Casimira of Poland and later to the Vatican. For his Polish employer, Scarlatti produced seven operas and an oratorio for production in the private theater in her palace in Rome. About 1720, Scarlatti left Rome, possibly to visit London for a production of one of his operas. He settled in Lisbon as the maestro of the royal chapel and music teacher to the Princess Maria Barbara. When Scarlatti's royal student married the heir to the Spanish throne in 1729, he accompanied her to Madrid, where he spent the rest of his life except for two short trips to Italy.

It was for the Princess Maria Barbara that Scarlatti composed the music for which he is remembered, the more than 550 keyboard works that we know as sonatas. The first appearance of these works was a publication of thirty of them as *Essercizi per gravicembalo* (1738). At this time Scarlatti was past fifty years of age, and recent research indicates that he wrote the bulk of his keyboard works in his late sixties and early seventies.

There are no original manuscripts of these works. The most important sources, aside from the early publication just mentioned, are manuscript collections that were copied for Maria Barbara. Fifteen such manuscript volumes are in Venice (containing 469 sonatas), and fifteen are in Parma (containing 463 sonatas). Various collections and reprints appeared in the nineteenth century, but it was not until 1906 that a complete edition of the sonatas was forthcoming. At that time Alessandro Longo edited the entire body of keyboard works, supplementing his work with a thematic index. Thus, for a time Scarlatti's sonatas were identified by L. numbers from Longo's chronological listing.

In 1953, Ralph Kirkpatrick published an extremely important study on the life and works of Scarlatti. Kirkpatrick established the fact that Longo's chronology was wrong to an extent that obscured Scarlatti's growth as a composer and compromised full appreciation of his stature. Furthermore, Kirkpatrick argued that 388 of the sonatas should be grouped in pairs in the same key, usually a slow sonata followed by a faster one. An additional 12 are to be grouped in triptychs. Kirkpatrick produced a new catalogue of the sonatas, one that uses K. numbers. Longo's working edition remains complete but is marred by the addition of the editor's dynamics, phrasing, and other markings. Kirkpatrick edited only sixty of the sonatas, but his work is exemplary. Since Kirkpatrick's work, other editors have followed his leadership, and various collections of critically edited sonatas have appeared.

Scarlatti used the binary form, each part marked to be repeated, almost invariably. Modulation takes place to the dominant before the first part ends, and the second part modulates back to the tonic. Occasionally, modulation to the parallel minor is substituted (L. 8; K. 461). Two or three thematic ideas, frequently closely related, are presented in the first section. The second section is usually modulatory before its return to the tonic. The return is effected early enough, so that one or two of the thematic ideas that appeared in the dominant in the first section can be restated in the tonic. The point in the structure at which the return to the tonic takes place has been designated by Kirkpatrick as the *crux*.

Scarlatti almost never uses a strict polyphonic texture, but motivic imitation frequently occurs (L. 452; K. 116), and the left-hand part often assumes a vital rhythmic role, even in monophonic sections (L. 359; K. 308). The left hand is often called upon to share in virtuosic display (L. 286; K. 427) or to provide accompanimental figuration of a quasi-melodic nature (L. 267; K. 52). Harmonic coloration in the form of notes added to chords sometimes creates bold dissonance, reminiscent of guitar effects (L. 429; K. 175; Example 5.3).

Example 5.3 Domenico Scarlatti: Sonata, K. 175, L. 429 mm. 1–4
Reprinted by permission of G. Schirmer, Inc.

Idiomatic characteristics include rapid scales, division of figuration between the hands (L. 461; K. 29), fast octaves, crossing of hands, execution of trills in a fast tempo (L. 241; K. 54), double notes, large skips, repeated notes (L. 215; K. 120), cadenza-like passages (L. 452; K. 116), profuse ornamentation in a rapid tempo (L. Supplement 24; K. 493), and connected melodic trills (L. 407; K. 115; Example 5.4). One could make a very long list of Scarlatti's keyboard devices, and many examples for each technique could be cited. Suffice it to say that Scarlatti was unusually imaginative in his use of idiomatic, virtuoso writing and that he helped establish the direction piano writing was to take. This fact is perhaps why Scarlatti sonatas remain so firmly established in the pianist's repertoire and why they are regarded as being so successful on the piano, notwithstanding the fact they were written for the harpsichord.

Within the framework of these sonatas, Scarlatti achieved a miraculous number of moods, traveling the entire gamut of musical expression. One finds moments of drama, grandeur, and brilliance as well as tenderness, serenity, and simplicity. The sonatas provide a seemingly inexhaustible source of fresh and compelling musical ideas, one that even today is far from being fully explored by keyboard performers.

Although the other Italian keyboard composers of the period did not come close to the genius of Scarlatti, their work is significant in that it exemplified the move toward the Classical sonata. Some wrote music that has a respectable degree of interest. Others wrote music that was unimaginative and shallow. The less gifted Italian composers are

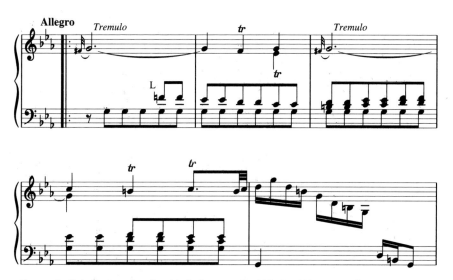

Example 5.4 Domenico Scarlatti: Sonata, K. 115, L. 407 mm. 47–51
Reprinted by permission of G. Schirmer, Inc.

usually cited as evidence whenever this period is criticized adversely. It is certainly true that many composers wrote works that seldom present an unexpected turn of melody, use stereotypical accompanimental figuration, and are mostly homophonic. Some of these composers, however, have not been explored in enough depth to determine if such writing represents them adequately. Moreover, even some of the less original compositions can serve as instructional pieces, adding acceptable alternatives to an overly familiar menu.

Azzolino Bernardino Della Ciaia (1671–1755) does not represent the *galant* style but rather used an earlier, more polyphonic texture. His six sonatas (1727) are in four sections, resembling toccatas.

Francesco Durante (1684–1755) published a volume of sonatas using the subtitles of etudes and divertimenti (1732). The etudes are imitative, and the divertimenti are in a fast virtuosic style.

Benedetto Marcello (1686–1739) was a man of many careers: lawyer, politician, poet, librettist, writer on the arts, and composer. His twenty sonatas follow the da chiesa pattern, using three, four, and five movements. They are of an unusually fine quality (Example 5.5).

Domenico Zipoli (1688–1726) centered his career first in Rome and then moved to Argentina, where he became organist at the Jesuit church in Cordoba. Sonatas for organ or harpsichord (1716) are of the da camera (dance suite) type.

Giovanni Benedetto Platti (1690–1763) spent his career in Germany at the court at Würzburg. He is one of the earliest composers to use the sonata-allegro structure in the sonata. Of his eighteen sonatas, twelve are based on the four-movement da chiesa type (slow-fast-slow-fast tempi). One sonata is of the da camera type, an opening allegro being followed by a sarabande, minuet, and gigue. The remainder are

Example 5.5 Benedetto Marcello: Sonata no. 7, lst movt. mm. 1–2

in three movements, following the pattern of the Italian operatic overture (fast-slow-fast tempi). Of these the first movements are in sonataallegro form with rather free developments and full recapitulations.

Giovanni Battista Pescetti (ca. 1704–66) wrote nine sonatas, of which six were published in London (1737). They are three-movement works with elements of fugal writing reminiscent of an earlier style.

Giovanni Battista Martini (1706–84) was a Franciscan padre who became maestro di cappella at the church of San Francesco in Bologna. He became one of the most famous musicians of the eighteenth century, not only as a composer but also as a teacher and author. Johann Christian Bach and Mozart were among his pupils, and he wrote two works well known in their day: *Esemplare ossia saggio fondamentale practico di contrappunto* (1774–75), a counterpoint text; and *Storia della musica* (1761–81), a three-volume history of ancient music. Martini wrote two collections of keyboard sonatas. The first set (1742) contains twelve that combine traits of both da chiesa and da camera types. In the second collection (1747) of six sonatas, three movements are used for each: fastslow-fast (Example 5.6).

Baldassare Galuppi (1706–85) was called *Il Buranello* after the island of his birth, Burano (near Venice). He was active in London and St. Petersburg, finally settling in Venice, where he was the principal maestro at San Marco. A prolific composer, he is believed to have written over ninety keyboard sonatas. Most remain in manuscript, but two sets were published by Walsh in London (1756 and 1759). The sonatas appear in any number of movements from one to five, but three-movement works are used most, a cantabile opening movement being followed by two faster, moderately virtuosic movements of light texture.

Domenico Paradisi (1707–91) achieved fame as an operatic composer in Italy before moving to London (1747), where he devoted the remainder of his career to teaching harpsichord. Twelve sonatas were published in London (1754) and Amsterdam (1770). They are in a twomovement pattern, either slow-fast or fast-fast, each movement in binary form.

Example 5.6 Giovanni Battista Martini: Sonata no. 2 (1742 set), lst movt. mm. 1–2

Domenico Alberti (ca. 1710–40) was a Venetian composer, harpsichordist, and singer, especially celebrated in London. His name is well known because it became curiously attached to the broken chord accompaniment pattern widely in use at the time, although the *Alberti bass* was probably not created single-handedly by Alberti. His eight sonatas published in London (1748) are usually in two movements, each using binary form.

Giovanni Marco [Giovanni Maria, Giovanni Placido] Rutini (1723–97) was a Florentine composer who traveled to Russia with an opera company managed by Giovanni Locatelli. He returned to Florence in 1761, settling there. It is estimated that he wrote as many as sixty sonatas. The set of six published in Prague (1748) exhibit binary forms, stereotypical figurations, and other expected *galant* traits.

Giovanni Maria Grazioli (1746–ca. 1802) became first organist of San Marco in Venice in 1785. He wrote two sets of six sonatas, all of them in three movements (fast-slow-fast). There are full recapitulations in some of them.

Ferdinando Gasparo Turini (ca. 1749–ca. 1812) was born in Prague, where his father was a court musician to Emperor Rudolf II. The emperor took an interest in Ferdinando, supporting his musical training in Venice and Rome. Turini became organist of Santa Giustina in Padua. The six sonatas of 1780 and the twelve of 1804 are more brilliant and imaginative than the norm (Example 5.7).

Domenico Cimarosa (1749–1801) was a famous Neapolitan composer of *opera buffa*. He went to Russia at the invitation of Catherine II (1791), later becoming Kapellmeister to the Austrian court in Vienna. He wrote thirty-two sonatas: one-movement, homophonic works of light texture.

Luigi Cherubini (1760–1842) was one of the most celebrated composers of his time, both in England and Europe. His career centered on the operatic scene in Paris, where he enjoyed enormous success as a composer. His six sonatas are in two movements, a sonata-allegro first movement followed by a rondo.

Finally, in passing, the name **Lodovico Giustini** (1685–1743) might be mentioned, for he wrote what is believed to be the earliest piano music, a set of twelve *Sonate da cimbalo de piano e forte detto volgarmente di martellati,*

Example 5.7 Fernando Turini: Sonata no. 4 (1780 set), lst movt. mm. 1–3

Op. 1 (1732). The works are in four or five movements, alternating slow and fast movements in the da chiesa style, but with the use of da camera style dance titles. The music itself is moderately distinguished. The score abounds in dynamic markings and uses every note from B to c *'''*.

Spain and Portugal

There exists a rather large hiatus between the keyboard music of six-teenth-century Spain and Portugal and the harpsichord school of the eigh-teenth century. That gap is filled somewhat by composers who wrote for the organ, such as **Juan Cabanilles** (1644–1712). Even so, there is rela-tively little information at the present time about the type and extent of keyboard music. It would appear that Domenico Scarlatti was the igniting spark, at least in the area of music for stringed keyboard instruments. Virtually nothing of significance is known about the harpsichord and clavi-chord music of the Iberian peninsula before his appearance on the scene. After Scarlatti, we have a handful of composers, some of whom were his students, who were influenced by him and who followed in his footsteps.

(José Antonio) Carlos de Seixas (1704–42) worked in Lisbon, writing sonatas, toccatas, minuets, and fugues. He used the term *toccata* for single movements similar to Scarlatti sonatas. His sonatas are sometimes single movements, too, but often works of between two and five movements.

Antonio (Francisco Javier José) Soler (Ramos) (1729–83) was the most significant of Scarlatti's successors. He studied with Scarlatti, and in 1752 he took holy orders at the monastery of the Escorial, where he spent the rest of his life. He wrote over one hundred single-movement sonatas, patterned after those of Scarlatti. Some are in groups of two or three. They are imaginative, delightful, and of high quality.

Manuel Blasco de Nebra (ca. 1750–ca. 1787) has remained almost completely obscure, for nothing is known of his life except that he was the organist at the cathedral in Seville. His only extant work is a set of six sonatas, each in two movements in a slow-fast arrangement. The movements are all in binary form, and, although they show considerable Scarlatti influence, they also sometimes exhibit the use of the longer, singing lines associated with Classicism.

Other Spanish and Portuguese composers of the late eighteenth and early nineteenth centuries are **Padre Rafael Angeles** (ca. 1731–1816), **Padre Narciso Casanovas** (1747–94), **Padre Felipe Rodiquez** (1758–1814), **Padre José Galles** (1781–1836), and **Sousa Carvalho** (d. 1798).

Germany and Central Europe

Although Italian and French composers led the way in the devel-opment of the galant style and the new structure of the sonata form, composers of northern and central Europe—notably those of Germany and Austria—effected various conceptual changes that resulted in a fully developed Classical style. Italy was still considered the artistic fountain-head by musicians in northern Europe, but the adoption of Italian practice took place with alterations that eventually proved to be quite significant. The seriousness of purpose and expressive intensity of the Baroque, although eschewed in theory by some, were, nevertheless, retained in practice by many composers in northern Europe as they adopted the new style and form. Thus, in the hands of these musicians the sonata became a longer, weightier composition, infused with expressive elements. Although the picture is far from one of uniform development, the ground was prepared for the emergence of the style and structure associated with Haydn and Mozart.

As was the case in Italy, there are composers who wrote in the "old" style, those whose work is a mixture of the old and the new, and those who concentrated on pushing as far ahead into the development of the "new" style as they could. Attention is once again drawn to the overlapping between the career of Johann Sebastian Bach, who is thought of traditionally as the end of the Baroque, and those of the first group of composers about to be considered, many of whom are contemporary with Bach and some of whom were born before him. As one might expect, those composers born before the turn of the eighteenth century represent, for the most part, a continuation of the traditional style.

Johann Joseph Fux (1660–1741) was an Austrian composer and theorist known primarily as the author of a treatise on counterpoint, *Gradus ad Parnassum* (1725). The treatise was widely studied by composers, including Haydn and Mozart. Fux wrote more than four hundred extant works in all forms, but most of them remain unpublished. For harpsichord there are four suites and seven sonatas. The sonatas are in two or three movements, often using a fast-slow-fast pattern. Fux, however, clung to the "old" style, making use of contrapuntal textures.

Johann Mattheson (1681–1764) was a German composer, writer, linguist, student of law, and director of music at the cathedral in Hamburg. He wrote extensively about music, including an early biography of Handel, a personal friend, and a biographical dictionary of musicians. As a composer, Mattheson wrote operas, oratorios, cantatas, harpsichord music, and sonatas for flute and violin. His style is "old," that is, contrapuntal. His harpsichord music is represented in *Harmonisches Denkmahl* (Harmonic Monuments; 1714), a set of twelve suites; and in *Die wohlklingende Fingersprache* (The Nicely Singing Finger-touch), a two-volume work (1735 and 1737) that contains twelve preludes and fugues. He also wrote a sonata for harpsichord (1713) as well as one for two harpsichords (1705).

Georg Philipp Telemann (1681–1767) was mostly self-taught. His distinguished career culminated as the Kapellmeister of the city of Hamburg (1721). As a composer he was incredibly prolific in all genres, having composed forty operas, forty-four passions, and about six hundred overtures. His harpsichord music shows elements of the "new" style without being entirely *galant*. It reflects both Italian and French influences. Representative are his *Fantasies pour le clavecin: Trois douzaines* (1732–33), a work that contains pieces of two or three voices in three or four sections. *Da capo* was often used in the three-section pieces, sometimes the next fantasie being really the B section of the one that immediately precedes it.

(Johann) Christoph Graupner (1683–1760) was trained in Leipzig and became Kapellmeister to Landgrave Ernst Ludwig of Hesse-Darmstadt. He is noted for having been offered the position at the Thomasschule in Leipzig (1722) before it was offered to Bach. Many of Graupner's works are still in manuscript or have been lost. He wrote about 50 concertos, over 80 overtures, 113 symphonies, and over 1,400 sacred works. Graupner wrote several sets of *Partien* (partitas) for harpsichord (1718, 1733, 1735, 1738, and 1740), using the expected order of dances but adding many optional dances after the sarabande and sometimes omitting the gigue. The dances are usually short and homophonic. Other harpsichord works include sets called *Monatliche Klavier Früchte* (Monthly Keyboard Fruits; 1722) and *Leichte Clavier Übungen* (Easy Keyboard Exercises; 1730).

Gottlieb (Theophil) Muffat (1690–1770) was the son of a well-known Austrian musician, Georg Muffat, studied with Fux, and spent his career as a court musician in Vienna. His *72 Wersetlsamt 12 Toccatas* (Seventy-two Versetl Followed by Twelve Toccatas; 1726) presented twelve toccatas followed by six very short fugues. The work was probably intended for organ and use in church, but the composer noted that it could also be used as a pedagogical aid for keyboard students. *Componimenti musicali peril cembalo* (1735–39) consists of six suites (ACSOG) and a chiacone. Each suite opens with a long movement called either overture, prelude, or fantasie. The music is heavily ornamented in the French style, and a composer's table of ornaments is supplied.

Johann Adolf Hasse (1699–1783) was a German composer known primarily for opera. He studied in Italy with Porpora and Alessandro Scarlatti. Hasse enjoyed an international career, finally settling in Dresdcn as the director of opera. In addition to writing for voice and theater, he wrote a significant amount of instrumental music. Six harpsichord sonatas were published in London (1758), and eleven other sonatas are known to exist, as well as a toccata and two other small pieces. His style of writing is very *galant*, possibly the result of his Italian training. About half of the sonatas are in the expected three-movement pattern (fast-slow-fast). Others are in two or four movements.

Johann Peter Kellner (1705–72) was from Thuringia, where he was Kantor at Gräfenroda. His work has been somewhat neglected in view of its apparent excellence. His style is very galant. Two sets of suites exist. *Certamen Musicum bestehend aus Preludien, Fugen, Allemanden* (1739–49) presents six suites that use only the allemande from the traditional group of dances. *Manipulus Musices, oder eine Handvoll kurtzweiliger Zeitvertrieb vors Clavier* (Musical Ideas, or a Handful of Amusing Pastimes for Keyboard; 1753–56) is a set of four suites in which none of the traditional dances appears. Three sonatas written in 1752 have apparently been lost. Kellner's son, Johann Christoph (1736–1803), also wrote a few harpsichord pieces that reflect the *galant* style.

The sons of Johann Sebastian Bach occupy a key position in this period of German music. It is not surprising that they would be scrutinized carefully by historians, since they were the offspring of one of the greatest creators of Western music. Bach's sons provide, moreover, a focal point for observing the differences between the "old" style and the "new," for they themselves were consciously aware of the stylistic differences between their work and that of their father, regarding their father's mode as somewhat old-fashioned. Finally, although history has not accorded any one of them the same elevated position it has Johann Sebastian, each one of them was, nevertheless, a successful professional musician in his day. Each won some degree of recognition, ranging from the relatively great fame of Carl Philipp Emanuel to the more modest careers of his brothers.

Three of Johann Sebastian's sons contributed significantly to the area of keyboard music: Wilhelm Friedemann, Carl Philipp Emanuel, and Johann Christian. A fourth son, Johann Christoph Friedrich (1732–95), known as the "Bückeburg Bach" because his career centered on that city, may be mentioned only in passing. Although he wrote several sets of sonatas and about six dozen short pieces in a *galant* style, these works are very lightweight. Many of them were designated as *leichte* (easy) and were probably intended to be used as teaching material.

Wilhelm Friedemann Bach (1710–84) was the eldest son of Johann Sebastian. He studied with his father, with August Friedrich Graun, as well as at the Thomaschule and the University of Leipzig. He held positions at the Sophienkirche (1733) and later the Liebfrauenkirche (1742) in Dresden and at the Liebfrauenkirche in Halle (1746). Considered to be perhaps the most gifted of Johann Sebastian's sons, he never realized his full potential, partly due to psychological instability triggered by a continuing conflict between his own liberal beliefs and the conservative life-style imposed upon him by his position in Halle. He attempted unsuccessfully to change jobs, finally quit his position unexpectedly (1764), moved to Berlin without employment (1770), and thus committed himself and his family to a life-style plagued by an instable income and ultimately poverty.

Wilhelm Friedemann's style is a mixture of the "old" and the "new." For harpsichord he wrote nine sonatas, ten fantasias, twelve fugues, and twelve polonaises. The sonatas are usually in three movements. There

Example 5.8 Wilhelm Friedemann Bach: Sonata no. 7, lst movt. mm. 1–4

are two theme areas in the expositions, complete recapitulations, and the use of stereotyped figurations. These are combined with contrapuntal devices and some thematic figurations typical of the "old" style. His fugues are not as long or elaborate as those of Johann Sebastian. The polonaises include several in a slow tempo that exhibit great expressive qualities (Example 5.8).

Carl Philipp Emanuel Bach (1714–88) was the most influential of Johann Sebastian's sons. Having received his musical training from his father, Carl Philipp studied law at the University of Leipzig and Frankfurt an der Oder. He went to Berlin (1738), and shortly after (1740) he was appointed chamber musician and clavecinist to Frederick the Great, in whose service Carl Philipp Emanuel remained for nearly thirty years. Carl Philipp Emanuel's final position was that of Kantor at the Johanneum school and music director of the five principal churches in the city of Hamburg (1767), a position in which he succeeded his godfather, Telemann.

While in the service of Frederick the Great, Carl Philipp Emanuel published his important treatise on keyboard playing, *Versuch über die wahre Art das Clavier zu spielen* (Essay on the True Art of Playing Keyboard Instruments; part 1 in 1743; part 2 in 1762). This work not only brought Carl Philipp Emanuel into prominence in the keyboard world of his day but also continues to be an invaluable reference work for students who wish to understand the style and performance practice of eighteenth-century Germany. It contains discussions of style and ornamentation, exploration of technical matters such as fingering, and detailed instructions on the realization of figured bass.

Carl Philipp Emanuel was a prolific composer, having devoted himself to writing all types of instrumental and sacred vocal music. Writing for keyboard was obviously an important area for him, for his keyboard pieces number over four hundred, many of which are sonatas. More than any other single composer, Carl Philipp Emanuel forms a link between the *galant* style of Italy and the Classicism of Haydn and Mozart.

As one surveys the overall output of Carl Philipp Emanuel, it becomes obvious that he not only adopted wholeheartedly the ideas of the "new" style but also used the sonata as a vehicle for all kinds of experimental features of his own devising. His experiments included tempo changes within movements, recitative-like sections, cadenzas, unorthodox key relationships between first and second themes in expositions, and writing out variations of the repeated sections of the first-movement sonata form. Especially significant is the use of the slow middle movement as an expression of personal emotion.

Carl Philipp Emanuel is associated with a movement in Germany at this time that valued emotional sensitivity in the arts. The terms *Empfindsamkeit* or *empfindsamer Stil* refer to this outpouring of expressiveness. Artists of all types tried to formulate a "natural" means of expressing human emotions, even going so far as classifying them. Thus, in music, each phrase, each element was to represent one or another emotion. Such expressiveness was intended to evoke gentle tears of melancholy during a performance. Carl Philipp Emanuel's scores abound in dynamic markings, and contemporary accounts of his playing refer to his remarkable range of dynamics, his subtle handling of phrasing, and the emotional manner he was able to project.

Carl Philipp Emanuel's favorite instrument was reported to have been the clavichord, possibly because of the expressive qualities of the *Bebung,* the vibrato generated by moving the key in order to vary the pressure of the metal tangent against the string. It is significant, however, that his late sonatas specify the fortepiano and that the expressive style that he evolved is a point of departure for so much piano music by later composers. Although his keyboard music is not heard frequently at the present time, his influence on what followed him was tremendous, and there seems to be increasing interest in his works on the part of many contemporary pianists.

A thematic catalogue was compiled by Alfred Wotquenne in 1905 (W. numbers). It was based on earlier work done by J. J. H. Westphal. A more complete and accurate catalogue by Eugene Helm (H. numbers) is still in progress, but much of the work in the area of keyboard music is completed.

Carl Philipp Emanuel wrote close to 180 sonatas and numerous works in other forms. Early sets of sonatas include six "Prussian" sonatas, dedicated to Frederick the Great (1742; W. 48; H. 24–29); six "Württemberg" sonatas, dedicated to Carl Eugene, Duke of Württemberg (1744; W. 49; H. 30–34 and 36); and six sonatas "mit veränderten Reprisen" (1760; W. 50; H. 126 and 136–40), the "changed reprises" referring to written-out variations for the repeats of the expositions and the repeats of the developments and recapitulations.

Perhaps the best known of Carl Philipp Emanuel's keyboard works is the set of six volumes entitled *Für Kenner und Liebhaber* (For Connoisseurs and Amateurs; 1779–87; W. 55–59 and 61; H. 130, 173, 186–89, 208, 243–47, 260–62, 265–71, 273–74, 276–79, 286–91). The first volume consists of six sonatas in *C, F, b, A, F,* and *G,* all in three movements (fast-slow-fast) except the second sonata (slow-slow-fast). Second movements are in a key closely related to the home key. The second movement of the sixth sonata features a cadenza-like, lyrical opening in unmetered rhythm (Example 5.9). The second and third volumes alternate rondos with sonatas, three in each category for each volume. The movements in the third sonata (*A*) of the second volume are joined by cadenza-like passages. The rondos are extensive, the principal theme returning at least three times. The fourth volume introduces two fantasias after three rondos that alternate with two sonatas. The fantasias are multisectional and contain unmetered sections, tempo changes, and key-signature changes; they almost always end with a free return of the opening section in the home key.

Example 5.9 Carl Philipp Emanuel Bach: *Für Kenner und Liebhaber*, 1, Sonata no. 6, 2nd movt. m. 1

Andantino

Example 5.10 Carl Philipp Emanuel Bach: *Für Kenner und Liebhaber*, 6, Fantasia no. 2 mm. 1–3

Volumes five and six present all three types: two rondos, two sonatas, and two fantasias in each volume (Example 5.10).

Other representative keyboard works are a set of light sonatas very much in the *galant* style, bearing the designation *à l'usage des dames* (for use by ladies; W. 54; H. 184–85 and 204–7; 1765–66), and six sonatas of three movements each, written as an illustrative supplement to the aforementioned treatise on keyboard playing, these works being known as the *Probestücke* (W. 63, 1–6; H. 70–75; 1753). There are, in addition, many sets of variations, fugues, and pieces with descriptive titles in French, such as "Les Langueurs tendres," "L'Irrésolue," and "La Journalière" (W. 117; H. 110–12; 1756).

Johann Christian Bach (1735–82) was Johann Sebastian's youngest surviving son. He studied with Carl Philipp Emanuel in Berlin after the death of Johann Sebastian and then went to Italy, where he worked with Padre Martini and absorbed completely the galant style. He pursued a successful career in London, where he anglicized his name to John and was appointed master of music to the queen. Johann Christian was influential in popularizing the early pianoforte, having played one of the first solo concerts on that instrument (1768). His compositions are written for piano or harpsichord in a *galant* style. Two sets of six sonatas in two and three movements constitute the main body of his solo keyboard works, Op. 5 (ca. 1768) and Op. 17 (1779). He often used lyrical thematic material in his fast movements, the so-called singing allegro that later became associated with Mozart. Development sections are usually minimal, but recapitulations are clear and complete. Minuets or sets of variations are sometimes used as final movements (Example 5.11).

As we enter the second half of the eighteenth century, we can no longer speak of forerunners of Classicism, for we are approaching the period of Haydn and Mozart, the two composers who are at the heart of the Classical period. Thus, most of the following group of composers may be considered the first echelon of minor Classical composers.

Georg Christoph Wagenseil (1715–77) studied with Fux and became a prominent musician at the Hapsburg court, being the teacher of Maria Theresa and her children. Wagenseil wrote operas, oratorios,

Example 5.11 Johann Christian Bach: Sonata, Op. 5, no. 3, Minuet mm. 1–4

symphonies, chamber works, and harpsichord concertos in addition to keyboard music. Early in his career he wrote dance suites. His approximately thirty sonatas (or *divertimenti,* as they are sometimes named) began to appear about 1754. They are usually in three movements: fast-minuet-fast or fast-slow-minuet. First movements are typically monothematic, resembling the two-part form of a Scarlatti sonata, but complete recapitulations are almost always present.

   Johann Gottfried Müthel (1718–88) studied with Johann Sebastian Bach just before the master's death. Müthel then traveled to Berlin, where he formed a close association with Carl Philipp Emanuel Bach and became organist at the Lutheran church in Riga. Dr. Charles Burney wrote highly of Müthel in a famous contemporary account entitled *Musical Tours in Europe.* Müthel's keyboard works consist of sets of variations and sonatas. The latter are in three movements, often unusually extended for the period. His style is emotional, employing many dynamic markings and crescendi, which suggests that the music may have been written for the pianoforte.

   Johann Gottfried Eckard (1735–1809) was a copper engraver by profession. He was taken by the piano manufacturer J. S. Stein to Paris (1758), where Eckard remained as a successful performing pianist and teacher. His published sonatas and variations (1763–64) are marked with crescendi, rinforzandi, mezza voce, tenuto, and other expressive devices associated with the piano rather than the harpsichord.

   Johann Schobert (ca. 1735–67) was active as a chamber musician to Prince di Conti in Paris (from 1760). Little is known of his early years, but the bizarre circumstances of his death have resulted in a macabre notoriety, for he and most of his family died as a result of eating poisonous mushrooms. His style of writing suggests that he may have been associated with the orchestral composers of the Mannheim school. Mozart admired Schobert's work and quoted sonata movements of Schobert in early concertos. Schobert wrote many sonatas in which the keyboard instrument was the prominent part, but another instrument (violin, flute, horn, etc.) was given an ad lib accompanimental role. Sets of such sonatas make up Opp. 5, 8, 14, 16, 17, 18, and 19.

Several other composers may be mentioned in passing. **Johann Ludwig Krebs** (1713–80); **Christoph Nichelmann** (1717–62); **Johann Philipp Kirnberger** (1721–83); and **Georg Benda** (1722–95). All wrote sonatas typical of the period, works that might well be worth looking into for the keyboard player intent on playing a diversified Classical repertoire.

CHAPTER SIX

Franz Joseph Haydn

The biography of Franz Joseph Haydn (b. Rohrau, Lower Austria, Mar. 31, 1732; d. Vienna, May 31, 1809) is full of uncertainties and periods of time of which little is known. Source material is provided from early biographical sketches that appeared shortly after Haydn's death and are based on conversations with the composer in his late years. Haydn's recollections seem less than clear, however, and it is probable that the biographers themselves added a measure of variation.

Haydn's ancestry has been a subject of debate, partly because the composer was born in a part of Europe with diverse populations: Austrian, Hungarian, Moravian, Slovak, and Croatian. Attempts have been made to link Haydn's family tree to several of these lineages as well as even that of the Gypsies. Recent research, however, has pointed to the fact that Haydn was of pure German stock. He was the second of twelve children born to Mathias Haydn, a wheelwright, and his first wife, née Anna Maria Koller.

Joseph Haydn went to Vienna in the spring of 1740 to become a choirboy at St. Stephen's Cathedral. He served in this capacity, receiving his education from the Kapellmeister there, until his voice broke, probably sometime around the age of sixteen. From this point until 1761, he worked in and around Vienna as a free-lance composer, performer, and teacher. He began to garner the support of wealthy, noble patrons in the mid-1750s, and his gradual rise as a young musician culminated in his being engaged in 1761 as the Vice-Kapellmeister to the household of Prince Paul Anton Esterházy, one of the richest and most influential of the Hungarian nobility. The following year Paul Anton died and was succeeded as head of the Esterházy domain by Nikolaus, the man for whom Haydn worked for nearly thirty years.

In the first years in this position at the Esterházy estate in Eisenstadt, Haydn was concerned mostly with composing instrumental music for the prince, because the Ober-Kapellmeister, Gregor Joseph Werner, was essentially a church musician and took charge of that area. In 1766, Werner's death left to Haydn the full responsibility for all performances at the court. The same year saw the completion of a sumptuous new palace far removed from Vienna, and Nikolaus took up permanent residence there, moving his household with him. Haydn was thus removed from the artistic stimulation of Vienna. Griesinger, one of Haydn's early biographers, quotes Haydn's autobiographical reflection: "I was set apart from the world. There was nobody in my vicinity to confuse and annoy me in my course, and so I had to become original."

Haydn continued his work thus until Nikolaus Esterházy died in 1790. Nikolaus was succeeded by his son, Anton, who did not inherit his father's taste for music. The staff orchestra was dismissed, only the wind band being retained. Although Haydn was kept on full salary, he was relieved of his duties. Haydn was thus free to return to Vienna, which he did. Meanwhile, Johann Peter Salomon, a London concert manager, heard of Nikolaus Esterházy's death while in Cologne embarking on a tour to secure soloists for his season. He went to Vienna and persuaded Haydn to undertake two visits to London (1791–92 and 1794–95). Otherwise, Haydn spent the remainder of his life in Vienna, returning to Eisenstadt during the summers.

Joseph Haydn himself was a man of few words. He was, however, kindhearted, friendly, and loved good humor. He was a lover of nature, but he also appreciated the refinement and luxury of the society in which he moved. For the most part he was well adjusted, accepting his social standing and adopting an optimistic view of reality. That strong religious belief was part of his philosophy is shown by his use of dedication mottos in his scores: *In nomine Domini* or *Soli Deo gloria* at their beginnings and *Laus Deo* at their closings.

Perhaps partly because of Haydn's basic stability as a person, he was able to apply himself with unusual diligence to his art, guiding his career from a modest beginning to a position of international eminence. From situations of great difficulty, he was able to draw advantage. When there seemed no place to turn for the solutions to musical problems, he was able to teach himself. He was, indeed, a self-made man. He was, nevertheless, liberal-minded with regard to the ideas of others and willing to experiment with new trends. He felt that, above all, his art was best used to bring pleasure to his fellow man.

Haydn came onto the scene at a time when he could stand at the crossroads of the Rococo and the *empfindsamer* styles. He was able to extract the best from existing styles and moved toward solidifying and clarifying the forms with which he worked. He gave importance and artistic stature to the galant style while at the same time avoiding the tendency toward sentimental exaggeration that could at times characterize the empfindsamer style. Among the composers whose influences may be traced in his works are Carl Philipp Emanuel Bach, Georg Teutter (the younger), Wagenseil, Monn, and Mozart. Influences from others, however, were only moderate in Haydn's creative life, and, as has been noted, his periods of relative isolation on the country estate of Nikolaus Esterházy not only separated him from the cosmopolitan atmosphere of Vienna but actually seemed to act as a stimulus for him to develop and perfect his own style.

Haydn commanded a full complement of moods and emotions in his music, from the joyous and gay to the tender and passionate. In keyboard writing, he often used folk-like melodies marked by diatonicism and simplicity. To the left hand, he usually assigned accompanimental figures. Ornamentation, especially in slow movements, was used as a means of compensation for the lack of a sustained tone in the instruments of the period. Brilliant passages exhibit instrumental rather than vocal characteristics, with arpeggios and broken chord figurations being prominent. Repetition and sequence are used more often than actual development.

The major compositions of Haydn's keyboard works are cast in sonata form. These works, although important in the history of keyboard literature, must take a second place in Haydn's overall output to both the symphonies and the string quartets. The sonatas, nevertheless, may be taken to represent the composer's development from his early years through 1794, the date of the final three sonatas being fifteen years before Haydn's death. The early sonatas, a group of about twenty, are in the galant style. They were labeled partitas in many instances by the composer himself and were probably used by Haydn as teaching pieces for students. The next group of sonatas, again a group of about twenty, is representative of a period of artistic change, often referred to as Haydn's *Sturm und Drang* (storm and stress) period. Experimental features that appear in the sonatas of this period include the selection of unusual keys, the use of minor keys as an expressive device, a high degree of contrast, and dramatic traits possibly influenced by the keyboard writing of Carl Philipp Emanuel Bach. The final group of sonatas, about twelve, shows the mature composer writing with complete assurance in his style, now totally refined and matured. These are compositions of increased dimension, representing the balance between skill and inspiration that enabled Haydn, along with Mozart, virtually to define Classicism in music.

The vast body of musical works that Haydn wrote has existed in a state of semiexploration until the twentieth century. Scholars have begun relatively recently to try to organize Haydn's output, searching for lost works, discovering works that may be spurious, attempting to determine chronology, and making the works available in critical editions suitable for performance preparation. As the total picture of the keyboard works began to emerge, one encountered a relatively complex scene.

The number of sonatas attributed to Haydn has varied, new ones having been brought to light and others having been judged to be spurious. The Breitkopf und Härtel "complete" sonatas was based on the catalogue that was prepared by Gottfried Christoph Härtel for the publication of the complete works of Haydn between 1800 and 1806. Haydn himself signed a preface statement that attests to the completeness of this collection, but the composer had by choice omitted a number of early works. This published edition contains thirty-four sonatas. Almost a century later Breitkopf und Härtel published the sonatas in a collected edition that was edited by Carl Päsler. This edition contained fifty-two sonatas and made reference to an additional eight "lost" sonatas, works for which we have no music but which Haydn himself listed in a catalogue he made of his own works, the so-called *Entwurf-Katalogue*. Päsler arranged the works in what he believed to be their chronological order.

Meanwhile, other publishers issued collections of Haydn sonatas, in many cases changing their order and often omitting some. Since there were no opus numbers for the works, the only other means of easy identification was by number or by key. Each had its problems. If one were to try to identify a sonata by number, one would have to specify the given publication, since numbering differed widely from publisher to publisher. If one tried to identify the sonata by its key, one was faced with the fact that often several sonatas were written in a given key.

In 1957, Anthony van Hoboken took over the Breitkopf und Härtel edition and published a Haydn catalogue. Works were given Hoboken numbers, often abbreviated on programs of performances simply as Hob. numbers. Insofar as the keyboard sonatas are concerned, Hoboken pretty much adopted the numbering of the Päsler listing of 1895. In 1958, the Haydn-Institut in Cologne began issuing a complete edition of the composer's works under the direction of Jens Peter Larsen and Georg Feder. About fifty volumes have been issued, and more are in progress. Keyboard music is in volumes XVI and XVII, and the editors use Hoboken's listing within these volumes.

Finally, there has appeared an even more recent revision. In 1963, Universal Edition published the work of Christa Landon. In the context of a working performance edition, Landon presented yet another chronology of the sonatas, one that rearranges the Päsler-Hoboken numbering (notwithstanding the fact that by Landon's own admission the chronology of the early sonatas is at this time virtually impossible to determine accurately). Landon throws out three sonatas included in the Päsler-Hoboken list on the grounds of doubtful authenticity. She includes in the regular chronology numbering for the eight "lost" sonatas on the theory that they may turn up and thus need a chronological niche reserved for them. (One of them actually has turned up and is printed in the Landon edition.) Finally, she adds five new works to her list of sonatas, two of them having been classified elsewhere by the Päsler-Hoboken catalogue, one of them a transposed, altered version of a sonata already in the Päsler-Hoboken list, and two newly discovered works. The following commentary is organized around the list of the sonatas developed by Landon. Since, however, the Päsler-Hoboken list is most often included in programming the works, the Hoboken numbers are indicated in addition in parentheses. Perhaps one day musicians can come to some general agreement as to which set of numbers to adopt for this body of literature, so that each sonata will bear but one identifying number. Communication will thus be greatly simplified.

The early sonatas of Haydn were probably composed as teaching pieces, many of them having been written when Haydn was earning his living as a free-lance musician around Vienna, before he went to work for Nikolaus Esterházy in 1761. Landon considers only the first fifteen sonatas early works, classifying sonatas 16–20 as transitional works leading to Haydn's mature style.

Although the early sonatas are in the galant style, they often show evidences of the spirited inventiveness for which Haydn's later works are particularly known. Most of them are in three short movements, each being some sort of binary form. The two-part structure often clearly shows a miniature sonata-allegro form, presenting after the double bar short, modulatory passages followed by a quasi-recapitulation in which opening material is restated in the home key. Such an arrangement occurs frequently in the first and third movements of these early works.

From the very beginning, Haydn showed a special affinity for the minuet and trio, including the movement in every sonata of the first group (L. 20, Hob. 18, is the first departure from this practice). The minuet and trio usually turns up as a second movement, occasionally as the finale. In only two cases is the minuet presented without a trio. In this form, Haydn begins to show his individuality and to exhibit a style that is characteristic of his later writing. Slow movements appear in only about a third of the early sonatas, most of them as a middle movement but twice as the opening movement. Variations are used but once, and then as an opening movement.

Identification	Key	No. of Movts.	Tempo Markings of Movts.
L. 1 (Hob. 8)	G	4	Allegro; Minuet (no trio); Andante; Allegro

The first movement contains a miniature, clear recapitulation ten measures after the double bar. All movements are very short. The Andante is but nine measures long; the final Allegro contains twenty-four measures.

Identification	Key	No. of Movts.	Tempo Markings of Movts.
L. 2 (Hob. 7)	C	3	Allegro moderato; Minuet and Trio; Finale (Allegro)

The first movement is only twenty-three measures long, its two-part form rounded. The trio is in *c*, a rounded two-part form. The Finale is the longest movement with a recapitulation thirteen measures after the double bar.

Identification	Key	No. of Movts.	Tempo Markings of Movts.
L. 3 (Hob. 9)	F	3	Allegro; Minuet and Trio; Scherzo (Allegro)

The first-movement motives are strong, using dotted rhythms and ornamental lines. The recapitulation is clear and occurs thirteen measures after double bar. The opening section of the Minuet balances a four-bar phrase with a six-bar phrase; the trio is in the key of *B-flat*. It is interesting to note the use of the term *scherzo,* also used later (1781) in the string quartets, Op. 33. The movement contains but twenty-four measures.

Identification	Key	No. of Movts.	Tempo Markings of Movts.
L. 4 (see note)	G	3	Allegro; Menuetto and Trio; Finale (Presto)

This sonata is not included in the Päsler-Hoboken catalogue but rather is listed as a separate clavier piece (Hob. XVI/G1, where the work is entitled *divertimento.* The first movement is the longest thus far encountered in this list. It has a twenty-eight-measure development that is modulatory and includes a retransition that employs a fragment of the opening theme. The trio of the minuet is in *C*. The Finale is in minuet and trio form with the direction of *da capo al fine* at the end of the section that serves as the trio. That section is in *g*, written with one flat in the key signature. The finale is also the opening movement of L. 5 (Hob. 11) and appeared elsewhere in manuscript as a separate piece.

Identification	Key	No. of Movts.	Tempo Markings of Movts.
L. 5 (Hob. 11)	G	3	Presto; Andante; Minuet and Trio

Landon believes this work to be three unrelated movements, assigning the opening Presto its proper niche as the finale of L. 4. The Andante in *g* is the longest movement thus far encountered: I: 20 measures :I: 43 measures :I. The modulatory section of twenty-one measures after the double bar uses fragments of the opening statement, and there is a clear recapitulation. The Minuet appears with alterations and another trio in the *Baryton Trio* (Hob. XI/No. 26). Its trio is in *e*.

Identification	Key	No. of Movts.	Tempo Markings of Movts.
L. 6 (Hob. 10)	C	3	Moderato; Minuet and Trio; Finale (Presto)

The first movement contains a modulatory section after the double bar that uses a fragment of the opening theme. There is a clear recapitulation. The second part of the Minuet is rounded, the trio being in *c* with two flats in the key signature. The Presto is in the same type of two-part structure as the opening movement and is relatively long (ninety-four measures).

Identification	Key	No. of Movts.	Tempo Markings of Movts.
L. 7 (Hob. XVI/01)	D	3	Tema (Moderato); Minuet; Finale (Allegro)

This is one of the works that Landon considers a sonata but that the Päsler-Hoboken catalogue had placed among other keyboard works. There does seem to be a sonata-like unity in the work in spite of the fact that the form of the opening movement, a theme and variations, is an unusual feature among the Haydn sonatas. The theme is cast in a two-part structure, as are each of the three variations. The last variation, employing triplet sixteenth notes, is the most brilliant. The following Minuet has no trio. The Finale is cast in a small sonata form and is an early example of the kind of brisk good humor that became a hallmark of Haydn's last movements.

Identification	Key	No. of Movts.	Tempo Markings of Movts.
L. 8 (Hob. 5)	A	3	Allegro; Minuet and Trio; Presto

Landon questions the authenticity of this work, particularly of the first and third movements, in spite of its early publication under Haydn's name in 1763 by Breitkopf und Härtel. In 1790, it was published by Cooper of London under Pleyel's name. The second theme of the first movement is in the dominant minor in the exposition, and a change of key signature is introduced into the text. There is no recapitulation of first-theme material. The last movement uses the same second-theme key relationship as the first, introducing a new key signature. There is a full recapitulation, introduced by an unprepared shift of tonality from *c-sharp* to *A*.

Identification	Key	No. of Movts.	Tempo Markings of Movts.
L. 9 (Hob. 4)	D	2	Moderato; Minuet and Trio

The first movement is in a clear, small sonata-allegro form. The trio of the second movement, also in *D,* is unusually long.

Identification	Key	No. of Movts.	Tempo Markings of Movts.
L. 10 (Hob. 1)	C	3	Allegro; Adagio; Minuet and Trio

The first movement has Haydn's characteristic cheerfulness with a development section after the double bar that uses more modulation than one expects in early Haydn. Modulation extends into the recapitulation, so that the opening theme is not heard in *C.* The recapitulation is somewhat obscured as a result. The Adagio presents a two-part form in a galant, singing style. The trio of the Minuet is in *c.*

Identification	Key	No. of Movts.	Tempo Markings of Movts.
L. 11 (Hob. 2)	B-flat	3	Moderato; Largo; Minuet and Trio

This work opens with the most extensive first movement encountered thus far in this list. There is a clear second-theme area, followed by a closing section. The development of both first- and second-theme material and the recapitulation are clear and complete. The second movement is more serious in mood and longer than any previous slow movement in the keyboard works. In *g,* it uses a two-part structure, but without any repeats. The trio of the Minuet is in *b-flat.*

Identification	Key	No. of Movts.	Tempo Markings of Movts.
L. 12 (Hob. 12)	A	3	Andante; Minuet and Trio; Finale (Allegro molto)

The first movement is highly ornamented and makes use of a triplet figure for both first- and second-theme areas. There is a short development that continues to use triplets and trills. The trio of the Minuet is in *a* and is a striking example of Haydn's early use of chromaticism. The last movement is in a truncated, miniature sonata-allegro form, there being no development but rather a seven-measure transition between the exposition and recapitulation, each marked to be repeated.

Identification	Key	No. of Movts.	Tempo Markings of Movts.
L. 13 (Hob. 6)	G	4	Allegro; Minuet and Trio; Adagio; Finale (Allegro molto)

This is the only early sonata for which an autograph exists. It is undated and of the first three movements only. The title on the autograph is *Partita per il clavicembalo solo*. There also exists a version of this work for piano trio (Hob. XV/No. 37), in Landon's opinion probably arranged by someone other than Haydn. The first-movement development includes both first and second themes. The recapitulation omits the first theme. An interesting technical feature is the chain of trills in the transition leading to the second theme. The trio of the Minuet is in *g*. The slow movement is also in *g* and makes use of continuous triplets decorated with trills, so that the entire movement is cast with a gently rocking perpetual motion. The Finale is in a miniature sonata-allegro form with a twenty-six-measure development and a full recapitulation.

Identification	Key	No. of Movts.	Tempo Markings of Movts.
L. 14 (Hob. 3)	C	3	Allegretto; Andante; Minuet and Trio

The first movement is reminiscent of the well-known Sonata in *C* (L. 48; Hob. 35), due to the fact that both employ an opening accompaniment figure of triplet broken triads, a device that is given almost no rest for the entire movement. The point of recapitulation is unclear, due to the altered statement of the first theme in *c*. The second movement is in *G* and uses a sonata-allegro form with a development that presents both first- and second-theme groups and a full recapitulation. The trio of the Minuet is in *c* with two flats in the key signature.

Identification	Key	No. of Movts.	Tempo Markings of Movts.
L. 15 (Hob. 13)	E	3	Moderato; Minuet and Trio; Finale (Presto)

The form of the first movement may emerge with some confusion for the listener, because a clear statement of opening-theme material takes place in *E* six measures after the development begins, and the material that follows does little to nullify the impression that the recapitulation has begun. The real recapitulation begins seventeen measures later, at which point the opening theme is stated again in *E*. The trio of the Minuet is in the parallel minor. The Finale is a wonderfully spirited sonata-allegro that makes use of juxtaposing brilliant arpeggio figurations in parallel major and minor keys.

Identification	Key	No. of Movts.	Tempo Markings of Movts.
L. 16 (Hob. 14)	D	3	Allegro moderato; Minuet and Trio; Finale (Allegro)

Although the first movement is in sonata-allegro form, the second theme is hard to identify because of the use of sequential melodic patterns. Such patterns are continued into the development section. The trio of the Minuet is in *d*. The Finale is in a two-part sonata-like form, but the development section hovers persistently around *d*, using material from the opening, and there is no statement of this material at the recapitulation point. Balance is maintained, however, by the closing measures of both exposition and recapitulation, which contain the opening-theme motive.

Identification	Key	No. of Movts.	Tempo Markings of Movts.
L. 17 (see note)	E-flat	3	Moderato; Andante; Menuetto and Trio

One of two sonatas (along with L. 18) published recently, having been brought to light by Georg Feder. No Päsler-Hoboken listing exists. Although the authenticity of the source (a manuscript from a former monastery in Rargern, Moravia) is not questioned, the manuscript is reported to show evidence of having been hastily copied and is full of apparent errors. This fact perhaps explains some of the roughness of detail evidenced in both works. Coupled with this crudeness, however, is a use of inventive ideas as thematic material and a keen sense of modulation. The opening movement of this sonata is unusually foursquare, making use of march-like, dotted-note rhythms. A long, modulatory development leads abruptly back to a condensed recapitulation. The second movement is in *c*, written with two flats in its key signature. It is in a two-part form that adds a final, short statement of the opening theme at the end of the second part. The minuet and trio are both rounded, the trio being in *c*.

Identification	Key	No. of Movts.	Tempo Markings of Movts.
L. 18 (see note for L. 17)	E-flat	2	Allegro moderato; Menuetto and Trio

The opening movement is unusually long. There is development of both the first- and second-theme groups, and a dramatic effect is achieved by using a long, modulating passage of broken chords drawn from the second theme. There is a full recapitulation. The trio of the Minuet is in *e-flat* and makes use of syncopation through a pattern of alternation between the left and right hands.

Identification	Key	No. of Movts.	Tempo Markings of Movts.
L. 19 (see note)	E	3	Adagio; Allegro; Finale (Tempo di Minuet)

This sonata is not listed in the Päsler-Hoboken catalogue. It was found recently by Jens Peter Larsen in Vienna in the library of the Gesellschaft der Musikfreunde. The work appears to be an early version of L. 57 (Hob. 47), where the opening Adagio of this work is marked *Larghetto*, transposed from *e* to *f*, and used as a second movement. The second movement of this work becomes the final movement of L. 57 and is transposed to *F*. The final movement of this work does not appear in the later sonata. The opening Adagio is a small but beautifully balanced sonata-allegro form. It ends on the dominant, which suggests moving without a break to the following movement. The first and second themes of the Allegro movement make use of identical motivic beginnings (four notes). Although the material that follows varies, one theme sounds very much like a variation of the other. Both are used in the development, and there is a full recapitulation. The final movement has a minuet-like character and is in two-part form. The first part is greatly extended, however, and ten measures after the double bar there occurs what might be regarded as a varied restatement of the entire first half, a quasi-recapitulation. There is no trio.

Beginning with L. 20 we encounter Haydn's mature style in the sense that the sonatas are no longer written as teaching pieces for students, nor by a composer in the process of finding his mature voice. We see, instead, Haydn in full command of his basic technique, and the composer explores new elements: the minor keys of the Sturm und Drang period, the conscious striving for expressiveness patterned after that of Carl Philipp Emanuel Bach, the growth of both the exposition and development sections, and the use of virtuosic devices. In L. 20, we have the appearance of the first dynamic markings, which would seem to indicate not only Haydn's increased interest in expressive aspects of the music but also the influence of the piano. By the time we come to L. 33, we find a great deal of dynamic direction (although it is suspected that the one crescendo in this sonata is a later addition).

With reference to the role of the early fortepiano, one might speculate that it was accepted as an instrument of worth theoretically, although it still must have been slow in becoming a frequently encountered item, even in areas where artistic life was vital. Imperfection in the instruments themselves, combined with a reluctance to invest too quickly in an expensive novelty, undoubtedly retarded the immediate widespread adoption of the fortepiano. Thus, we find Haydn now writing music, some of which suggests harpsichord, some of which suggests fortepiano, and much of which was probably meant to be played on either. It should be remembered in this context that many musicians would regard the timbre of the early fortepiano as being as close to the sound of the harpsichord as it is to the sound of the present-day piano.

Identification	Key	No. of Movts.	Tempo Markings of Movts.
L. 20 (Hob. 18) (ca.1766)	B-flat	2	Allegro moderato; Moderato

Landon states of her own chronology that this sonata is probably placed too early, showing evidences of later writing. The first movement is in the usual sonata-allegro form with development of both first and second themes and a full recapitulation. The second movement has a minuet-like character and is in three-four time but is cast in sonata-allegro form with fairly elaborate ornamental decoration being a part of the texture. The autograph of part of this movement is extant.

The sonatas L. 21–27 are the "lost" sonatas. Proof of their existence comes fromHaydn's own holograph catalogue of his works, the Entwurf-Katalogue (1765) that Haydn drew up as a response to Prince Esterházy's letter of reprimand, one that urged Haydn to "apply himself to composition more diligently than heretofore." The letter was undoubtedly inspired by complaints from Haydn's immediate superior, Gregor Joseph Werner, who was uncomfortable with Haydn's professional strength, especially in the area of church music.

The Entwurf-Katalogue was used as the basis of a more complete catalogue Haydn drew up in 1805 with Johann Elssler, son of Haydn's longtime copyist Joseph Elssler. The Entwurf-Katalogue lists each of the "lost" sonatas as a *Divertimento per cembalo solo* and from two to four opening measures are recorded as a means of identification. The keys of the sonatas are as follows:

L. 21—*d*
L. 22—*A*
L. 23—*B*
L. 24—*B-flat*
L. 25—*e*
L. 26—*C*
L. 27—*A*

Sonata L. 28 in *D,* too, is one of the "lost" items, but part of it turned up in the sale of a private collection in 1961. The twenty-one final measures of the first movement and a minuet and trio, probably a second movement, are thus extant. The trio projects an almost military mood, with an effective use of dotted rhythms and rests.

Identification	Key	No. of Movts.	Tempo Markings of Movts.
L. 29 (Hob. 45) (1766)	E-flat	3	Moderato; Andante; Finale (Allegro di molto)

According to Landon, the placing of this sonata so much earlier than the listing in the Päsler-Hoboken catalogue is based on the fact that there is an autograph of the work dated 1766, although the piece was not issued by Breitkopf und Härtel until 1788. The entire sonata is perhaps more virtuosic than any so far in this list. The first movement is in sonata-allegro form with an unusually well-marked second theme. The movement centers on keyboard display, using arpeggio figuration and Alberti bass. A lovely, flowing second movement in *A-flat* features two- and three-voiced textures in sonata-allegro form. Virtuoso writing returns in the final movement, also in sonata-allegro form, the second theme making use of repeated notes and an alternating-hand technique. The development shows unusual dramatic power, foreshadowing Beethoven.

Identification	Key	No. of Movts.	Tempo Markings of Movts.
L. 30 (Hob. 19) (1767)	D	3	Moderato; Andante; Finale (Allegro assai)

The first movement is quite extended with a second theme that is introduced by a repeated-note accompaniment. There is an unusually long closing section. The development uses both first and second themes, and there is a full recapitulation. The second movement uses a motivic opening. Its second theme is stated in the tenor register, and the first part ends with a dialogue alternating between melodic fragments stated in the tenor register and the opening motive in a high soprano range. A development follows the double bar. The recapitulation omits the first ten measures of the exposition but is complete otherwise. The last movement marks the first appearance in this list of a rondo type that is to be encountered frequently in the last movements of later Haydn sonatas. Its plan is as follows:

                                              Key
    A |: a :|: b :| D
    B |: c :|: d :| d
    A |: a :|: b :| D (varied)
    C |: e :|: f :| A
    A |: a :|: b :| D (varied further)
    Coda

Curiously, the coda, too, is marked to be repeated. The mood is one of spirited joy.

Identification	Key	No. of Movts.	Tempo Markings of Movts.
L. 31 (Hob. 46) (ca. 1767)	A-flat	3	Allegro moderato; Adagio; Finale (Presto)

The opening movement is cast in a large sonata-allegro form with a clearly defined second subject and a long closing section in the exposition. An extensive development achieves excitement by an extended use of broken chords divided between the hands. The first and second themes, as well as transition and closing-section material, are used in the development. A false recapitulation in *f* serves as a transition to the real recapitulation in *A-flat*. The Adagio, an extended movement in a free two-part form, is so full of original lyricism and coloristic experimentation that it is difficult to convey its power. Opening with a cantabile left-hand solo in two voices played above c′, Haydn adds still another melodic level above this one in the right hand. The three voices are expanded to four in a passage in which soprano and alto echo each other's trill figuration (Example 6.1). In the development-like section after the double bar, voice writing continues through modulatory maneuvers. A return to the home key of *D-flat* is clear, but the final section is a rewritten version of the opening one. Seven measures before the end of the movement, Haydn makes an excursion in *A* (still written in flats!), returning to *D-flat* four measures before the end of the movement. The Finale is a spirited compact sonata-allegro form. It is obviously planned to provide a brilliant conclusion to the work, for virtuosic elements, this time in the form of rapid scale passages, predominate. The recapitulation extends these scale passages in order to build excitement before the final cadence of the sonata, a device that the composer begins to use with some degree of regularity henceforth.

Identification	Key	No. of Movts.	Tempo Markings of Movts.
L. 32 (Hob. 44) (ca. 1769)	g	2	Moderato; Allegretto

The opening movement is essentially lyrical and expressive with very little display but with many opportunities to emphasize the pathos of the minor mode. Most of the development section centers on *c*. An unusually expressive passage occurs in measure 15 and the few measures that follow. In it, Haydn, having just introduced the second theme, causes the figure to rise sequentially with suspension devices. An expressive cadenza, marked *Sempre più adagio*, is included in the recapitulation (Example 6.2). The Allegretto is based on a minuet and trio concept but offers several significant innovations: the trio theme in *g* is derived from the motive of the minuet in *G;* the trio has no repeat signs, and although the first four measures are repeated in a written-out form, the remainder of the section is irregular; there is a short transition leading back to the minuet; the restatement of the minuet is completely written out, the material being varied; the movement ends with a restatement of the trio version of the main idea in *G,* the seventeen-measure section that acts as a coda.

Example 6.1 Franz Joseph Haydn: Sonata, L. 31, Hob. 46, 2nd movt. mm. 13–14 Edited by Christa Landon. © 1964, 1966 by Universal Edition A.G.,Wien, assigned 1973 to Wiener Urtext Edition, Musikverlag Ges.m.b.H. & Co., K. G., Wien. © renewed. All rights reserved. Used by permission of European American Music Distributors Corporation, sole U.S. and Canadian agent for Wiener Urtext Editions.

Example 6.2 Franz Joseph Haydn: Sonata, L. 32, Hob. 44, 1st movt. mm. 67–69 Edited by Christa Landon. © 1964, 1966 by Universal Edition A.G.,Wien, assigned 1973 to Wiener Urtext Edition, Musikverlag Ges.m.b.H. & Co., K. G., Wien. © renewed. All rights reserved. Used by permission of European American Music Distributors Corporation, sole U.S. and Canadian agent for Wiener Urtext Editions.

Moderato

Example 6.3 Franz Joseph Haydn: Sonata, L. 33, Hob. 20, 1st movt. mm. 13–14
Edited by Christa Landon. © 1964, 1966 by Universal Edition A.G., Wien,
assigned 1973 to Wiener Urtext Edition, Musikverlag Ges.m.b.H. & Co., K. G.,
Wien. © renewed. All rights reserved. Used by permission of European
American Music Distributors Corporation, sole U.S. and Canadian agent for
Wiener Urtext Editions.

Identification	*Key*	*No. of Movts.*	*Tempo Markings of Movts.*
L. 33 (Hob. 20) (1771)	c	3	Moderato; Andante con moto; Finale (Allegro)

This work is perhaps the most famous example of Haydn's so-
called Sturm und Drang period, and it is the first sonata to include a sizeable number of dynamic markings, including a curious passage in
measure 14, where dynamic markings of *f* and *p* alternate on successive
notes (Example 6.3). The exposition and recapitulation of the first
movement both contain a cadenza, marked *Adagio*, as a bridge between
the first- and second-theme groups. The development relies mostly on
first-theme, transition, and closing material. The recapitulation is somewhat shortened. The second movement in *A-flat* is another in the line of
those employing lyrical, long melodies with one- or two-voiced accompaniments that contain a fair amount of linear definition. The two-part
form presents some developmental characteristics after the double bar.
The final movement is in sonata-allegro form, and, as has been noted in
other last movements, the recapitulation is extended in order to build a
feeling of dramatic tension. There is, too, a final statement of the first
theme, which gives the closing measures a coda-like quality.

Identification	*Key*	*No. of Movts.*	*Tempo Markings of Movts.*
L. 34 (Hob. 33) (ca. 1772)	D	3	Allegro; Adagio; Tempo di Minuet

No dynamic markings are present in this sonata, although both the
Landon and Päsler-Hoboken lists place it later than the one in *c*. The
opening movement is in sonata-allegro form, and a one-phrase section
marked *Adagio* appears in both the exposition and the recapitulation just
before the closing sections. The beginning of the second theme is not as

clearly marked as in some previous works. The development uses mostly first-theme and closing-section material. The second movement in d
is remarkable in its use of a motivic first theme; melodic fragments in
dialogue in extreme registers (meas. 7, 8, 48, 49); and its use of rests—
all characteristics that Beethoven later adopts in several early sonata slow
movements (Op. 2, no. 3, and Op. 7, for example). The form of the second movement could be regarded as sonata-allegro if one allows for an
unusually short development section of only eight measures and an
extensively varied recapitulation. The movement ends on a dominant
arpeggio that leads to the final movement. The last movement follows
the rondo-type plan outlined for the final movement of L. 30 (Hob. 19),
both departures from the main theme being in d.

Identification	Key	No. of Movts.	Tempo Markings of Movts.
L. 35 (Hob. 43) (ca. 1772)	A-flat	3	Moderato; Menuetto and Trio; Rondo (Presto)

The opening movement, written in two-four time, employs dotted
rhythms for the first theme and broken triad triplets for most of the second theme and closing section. These accompanimental triplets are present for much of the development, thus giving the movement a kinship
with the opening movements of sonatas L. 14 and 48 (Hob. 3 and 35). A
recitative-like passage, marked *Adagio*, serves as a transition back to the
recapitulation. The second movement is a relatively undistinguished,
small one, both the minuet and trio being in *A-flat*. The final movement
is labeled *Rondo* and represents the first use of this term in this listing of
sonatas. The form, while psychologically centered on the return of the
main theme, is interesting in that the departures hardly have the sound
of contrasting material, being so closely allied with the opening motive
so as to sound like either a variant of it or an embryonic development.
One alternate section in f near the middle of the movement clearly presents something new.

Identification	Key	No. of Movts.	Tempo Markings of Movts.
L. 36 (Hob. 21) (1773)	C	3	Allegro; Adagio; Finale (Presto)

This work and the next five sonatas were published as a set in 1774,
having been written the previous year. It was the first publication of any
of the sonatas. These works probably influenced Mozart's early set of
sonatas (K. 279–84), also written in 1774. The opening movement of
this sonata is characterized by continued use of dotted rhythm in both
the first- and second-theme groups and for much of the development, a
section that uses both theme groups and is within a few measures of
being as long as either the exposition or the recapitulation. The second

movement in *F* makes use of a wide variety of rhythmic values in long lines of cantabile melody, sometimes with imitative patterns between the hands. In two-part form, the movement presents a section of departure after the double bar that ends after eleven measures and is followed by a full statement of that segment of the piece that had occurred before the double bar. The Finale is in a two-part sonata-like form, but, other than the fact that the modulations take place at expected points, there is no real difference between the first-theme and second-theme material, one growing quite naturally out of the other. The mood of the movement is that of uninhibited cheer.

Identification	Key	No. of Movts.	Tempo Markings of Movts.
L. 37 (Hob. 22) (1773)	E	3	Allegro moderato; Andante; Finale (Tempo di Minuet)

The opening movement presents an exposition in which the second theme is not clearly marked but rather grows out of a modulatory transition passage. There is a long development that touches upon most of the materials used in the exposition. A full recapitulation follows, including a cadenza-like passage marked *Adagio* after the restatement of the first theme. The cadenza is followed by the restatement of the transition passage that is now extended, making use of a surprising succession of diminished-seventh harmonies. The Andante in *e* makes continuous use of a sixteenth-note triplet figuration, giving the feeling of a gentle perpetual motion. The two-part form presents a short development-like section after the double bar and a full recapitulation. The last movement is an extended minuet and trio, the trio to be played a second time after a written-out, slightly varied da capo. Still another written-out varied statement of the minuet occurs after the second playing of the trio.

Identification	Key	No. of Movts.	Tempo Markings of Movts.
L. 38 (Hob. 23) (1773)	F	3	Moderato Adagio Finale (Presto)

This sonata has been singled out often as an unusually clear example of Haydn's influence on Mozart, for the similarity between the slow movement of this work and that of K. 280 is striking (Examples 6.4 a–b). The opening movement presents a sonata-allegro plan with an unusually long and brilliant second-theme group. The development features a passage of broken chords in which alternation of the hands adds to the technical display. The recapitulation adds a cadenza-like interlude with a pedal-point trill on C. The Adagio in *f* is built around an accompaniment of broken chords in triplets, over which is stretched a lovely, long melodic line. It is in two-part form with almost no literal repetition of

Example 6.4a Franz Joseph Haydn: Sonata, L. 38, Hob. 23, 2nd movt. m. 1

Example 6.4b Wolfgang Amadeus Mozart: Sonata, K. 280, 2nd movt. m. 1

the first part after the double bar, even though the expected transposition takes place. The final movement is cast in a two-part form with sonata-allegro features. The development-like section takes up almost a third of the number of measures in the movement, and there is a full recapitulation. The structure is completely monothematic, however, the opening theme serving also as the second theme in a slightly altered form.

Identification	Key	No. of Movts.	Tempo Markings of Movts.
L. 39 (Hob. 24) (1773)	D	3	Allegro; Adagio; Finale (Presto)

The opening movement is in a two-part sonata-allegro form that combines a relatively lyrical first theme with a more display-oriented second theme. The development works with both ideas and is but four measures shorter than the exposition. A full recapitulation is followed by a nine-measure coda. The Adagio in *d* is full of breathtaking beauty and originality. Probably using a two-part structure as a point of departure, it is essentially through-composed with elements of expressiveness and fantasy throughout: the staccato effects of the opening theme; the cadenza at measure 21; and the suspense generated by the bridge that leads to the last movement without interruption. The Finale presents a theme in two-part form, followed by a variation of the theme, in turn followed by a coda-like section using portions of the theme as it was stated in its original form.

Identification	Key	No. of Movts.	Tempo Markings of Movts.
L. 40 (Hob. 25) (1773)	E-flat	2	Moderato; Tempo di Minuet

The exposition of the opening movement presents a wide variety of materials in a texture that continuously juxtaposes groups of notes with greatly different time values. A case could be made for the presence of three themes in the exposition, two of them clearly marked after the modulation to *B-flat*. All three are used in the development section. The second movement is in a two-part form, its dotted rhythm conveying a sense of dignity.

Identification	Key	No. of Movts.	Tempo Markings of Movts.
L. 41 (Hob. 26) (1773)	A	3	Allegro moderato; Minuet al Rovescio; Finale (Presto)

The second-theme area of the exposition of the first movement settles into a final cadence in *E* only three measures before the double bar, having spent the preceding thirteen measures moving around *E* or *e* without ever coming to rest. As a result, it sounds as if there is no real second theme, although a wide variety of material is presented. The development is as long as the exposition, uses most of the various fragments presented in the exposition, and is intensely emotional. The title *Minuet al Rovescio* refers to the fact that the piece is designed to be played in retrograde. Both the minuet and trio turn out to be uncomplicated pieces, both rhythmically and harmonically. The final movement, a twenty-six-measure miniature in two-part form, provides but token balance for the impressive first movement.

Identification	Key	No. of Movts.	Tempo Markings of Movts.
L. 42 (Hob. 27) (1776)	G	3	Allegro con brio; Minuet and Trio; Finale (Presto)

This sonata and the five that follow compose a group of six sonatas that appeared in 1776. Its first movement is regular, presents little variety of material, and makes much use of Alberti bass. The Minuet and Trio seem less inventive than previous examples. The last movement presents a twenty-four-measure theme in two-part form and follows it with several variations, the first two variations conforming strictly to the original structure and those that follow becoming more free.

Identification	Key	No. of Movts.	Tempo Markings of Movts.
L. 43 (Hob. 28) (1776)	E-flat	3	Allegro moderato; Minuet and Trio; Finale (Presto)

The first- and second-theme areas are clearly defined in the exposition, the second theme being interrupted by a half cadence marked *Adagio*. There follows yet another thematic idea decorated with trills. The development is somewhat shorter than usual for Haydn at this stage, but still long enough to touch upon all three ideas from the exposition. An unusually interesting minuet is followed by a trio in *e-flat*. The last movement is very similar in mood and form to that of L. 42: a joyous two-part theme is followed by several variations interspersed with statements of the theme in its original form.

Identification	Key	No. of Movts.	Tempo Markings of Movts.
L. 44 (Hob. 29) (1774–76)	F	3	Moderato; Adagio; Tempo di Minuet

Of the 1776 set of six sonatas (L. 42–47), this is the only one that has dynamic markings in the early sources. Dramatic effects give the opening movement great interest: dynamic markings, including a crescendo; a second theme that utilizes a very fast, ascending arpeggio, which includes the interval of a major seventh; moments of highly disjunct texture (m. 14); a written-out trill figuration that suddenly doubles in speed (mm. 22–23); and a development section that employs a dramatic exploration of minor keys such as *c* and *d*. The Adagio is cast in sonata-allegro form. Its use of motivic elements and rests and its serious mood make it a worthy forerunner of the profound slow movements of Beethoven. (It seems akin in key and spirit to the Largo of Op. 31, no. 2.) The final movement is a minuet and trio with significant formal alterations. There is no da capo after the trio, but rather at that point the minuet is written out in a varied form and marked with repeat signs. There follows still another repetition of the minuet, this one with the repeats written out in varied form. A plan of the form of this movement would be:

Minuet   ‖: A   :‖: B   :‖

Trio   ‖: C   :‖: D   :‖

Minuet   ‖: A (varied)   :‖: B (varied)   :‖:
           AA (varied further)   BB (varied further)

Identification	Key	No. of Movts.	Tempo Markings of Movts.
L. 45 (Hob. 30) (1776)	A	3	Allegro; Adagio; Tempo di Minuet (with variations)

The spirited opening is reminiscent of the style of Carl Philipp Emanuel Bach in its use of dotted rhythms. The development section uses sequential movement by descending fifths as well as some rapid passagework wherein the two hands play the same notes an octave apart. There is no closing section to the recapitulation, but rather a recitative-like arpeggio leads to an improvisatory adagio of only twenty measures in length. Here, a staccato bass provides an accompaniment for the long, lyrical melody. The Adagio, also in *A*, ends on the dominant. The final movement presents a small minuet in the usual two-part form and follows it with six variations of very regular structure.

Identification	Key	No. of Movts.	Tempo Markings of Movts.
L. 46 (Hob. 31) (1776)	E	3	Moderato; Allegretto; Finale (Presto)

The opening movement contains a number of lyrical moments contrasted with those of rhythmic vitality. The Allegretto in *e* substitutes for a slow movement and is also lyrical in character, ending on dominant harmony. The final Presto states a lively theme in two parts. It is followed by four variations, one of them in *e* being free enough harmonically to serve as a middle section. The movement ends brilliantly.

Identification	Key	No. of Movts.	Tempo Markings of Movts.
L. 47 (Hob. 32) (1776)	b	3	Allegro moderato; Minuet; Finale (Presto)

The opening Allegro presents a first theme that is dignified and uses both ornaments and dotted rhythm. The second theme is more brilliant and impassioned. The development section is short and exploits the opening theme. The Minuet is in *B* with a trio in *b*. The final movement is a vigorous, strong, sonata-allegro that employs repeated notes, octaves, and brilliant passagework.

Identification	Key	No. of Movts.	Tempo Markings of Movts.
L. 48 (Hob. 35) (ca. 1777–79)	C	3	Allegro con brio; Adagio; Finale (Allegro)

Sonatas L. 48–52 were combined with L. 33 (Hob. 20) and published by Artaria in Vienna in 1771. Landon 48 is one of the best-known sonatas in the student's repertoire. Both the first and second themes use broken chord figuration in triplets, and the figurations occur again in the development section. The Adagio is lyrical in mood and in a two-part structure. The Finale is a rondo-type with a section in *c* that acts as an important departure before the final return of the main theme.

Identification	Key	No. of Movts.	Tempo Markings of Movts.
L. 49 (Hob. 36) (ca. 1777–79)	c-sharp	3	Moderato; Scherzando; (Allegro con brio); Minuet and Trio (Moderato)

Another sonata in a minor key, this work exemplifies the concept of a Sturm und Drang period in Haydn's works. The exposition of the first movement is closely knit, for a vigorous opening motive is presented as a first theme, a portion of it returns to serve as the second theme, and the closing section makes use of the head of the same motive. The publisher of this sonata, Artaria, wrote a letter to Haydn mentioning the similarity between the second movement of this work and the first movement of L. 52 (Hob. 39) (Examples 6.5a and b). The Scherzando is a short set of double variations with the plan ABAB′A′, where each return of both A and B is varied. The tonality alternates between *A* and *a*. The final, graceful Minuet and trio are in *c-sharp* and *C-sharp*.

Example 6.5a Franz Joseph Haydn: Sonata, L. 49, Hob. 36, 2nd movt. mm. 1–4

Example 6.5b Franz Joseph Haydn: Sonata, L. 52, Hob. 39, 1st movt. mm. 1–4

Identification	Key	No. of Movts.	Tempo Markings of Movts.
L. 50 (Hob. 37) (1777–79)	D	3	Allegro con brio; Largo e sostenuto; Finale (Presto ma non troppo)

One of Haydn's best-known sonatas, the first movement is brilliant and dramatic with a development section that poses difficult left-hand passagework. The Largo is a free, two-part form that is reminiscent of French overture style with its free-part writing and dotted rhythms (Example 6.6). In *d*, it ends on a half cadence and leads without pause to the finale. The last movement presents a rondo pattern (ABACA) in which the B section is in *d* and the C section is in *G*. The final statement of the main theme is made more brilliant by adding rapid bass figuration.

Identification	Key	No. of Movts.	Tempo Markings of Movts.
L. 51 (Hob. 38) (1777–79)	E-flat	3	Allegro moderato; Adagio; Finale (Allegro)

The opening sonata-allegro movement contains strong motives of great rhythmic variety, where elements of lyricism are combined with cadenza-like passages of great brilliance. An unusual adagio in *c* using

Largo e sostenuto

Example 6.6 Franz Joseph Haydn: Sonata, L. 50, Hob. 37, 2nd movt. mm. 1–2 six-eight time follows. Its structure is close to being a miniature sonata-allegro but with several significant alterations: the repeat of the exposition is written out with variations; the six-measure development is hardly more than a transition; and the recapitulation closes on a dominant pedal point. The final movement, although marked as an allegro, seems very much like a minuet with a trio section in *A-flat*.

Identification	Key	No. of Movts.	Tempo Markings of Movts.
L. 52 (Hob. 39) (1780)	G	3	Allegro con brio; Adagio; Prestissimo

The opening movement is a rondo (ABACA), each section being cast in a two-part form. Whenever A reappears, it is varied. The B section is in *g,* and C is in *e*. The second movement is an elaborate, serious adagio in binary form. It is highly decorated, making use of several types of ornamentation, running scale passages, and, at one point, octaves. The second part is not marked to be repeated, but it does present a long section near its end that combines elements of development with a cadenza and might be viewed as a foreshadowing of Beethoven's developmental codas. The return to the home key of *C* is prepared by double trills at the interval of a major sixth, played with crossed hands! The final movement is in six-eight and presents a playful sonata-allegro in which the same motive is used as both the first and second subjects. Both sections of the sonata-allegro structure are marked to be repeated.

Identification	Key	No. of Movts.	Tempo Markings of Movts.
L. 53 (Hob. 34) (1781–82)	E	3	Presto; Adagio; Vivace molto

Although this sonata was published with two earlier ones, L. 34 (Hob. 33) and L. 35 (Hob. 43), about 1783, it is placed later by Landon by virtue of her evaluation of its stylistic traits. Its opening movement has drama and drive, using the same idea for both the first and second themes. A short extension of the closing section at the end of the recapitulation combines with a restatement of the first theme to form a coda. The Adagio in *G* is cast in a two-part, sonata-allegro form. Its mood is serious, and it uses cadenza-like figurations in thirty-second notes as an integral part of each section. A recitative-like series of chords in the closing measures comes to rest on the dominant of *e,* preparing the way for the final movement without a break. The presto consists of alternating sections of similar character (ABACA), where A is in *e* and B is in *E*. Each section is cast in its own small two-part form. Sometimes each part is marked with a repeat sign and sometimes the repeat is written out with melodic variations. Alberti basses function throughout the movement.

Identification	Key	No. of Movts.	Tempo Markings of Movts.
L. 54 (Hob. 40) (1782–84)	G	2	Allegro innocents; Presto

Landon 54–56 were published together in 1784 in Berlin. Four years later a Viennese publisher brought out the same works for violin, viola, and violoncello. This fact gave rise to speculation as to whether these three sonatas were arrangements of string trios, in spite of the fact that the keyboard versions were published first. Evidence that supports the priority of the keyboard works includes a firsthand report that Haydn played the sonatas as keyboard works in 1785. Furthermore, Haydn's usual instrumentation for original works for string trio was two violins and violoncello rather than the instrumentation used for these works. The opening movement of L. 54 is a simple rondo-type cast as ABABA, where the A sections are in *G* and the B sections are in *g*. Each section presents a small two-part form, employing the usual repeat signs. Whenever a section returns, it is given fairly elaborate ornamental variation. There are a great number of dynamic markings, including many sforzatos that Landon reports as appearing in an inconsistent manner in the first edition. The Presto is similar to the first movement both in spirit and in design. A two-part structure with each part marked to be repeated forms the first section in *G*. There follows a through-composed section in *e*. The first section returns in a varied form that utilizes rapid figuration to produce a brilliant effect.

Identification	Key	No. of Movts.	Tempo Markings of Movts.
L. 55 (Hob. 41) (1782–84)	B-flat	2	Allegro; Allegro di molto

The two-four time of the first movement results in a tempo that underscores its near-virtuosic elements. Measures 25–35, occurring just after the opening of the second theme, offer an imaginative modulatory excursion. After the exposition has ended clearly in *F*, the development opens in *D-flat*, a surprising relationship, but one that Mozart uses in exactly the same way at the same structural point in the Sonata, K. 570 (1789). The second movement presents a vigorous theme in the form of a dialogue between the two hands. It sets the mood for the entire first section in binary form with the usual repeats. The texture here seems born as much of contrapuntal thinking as of galant-style homophony. There follows a quasi-developmental section in *b-flat*. In the return to the first section, the repeats are written out with figural variations that add brilliance but weaken somewhat the contrapuntal effect of the first statement.

Identification	Key	No. of Movts.	Tempo Markings of Movts.
L. 56 (Hob. 42) (1782–84)	D	2	Andante con expres- sione; Vivace assai

The opening movement is a set of variations. The theme is in two-part form with the expected repeats, but it is filled with rests and arpeggiated flourishes. The same structure is used for each of two following variations, the second one being in *b-flat*. A three-measure interlude prepares the way for the final variation. It uses no repeat marks but is based on the second half of the theme, achieving at this point the most florid texture of the movement. The final movement is a joyous vivace cast in a form unusual for Haydn. An eight-measure theme marked to be repeated is first presented. There follows a long developmental section in which elements of the theme are fragmented and transposed. There is a return to the home key at measure 61, but the original theme is not stated. Rather, fragments continue to be juxtaposed and extended until the end of the piece. This entire section is marked to be repeated. One is reminded of the structure of the last movement of Beethoven's Op. 10, no. 2, wherein the same general pattern is used, albeit thematic return at the point where the home key comes back is clearer in the Beethoven work than it is here. A delightful aspect of the movement is that the absence of a clear return of the theme keeps the interest high until the very end of the piece.

Identification	Key	No. of Movts.	Tempo Markings of Movts.
L. 57 (Hob. 47) (1788)	F	3	Moderato; Larghetto; Allegro

The second and third movements of this work appear in an earlier version as the first and second movements of L. 19. The first movement is thus the only movement new to this sonata, and Landon indicates historical reasons that cast a shadow of doubt on its authenticity. If the first movement is indeed Haydn, it represents the composer in an uncharacteristic mood. The long, lyrical lines of the movement are somewhat undistinguished. There is no clear second theme, the modulation to the dominant in the exposition seeming to take place in a quasi-sequential passage. A bit of melodic syncopation, later picked up in the development section, is also introduced with the arrival of the dominant, but its presence is hardly enough to impress the listener as more than a passing idea. The development, too, seems to lack Haydn's usual sense of excitement. The second and third movements are almost exactly the same as they appear in L. 19. Revision by Haydn amounted to little more than editing: ornamentation written out more clearly here and there or a note or two added or deleted in a chord occasionally. For a general description of these movements, the reader is referred to the discussion of L. 19.

Identification	Key	No. of Movts.	Tempo Markings of Movts.
L. 58 (Hob. 48) (1788–89)	C	2	Andante con espressione; Rondo (Presto)

This sonata was written especially for a collection published by the Leipzig firm of Breitkopf and Härtel. It may have been intended exclusively for the pianoforte, a point open to challenge in this sonata but less so in L. 59, which follows. The first movement is in an unusual form. It begins regularly with a highly ornamented binary theme in C, each part marked to be repeated. There follows a section in c that begins with the same opening motif but proceeds differently. Then comes a return to the section in C, still more highly varied. Haydn uses no repeat signs at this point, but the second half is followed by a written-out repeat, employing even more elaborate variation. Then a change in key signature announces the arrival of c once again. In spite of the fact that the opening phrase of this new section is the same as that of the earlier section in c, the idea unfolds in a different manner, one of a quasi-development nature. The movement ends with a return to the section in C, but the statement of its theme is so shortened that it acts more as a coda than as a final recapitulation. Schematically, the movement might be represented as follows:

					Key
‖: A	:‖: B	:‖			C
‖ C	‖				c
‖ A′	‖ B′	‖	B″	‖	C
‖ D	‖				c
‖ A″	‖ Coda				C

The second movement is a cheerful rondo (ABACABA) in which the same motivic figure permeates all sections. The C section is in c and sounds quasi-developmental in its use of the principal motive. The relationship of the A and B sections is that of the two parts of a binary form rather than that of contrasting ideas as might be presented in an exposition. In the overview, this sonata suggests that the composer was trying to gain new perspectives on traditional forms, a kind of endeavor that, had he pursued it, might have led to completely new structural concepts.

Identification	Key	No. of Movts.	Tempo Markings of Movts.
L. 59 (Hob. 49) (1789–90)	E-flat	3	Allegro; Adagio e cantabile; Finale (Tempo di Minuet)

A letter of Haydn to Marianne von Genzinger, to whom this work is dedicated,recommends that the sonata be played on a fortepiano, one made by the Schantz workshop. The opening movement is an extended sonata-allegro form, the exposition alone running over sixty measures and including a long closing section. The development, of equal length, works the first theme, the second theme, and closing-section material. Figuration that was prominent in the closing measures of the exposition assumes great importance in the retransition to the recapitulation. A long cadenza then introduces the recapitulation. A coda of twenty-three measures, almost developmental in nature, closes the movement. The Adagio in *B-flat* is a long, serious piece with a highly ornamented line and surprising excursions into *b-flat* and *G-flat*. Cast in an ABA pattern, the opening A section takes its point of departure from binary form but uses no repeat signs, the second half being followed by a written-out repeat with variants. The middle section is also in two-part form, but only the first part is repeated. It uses an accompaniment of sixteenth notes grouped in sets of six, with a melody that is alternately below and above the accompaniment, the left hand crossing over where necessary. A coda of sixteen measures closes the movement. The Finale is quasi-rondo in form (ABACA), notwithstanding the direction of *Tempo di Minuet*. Each section is cast in binary form, some of the two parts marked to be repeated. Schematically, its structure can be seen easily:

A	‖:	a	:‖:	b	:‖
B	‖:	c	:‖:	d	:‖
A	‖	a	‖		
C	‖:	e	:‖	f	‖
A	‖	a	‖	b	‖

The C section is in the parallel minor. Throughout, the mood is bright, but figural display is kept at a minimum.

Identification	Key	No. of Movts.	Tempo Markings of Movts.
L. 60 (Hob. 50) (1794–95)	C	3	Allegro; Adagio; Allegro

This is the first of the final three sonatas, all composed in London. The first movement is brilliant and virtuosic. The opening motive permeates the entire movement, including the second-theme area and the development section. Rapid runs are used in counterpoint with it, and these become material for development. In the presentation of the second theme in the recapitulation, the measures at the beginning of the theme that contain the characteristic motive are omitted. The Adagio belongs to a type encountered in L. 39, 44, and 51 (Hob. 24, 29, and 38) in that it is through-composed and of profound mood. The underlying structure may be thought of as sonata-allegro with a short modulatory section (mm. 24–33) acting as the development. The final movement is in an extended two-part form. Both sections are repeated, but Haydn writes out the exact repeat rather than using repeat signs. The two parts are related thematically, much like the two parts of a minuet. The opening theme is not, however, repeated verbatim at the end of the second part; thus, the movement is not rounded.

Identification	Key	No. of Movts.	Tempo Markings of Movts.
L. 61 (Hob. 51) (1794–95)	D	2	Andante; Finale (Presto)

The opening movement presents a somewhat altered version of a sonata-allegro form. It uses no repeats. The first theme has two distinct sections, the second of which is omitted in the recapitulation but used in the development. The second-theme area is fully recapitulated, but the materials are presented in a slightly different order. The development is unusual in that it opens in the home key and is identical to the recapitulation for its first ten measures. Notwithstanding all of these alterations, sonata-allegro form is clearly evident. The Finale uses a two-part form that resembles the concept used for the Finale of L. 60 (Hob. 50). The first of the two parts is marked to be repeated. The second part has its exact repeat fully written out. In spite of the rapid tempo, the movement is essentially lyrical in mood and makes use of a great number of dissonant devices on downbeats, such as appoggiaturas and suspensions. The result is a series of strikingly bold sounds.

Identification	Key	No. of Movts.	Tempo Markings of Movts.
L. 62 (Hob. 52) (1794)	E-flat	3	Allegro; Adagio; Finale (Presto)

This sonata is one of Haydn's most famous and is considered by many to be his most forward-looking keyboard work. Its opening movement presents a large-scale sonata form with repeat indications for only the exposition. The movement combines majesty, virtuosity, and dramatic gesture, relying heavily on contrasting dynamics, moods, and rhythms. (See, for example, mm. 36–39.) It ends brilliantly. The Adagio is written in a key one-half step above the key of the sonata (*E*), an unusual relationship. It is a serious piece, based on a dotted-rhythm motive presented in the opening measures, and in this respect fore-shadows the slow movements of many Beethoven sonatas (Op. 2, no. 3; Op. 31, no. 2; Op. 81a, and others; Example 6.7). The form of the movement is a cross between a minuet and trio and a sonata-allegro:

$$\lVert: \text{A} :\rVert: \text{B} :\rVert \; \text{C} \; \vert \; \text{A} \; \vert \; \text{B} \; \vert$$

The section marked C is developmental but is also rhapsodic in its use of cadenza-like runs, rests, and long note values. The final presenta-tion of A and B is varied from the original, being, in general, more florid. The presto is a brilliant sonata-allegro movement that presents Haydn in his most good-natured, virtuosic mood. It is a fitting close to the sonata in that, although its mood is less serious than that of the opening move-ment, the movement is, nonetheless, just as substantial and important.

Example 6.7 Franz Joseph Haydn: Sonata, L. 62, Hob. 52, 2nd movt. mm. 1–4 Edited by Christa Landon. © 1964, 1966 by Universal Edition A.G.,Wien, assigned 1973 to Wiener Urtext Edition, Musikverlag Ges.m.b.H. & Co., K. G., Wien. © renewed. All rights reserved. Used by permission of European American Music Distributors Corporation, sole U.S. and Canadian agent for Wiener Urtext Editions.

Several solo keyboard works of Haydn not conceived as sonatas may be mentioned. The Fantasia in C (1789) is a single movement that is akin to an opening movement of a sonata. It is based on the melody of a German folk song, "Ich wünchet' es wäre Nacht" (also used by Mozart at the age of ten in his *Galimathias Musicum*). The musical ideas of the Fantasia are orchestral but presented with pianistic devices such as crossing the hands, arpeggios, and passage work distributed between the two hands. An unusual effect is achieved by sustaining notes in the bass until they die away (*tenuto intanto finchè non si sente più ilsono*).

The *Andante con Variazioni* (composed in 1793, published in 1799) is a set of double variations, written in *f* in the style of a funeral march and in *F*. Each idea is varied twice. The first variation is characterized by a syncopated, half-step melodic progression. The second variation uses a more contrapuntal texture. The coda is introduced by abrupt, unprepared modulations that contain traces of the theme and proceed with bold harmonic invention.

Other works that may be noted in passing are the *Menuetto con Variationi* in *A* (written before 1771); *Arietta con Variationi* in *E-flat* (written before 1774); Capriccio in *G* (1789), a lighthearted, rondo-like piece that suggests an improvisation; and *Tema con Variationi* in *C* (1790).

CHAPTER SEVEN

Wolfgang Amadeus Mozart

Wolfgang Amadeus Mozart (b. Salzburg, Jan. 27, 1756; d. Vienna, Dec. 5, 1791) was baptized Joannes Chrysostomus Wolfgangus Theophilus on the day after his birth. Since the infant was born on the feast day of St. John Chrysostom, the first two names were given in honor of the saint. Theophilus came from the name of the baby's godfather, Joannes Theophilus Pergmayr. The German equivalent of Theophilus is Gottlieb, a name Mozart sometimes used, and the Italian version is Amadeus, the name that Mozart preferred and by which he came to be identified in the world of music.

Mozart's father, Leopold, was an able violinist and a composer of church music, symphonies, concertos, and sonatas. In addition, Leopold wrote a well-known treatise on violin playing, *Versuch einer gründlichen Violinschule* (1756). Mozart's mother was Austrian, born Anna Maria Pertl. She gave birth to seven children, but only Wolfgang Amadeus and his elder sister, Anna Maria (generally referred to as Nannerl by the family), survived infancy.

Mozart exhibited pronounced musical ability at a very early age and with his father's guidance began to give performances by the age of five. Both Amadeus and Nannerl played before Maria Theresia in 1762. She sent them a set of court clothes, which the children wore when they posed for paintings by Lorenzoni and Carrogis de Carmontelle over the next few years. There followed a series of tours in which the two gifted children were exhibited. During the five months in Paris, they played for Louis XV. There followed fifteen months in London, later fifteen months in Vienna (1767–68), and three trips to Italy in 1770, 1771, and 1772. During these formative years, Mozart was exposed to the styles of various counties, and he thus developed into an international composer, having absorbed the lyricism of Italian opera, the intensity of the Austrian and German traditions, and the stylishness of Paris and London. The childhood tours were highly successful, bringing recognition from dignitaries and attracting large audiences. The pope conferred upon Mozart the Order of the Golden Spur. Mozart was elected a member of the Bologna Philharmonic Academy; and in Milan he directed twenty consecutive performances of an early opera, *Mitridate, rè di Ponto.*

In 1769, Mozart was appointed Konzertmeister to the archbishop of Salzburg. In 1772, however, Hieronymus, count of Colloredo, a man of little taste for music, ascended to the position of archbishop, and Mozart's position became increasingly uncomfortable. In 1777, Mozart took a leave of absence to journey to Paris, where a symphony was performed at one of the Concerts Spirituels. Local arguments over style and taste resulted in little attention being paid to Mozart.

Moreover, Mozart's mother, who had accompanied him, became ill with fever and passed away. Mozart returned to Salzburg after this disappointing trip and resumed his duties as Konzertmeister, also becoming court organist in 1779.

Service under the archbishop of Salzburg finally became unbearable, and Mozart decided to move to Vienna (1781), where a commission for an opera by the emperor seemed to offer great promise. There followed intermittent successes with productions of *Die Entführung aus dem Serail* (The Abduction from the Harem), *Der Schauspieldirektor* (The Impressario; 1786), and *Le nozze di Figaro* (The Marriage of Figaro; 1786). The warm reception accorded *Don Giovanni* (Don Juan) at its premiere in Prague (1787) and a fear that Mozart would accept invitations to move to England prompted the emperor to offer Mozart the appointment of "chamber composer" at a salary of 800 florins, a niggardly sum when compared to the 2,000 florins Gluck was receiving just before his death.

Mozart accompanied Prince Carl Lichnowsky to Berlin (1789), en route playing at the Dresden court and in the Thomaskirche at Leipzig. An unverified offer from Friedrich Wilhelm II of Potsdam would have resulted in a salary of 3,000 thaler and the appointment of First Royal Kapellmeister. Mozart reportedly refused the offer out of loyalty to the Austrian emperor. Money matters became of great importance, however, for Mozart enjoyed a free-spending life-style, and his wife, Constanza (née Weber), was reported to have been somewhat imprudent in her managing of the household. As a result, money troubles plagued Mozart from the time of his marriage to the end of his life.

Two more short trips complete Mozart's career, the first to Frankfurt for the coronation of Emperor Leopold II and the second to Prague for the coronation of Leopold as King of Bohemia. By 1791, in the middle of the production of *Die Zauberflöte* (The Magic Flute; 1791), Mozart was already exhausted from traveling and overwork. His short life ended, it is believed, from an attack of malignant typhus.

The art of Mozart, as evidenced in his brief life of thirty-six years, was entirely spontaneous, being unhindered by theory and unhampered by prevailing tenets of the time. His creative ability was the most spectacular known to music, with consummate achievements in such different fields as opera, symphony, chamber music, and solo literature—both vocal and instrumental. His sense of form was well-nigh perfect and intuitive. The quality of his musical detail was virtually faultless.

Of all the composers of unquestionable greatness, Mozart was the least distinguished by national characteristics. He represented an amalgamation of all Western music, a universal language, not a local dialect. However, Mozart's three visits to Italy and the associations growing out of those visits resulted in music that reflected Italian polish, refinement, and spirit. Mozart formed a close friendship with Johann Christian Bach, and Haydn was greatly admired. Unlike Haydn or Beethoven, Mozart took no special notice of nature as a source of inspiration. Although Mozart's music often seems bright and serene to the casual listener, it harbors beneath its surface qualities that are deep and profound with underlying tenderness and melancholy.

Mozart was one of the greatest keyboard virtuosi of his time. The ideals of his clavier style, however, were quite different from those that were to evolve in the nineteenth century. He lived to witness only the early stages of a new concept of piano playing, one that emphasized sonority, legato touch, and more concern with virtuosity. Mozart was highly critical of this trend in the playing of others, especially Clementi, continuing to prefer lightness of touch, refinement, and elegance as ideals to be sought at the instrument.

The only works of Mozart actually composed for the harpsichord were early concerto arrangements. He first used pianofortes made by Späth of Regensburg. When Mozart became acquainted with the instruments made by Andreas Stein of Augsburg, however, these instruments were preferred. Thus, it was for an instrument of delicate, penetrating tone with an easy action that Mozart conceived his works after 1777. Early pianoforte works were improvised first, being written out later, usually as material for pupils or publishers.

A catalogue of Mozart's works by Ludwig von Köchel was published in 1862. This listing became the means of identifying Mozart's works for the next several decades. Alfred Einstein revised Köchel's numbering, presenting what amounted to a new chronology in 1937 with further corrections in 1947. By the time Einstein had revised the original Köchel numbering, however, its use had become traditional to a great extent. Thus, most editions continue to use K numbers, as do keyboard players in speaking of the music. The Einstein numbering is often found in recent critical editions and in scholarly literature about the music. Both numbers are included in this presentation, the K numbers being given first and the Einstein numbers following in parentheses.

The early sonatas stem from the light, cheerful style associated with the galant movement in Italy. Other models for the young composer may have been keyboard works of Johann Schobert, Carl Philipp Emanuel

Bach, and especially Johann Christian Bach. Mozart may have known, in addition, the six Haydn sonatas published in 1774 as Op. 13. Haydn's influence is particularly strong in K. 280, 281, and 282 (189e, 189f, and 189g). The early Breitkopf und Härtel catalogue lists six youthful sonatas from 1766, works that have been lost.

The first extant sonatas are the six written down in 1774–75. It is believed that these works had been played for several years, having been presented in concerts in Mannheim and Paris. The use of many dynamic markings suggests the piano, the instrument that Mozart was to play in forthcoming concerts in Munich. The first five sonatas of this set, K. 279–83 (189d, e, f, g, and h), were composed in Salzburg, and the sixth, K. 284 (205b), in Munich. Only the sixth was published by Mozart, although the set was originally intended as a series, for a key sequence at intervals of the fifth, three down from *C* and two up, was used.

Identification	Key	No. of Movts.	Tempo Markings of Movts.
K. 279 (189d) (1774–75)	C	3	Allegro; Andante; Allegro

All of the movements are in sonata-allegro form, the last movement especially showing influences of Haydn. The first two movements employ the device of changing the order of presentation of patterns in recapitulations, including the omission of some of the music presented in expositions.

Identification	Key	No. of Movts.	Tempo Markings of Movts.
K. 280 (189e) (1774–75)	F	3	Allegro assai; Adagio; Presto

The first movement contains an unusual chromatic passage in triplets. A new theme is presented in the development. The close relationship between the second movement of this work and the second movement of Haydn's Sonata, L. 38 (Hob. 23), has been noted in the discussion of the Haydn piece. Similarities are apparent not only in the key (*f*) and rhythmic patterns of the movement but extend even to the contrast between the first and second ideas and the treatment of the material in the development-like section after the double bar. The last movement, an unusually brief sonata-allegro structure, seems less Haydn-like.

Identification	Key	No. of Movts.	Tempo Markings of Movts.
K. 281 (189f) (1774–75)	B-flat	3	Allegro; Andante amoroso; Rondo (Allegro)

The first movement opens with a trill followed by a triplet figuration, exemplifying the florid elegance of the piece. The second movement is reminiscent of an Italian opera aria. The final movement is a rondo in which small bits of development appear within the departures from the main idea. It is the most extended last movement in the sonatas up to this point and forecasts Mozart's more mature writing.

Identification	Key	No. of Movts.	Tempo Markings of Movts.
K. 282 (189g) (1774–75)	E-flat	3	Adagio; Menuetto I, II; Allegro

The use of an opening adagio movement in binary form is reminiscent of a pattern that occurs several times in the Haydn sonatas, as is the use of two minuets as a second movement. The minuets exhibit numerous fortepiano contrasts, and a da capo is indicated after the second one. The finale is in a miniature sonata-allegro structure with a short development section and a full recapitulation.

Identification	Key	No. of Movts.	Tempo Markings of Movts.
K. 283 (189h) (1774–75)	G	3	Allegro; Andante; Presto

The opening movement is one of Mozart's best known, for it is popular in the teaching studio. It features a famous, lyrical opening and offers some moments of technical display, such as the octaves and broken thirds that serve as a transition to the second theme. The unusually short development section (only eighteen measures) presents material that is only casually related to that of the exposition. There is a full recapitulation. The adagio is in sonata-allegro form with both parts marked to be repeated. A tiny coda ends the piece. The most virtuosic movement of the sonata is the Presto. It, too, is cast in sonata-allegro form and stands on a par with Haydn's more ambitious finales, striving for both technical display and excitement.

Identification	Key	No. of Movts.	Tempo Markings of Movts.
K. 284 (205b) (1774–75)	D	3	Allegro; Rondeau en Polonaise; Andante (Theme and 12 Variations)

Although this work was written in Munich in 1775, it shows the influence of the French clavier music of the day in its brilliance and in the title of the second movement. The use of the polonaise was particularly fashionable in Paris at this time as a way of honoring Louis XV's wife, Maria Leczinska (Example 7.1). An opening fanfare in octaves invokes the spirit of the first movement, which is brilliant and orchestral-sounding. The development section is relatively short. The second movement is cast in a rondo pattern (ABACBA), the final return of A being highly varied. The theme that serves as the basis for the variations is in the expected two-part structure, each part marked to be repeated. Variations 1 and 2 increase the pace of the movement by using triplet eighth notes in the right and left hands respectively. Variations 3 and 4 continue in this direction by using sixteenth notes. Variation 6 features figuration to be played by crossing the hands. Variation 7 is in minor, reported to be Mozart's first use of the minor mode for a variation. Variation 8 features octaves. Variation 9 is imitative with a few measures of canon. Variation 10 uses tremolo patterns. Variation 11 is an adagio cantabile, and it represents Mozart's frequent use of a slow variation as the penultimate one. Its repeats are written out and highly ornamented. Variation 12 provides a lively finale to the set.

Identification	Key	No. of Movts.	Tempo Markings of Movts.
K. 309 (284b) (1777)	C	3	Allegro con spirito; Andante un poco adagio; Rondo (allegretto grazioso)

This sonata was written for Rose Cannabich, daughter of the director of the famous Mannheim orchestra. The work is larger in scope than previous keyboard sonatas, with the possible exception of K. 284 (205b). Like the K. 284, the K. 309 contains many orchestral effects. It goes beyond the earlier sonata, however, in its attempt to bring together widely diversified material and in the second and third movements to experiment with a freer approach to structure. The opening of the first movement presents a brilliant motive stated in octaves. An unusual number of rapidly contrasting dynamics are exhibited here and in the second movement. Measures 49–50 present accents on weak beats. The second theme is of unusual delicacy and charm, providing a sharp contrast to material that precedes and follows. The second movement is said

Example 7.1 Wolfgang Amadeus Mozart: Sonata, K. 284, 2nd movt. mm. 1–4

to be a portrait of Rose Cannabich. Its opening eight-measure theme is stated four times, each with more elaborate variations. An intervening second theme forms a departure. It is followed by yet another variation of the first theme, a varied statement of the B section, and a final return of A in its most elaborate statement. The rondo pattern used in the final movement is ABACBA with a coda-like section that uses portions of B and a final statement of A just before the end of the piece. A is melodious and gentle; B, by contrast, uses brilliant passagework and tremolos. Present also are passages likely to be perceived by the listener as transition or closing sections. These, combined with some irregularity of balance, give the overall impression of an expanded movement of great freedom.

Identification	Key	No. of Movts.	Tempo Markings of Movts.
K. 311 (284c) (1777)	D	3	Allegro con spirito; Andante con espressione; Rondo (Allegro)

This work was written before Mozart went to Paris, while the composer was still in either Munich or Mannheim. The opening movement experiments with the arrangement of the material presented in the recapitulation. The transition between the first and second themes in the exposition appears in an extended form in the development and leads to a statement of the second theme in the tonic, this presumably being the beginning of the recapitulation. The exposition material then continues to be recapitulated as one might expect with the exception of the final phrase, an idea that had been used extensively in the opening of the development. The first theme then appears unexpectedly just before that final phrase ends the movement. The second movement presents a songlike melody of eight measures with a three-measure codetta. It is repeated and alternated twice with a contrasting section of equal lyric beauty and rounded off with elements of the A section. The final movement is a large rondo (ABACABA) with a cadenza interspersed between C and the return of A. The movement is brilliant and dramatic, suggesting orchestral textures.

Identification	Key	No. of Movts.	Tempo Markings of Movts.
K. 310 (300d) (1778)	a	3	Allegro maestoso; Andante cantabile conespressione; Presto

This sonata was written in Paris, shortly after the death of Mozart's mother there on July 3, 1778. The work's minor key and dramatic power reflect the emotional stress through which the composer was passing. The opening movement exhibits rhythmic drive through the repeated triads that serve as an accompaniment to the first theme. The second theme also features nonstop sixteenth-note patterns. Even the closing section does not relent but rather combines elements of both the first and second themes. The development uses mostly first-theme material, treating it in a free, contrapuntal style and combining it with ostinato-like sixteenth-note patterns in the bass (Example 7.2). It is a section filled with darkness and intensity. The recapitulation is regular except for an outburst of diminished-seventh arpeggios before the final closing section.

The second movement in *F* is conceived in a large sonata-allegro form. The opening section is given length and importance by the inclusion of both a significant transition theme before the modulation to the dominant, and an extended closing section that features a highly decorated second-inversion tonic chord. The development is free, making use of the most casual allusion to the opening theme and later to the transition material. It is somewhat turbulent and features exposed seconds in a right-hand accompaniment figure (Example 7.3). The recapitulation is regular. The final movement is cast in an overall ABA form. It returns to the drive of the opening movement with material presented in virtually perpetual motion, continuing through two segments of the A section. Perilous skips and parallel thirds (in the bass, also!) and fourths give the movement a wild, distraught quality. The B section is in a two-part form, each marked to be repeated. It is in *A* and provides momentary relief from the emotional turbulence characteristic of the piece.

Identification	Key	No. of Movts.	Tempo Markings of Movts.
K. 330 (300h) (1781–83)	C	3	Allegro moderato; Andante cantabile; Allegretto

This sonata, written in the same year as the K. 310, provides an amazing contrast to the previous work, for it seems to be born of lovely, elegant melodies, and its mood is seemingly effortless and completely at peace with the world. The opening movement contains an exposition in which there is an unusually long, lyrical closing section. The development is not clearly connected with what has gone before in the exposition but rather seems to grow out of it, discovering new melodies in the process. The development is short and does not reach great dramatic heights. The recapitulation is regular. The aforementioned closing section is now decorated with trills, rendering it a much more difficult passage this time around. The movement ends with the opening measures of the development, reharmonized in the tonic key. The second movement in *F* is outwardly in an ABA form with a coda based on B, each section being in a two-part form with each section marked to be repeated. The thematic material of the B section in *f* is, however, so closely related

Example 7.2 Wolfgang Amadeus Mozart: Sonata, K. 310, 1st movt. mm. 58–60

Example 7.3 Wolfgang Amadeus Mozart: Sonata, K. 310, 2nd movt. m. 44

to that of A that it sounds almost like a reworking of the opening theme in the parallel minor key. When the B section returns as a coda, it is in the major mode. The movement is one of reserved emotional intensity, but its musical ideas are superb. The last movement is in sonata-allegro form with themes that are somewhat rondo-like in character in that they are easygoing with short, regular phrases. The development section, as in the first movement, is remotely connected thematically with the exposition. The recapitulation is regular.

Identification	Key	No. of Movts.	Tempo Markings of Movts.
K. 331 (300i) (1781–83)	A	3	Andante grazioso (with variations); Menuetto; Alla Turca (Allegretto)

For all its familiarity, this sonata is unique in that it contains no movement in sonata form, the theme and variations serving to provide an imposing first movement. Beethoven followed suit later in his Op. 26. The theme of the first movement is said to be a German folk song called "Rechte Lebensart." Very likely Mozart provided the delicate slurring of the opening motive, as well as the accents and dynamic changes, all of which give the music so much of its character. Variations 1 and 2 provide increasing rhythmic activity through the use of more rapid note values. Variation 3 is in the parallel minor and poses melodic octave sequences that are tricky to play. Variation 4 returns to A and offers passagework to be played by crossing and uncrossing the hands. Variation 5 is slow with highly decorated lines, and the final allegro foreshadows the mood of the last movement. One may note that the variations' types and the order of presentation are similar to features described in the final movement of K. 284 (205b). The minuet and trio offers a perfectly regular structure. Its charm comes from some irregularity of phrase groups and from several unexpected leaps in the legato line. The trio is almost ländler-like, making use of cross-hand technique to present fragments of the melody in a high register. The Alla turca presents a sectional pattern that features returns varied to elicit ever-increasing excitement. Turkish music was construed in this period to include drums and cymbals. Thus, the finale, which seems to come from the theater, imitates percussion effects in the bass and through the use of repeated chords embellished with rapid acciaccatura-like grace notes. The brilliant coda was added later, in 1784.

Identification	Key	No. of Movts.	Tempo Markings of Movts.
K. 332 (300k) (1778)	F	3	Allegro; Adagio; Allegro assai

The first movement of this work is characterized by quicksilver changes in mood. The first theme of the exposition is singing. A transition theme in *d* is highly dramatic (Example 7.4). The second theme projects both humor and lyricism. This, in turn, leads to a section of great rhythmic vitality with alternate fortepiano dynamic indications (Example 7.5). The development section begins with a new lyrical theme and later utilizes the passage that had featured rhythmic vitality and rapidly changing dynamics. The recapitulation is regular. The second movement is in a truncated sonata-allegro form in that there is an exposition and recapitulation but no development. The main theme is stated in both its major and parallel minor, *B-flat* and *b-flat*. The second theme achieves its interest by the use of repeated notes in the bass and rests in the upper melodic parts. The final movement is cast in a brilliant sonata-allegro form. The first theme is built from a virtuosic, descending arpeggio figure. The second theme is in *d*. The development features both first- and second-theme materials. The movement ends quietly, its brilliance notwithstanding.

Example 7.4 Wolfgang Amadeus Mozart: Sonata, K. 332, lst movt. mm. 23–26

Example 7.5 Wolfgang Amadeus Mozart: Sonata, K. 332, 1st movt. mm. 60–65

Identification	Key	No. of Movts.	Tempo Markings of Movts.
K. 333 (315c) (1778–79)	B-flat	3	Allegro; Andante cantabile; Allegretto grazioso

There is some question as to whether Mozart wrote this work near the end of his stay in Paris or upon his return to Salzburg. It certainly stands as one of the more ambitious of the sonatas, combining elements of musical intensity with large-scale structures and technical brilliance. The opening movement is filled with an abundance of lovely lyricism. It is gracious and unhurried until it reaches the development. Here, in a section that opens in *f*, the composer achieves dramatic intensity of great power without ever sacrificing the basic lyrical mood of the movement. The recapitulation is regular except for an extension of the section just before the closing theme. The second movement is in sonata-allegro form. The exposition is fairly long for a second movement, employing both a transition theme and an extended second theme. The development is only nineteen measures long, but in it the composer exhibits a striking use of chromaticism combined with an emotionalism that is unusually intense, even for Mozart (Example 7.6). The recapitulation is more highly decorated than the exposition but otherwise regular. The final rondo is close to being the type of sonata-rondo concept associated with Beethoven (ABACABA). The movement proceeds as expected until the second departure from the main theme. At this point, Mozart presents two themes, one in *g* and one in *E-flat,* and also begins to develop the principal theme of the movement. The imposing structure is extended by the addition of a written-out cadenza. It is introduced by a passage that sounds very much like the orchestral tutti of a concerto, and the cadenza is sufficiently long to form virtually another section, one that leads to the final statement of the main theme. A short coda closes the movement.

Identification	Key	No. of Movts.	Tempo Markings of Movts.
K. 475 (475) and K. 457 (1785 and 1784)	c	Fantasia and Sonata	Sonata in 3 movts: Allegro; Adagio Molto allegro

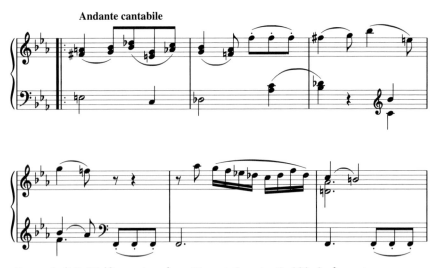

Example 7.6 Wolfgang Amadeus Mozart: Sonata, K. 333, 2nd movt. mm. 32–37

These two works were published together, although they were written at different times. Both works are dedicated to Therese von Trattner, a pupil. The set is considered to be one of the most emotionally profound and forward looking of the keyboard works. The Fantasia is in five sections: Adagio, Allegro, Adantino, Piu allegro, and Tempo primo. The opening Adagio presents a strong motive and develops it by passing through a number of keys and chords, many of which remain unresolved, over a chromatically descending bass. The section finally resolves to *b* before stating a two-part songlike theme in *D*. The Allegro that follows begins dramatically, passes through *F* with more lyrical material, and ends with a cadenza. The Andantino, still another songlike section, is in *B-flat* and in its third and fourth measures provides the germinal idea for the following stormy Più allegro. The storm subsides as the passagework becomes somewhat fragmented before the final Tempo primo returns, once again presenting the opening idea.

The opening motive of the first movement of the sonata invites comparison to Beethoven, not only because of its brusque, strong character but also because it is so similar to the opening of Beethoven's Sonata Op. 2, no. 1. Both ideas are possibly borrowed from the orchestral gesture known as the "Mannheim rocket" (Example 7.7). Mozart's contrasting idea, however, is equally important, and it provides a good example of the chromaticism that has come to be associated with his style. The exposition contains two themes in *E-flat,* albeit they are similar in that they are both lyrical. The exposition closes with a return of the Mannheim rocket. In the recapitulation, the first of the two lyrical themes is referred to only in passing, now in *D-flat,* while the second of the two themes is given a full statement in *c.* A coda brings the movement to a subdued conclusion.

The Adagio is in an extended ABA form. The A section is rounded so that it in itself becomes a small aba structure. The middle section presents a theme of almost Schubertian character in *A-flat.* After a cadenza, the theme is repeated in *G-flat.* Tune detectives are fond of pointing to the similarity of the melodic line between this theme and the main theme of the second movement of Beethoven's Sonata, Op. 13 (Examples 7.8 a–b).

Example 7.7 Wolfgang Amadeus Mozart: Sonata, K. 457, 1st movt. mm. 1–4

After a section filled with chromatic inflection, the A section returns, now shortened but also offering a cadenza. The form of the final movement is difficult to categorize. It probably resembles a rondo more than any-thing else (ABACBACcoda). Frequent breaks in the flow of the music, however, and the almost fragmentary return of the main theme in its last appearance, give the movement a searching restlessness. The mood of the music is persistently elusive and disturbed, but it works admirably as the final dramatic touch for this sonata.

Identification	Key	No. of Movts.	Tempo Markings of Movts.
K. 545 (545) (1788)	C	3	Allegro; Andante; Rondo

This work is perhaps Mozart's most famous insofar as the general public is concerned, yet it was not published during Mozart's lifetime. It was intended to be used as teaching material. The opening movement presents a scaled-down sonata-allegro form with a recapitulation that arrives in the subdominant. The Andante uses an Alberti-bass accompa-niment almost without interruption throughout. The opening melody resembles the aria "Dalla sua pace," composed in the same year as this work for the Viennese production of *Don Giovanni*. The Rondo is almost

Example 7.8a Wolfgang Amadeus Mozart: Sonata, K. 457, 2nd movt. m. 24

Example 7.8b Ludwig van Beethoven: Sonata, Op. 13, 2nd movt. m. 1–2

Haydn-like in its use of short sections alternating with frequent returns of the opening theme. This movement was also used with slight revisions as the last movement of the Sonata in *F,* K. Anh. 135 and 138a (547a).

Identification	Key	No. of Movts.	Tempo Markings of Movts.
K. 570 (570) (1789)	B-flat	3	Allegro; Adagio; Allegretto

This late work was published in its first edition (1796) with a violin part that has been deemed spurious. The opening movement presents interesting alterations to the traditional sonata-allegro key arrangement. A second theme appears in the subdominant (*E-flat;* measure 23). Then the more traditional dominant is prepared. With its arrival, however, comes a restatement of the opening theme, now presented with a countermelody. The development opens in a remote key (*D-flat*) with the theme first presented in the exposition in the subdominant. The development expands the material through several keys, continuing with a presentation of the second version of the main theme. The recapitulation places the subdominant theme once again before the tonic presentation of the opening theme with its countermelody. The Adagio is a dignified rondo-type with two departures, in *c* and *A-flat,* and a particularly beautiful coda. It shows spiritual kinship to the seriousness usually associated with Beethoven's slow movements. The final Allegretto is also a rondo (ABACDA coda). Its mood is genial and suggests humor through the use of syncopation in both the A theme and the C section. The D section features disjunct groups of repeated notes. Both C and D are combined ingeniously in a brilliant coda.

Identification	Key	No. of Movts.	Tempo Markings of Movts.
K. 576 (576) (1789)	D	3	Allegro; Adagio; Allegretto

This work is the last of the completed sonatas, one of a planned set of six to be written for the oldest daughter of the king of Prussia. The work represents Mozart's most sophisticated pianistic thinking, combining an emphasis on contrapuntal devices with idiomatic keyboard writing. The opening Allegro presents a canon based on the first theme at the point where a second theme is expected. A curtailed second idea follows. Canonic passages are featured in the development. They pass through several keys: *B-flat, g, F-sharp,* finally coming to rest in the dominant (*A*). In the recapitulation, the order of the second-theme fragment and the canon is reversed so that the latter may provide a brilliant passage before the quiet ending. The songlike Adagio (ABA) contains an extended middle section in *f-sharp,* leading to imitative scale-like figurations that pass from one hand to the other. The coda is based on the B theme. The innocent first theme of the Allegretto becomes a technical tour de force in measure 9 when triplets are suddenly introduced in the left hand. As in the first movement, the point at which a contrasting theme is expected is used to introduce a developmental statement of the opening theme. A short, contrasting theme finally arrives just a few measures before the first theme is restated in measure 65. The movement then proceeds one more time through this sequence of events, restating the first theme in the home key of *D* but modulating to new areas for both the development area and the contrasting theme. A final joyous statement of the opening theme, once again in *D*, brings the movement to a close. The returns of the main theme in the home key give the movement a rondo-like quality, but the use of development sections as contrasting sections instead of the presentation of new material gives the movement more tension and unity than the typical rondo and injects elements of the sonata-allegro structure.

There remain for consideration five miscellaneous works in the sonata category that are often not included in collections of the sonatas, even "complete" ones. Two are irregular with regard to original publication. Two are single movements, possibly representing incomplete works.

Identification	Key	No. of Movts.	Tempo Markings of Movts.
K. 533 (movts. 1 and 2) (533) (1788) and K. 494 (movt. 3) (494) 1786 (published in 1790)	F	3	Allegro; Andante; Rondo

The opening movement is essentially lyrical in character, but it achieves a texture unusual in Mozart's keyboard style due to an almost constant use of imitation between the hands. The development is long and involved, but the recapitulation is shortened in order to allow for a coda. Highly chromatic writing appears in transitional sections, just after the recapitulation begins and at the beginning of the coda. The Andante shares an unhurried pacing with the opening movement. Slow-moving and diffuse almost to the point of losing momentum, it is nonetheless possessed of an extraordinary palette of harmonic changes, so that the ear is constantly urged to seek what is to come next. Sonata-allegro structure is used for the movement. The Rondo, written earlier, was published as the third movement of this sonata with the addition of a twenty-seven-measure cadenza (mm. 143–69). Like the other two movements, it is deliberate, presenting an unhurried mood. The middle section and the opening of the cadenza share a kinship with the first movement through the use of polyphonic texture.

Identification	Key	No. of Movts.	Tempo Markings of Movts.
K. 547a (1788)	F	2	Allegro; Allegretto

The opening Allegro was originally the first movement of a teaching sonata (*für Anfänger*) for violin and piano, K. 547 (547). The Allegretto is a transposition of the second movement of the K. 545 (545) with a few changes of detail and a new ending. Both movements have been transplanted skillfully by Mozart, so that they work well together, notwithstanding the fact that their existence as this work represents a pastiche.

Identification	Key	No. of Movts.	Tempo Markings of Movts.
K. 312 (590d) (1789–90)	g		sonata-allegro movement

The autograph of this movement was given to Mendelssohn on the occasion of his engagement to Mlle Jeanrenaud. Some scholars believe it was written earlier than is indicated here, about 1774. The movement presents a regular sonata-allegro structure, using some imitation between the hands of the first-theme material. The development section modulates freely.

Identification	Key	No. of Movts.	Tempo Markings of Movts.
K. 400 (372a) (1781)	B-flat		incomplete sonata movement

Mozart stopped writing this movement at the beginning of the recapitulation (m.90). A convincing final section was provided by Abbé Maximilian Stadler (1748–1833). The date of the work has been surmised from the fact that there is similarity between the musical material of this work and two violin sonatas composed in 1781, the K. 379 (373a) and 380 (374f). Also notated in the score in the development section over two successive phrases are references to Sophie and Constanze Weber, daughters of the family with whom Mozart spent the summer of 1781. The composer married Constanze in 1782.

Mozart wrote eighteen sets of variations, of which fourteen were unquestionably completed by the composer. They represent his more "popular" side by standards of his own day. Thus, the themes used as a basis for the variations are quite simple and melodious. The structures retain a stereotyped pattern, and slow variations depend upon ingenious melodic ornamentation for effect rather than profound emotional expression. Ironically, the sets of variations are much less popular today than his more "serious" sonatas. Many of the variations were improvised first. Most of them are based on borrowed themes, some operatic, some from lighter theater music, a few from folk sources or other composers' works.

Mozart's procedure is very predictable, and it has already been described in discussions of the variation movements of the K. 284 (205b) and K. 331 (300i). The theme is stated, oftentimes with a moderate amount of embellishment. All the themes except four are cast in two-part form, each part marked to be repeated. The variations follow the structural pattern of the opening theme almost without exception. The variations are figural, restating the theme and employing various devices such as shorter note values to increase movement (usually present in the first few variations after the theme is stated), triplet figuration, passage-work that requires alternation or crossing of hands, octaves, broken octaves, trills, and dotted rhythms. The penultimate variation is usually slow, often highly ornamented with cadenza-like passages. The final variation almost always employs brilliant passagework and a rapid tempo. In eight of the sets there is either a restatement of the original theme or some reference to it after the final variation, a practice that Mozart uses more consistently in the later sets of variations. Written-out cadenzas frequently suggest improvised theatrical flourish, joining variations, particularly near the ends of the sets or as a set-up for the final variation. For example, such cadenzas occur in K. 274 (315d), 352 (374c), 398 (416e), 455 (455), and 500 (500).

Pianists persist, by and large, in programming the sonatas instead of the variations, and, as a result, one rarely encounters a set of Mozart variations on recital programs. Although admittedly less concentrated than the sonatas, the variations are also probably more neglected than they deserve to be. Perhaps the most popular set is the K. 265 (300e), *Ah, vous dirai-je Mamam,* known in English-speaking countries as "Twinkle, Twinkle, Little Star." More ambitious sets that are occasionally performed are the K. 353 (300f), a set of twelve variations based on the French song "La Belle Françoise"; K. 354 (299a); twelve variations on "Je suis Lindor," a song from the first act of Beaumarchais's *Le Barbier de Seville* by Nicholas Dezède; K. 455 (455), a set of ten variations on a musical number entitled "Unser dummer Pöbel meint" from the comic opera *La Rencontre imprévue* (originally produced under the title *Die Pilgrimme von Mekka*) by Christoph Willibald Gluck; and K. 573 (573), a set of nine variations based on a minuet of Jean Pierre Duport. Deserving more frequent performance is a fine set of twelve variations that Mozart wrote on a theme that is probably original, K. 500 (500).

There are numerous works by Mozart in other forms. Many of them are small pieces, mostly minuets and allegro movements, a number of them dating from the composer's youth. Of the mature, longer works, several fantasias or fantasia-like works should be noted. The Fantasia in *c*, K. 475 (475; 1785), published with the sonata, K. 457 (457), has already been discussed. The K. 397 (385b) in *d* (1782 or 1786–87) is a fantasia that is both short and accessible, so it has achieved a degree of popularity as a useful, attractive work of intermediate difficulty. After a somber introduction of arpeggios, its opening section presents an adagio made up of dramatic material interrupted by two cadenzas. A cheerful closing section, an allegretto in *D*, is believed to have its final ten measures added by someone other than the composer. The Fantasia in *c*, K. 396 (385f; 1782), was originally written for piano and violin and is believed to have been completed by Abbé Stadler. The work approaches a sonata-allegro structure, Mozart probably having provided only the exposition. The opening gestures of the work are extremely grandiose, so much so that, indeed, suspicions as to the authenticity of even that portion attributed to Mozart have been aroused. The K. 394 (383a) in *C* (1782) is known as both a fantasia and as a prelude and fugue. After an opening introduction, an andante uses ascending arpeggio figurations over stepwise progression in the bass to achieve considerable intensity. A three-voiced fugue follows, its countersubject creating dissonant intervals of seconds, sevenths, and ninths. A fantasia-like work in *C* called Capriccio, K. 395 (300g; 1777), presents several contrasting sections, uses extended improvisatory figuration on diminished-seventh harmonies, and closes with the section marked *Capriccio*.

Two other significant works cast as single movements are the Rondo in *a*, K. 511 (511; 1787), and an adagio in *b*, K. 540 (540; 1788). Both are built around slow-moving themes. The main theme of the Rondo is chromatic and emotionally intense. The two departures, in *F* and *A*, are closely related in rhythm to the main idea and provide both a brighter mood and more movement. There is a long, chromatic transition section back to the final statement of the main theme and an extended coda that is filled with anguish. The Adagio is cast in sonata-allegro form. It presents material that is fragmented by frequent breaks in texture for dramatic effect. Its harmonic progressions are often daring, and a considerable amount of chromaticism is to be found, especially in the development section. A coda modulates effectively and unexpectedly to *B*.

Among other miscellaneous works of interest is a set of pieces that resembles a Baroque dance suite, K. 399 (385i; 1782). It has been assumed that the cycle remained incomplete, for only three pieces were completed, an overture in the French style that features dotted rhythms and powerful chords, an allemande, and a courante. A fragment of the sarabande also exists. The group moves from its opening in *C* to *c*, *E-flat*, and *G*. It is possible that had the work been completed there would have been a return to the opening key of *C*.

Other single-movement works include two rondos written in 1786, K. 485 (485) and K. 494 (494); a gigue in *G*, K. 574 (574; 1789); a funeral march in *c*, K. 453a (453a; 1784); and two fugues that were completed by Abbé Stadler, K. 401 (375e; 1782), and K. 153 (375f; 1783).

CHAPTER EIGHT

Ludwig van Beethoven

Ludwig van Beethoven (b. Bonn, Dec. 16, 1770; d. Vienna, Mar. 26, 1827) represents the change from Classicism to Romanticism perhaps more clearly than any other composer of the turn of the nineteenth century. On one hand, he chose to cast almost a third of his compositions in sonata form. On the other, his imagination and his fascination with experimentation drove him into a never-ending search for innovative ways of using traditional structures, all the while enhancing emotional intensity. The balance he achieved between the rigor of traditional discipline and the freedom associated with emotional outburst or inner serenity represents his special genius and provides a continuing source of reflection for those who study his work.

Beethoven descended from a musical family of Flemish origin (hence the prefix van) on his father's side. Both his grandfather, Ludwig, and his father, Johann, were musicians in the court of the elector of Cologne at Bonn. Each married a local girl, Marie Poll becoming Beethoven's grandmother, and Marie Magdalena Laym (a widow, née Keverich), his mother.

Beethoven's father was a stern, often intemperate man who saw in young Ludwig's musical talent a means to making money by exhibiting him as a child prodigy. Thus, Ludwig was held to a severe schedule of music instruction in both piano and violin. His teachers included his father; Jean-Baptiste Van der Eiden, the court organist; and the latter's successor, Christian Gottlob Neefe, with whom Beethoven studied Bach's *Well-Tempered Clavier.*

Beethoven's first appearance as a pianist was in 1778 in Cologne. (The child was advertised as being six years of age.) By 1782, Beethoven was formally installed as Neefe's deputy in the position of court organist and by 1784 was given a small salary for the position by Elector Max Franz. In 1787, at the age of seventeen Beethoven visited Vienna, where he played for Mozart, who is said to have commented that the young man should be watched, for one day he would make his mark on the world.

Notwithstanding Beethoven's reputation as a formidable improvisor, the number of compositions he wrote before the age of twenty-one is surprisingly small. These include the three piano quartets, most of the Op. 33 Bagatelles, the two rondos that were later revised and published as Op. 51, and several sonatinas. Thus, Beethoven was very much a budding composer in 1792 when Haydn, traveling through Bonn, heard a cantata Beethoven had written (now lost) and praised it. Probably at the urging of Beethoven's friend, Count Waldstein, the elector decided to send Beethoven to study in Vienna, then considered to be the musical capital of central Europe. Beethoven accepted the opportunity to further his musical goals but found Haydn neglectful and indifferent as a teacher. As a result, Beethoven sought theory lessons from Johann Schenk surreptitiously. In 1794, Haydn went to London, so Beethoven began studying openly with Johann Georg Albrechtsberger, who after a time proffered the verdict that Beethoven was a poor student who learned nothing and would never do anything in a decent style.

In 1795, Beethoven made his first appearance as a pianist in Vienna, probably playing his *B-flat* concerto (Op. 19). Beethoven's approaching deafness was diagnosed as early as1798, and over the next sixteen years his hearing deteriorated to the point that his final appearance as a pianist was made in 1814. After 1819, he communicated only through conversation books.

Beethoven was much admired by the ruling class of Viennese society. They recognized his genius and appreciated his simplicity, directness, and noble spirit. Beethoven, on the other hand, was a champion of independence and freedom, and he steadfastly refused to be subservient to his powerful admirers. As Beethoven's deafness became pronounced, he became more eccentric, suspicious, and morose, with frequent outbursts of temper. The Viennese aristocracy remained, however, remarkably loyal and respectful.

The keyboard works form a central core in Beethoven's creative life. His compositional process was one that depended heavily upon metamorphosis, polishing, and testing initial ideas until they were refined to their final version. Beethoven's sketchbooks give us clear insight into this process. By the same token, the keyboard became a proving ground for much of his compositional development. Thus, much of the composer's musical thinking appears first in keyboard works and later becomes evident in other instrumental forms. The keyboard works, too, represent Beethoven's creativity at all stages of his professional life, from the earliest beginnings in Bonn as a teenager right up through his final years. Finally, it is as a pianist that Beethoven gained his reputation as a virtuoso performer.

Beethoven's power and energy undoubtedly taxed the limits of light-actioned Viennese instruments of the day. His penchant for sudden accents, thick bass textures, and intense sonority was suited to the piano of the nineteenth century rather than the instrument Beethoven worked with for most of his productive years. The piano that John Broadwood shipped to him in 1818 went a considerable way toward meeting the composer's demands, and Beethoven was grateful to Broadwood for the instrument and proud of it. He was, however, almost totally deaf by the time it arrived.

The Thirty-two Piano Sonatas

The sonatas represent perhaps more clearly than any other body of works the innovative processes that are at the core of Beethoven's creativity. From the beginning works, Beethoven shows us many of the directions he will explore, and one can follow his thinking about structure, key relationship, emotional content, and sonority through the sonatas.

The four-movement sonata pattern, heretofore reserved mostly for the quartet and symphony, now became a viable option for piano works. Although Beethoven also used the three-movement and sometimes two-movement plans, the four-movement sonata, with the dance movement as the third movement (later sometimes the second), gave the overall structure more significance, placing it on an equal level with larger sonata-type works.

The sonata-allegro arrangement, as exemplified in individual movements, was also altered in concept. Expositions were expanded by the addition of more thematic material, by development of that material within the confines of the exposition, and often by use of greater contrast between the thematic units. Development sections became more dramatic, more modulatory, and often worked with more than one theme. Recapitulations often contained passages in which themes were presented differently from their counterparts in the exposition. Codas occur frequently and in their most imposing form are extended to the point of rivaling development sections in both complexity and emotional intensity.

The slow movement emerged as a vehicle for Beethoven's inner spiritual quest. Sweet cantabile melodies were often abandoned in favor of heavy, slow-moving, motivic gestures. Beethoven frequently used rests to enlist silence, thus suggesting a meditative mood. High and low registers oftentimes suggest spaciousness or great distance, which could translate into philosophical concepts such as infinity. Slow movements are often lengthy, providing a center of stability in the overall sonata structure. In later works, the slow movement sometimes comes close to being the focal point of the entire work (in Opp. 106, 109, and 111, for example), and Beethoven experiments with combining it with the variation (Opp. 109 and 111) and the fugue (Op. 110).

Beethoven was not the first to employ the term *scherzo* in the context of the sonata structure. Haydn had used the term as a minuet and trio substitute in his Op. 33 string quartets. As early as Op. 2, no. 2, Beethoven began to employ the concept for movements that were more lively than the minuet and trio but still retained its basic structure. By the Op. 2, no. 3, he began to apply a series of small alterations to that traditional form, and he continued to fuss with the concept in one way or another throughout the sonatas. Thus, the dance-based movement may appear as a minuet, as a scherzo, or as neither with only a tempo marking. He may place it as a middle movement in a three-movement work, as a second or third movement in a four-movement work, with or without traditional repeats, and with or without a written-out da capo. The accompanying chart summarizes these variants.

The final movements of Beethoven's sonatas were conceived from the beginning as larger, more serious movements than those typically found in Classical sonata structure. In only a few cases could the last movement of Beethoven's three- or four-movement sonatas be considered "slight." Opus 2, no. 1, presents a dramatic sonata-like structure, and Op. 2, nos. 2 and 3, offer lengthy rondos. In the Op. 27 sonatas, we see the first clear indication of Beethoven's shifting the focal point of the work away from the first movement toward the final movement. In both of these works the longest, most imposing concept is reserved for the last movement. Then for a time, a nearly equal balance of importance between the first and last movements exhibits itself. The last sonatas tend, once again, to favor last-movement importance. Clearly the final movements are the weightiest in the Opp. 101 and 109 sonatas, and arguments for that perception could be made for the Opp. 106 and 110. Two-movement works are harder to pin down in this regard, but certainly the final movement of the Op. 111 should be considered at least an equal of the powerful first movement.

The two forms most often used by Beethoven for last movements are the rondo (in about half the sonatas) and the sonata-allegro (in about a quarter of the sonatas). Mixing the two in some manner occurs frequently. The ABACABA pattern, where the B sections appear first in a related key and then in the home key (much like the second-theme areas of the sonata-allegro structure), is sometimes even referred to as "sonata-rondo" form. This pattern appears often, as well as arrangements in which the C section takes on a development-like character, manipulating material presented in the A or B sections. In the last movements of the Op. 10, no. 2, and the Op. 54, Beethoven writes a perpetual-motion piece that strongly resembles a sonata-allegro structure, albeit each movement is tightly knit and tends to revolve around a single idea.

Beethoven attempted to infuse into the overall sonata structure elements of both the formal theme and variation and the fugue. Variations as a first movement had been used by both Haydn (L. 7 and 56) and

Minuet and Trio Structure

da capo

$$\|:\ A\ :\|:\ B\ :\|:\ C\ :\|:\ D\ :\|\ A\ \|\ B\ \|$$

Op. 2, no. 2	(Menuetto)	3rd movt. of 4; regular structure
Op. 2, no. 2	(Scherzo)	3rd movt. of 4; regular structure
Op. 2, no. 3	(Scherzo)	3rd movt. of 4; no repeat signs in D (repeat written out)
Op. 7	(Allegro)	3rd movt. of 4; D through-composed with no repeat signs
Op. 10, no. 2	(Allegretto)	2nd movt. of 3; C, D, da capo written out with variants
Op. 10, no. 3	(Menuetto)	3rd movt. of 4; C and D combined; repeat written out with variants
Op. 14, no. 1	(Allegretto)	2nd movt. of 3; A and B combined with no repeats; D no repeats; coda
Op. 22	(Menuetto)	3rd movt. of 4; regular structure
Op. 26	(Scherzo)	first appearance as 2nd movt. of 4; A no repeat (written out)
Op. 27, no. 1	(Allegro molto e vivace)	2nd movt. followed by combined 3rd and 4th; da capo written out with variant
Op. 27, no. 2	(Allegretto)	2nd movt. of 3; A not repeated
Op. 28	(Scherzo)	3rd movt. of 4; A and D not repeated (written out repeats with variants)
Op. 31, no. 3	(Scherzo)	2nd movt. of 4; notwithstanding its title, the movement is in duple time and sonata-allegro form
Op. 101	(Lebhaft. Marsch-mässig)	2nd movt. of 4; march-like character; duple time; D not repeated; transition to da capo
Op. 106	(Scherzo)	2nd movt. of 4; through-composed with no repeats; generally ABA with interludes
Op. 110	(Allegro molto)	2nd movt. followed by combined 3rd and 4th; duple meter; C and D combined and through-composed; da capo written out with B repeated; short, transitional coda.

Mozart (K. 331), so the set of variations that serves as the opening movement of Op. 26 is not an innovation. One can also find sets of variations used as last movements (Mozart K. 284). More innovative is the concept of using a slow theme and variations as a psychological summing up, creating a sense of transcendental intensity (Opp. 109 and 111). The fugue appears at various points in Beethoven's sonatas: as the development section of the sonata-allegro movement that closes Op. 101; as the climactic final movement of Op. 106; as the basis of one of the variations in the last movement of Op. 109; and mingled with the slow movement in the fantasy-like closing sections of Op. 110.

Beethoven also applies strong unifying devices to the sonata structure. Cyclicism, the unexpected appearance of thematic material from one movement at some other place in the sonata, is one of them. An argument can be made for its first occurrence as the final movement of Op. 27, no. 1, where a segment of the slow movement appears before the coda of the final movement. One must, however, take note of the use of the term *Tempo I* at that point where the slow material returns. This might mean that Beethoven thought of the slow and faster material as one movement, a kind of foreshadowing of the concept of the last movement of the Op. 110. Less subject to dispute is the cyclicism in Op. 101, where the opening phrase of the first movement of the sonata later becomes a link between the slow third movement and the last movement.

Yet another unifying device is the use of material from a slow introduction throughout an ensuing sonata-allegro structure. This takes place in the opening movements of the Opp. 13; 31, no. 2; and 81a. Beethoven often projects a strong sense of unity within a movement by developing motivic material in all sections of the structure. A notable example of this technique is the first movement of the Op. 10, no. 3, where the first four notes of the opening theme are almost constantly present in some guise throughout the movement.

Beethoven continued to rethink and reshape the sonata structure in both its internal and overall components from his earliest works right on through his final ones. The sonata was for him a living, changing, growing entity. That his thinking managed to be not only innovative but also artistically successful in almost every case is a mark of his genius.

Identification	No. of Movts.	Tempo Markings of Movts. and (Key)
Op. 2, no. 1 (1795)	4	Allegro *(f);* Adagio *(F);* Menuetto *(f);* Prestissimo *(f)*

The first of three sonatas dedicated to Joseph Haydn, this sonata shares the key of *f* with the Op. 57, a fact that has suggested comparison to some. The Op. 2, no. 1, has even been called the *Little Appassionata*. Other similarities between the two sonatas may be observed, although they may be coincidental: the opening themes of both works are based on the tonic triad arpeggio; the opening movements share second themes that are so similar to first themes that arguments could be made to support the contention that the themes are, in fact, the same idea in different guises; the final movements of both sonatas are large, somewhat modified sonata-allegro structures, both tempestuous and rhythmically driving.

The opening Allegro of the Op. 2, no. 1, is a very compressed sonata-allegro structure with a six-measure codetta. To be noted is Beethoven's use of the sforzando, especially as a means of setting up patterns of syncopation. The second theme might be thought of as a free inversion of the first-theme idea. It appears in *A-flat* in the exposition with a reiterated lowered sixth degree of the scale, suggesting *a-flat*. In the closing theme of the exposition the third degree of the *A-flat* scale is lowered.

The second movement is galant in spirit and in this regard does not herald Beethoven's later concepts regarding slow movements. Its structure resembles a two-part sonata-allegro structure, one in which the development has been truncated but in which the exposition and the recapitulation remain intact with the traditional key relationships in place, except for a six-measure excursion into *d* that appears in the exposition. There is a three-measure codetta. This truncated sonata-allegro structure is noted at this point, because Beethoven returns to it, or a slightly altered version of it, in the slow movements of the Opp. 10, no. 1; 31, no. 2; and 81a.

The Menuetto with its trio is in a strict form, and the final movement uses a sonata-allegro form with a middle section that presents new thematic material substituting for the development. This middle section is in a two-part form, each part being presented with written-out repeats and variations. An imaginative retransition to the recapitulation provides brief developmental play based on the opening subject of the movement.

Identification	No. of Movts.	Tempo Markings of Movts. and (Key)
Op. 2, no. 2 (1795)	4	Allegro vivace *(A)*; Largo appassionato *(D)*; Scherzo, Allegretto *(A)*; Rondo, Grazioso (A)

The exposition of the opening movement points clearly to the composer's interest in enlarging the scope and function of the opening section of the sonata-allegro structure. Three motivic ideas join to form an opening theme (Examples 8.1a–c). A carefully prepared modulation is to the dominant minor rather than the dominant major. The second theme itself modulates from *e* through *G* and *B-flat*, reaching its climax on a VII_7 in *e*. At this point, the opening theme's first motive returns followed by a closing section that presents a third theme. Beethoven thus mixes the concepts of stating thematic material with elements of development, such as modulation, fragmentation, and unexpected reappearances.

Example 8.1a Ludwig van Beethoven: Sonata, Op. 2, no. 2, 1st movt. mm. 1–4

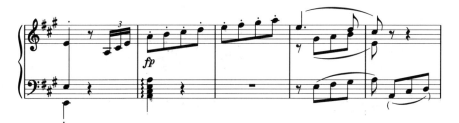

Example 8.1b mm. 8–12

Example 8.1c mm. 32–35

From *Beethoven: Klaviersonaten,* ed. by B. A. Wallner. Copyright G. Henle Munich.

The development section is based on the first and second motives of the opening theme. It opens in *C* and functions in and around that key with passages in *F, d,* and *a.* Beethoven even changes the key signature, eschewing sharps or flats to facilitate his notation of this section. In the retransition, *E* enters as the dominant of *a* and functions to return the piece to *A* in the recapitulation, at which point Beethoven reinstates the appropriate three sharps in the key signature. The relationship of key centers separated by the interval of a third is already very significant in the concept of this movement. It is a relationship that Beethoven continued to explore throughout his creative life.

Counting numbers of measures in a musical work can be both sterile and misleading, but here comparison with the Op. 2, no. 1, points to the enlarged concept of the sonata-allegro structure in the second work. (Both works are in two-four time, the Op. 2, no. 1, written as *C.*

	Op. 2, no. 1	*Op. 2, no. 2*
Exposition	48	121
Development	51	104
Recapitulation	51	112

The seriousness of the second movement is suggested by its tempo marking, *Largo appassionato.* Of the possible slow tempo indications, largo was considered to be the slowest, indications moving up through lento, adagio, and andante. It is interesting to note that Mozart never used largo as an indication in his keyboard sonatas and Haydn used it only once (L. 50), as a direction for the short French overture that serves to introduce the final movement.

Beethoven opens the slow movement with a theme that suggests string-quartet writing: the use of four voices; a relatively static sustained melody; and a pizzicato-like moving bass, not only marked *staccato* but also painstakingly written with rests between each note (Example 8.2). The middle section opens in *b,* modulates to *f-sharp,* and then offers an eloquent moment of serenity as it moves unexpectedly to the key of the Neapolitan sixth, *G.*

Beethoven's use of the coda as a point of departure for a new and unexpected section becomes an important distinguishing characteristic of his musical thinking. Both the slow movement and the final movement of the Op. 2, no. 2, show us this thinking in an embryonic form.

Example 8.2 Ludwig van Beethoven: Sonata, Op. 2, no. 2, 2nd movt. mm. 1–2
From *Beethoven: Klaviersonaten,* ed. by B. A. Wallner. Copyright G. Henle Munich.

The structure of the slow movement balances with almost perfect symmetry up to the point of the surprise section (m. 58).

Op. 2, no. 2; second movement							
A Section			*B Section*	*A Section*			*Coda-like*
a — b — a			c	a — b — a			
8	4	7	12	8	4	7	7

Number of measures

The section noted as coda-like has the feel and cadential preparation one might expect in a Classical coda, and the listener is completely prepared for a final cadence in *D* in the eighth measure. Instead, the opening theme returns dramatically in *d*, marked *fortissimo* (Example 8.3). The passage wanders off into *B-flat* briefly before returning to the dominant of *D*. A final, varied statement of the opening theme in *D*, followed by yet another six-measure coda, brings the movement to a close. The developmental coda as Beethoven ultimately conceived it is not yet fully formed in the composer's mind at this point, but the unexpected excursion that concludes the movement is a clear forerunner.

The third movement is marked *Scherzo*, Beethoven's earliest use of the term in the sonatas. Johann Sebastian Bach had used it in his third partita as a dance movement, and Haydn used it in the Op. 33 string quartets (1782) as an accelerated, lighthearted minuet and trio substitute, four times as the second movement, and twice as the third movement. Beethoven borrows Haydn's concept here, presenting the scherzo in strict minuet and trio form.

The Rondo, which serves as the final movement, starts off by conforming reasonably well to the pattern of ABACABA. Each time the A theme returns, its opening arpeggiated figure is more elaborate. The C section is in the parallel minor key and is in a two-part form. Each part

Example 8.3 Ludwig van Beethoven: Sonata, Op. 2, no. 2, 2nd movt. mm. 58–59

From *Beethoven: Klaviersonaten*, ed. by B. A. Wallner. Copyright G. Henle Munich

is repeated, the first part indicated by the use of repeat signs and the second by being written out. At the final presentation of the A theme, Beethoven once again interjects the unexpected. A varied version of the theme is only in its second phrase when it wanders off into *F.* It returns to *A* in a fragmented form, is interrupted by a return of the theme from the C section, now in *B-flat,* and is finally permitted a closing statement in *A.* As in the second movement of the sonata, Beethoven presents here an incipient developmental coda.

Identification	No. of Movts.	Tempo Markings of Movts. and (Key)
Op. 2, no. 3 (1796)	4	Allegro con brio *(C);* Adagio *(E);* Scherzo, Allegro *(C);* Allegro assai (C)

This sonata is the most overtly brilliant of the Op. 2 set. As in Op. 2, no. 2, Beethoven offers a first-movement exposition of extended scope. Here the composer presents two distinct second themes. Both are lyrical in contrast to the motivic first theme, the first in the dominant minor and the second in its parallel major (Examples 8.4 a–b). A return of the first-theme material serves to reinstate virtuosic brilliance, and a closing theme built on a series of cadences both rounds off the exposition and opens the development. The development section is based

Example 8.4a Ludwig van Beethoven: Sonata, Op. 2, no. 3, 1st movt. mm. 27–28

Example 8.4 b Ludwig van Beethoven: Sonata, Op. 2, no. 3, 1st movt. mm. 47–48

From *Beethoven: Klaviersonaten,* ed. by B. A. Wallner. Copyright G. Henle Munich.

entirely on this cadence figure and opening-theme material. The recapitulation presents all sections found in the exposition, including both second themes. As the recapitulation nears its conclusion, a startling, sudden jump to *A-flat* suggests an extended coda. We are led, instead, to a cadenza, much as one might expect to find in a keyboard concerto. A brief statement of first-theme material brings this movement to a brilliant close.

The adagio movement is written in *E,* a key a major third away from the home key of the sonata. The two-four time signature possibly presents a problem for its interpreter, for the two themes around which the movement revolves are written in sixteenth and thirty-second notes, both values tending to move quickly if one adheres to the adagio quarter note. Many performers have thus been convinced that the repose suggested by the musical material can be achieved only by applying an adagio beat-flow to the eighth note, essentially rendering the movement in four counts per measure rather than two. The problem can also be addressed by maintaining the two counts per measure but playing the movement somewhat slower than the term *adagio* might suggest.

The opening theme of the Adagio makes use of both dotted rhythm and rests between motives (Example 8.5). This theme alternates with an improvisatory-like section that is stated first in *e* and, in its second appearance, in *C.* The movement is, however, not at all symmetrical in its alternation of these sections, for the first statement is thirty-one measures in length while the second is but twelve measures long. A final, slightly varied statement of the opening theme closes the movement. Worth noting is the early example of register shifts, here displacing a melodic phrase from a high monophonic upbeat down three-and-one-half octaves (m. 80).

The Scherzo offers only slight modifications to the traditional form. The second part of the trio has a written-out repeat, probably so notated in order to accommodate alterations in the last five measures of the section. There is a twenty-three-measure coda that follows the da capo.

Example 8.5 Ludwig van Beethoven: Sonata, Op. 2, no. 3, 2nd movt. mm. 1–2
From *Beethoven: Klaviersonaten,* ed. by B. A. Wallner. Copyright G. Henle Munich.

The underlying structural concept of the Allegro assai is undoubtedly that of sonata-rondo (ABACABA), but by now it is not surprising that Beethoven adds some unusual features to the expected pattern. In the second appearance of the A theme, Beethoven moves into a development of the theme four measures after it is begun (m. 73). After twenty-six measures of developmental play, a middle-section theme in *F* is announced. Although its opening phrase suggests a new theme, material that has close ties with both the original statement of the A theme and a portion of the B theme is soon recalled. The expected final statement of A never really takes place. Instead, a series of trills and fragments from the A theme combine to create the impression of a concerto-like cadenza, although, unlike in the first movement (where bar lines are temporarily abandoned), the cadenza here remains measured. A series of fermatas and interpretive directions slow the movement down to a virtual standstill before a final burst of energy. The device of letting a movement wind down, just before bringing it to a brilliant conclusion, seems to have pleased the composer, for similar endings can be found in Op. 27, no. 1; Op. 81a; and the last movements of both the first and fifth piano concertos (Opp. 15 and 73).

Identification	No. of Movts.	Tempo Markings of Movts. and (Key)
Op. 7 (1796–97)	4	Allegro molto e con brio (*E-flat*); Largo, con gran espressione (*C*); Allegro (*E-flat*); Rondo, Poco allegretto e grazioso (*E-flat*)

The first movement exhibits a number of characteristics already noted in the Op. 2 set. The exposition here is filled with so much material that central themes become almost inundated with significant contrasting material. Thus, the opening motive, accompanied by a triplet figure in the left hand, is paired with a melodic triplet motive of equal importance. The transition to the dominant sounds like development of the opening idea. The second theme is paired with a more lyrical idea that is, in turn, combined with the triplet figure. This material is developed for about thirty measures (beginning at measure 81), and for a time the key of *C* plays an important role. The triplet figure is used to build a closing section (m. 93). The exposition finally ends with cadences written in a rhythm heard earlier as a transition to the second theme.

These observations point to the fact that the composer achieves a remarkable degree of unity through manipulating and juxtaposing rhythmic and melodic material but at the same time creates the impression of an almost improvisatory style, moving quickly from one idea to the next. Each seems to grow effortlessly out of the material of its predecessor. Thus, the sections that might be labeled first theme, transition, second theme, and so forth become so obscured that a seemingly through-composed, rapturous composition emerges.

The development section is straightforward, using material from the opening ideas of the exposition and its final cadence. The recapitulation leaves virtually all of the material intact. A coda of forty-nine measures is announced with an unexpected statement of the opening theme in *c* (m. 313). The return to *E-flat* is, however, swift and decisive.

The second movement employs the term *largo*, as did the second movement of the Op.2, no. 2, with the additional notation of *con gran espressione*. The solemnity of the opening theme is enhanced by the use of rests for half of each measure (Example 8.6). A contrasting section in *A-flat* makes use of a staccato bass figure, reminiscent once again of the Op. 2, no. 2. Extreme register shifts, monophonic textures, and great dynamic contrasts suggest orchestral effects. A return to the opening theme in a slightly altered form is followed by a short coda. As in the Op. 2, no. 3, the key of the slow movement is at the interval of a third away from the key of the sonata, this time a minor third (instead of major).

The third movement is designated neither a scherzo nor a minuet and trio, but its structure conforms to the pattern associated with those titles. The second half of the trio bears no repeat signs, and here (unlike the scherzo movement of the Op. 2, no. 3) the repeat is not written out in the music itself.

The form of the Rondo is regular: ABACABA-coda. Each time A reappears it does so with a more elaborate figural variation. The middle section (C) is a miniature two-part form in *c* with each part marked to be repeated. The coda provides a half-step upward shift of the A theme to *E*. The effect is short-lived, however, and the movement unwinds to end quietly in *E-flat*.

Example 8.6 Ludwig van Beethoven: Sonata, Op. 7, 2nd movt. mm. 1–4
From *Beethoven: Klaviersonaten*, ed. by B. A. Wallner. Copyright G. Henle Munich.

Identification	No. of Movts.	Tempo Markings of Movts. and (Key)
Op. 10, no. 1 (1796–98)	3	Allegro molto e con brio (*c*); Adagio molto (*A-flat*); Finale, prestissimo (*c*)

The first two sonatas of the Op. 10 set exemplify Beethoven's return to a shorter, less-imposing sonata concept. Not only is there a breaking away from the four-movement pattern but also a compactness within most of the movements, the composer eschewing lengthy codas, extended developments, and other internal devices that serve to enlarge the structure. This is a reversal of the thinking exemplified in the first four sonatas (the Op. 2 set and the Op. 7). This conceptual shifting continues to occur throughout the thirty-two sonatas, so that we are presented with a series of changing concepts, Beethoven envisioning the sonata at one time as a work of heroic dimension, at another time as small and intimate; sometimes traditional, and at other times a vehicle for bold experimentation.

The opening movement of the Op. 10, no. 1, has few surprises. The development begins briefly with material from the very opening of the work but then utilizes a new, lyric theme. The Adagio molto presents the same two-part structure described in the discussion of the slow movement of the Op. 2, no. 1, adding to it a twenty-measure coda. The Adagio must be played very slowly to accommodate the ornamental sixty-fourth notes that occur in the second theme. As in the slow movement of the Op. 2, no. 3, reconciliation between the tempo marking of *adagio* and its application to the quarter note in two-four time may prove difficult. The final movement is a very compressed sonata-allegro form with a development only twelve measures in length.

Identification	No. of Movts.	Tempo Markings of Movts. and (Key)
Op. 10, no. 2 (1796–98)	3	Allegro (*F*); Allegretto (*f*); Presto (*F*)

This sonata well represents Beethoven in high spirits, Beethoven the humorist. The first movement contains several musical jokes. The development is built mischievously from the last three cadence notes of the exposition, eschewing all other thematic material from the exposition. To this idea is added a new theme. At the end of the development a painfully obvious dominant preparation leads to a fake recapitulation in the wrong key of *D*. An unusually lengthy rest occurs at the point where the music gets back to the right key (mm. 129–30), as if the performer had to have an extra second to figure out how to get back on track. Beethoven marks both the exposition and the development-recapitulation sections of the movement to be repeated, a procedure he had not used in the preceding three sonatas (Op. 2, no. 3; Op. 7; and Op. 10, no. 1).

The second movement is in minuet and trio form with the repeats of both sections of the trio written out with slight variants. The da capo is also written out, varied to feature syncopation. The structure of the final movement looks on the page to be one of two parts, each marked to be repeated. Within that framework lies the outline of a free sonata-allegro form. The movement opens with imitative entrances that suggest fugal writing, but the texture quickly evolves to a more homophonic mode. The opening section of thirty-two measures is monothematic. The second section opens with a development of the main idea that once again features free imitation. A return to *F* in measure 87 serves as a quasi-recapitulation, albeit thematerial is significantly different from the way it first appeared, rewritten to incorporate virtuoso display. The end of the movement is abrupt and somewhat surprising. The movement is built of perpetual eighth- and sixteenth-note patterns, leaving an impression of buoyant energy.

Identification	*No. of Movts.*	*Tempo Markings of Movts. and (Key)*
Op. 10, no. 3 (1796–98)	4	Presto *(D);* Largo e mesto *(d);* Menuetto, Allegro *(D);* Rondo, Allegro *(D).*

After the excursion into the two shorter, lighter works, Op. 10, nos. 1 and 2, Beethoven here returns to the four-movement, large sonata structure, underscoring many of the procedures noted in the Op. 2 set and the Op. 7. The first movement presents a theme that opens with four descending notes of the *D-major* scale. These four notes become motivic throughout the movement, appearing everywhere in the exposition, the development, and of course the recapitulation. They are sometimes inverted, going up instead of down, sometimes used imitatively, but there is hardly a passage in the piece in which their presence is not heard, the four-note idea acting as a powerful unifying device.

The second movement is a serious sonata-allegro structure with a developmental coda. So magnificent is this movement that many musicians have come to regard it as the most profound slow movement Beethoven wrote before 1800. To be noted as especially colorful is the "orchestral" quality at the end of the middle section (Example 8.7). This texture is used again in the coda. The movement ends with the use of wide-range register shifts and rests.

The Menuetto offers a trio that is through-composed with no written-out repeats. The final Rondo is rather free. As in the first movement, an opening motive, this time of only three notes, acts as a unifying device for different departures. Sections can be delineated each time this motive returns, but the use of fermatas, little cadenzas, and developmental techniques in alternate sections give the movement an improvisatory

Largo e mesto

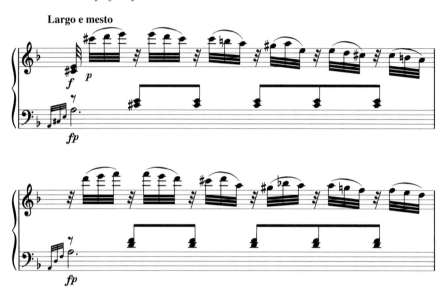

Example 8.7 Ludwig van Beethoven: Sonata, Op. 10, no. 3, 2nd movt. mm. 38–39

From *Beethoven: Klaviersonaten,* ed. by B. A. Wallner. Copyright G. Henle Munich.

feeling. Although the expected rondo pattern is suggested, labeling sections in order to make the movement fit a mold seems contrary to the spirit of the piece.

Identification	No. of Movts.	Tempo Markings of Movts. and (Key)
Op. 13— Grande Sonata Pathétique (1798–99)	3	Grave-Allegro de molto e con brio (c); Adagio cantabile (A-flat); Rondo, Allegro (c)

After having observed that up to this point Beethoven expanded the sonata concept in four-movement works or treated it somewhat more lightly in three-movement works, we now encounter the first of several three-movement sonatas in which the intensity and dramatic content clearly herald a serious, important work. Indeed, this three-movement, intense, dramatic combination is to serve the composer in the Op. 27, no. 2; Op. 31, no. 2; Op. 53; Op. 57; and Op. 81a. Curiously, each of the works born of this concept is among the most frequently performed of the sonatas, and all of them have nicknames, albeit only the Op. 13 and Op. 81a carry names endorsed by the composer. In the case of the Op. 13, Beethoven's approval was only implied. Beethoven was aware before publication of the work that the designation *Pathétique* was to be

Allegro molto e con brio

Example 8.8 Ludwig van Beethoven: Sonata, Op. 13, 1st movt. mm. 137–41
From *Beethoven: Klaviersonaten*, ed. by B. A. Wallner. Copyright G. Henle
Munich.

added by the publisher as a way of stimulating interest, and the composer apparently offered no objection.

The term *Pathétique* suggests that the music is emotional and
intense. The first movement lives up to this promise. The slow introduction is filled with abrupt dynamic contrasts and heavy-textured
chords in dotted rhythm, possibly a throwback to the French overture
style. The introduction becomes an integral part of the movement inasmuch as it returns in its original tempo to introduce the development
section and again as a link to a short coda. Moreover, the motive from
the introduction is used in the development section, where its opening
phrase is to be played allegro (Example 8.8). The second theme of the
exposition opens in *e-flat* in the exposition and *f* in the recapitulation,
although in each case the more traditional keys of *E-flat* for the exposition and *c* for the recapitulation are in place by the time the extended
closing sections arrive. Of the many dramatic devices in the movement
are the use of bass tremolos throughout the movement and the introduction of overlapping half notes in a very low register at the climax of
the development (Example 8.9).

The second movement is one of Beethoven's best-known slow
movements. It is built around an unusually attractive melody with two
departures and a short coda. The main melody is consistently written
with curious phrase groupings, unusual enough to be ignored frequently by performers. The final Rondo is in the expected form: ABACABA-
coda. The composer returns to the use of low registers to create dramatic effects (mm. 107–8) and in the coda uses a series of rapid-fire
sforzandi to create a virtual frenzy (mm. 193–94ff). A surprise departure
into *A-flat* is combined with rests, a fermata, and extreme dynamic contrasts to bring the movement to a suspenseful moment before a forceful,
final, descending scale.

Identification	No. of Movts.	Tempo Markings of Movts. and (Key)
Op. 14, no. 1 (1798–99)	3	Allegro *(E)*; Allegretto *(e)*; Rondo, Allegro comodo *(E)*

Example 8.9 Ludwig van Beethoven: Sonata, Op. 13, 1st movt. mm. 178–83
From *Beethoven: Klaviersonaten*, ed. by B. A. Wallner. Copyright G. Henle
Munich.

Both of the Op. 14 sonatas, like the Op. 10, nos. 1 and 2, represent
a smaller, lighter concept of the genre. The first movement of this sonata
particularly exhibits passages that suggest part writing for string quartet
(mm. 8–9). The development section is built almost entirely on a new
melodic idea, introduced after the first four measures. A short, nondevelopmental coda ends the movement. The Allegretto is a minuet-and-
trio-like movement. There are no marked repeats in the piece except
for the second half of the trio (*Maggiore*) section. A short coda follows the
da capo. The final Rondo is very regular (ABACABA), the sections being
both quite evident and brief.

Identification	No. of Movts.	Tempo Markings of Movts. and (Key)
Op. 14, no. 2 (1798–99)	3	Allegro *(G)*; Andante *(C)*; Scherzo, Allegro assai *(G)*

Like the Op. 14, no. 1, this sonata exhibits quartet-like writing in
its first movement (mm. 47–49). The development section is somewhat
longer here and utilizes the opening motive from the exposition extensively as well as the second theme. The second movement represents
Beethoven's first incorporation of a formal set of variations into the
sonata. Such a marriage seems quite innocuous in this work, but, as the

composer continues to work with this combination, it becomes an increasingly powerful force for shaping the sonata concept. This movement modestly presents a two-part theme with its second part marked to be repeated. This pattern is followed through two variations. A third variation without repeats and a short coda end the movement. The last chord is a "surprise" ending, being marked *fortissimo* after three measures of pianissimo. The final scherzo movement is generally in ABA form, although the return of A is considerably shortened and is followed by a lengthy coda based on B material. The jovial spirit of the movement is sustained by the use of short motives that often end staccato.

Identification	No. of Movts.	Tempo Markings of Movts. and (Key)
Op. 22 (1799–1800)	4	Allegro con brio (*B-flat*); Adagio con molto espressione (*E-flat*); Menuetto (*B-flat*); Rondo, Allegretto (*B-flat*)

After having developed the four-movement sonata concept in the Op. 2 set and the Op. 7, and after having shown striking originality in four movements of Op. 10, no. 3, Beethoven has raised the level of expectation for his treatment of the four-movement sonata to a very high level. This fact has not served the Op. 22 very well, for, although it is a well-constructed work that rests comfortably within Beethoven's style, it is not a work that represents the composer penetrating new frontiers. As a result, some observers have found the work mundane.

Even so, the Op. 22 should not be dismissed too quickly. Its opening movement offers a lengthy, well-constructed development section. The slow movement is elegant with its nine-eight time signature and long-flowing, ornamental lines. It is, incidentally, in sonata-allegro form with a fine development and a short coda. The minuet, although in perfectly regular form, has considerable charm. The final Rondo is built on a lovely, lyrical theme that becomes considerably varied in its last two appearances and in the coda. Although it is true that Beethoven presents us with few or no experimental features in the Op. 22, his musical thinking, nevertheless, is on very solid ground throughout the work. The sonata deserves higher marks than it has been accorded in many quarters.

Identification	No. of Movts.	Tempo Markings of Movts. and (Key)
Op. 26 (1800–1801)	4	Andante con Variationi (*A-flat*); Scherzo, Allegro molto (*A-flat*); Marcia Funebre sulla morte d'un Eroe (*a-flat*); Rondo (*A-flat*)

The next three sonatas, all from around 1800, are experimental in that the sonata concept is adjusted in various ways. In the Op. 26 there is no sonata-allegro form in any of the four movements. Beethoven was not the first to use a theme and variations as the opening movement of a sonata, for Haydn employed such an arrangement in a late sonata (Hob. 42; L. 56), as did Mozart in the K. 331. The theme of the Op. 26 is in rounded two-part form. There are no repeat signs in the movement. The five variations that follow stay close to the harmonic profile of the theme with fragments of the original melody frequently emerging. The third variation is in *a-flat*. The final variation presents the theme pretty much intact, set in florid figuration, much of which is a slow written-out trill pattern. This texture is a foreshadowing of the extended trills that the composer is to use in the variation movements of the Opp. 109 and 111.

Beethoven writes out the repeat for the first part of the Scherzo and leaves a note for the performer not to repeat the section. The movement is very rapid and virtuosic. The appearance of a funeral march in the sonata structure forecasts its use in the third symphony (*Eroica*), Op. 55, a few years later. The structure of the funeral march is ABA, where the B section is in a two-part form, each part marked to be repeated. Noteworthy are the imitations of drum rolls in the B section. A short but intensely emotional coda ends the march.

The final movement is a tightly knit Rondo (ABACABAcoda) where the last statement of the theme and the coda combine. Most of the movement is driven by sixteenth notes, giving the effect of perpetual motion. The use of a funeral march as the third movement of a four-movement sonata, and following it with a compact, short perpetual-motion movement, was also done by Chopin in his second sonata, Op. 35 (*b-flat*). Although historic evidence has suggested that Chopin was not a great admirer of Beethoven, preferring the music of Mozart and J. S. Bach instead, the similarity of the concepts of the last two movements of Beethoven's Op. 26 and Chopin's Op. 35 seems to point to more than coincidence. It may even be logical to assume that Chopin knew the Op. 26 and admired it at least to the extent of using its concept and arrangement of movements.

Identification	No. of Movts.	Tempo Markings of Movts. and (Key)
Op. 27, no. 1 (1800–1801)	3 or 4	Andante, Allegro, Tempo I (*E-flat*, *C*, *E-flat*); Allegro molto e vivace (*c*); Adagio con espressione (*A-flat*); Allegro vivace (*E-flat*)

Beethoven himself sets the stage for this work with the subtitle *Sonata quasi una fantasia.* Improvisatory characteristics abound in the work: the multiple-tempo pattern of the first movement; the joining of all movements by specific instructions from the composer, *attacca subito* with the tempo of the following movement being noted; a cadenza before the final Allegro vivace; and the return of the Adagio material with yet another cadenza just before the final presto. There is no sonata-allegro structure in the work, although the Allegro vivace comes very close to being one.

The opening movement presents its andante material in the keys of both *E-flat* and *C*. New material, also in *C*, is presented in a brilliant, short middle section marked *Allegro*. The *E-flat* Andante comes back at Tempo I in a curtailed form before leading to the second movement in *c*. Here the spirit is that of a rapid scherzo, in minuet and trio form, the da capo being written out so that a syncopated variation can be embedded in the material.

The Adagio acts as a slow, short interlude leading to the final Allegro vivace. The Adagio comes back near the end of the sonata, just before the final coda, marked *Presto*. At this point, Beethoven marks the adagio material *Tempo I,* just as he had for the return of the opening material in the first movement (Example 8.10). This tempo marking may suggest that the composer conceived the contrasting sections as a unity, much the same way the final sections of the Op. 110 were to be structured some twenty years later. Curiously, however, the key structure does not quite square with this concept, for the original Adagio is in *A-flat*, a key related to the key of the sonata and one befitting a separate slow movement. The return of the Adagio near the end of the work is in *E-flat,* the home key of the Allegro vivace. If the arrangement of the Adagio and the Allegro vivace were to be viewed as two separate movements, connected by a cadenza, then the return of the material near the end of the work becomes an early example of cyclicism, not yet as clear as that in the Op. 101, but perhaps the predecessor of the cyclicism to be found in the composer's Symphony no. 5, Op. 67, where third-movement material also appears in the last movement.

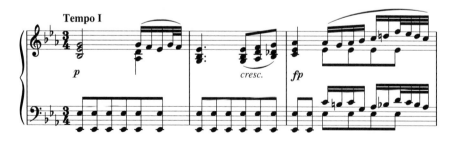

Example 8.10 Ludwig van Beethoven: Sonata, Op. 27, no. 1, last movt. (Allegro vivace) mm. 256–58

From *Beethoven: Klaviersonaten,* ed. by B. A. Wallner. Copyright G. Henle Munich.

The Allegro vivace itself is in sonata-rondo form (ABACABcoda), where the C section is a full-flown development of the opening theme. There is no final return of A, the coda being composed of the afore-mentioned return of the Adagio followed by a short, closing presto. Thus, the movement tends to lean toward a sonata-allegro structure by virtue of the development section (C) and the fact that the two presen-tations of B material are in the dominant and tonic, respectively.

Identification	No. of Movts.	Tempo Markings of Movts. and (Key)
Op. 27, no. 2	3	Adagio sostenuto (*c-sharp*);
(1801)		Allegretto (*D-flat*); Presto (*c-sharp*)

Notwithstanding the fact that this composition is known through-out the world as the *Moonlight Sonata,* the designation is not from the composer. Beethoven did, however, indicate *Sonata quasi una fantasia.* Here the experiment takes a different turn from that explored in its companion piece, the Op. 27, no. 1. Although improvisation may be suggested by the introduction to the first movement and the persistent use of the triplet figure, quite a different effect ultimately evolves because of the high degree of unity achieved by the unrelenting, slow triplets. One mood is thus sustained and unbroken throughout the movement, thereby establishing a serene but intense emotionalism. Underlying this unity and intensity is an embryonic sonata-allegro struc-ture. After five measures of introduction, the opening theme fragment appears in *c-sharp.* Ten measures later comes a second theme fragment revolving around the note *B.* Its parallel spot in the return (recapitula-tion) revolves around *C-sharp.* A middle section in *f-sharp* begins by pre-senting an extended statement of the opening theme and evolving into a series of theme fragments and arpeggios over a *G-sharp* (dominant) pedal point. A coda based on the opening motif closes the movement. The composer's instructions are to *attacca subito il sequente.*

The Allegretto that follows is clearly a minuet and trio in strict form. The first-section repeat is written out with a bit of variation. The composer calls attention to the absence of repeat signs with a reminder to the performer *La prima parte solamente une volta.* The large, dramatic sonata-allegro form is saved for the final movement, shifting the focal point of the work away from the first movement, as was also the case in the Op. 27, no. 1. Never before, however, has this shift of emphasis been so clear in Beethoven's sonatas, and the tendency will reappear decid-edly in the Op. 101 and the Op. 109 and to a lesser extent in the other late sonatas, Op. 106, Op. 110, and Op. 111.

The tranquil intensity held in check throughout the first movement of the Op. 27, no. 2, is unleashed and mushrooms into a wild frenzy in the final movement. Even the quieter moments of this movement are used to set the stage for yet another outburst. The development section utilizes both first and second themes of the exposition, as does a lengthy coda that combines them with cadenza-like material.

Identification	No. of Movts.	Tempo Markings of Movts. and (Key)
Op. 28 (1801)	4	Allegro *(D);* Andante *(d);* Scherzo-Allegro vivace *(D);* Rondo-Allegro, ma non troppo *(D)*

Popularly known as the *Pastoral* sonata, this work once again shows us how quickly Beethoven's musical thinking shifted from the experimental fantasy of the Op. 27 set back to a self-contained expressiveness in a more traditional structure. The lyricism of all the themes in the exposition of the opening movement blend into a texture of gentle contours, sustaining a mood that the development interrupts only briefly at its climax. The coda to the movement is short and nondevelopmental.

The second movement presents a quartet-like texture with a staccato bass line, as did the second movement of the Op. 2, no. 2, but here the tempo moves more quickly and the part writing is more relaxed. The overall structure of the movement is that of a minuet and trio with a written-out da capo that provides figural variations as each section is repeated. A short coda that recalls material from the trio section closes the movement.

The Scherzo is perfectly regular in form, albeit Beethoven writes out the repeat of the second half of the trio in order to provide the melody with a different harmonization. The main theme of the Rondo may have inspired the sonata's nickname, for it has a ländler-like quality. The main body of the movement is perfectly regular in structure (ABACABA). The final statement of the principal theme is in *G* and provides a coda-like feeling. It sets the stage for a surprising burst of energy, a presto based on the main theme, now in *D*, which provides a flourish of unexpected brilliance with which to end the work.

Identification	No. of Movts.	Tempo Markings of Movts. and (Key)
Op. 31, no. 1 (1801–2)	3	Allegro vivace *(G);* Adagio grazioso *(C);* Rondo, Allegretto *(G)*

Several authors commenting on the sonatas of Beethoven have shortchanged this sonata, and the suspicion is aroused that comments about the poverty of musical ideas or the redundancy in the work are born of failure to recognize its humorous spirit, a subtle spoof on the clichés of the day. Indeed, the work opens with a first movement that is filled with imagination and funny surprises: the constant shift of dynamic levels in the opening theme, the careful dominant preparation that moves to the wrong key a whole step flat (Example 8.11), the overkill of the dominant preparation that finally brings the piece back

Example 8.11 Ludwig van Beethoven: Sonata, Op. 31, no. 1, 1st movt. mm. 10–14

From *Beethoven: Klaviersonaten*, ed. by B. A. Wallner. Copyright G. Henle Munich.

to G (mm. 39–44), only to have the key slip away once again (mm. 52–57). The entire second-theme area remains persistently in *b* rather than the dominant right up to the end of the exposition. The recapitulation, too, remains stubbornly dominant-resistant. Not until the coda is the "lesson" finally mastered, where, like an intimidated student, the tonic is made to answer correctly to dominant preparation time and again, even down to the final echo.

The second movement is cast in a typical rondo form with a coda. Its character is extraordinary in that it is a compendium of figural, ornamental gestures. The nine-eight time signature conveys a slow, undulating motion, and the composer's directions suggest it be played *grazioso*. The resulting effect is one of consummate elegance and grace. Twice the return of the main theme is ushered in with written-out cadenzas. The trill, which is an integral part of the main theme, becomes particularly prominent in a sizeable coda.

The final Rondo, like the first movement, is filled with humor and high spirits. The opening phrase of the main theme forms the basis of the middle section, which is developmental in character. The final return of the main theme is hesitant, made so by tempo changes and long rests. A presto then leads to the closing chords, which evoke humor right to the end of the piece.

Identification	No. of Movts.	Markings of Movts. and (Key)
Op. 31, no. 2 (1801–2)	3	Largo, Allegro *(d);* Adagio *(B-flat);* Allegretto *(d)*

Beethoven himself referred to Shakespeare's play *The Tempest* in the context of this sonata. Thus, the composer is partly responsible for the nickname by which this work is generally known. The opening Largo acts like an introduction but also presents the motive that becomes the most important unifying device of the first movement. It appears as an integral part of the main theme (Examples 8.12 a–b), and it forms the

Example 8.12 Ludwig van Beethoven: Sonata, Op. 31, no. 2, 1st movt. (a) mm. 1–2; (b) mm. 21–22

From *Beethoven: Klaviersonaten*, ed. by B. A. Wallner. Copyright G. Henle Munich.

Example 8.13 Ludwig van Beethoven: Sonata, Op. 31, no. 2, 1st movt. mm. 143–48

From *Beethoven: Klaviersonaten*, ed. by B. A. Wallner. Copyright G. Henle Munich.

basis of much of the development section. Furthermore, the motive in its largo form appears as a link between the exposition and the development, as well as at the beginning of the recapitulation, where it is extended to form longer recitative-like statements (Example 8.13). The composer's pedal indications in this passage have been a source of speculation and controversy among interpreters, for Beethoven's markings seem to invite some blurring of the recitative-like melody. Beethoven combines the dramatic effect of the tempo changes with a driving intensity in the Allegro sections. The overall dimensions of the movement are kept reasonably small, the development being rather short and there being only a few arpeggios that act as a coda.

The Adagio is one of the composer's most marvelous slow movements. The entire movement is filled with orchestral effects such as the contrast between the rich, low chords and the upper-register monophonic motive (Example 8.14), or the percussion-like tremolo of the next section. The structure of the movement is that of the large two-part form encountered previously in the second movement of the Op. 2, no. 1, and the Op. 10, no. 1. A coda based on the opening motive exploits register contrasts to the fullest. This movement provides a good example of the fact that mere observation or recounting of salient details falls short of touching the magic that is at the heart of the music. The composer here, indeed, created a composition in which the totality in terms of musical expression is far greater than the sum of its parts.

The Allegretto is virtually a perpetual motion in that there is a nonstop flow of sixteenth notes from the beginning to the end of the movement. Cast in a sonata-allegro form, the movement presents a lengthy development section based entirely on the opening theme and a coda that is developmental and offers a final climactic statement of the opening theme. Perhaps surprisingly, the sonata ends quietly and almost abruptly.

Identification	No. of Movts.	Tempo Markings of Movts. and (Key)
Op. 31, no. 3 (1801–2)	4	Allegro (*E-flat*); Scherzo, Allegro vivace (*A-flat*); Menuetto, Moderato e grazioso (*E-flat*); Presto con fuoco (*E-flat*)

This sonata is Beethoven's only large-scale sonata in which three of the four movements are cast in sonata-allegro form. The composer's thinking in this matter is paralleled by the Symphony no. 4, Op. 60, in which all four movements are in that form. A tentative, gently playful

Example 8.14 Ludwig van Beethoven: Sonata, Op. 31, no. 2, 2nd movt. mm. 1–5

From *Beethoven: Klaviersonaten*, ed. by B. A. Wallner. Copyright G. Henle Munich.

opening on a supertonic chord in its first inversion resolves eight measures later to *E-flat*. The ambiguous quality of this motive and its seemingly hesitant resolution provide material for the transition to the development later as well as for the development itself. It also forms the basis of the coda. Contrasting material presented by the second-theme area is touched upon briefly in the development. The movement remains energetic and jovial throughout.

The use of the title Scherzo for the second movement is one of spirit only, for Beethoven substitutes a sonata-allegro structure for the expected minuet and trio form as well as a duple meter rather than the expected triple one. A rapidly moving staccato bass figure provides energy beneath the opening melodic line, continues in both hands as an integral part of the second theme, and appears as left-hand double notes in the closing section. The development maintains this figure, combining it at one point with comical, little eruptions in sixty-fourth notes (mm. 90–95). There is no coda.

The Menuetto is traditional in structure and provides a respite from the high energy of the other three movements. It has a small coda. The final Presto, written in six-eight time, is constructed in such a way that it is heard as a rapid two-four movement, permeated with nonstop triplet figuration. Relief from the triplet drive is provided only by stops at cadence points at the end of the exposition, as well as near the conclusion of the development, and in the coda. This incessant triplet-like drive has led musicians to characterize the movement as a tarantella, and it provides a brilliant, strong, conclusion to the sonata.

Identification	No. of Movts.	Tempo Markings of Movts. and (Key)
Op. 49, nos. 1 and 2 (1795–98)	2 each	no. 1 Andante *(g);* Rondo, Allegro *(G)* no. 2 Allegro, ma non troppo *(G);* Tempo de menuetto *(G)*

Composed almost a decade earlier, these works bear the German word *leichte* in their title, "easy" suggesting their possible use as teaching material. Indeed, they have become staples in students' repertoire. Although they represent sterling examples of the composer's musical thinking, they are not remarkable in structure, nor do they find Beethoven in a particularly innovative mood. Both first movements are in typical sonata-allegro structures. The Rondo of the first of the set is a bit lopsided in that the first departure from the theme is in *B-flat* (a major third away from the home key) and is followed by a very short new theme in *g*, all before the first return of the main theme. The structure of the second sonata's minuet is more a little rondo with two departures and a coda than it is a minuet and trio. It is reported that this little piece enjoyed a faddish popularity in Vienna during Beethoven's lifetime.

Identification	No. of Movts.	Tempo Markings of Movts. and (Key)
Op. 53	2 or 3	Allegro con brio *(C);*
(1803–4)		Introduzione, Adagio molto *(F);*
		Rondo, Allegretto moderato *(C)*

Beethoven's dedication of this work to his lifelong friend, Count Waldstein, was a gesture of affection and tribute, but even the composer could not have predicted that the dedication would be carried over into the vernacular and that the work would be known generally as the *Waldstein Sonata.* Deservedly one of the most popular of the sonatas, it ranks near the top in large-scale conception, originality, and virtuoso display.

The opening theme of the first movement arrests attention with a series of rapid *C* chords in the low register of the keyboard that deftly end up in the dominant key. Drama and color are added when the entire sequence of chords is repeated in *B-flat*, ending up in *F* (Example 8.15).

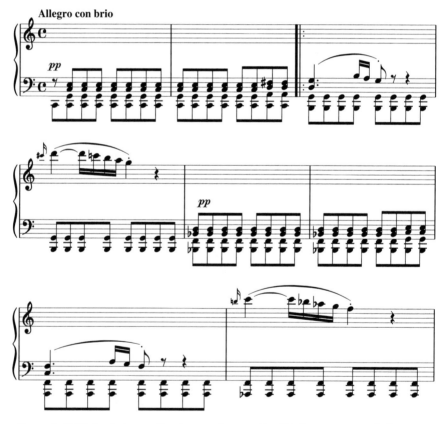

Example 8.15 Ludwig van Beethoven: Sonata, Op. 53, 1st movt. mm. 1–8
From *Beethoven: Klaviersonaten,* ed. by B. A. Wallner. Copyright G. Henle Munich.

The composer shifts quickly to the parallel minor and uses it as a subdominant to return to *c*. Then with a shift back to the parallel major he is ready to restate the main theme. All of these key changes take place in the first thirteen measures of the piece and are representative of the virtuoso display of compositional techniques, especially with regard to key relationships, the composer stages throughout the movement. The miracle is that the virtuosity is so consummate that the listener is aware only of a general sense of drama, excitement, and remarkable color change, but never of any forced modulation or contrivance.

The second-theme area consists of two distinct ideas, a chorale-like, sustained melody and a series of triplet arpeggios first introduced as an ornamental decoration to the chorale-like melody, but then becoming new material punctuated with syncopation. In the exposition these themes revolve around the mediant key of *E* rather than the dominant. There is a climactic cadence in *E* before a lengthy closing section in which the *E* tonality seems to veer toward *a*.

The development section makes use of both the opening theme and the triplet figuration of the second theme, and modulation remains important as a device. At one point the triplet figuration in a frenzy of excitement passes through *e-flat*, a dominant-seventh chord on *f-sharp*, *b*, a dominant-seventh chord on *G*, *c*, *D-flat*, a diminished-seventh chord built on *C*, to a dominant seventh on *G*, which ultimately acts as the dominant of the home key, albeit *C* does not return until after a prolonged, dramatic retransition that utilizes a drum-like ostinato figure in the low register (Example 8.16).

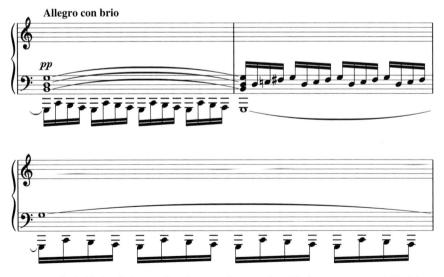

Example 8.16 Ludwig van Beethoven: Sonata, Op. 53, 1st movt. mm. 142–44
From *Beethoven: Klaviersonaten*, ed. by B. A. Wallner. Copyright G. Henle Munich.

The movement ends with a developmental coda that is both lengthy and climactic. The Op. 53 and the Op. 57 represent the epitome of the developmental coda in the composer's thinking. The coda is no longer acting as a mere closing section but rather as an important counterbalance to the development section itself. Developmental tension is built in almost equal measure, the only difference being that in both codas the returns to the home keys are given even more elaborate preparations.

The original slow movement of the Op. 53 was rejected by the composer and issued separately as an Andante in *F.* Known popularly as the *Andante favori,* the original movement was never given an opus number. (Along with other works without opus numbers, it was assigned an identifying catalogue number—in this case, WoO 57—in George Kinsky's *Das Werk Beethovens, thematisch-bibliographisches Verzeichnis seiner sämtlichen vollendeten Kompositionen,* completed by Hans Halm and published in 1955. WoO stands for *Werk ohne Opuszahl,* or "work without opus number.") The shorter composition used by Beethoven for the Op. 53 is improvisatory in nature and lives up to the composer's designation of *introduzione* in that, after offering a miniature ABA form, it moves into a cadenza-liketreatment of the opening motive, preparing the listener for the return of *C* with the onset of the final movement.

The Rondo (ABACABcoda) presents the most extended structure in this form of any of the sonatas. Beethoven's sketchbooks show us how painstakingly the composer evolved the apparent effortlessness of the opening theme (Example 8.17). In its first statement and each of its subsequent two appearances, it is presented more than once in increasingly elaborate settings. The continuous trill on the dominant note renders the last appearance of the theme both virtuosic and emotionally intense.

As in the Op. 31, no. 2, long pedal indications from the composer pose performance challenges for today's pianist. Some publications have modified the long indications, editors assuming that the mixture of tonic and dominant harmonies that results from Beethoven's markings will not work on modern instruments. Performers who are offended by the blend of harmonies sometimes attempt to use half-damping to simulate the intent of the composer in a modified form. Others prefer to be faithful to the score, trying to balance sonorities with enough finesse to make Beethoven's pedaling work.

The departures from the Rondo theme are multisectional. The first departure offers a triplet figuration strongly reminiscent of the first movement as well as an octave motive in *a.* The second departure offers both a sturdy, forte theme in *c* and a lengthy development of the Rondo theme. Here the composer exploits the opening rhythmic motive of the Rondo by placing it in the left hand against an arpeggio figure and, again reminiscent of the development of the first movement, taking it through a variety of keys (Example 8.18). The almost thirty measures of

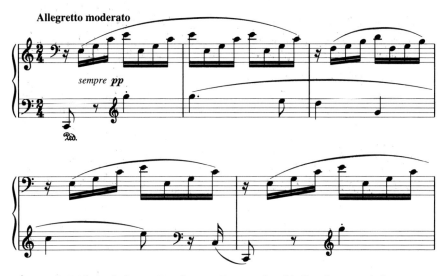

Example 8.17 Ludwig van Beethoven: Sonata, Op. 53, Rondo, mm. 1–5
From *Beethoven: Klaviersonaten,* ed. by B. A. Wallner. Copyright G. Henle Munich.

Example 8.18 Ludwig van Beethoven: Sonata, Op. 53, Rondo, mm. 251–52
From *Beethoven: Klaviersonaten,* ed. by B. A. Wallner. Copyright G. Henle Munich.

dominant preparation before the return of the Rondo theme is even exceeded by the thirty-five measures of dominant harmony that link the return of the first departure to the coda.

The final return of the Rondo theme is combined with a coda marked *Prestissimo* and designed to push virtuosic devices to the limit. A passage of rapid octaves confronts the performer at one point (Example 8.19), often dealt with by assigning some of the octaves to both hands or by using glissando octaves. The prolonged trill returns as an ornament, as the main Rondo theme is restated in several keys. The movement ends with a final burst of energy in *C.*

Prestissimo

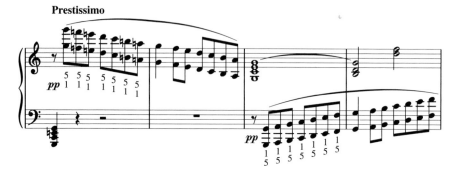

Example 8.19 Ludwig van Beethoven: Sonata, Op. 53, Rondo mm. 465–68
From *Beethoven: Klaviersonaten*, ed. by B. A. Wallner. Copyright G. Henle Munich.

Identification	No. of Movts.	Tempo Markings of Movts. and (Key)
Op. 54 (1804)	2	*In Tempo d'un Menuetto (F)*; Allegretto (*F*)

This sonata is almost like an entr'act between the two giants, the Op. 53 and Op. 57. It is by comparison unpretentious and brief, but by no means should it be regarded as stylistically inferior or as a teaching piece. The opening movement presents two ideas, the first built around a dotted rhythm and the second based on triplet octaves. There is free alternation of these two ideas in a loosely structured ABABA pattern. The Allegretto is not unlike the final movement of Op. 10, no. 2, in structure. There are two parts, both marked to be repeated. The opening section is short, monothematic, and presents a perpetual-motion figure. The second section opens in *A*, is developmental using the same material, and finally returns to *F* with a recapitulation of the opening in a varied form. One senses that there is an underlying sonata-allegro structure at the foundation of the movement, notwithstanding its terseness and lack of contrasting material.

Identification	No. of Movts.	Tempo Markings of Movts. and (Key)
Op. 57 (1804–5)	3	Allegro assai (*f*); Andante con moto (*D-flat*); Allegro ma non troppo (*f*)

For many musicians the *Appassionata,* as this work is called, epitomizes the elements of Beethoven's mature style. The contrasts of turbulence and serenity; the strength and scope of structure; the mastery of thematic manipulation; the flashes of color; the virtuosic power—all combine in remarkable balance to produce a work of consummate drama and

Example 8.20a Ludwig van Beethoven: Sonata, Op. 57, 1st movt. mm. 1-2

Example 8.20b mm. 5–6

Example 8.20c ; m. 10

From *Beethoven: Klaviersonaten*, ed. by B. A. Wallner. Copyright G. Henle Munich.

emotional intensity. The Op. 53 and this work stand as twin peaks of the keyboard literature of the first decade of the nineteenth century.

The opening theme is presented two octaves apart in single lines in *f*, the registration creating a distinct, somber mood. Without any preparation, the theme is restated a half step higher in *G-flat*. The tension created by this dual allegiance forms the basis for the emotional unrest of the entire movement, the half-step relationship between *f* and *G-flat* appearing in new form in an important motivic figure that uses the half-step relationship between *D-flat* and *C* (Examples 8.20 a–c). The second-theme area also struggles with a half-step battle, here between the third degree of the scale of *A-flat*, the key in which a theme remarkably similar to the opening one appears, and its parallel minor, which is used to mount the most stormy passagework of the exposition.

Unlike the exposition of the Op. 53, which is marked to be repeated, the exposition of the Op. 57 flows deftly into the development as *a-flat* is transformed to *E* and its parallel minor. The development section

Example 8.21 Ludwig van Beethoven: Sonata, Op. 57, 1st movt. mm. 141–43
From *Beethoven: Klaviersonaten,* ed. by B. A. Wallner. Copyright G. Henle Munich.

utilizes both opening-theme material as well as the first part of the second theme. The retransition provides a cadenza-like passage built on a diminished-seventh chord derived from the leading-tone harmony of *f.* The reiteration of this sound and its transformation to a dominant ninth with a repeated-note pedal point on *C* in the bass creates almost unbearable tension.

The repeated-note bass continues well into the recapitulation, where at one point it divides into a repeated-note diminished-fifth interval, creating a sound that still carries ominous impact today, almost two centuries after it was written (Example 8.21). As in the Op. 53, the coda of the first movement of the Op. 57 is virtually as long and as dramatic as the development section itself. Both first and second themes appear and are developed. The cadenza-like figuration used at the end of the development in the retransition is presented in the coda even more elaborately. It could easily be argued that this passage in the coda is the climactic one of the movement. After a final burst of energy, marked *Più allegro,* the movement ends quietly, forming a transition to the serenity of the second movement.

The formal structure of the Andante con moto forms a very beautiful contrast to the elements of improvisation inherent in the first movement. Whereas the first movement flowed freely from section to section, the second presents a two-part theme and a set of variations, all sections being carefully repeated. The theme is chorale-like with a relatively static melodic line. Each of the three variations that follow increases the flow of the movement by adding more florid figuration. In the final vari-

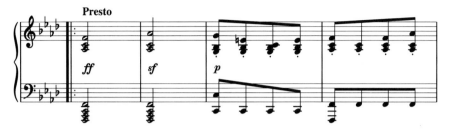

Example 8.22 Ludwig van Beethoven: Sonata, Op. 57, 3rd movt. mm. 308–11
From *Beethoven: Klaviersonaten*, ed. by B. A. Wallner. Copyright G. Henle Munich.

ation, syncopation adds to the interest, and the repeats are written out
rather than marked with repeat signs, so that the two hands can trade
material when the section is repeated. The movement ends with a quiet
restatement of the theme in a form fairly close to the original statement.
The final cadence is interrupted by diminished-seventh arpeggios that
set the stage for the unrest of the final movement marked *attacca*.

The last movement is a veritable whirlwind of continuous motion.
Cast in sonata-allegro form, it utilizes nonstop sixteenth-note figuration
of some kind in virtually every measure, except for a brief respite near
the end of the development section and at the opening of the final, fren-
zied presto. There is a marvelous, subtle link between the opening
theme of the first movement and the opening theme here in that a quick
shift from *f* to *G-flat* takes place in both themes. There is no marked contrast between the thematic ideas in the exposition of the final movement,
although two other thematic fragments are presented after the opening
idea, one of them being in the dominant minor. Unity is intensified by
presenting the opening thematic fragment both between the two other
fragments and again at the end of the exposition.

The sonata-allegro structure undergoes an interesting shift of focus
in that the composer places no repeat sign at the end of the exposition
yet marks the lengthy development and full recapitulation to be repeated. Executing the repeat not only lengthens the movement considerably
but also provides a challenge in terms of endurance for many pianists.
The development section is based almost entirely on the opening theme.

The coda, marked *Presto*, opens with two accented chords of punc-
tuation and continues with a series of rapid-fire staccato chords in eighth
notes (Example 8.22). Two short sections, each marked to be repeated,
are constructed so as to bring the excitement to an almost unbearable
height. The composer, however, takes the drama even one step further
with the return of the main theme, now at a breakneck speed and punctuated with syncopated sforzandi. This coda would have many musicians'
vote as the most intensely dramatic conclusion of any of the thirty-two
sonatas.

Identification	No. of Movts.	Tempo Markings of Movts. and (Key)
Op. 78 (1809)	2	Adagio cantabile, Allegro ma non troppo *(F-sharp);* Allegro vivace *(F-sharp)*

After the monumental sonatas of the period between 1804 and 1805, a break of about four years takes place in the creation of keyboard sonatas, Beethoven's creativity in this genre having been more or less continuous during the preceding ten years. The years 1809–10 see the composition of this sonata, the Op. 79, and the Op. 81a before another hiatus takes place. The Op. 78 is small in concept but filled with beauty and charm. Its opening adagio is but four measures long and, unlike the introductions to Op. 13 or Op. 31, no. 2, provides no significant thematic germs but rather acts as an improvisatory moodsetter. The sonata-allegro structure that follows is compact and regular with only eighteen measures of development and a short extension of the closing section of the recapitulation as a codetta. Both the exposition and the development-recapitulation are marked to be repeated.

The Allegro vivace opens with a series of short phrases that skirt resolution to the home key for eleven measures. The effect is heightened by the boldness of the opening phrase that starts forte with an augmented-sixth chord and ends with a dominant seventh in its third inversion. This high-spiritedness is maintained throughout the movement and is intensified by unexpected key manipulations and a series of passages built on broken dominant figurations that are both irregular in construction and never appear the same way twice. The overall form of the movement is that of a rondo with but one departure. The B section appears twice and seemingly can't make up its mind whether to be in major or the parallel minor, the first time revolving around *D-sharp* and the second around *F-sharp.* The movement closes after a short cadenza and a codetta.

Identification	No. of Movts.	Tempo Markings of Movts. and (Key)
Op. 79 (1809)	3	Presto alla tedesca *(G);* Andante *(g);* Vivace *(G)*

The composer calls this work a sonatina, and indeed all three movements are diminutive in structure and concept. He furthermore leaves no doubt about the energetic, ländler-like character of the opening movement, for he marks it *Presto alla tedesca.* The movement is in regular sonata-allegro form with a development that features cross-hand syncopation and a short nondevelopmental coda. The Andante that follows has a barcarolle feeling, being written in nine-eight time. It is in ABA form. The final Vivace is based on two themes: a central one that appears and returns in *G* and a short contrasting one in *C*. The opening theme is in a two-part structure, returning in variation much as a rondo theme might, and even being developed a bit at one point. The contrasting theme is in the middle, so if hard-pressed one might describe this movement's structure generally as ABA, but other structural elements coexist, as noted.

Identification	No. of Movts.	Tempo Markings of Movts. and (Key)
Op. 81a (1809–10)	3	*Das Lebewohl.* Adagio, Allegro *(E-flat); Abwesenheit,* Andante espressivo *(c); Das Wiedersehen,* Vivacissimamente *(E-flat)*

The descriptive titles of the movements of this sonata are provided by Beethoven; he also noted that the departure referred to at the beginning of the first movement was that of the Archduke Rudolf on May 4, 1809. The postillion-like motive that opens the work moves from the tonic through the dominant to the submediant, thus using a deceptive cadential progression ending with a *c* chord to suggest the underlying sadness attending the excitement of the journey. Midway through the sixteen-measure introduction marked *Adagio,* Beethoven provides an even more remarkable harmonization of the motive, ending up in *C-flat,* the enharmonic equivalent of *B.*

The ensuing sonata-allegro is marked in cut time, so its energy is high. The adagio introduction never returns at its original tempo, unlike the slow introductions to the first movements of the Op. 13 and the Op. 31, no. 2. The postillion theme reappears frequently, however: near the end of the exposition; in an altered form throughout the development, where it is combined with fragments of the opening motive of the allegro; and as the basis of a long coda, where it is momentarily canonic.

Certainly one of the most notorious features of this movement among performers is the double-note passagework, one set of double notes appearing in the exposition (Example 8.23) and one in the recapitulation. These passages seem to provide for many performers a never-ending challenge in terms of accuracy and security. One can even imagine a sly smile crossing the composer's face as he conceived passages that he suspected would be drilled many times by even the most experienced keyboard players. One might even go so far as to suggest that Beethoven had a conscious penchant for placing nasty technical hurdles near the beginnings of expositions, other examples being the double thirds that open the Op. 2, no. 3, and the broken sixths that appear near the beginning of Op. 10, no. 3.

The structure of the second movement is remarkable for its harmonic deftness. The composer uses the half diminished-seventh and the

Example 8.23 Ludwig van Beethoven: Sonata, Op. 81a, 1st movt. mm. 31–34
From *Beethoven: Klaviersonaten,* ed. by B. A. Wallner. Copyright G. Henle Munich.

diminished-seventh chords to create not only the mood of loneliness suggested by *Abwesenheit* (Absence) but also as harmonies capable of multiple resolutions. Thus, a kaleidoscopic series of key relationships is set up that passes through *g, f, b-flat,* and fleetingly *A-flat* and *D-flat* before coming to rest in a transition passage in *c,* which in turn drifts off into the dominant of *E-flat* to prepare the way for the final movement. The second movement might give the general impression of being in ABAB(Acoda), but such a schematic does not take into account that returning sections are never in the same key, and often sections or phrases begin in one key and end in another. The composition thus is masterful in suggesting a psychological feeling of aimlessness, or being at "loose ends," a state that might indeed accompany the loneliness brought on by the absence of a loved one.

A burst of energetic arpeggio figuration provides an introduction to the sonata-allegro structure of the final movement. Here the tonic-dominant undulation of the first theme acts almost as a paraphrase of the postillion motive that opened the sonata. A short development section uses both A and B themes. The brilliance of the close of the recapitulation suggests finality so strongly that listeners are often unprepared for the poco andante that follows and acts as a short coda. A final return to the more rapid tempo provides a virtuoso flourish with which to end the movement, surely one of the most brilliant and joyful of any of the last movements of the thirty-two sonatas.

Identification	No. of Movts.	Tempo Markings of Movts. and (Key)
Op. 90 (1814)	2	*Mit Lebhaftigkeit und durchaus mit Empfindung und Ausdruck (e); Nicht zu geschwind und sehr singbar vorgetragen (E)*

In this sonata, Beethoven gives us tempo and expressive directions in some detail in German rather than the traditional Italian for the first time. The composer never abandons Italian directions entirely, however, sporadically combining the two languages in the Op. 101 and the Op. 109. Most of the directions for the Opp. 106, 110, and 111, however, remain in the traditional Italian. Musicians have speculated as to the significance of the more detailed German directions, many believing that using German points toward the composer's extremely personal involvement in the expressive aspects of his late music.

Another four-year sabbatical from writing keyboard sonatas had taken place since the composition of the Op. 81a, and although the Op. 90 is short, it shows clearly the direction the composer's writing is to take, one that is born of acute awareness of the inner life and its quests. Expressive values in the music are placed in ever-increasing control over all other aspects. Although virtuoso elements, dramatic gesture, and even the calculated roughness in which Beethoven has sometimes reveled are still present in the final sonatas, these are all combined with a fountainhead of spiritual energy from deep within the composer. The perception of this development in the composer's style has built a firm, well-founded belief among musicians and listeners that "late" Beethoven is music of great depth and spirituality, representing in music the eternal enigmas of life itself.

The structures of both movements of the Op. 90 are regular and offer few surprises. The opening sonata-allegro is compact and presents an exposition that ends in the dominant minor. The recapitulation is ushered in by some canonic imitation that uses first augmentation and then diminution of the main motive of the movement. The coda is only a few measures long. The second movement is a rondo that seems to proceed leisurely due to the fact that the main theme is stated twice each time it appears. The last statement is varied and developed slightly to produce a coda-like effect.

Identification	No. of Movts.	Tempo Markings of Movts. and (Key)
Op. 101 (1816)	4	*Etwas lebhaft und mit der innigsten Empfindung (A); Lebhaft, Marschmässig (F); Langsam und sehnsuchtvoll (a); Zeitmass des ersten Stückes–Geschwinde, doch nicht zu sehr, und mit Entschlossenheit (A)*

Many compositional ideas that appeared in earlier works come together in this sonata. As in the Op. 27 pair, the first movement is of modest proportions, setting the stage for the importance of the final movement. Whereas the cyclicism in the Op. 27, no. 1, may be open to question, it is clearly a unifying device in this work. The last two movements are joined by both a cadenza and the insertion of the opening phrase of the sonata. Finally, Beethoven's penchant for regarding the sonata as an umbrella under which other structures might flourish gives birth in this work to the inclusion of a fugue as the development section of the sonata-allegro form of the final movement.

The opening movement is transcendental in its lyricism, so much so that pianists have often been known to refer to this sonata as the "most romantic" of the thirty-two. The sonata-allegro of the first movement is so compact that it is not possible to identify a clear second theme. An exposition of but thirty-four measures ends in the dominant and leads to a development of only twenty-three measures. A short coda closes the movement. The uninterrupted melodic intensity of the movement contributes to the effect of a single mood, sustained from beginning to end, and in this regard is reminiscent of the opening movement of the Op. 27, no. 2.

The march that follows is full of angular skips, its dotted rhythm underscoring a rough-and-tumble ruggedness (Example 8.24). It is cast in ABA form, the middle section being written in *B-flat*, in two-part form, and for the most part with two voices in canonic imitation. There is a short transition to the da capo section but no coda.

The next section serves as a slow movement, but its effect is very much that of a connecting improvisation. The section is truly through-composed, using the opening motivic figure as its focal point (Example 8.25). A free

Example 8.24 Ludwig van Beethoven: Sonata, Op. 101, 2nd movt. mm. 1–4

From *Beethoven: Klaviersonaten*, ed. by B. A. Wallner. Copyright G. Henle Munich.

cadenza leads to a statement of the opening two phrases of the sonata, which, after a brief hesitation, is followed by a short presto cadenza. The final movement arrives with an introduction on the dominant of *A*. The remarkable fact is that the entire movement with all three of these facets is only thirty-three measures in length. A recounting of what happens in these measures falls pitifully short of conveying the power and magic of this interlude, for it is certainly one of the composer's most concentrated statements, a combination of intense beauty and profundity.

The final movement opens with a theme that is imitative and thus foreshadows the fugue that is to come. The second theme of the exposition, although in the expected dominant key, is fragmentary and fleeting, leading after only ten measures to a closing section based on the opening theme and its imitation. The exposition is marked to be repeated.

The development opens with a short introduction. An abrupt change of tonality to the parallel minor announces the beginning of the fugue, its subject clearly based on the opening theme of the exposition. As the second voice enters with a tonal answer, the key shifts to *F.* The third voice enters in *d,* and the final voice, like the first, is in *a.* Although

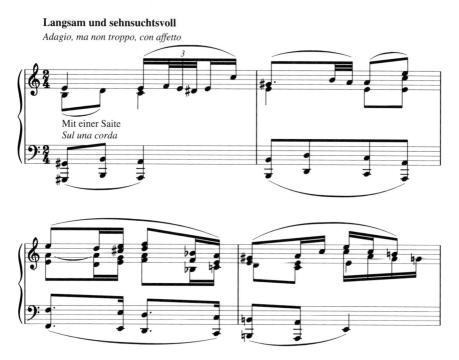

Example 8.25 Ludwig van Beethoven: Sonata, Op. 101, 3rd movt. mm. 1–4
From *Beethoven: Klaviersonaten,* ed. by B. A. Wallner. Copyright G. Henle Munich.

the four-voiced texture remains in use throughout the fugue, the approach to the counterpoint is influenced by the use of idiomatic keyboard figurations such as scalar runs and double notes. The composer seems to take delight in pushing what is physically possible to play at the keyboard to the outer limits. There is, moreover, an angularity to the part writing that results in a vigorous, almost gruff, vitality. The fugue ends with a written-out cadenza on the dominant of *A*, ushering in what is surely one of the most glorious returns to the tonic in the entire literature. At the end of the recapitulation, a playful coda threatens to return to fugal entries but settles instead for bringing the work teasingly to a close.

Identification	No. of Movts.	Tempo Markings of Movts. and (Key)
Op. 106 (1817–18)	4	Allegro (*B-flat*); Scherzo, Assai vivace (*B-flat*); Adagio sostenuto (*f-sharp*); Allegro risoluto (*B-flat*)

The notation *Grosse Sonate für das Hammerklavier* appears as part of the title of this work. The term *Hammerklavier* is simply the German word for the piano, so in a sense, any Beethoven sonata might have been so designated, especially the later ones. The label has attached itself to this particular work only, however, so that musicians speak of the *Hammerklavier Sonata*, referring to this work and none other. One suspects a vague psychological connection between the imagery of an emerging piano, one gaining in strength and power of tone, and the heroic demands of this work on both the instrument and the performer.

The Op. 106 is the longest sonata of the thirty-two, and many regard it as the most formidable. Its technical challenges, as represented by the fugue, are unique and among the greatest in keyboard literature. Similarly, the work's musical challenges, as represented by the Adagio sostenuto, demand that the performer, as well as the listener, enter a world so intensely profound that, once again, parallels in the literature can scarcely be found. This work is Beethoven's final essay in the monumental sonata structure, a concept of an expanded, four-movement work that had begun its growth as early as the Op. 2 set and had been evident throughout the production of the sonatas, as exemplified in the Op. 7, Op. 10, no. 3, Op. 22, Op. 28, and Op. 31, no. 3. In the Op. 106, the concept reaches its zenith.

Although the sonata-allegro structure of the first movement is reasonably regular, several interesting features are present: the strength of the opening motive, destined to become one of Beethoven's best-known musical signatures and probably copied by both Mendelssohn and Brahms (Example 8.26a–c); the unusual key relationship in the exposition, where the second-theme area is in the submediant major (*G*); the playful imitation of thedevelopment, which suggests fugue-like entries

Example 8.26a Ludwig van Beethoven: Sonata, Op. 106, 1st movt. mm. 1–2

Example 8.26b Felix Mendelssohn: Sonata, Op. 106, 1st movt. mm. 1–2

Example 8.26c Johannes Brahms: Sonata, Op. 1, lst movt. mm. 1–2

and canonic imitation; and the frequent change of key signature throughout the movement to accommodate the fluidity of modulation. The movement exhibits other late Beethoven traits as well, such as high-ly disjunct writing, often in extreme registers; long trills; and rapidly changing dynamic contrasts. A short coda closes the movement.

The structure of the Scherzo might be regarded as the final reso-lution to all of the fussing with the concept the composer has exhibited throughout the sonatas. This is the last time the composer used the term *scherzo* in the thirty-two sonatas. Here he returns to the concept of a rapid three-four meter with an underlying minuet and trio structure. There are, however, no repeats. Everything is written out, including the

Example 8.27 Ludwig van Beethoven: Sonata, Op. 106, 3rd movt. mm. 1–5
From *Beethoven: Klaviersonaten*, ed. by B. A. Wallner. Copyright G. Henle Munich.

da capo, and when material is repeated it is usually varied. The return of the main section is preceded by an improvisatory section that closes with a prestissimo cadenza. The entire movement ends with a coda filled with surprise and outburst.

The Adagio sostenuto is also marked *Appassionato e con molto sentimento*. It is cast in a large, free sonata-allegro form. The *f-sharp* tonality, a major third below the home key of the sonata, is clearly established by a chorale-like opening theme in which neither phrase structure nor harmonic tension and release are presented in easily discernible patterns. The result is an almost subliminal meditation (Example 8.27). The shifts to *G* in measures 14 and 22 recall a similar procedure in the slow movement of the Op. 2, no. 2, for both the keys involved and their relationships are the same (Examples 8.28 a–b). The long exposition contains a variety of material. After the opening chorale-like theme comes an improvisatory passage of figural writing, which, in turn, leads to a section in the key of *D* in which the crossing of the hands is prominent. Here the composer changes the key signature appropriately to one with two sharps. More chorale-like chords return near the end of the exposition to form a closing section.

The entire development section is only fifteen measures long, acting as but a brief interlude between the extended outer sections. Beethoven changes the key signature back to that of three sharps at the opening of the development. As modulation occurs in the next few measures, appropriate key signatures are adopted. Thus, three measures into the development, the signature shifts to three flats. Five measures later are four measures without flats or sharps in the signature to accommodate a modulation back to the dominant of *f-sharp*. The appropriate key signature of three sharps returns for the recapitulation.

The recapitulation of the chorale-like opening is presented with such elaborate figuration that it is scarcely recognizable. Yet measure by measure one can follow the harmonic progression that had been pre-

Largo appassionato

Example 8.28a Ludwig van Beethoven: Sonata, Op. 2, no. 2, 2nd movt. mm. 25–27

Adagio sostenuto

Example 8.28b Ludwig van Beethoven: Sonata, Op. 106, 3rd movt. mm. 13–15
From *Beethoven: Klaviersonaten*, ed. by B. A. Wallner. Copyright G. Henle Munich.

sented in the exposition (Example 8.29). As ensuing sections of the recapitulation occur, they become more nearly like their counterparts in the exposition, albeit the key relationship is predictably altered. The point at which the composer changed the key signature to two sharps to accommodate the key of *D* in the exposition is paralleled in the recapitulation by a change to *F-sharp* with the appropriate six sharps. An extended coda begins in *G* and states both the cross-hand theme and the chorale-like opening theme before the movement concludes.

The Adagio is a puzzling movement in that its improvisatory nature, its frequent lapses into thematic material without strong motivic features, and the masking of its structure by elaborate variation of returning sections all add up to a movement that is difficult to follow for the majority of listeners. This experience has to be reconciled with the movement's reputation for being one of the most profound, spiritual expressions of the composer, a reputation born of abundant testimony by famous musicians of the past. As a guardian of spiritual revelation, the movement, like most keepers of the flame, does not give up its truths easily, not until an earnest quest on the part of the seeker, in this case the listener, has been undertaken.

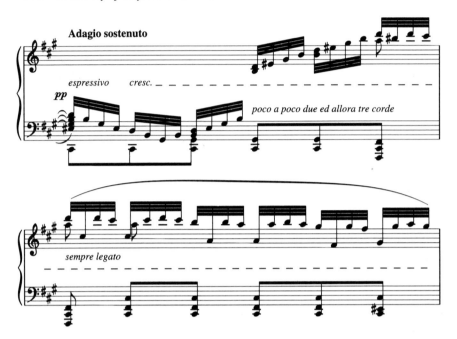

Example 8.29 Ludwig van Beethoven: Sonata, Op. 106, 3rd movt. mm. 87–88
From *Beethoven: Klaviersonaten,* ed. by B. A. Wallner. Copyright G. Henle Munich.

The series of fragments that connect the Adagio to the fugue give the impression that the composer has decided to share with his listeners his musical stream of consciousness. The process begins with vague, improvisatory sounds and seems to fasten on at least one musical theme, perhaps rondo-like in character, which is then broken off. Energy is invoked with a series of broken chords that lead to the Allegro risoluto and, five measures later, the introduction of the fugue subject (Example 8.30).

To recount the academic features of the three-voiced fugue does not begin to convey the extraordinary character of the music. The disjunct leap and the trill at the head of the subject immediately set the stage for music of high energy, ruggedness, and extreme intensity, all of which are magnified as the fugue progresses. Technically, the music is as challenging as anything in the literature, and the listener is hurled into a wild panorama of sound and fury, one that stretches the performer and the instrument to the absolute limits. Leaps, trills, double notes, sforzandi, octaves, and syncopation abound. About two-thirds of the way through the fugue (m. 250), a second exposition of a quiet nature forms a contrasting section. The energy soon returns, however. A long trill on the dominant leads to a final brilliant ending. The intensity and complexity of the fugue combine to form an incredible climax

Allegro risoluto

Fuga, a tre voci, con alcune licenze

Example 8.30 Ludwig van Beethoven: Sonata, Op. 106, 4th movt. mm. 16–20
From *Beethoven: Klaviersonaten,* ed. by B. A. Wallner. Copyright G. Henle Munich.

to this monumental sonata, a work that continues to defy both performer
and listener almost two centuries after its creation.

Identification	No. of Movts.	Tempo Markings of Movts. and (Key)
Op. 109 (1820)	3	Vivace, ma non troppo *(E);* Prestissimo *(e);* Gesangvoll, mit innigster Empfindung *(E)*

The focus of this three-movement work is directed toward the final
movement, a theme and six variations. Accordingly, the opening movement's sonata-allegro structure, like that of the Op. 101, is very compressed. Unlike the Op. 101, however, there is great contrast between
the eight measures that form the opening theme and the adagio espressivo that serves as a second section of the exposition. The former moves
quickly in reiterated figuration formulated into irregular phrase lengths.
The latter, although written in measured notation, moves as if it were a
free, improvised cadenza, linking short melodic fragments with arpeggio-like material that sweeps the entire range of the keyboard. The
development section makes use only of the first-theme material. It
builds using a series of syncopated sforzandi so that its climax coincides
with the onset of the recapitulation. The restatement of the opening
measures is presented now in more extreme registers. The adagio, too,
is fully rewritten, touching momentarily on a rich, mighty arpeggio figuration in *C.* A short, expressive coda based on the opening theme closes the movement.

The Prestissimo also uses sonata-allegro form as its point of departure. The speed of the movement is such that the six-eight meter sounds like two sets of triplets per measure in two-four time. The movement is characterized by drive throughout. As the exposition ends, what seems to be the beginning of a development section leads to a respite from the eighth notes, evolving into a chorale-like texture. A curious half cadence in *b* ushers in the recapitulation, leaving the development with a sense of incompleteness. A full recapitulation is closed by a series of chords that bring the movement to a strong, punctuated final cadence.

The expressive, slow movement of the sonata is reserved for the final set of variations. The theme is chorale-like, serious, and in two-part form, each section marked to be repeated. It undergoes a series of startling transformations during the course of the six variations. Each variation follows the underlying harmony of the theme, the most traceable common ground, although melodic fragments, especially one based on a falling major third, are also in evidence throughout. In variations 2, 3, 5, and 6, the repeats of the theme are written out, thereby adding still another dimension of variation. Variation 3 is the most brilliant technically. Variation 4 is freely imitative, and variation 5 is fugue-like. The final variation sets the theme amid continuous trill figurations (Example 8.31), an idea for suggesting transcendentalism that Beethoven had

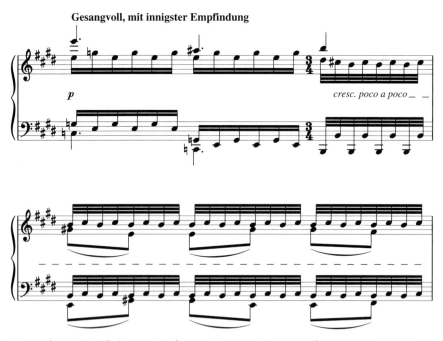

Example 8.31 Ludwig van Beethoven: Sonata, Op. 109, 3rd movt. mm. 160–61
From *Beethoven: Klaviersonaten*, ed. by B. A. Wallner. Copyright G. Henle Munich.

already used in the final variation of the first movement of the Op. 26 and was to use again near the end of the Op. 111. The movement closes with a restatement of the theme as it first appeared, now without repeats, thus suggesting a full cycle has been achieved. The final movement is one of the composer's most remarkable sets of variations in terms of originality and depth of expression.

Identification	No. of Movts.	Tempo Markings of Movts. and (Key)
Op. 110 (1821)	3	Moderato cantabile molto expressive *(A-flat)*; Allegro molto *(f)*; Adagio ma non troppo *(a-flat)* – Fuga, Allegro ma non troppo *(A-flat)*

If Beethoven had written this work twenty years earlier, he might have been consistent and entitled it *quasi una fantasia*, as he did with the Op. 27 pair. Features that suggest this designation are a relatively compact sonata-allegro first movement, although not as condensed as the first movements of either the Op. 101 or the Op. 109; a free, improvisatory introduction to the third movement; and a final movement in which two strikingly contrasting sections, an arioso and a fugue, alternate. The fugue itself undergoes a metamorphosis in the final pages of the work.

The opening ideas of the first movement have as their hallmark a high-flown, lyric quality. This mood is so pronounced that, as the exposition moves to the dominant key, it is difficult to distinguish the contrasting second theme. The development is only sixteen measures long and, once again, uses first-theme lyricism as its basis. There is a complete recapitulation that flows into the short coda that closes the movement.

The structure of the second movement is that of a minuet and trio. It might have been called a scherzo, for the rapid tempo, the duple meter, the use of syncopation, and an unexpected two-measure rest give the movement a jovial, witty quality. The middle section is famous for its tricky, descending passagework, combined with a syncopated, cross-hand accompaniment. The following improvisatory passage that leads to the first arioso section contains curious repeated notes that may be an imitation on the piano of the expressive device of *Bebung*, associated with the clavichord (Example 8.32). Its use suggests deep contemplation, a mood that is intensified in the arioso section. Actually, Beethoven does not label the first appearance of the slow, songlike section in *a-flat arioso*, but, when it reappears in *g* after the first fugue, the composer gives the direction *L'istesso tempo di Arioso*, thereby implying that the earlier section was, in fact, an arioso.

The fugue appears first in *A-flat* between the two arioso statements. It is in three voices with frequent octave doublings of the lowermost

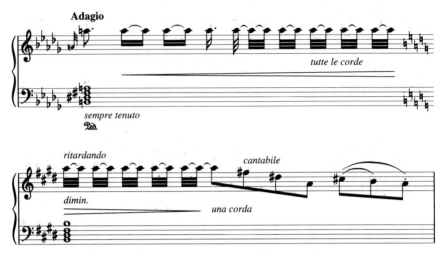

Example 8.32 Ludwig van Beethoven: Sonata, Op. 110, 3rd movt. m. 5
From *Beethoven: Klaviersonaten,* ed. by B. A. Wallner. Copyright G. Henle Munich.

Example 8.33 Ludwig van Beethoven: Sonata, Op. 110, 3rd movt. mm. 27–29
From *Beethoven: Klaviersonaten,* ed. by B. A. Wallner. Copyright G. Henle Munich.

voice. Its mood is one of well-being and grace (Example 8.33), and it has little in common with the wild impetuousness of the fugue in the Op. 106. When this fugue returns, after the restatement of the arioso section, it does so in *G* with the inversion of the fugue subject. Passing through a section marked both *Meno allegro* and its German equivalent *Etwas langsamer,* the fugue subject is transformed by free diminution into an accompanimental figure. There is a return to *A-flat,* and, as the fugue becomes virtually homophonic, its subject enters anew in an ecstatic, lyrical statement and continues to expand, reaching a glorious climax at the final cadence of the work.

Identification	No. of Movts.	Tempo Markings of Movts. and (Key)
Op. 111 (1821–22)	2	Allegro con brio ed appassionato (*c*); Arietta –Adagio molto semplice e cantabile (*C*)

Example 8.34 Ludwig van Beethoven: Sonata, Op. 111, 1st movt. mm. 1–2
From *Beethoven: Klaviersonaten*, ed. by B. A. Wallner. Copyright G. Henle Munich.

The final sonata of the thirty-two exemplifies beautifully the composer's continuing use of the sonata as a vehicle for new ideas. Here he presents a two-movement work in which the movements provide a balance for each other, both being strong, lengthy, serious compositions. At the same time, they offer the ultimate contrast, the first acting as an expression of turbulent drama and the second as an essay in transcendentalism.

The introductory maestoso avoids resolution to *c* through the use of diminished-seventh chords and half cadences (Example 8.34). This procedure creates a feeling of restlessness that is momentarily put aside with the arrival of the tonic on the downbeat of the exposition. The strong opening motive of the Allegro seems to grow out of the introduction and permeates the entire exposition with only a contrasting figuration in *A-flat* serving as a second theme (m.50). The twenty measures that act as a relatively short development section are based entirely on the main motive. For about eight measures it seems as if a fugue might develop, but the composer abandons the idea in favor of more homophonic figural writing. The full recapitulation presents the contrasting second-theme fragment in *C* (m. 116). A coda acts as a tranquilizer, bringing the movement to a calm close in *C* in preparation for the arietta.

It is interesting to note that Beethoven uses the term *arietta* in this movement, denoting a small aria, whereas in the Op. 110 he had used *arioso*, suggesting the recitative-like quality of the music. Indeed, the opening theme of this movement is built on two eight-measure phrases, each marked to be repeated. The first three variations conform to the formal pattern. Each of these variations doubles the sense of forward motion by continuous use of smaller rhythmic values. Thus, the arietta moves in dotted eighth notes in its original statement; variation 1 uses eighths and sixteenths; no. 2, sixteenths and thirty-seconds; and no. 3 employs sixty-fourth notes. Beethoven cautions against slowing the tempo by placing *L'istesso tempo* at the openings of each of these variations.

The repeats in variation 4 are written out and varied, providing yet another figural pattern. At the end of variation 4 an extension of the figuration leads to an improvisatory section in which a free treatment of the theme is accompanied by a long trill, a forecast of the final variation. There is then a short section built around the key of *c* with an appropriate change in key signature. As the *C* signature returns, the theme is once again structured more closely to its original form. The final variation uses only the first half of the theme, instituting a return of the long trill in its repeat and adding a short coda in which the motion is slowed, and the soaring mood suggested by the high trills is returned to earth.

A description of what happens in this set of variations does not begin to touch upon the effect the movement can produce, for it has the potential of creating a musical experience that incorporates both profound meditation and exalted revelation. It is not possible to know if Beethoven consciously wrote this movement as a capstone to the body of works for solo piano in sonata form, but it seems almost as if he planned for this movement to be a summation of his spiritual energy and his creative life. The movement is, in fact, a miraculous capsulization of Beethoven's musical essence and as such stands as a fitting closing statement to the thirty-two sonatas.

The Variations

Beethoven wrote sets of variations his entire career, his output spanning a period of time even greater than that of the sonatas. Most of the variations are either on melodies from popular theater works by composers such as Dittersdorf, Salieri, or Paisiello or on well-known traditional melodies, such as the sets on "God Save the King" and "Rule Brittania."

In all, there are twenty sets of variations for solo keyboard and two additional sets of late variations on folk tunes with flute or violin obbligato, Opp. 105 and 107 (ca. 1818). These folk-tune sets have not traditionally been part of the pianist's repertoire, but ever-increasing recognition of the superfluous nature of the obbligato part has caused some historians to argue that performance by a solo pianist is valid.

Several sets of variations stand out as works that go well beyond the usual variation concept of the period, that of providing entertaining, light musical commentary on a familiar tune. The most outstanding of those that exceed expectations is the Op. 120, the *Thirty-Three Variations on a Waltz by Anton Diabelli*. A well-known music publisher, Anton Diabelli (1781–1858), contacted fifty composers to write a variation on a slight waltz he had written, a giddy little tune that borders on being downright insipid. He planned to publish the contributions as a single set of variations, presumably garnering sales because of the stellar names associated with the project. Most of the composers submitted their contribution in a timely manner, and Beethoven, indeed, began work around 1819. Not until 1823, however, did Beethoven respond to Diabelli, not with a single variation on the tune but rather with an imposing set of variations, one that has taken its place along with Johann Sebastian Bach's *Goldberg* set as one of the monuments of the literature. The Op. 120 brings together many elements of Beethoven's style in a tour de force: virtuosity, humor, profound introspection, and contrapuntal complexity. The set achieves its climax in variations 21, a slow movement marked *Largo molto espressivo,* and 32, a fugue marked *Allegro.* The work ends with a serene variation marked *Tempo di Menuetto,* a moderato movement that seems curious after the energy-driven fugue.

Perhaps the most frequently performed set of the composer's variations is the *Thirty-two Variations on an Original Theme, c* (WoO 80; 1806). Here the short, eight-measure theme is built on a passacaglia-like bass line that descends in half steps. The variations follow the harmonic pattern virtually without exception, and, because the progression is both short and without repetition, the variations seem to pass by in rapid-fire fashion. A short coda closes the work after the last variation.

The *Fifteen Variations and a Fugue on an Original Theme, E-flat,* Op. 35 (1802), are known as the *Eroica* variations, for the theme from the set appears in the Symphony no. 3, Op. 55, the *Eroica* (1803). One of the unusual features of the work is the way the theme is presented. The composer opens the piece by introducing only the bass line of the melody. One voice is added at a time, each with repetition, until a four-voiced texture is formed. Only then is the theme stated. Fifteen variations follow, the last variation an expressive largo. The brilliant fugue that follows draws its subject from the first four notes of the bass line at the beginning of the work.

Of the miscellaneous piano pieces, note should be taken of the sets entitled Bagatelles, Opp. 33, 119, and 126. These small pieces are arranged in groups and represent early examples of the type that came to be known as the *character piece.* They are thought to have been a conceptual guide for later composers who worked with the genre. Rounding out the list of significant works are three rondos, the so-called "Rage over a Lost Penny," Op. 129 (1795), and the two that compose the Op. 51 (?1796–98); a fantasy Op. 77 (1809); a polonaise, Op. 89 (1814); the Andante in *F* (*Andante favori*), WoO 57 (1803), and a set of six *Ecossaises,* WoO 86 (1825). There are, in addition, perhaps two dozen small pieces often used in the teaching studio. One of these is among Beethoven's best-known works: *Bagatelle für Elise,* WoO 59 (1808, 1810).

CHAPTER NINE

The Turn of the Nineteenth Century

The nineteenth century is connected with the concept of Romanticism in music. Although musicians use the term constantly in reference to music of the period, defining it succinctly is far from easy, for it embraces an adherence to both freedom and contradiction. Philosophically, the Romantic impulse represents a turning away from dedication to the belief that reason and its use by human beings can result in reaching a solution to their problems. Rather, Romanticism seeks realization and identity through exploration of an inner emotional life and courts the freedom to express emotional states freely, even at times passionately and wildly. Thus, orderliness of logic, balance of structure, and containment of excess are all thrown aside to some degree in the headiness of emotional expression. Moreover, inscrutable or exotic worlds that are unknown, unpredictable, or perceivable only by exercising the imagination were sought out. Of these, nature was deemed an example of limitless strength and constant change and capable of violence and surprise. Legend concerned itself with gods and goddesses who combined formidable power with human appetites and frailties. Antiquity, dimly perceived through folklore or haphazard research, provided a vehicle for embellishment. Religion with its concepts of life, death, good, evil, the hereafter, and salvation offered eternal, unsolvable mysteries. Fascination with the less-exalted side of eternal mysteries resulted in focus on the spooky or the macabre. Finally, of paramount importance was the exploration of the human heart in its quest for love, a process that was seen to embrace various intense, emotional states such as yearning, ecstasy, frustration, rejection, denial, and despair.

The protagonist most often assumed the role of a hero, brave and innocent, battling adversities, and imbued with transcendental ideals. If circumstances resulted in ultimate defeat, nothing less than full-blown tragedy was the result. Those caught between the forces of good and evil were regarded as exalted symbols of the human condition. Even small-scaled visions and homespun characters were assumed to be somehow representative of a universal experience, one in which all potentially shared. Fantasy was exaggerated for effect, often slightly past the threshold of aberration. Dramatic gesture, whether grand or intimate, was frequently extreme enough to strain verisimilitude. Extramusical concepts became de rigueur as a means of pinpointing what the music was attempting to convey. These concepts ranged from detailed description of a series of events to the mere suggestion of a mood or setting.

The evolution of such aesthetic goals took place gradually in all of the arts. In music, experimenting with sonic effects suggested fantastic and mysterious realms. Pursuit of emotional goals often eroded structural regularity. Moreover, new concepts, represented by the tone poem and the character piece, molded structure by following a story line, transforming thematic motives to express a variety of emotional states or capturing a mood in a brief miniature. Modified use of the harmonic vocabulary that was already in place served composers well, for they were able to evoke the emotionalism and fantasy they sought by exploring new relationships between keys, effecting startling modulations, as well as altering chord progressions with an increased emphasis on dissonance and chromaticism. In melody, legato, singing lines became more prominent, and these were decorated with fanciful cadenza-like passagework. Rhythmic innovations were less striking, but fresh uses of metered rhythm resulted from interest in highly stylized versions of the waltz, polonaise, mazurka, fandango, and other folk or dance music.

Instrumental music assumed an ever-increasing role. Orchestras swelled in size, and the importance of the orchestral conductor was enhanced. The real idols of the time, however, were the instrumental virtuosi. They were generally composer-performers, and they became focal points of adulation as artist-heros. Leading the virtuoso violinists was Niccolò Paganini, and leading the pianists was Franz Liszt. The rise of the instrumental virtuoso-idol coincided with the physical refinement of the piano to an instrument of power, beautiful tone, and reliability. Many of the great composers of the nineteenth century were trained as virtuoso pianists and regarded the piano as the instrument for their most personal work, often using it as a vehicle for refining ideas that later appeared in other guises.

As traditional structural concepts were subjected to the evolution of nineteenth-century aesthetics, their characteristics often changed and in some cases their importance. Contrapuntal writing was approached with considerably more freedom and used less consistently. Structures born of contrapuntal rigor, such as the fugue, passacaglia (chaconne), or invention-types, were generally used much less frequently and, when invoked, were approached with a cavalier regard for strict contrapuntal practice. Formal sets of themes with variation were still used but often as vehicles for ordering up a sequence of virtuoso displays or for exploring techniques of thematic transformation. In longer works that broke away from expected structural patterns, thematic transformation provided a means of achieving unity.

The sonata, which entered the nineteenth century at its zenith, was now suddenly encountered much less frequently, and works entitled sonatas became freer, varying considerably in the degree of adherence to the traditional eighteenth-century structure. Influences, however, of both the multimovement concept or the sonata-allegro pattern appear often in works that bear another title, such as fantasia, rhapsody, ballade, capriccio, or toccata.

The term *fantasia* would seem to convey a concept born of freedom of expression, and it became associated with several types. It was used, as noted, in connection with multimovement sonata-like works, exemplified by the fantasias of Mendelssohn, Schubert, and Schumann. It is often encountered as a title for small works, generally thought of as character pieces, such as the fantasy pieces of Schumann, Op. 12, or of Brahms, Op. 116. Finally, it appears as a title for works that freely embellish material borrowed from other sources, usually theater works such as opera. Liszt provided many examples of such embellished transcriptions, such as the work based on Bellini's *Norma* or the one on Mozart's *Don Giovanni*. Such pieces are also sometimescalled *reminiscences* or *paraphrases*.

The emergence of a lengthy, single-movement piano work in a free structure mirrored the development of the orchestral tone poem. Strangely, however, the term *tone poem* is applied to solo keyboard music relatively rarely. Rather, such pieces draw their titles often from specific descriptive or literary references, such as the "Vallée d'Obermann" of Liszt, or by making use of a fanciful, more general term, such as Chopin's ballades or Schumann's "Humoresque." Some might view such works as simply unusually long character pieces, but in doing so no distinction is made between the short, succinct character piece, which seeks to express a single emotional state, and these multisectional works, which embrace a series of contrasting moods.

The term *character piece* has come to be used to describe the shorter keyboard pieces of the nineteenth century. Several examples of the use of the specific term may be cited: Mendelssohn calls his Op. 7 *Charakterstücke*, and Schumann attached the term as a subtitle to his *Davidsbündlertänze*, Op. 6. Lesser-known composers who used the term were Johann Wilhelm Hässler (1747–1822) and Heinrich Marchner (1795–1861). It is not entirely clear why this particular term has emerged to designate the small piano piece of the period in place of possible others, for composers also frequently used such titles as *fantasy, rhapsody,* or *lyric piece*. As a catchall term, *character piece* has even come to include small pieces that have served in other capacities, such as the *prelude* or *etude*, as well as pieces based on dance forms, such as the *waltz* or *mazurka*.

The sets of bagatelles of Beethoven are often cited as the first important character pieces. Almost all prominent composers since Beethoven contributed to the genre. Some composers arranged the pieces in sets with the underlying suggestion that they be played together. This implication is particularly clear when there is a carry-over of thematic material from one piece to another or a cyclic return of material near the end of the set, such as *Papillons*, Op. 2, and *Davidsbündler-tänze*, Op. 6, of Schumann. Other sets of pieces are sometimes broken up in performance, the pianist choosing and grouping compositions according to personal taste. One finds, for example, the four pieces of Brahms's Op. 119 sometimes played together as a set but also one or another of the pieces offered separately, sometimes combined with other short pieces of Brahms drawn from other groups. Sets of more extended character pieces, such as the impromptus, Op. 90, of Schubert, or the *Suisse* from the *Années de Pélerinage* of Liszt, are played in their entirety infrequently. There is thus no rigid protocol among performers regarding the program arrangement of character pieces, although one can observe periodic trends.

Structures of character pieces vary but most often are formed of some simple block arrangement of sections, such as ABA or AB often with parts marked to be repeated. Very short pieces often defy analysis in terms of block arrangements and are sometimes described as being "through-composed." Such pieces can be found with some degree of frequency in the works of Schumann and to a lesser extent of Mendelssohn, Chopin, and Brahms.

Equally variable is the degree to which a character piece may be involved in extramusical suggestion. The most explicit compositions are those that are based on a literary text, such as the first Brahms Ballade from Op. 10 or the three pieces from Ravel's *Gaspard de la nuit*. Descriptively less specific are titles that suggest extramusical pictures but nothing more. Most of the pieces of Debussy fit this category, as well as many of Schumann and Liszt. Examples are Debussy's *Reflets dans l'eau* (Reflections on the Water), Schumann's *Bittendes Kind* (Entreating Child), and Liszt's *Les Cloches de Genève* (The Bells of Geneva). Finally, there are those compositions that suggest a mood in the most general sense, such as *nocturne* or *capriccio*. It is interesting to note that some composers wrote in all categories of descriptive pieces, while others, it seems, eschewed descriptive detail and chose to use only more general titles. Chopin and Brahms, for example, seemed reluctant to attach descriptive titles to their works other than the ones that suggest an overall mood, such as capriccio, rhapsody, or nocturne.

Composers of the turn of the nineteenth century began to embrace Romantic concepts but slowly and intermittently. Many continued to use the older concepts, such as the sonata, but also wrote shorter works that might be considered character pieces. Some combined titles that suggested the new aesthetics with traditional arrangements of sections. Mendelssohn's capriccios and Schubert's impromptus, for example, are cast mostly in traditional molds, notwithstanding the freedom implied in their titles. Pieces began to emerge that implied mood or exotic settings, such as the nocturne or the barcarolle. Gradually, such works began to incorporate more freedom through the addition of introductions, transitions, developmental departures, or codas. Teaching material often figured prominently in composers' efforts, and the etude in particular saw a rapid rise in popularity due to high interest in exploring the technical limits of the emerging modern piano.

Two composers whose careers lie mostly in the late eighteenth century are **Johann Wilhelm Hässler** (1747–1822) and **Daniel Gottlob Türk** (1750–1813). Hässler's long career included concertizing widely in Germany as well as teaching and playing in London (1790–92) and Moscow (1794–1822). His voluminous catalogue consists mostly of sonatas, many of them easy enough to be useful as teaching material. He also wrote sets of pieces with titles that suggest forward-looking concepts, such as *5 Pièces caractéristiques*, Op. 27, and *Caprice, divertissement, romance, et presto*, Op. 35. He produced sets ofpieces that used all of the keys: two sets of etudes in waltz form, Opp. 24 and 49; and *360 préludes . . . dans tous les tons majeurs and mineurs*, Op. 47 (1817). Türk's work, on the other hand, was focused almost exclusively on the sonata and didactic material. Many of the forty-eight sonatas (1776–93) are designed for students (*leichte*). The *Clavierschule* (1789) became one of the most famous teaching manuals for keyboard instruments of its time.

Muzio Clementi

Muzio Clementi (b. Rome, Jan. 23, 1752; d. Evesham, Worcestershire, England, Mar. 10, 1832) received his early training in Rome and at the age of thirteen was appointed organist at a church close to his home, St. Lorenzo in Damaso. Soon thereafter, however, Clementi's playing attracted the attention of an English traveler, Peter Beckford (1740–1811), who states in his own account that he "bought Clementi of his father for seven years." Clementi was taken to the Beckford estate in Dorset, where the young man spent the next seven years in relative isolation, studying and practicing the harpsichord.

Upon securing his freedom in 1774, Clementi went to London, where he began to build his career as a keyboard performer, conductor, and composer. In 1780, he embarked upon a tour that took him to Paris, Vienna, and Lyons. In Vienna, Clementi participated in a famous competition with Mozart, ordered by Joseph II on December 24, 1781, for the amusement of the grand duke and duchess of Russia, who were guests of the emperor. No clear winner of the event emerged, a fact that may have nettled Mozart, for in a well-known letter dated January 12,

1782, Mozart wrote to his father that Clementi's playing was technically strong but without taste or feeling. According to Clementi's pupil, Ludwig Berger, Clementi found Mozart's playing, on the other hand, filled with spirit and grace.

The balance of Clementi's career alternated between professional activities in London and professional concert tours abroad. Clementi became an extremely fashionable keyboard teacher of both younger professionals and members of London society. Among his prominent students were Johann Baptist Cramer and John Field. Clementi was also a successful businessman, working with a series of partners to amass a small fortune from music publishing and instrument making. He continued to perform and conduct right up until his retirement in 1830.

Clementi's keyboard works span a period of fifty-five years, and his style reflects the changes that took place in general during that period. Thus, early Clementi is very much in the *galant* style, and gradually his works evolve to a late style that might be compared to that of late Beethoven or early Romantic composers. Throughout these changes, Clementi embraced a marked fondness for writing sections of music that alternately featured virtuoso display, strong dynamic contrast, and contrapuntal textures. Even Mozart recognized Clementi's adeptness in executing double notes, a skill that resulted in the frequent inclusion of double notes in passagework. Clementi also periodically experimented with structural alterations of the sonata form, the use of profuse ornamentation, and chromatic harmonies.

Gaining a comprehensive overview of Clementi's keyboard works is difficult, for the composer's commercial interests resulted in some works being published under several opus numbers, early works being published with late opus numbers, and transcriptions of works for other media being published as original keyboard works. By far the majority of Clementi's keyboard works are cast in sonata form. Researchers differ with regard to the exact number of the sonatas, but it seems to be somewhere around seventy, spanning a period of approximately fifty-five years. Opuses 2 and 3, sets of six sonatas each, most of which date from the 1770s, strongly reflect the Italian Classical style. Most of the sonatas are in two movements. Opuses 7–10, twelve sonatas in three movements from the early 1780s, incorporate fugal writing and virtuoso display.

Many sonatas of Clementi are worthwhile and need to be explored by pianists. Outstanding among them are the Op. 13, no. 6, in *f;* the Op. 24, no. 2, in *B-flat*, which opens with a motive similar to that Mozart used ten years later in the overture to *Die Zauberflöte* (The Magic Flute); the Op. 25, no. 5, in *f-sharp;* and the Op. 34, no. 2, in *g*, which opens with an introduction reminiscent of the Op. 13 (*Pathétique Sonata*) of Beethoven. The three sonatas that make up Op. 40 (1802), in *G, b,* and *d-D,* are all highly sophisticated works of multiple, contrasting themes, extended development sections, and expressive slow movements (Example 9.1). The one in *G*, incidentally, is Clementi's only sonata in four movements. The final set of three sonatas, Op. 50 (probably written about 1805 but published first in 1821), contains equally extended works, the last sonata in *g* having achieved some note from its poetic title, *Didone abbandonata*.

The last significant work of Clementi is the *Gradus ad Parnassum* (1817), a collection of one hundred pieces that were written, revised, and collected by the composer over a period of forty-five years. The work represents a summing up of Clementi's keyboard creativity, for it includes preludes, canons, fugues (including revisions of those in the sonatas Opp. 5 and 6), sonata-like movements, and programmatic pieces with titles such as *Scena patetica* (no. 39) and *Bizzarria* (no. 95). It also-contains many exercises, probably intended as preparatory material for the compositions. Unfortunately, twenty-nine of these exercises were assembled by Carl Taussig in about 1865 and published as the *Gradus ad Parnassum*. The importance and musical significance of the complete work was thus distorted, and generations of pianists have regarded it as nothing more than a technical manual.

Other works of Clementi should be mentioned in passing. The set of sonatinas, Op. 36, is a staple in the teaching studio and is possibly the music by which most pianists know Clementi. These six sonatinas were originally published as a supplement to Clementi's important treatise, *Introduction to the Art of Playing the Piano Forte* (1826). A Toccata, Op. 11 (ca. 1784), is an essay in double notes, possibly a forerunner of Schumann's Op. 7 (1833). There are also four sets of variations; capriccios, Opp. 17 and 47; two sets of twelve waltzes to be accompanied by triangle and tambourine, Opp. 38 and 39; and miscellaneous smaller pieces.

Jan Ladislav Dussek (1760–1812) received his education in Prague from his father, a noted musician and teacher. By the time he was nineteen, Jan Ladislav embarked upon a career as a pianist and teacher, one that embraced many tours and residencies of several years in a number of geographical locations. After short periods of time in Russia, Lithuania, Germany, and France, Dussek spent ten years in London, where he was a partner with his father-in-law in a music publishing business.

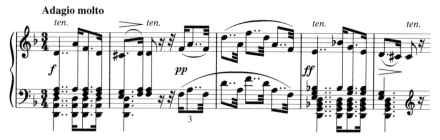

Example 9.1 Muzio Clementi: Sonata, Op. 40, no. 3, lst movt. mm. 1–5

Upon its bankruptcy, he fled to Hamburg to escape his creditors, then returned to Prague, traveled for a period of time with Prince Louis Ferdinand of Prussia, and ended up in the service of Talleyrand in Paris. Throughout his varied career, Dussek garnered considerable admiration, both as a performer and a composer. Some believe that it was Dussek who first started the tradition of placing the pianist's profile to the audience in public concerts.

Like Clementi, Dussek wrote mostly sonatas that stylistically move from a Classical style similar to that of Haydn to a more Romantic style that might be compared to those of the better-known composers of the early nineteenth century. There are about forty sonatas, a number of them arranged from works written for small groups of instruments. Research by Howard Allen Craw has resulted in clarification of the confusionthat has surrounded the opus numbers of Dussek's works, and "C" numbers may now be used to identify the composer's output. Several sonatas include programmatic reflections of events in Dussek's life. There is, for example, a Sonata, Op. 44, C. 178, in *E-flat* (1800) subtitled "The Farewell," written before Beethoven's more famous *Lebewohl Sonata* in the same key, Op. 81a. Dussek's sonata, Op. 61, C. 211, is subtitled *Elegie harmonique sur la mort du prince Louis Ferdinand de Prusse* (1807), and his Op. 64, C. 221, has two descriptive titles attached to it: *Le retour à Paris* and *Plus ultra* (1807).

Other works of Dussek include three preludes, six sonatinas, a fantasy, as well as a few sets of variations and a few character pieces. Like many of his contemporaries, Dussek wrote a piano method, *Instructions on the Art of Piano Playing* (1796). Dussek's music was very popular during his lifetime. It suffered a decline after his death, but at various times revivals have been attempted, one between 1860 and 1880, when Breitkopf und Härtel issued a new edition of his piano sonatas, and more recently since 1950, when many scholars and musicians have once again pointed to Dussek as a neglected composer of considerable worth.

Daniel Steibelt (1765–1825) pursued a controversial career in Paris, London, the cities of central Germany, and St. Petersburg. Apparently vain, arrogant, and perhaps even dishonest, he attracted admirers of his virtuoso piano playing and fashionable compositions, but he also reaped much criticism. A prolific composer in all genres, he reportedly composed more than 180 sonatas as well as numerous variations, preludes, divertissements, caprices, rondos, fantasias, and other pieces with descriptive titles. A set of etudes, Op. 78, is the only work still occasionally encountered (Example 9.2).

Johann Baptist Cramer (1771–1838) was born in Germany but was taken to London at an early age. There he studied with Clementi for a few months, played concerts, established a publishing business, and built his career with frequent, extended trips to the Continent. During his journeys, he met and befriended most of the prominent musicians of his

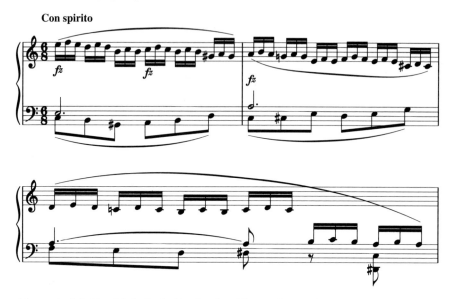

Example 9.2   Daniel Steibelt: Etude, Op. 78, no. 2 mm. 1–3

day, including Haydn and Beethoven. Cramer was universally admired as a pianist, and his compositions, although conservative, were highly regarded. His strength as a composer was in creating inventive passagework for the piano, and in this area he foreshadowed what was to follow in the works of Mendelssohn, Chopin, and Liszt. Cramer wrote more than one hundred sonatas, thirty-three sets of variations, and a large number of character pieces. The work for which he is remembered, however, is a set of eighty-four studies, published in two parts (1804 and 1810). Most of these pieces are short works, each dealing with a technical problem that can be easily recognized. The pianistic writing is imaginative and moderately challenging and fits the hand well. Beethoven annotated twenty-one of these studies for use by his nephew, Carl, and Schumann reviewed them favorably. Although they are seldom regarded as concert pieces now, Cramer himself played them in public, and they have remained firmly entrenched in the literature as traditional material with which to train pianists (Example 9.3).

Václav Jan Křtitel Tomášek(1774–1850) is the leading Czech composer of the time, strongly influencing the transition from Classicism to Romanticism. Although his training and career were centered in Prague, he was sought out by many musicians whenever they visited the city: Clementi, Clara Schumann, Paganini, and others. Tomášek possessed a sharp critical sense that kept him removed from many of the more ephemeral fashions of the day. In his autobiography, for example,

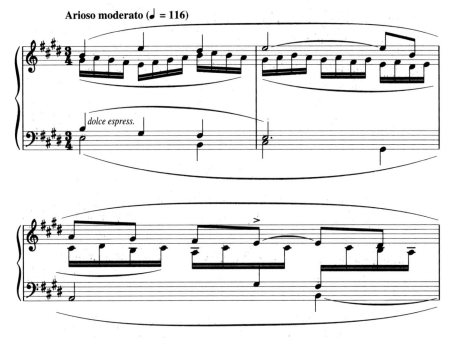

Example 9.3 Johann Baptist Cramer: Etude no. 41 mm. 1–3
Reprinted by permission of G. Schirmer, Inc.

he wrote: "Everyone tours Europe with a couple of memorized Chopin studies and a few of the so-called fantasias of Thalberg, not to glorify art, but solely to attract reviews, which, via hireling newspapers, may be used to advertise the newcomer as something extraordinary. . . . The piano has now become a coffin wherein true musicianship shall sleep until a musical spring wakens it from slumber, once again to admit it to a lost musical paradise."

Tomášek's early sonatas and variations reflect Classicism, particularly the style of Mozart, whom he admired. In 1807, he began to turn his attention to writing character pieces, using a style born of the lyricism associated with Romanticism. Influential in development of the character piece, therefore, are Tomášek's forty-two lyrical *Eclogues*, in sets of six each, Op. 35 (1807), Op. 39 (1810), Op. 47 (1813), Op. 51 (1815), Op. 63 (1817), Op. 66 (1819), and Op. 83 (1823). More technically demanding are the fifteen *Rhapsodies*, Op. 40 (1810), Op. 41 (1810), and Op. 110 (n.d.). He also wrote six *Allegri capricciosi*, Op. 52 (1815) and Op. 84 (after 1823); and three improvisatory *Ditirambi*, Op. 65 (1818).

Johann Nepomuk Hummel (1778–1837) was a child prodigy who studied with Mozart and, taken by his father, toured Scotland, England, and the Continent for several years. He returned to Vienna to build a career. For several years (1804–11), he was Haydn's successor in the

Esterházy household, a position in which Hummel was not entirely comfortable, for although he was recommended by Haydn for the post after Haydn's retirement, filling the shoes of so beloved a figure as Haydn was far from easy. He returned to Vienna as a free-lance musician for a time, building a reputation on a par with that of Beethoven, with whom he maintained a cordial, but sometimes stormy, friendship. Hummel became the Kapellmeister at Weimar (1819), where, along with Goethe, he enjoyed celebrity status. Several more tours rounded out his career, to Russia (1822), where he met John Field; Poland (1828), where he met Chopin; France; the Netherlands; and three times to England.

Hummel was regarded as one of the most important musicians of his time. His performances were generally praised for their clarity, beauty, and carefully controlled virtuosity. As a teacher he counted among his students some of the most famous musicians of the early nineteenth century, including Hiller, Mendelssohn, Henselt, and Thalberg. Hummel's work as a composer was highly regarded, and he wrote extensively in all genres of the time, except the symphony.

Hummel represented the epitome of a declining Classical style, even in his lifetime. As a performer he preferred the light-actioned, more transparent Viennese piano. As a teacher, he used his own works as material but emphasized an older tradition, focusing on counterpoint and conservative structural integrity. As a composer, he lived to see his self-contained style become old-fashioned, as aesthetics that valued passion and freedom took over. Hummel brought his style, however, to a high degree of refinement, and it represents admirably the full bloom of Classicism in its final stages.

Hummel was an astute businessman, and during his lifetime he did much to enhance the rights of composers, fighting for international copyright codes and fair practices. There is considerable confusion regarding the chronology of Hummel's works, partly because he managed publication with an eye to good business and partly because Hummel's style does not undergo monumental change. Six sonatas were published during Hummel's lifetime and span a period between 1792 and 1825. Of interest is a set of twenty-four preludes, Op. 67 (1814–15), alternating relative major and minor keys in the same order Chopin later adopted, and a set of twenty-four etudes, Op. 125 (1833), one for each key but combining parallel major and minor keys. Titles of other piano works suggest that Hummel was au courant with his time, notwithstanding his conservatism, for included in a listing of his works are many sets of variations, rondos, bagatelles, fantasias, and capriccios (Example 9.4). Of all of these, only the Rondo in *E-flat*, Op. 22, has remained in the repertoire.

Of tremendous importance to Hummel during his lifetime and to historians now is his three-volume pedagogical work on piano playing, *Ausführlich theoretisch-practische Anweisung zum Pianoforte Spiel* (Introduction

Example 9.4 Johann Nepomuk Hummel: Fantasie, Op. 18, opening

to the Theory and Practice of Learning to Play the Pianoforte; written about 1822, published in 1828). The work presents the usual array of finger exercises and technical patterns but also offers observations on many matters of style and interpretation, mixing traditional performance practices of Classicism with more up-to-date concepts. For example, it provides clear documentation, perhaps the earliest, that, at least in Hummel's opinion, the trill should begin on the main note rather than the upper auxiliary.

John Field (1782–1837) was born in Dublin, received early musical training there, and made a debut as a pianist at the age of ten. The following year, Field was taken to London, where he studied with Clementi and served as an apprentice in Clementi's piano firm, demonstrating and selling pianos. Clementi is reported to have treated Field unfairly, limiting his performances and publishing several early piano pieces anonymously. Field's period of working for Clementi came to an end about 1800, and he was able to start building a reputation in London as a pianist, teacher, and composer. In 1802, however, Clementi persuaded Field to join him in an extensive European tour, which included Paris, Vienna, and St. Petersburg. Once again there is evidence that Clementi exploited Field, not providing proper clothing, nor remitting a fair portion of the income generated by the tour. Field stayed behind in St. Petersburg, possibly to escape from Clementi's suppression but also possibly to act as a representative for Clementi's firm. Field was enormously successful in Russia, becoming fashionable as a pianist and teacher first in St. Petersburg and later in Moscow. In 1831, he returned to London, partly in order to undergo an operation for cancer and partly to renew musical activities there. In 1833, concerts were arranged in Belgium, France, Switzerland, and Italy. In Naples, Field became ill once again. He was able to revive enough to return to Russia (1835) for his final days.

Field was influential in establishing a new aesthetic in piano playing, one that eschewed bombast and display in favor of tenderness and intimacy. The search for a type of character piece that featured this style resulted in his creating the *nocturne,* a title he settled on after experimenting with

Un poco allegretto

Example 9.5 John Field: Nocturne no. 3 mm. 1–3

several other names. Field's first nocturne was published in 1812, almost
two decades before Chopin used the title. Field's nocturnes clearly
establish the mood and texture associated with the genre. Typically an
elaborate but intimate right-hand melody is spun over a subservient left-
hand accompaniment pattern. Delicacy and soulful expression attend
the melodic unfolding. The structure of the piece, although often recognizable as ABA or another block arrangement, is subservient to the
mood and is kept from rigidity through the use of passage work, transitions, or cadenzas.

Field produced fifteen nocturnes between 1812 and 1836, after he
settled in Russia. These are the pieces by which he is remembered, and
they remain marginally in the repertoire of pianists (Example 9.5). Field
also wrote four sonatas, many sets of variations, rondos, and other character pieces. The chronology of Field's works was established in 1961
through the research of Cecil Hopkinson. Compositions Field wrote
before going to Russia tend to reflect Clementi's influence and are less
individual. They are, however, worthy of more attention from pianists
than they currently receive.

Frédéric Kalkbrenner (1785–1849) achieved fame as both a pianist
and teacher in London and Paris. It was Kalkbrenner to whom Chopin
dedicated his first piano concerto, Chopin having admired Kalkbrenner
to the point of considering study with him soon after arriving in Paris.
Kalkbrenner wrote thirteen sonatas; six rondos, which he subtitled *Essais*

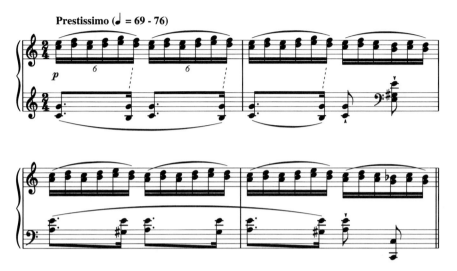

Example 9.6 Frédéric Kalkbrenner: Etude (Toccata), Op. 182, no. 2 mm. 1–4

sur différents caractères (Essays upon Different Characters), Op. 34 (1817); as well as numerous fantasies, variations, and romances. Like most of his contemporaries, he wrote a piano method, Op. 108, one that made use of a mechanical device to keep the forearms in position. There are also numerous etudes (Example 9.6). One set of etudes uses all keys, Op. 20 (1816), as does a set of preludes, Op. 88 (1827), which predates Chopin's preludes, Op. 28, by almost a decade.

Carl Maria von Weber

Carl Maria von Weber (b. Eutin, Nov. 18[?], 1786; d. London, June 5, 1826) was born into a family that had formed itself into a traveling theater troupe. He thus studied with a number of teachers in different locations, including Michael Haydn. Weber began to see his operas produced when he was still in his teens. His first important post was that of Kapellmeister in Breslau (1804). From there, Weber moved to jobs or activities in Stuttgart, Darmstadt, and Berlin, finally reaching Prague (1813), where he was appointed director of the Prague opera. He worked in Prague for three years to build the standards of the opera and to introduce German opera to a reluctant public. After three years, Weber resigned the post but accepted one of similar challenge in Dresden (1817). Through the years, Weber made periodic visits to Berlin for concerts, where his reputation grew steadily. The high point of his popularity in Berlin was the production of his opera, *Der Freischütz* (The Free-shooter; 1821), which, as a Romantic opera based on German folklore, rapidly gained popularity across Germany and eventually throughout Europe. Weber was never very robust physically, and he developed tuberculosis at an early age. Being warned by doctors of his impending death, he, nevertheless, undertook a journey to London, where Covent Garden had commissioned a new opera, *Oberon*. The opera was premiered on April 12, 1826, and, although Weber hoped to return home to his family, he was overtaken by his condition and died in London a few weeks later.

Weber's career embraced many facets. As a journalist and composer, he set the stage for the Romantic movement and is considered by many to be the spiritual father of Romanticism. He was a fine pianist and possessed an unusually large hand, one capable of playing four-note chords spanning the interval of a tenth. He used this physical advantage to great effect and regarded the piano as a means of evoking orchestral-like sonorities, preferring color and expressiveness to mere virtuoso display. His piano style is derived from those of Clementi, Cramer, and Dussek, but Weber's genius for writing opera gave rise to exceptional gifts in creating melodic lines and passagework for the keyboard and imparted a sense of drama to his longer, more serious keyboard works.

In addition to opus numbers, identification of Weber's works was provided in a thematic catalogue prepared in 1871 by Friedrich Wilhelm Jähns (1809–88). The most significant keyboard works are the four sonatas: *C*, Op. 24, J. 138 (1812); *A-flat*, Op. 39, J. 199 (1814–16); *d*, Op. 49, J. 206 (1817); and *e*, Op. 70, J. 287 (1819–22). The structures in the sonatas are traditional. All except Op. 49 are written in four movements, with an opening sonata-allegro, a slow second movement followed by a dance movement, and a lively, often virtuoso, finale. Within the traditional frameworks, Weber uses strongly contrasting material and often dramatic gestures. The first sonata, perhaps the least unified of the four, has a famous final movement, a rondo in perpetual motion that is sometimes performed separately. Similarly, the last movements of the third and fourth sonatas are sometimes presented singly as the *Allegro di bravura* and *La Tarantella*, respectively. The fourth sonata is regarded as the finest of the group, the quality of writing being the most consistently interesting. The composer provided clues to its programmatic references, being linked vaguely with depression, mental instability, and death.

Other significant works of Weber include the famous *Aufforderung zum Tanz* (Invitation to the Dance), Op. 65, J. 260 (1819), a rondo in *D-flat* with a program in which, after an introduction, a lady is approached, asked to dance, and accepts. Less well known but worthwhile are the *Movimento capriccioso*, Op.12, J. 56 (1808); *Grande Polonaise*, Op. 21, J. 59 (1808); *Rondo brilliante (La gaité)*, Op. 62, J. 252 (1819); and *Polacca brilliante (L'hilarité)*, Op. 72, J. 268 (1819). Eight traditional sets of variations show less originality.

Carl Czerny (1791–1857) studied first with his father, a professional pianist and teacher. At the age of ten, Carl was taken to Beethoven, who accepted him as a pupil, using as a textbook the *Versuch* of C. P. E. Bach. As a young musician, Czerny performed frequently in Vienna, specializing in the works of Beethoven, which, it is reported, he played in their entirety. Having no taste for public performance or touring, Czerny remained in Vienna, concentrating on composing and teaching. There he was sought out by many of the famous musicians of the day, including Hummel, Clementi, and, later, the young Chopin. Czerny had many famous students, including Kullak, Thalberg, and Liszt. Although Liszt was only nine years old when he went to study with Czerny and stayed less than two years, Czerny's influence on the young musician was enormous, for Czerny imparted discipline to Liszt's playing that served as the basis for later development as a virtuoso.

Czerny was a prolific composer in all genres, but his compositions reflect the stylish taste of the day and are mostly shallow and uninspired. For solo piano, Czerny produced about thirteen sonatas, twenty-eight sonatinas, and numerous sets of variations, character pieces, potpourris, and arrangements. Of these the first sonata in *A-flat*, Op. 7, and a set of variationson a theme by Rode (*La ricordanza*), Op. 33, are of moderate interest and receive an occasional performance. The sonata, incidentally, was highly regarded in its day and often played by Liszt. The Czerny Toccata, Op. 92, may be mentioned in passing, for it features double notes and is possibly a forerunner of Schumann's Op. 7.

The area in which Czerny has achieved immortality is that of didactic works for the developing pianist. Czerny's exercises and studies cover virtually every facet of preparation for virtuoso pianism, and they range from moderately easy to very difficult. Many of the exercise sets are arranged in an order of progressive difficulty. Well known among the many sets of studies are *The School of Velocity*, Op. 299; *School of Legato and Staccato*, Op. 335; *School for the Left Hand*, Op. 399; *110 Easy and Progressive Etudes*, Op. 453; and *The Art of Finger Dexterity*, Op. 740. Czerny also wrote several comprehensive didactic worksincluding *School of Extemporaneous Performance,* in two volumes: 1, Op. 200, and 2, Op. 300; *Complete Theoretical and Practical Pianoforte School*, Op. 500, which he dedicated to Queen Victoria, incidentally; and *School of Practical Composition,* in three volumes, Op. 600.

Ján Václav Voříšek (1791–1825) was a student of Tomášek in Prague and then, partly motivated by a personal enthusiasm for the work of Beethoven, moved to Vienna, where he spent the balance of his career. Voříšek worked there as a civil servant in the Imperial War Department, and he held the post of conductor of the Gesellschaft der Musikfreunde. He met Moscheles, Hummel, and Beethoven and became a personal friend of Schubert, who is reputed to have been influenced by his piano music. His best-known work is a piano sonata in *b-flat*, Op. 20, a three-movement work in a style that resembles Beethoven's. Also significant are his character pieces: twelve rhapsodies,

Op. 1, works that Beethoven mentioned favorably in a meeting with Tomášek, and aset of six impromtus, Op. 7 (1817), that were published before those of Schubert.

Other composers of the time should be mentioned briefly. **Joseph Wölfl** (1773–1812) was almost as celebrated as Beethoven in Vienna. He wrote some thirty sonatas in a style resembling early Clementi, sets of variations, rondos, and a piano method, Op. 50. **George Frederick Pinto** (1785–1806) exhibited remarkable originality in his short life, reflecting Mozart, Dussek, and anticipating Beethoven. For solo piano he wrote nine sonatas, one with a fantasia, and a few other shorter works. **Johann Peter Pixis** (1788–1874) was a successful performing pianist and piano teacher, centering his career in Paris and Baden-Baden. He wrote many works in Classical structures, to which he added virtuoso devices popular at the time. Among his works are three sonatas, many sets of variations, fantasias, polonaises, capriccios, and other character pieces. **Ignaz Moscheles** (1794–1870) built a career as a performing virtuoso in Vienna, then moved to London (1825), and later to Leipzig, where he became the leading piano faculty member in Mendelssohn's newly founded conservatory. His most important piano works are six grand sonatas, of which the *Sonate mélancolique* in *f-sharp*, Op. 49 (1814), is best known. He also wrote many character pieces and didactic works, among which is a set of twenty-four etudes, Op. 70 (1825–26; Example 9.7); *Charakterische Studien*, Op. 95 (1836); and the collaboration with Fétis on *Méthode des méthodes* (1840), a method book and anthology of etudes to which Chopin contributed.

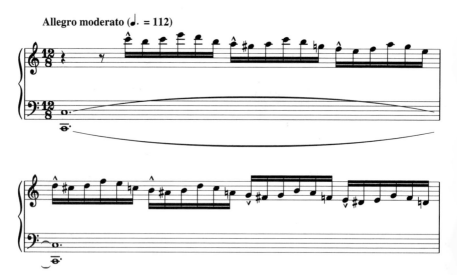

Example 9.7 Ignaz Moscheles: Etude, Op. 70, no. 1 mm. 1–2
Reprinted by permission of G. Schirmer, Inc.

CHAPTER TEN

Franz Peter Schubert

Franz Peter Schubert (b. Liechtental, Jan. 31, 1797; d. Vienna, Nov. 19, 1828) was born in a suburb of Vienna. Of Moravian lineage, his father was a schoolmaster, and his mother was the daughter of a local locksmith originally from Silesia. The couple maintained a small, three-room apartment, into which were born fourteen children, five of whom lived. Franz was the fourth surviving infant.

Schubert's early musical training was provided by his father and his older brother, Ignaz. Since the boy showed considerable talent, he was taken to Michael Holzer, choirmaster of the local church, for instruction in singing, organ, and counterpoint. In 1808, when Franz was eleven, he was admitted to the Imperial Court Chapel as a choirboy. The Stadtkonvict, the boarding school that trained the choristers, boasted a distinguished faculty that included Salieri, but the atmosphere was one of strict discipline and meager nourishment. Still, the musical life at the school was noteworthy, and the years Schubert spent there form the bulk of his formal training as a musician. Fortunately, that training included orchestral and chamber-music playing in addition to vocal instruction.

As a composer, Schubert expressed himself most easily in song. His first song, "Hagars Klage," was written just after his fourteenth birthday, and he created dozens of masterful lieder when he was still a teenager. He wrote 144 songs in the year 1815 alone. Although Schubert wrote instrumental music from the beginning of his creative life, his development in this area was slower and less sure. Large forms, developmental techniques, and to some extent the short motivic themes characteristic of instrumental writing of the day came less naturally to Schubert, and early works tend to reveal the young composer's struggle to achieve complete ease of expression.

Schubert spent his life in the city of Vienna, except for a couple of summers when he traveled to Hungary to serve as a music teacher in the Esterházy household. Earning a living was never easy for him. He taught school for a couple of years after he left the Stadtkonvict, but he was an unsuccessful applicant for several music positions both in and out of Vienna. By 1821, publishers began to be interested in his songs, and, during the few remaining years of his life, sales of his songs and some of his piano music were good. The publishers paid paltry sums to Schubert, however, and he often had to rely on the generosity of friends and family for basic subsistence.

Notwithstanding Schubert's financial plight, he became a local celebrity to a segment of Viennese society. His many friends included some prominent families, writers, and other musicians. They both admired and liked Schubert, and they often arranged for performances of his music both publicly and privately. Such events paid little but added to Schubert's reputation as a gifted composer. These performances, too, tended to concentrate on the songs and smaller instrumental works. Had Schubert lived beyond the age of thirty-one, he might, indeed, have garnered more recognition, and he might have had the pleasure of hearing some of his major compositions performed. Schubert's health began to decline, however, as early as 1823, and in 1828 he became a victim of the epidemic of abdominal typhus that was sweeping Vienna. Almost ten years later, Robert Schumann unearthed much unpublished, unperformed music of Schubert, including some of his greatest masterworks.

Schubert's musical style contains a mixture of the traditional and the forward looking, the formality of schooled composition and the freedom of spontaneous improvisation. This combination of diverse elements has led to more than one approach in attempting to capture its essence. Most observers agree that song writing and vocal expression lie at the center of Schubert's musical thought. In listening to his music, one is never very far from a glorious melody that, however produced, suggests singing. In this mode, Schubert is his warmest, most personal, and most characteristic.

Not far behind the vocal writing comes music born of the dance. Waltzes, minuets, and ländler not only exist as separate pieces but also appear constantly as thematic material in the context of longer works. In this music we find the composer charming, affable, and given to frequent merriment.

Coexisting with the song and dance-like writing is a style born of Schubert the serious musician and thinker. Whereas the songs and dances seem to emanate from Schubert spontaneously and virtually effortlessly, the more formal writing is born of considerable deliberation, and, indeed, the composer was obliged to spend some time polishing the rough edges. One can trace this process in the instrumental works by noting an increasing mastery of form, developmental techniques, and transitional material as well as the increasing sophistication with which Schubert uses his thematic material. The effect of this growth can be noted in the fact that many of Schubert's early, large-scale instrumental works are less skillfully wrought than later compositions. This has resulted in a tendency to program late sonatas, symphonies, and chamber works more often than early works.

Schubert did not share with Beethoven the compulsion to experiment with structure. Schubert seems content to use the sectional forms of the day, but he achieved his artistic goals by injecting into those forms his own special kind of lyricism. Although he often exhibited considerable development of musical ideas, he had a tendency to restate themes, either adding figural variation, new harmony, or simply moving to a new key. Schubert's gift for sudden, unexpected modulation or shifting from major to minor was unerring, and even today our ears seem never to tire of the apparent freshness of these changes.

Contemporary accounts suggest that Schubert was an accomplished pianist. He often performed in the formal and informal evenings built around his music, and, in an environment given to comparison of pianists of the day, he drew favorable commentary from his peers.

In view of this fact, it often comes as a surprise to those who attempt to play his keyboard music that it seems to lie in the hands less comfortably than the music of many of his contemporaries. Chordal passages are often attended by difficult skips and thickness of texture. Accompaniment figures are sometimes rather awkward or laid out in such a way as to make subdued playing extremely difficult. Schubert's fondness of writing as if the piano were an orchestra leads to problematic shifts in register or in texture. These difficulties in performance have led pianists to realize that successful projection of a piece of Schubert requires an unusual amount of effort in polishing details, and, until an extremely high level of refinement is achieved, the music tends to sound less than satisfying. Solving this challenge is often made more difficult by the fact that Schubert remains unhurried in the unfolding of his musical material most of the time. Attention must therefore be given to pacing and highlighting the musical events in such a way that the composition does not seem too lengthy. These are problems that prevent many pianists from delving deeply into the Schubert literature, but those who overcome the initial barriers and enter into Schubert's magical world have testified eloquently and fervently that the musical and emotional rewards are unsurpassed.

The fact that so little of Schubert's music was published during his lifetime, coupled with the existence of a fair number of fragments, revisions, and even lost compositions, has resulted in considerable chronological inaccuracy in the sequence of opus numbers. Otto Deutsch remedied this situation in 1913 with the publication of a carefully researched chronology of Schubert's works along with a great number of other documents pertaining to his life. Most of Schubert's works thus carry two sets of identifying numbers, the chronologically unreliable opus numbers and D (Deutsch) numbers. Some works have only D numbers.

A number of recent publications have made available to the performer critical editions of most of Schubert's keyboard works. These editions are helpful in eliminating errors and the surplus of interpretative markings found in many earlier editions. Even a clean edition of Schubert's music, however, does not always clarify a number of performance problems, particularly in the areas of phrasing and articulation.

The Sonatas

Whereas Schubert approached song writing with relatively few highly structured models provided by important composers of the immediately preceding generations, it was not so in the realm of the keyboard sonata. Haydn, Mozart, Beethoven, and Clementi, to name but four, all wrote important sonatas and in doing so left a legacy of expectation with regard to the form. It could be argued that Schubert's originality in dealing with the sonata has been underestimated because his sonatas have been measured against those expectations too vigorously. It is almost impossible to avoid comparing Schubert's sonatas to those of Beethoven, and yet doing so too often results in the perception that Schubert worked hard as a composer to match Beethoven's monumental achievements in sonata writing but never quite reached the same exalted level, although the late sonatas of Schubert come very close in their own way. More than a century and a half after Schubert's death, his sonatas are still being reevaluated by writers and performers in an attempt to escape the long shadow of Beethoven.

Two early sonatas (D. 157 and D. 279) date from 1815, written when Schubert was eighteen and composing his second symphony. This is also the year in which the famous song "Erlkönig" was created. Both sonatas contain three movements, the last in both cases being a minuet and trio in a related key, but not the home key. This fact has led most musicians to believe both works lack final movements. The second and third movements are actually the strongest in the case of the earlier work in *E* (D. 157). The first movement of the one in *C* (D. 279) presents some striking modulations and a recapitulation that begins in the subdominant, a procedure that Schubert uses several times in his sonata forms.

The Sonata in *E* of 1816 (D. 459) was first published in 1843 under the title of *Fünf Klavierstücke*. In 1928, a manuscript was discovered of the first two movements inscribed "Sonata, August, 1816." Whether or not the final three movements were actually conceived as part of the work remains a question. As the work stands, the second and fourth movements are both scherzos with trios, and the slow movement is in the middle. The first scherzo combines elements of sonata-allegro form with minuet and trio form in that the section before the trio ends in the dominant and the da capo, written out, closes in the tonic. The trio is unusually short and has no section marked to be repeated. The middle movement, an adagio in *C,* is a sonata-allegro form without development (truncated). The outer movements are in sonata-allegro form with no particular surprises. The final movement is marked *Allegro patetico,* and sixteenth-note sextuplets figure prominently throughout, adding an element of brilliance.

In 1817, Schubert produced three sonatas that remain very much in the pianist's repertoire and five others that contain problems of various kinds. Of the latter group, the Sonata (D. 557) is a three-movement work that opens in *A-flat* and has the final two movements in *E-flat,* thereby giving rise to the suspicion that the final movement either is missing or was never written. The Sonata (D. 567) is but a first draft of the completed D. 56 in *E-flat.* There is a fragment in *E* (D. 994) and yet another work in *e* that was never assembled by Schubert but rather published piecemeal, eventually being restored by Kathleen Dale in 1928 (D. 566 and 506). Finally the Sonata in *f-sharp* (D571 and 570) is problematic in terms of number and order of movements, Schubert having stopped writing at the recapitulations of both the first and last movements.

Identification	No. of Movts.	Tempo Markings of Movts.and (Key)
Op. 164	3	Allegro ma non troppo *(a);*
(D. 537)		Allegretto quasi andantino *(E);*
(1817)		Allegro vivace (a)

The first movement opens with two five-measure phrases that are followed by phrase groups of irregular lengths. The mood is energetic and almost developmental (Example 10.1). The development itself is built almost entirely on a two-note motive introduced in the final measures of the exposition, a procedure similar to that used by Beethoven in the first movement of the Op. 10, no. 2. The second movement presents an opening, lyrical theme over a pizzicato-like accompaniment. A faster version of this theme in the key of *A* serves also as the opening theme of the last movement of the posthumous sonata in *A* (D. 959; Examples10.2a–b). In the D. 537, the theme appears in altered form twice after its initial statement. Two departures intervene, the first presenting flowing sixteenth notes in *C* and the second a march in *d* with staccato bass chords. The final movement could be thought of as a rondo with the pattern ABABA, where the two B sections contain several themes. Since the two B sections are also a fifth apart, the first closing in *E* and the second in *A,* the movement can also be thought of as a truncated sonata-allegro, especially since the final appearance of the A section is coupled with coda-like material. This work is one of the most effective of the early sonatas and enjoys moderate popularity with performers.

Allegro, ma non troppo

Example 10.1 Franz Schubert: Sonata, D. 537, 1st movt. mm. 1–5
Edited by Erwin Ratz. Used by kind permission of European American Music
Distributors Corporation, sole U.S. and Canadian agent for Universal Edition.

Identification	No. of Movts.	Tempo Markings of Movts.and (Key)
Op. 122	4	Allegro moderato (E-flat);
(D. 568)		Andante molto (g); Menuetto,
(1817)		Allegretto (E-flat);
		Allegro moderato (E-flat)

This work is the first large, four-movement work encountered in
the keyboard sonatas. The incomplete earlier version in *D-flat* (D. 567)
gives us an opportunity to study Schubert's process of revision in detail.
Although the work is large in dimension, the prevailing mood is lyrical.
Both outer movements are in sonata-allegro form, and both offer essentially singing themes throughout. The development of the first movement is relatively short, and there is no coda. The final movement offers
a more extended development section and a few additional measures to
close the composition. The second movement presents a slow, lyrical
theme with a more dramatic contrasting section in octaves and repeated
chords. The contrasting section comes twice, the first time touching on
related keys and the final time in the home key (g). Thus, a truncated
sonata-allegro form with an incomplete reference to the first theme acting as a coda seems to be the format of the movement. The minuet and
trio that acts as the third movement is lyrical and concise. Overall, this
work is quite satisfying and offers some of Schubert's loveliest lyricism,
although for some reason it has not enjoyed great popularity with performers, possibly because it offers relatively few big, dramatic moments.

Example 10.2a Franz Schubert: Sonata, D. 537, 2nd movt. mm. 1–4

Example 10.2b Sonata, D. 959, 4th movt. mm. 1–4
Edited by Erwin Ratz. Used by kind permission of European American Music
Distributors Corporation, sole U.S. and Canadian agent for Universal Edition.

Identification	No. of Movts.	Tempo Markings of Movts.and (Key)
Op. 147	4	Allegro ma non troppo *(B);*
(D. 575)		Andante *(E);* Scherzo, Allegretto
(1817)		*(G);* Allegro giusto *(B)*

Although this work was written in the same year as the D. 568 and
is of about the same length, it is more restless and shows the composer
in a more innovative mood. The dotted rhythms of the opening movement convey great energy, and the fact that Schubert changes the key
signature three times during the exposition points to harmonic boldness, the most striking shift, from *B* to *G*, occurring just fourteen measures after the piece opens. The short development section is based on
the dotted rhythm of the opening motive, and the recapitulation opens

in the subdominant. The second movement presents a songlike theme in *E* with interesting, fleeting excursions into *C* and *d*. A middle section opens with a staccato octave accompaniment in *e*. The return of the main theme is varied, and there is a short coda. The Scherzo is regular in structure, but it contains some colorful key relationships. The first section of the Scherzo itself closes in the expected dominant key (*D* in this case). It is followed by a second-section opening in *B-flat*. Similarly, the first part of the trio closes in its dominant (*A*), and the next section opens with a major chord built on *F-sharp*. The final sonata-allegro movement is light and cheerful. It offers charming themes composed of short motives and a modest, delicate development section. This work thus ends pleasantly but certainly not imposingly.

The two sonatas from 1818 are both incomplete. The first in *C* (D. 613) exists as an apparent first and last movement, neither of which have a recapitulation. Maurice J. E. Brown has argued for the inclusion of an Adagio in *E* (D. 612) with these two movements as a slow movement inasmuch as it was written at about the same time, although it was originally published separately. The second sonata of 1818 is more nearly complete, lacking only a first-movement recapitulation. The fact that it is in *f* has inspired associations with the Op. 57 of Beethoven, and indeed the opening theme relies on monophonic parallel lines in each hand an octave apart, thus setting forth a texture vaguely reminiscent of the Beethoven work. Both first themes also feature trills. The two middle movements of the work are the Adagio in *D-flat* (D. 505), the connection between that particular adagio and this sonata having been established by Otto Deutsch, and a sprightly Scherzo and Trio in *E*. The opening theme of the final movement of the work is built from a series of sixteenth notes in the lower register of the keyboard, providing a texture that once again recalls the Op. 57 of Beethoven, this time the opening theme of the last movement. This movement, also in sonata form, is, however, far less imposing than its *Appassionata* counterpart, and it makes fewer demands on the performer. This sonata, nevertheless, is both imaginative and evocative, and it probably should be played more often than it is, even if performance means reconstruction of the opening movement's recapitulation. The following year, 1819, Schubert began a sonata in *c-sharp*, but only the exposition of the first movement is extant (D. 655).

Identification	No. of Movts.	Tempo Markings of Movts. and (Key)
Op. 120 (D. 664) (?1819)	3	Allegro moderato (*A*); Andante (*D*); Allegro (*A*)

This work was published shortly after Schubert's death, along with the Piano Quintet in *A* (D. 667), "Die Forelle" (The Trout). The popularity of this sonata is well deserved, for it combines Schubert's special gifts for writing charming song and dance music with a succinct, well-balanced structure and nicely placed dramatic climaxes. The first and last movements are clearly in sonata-allegro form, each ending with a short restatement of the opening theme of the movement acting as a coda. Each movement opens with a lyrical, songlike melody and uses dance-like material as a second theme. Both movements contain well-constructed development sections that reach a point of climax before the onset of the recapitulation. The last movement recapitulation opens in the subdominant. The middle movement is also probably born of sonata-allegro form, although the middle section that serves as a development consists of little more than the opening theme stated in the subdominant with a slight extension that builds to a dramatic high point. The return of the main theme in the recapitulation includes a charming echo-like imitation of its basic rhythmic pattern.

Identification	No. of Movts.	Tempo Markings of Movts. and (Key)
Op. 143 (D. 784) (1823)	3	Allegro giusto *(a);* Andante *(F);* Allegro vivace *(a)*

This work was written after a lapse in sonata writing of several years, although the *Wanderer Fantasy* (D. 760) was produced the preceding year in 1822. The D. 784, like the D. 664 of 1819, is one of Schubert's most successful popular works. Schumann singled it out for special praise. There is a universal appeal in the sombre opening material of the first movement, and it is contrasted with a second theme of extraordinary serenity (Example 10.3). Of special merit is the development, for it combines several motives set forth in the exposition with great skill and beauty. The lyrical melody of the second movement is punctuated with a short rhythmic motive that is almost like a soft drum roll. This figure is used both to lead into the short, climactic middle section and as the basis of a coda that touches on several remote keys. The final movement is built on two contrasting sections: a triplet figure that suggests urgency and drive and a lilting Viennese waltz. The former modulates each time it appears, and the latter is simply transposed each time, so that it appears in three different keys. The effect is magical. The final statement of the opening material is presented in octaves in both hands in imitation. The composer thus surprises the performer with a difficulty that is both formidable and somewhat out of proportion to the demands of the rest of the movement (Example 10.4). Many performers, knowing that this passage lies ahead at the very end of the movement, adopt a conservative basic tempo in the beginning rather than being forced to slow down the momentum of the piece in its final measures.

Example 10.3 Franz Schubert: Sonata, D. 784, 1st movt. mm. 9–14
Edited by Erwin Ratz. Used by kind permission of European American Music Distributors Corporation, sole U.S. and Canadian agent for Universal Edition.

Example 10.4 Franz Schubert: Sonata, 784, 3rd movt. mm. 260–62
Edited by Erwin Ratz. Used by kind permission of European American Music Distributors Corporation, sole U.S. and Canadian agent for Universal Edition.

Schubert wrote three sonatas in 1825, one of which, the D. 840 in C, was not completed, lacking endings to both the third and fourth movements. The quality of the writing in the first two movements is such that the work has garnered considerable interest from research musicians, many of whom bemoan the fact that it was never finished. Ernst Krenek and Walter Rehberg have both provided endings for the movements but in doing so demonstrated enough difference in approach so that performers have not been comfortable with accepting either version and, indeed, have perhaps been led to the conclusion that satisfactory posthumous reconstruction of these movements' endings is not really possible. In any case, no version of the work has found its way to being included on performer's programs with any degreeof frequency. Curiously, the work was published in 1862 under the title *Reliquie*, a poetic reference to its incompleteness. The nickname has been more or less adopted.

Identification	No. of Movts.	Tempo Markings of Movts.and (Key)
Op. 42	4	Moderato *(a)*; Andante poco moto
(D. 845)		*(C)*; Scherzo, Allegro vivace *(a)*;
(1825)		Rondo, Allegro vivace *(a)*

The last of the three sonatas in *a* received more attention during Schubert's lifetime than almost any of the other sonatas, having both been performed on several programs and reviewed by the press. The reviews, although generally favorable, comment with some degree of concern about the sonata's length, a factor that still challenges performers and listeners, both in this work and the remainder of the late sonatas. The opening movement is built on two ideas, the first a lyrical line introduced monophonically and the second a rhythmic figure that is introduced in *a* before it is transformed into the second theme in the relative major. Its reappearance in the recapitulation is in *A*. The development section concentrates on the first theme, and its use in the recapitulation is canonic. The movement is thus notable for a tightly knit use of material. The second movement presents a two-part theme with a set of five variations, all elaborating on the theme with increased complexity. A short coda is built on the triplet figuration of the final variation. A charming, but totally regular, scherzo and trio follow. The final movement is labeled a rondo by the composer, and, although the movement is indeed built around the repeated return of a main theme, there are other elements in the movement that make it unusual: the second departure from the main theme is that theme developed, and even the middle section in the parallel major grows out of a four quarter-note grouping of the main theme. This movement reflects the first movement of the sonata in its economic use of material.

Identification	No. of Movts.	Tempo Markings of Movts. and (Key)
Op. 53	4	Allegro vivace *(D)*; con moto *(A)*;
(D. 850)		Scherzo, Allegro vivace *(D)*;
(1825)		Rondo, Allegro moderato *(D)*

Published during Schubert's lifetime as his "second sonata," this work is dedicated to a pianist of the day, Carl Maria von Bocklet. The desire to please a performer of note possibly accounts for the vigorous opening of the first movement and a second theme that is equally energetic, displaying a jaunty military-like tune and interrupted by a striking leap without warning from *A* to *G*. The development section, based on first-theme material, never relents, and the movement ends with a coda in which the urgency of the first theme is heightened by the intrusion of a German augmented-sixth chord. Schubert offers the listener virtually none of the songful lyricism for which he is so famous in the first movement, a fact that has caused some critics to complain about its quality. The movement is, however, beautifully balanced and masterfully constructed. It simply represents Schubert in an unusually ebullient, vigorous frame of mind. Although the second movement opens with the long-awaited Schubertian lyricism, its second section is built on an energetic syncopated figuration that is in sharp contrast to the opening

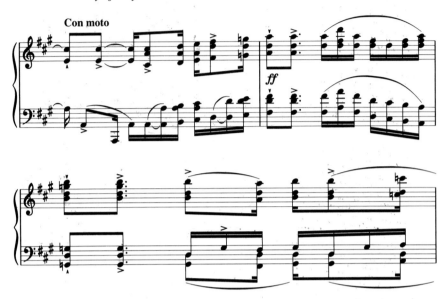

Example 10.5 Franz Schubert: Sonata, D. 850, 2nd movt. mm. 45–47
Edited by Erwin Ratz. Used by kind permission of European American Music
Distributors Corporation, sole U.S. and Canadian agent for Universal Edition.

(Example 10.5). Even the lyrical main theme has an unsettled quality
about it in its penchant toward frequent modulation, both in its original
appearance and when it returns. The syncopated section, too, is presented a second time, and the final appearance of the main theme is in
counterpoint with rhythmic elements borrowed from the syncopated
theme. This coupling provides the basis for a short coda as well.

Dotted-note rhythm formed into long, iambic upbeats generates
energy for the Scherzo. This pattern is present throughout the unusually long scherzo section, even when it is turned into a lilting waltz. The
trio offers a sharp contrast in terms of rhythmic organization but
becomes equally caught up in its quarter-note pattern. The final movement offers opening material that is deceptively simple, utterly charming, and completely Schubertian (Example 10.6). Two departures from
this theme are presented, the first built on rapid sixteenth-note patterns
and the second, with its own ABA structure, formed of more lyrical
repeated eighth notes. The final return of the main theme is varied with
passagework, but the sonata ends quietly with a recalling of the simplicity of the opening. In 1834, shortly after Schubert's death, Schumann
wrote a short review of this sonata in which he characterized the last
movement as comical or humorous. Its very special mood, indeed,
invites speculation, although most writers have disagreed with
Schumann as to the exact nature of the expression, opting instead for

Example 10.6 Franz Schubert: Sonata, D. 850, 4th movt. mm. 1–4
Edited by Erwin Ratz. Used by kind permission of European American Music
Distributors Corporation, sole U.S. and Canadian agent for Universal Edition.

lightheartedness and gaiety. It is, however, to be noted that overall the
sonata moves from the serious, nonstop intensity of the first movement,
by degrees through the middle two movements, to the much more carefree, relaxed expression in the final movement.

Identification	No. of Movts.	Tempo Markings of Movts.and (Key)
Op. 78	4	Molto moderato cantabile *(G);*
(D. 894)		Andante *(D);* Menuetto, Allegro
(1826)		moderato *(G);* Allegretto *(G)*

This work was the last of the sonatas to be published during
Schubert's lifetime, and it appeared not as a sonata but rather as four
separate pieces: Fantasie, Andante, Menuetto, and Allegretto. The work
is dedicated to Schubert's close friend Joseph Spaun. Schumann's praise
of the work is terse but extravagant, for he dubbed it Schubert's "most
perfect" sonata in "form and spirit." Other contemporary reviews were
more moderate but generally warm, and writers since have almost
always regarded this work with enthusiasm. This is perhaps curious
inasmuch as the work gives the impression of leaning heavily on sustained lyricism almost to the point of neglecting more sharply etched,
vigorous musical ideas. The performer must be completely dedicated to
the gentle beauty of the work and must draw the audience into a world
that is predominantly serene. When this difficult task is successfully
accomplished, the resulting communion is richly rewarding.

The opening movement's first theme is characterized by two-bar
phrases based on sustained chords (Example 10.7). The second theme
is more dance-like with its dotted-rhythm accompaniment figure, but it,
too, is built on phrases that open with long, downbeat sounds, this time
using accented, dotted quarter notes. The dotted rhythm of the second-theme accompaniment provides the most dramatic moment in the
exposition. The development reaches two high points, both drawn
from the opening theme, powerful but once again characterized by sustained sounds. The same material is used for the coda that brings the

Molto moderato e cantabile

Example 10.7 Franz Schubert: Sonata, D. 894, 1st movt. mm. 1–2

Edited by Erwin Ratz. Used by kind permission of European American Music Distributors Corporation, sole U.S. and Canadian agent for Universal Edition.

Andante

Example 10.8 Franz Schubert: Sonata, D. 894, 2nd movt. mm. 30–34

Edited by Erwin Ratz. Used by kind permission of European American Music Distributors Corporation, sole U.S. and Canadian agent for Universal Edition.

movement to a quiet close. The scheme of the Andante is ABABA. The opening theme is a two-part song that is varied each time it comes back. The alternate sections provide some of the most dramatic motivic writing in the sonata (Example 10.8). The Menuetto contrasts a vigorous opening with lilting melodies of waltz-like character. The mood of the trio is especially endearing. The final Allegretto is cast in rondo form: ABACA. Each of the sections has an ABA structure of its own. The central theme is a gentle pastoral song, and both departure themes convey the spirit of country dances. A coda based on the opening theme brings the work to a quiet close.

The last three sonatas were written only a few weeks before Schubert's death in a remarkably short time, probably about four weeks. There is evidence that the composer played them for friends in late September 1828, that he sought to have them published, and that he intended to dedicate them to Hummel. The three sonatas were, in fact, not published until 1838, ten years after Schubert's death. At first they did not inspire the admiration they now enjoy. Even so ardent an admirer as Schumann had relatively little reaction to them in his reviews, and

Example 10.9 Franz Schubert: Sonata, D. 958, lst movt. mm. 1–8
Edited by Erwin Ratz. Used by kind permission of European American Music
Distributors Corporation, sole U.S. and Canadian agent for Universal Edition.

for the rest of the century many writers characterized the music as a
product of the composer's waning energy. More recent analysts have
forcibly reversed this assessment, regarding these works as supernal
expressions, an apotheosis of the composer's musical thinking, perhaps
even prophetically visionary of his impending death. Although all three
sonatas are treated with equal reverence, the last one in *B-flat* (D. 960)
has achieved a most-favored status among performers.

Identification	*No. of Movts.*	*Tempo Markings of Movts.and (Key)*
D. 958 (1828)	4	Allegro *(c);* Adagio *(A-flat);* Menuetto, Allegro *(c);* Allegro *(c)*

The first movement balances beautifully an opening that is orchestral and motivic (Example 10.9) with a second theme that is delicate and
songlike. The development is masterful in that its material never quotes
directly from themes presented in the exposition but rather seems to
grow inexorably out of them. One main idea that evolves is a chromatic line, presented most often in the low registers of the keyboard. It is
both ominous and grim, and it returns in the coda to close the movement. As with the two preceding sonatas, the second movement is cast
in an ABABA structure with the A being a songful melody that is varied
with each return and the B sections providing a more lively, dramatic
contrast. In this movement the B sections are unusually dark and

Example 10.10 Franz Schubert: Sonata, D. 958, 2nd movt. mm. 28–30
Edited by Erwin Ratz. Used by kind permission of European American Music
Distributors Corporation, sole U.S. and Canadian agent for Universal Edition.

threatening, employing octaves in repeated-note patterns (Example
10.10). The Menuetto, too, seems rather somber, its only relief being the
small trio section. The final movement is cast in sonata-allegro form, but
there are no repeats indicated. The unrelenting energy of the six-eight
time suggests a tarantella. Except for a closing section of the exposition
and recapitulation where the music catches its breath for a few measures,
the movement drives hard from beginning to end, and it ranks high on
the list of the composer's works in terms of nonstop excitement. It
would be easy to see why some might find this sonata an expression of
Schubert's darkest, most troubled mood.

Identification	No. of Movts.	Tempo Markings of Movts.and (Key)
D. 959 (1828)	4	Allegro *(A);* Andantino *(f-sharp);* Scherzo, Allegro vivace *(A);* Rondo, Allegretto *(A)*

Like the D. 958, this work opens with a motivic gesture. In measure
7, triplet eighth notes are introduced as an extended upbeat to the main
motive. These triplets return after the songlike second theme to form the
basis of passagework that leads to the exposition's climax. The development section is interesting in that it uses the lyric second theme almost
entirely, referring to the opening material only once near the middle of the
section. The opening does, however, return to provide the basis of a coda.

Example 10.11 Franz Schubert: Sonata, D. 959, 2nd movt. mm. 111–13
Edited by Erwin Ratz. Used by kind permission of European American Music
Distributors Corporation, sole U.S. and Canadian agent for Universal Edition.

The second movement is virtually unique in Schubert's expression
because of its middle section. The ABA structure opens with a lovely
plaintive melody. As it comes to an end, we move into a new section, a
cadenza-like passage presented in sixteenth notes. Soon these give way
to thirty-second notes that outline a series of descending diminished-seventh chords over a pedal point on *G*. The arrival of the key of *c* suggests
that a new theme is about to be stated, but this, too, gives way to trills
and further modulation to *e* and *c-sharp*. By now, a storm of improvisatory frenzy erupts (Example 10.11). A retransition of thirty-six
measures, punctuated with sforzando chords and a beguiling shift from
c-sharp to *C-sharp*, ultimately ushers in a return of the first theme, now
stated with a more active accompaniment as well as a nervous triplet
sixteenth-note figure. The dramatic contrast in this slow movement is so
intense that it is difficult to think of anything else in the keyboard literature quite like it. It also serves to make the disjunct triads in *A* that open
the scherzo and trio sound unusually giddy. The thematic idea that
opens the Rondo was used by Schubert as the basis for the second
movement of the early Sonata in *a* (D. 537). The transformation of the
material includes a tempo change as well as subtle rhythmic alterations
that render the theme more flexible, changing it from a straightforward
song to music filled with dance-like turning and swaying. The activity is
increased as the theme is repeated with an added triplet eighth-note figuration. The triplets continue right on through a long B section and the
return of A. The middle section is a development of the A theme, giving

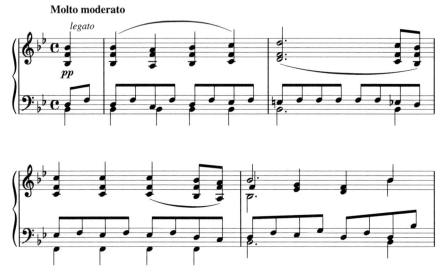

Example 10.12 Franz Schubert: Sonata, D. 960, 1st movt. mm. 1–4
Edited by Erwin Ratz. Used by kind permission of European American Music
Distributors Corporation, sole U.S. and Canadian agent for Universal Edition.

the movement a sonata-like feeling. Material from both the A and B sections form the basis of a coda marked *Presto,* and as the work closes the
motive that opened the first movement reappears, making the sonata
cyclic. Of the three posthumous sonatas, the *A* probably presents the
best balance of material, for it includes Schubert's lyricism, his dance-like
gaiety, and his orchestral-like dramatic gestures, all presented in expertly proportioned movements. It deserves more attention from performers than it seems to be getting.

Identification	No. of Movts.	Tempo Markings of Movts.and (Key)
D. 960 (1828)	4	Molto moderato *(B-flat);* Andante sostenuto *(c-sharp);* Scherzo, Allegro vivace con delicatezza *(B-flat);* Allegro ma non troppo *(B-flat)*

The final sonata has the well-deserved reputation of being the
quintessence of all things Schubertian. From its broadly lyrical opening
theme (Example 10.12) to the final burst of joyful energy that character-
izes the last movement's coda, it is a compendium of the composer's most
effective musical utterances. Particularly striking is the key change to *G-
flat* twenty measures after the first movement begins. The return to *B-
flat* fifteen measures later is a small miracle in that its power to evoke a
warm feeling of well-being, as if the sun had just emerged from behind

a cloud, seems undiminished even after a century and a half. The exposition contains twenty-two measures written with a key signature of three sharps, a passage that opens with a new melody in *f-sharp*, hovers around *b*, and passes quickly through *d* before it returns to *b-flat*, just at the point where that key slips deftly to its dominant and offers still another dance-like theme. The exposition of the first movement is thus filled with variety and richness. The development uses both the opening melody of the movement and the dance-like theme. Although there is a climactic moment near the middle of the development, the most memorable moments of this section are the intimate ones of the retransition where both themes are presented very softly and punctuated with long trills written in very low registers of the keyboard. Every section of the long exposition is recapitulated, and the movement ends with a quiet restatement of the opening theme.

The second movement in *c-sharp* presents an opening melody that initially hovers around the dominant note, thereby allowing the composer to surround it with a dotted-rhythm accompaniment figure that is hypnotic in its effect. The rhythm is unwavering, even as the melody moves around. The middle section is built on a broad lyrical theme that begins in *A* both times but tracks quite differently each time and is a tour de force of expert modulations. A more complex rhythmic figuration attends the restatement of the opening section, providing nonetheless the same hypnotic undergirding. The Scherzo provides a wonderful combination of song and dance material as well as a trio that is disarmingly charming in its simplicity. The final movement lies somewhere between a rondo and a sonata-allegro form. The beguiling opening theme returns between departures, to be sure, but the first departure is lengthy, presenting as much new material as did the exposition of the first movement, and the second departure offers a middle section that is, in fact, a development section based on the opening theme. There is a full recapitulation after the development, and a short coda marked *Presto* closes the sonata. This work has achieved the status of the crown jewel of the Schubert sonatas, and indeed, if one must single out a work for such an honor, this seems as good a choice as any, for its greatness cannot be questioned, and it represents Schubert in all his glory. It would be a shame, on the other hand, to stop with a study of this work, as many musicians have a tendency to do, for there are others that offer their own beauty and are in their own way just as rewarding.

The *Wanderer Fantasy*

The *Wanderer Fantasy* (D. 760) was composed in 1822, a year in which Schubert wrote no other extended keyboard work. The title of the work comes from the fact that Schubert borrowed a piece of melody used in his song "Der Wanderer," specifically that used to set the line

Allegro con fuoco ma non troppo

Example 10.13a Franz Schubert: Fantasie (*Wanderer*), D. 760 1st movt. mm. 1–3

Adagio

Example 10.13b   2nd movt. mm. 1–2

"Die Sonne dänkt mich hier so kült." All four movements of the fantasy are based on the song rhythmically, and the slow second movement draws even more directly from this source (Examples 10.13a–d). The opening movement acts very much like a sonata-allegro structure up through the development section, with both the opening theme and the more lyrical second theme being generated from the same idea. There is no recapitulation, however, and a dramatic transition leads without pause to the slow second movement, which presents its melody with a set of variations. A presto movement follows without any break and is basically a scherzo and trio. The final movement acts very much as if it wants to be fugal in its opening entries but settles for a series of octaves, tremolos, arpeggios, and rapid scales to bring the work to a brilliant conclusion.

The *Wanderer Fantasy* considerably expands Beethoven's concept of cyclicism within the framework of the sonata structure by letting the thematic germ permeate every movement. Furthermore, it weds the four-movement sonata structure with the concept of a longer free form, keeping elements of traditional structures, such as sonata-allegro and minuet and trio, in place. It is the earliest of a series of famous sonata-like fantasies, or fantasy-like sonatas, examples of which come from Mendelssohn, Schumann, and Chopin and culminate with the Sonata in *b* of Liszt. In the bargain, Schubert gives us one of his most satisfying and brilliant keyboard works.

Example 10.13c 3rd movt. mm. 1–7

Example 10.13d 4th movt. mm.1–4

Character Pieces

The smaller pieces of Schubert may very well be regarded as character pieces, albeit there are no extra musical references or literary sources that are attached to any of them. The semi-improvisatory nature suggested by the titles—Impromptu, *Moments musicals* (Schubert's incorrect French seems to delight many scholars, so it is often retained)—is the extent to which mood is indicated. The two sets of four impromptus (Op. 90, D. 899; Op. 142, D. 935) and the three late pieces, known simply as *Klavierstücke* (D. 946), are all somewhat longer than might be expected for the character piece, and they utilize a variety of structural formats.

The first Impromptu from the Op. 90 (D. 899) in *c* presents its opening theme in single notes and repeats it with a chordal harmonization. A more lyrical theme built on the same idea serves as a contrasting theme, and a third melody, not far removed from the spirit of the first two, is accompanied with repeated bass chords. Thus far, the structure could be thought of as a sonata-allegro exposition. What follows, however, does not conform to the sonata-allegro pattern, for after a short transition the sequence of events is repeated with some variation both in figuration and key relationships. A final statement of the opening theme brings the work to a close.

The second Impromptu in *E-flat* is one of the most frequently-played of Schubert's short pieces, for it is brilliant without being excessively difficult, and it offers a clear ABA structure with a B section of nicely contrasting material. The opening perpetual motion of scales is repeated exactly in its return, and there is a short coda. The third piece is in *G-flat,* albeit one occasionally encounters the piece in a transposed version in *G,* a facilitation, one suspects, for the poor reader, but one that violates the color of the music and damages the physical sensation of playing it in a key that involves many black keys on the keyboard. The piece is a song without words, both in mood and structure. The final Impromptu carries a key signature of *A-flat,* but Schubert adds appropriate C-flats and F-flats measure by measure to render the opening theme first in *a-flat.* The composition, also in ABA form, settles finally for the major mode.

The second set of impromptus, Op. 142 (D. 935), was reviewed by Schumann in 1838 at the time of their publication. He felt that the set should be thought of as a sonata. His case rests on the fact that the first and last impromptus are both in *f,* that the second of the set is in minuet and trio form, and that the third is an andante with five variations, a form that could possibly serve as the slow movement of a sonata but that is unusual when regarded as an impromptu. The last impromptu is a rondo with an unusually long middle section, so it, too, would be appropriate for a sonata structure. The first movement, however, is similar to the first of the Op. 90 set in that it starts out acting like a sonata-allegro structure but then evolves into a large two-part form, a truncated sonata-allegro form at best, with a final statement of the opening theme at the end to serve as a coda. Schubert was not in the habit of experimenting with first-movement structure in his sonatas. This observation weakens Schumann's case considerably, and most performers continue to regard the four as distinct pieces, often exercising the option of programming them separately. The theme (and variations) especially is programmed by itself, for its melody is one of Schubert's most famous, appearing also in the *Rosamunde* ballet music.

The three pieces (D. 946) written in 1828, the last year of Schubert's life, were not published until 1868 and then simply as *Klavierstücke,* although there is evidence to suggest that Schubert had planned another set of four impromptus but had been able to complete only these three. The first one in *e-flat* combines an opening, driving triplet section with an andante in *B* as a middle section. Schubert apparently planned two departures to the opening material, the second an andantino in *A-flat,* but he canceled the second episode. Although it is printed in some editions, performers seldom use it. The second piece in the set does, however, have two episodes, resulting in a five-part form ABACA. The opening allegretto is a gentle, melodic pastorale in six-eight time, and the two contrasting episodes are in *c* and *a-flat,* providing darker moods.

This is the longest of three pieces. The final piece features lively syncopation in its opening allegro in *C* and a sustained, contrasting middle section in *D-flat*. The episode is written in three-two time, and the basic rhythmic structure of literally every measure is two half notes followed by two quarters. A brilliant coda ends the third piece.

There has been some feeling among writers that the *Klavierstücke* do not have as much musical value as the other sets of impromptus. It is true that the structures of all three are laid out in sectional fashion without much attempt at transition and that there is very little development of any of the thematic ideas. On the other hand, the same charges could be leveled at several of the other well-known impromptus, both the *E-flat* and the *A-flat* of the Op. 90 set, for example. In defense of the *Klavierstücke,* one could point to much that is attractive: the high energy of both the first and third pieces, the wonderful color created by the low tremolos of the episode in *c* in the second piece, or both the tremolos and the cadenza-like runs that frame part of the middle section of the first piece. Highlighting the beauties of these pieces is more appropriate than criticizing their possible weaknesses, for they are certainly worth playing, and performers have tended to neglect programming them, which is a pity.

Following along the same lines, but somewhat smaller, are the six *Moments musicals* (D. 780). They were published in 1828, and the fanciful title may have come from the publisher rather than Schubert, for two of the pieces were published earlier with different titles: no. 3, one of Schubert's most famous pieces, as *Air russe,* and no. 6 in *A-flat* as *Plaintes d'un troubadour.* These six pieces appear to be somewhat less demanding than the impromptus, but polished, sensitive performance of these supposedly easier pieces takes great control, and projecting their undeniable charm can sometimes be elusive.

The same observation might be made about the dance music that Schubert wrote for keyboard. Dozens of waltzes, minuets, ländler, ecossaises, and galops were probably improvised by Schubert for social occasions and later written down. Some are organized into sets that lend themselves to performance together, such as the twelve *Grazer Waltzer,* Op. 91 (D. 924), while others seem to be more carelessly placed together in groups of two, three, four, six, or whatever was convenient. The small pieces themselves are almost always in binary form, each part marked to be repeated, quite often each part only eight measures long. These little pieces exemplify wonderfully Schubert's gift for tossing off melodies. Time after time the tunes seem familiar even as one hears them for the first time, and yet they remain amazingly fresh and powerful in their ability to delight the listener. It is easy to see why Ravel used two of the sets, *Valses sentimentales,* Op. 50 (D. 779), and *Valses nobles,* Op. 77 (D.969), as sources of inspiration for his own *Valses nobles et sentimentales* (1911). Schubert's dances have long been well established in the teaching studio, but their musical value is certainly high enough to be included on concert programs as well, a practice not often encountered.

There are about a dozen other miscellaneous works of Schubert. Worthy of mention are two fantasies, the first (D. 993) in a simple ABA form and the second, discovered in 1962, in a more extended structure, somewhat like that of Mozart's K. 475. The entire composition grows out of motivic material presented in the opening section and includes a polonaise, sections of brilliant passagework, and a return of the opening section at the end. There are also two sets of variations: the first, dating from 1815 (D. 156), presents ten variations on an original theme, and the second, dating from 1817 (D. 576), uses a theme of Schubert's contemporary, Anselm Hüttenbrenner, as the basis for thirteen variations.

CHAPTER ELEVEN

Felix Mendelssohn

Felix Mendelssohn (b. Hamburg, Feb. 3, 1809; d. Leipzig, Nov. 4, 1847) was born into a prominent family. He was the great grandson of a Jewish schoolmaster, Mendel, who was converted to Christianity and insisted that his children be reared in the Christian faith. His grandfather was the famous philosopher Moses Mendelssohn, a scholar who has been called "the modern Plato." His father, Abraham, moved to Berlin in 1812 to escape the French occupation of Hamburg. In Berlin, Abraham met and married Felix's mother, Lea Salomon-Bartholdy. The full proper name of the composer is Jacob Ludwig Felix Mendelssohn-Bartholdy.

Mendelssohn was devoted to his family, and his home life was one of refinement and social position. His education was carefully planned. His mother taught early piano lessons to both Felix and his older sister, Fanny. Felix was precocious and excelled in languages and painting as well as music. It became apparent, however, that music was Felix's most intense interest, and piano study was continued with Ludwig Berger in Berlin and, for a short time in Paris when Felix was seven, with Marie Bigot. He also studied theory with Carl Friedrich Zelter, and at the age of ten he entered the Berlin Singakademie as an alto. The same year the Singakademie performed a composition by Mendelssohn based on the text of the nineteenth psalm. By 1826, he had reached complete maturity in his composition, for he wrote the overture to Shakespeare's *A Midsummer Night's Dream*.

One of the best pianists of his age, Mendelssohn had a style of playing that was characterized by a facile technique and phenomenal memory. A conductor of great authority, he worked consistently and constantly in the cause of worthwhile music. A significant contribution in this regard took place on March 11, 1829, when at the age of twenty he conducted Johann Sebastian Bach's *St. Matthew Passion* at the Singakademie, the first performance anywhere since Bach's death.

He also made his first journey to England at the age of twenty. There he conducted his first symphony in *c*, Op. 11, dedicating it to the London Philharmonic Society, which in turn made him an honorary

237

member. On the same tour, he played Weber's *Concertstück* and Beethoven's *Emperor* Concerto, Op. 73. In 1833, he began conducting at the Lower-Rhine Music Festival in Düsseldorf and soon after accepted the position of Kapellmeister, taking charge of the church music, the municipal opera, and two singing societies. Two years later he was offered the position of music director of the celebrated Gewandhaus orchestra in Leipzig. In 1841, Friedrich Wilhelm IV appointed Mendelssohn to take charge of the major orchestral and choral concerts of the city of Berlin, conferring on him the title of Royal General Musical Director. Mendelssohn eventually became frustrated, however, with the Berlin appointment because of local jealousies and politics. The remainder of Mendelssohn's career was centered on concertizing both on the Continent and in London, where he was especially successful, and activities associated with his positions in central Germany.

Mendelssohn was one of the first to bring discipline into the orchestra, insisting that the performance be faithful to the written score. He was especially noted for bringing the orchestra at Leipzig to a very high level. As a successful musician he enjoyed high visibility, and he numbered among his friends many celebrated writers and musicians: Weber, Goethe, Halévy, Herz, Kalkbrenner, Meyerbeer, Rossini, Paganini, Berlioz, Liszt, Chopin, Field, Spohr, Hiller, Cherubini, and Wagner.

Mendelssohn's feverish schedule, however, was a mixed blessing, for in later life he grew somewhat irritable because of overwork and nervous strain, and he was often impatient with others' viewpoints. Although he married in 1837 and enjoyed a harmonious home life, he persisted in working himself to the point of exhaustion. The death of his sister, Fanny, on May 14, 1847, threw him into depression, and his overwrought nervous system collapsed six months later. He was thirty-eight years old.

Valuation of Mendelssohn's work as a composer has varied since his death. At first Mendelssohn's brilliance and the high visibility of his career resulted in worldwide lamentation of his premature passing. Mendelssohn societies, scholarships in his name, and musical events all contributed to enshrining his memory. As the century progressed, however, musical taste evolved in a direction that tended to devalue Mendelssohn's work. His strengths continued to be recognized: superbly crafted compositions, filled with glittering brilliance and contrapuntal ingenuity and deft at evoking a unique quality of elfin-like delicacy. Weaknesses, however, also began to be cited. He was thought to be incapable of grand dramatic gestures, and, as the aesthetics of Wagner and Liszt began to dominate the musical scene, Mendelssohn's music was regarded more and more as lacking true depth of feeling. Moreover, in the wake of increasing interest in the harmonic complexities of chromaticism, altered chord progressions, and modulation, Mendelssohn's

Andante sostenuto

cantabile

Example 11.1 Felix Mendelssohn: *Songs without Words*, "Venetian Boat Song," Op. 17, no. 6 mm. 7–9

music began to sound somewhat naive harmonically. His slow music, especially exposed in this regard, began to be regarded as too sentimental. Thus, most references to Mendelssohn carefully make the point that, in spite of his obvious skill, he cannot be regarded as being on the same level as Mozart, Schubert, or Beethoven, even though a few works are so successful that they suggest genius of such caliber. It is quite possible that, as a result of this devaluation, Mendelssohn is more neglected by performers than he ought to be.

Songs Without Words

The catalogue of Mendelssohn's published works for solo piano is extensive, and there are a number of pieces that are still in manuscript. Even so, only a handful of pieces appear on concert programs with regularity. Among the most frequently encountered pieces are the *Lieder ohne Worte* (Songs without Words), for they remain a staple in the teaching repertoire and are performed frequently on student programs. Originally published between 1829 and 1845 in eight sets of six each, the body of forty-eight was increased to forty-nine by the discovery of another in 1951 in the Bodleian Library of Oxford University. The title itself is apparently Mendelssohn's creation, for it appears early in his correspondence but is not to be found elsewhere. The concept combines the art song and the character piece, the keyboard player being responsible for both the vocal line and the accompaniment. The entire gamut of moods typical of the art song is encompassed. Some are lyrical, others are playful, and a few are agitated or chorale-like. Structures are kept simple, binary or ternary, often with introductions or codas. There are a few programmatic references: three Venetian boat songs (Example 11.1), a hunting song, a spring song, a spinning song, a funeral march, and folk songs. Most of the songs make but modest technical demands in terms of virtuoso devices, but achieving beautiful balance of texture, shape of phrase, and appropriate rhythmic flexibility in these miniatures is often deceptively difficult.

Andante sostenuto

Example 11.2 Felix Mendelssohn: *Variations sérieuses*, Op. 17 mm.1–4

Variations

In the realm of the serious, extended concert piece, the *Variations sérieuses*, Op. 54, is by far the most popular (Example 11.2). An original theme, consisting of two eight-measure sections, is followed by seventeen variations and a brilliant coda. The variations provide a compendium of Mendelssohn's stylistic characteristics: rapid passagework (nos. 8 and 9); quick octaves, arpeggios, and chords (nos. 7 and 12); delicate staccato (nos. 4 and 13); songlike lyricism (no. 11); and brief excursions into contrapuntal textures (no. 10). The work is masterfully paced. The theme is concise; the variations move quickly from one to the next and may be grouped in pairs at times (nos. 1 and 2; nos. 8 and 9; nos. 16 and 17); the slow, contrasting sections are well placed (nos. 10 and 14); and tension throughout the work culminates in climactic brilliance near the end of the piece (no. 17 and coda). Two other sets of variations, both on original themes, Op. 82 and Op. 83, are worthwhile but are considerably shorter and offer less-impressive material. Also planned very much like a set of variations is the Op. 15, *Fantasie on a Irish Song* ("The Last Rose of Summer"). Here, frequent shifts between fast and slow tempi and recitatives result in an informal, improvised character.

Sonata Types

Of the compositions that can be related to the sonata structure, the Fantasia in *f-sharp*, Op. 28, is the most frequently played. The work is also known as the *Sonate écossaise* (*Scottish Sonata*). This linkage between the concepts of the fantasy and the sonata calls to mind the Op. 27 set of Beethoven, and, as in the Beethoven set, the most imposing movement is shifted away from the first to the last. Here, the last movement makes use of sonata-allegro structure. The opening movement simply alternates between rapid arpeggio-like figurations marked *agitato* and a songful andante (Example 11.3). The Allegro con moto that serves as a middle

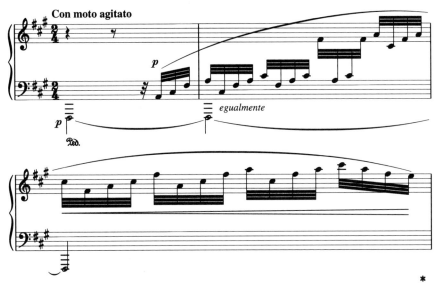

Example 11.3 Felix Mendelssohn: Fantasia, Op. 28, 1st movt. mm. 1–3

movement feels very much like a minuet and trio or scherzo, notwithstanding its duple meter, unusually long middle section, and written-out
da capo. The final Presto offers considerable brilliance, its attractiveness
undoubtedly contributing to the fact that the work has a relatively secure
place in the performing repertoire.

One might hope that the keyboard sonatas of Mendelssohn would
turn out to be among his strongest compositions. Although they were
written in his teens, a time when Mendelssohn's precocity enabled him
to write masterworks, they show promise rather than fulfillment. The
Op. 105 in *g*, the earliest of Mendelssohn's published works, was written
at age eleven. It is a three-movement work of both modest proportion
and difficulty. The two outer movements are in a scaled-down sonata-
allegro form, the last movement offering an exceedingly short development section. The middle movement is a free, ternary improvisation,
possibly the most imaginative writing in the work.

The sonatas in *E,* Op. 6, and *B-flat,* Op. 106, were written a few
years later, when Mendelssohn was seventeen and eighteen. Here, the
influence of Beethoven is obvious, so much so that the Op. 6 is frequently compared directly to the Op. 101 of Beethoven and the Op. 106
to the Beethoven sonata bearing the same opus number, the *Hammerklavier.* (It has been suggested that the editor of Mendelssohn's complete
works, Julius Rietz, in assigning opus numbers to those works published
posthumously, noted the similarity and accordingly chose Op. 106 for
the Mendelssohn work.)

To turn to the Op. 6 first, the work opens with a movement that uses the meter, the same key, the same rhythmic pattern, and the same general mood as Beethoven's Op. 101. Both first movements also are cast in a free sonata-allegro structure that share unusual features, notably with but little contrast between the first and second themes, an exposition that is not repeated, and a recapitulation in which there is a moderate amount of rewriting of the thematic material. Instead of a march for the second movement, as Beethoven used in Op. 101, Mendelssohn uses a minuet and trio in *f-sharp*. Other features of the work also suggest late Beethoven sonatas: a recitative to open the third movement suggests Beethoven's Op. 110; the return of a fragment suggesting the first movement calls to mind the cyclicism of Op. 101; and the focus on the final movement as the most substantial, although Mendelssohn does not introduce fugal writing into the final movement, as Beethoven did in Opp. 101, 109, and 110, but rather settles for a free sonata-allegro structure.

The Op. 106 is more foursquare than the Op. 6. Although the rhythmic figure that opens the first movement is not exactly like that of the *Hammerklavier,* it is close enough to bring to mind the Beethoven work (see Example 8.26a–b). The first movement's sonata-allegro structure tapers off with repeated notes on B-flat to introduce the Scherzo, composed of staccato, pianissimo figurations in *b-flat*. Here, Mendelssohn utilizes his almost unique ability to create music of elfin grace and charm. The Scherzo thus becomes the best movement of the work. The slow movement is a simple ABA song. The buildup transitional passage to the final movement recalls the opening theme of the sonata, and the middle section of the final movement's sonata-allegro form makes reference to the theme from the Scherzo.

Although there is much to recommend the sonatas of Mendelssohn, there is also much that is awkward, both structurally and, surprisingly, even pianistically. This, coupled with the fact that the thematic material does not represent the composer at his best, has resulted in the sonatas not being played very often.

Preludes and Fugues

The neglect of some other works, however, cannot be so easily justified. Among these are the six preludes and fugues, Op. 35, written between 1832 and 1837. There seems to be no key scheme to the set, although the middle four show relative-major and -minor relationships (*D* and *b; A-flat* and *f*). The opening composition in *e* is possibly the most extended. The prelude is very much in the style of a song without words, arpeggios surrounding an intense melody. The four-voiced fugue begins calmly, but as it progresses it increases in excitement and texture. Octaves are added as the counterpoint becomes increasingly

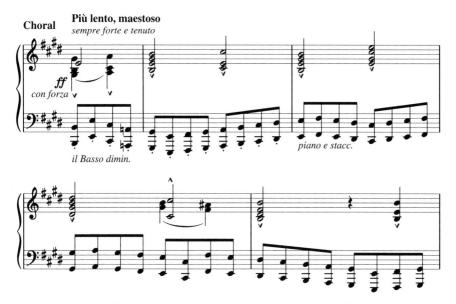

Example 11.4 Felix Mendelssohn: *6 Preludes and Fugues*, Op. 35, Fugue no. 1 mm. 104–8

free. At the height of the composition, a glorious chorale, accompanied by running octaves, breaks forth (Example 11.4). A final section rapidly reduces the intensity and excitement to the composure of the opening. The composition is one of Mendelssohn's most effective works.

The second pair in *D* opens with a piece that calls to mind a chorale prelude, for it creates its texture from an octave base line moving in eighth notes; a middle part moving in sixteenth notes; and a melodic line in the upper part, moving mostly in quarter and eighth notes. The slow fugue that follows is interesting in that the opening notes of the subject outline, not the tonic, but rather the submediant triad. The fugue, in four voices, is the shortest of the Op. 35.

Number 3 in *b* opens with a prelude that is gigue-like in character. The fugue that follows is in three voices, marked *Allegro con brio*, the first really fast fugue in the set. The prelude in *A-flat,* no. 4, is written as a duet over an accompaniment figure. The fugue subject brings to mind the subject of the fugue in *A-flat* in the first volume of the *Well-Tempered Clavier.* A double fugue, the second exposition, introduces its subject in measure 46. The prelude of no. 5 in *f* is another song without words, made unusually intense by an accompaniment of repeated chords in both the right and left hands. The four-voiced fugue that follows is in six-eight time marked *Allegro con fuoco.* Its driving repeated-note subject sets the stage for free contrapuntal writing that is put at the service of brilliance and excitement, as repeated chords and octaves make their appearance. The final prelude, marked *Maestoso moderato,* presents a sustained melody with an elaborate accompaniment of octaves and double notes. The fugue that follows has a subject that climbs the *B-flat* scale in sixteenth notes and then, after a rest, breaks off into dotted-note fragments. The key of *B-flat,* the running, diatonic subject, and the intrusion of rests in the middle of the subject all combine to call to mind the subject of the *Hammerklavier* fugue of Beethoven. The influence is certainly possible when we remember Beethoven's influence in Mendelsson's sonatas. Once again the composer feels free to use octave doublings and fill in chords in order to achieve a rich harmonic texture and excitement.

A separate prelude and fugue in *e* should also be mentioned. Although the two pieces were written at different times, the prelude in 1841 and the fugue earlier in 1827, they go together to form an effective pair. The fugue subject is unusually bold with its opening drop of a major seventh followed by ascending dotted-rhythm figuration. Although perhaps not the equal of the set in *e* of the Op. 35, this pair offers considerable dramatic intensity and excitement and should be played more often than it is.

Preludes and Etudes

The six pieces that make up the Op. 104 are grouped into three preludes and three etudes, although they are all similar in their concentration on arpeggios, runs, and passagework. The opening prelude might well be a study for octaves and staccato, the second a left-hand study, and the third a composition for perfecting continuous scales divided between the two hands. The three etudes in turn concentrate on right-hand arpeggios, on triplet passagework, again mostly for the right hand, and, last, on difficult skips in left-hand accompaniment combined with a staccato right hand. A separate etude in *f* was written for the method book put out by Moscheles and Fétis in 1837. Marked *Presto agitato,* the piece presents an active melody supported by arpeggios divided between the two hands. Although these pieces cannot be considered as important for the pianist as the Chopin etudes, they, nevertheless, are technically challenging and musically interesting. Their almost total neglect is undeserved.

The Character Pieces, Op. 7

In Mendelssohn's works, we find the use of both the terms *character piece* and *capriccio*. As noted earlier, it is difficult to discern just why the former term evolved into a label for the genre of the short piece and the latter remained simply a title for individual works. If Mendelssohn's use of the terms were taken into consideration by itself, one might conclude that there is little or no difference between the designations, for certainly there is no structure associated consistently with either term.

The seven character pieces that make up the Op. 7 vary in length and texture. Key relationships also seem tenuous, although all of the pieces are in keys that use sharps. The first, in *e*, presents a concise binary form, its contrapuntal texture being reminiscent of any one of several two-part preludes from the second volume of the *Well-Tempered Clavier.* The second piece is driving, scherzo-like, and in a short AABA form. Number 3 is marked simply *Allegro vivace* but is in reality a full-blown fugue. The fourth piece consists of an energetic array of sixteenth-note themes, structured into a loose sonata-allegro form. Number 5 is a ricercare-style fugue, which opens with a controlled slow-moving subject and grows in both activity and intensity. The two-part Andante that follows is chorale-like, and the final piece is yet another of those light scherzo-like presto movements that have become Mendelssohn's calling card. One senses neither a strong unity within the set of pieces nor a clear overriding profile. By the same token, the pieces do not stand alone very successfully. This lack of focus, coupled with the fact that the pieces are quite demanding, given the highly contrapuntal textures of several of them, has kept the set from being among the favorites of performers, notwithstanding the perception that, taken individually, the pieces represent Mendelssohn at his best.

Capriccios

Mendelssohn was obviously drawn to the title *capriccio,* for he used it throughout his career for compositions of moderate length and seriousness of purpose. Although a case for an association between the capriccio and the sonata-allegro structure might possibly be made, so many exceptions are encountered that the comparison becomes tenuous. Nor is the suggestion of happy impulsiveness associated with the meaning of *capriccio* or *caprice* always present. Moreover, although many of the caprices are difficult, their paramount reason for being is not virtuoso display, as in the case of the Paganini caprices. Thus, one is forced to conclude that in Mendelssohn's case, the use of the term itself was a manifestation of whim, or, one might add bemusingly, capriciousness.

Of the ten pieces to which the designation *capriccio* is added, two were written by Mendelssohn as a teenager. The earlier is the famous Rondo capriccioso, Op. 14. A slow introduction is followed by a scherzo-like Presto based on two themes. The opening one in *e* is highly articulated with short phrases and staccatos, and a second one in *G* is somewhat more cantabile in nature. The initial presentation of these themes suggests the exposition of a sonata-allegro form with even the key relationship being traditional. There are hints of development, but then the composition turns into one devoted completely to a display of rapid passagework. The two themes are never recapitulated, although reference is made to them in a coda. The capriccio, Op. 5, is shaped into a simple ABA pattern, its middle section providing lyrical contrast to the opening motivic theme. The coda is based on the theme of the middle section.

The three pieces that make up the Op. 16 are shorter and seem to be more diverse than the other caprices. Perhaps this accounts for the duplicity in the title of the set, *Three Fantasies or Caprices*. The opening one consists of an opening and closing andante in *a*. Between these sections is a two-part Allegro vivace in *A*. The second is marked *Scherzo*. It is an attractive, short piece of moderate difficulty and has gained a reputation as an excellent teaching piece. The third, equally short, is a flowing andante in *E*.

The Op. 33 set of capriccios is one of the most attractive. The first and third pieces combine a slow introduction with a fast sonata-allegro structure, each traditional to the point of indicating a repeated exposition. The middle capriccio is also based on sonata-allegro structure, but it is more continuous with no introduction, repeat signs for the exposition, and no coda. It offers a longer development section, however, than its companions. There seems little to suggest that these three caprices were planned as a set to be played together. The keys of *a*, *E*, and *b-flat* do not contribute to unity very strongly, nor does the sequence of tempi suggest the typical fast-slow-fast pattern, even though the middle caprice, marked *Allegro grazioso*, is slightly slower and calmer in character than the outer movements. Separately, however, they stand successfully as interesting concert pieces, conceivably in the same league with the longer Chopin waltzes or nocturnes and many of the longer character pieces of Liszt.

Two other compositions make use of the capriccio designation, the Capriccio, Op. 118, of 1837, and the Scherzo a capriccio (1835–36) in *f-sharp*. The former is much like the first and third capriccios of the Op. 33 in structure, combining a slow introduction in *E* with a rapid movement in *e* in sonata-allegro form. The Scherzo a capriccio begins like a scherzo and trio, but the second portion of the trio includes a development of the material from the Scherzo as well as a fairly long retransition passage. After the return of the scherzo in a written-out da capo, a long coda closes the work. Thus, the traditional scherzo and trio structure is considerably enlarged and embellished.

Other Piano Works

Another extended work reminiscent of the capriccios is the 1838 work in *b* entitled Andante cantabile e Presto agitato. Once again, a slow introduction spins its cantabile melody and is followed by a fast, virtuoso-style piece. It proceeds very much like a sonata-allegro structure with a relatively short development section. At the end of the recapitulation, however, the development section is repeated in its entirely in the home key. This, in turn, is followed by a recitative-like section that acts to introduce the real coda, based on figuration from the development section. The movement is thus cleverly extended and tension heightened for the final pages.

Mendelssohn's turn at didactic material is represented by the *Sechs Kinderstücke,* Op.72 (1842), originally composed as Christmas pieces in London. These pieces are short and reasonably charming, but there appears to be little alteration of the style found in the *Songs without Words.* Thus, they are not entirely appropriate for lower-level students, and, by the time students get to the point technically where they can play these pieces, they would rather attempt the *Songs without Words,* which are more substantial and impressive compositions. The Op. 72 set is thus not so useful as teaching material as one might imagine.

Other short pieces round out Mendelssohn's solo works for piano: a *Perpetuum mobile.* Opus 118; two short *Clavierstücke* in *B-flat* and *g;* a barcarolle in *A;* and a short scherzo in *b* without a trio section.

CHAPTER TWELVE

Robert (Alexander) Schumann

Robert Schumann (b. Zwickau, Saxony, June 8, 1810; d. Endenich, nr. Bonn, Jul. 29, 1856) is considered by many to be at the very heart of the Romantic movement in music, partly because of his close association with the literature of the period and his own literary interests. Schumann was the youngest son of a bookseller and publisher. His early education was broad, for he attended the Zwickau Gymnasium between 1818 and 1820. Early music study was with the organist of the Zwickau Marienkirche, Johann Gottfried Kuntzsch, a musician whose achievements are modest at best but who had enough insight with regard to the young Schumann's potential to have prophesied immortality for him. Robert, on the other hand, seemed equally interested in music and literary pursuits. He started to compose at age seven, and by the time he was eleven he was attempting to create large works for chorus and orchestra. By the same token, at age fourteen he contributed to *Bildergallerie der berühmtesten Menschen aller Völker und Zeiten,* a biographical dictionary brought out by his father. At seventeen he was setting his own poems to music.

Between 1828 and 1830, Schumann was enrolled as a law student first at Leipzig University and later at Heidelberg, but in 1830 he returned to Leipzig and enrolled in the piano class of Friedrich Wieck, at the same time studying composition with Heinrich Dorn, a young composer who was only six years older than Schumann himself. It was during this period of intense piano practice that Schumann, eager to perfect his technique, injured his hand during an experiment in which he attempted to strengthen the fourth finger by suspending it in a sling while continuing to use the others. Having thus put an end to his aspirations for a career as a virtuoso performer, Schumann concentrated on composing, writing, and furthering his academic education.

It was during this period that Schumann joined with several others, including Friedrich Wieck, to found the *Neue Zeitschrift für Musik,* a periodical devoted to music deemed worthwhile and serious as opposed to that judged superficial. Schumann edited the journal for ten years, from 1834 to 1844, and guided it through a move to Vienna, where it did not flourish, and a return to Leipzig. Writing under several pseudonyms (Florestan, Eusebius, Master Raro, and the numerals 2 and 12), Schumann created a legacy of essays and criticisms that are considered to be the epitome of musical journalism and that intelligently chronicle much of the artistic thought and concern of his age. Among his most famous essays are those on Chopin, one of the earliest tributes to that composer, and Brahms.

In 1840, Robert was able to consummate his love for Clara Wieck, Friedrich's daughter, in marriage. Father Wieck had opposed the marriage for several years, for he felt that Robert's financial status was insecure and that marriage would interfere with Clara's concert career. The same year, Schumann was awarded a doctor of philosophy degree from the University of Jena. In 1843, Mendelssohn invited Schumann to join the faculty at the newly founded Leipzig Conservatory, but Schumann did not fare particularly well in this academic setting. Although he introduced the pedal piano there in order to provide a mode of practice for organ students who were without practice instruments, Schumann left the conservatory as early as 1844, possibly because Mendelssohn did not fully appreciate the extent of Schumann's gifts. The Schumanns moved to Dresden for six years, where Robert taught privately and composed. In 1850, Robert accepted the position of music director of the city of Düsseldorf, a post being vacated by Ferdinand Hiller, but Schumann's tenure in this position, too, was to be short-lived.

As early as 1833 signs of mental disorder had appeared. By 1845, even more alarming symptoms were apparent. It is thus not surprising that by 1853 Robert had to give up his new post. In 1854, he attempted suicide by throwing himself into the Rhine River. He was subsequently confined to an institution at Endenich, where he had but few lucid moments during the final two years of his life.

Schumann's creative impulse was very closely tied to literary sources. As both a journalist and a composer, he worked in a world, part real and part imaginary, that was intertwined with the characters and events of the literature he knew and loved. Jean Paul (Richter; 1763–1825) and E. T. A. Hoffmann (1776–1822) were particularly strong influences, and Schumann followed a trend these writers, among others, established of dividing their egos into multiple personalities, each representing a different mood. In both Schumann's journalism and music, there are frequent references to Florestan, the enthusiastic, aggressive side of his nature; to Eusebius, the more passive, dreamy side; and to Raro, the personality in balance, representing wisdom and maturity. The names Schumann created were often, in themselves, coded references to other aspects of his life. Thus, his love for Clara Wieck is represented by the joining of the last two letters of her name, the R and the A, with the first two of his own name, the R and the O. Schumann created an imaginary social organization dedicated to the fight for preserving the new music he considered serious and worthwhile. Borrowing from the story of David and Goliath in the Bible, Schumann imagined a group of ardent defenders that he called the Davidsbündler (League of David). Members of this group in Schumann's mind included Felix Meritas, a coded name for Mendelssohn; Jeanquirit, his name for Stephen Heller; and several representations of Clara herself: Chiara, Chiarina, and Zilia. One can only guess the extent to which the vividness of this ever-present imaginary world eventually contributed to Schumann's own mental health problems.

Schumann also used the concept of coding in the actual formation of his thematic material. In his Op. 1, *Theme on the Name ABEGG*, he took the letters of the name of a family he knew and, by applying them to musical notation, created the melodic idea on which his theme is based. (The German designation *B* isthe English equivalent of B-flat.) Similarly, the four notes on which *Carnaval, Op.* 9, is based were drawn both from the German town of ASCH, the hometown of Ernestine von Fricken, a fellow student of Wieck, and, in a different order, SCHA, from letters present in Schumann's own name. (Here, the German designation *S* equals E-flat, and *H* is B.) These are two of the more obvious examples of thematic coding. More obscure ones appear in many of the keyboard works, and finding them in their various guises is a study that has fascinated generations of scholars.

The musical style that emerged from these literary references and coded manipulations is perhaps surprisingly personal, one given particularly to warmth and sensitivity. Schumann is at his very best in the expressive, short character piece, where a single mood is explored. In these works, his attention to detail is well-nigh perfect, his harmonic language beautifully subtle and ever fresh-sounding, and his ability to capture the essence of emotional expression often breathtaking. This is the reason his collections of short character pieces, particularly those meant to be played together by virtue of thematic linkage, are so successful. *Papillons, Op.* 2; *Davidsbündlertänze, Op.* 6; and *Carnaval, Op.* 9, come to mind immediately. Even when the composer puts together in one piece several sections composed of these short utterances, arranging them in ABA, ABAB, or similar patterns, the result is solid, first-rate Schumann. Here, one can cite examples such as *Fantasiestücke, Op.* 12, and *Kreisleriana, Op.* 16. Whenever Schumann moves into larger structures, however, one senses difficulty in maintaining the same ease of expression, and his success rate becomes more open to question. Some of these longer works seem overextended, burdened by awkward transitions or passages of questionable inspiration. There are those who have leveled such criticism at the Sonata in *f-sharp*, Op. 11, and the "Humoresque," Op. 20, for example. In these works, such alleged weaknesses stand beside sections of undeniable beauty. Many performers feel that the works can be paced in such a way as to minimize the problems, and thus the beautiful moments in the works can still be enjoyed. Other performers pass such works by, opting instead to concentrate on works that are undeniably without flaws. Nor should it be thought that Schumann's movements in extended forms are always problematic. The Fantasia, Op. 17, is a good example of a sonata-like work in which all three movements are long and yet succeed admirably.

In addition, there is a body of Schumann's keyboard works that is simply not played very much because these pieces are deemed inferior to his best efforts. The temptation to associate these less successful compositions with his mental deterioration is strong, but in fact such works are scattered throughout his creative career. A list of such works might include the two sets of Paganini Caprices, Opp. 3 and 10; the *Impromptus on a Theme of Clara Wieck,* Op. 5; the Allegro in *b,* Op. 8; or the Sonata in *f,* Op. 14. A greater concentration of such problematic works do indeed occur toward the end of the composer's career. Many performers at one time or another have felt the desire to "rediscover" one or more of these works, for they all contain passages of beauty and, at least to some extent, are worthy of being played. Most such adventurers, however, suffer a lessening of interest sometime after the initial excitement has worn off and eventually return to playing the better-known, time-tested compositions.

Other features of Schumann's style of writing for the piano include extended passages of syncopated rhythm that oftentimes give the impression of dislocating the strong beats, attention to inner voice levels to the extent that frequently several levels of texture exist simultaneously, a carefully crafted symbiosis between technical demands and musical content, and an emotional gamut that extends from the most intimate tenderness to wide-open, almost aggressive ebullience, often within the same composition. A particular challenge many performers associate with Schumann is one born of his habit of transposing entire sections of a work and, in doing so, changing a host of seemingly unimportant details such as chord voicing, arpeggio position, or accompaniment patterns. Keeping these changes on track, especially in memorized performance, requires intensive study for most musicians.

Several performance problems are also associated with Schumann's keyboard music. His metronome markings seem often at odds with the musical content, as perceived by most musicians. Much of the time the markings seem excessively fast. The question of whether or not to play entire works is one that is answered in various ways by different performers. In the case of those works in which thematic material is cyclic, such as *Davidsbündlertänze,* Op. 6, or *Carnaval,* Op. 9, there is little question but that the work should be programmed in its entirety. But there are several other works in which such thematic linkage is not as clear. The propriety surrounding these works is less clear-cut. The *Phantasiestücke,* Op. 12, and the *Noveletten,* Op. 21, are heard both as complete cycles and as individual pieces. Groups of shorter pieces, such as *Kinderszenen,* Op. 15, or *Waldszenen,* Op. 82, tend to be played in their entirety in the concert hall, but, when used as teaching material, the individual pieces are often programmed separately. *Bunte Blätter,* Op. 99, composed over a period of several years with subdivided groupings by the composer, is almost never played completely, and performers tend to want to change the order of the pieces due to the fact that the ones that appear toward the end of the set are all much weaker musically than those that open the work. Thus, in Schumann, how the works are programmed depends upon a number of circumstances, and in many instances there is no clear-cut tradition.

Character Pieces

The first set of character pieces is the *Papillons,* Op. 2. The work was written between 1829 and 1831, when Schumann was at Heidelberg University at least part of the time. Research into Schumann's letters and notebooks reveals clearly that the work is based on the penultimate chapter of a novel by Jean Paul entitled *Fliegeljahre.* The chapter describes a ballroom scene, and Schumann's references to characters and events are quite specific. The title *Butterflies* seems to convey to Schumann himself a sense of lightness, fluttering, and gaiety. The work is composed of twelve short pieces, mostly dances, several waltzes, and a polonaise, set with an introduction and occasional scene music. The final piece presents the first waltz again and then fragments of it over a long dominant pedal, suggesting that the party is finally unwinding. Six accented notes have been interpreted as the striking of the clock as the all-night revelers finally turn in. A very long dominant-seventh chord is dissipated by releasing one note at a time. The *Papillons* is attractive, technically accessible, and enjoys considerable popularity.

The *Intermezzi,* Op. 4, consists of six short pieces, slightly longer than most of the *Papillons.* All of the pieces except the fourth one are based on an ABA structure, sometimes with developmental retransitions leading to the return of the A section or with short codas. The fourth piece, the shortest of the group, is through-composed. All of the pieces are marked either *Allegretto, Allegro,* or *Presto,* so there is no true slow-movement, although no. 5 serves as such, for it is marked *Allegro moderato* and presents a lyrical melody. It, too, is likely to impress listeners as containing the most inspired musical ideas. There is no obvious cyclicism in the work, although the rhythmic figurations and melodic fragments of the opening sections of nos. 2 and 6 bear strong resemblance to each other. Schumann does, however, quote the opening phrase of the *ABEGG Variations,* Op. 1, in the middle of the last piece. The *Intermezzi* are not very often played, and they very likely merit more attention from musicians than they receive, although probably no one would argue that the set represents Schumann at his most exalted level of inspiration.

Each of the next two works, *Impromptus on a Theme of Clara Wieck,* Op. 5, and *Davidsbündlertänze,* Op. 6, exists in two editions, all dating from 1837. (The second edition of the Op. 6 is titled simply *Davidsbündler.*) In the case of the *Impromptus,* the rewrites in the second edition are substantial. Textures are changed, chords are filled in, and rhythmic notation altered. The differences between the two versions of the *Davidsbündler* are less striking, being confined to occasional small details, even nonmusical ones, such as the placing of "F" or "E" at the ends of certain pieces for Florestan or Eusebius. Most musicians perform the music of the second edition on the assumption that this version represents Schumann's more polished thoughts. A few performers have argued, however, that the process of refinement led Schumann away from his original impulses, ideas daring for their time, into more mundane patterns of expression, easily acceptable but also more predictable.

By calling the Op. 5 *impromptus,* Schumann has possibly suggested a set of character pieces based on a variety of themes. The Op. 5, however, gives the impression of a theme and variations. The opening, indeed, is reminiscent of the opening measures of the *Eroica Variations,* Op. 35, of Beethoven, both works presenting only the bass line of the theme first. Beethoven builds to his presentation of the theme by adding voices one at a time, while Schumann cuts directly to the theme after the bass line is stated. By including the statement of the theme in the numbering of the variations in the first edition, Schumann comes up with twelve variations. The second edition assigns no number to the theme, and no. 11 of the earlier set is dropped altogether, resulting in but ten numbered variations. The variations follow the two-part profile of the theme in each case, except for no. 11 from the first edition and the final variation. In these cases the structure is expanded into an ABA pattern that seems more consistent with the use of the term *impromptu.* Both versions end by returning to a statement of the bass line of the theme. In the first edition, the melody never appears at the end, and the work closes softly with the barren sound of the interval of a second that resolves. The second edition presents a portion of the melody again after the bass line is stated in octaves, and a more traditional ending is provided by using full tonic chords. For all its interesting features on paper, the Op. 5 is not very popular with performers. One might be tempted to point to the fact that Clara's theme is not very striking, but this line of thinking does not account for the masterworks that great composers can and do create from thematic material that is somewhat commonplace. (Beethoven's *Diabelli Variations* or even Schumann's own *Études symphoniques* can be cited as cases in point.) Whatever the reason, Schumann has created here a work that has not, by and large, inspired pianists to want to play it.

The *Davidsbündlertänze*, on the other hand, form an undisputed masterwork. These eighteen short pieces represent the composer at the peak of his creative powers, combining virtuoso writing of great imagination, such as nos. 6 and 13, with inspired poetic lyricism, as in nos. 7 and 14. The opening motive of the first piece was borrowed by Schumann from a piece of Clara, a mazurka that appears in the second set of her *Soirées musicales*, Op. 6, and the thematic material throughout *Davidsbündlertänze* is thought to be born of considerable encoding. Many of the pieces have above the first bar a word or two that suggest not so much tempo but often mood or character. Examples are *Mit Humor* (humorously) for nos. 3 and 12, *Ungeduldig* (impatiently) for no. 4, and *Frisch* (fresh) for nos. 8 and 15. The first edition contains several insightful markings that Schumann deletes from the second edition. Before no. 9, for example, Schumann writes in the first edition, "Hierauf schloss Florestan und es zuckte ihm schmerzlich um die Lippen" (At this point Florestan paused and his lips trembled sorrowfully), and at the opening of the final piece, "Ganz zum Überfluss meinte Eusebius noch Folgenden; dabei sprach aber viel Seligkeit aus seinen Augen" (Quite reluctantly Eusebius added the following, all the while great happiness shone in his eyes).

The work is cyclic in that music from no. 2 returns in no. 17, growing out of an almost impressionistic setting marked *Wie aus der Ferne* (As from out of the distance). The theme builds to an ending befitting the entire cycle, cadencing in *b*, a key that has appeared prominently throughout the work, including the original statement of the thematic material in no. 2. Then Schumann gives us Eusebius' postscript, and it is understandable that he added it "reluctantly." It is in *C*, a key that has been all but absent from the entire work, and the music is simple, appearing to be almost innocuous. The effect, however, is unbelievably breathtaking and magical. There is quite possibly no finer example of Schumann's sense of poetic transcendence than this ending (Example 12.1).

The *Carnaval*, Op. 9, is a set of twenty-one character pieces. Schumann draws inspiration from describing the party atmosphere that takes place before the beginning of Lent. In Europe this festivity is known generally as the carnival season, and in the United States its manifestation takes place most clearly as the Mardi Gras in New Orleans. The scenes that *Papillons*, Op. 2, reflect are set at this season, and the title of the Op. 26, *Faschingsschwank aus Wien* (Carnival Prank in Vienna), is a third reference to it.

Amid the revelry, Schumann focuses on a variety of characters. Four stock personas from the theater tradition appear: Pierrot (no. 2), who clowns clumsily in his whitened face and loose-fitting pantaloons and jacket; Arlequin (no. 3), who wears a mask and spangled, diamond-patterned tights of many colors; and together Pantalon and Colombine (no. 15), the comic old father and his pretty daughter, who incidentally

Example 12.1 Robert Schumann: *Davidsbündlertänze*, Op. 6, no. 18 mm. 1–9

is Arlequin's sweetheart. Also described are Schumann's alter egos, Florestan and Eusebius (nos. 6 and 5); Chiarina, or Clara (no.11); Estrella, or Ernestine von Fricken, a pupil of Friedrich Wieck (no. 13); Chopin (no. 12); and Paganini (no. 17). Other pieces simply help set the scene: the "Préambule" (no. 1), "Valse noble" (no. 4), "Reconnaissance" (no. 14), "Valse allemande" (no. 16), and so on. The final piece, "Marche des 'Davidsbündler' contre les Philistins," is the longest, most imposing of the set and symbolically depicts Schumann's imaginary brotherhood of musicians of good taste at war with those deemed to be less discriminating.

The encoding of much of the thematic material of *Carnaval* has been previously mentioned. Schumann presents the versions of ASCH and SCHA as "Sphinxs," a silent segment inserted between nos. 8 and 9. The combinations Schumann uses are seen as double whole notes in the bass: E-flat, B, C, A, then A-flat, C, B, and finally A, E-flat, C, B. Virtually all performers ignore the "Sphinxs." There is, however, a famous early recording by Rachmaninoff in which he transforms the notes into great, ominous-sounding tremolos.

Other thematic linkages occur as well. "Florestan" (no. 6) contains a segment of the opening theme of *Papillons,* Op. 2. Music from the "Préambule" returns near the end of the work in both the "Pause," a short movement leading up to the final march, and the march itself. Schumann's capturing of Chopin's lyrical style in no. 12 is well-nigh perfect, although there is no direct quotation from Chopin (Example 12.2). Similarly, the music of Paganini imitates virtuoso violin techniques, providing the pianist, incidentally, with one of the most difficult moments

Example 12.2 Robert Schumann: *Carnaval*, Op. 9, "Chopin," mm. 1–4

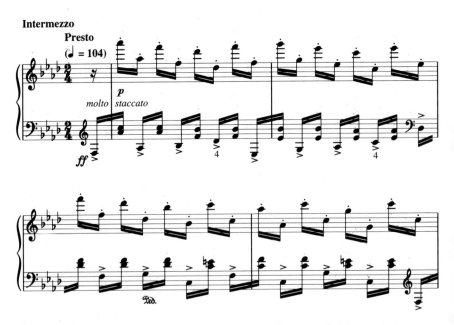

Example 12.3 Robert Schumann: *Carnaval*, Op. 7, "Paganini," mm. 1–4

Example 12.4 Robert Schumann: *Carnaval*, Op. 7, "Chiarina," mm. 1–6

technically in the work (Example 12.3). Appropriately, "Chiarina" is marked *Passionato*, and its music is both ardent and longing (Example 12.4). In short, there is such an abundance of inspired writing in *Carnaval* that its standing as one of the most beloved, frequently played keyboard works of the nineteenth century remains unchallenged.

The *Phantasiestücke*, Op. 12, consists of eight character pieces, generally somewhat longer than those encountered in the other sets. Five of the pieces (nos. 2, 4, 5, 7, and 8) are cast in ABA form, and each section is sizeable. In some cases (nos. 2 and 4, for example), the opening A section itself can be subdivided into several sections. Evidence points to the fact that Schumann conceived the *Phantasiestücke* as a group to be played together, but performers have not always felt compelled to present the group in its entirety. Thus, one frequently encounters performances of a group of several pieces from Op. 12, or occasionally a single piece. The length of the individual pieces makes this choice possible, and the fact that there is no thematic link between the pieces undoubtedly contributes to the feeling that the work has less unity than other sets such as *Davidsbündlertänze* or *Carnaval*. On the other hand, the *Phantasiestücke* provide excellent contrast of mood and tempo when played together, and most musicians would agree that they represent Schumann at a very high level of inspiration. Some of the pieces are among Schumann's finest (nos. 1, 2, 3, and 5, for example). Other pieces may not quite come up to that standard in the opinion of some, another reason why performers sometimes pick and choose.

Example 12.5 Robert Schumann: *Phantasiestücke*, Op. 12, "Des Abends" mm. 1–4

There are several examples of rhythmic devices typical of Schumann in this set. "Des Abends" (In the Evening), the opening piece, presents a fascinating cross-rhythm between the hands (Example 12.5). In "Aufschwung" (Soaring), a similar disparity between the hands occurs in the second part of the A section. In the middle section of "In der Nacht" (In the Night), the accompaniment figuration is slightly displaced (Example 12.6).

The *Phantasiestücke* contains many moments of special beauty: the gentle sensitivity of "Des Abends," the exuberance of "Aufschwung," the stormy passion of "In der Nacht," and the flighty fantasy of "Traumes-Wirren" (Dream Visions). Special note should be made of "Warum" (Why), as beautiful as any of Schumann's most inspired lieder. There is yet another piece originally planned for the set, but deleted by Schumann, entitled "Feurigst" (Fiery). Although the piece is easily recognizable as Schumann, most would probably agree with the composer's decision to discard it.

Kinderszenen, Op. 15, consists of thirteen short character pieces, each with a descriptive title, the titles having been added by Schumann after the pieces were written. They are suitable either for performance as a set or, as often done, for use as separate teaching pieces. Written in 1838, the music represents Schumann at his best, and many of the pieces are extremely well known. "Von fremden Ländern und Menschen" (From Foreign Lands and People) is frequently heard as an encore piece, and "Träumerei" (Dreaming) contains one of Schumann's most famous melodies. Almost all of the pieces are in miniature ABA form, for even those structures that appear to be two-part, each part marked to be repeated, use a return of opening material near the end of the second section. There is no explicit evidence that Schumann intended the set to be played together, and yet it can be noted that Schumann's pattern of ending cyclic sets with a poetic afterthought is repeated here. (The

Etwas langsamer
Un poco più lento

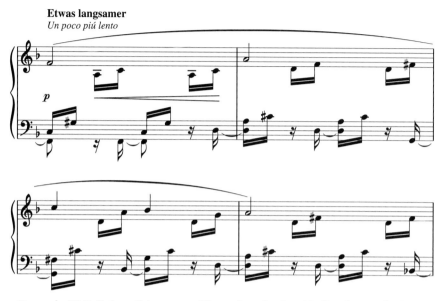

Example 12.6 Robert Schumann: *Phantasiestücke*, Op. 12, "In der Nacht," mm. 69–72.

Davidsbündlertänze ended with such an arrangement.) Although cyclicism is not present in *Kinderszenen,* there is the addition of a thirteenth piece entitled "Der Dichter spricht" (The Poet Speaks), a slow, dreamy final statement in which, as in the *Davidsbündlertänze,* Eusebius has the last word.

Kreisleriana, Op. 16, is a set of eight pieces based on the writing of E. T. A. Hoffmann. In Hoffmann's novel *Kater Murr,* Kapellmeister Kreisler, the city musician for a small town, relates incidents from his life that are then retold from the point of view of the household cat, a remarkably experimental literary concept for its time. The pieces that make up the *Kriesleriana* are appropriately contrasting in mood and character, nos. 2, 4, and 6 providing poetic lyrical contrast to the livelier nos. 1, 3, 5, 7, and 8. The structures are predominantly sectional: nos. 1, 3, 4, and 5 are clearly ABA; nos. 2, 6, and 8 contain two departures, resulting in ABACA; no. 7 presents a small arch form, ABCBA. Number 2 has a lengthy retransition before the final appearance of A, and no. 3 closes with a brilliant coda. The lengths of the pieces are more in line with the more extended concept represented by the pieces of the *Phantasiestücke* rather than the short miniatures of *Papillons* or *Davidsbündler.* Thus, the eight pieces of *Kreisleriana* take as long to perform as the eighteen of the *Davidsbündlertänze.* The literary reference of *Kreisleriana* has convinced most musicians that the set of pieces should be performed together rather than separately, even though there is no thematic cyclicism in the work.

Most would agree that the quality of the music is extremely high and that *Kreisleriana* is one of Schumann's most beautiful and successful works.

The concept of writing extended compositions made up of a number of contrasting sections comes to full fruition in the next three opus numbers: "Arabesque," Op. 18; "Blumenstück" (Flower Piece), Op. 19; and "Humoresque," Op. 20, all written in 1838. In the case of the first two works, the format is of modest length, presenting five and eight sections respectively in a loose rondo-style arrangement. "Arabesque" uses a slow retransition before the second return of the main theme and a dreamy coda. The arrangement of "Blumenstück" is a bit unusual in that the second section becomes the returning theme in the rondo concept. "Humoresque" expands the concept of multiple, contrasting sections into a composition that begins to take on a size that might compare with works such as *Carnaval,* and the arrangement seems to work less well than it did for "Arabesque" and "Blumenstück." Schumann provides excellent musical material in the two shorter works, and the compositions exemplify a skillful balance of unity and contrast. The "Humoresque," however, is much more problematic.

Opening with a lyrical theme, "Humoresque" first presents an arch form ABCBA, where B is a lively contrast and C moves along even more. There follows a small experimental section in that Schumann writes an inner-voice melody in quarter notes and half notes that is accompanied by right- and left-hand figuration moving in eighth and sixteenth notes. All the parts cannot be played by two hands, and the implication is that the inner voice is to be heard inwardly by the player but should not be played (Example 12.7). A contrasting section, march-like in character, is presented several times, eventually evolving toward simple, heavy chords. Then there is a return of the preceding section, this time without the notation of the silent inner voice. There follow yet three more ABA arrangements, one in which the outer sections are marked *Einfach und zart* (simple and tender), and the B section is a rapidly moving intermezzo, one of contrasting sections marked *Innig* (inwardly expressive) and *Schneller* (faster), and one marked *Sehr lebhaft* (very lively). A short transition marked *Stretto* leads to a majestic section of octaves and repeated chords marked *Mit einigem Pomp* (somewhat pompous). Finally, a slow section marked *Zum Beschluss* (in conclusion) presents material that is reminiscent of a phrase from the middle part of the theme with the silent inner voice and running figures used in the intermezzo. The relationships here are tenuous, however, unlike the clear cyclicism of *Davidsbündler.* The similarities might even be accidental. Twelve bars marked *Allegro* finish off the composition in an attempt to end with a flourish.

It is difficult to identify clearly why "Humoresque"does not work better than it does. Much of the material is undeniably inspired and beautiful. Some musicians have complained that the piece deteriorates

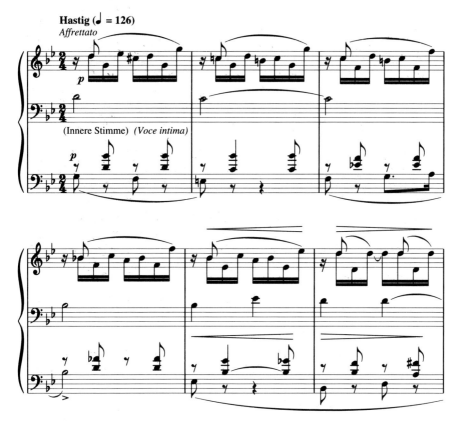

Example 12.7 Robert Schumann: "Humoresque," Op. 20 mm. 152–56

toward the end, presenting too many slow sections of questionable quality. Schumann was obviously delighted with his piece, for in a frequently quoted letter to Clara of March 11, 1839, Robert writes: "I have been sitting the whole week at the pianoforte, composing, laughing and crying all at once; you will find this all beautifully depicted in my Op. 20, the 'great Humoresque.'" Performers have generally not shared Schumann's enthusiasm for the work, however, for it remains one of the composer's less frequently played pieces.

The *Noveletten*, Op. 20, were composed in 1838, a year earlier than the preceding three works. The work is made up of eight character pieces of moderate length. One is reminded immediately of the format of *Kreisleriana*. As in the earlier work, the pieces are built on contrasting sections, each presenting a main idea with one or two departures between returning sections of the main theme. The departures frequently are marked with a separate tempo and structure indication such as *Trio* (nos. 1 and 8) or *Intermezzo* (nos. 2 and 3). Schumann's dreamy

side, Eusebius, is not very much in evidence in the *Noveletten,* for virtually all of the tempo markings are on the vigorous side, with one or two
of the departure sections being marked only *Etwas langsamer* (somewhat
slower). One suspects that the party atmosphere of the carnival season
is once again in Schumann's mind, for no. 4 is marked *Ballmässig, sehr
munter* (in the manner of a ball, very vigorous); no. 5, *Rauschend und fest-
lich* (noisy and festive); and nos. 3 and 6 call for humor. As in the *Davidsbündlertänze* the concept of music *aus der Ferne* (from the distance) is
evoked near the end of the set of pieces, here as part of the second trio
of no. 8. Following that trio is a section marked *Fortsetzung und Schluss*
(continuation and ending) that is almost like a ninth piece, for it presents
a chordal theme with its own contrasting departures. Its middle section
is, however, linked thematically to the second trio of no. 8, notwithstanding its apparent independent structure. Curiously, the *Novelletten*
do not rank high on the list of Schumann's most frequently heard works,
and often performers play them individually. To be sure, there is no
cyclic return to ensure its being conceived as a unified work, but Schumann's description of it as a set of "longish connected tales of adven-
ture" suggests that thinking of it as one thinks of *Kreisleriana,* for
example, might be appropriate, even though there is no known literary
reference to back up the claim.

Three more sets of character pieces come from the 1838–39 period,
Nachtstücke, Op. 23; *Drei Romanzen,* Op. 28; and *Scherzo, Gigue, Romanze,
und Fughette,* Op. 32, but none of them are as successful as the previously
discussed works from those years. The *Nachtstücke* (Night Pieces) had several working titles: *Funeral Processione, Strange Company, Nocturnal Carouse,*
and *Round with Solo Voices.* The last working title gives us a clue as to the
composer's thinking about the rather puzzling structural relationship of
the four pieces composing the set. The first piece presents a theme made
up of a series of short chords, and the opening themes of the second and
fourth pieces are similar enough to that theme to arouse the suspicion
that they are meant to be thought of as free variations. What follows that
theme in both cases does not seem to be particularly related to material
in the opening piece, however, so the connection becomes tenuous. The
third piece stands apart from this material and represents the most effective contrasting music in the work. Pieces 1, 2, and 4 have contrasting
middle sections, but in nos. 1 and 4 the contrasting sections are short and
not very well established, and the departures of no. 2 never move very far
away from giving the impression of a constant flow of eighth notes. These
relationships contribute toward a sameness in the work that performers
find hard to dispel.

The *Drei Romanzen,* Op. 28, are short, sectional pieces. The first
two of the set are less extended and the most successful. Number 1 is in
ABA form and presents a songlike melody over a figured accompaniment divided between the two hands. Number 2 is based on a lyrical

melody in the tenor register, written on an added bass clef fixed between the usual treble and bass ones. The melody is played with the thumb side of the right hand. The piece evokes in miniature the quintessence of Schumann's lyrical style and has gained considerable popularity, being often used as a teaching piece. The final piece is an extended rondo arrangement with two intermezzi, and it seems to suffer from the fact that its unity is diffused with too many musical thoughts. The four pieces that make up the Op. 32 are not often given much attention. The Gigue and the Fughette are much like small teaching pieces, both written in triple meter and neither long enough to permit much intricacy. The Scherzo and Romance are longer but not much more substantial in musical interest. Surprisingly, the romance is not a lyrical expression, but rather scherzo-like in its staccato, impetuous texture.

The decade 1829–39 had witnessed a steady stream of Schumann's creative energy directed toward writing solo keyboard music. Then there is a hiatus of about eight years, when the composer, embarking on his typically manic creative pattern, turned his attentions to writing songs and orchestral, choral, and chamber music. This shift away from solo piano music took place just as his marriage to Clara was consummated, and one might speculate that writing for the piano was psychologically tied up with Schumann's frustration and longing for the time when his life with Clara could become a reality. The only exception to this break is the set of pedal piano pieces he wrote in 1845 as material to be used for the practice instruments at the Leipzig Conservatory, which possessed no organ. By the time Schumann returned to writing with regularity for solo keyboard, he was at a point in his life when signs of his eventual mental deterioration had begun to show themselves periodically. This may account for the fact that the creative flame never burned with as much consistency in these later works, notwithstanding a few exceptions.

In 1848, Schumann wrote the forty-three small character pieces he entitled *Album für die Jugend* (Album for the Young), Op. 68. Using miniature binary and ternary forms, he created a veritable treasure house of teaching material. Each piece bears a descriptive title, and many of the pieces succeed admirably in painting an imaginative musical picture. Although the level of technical difficulty is somewhat variable, almost all of the pieces are quite accessible to the piano student. Favorites in teaching studios include "Wilder Ritter" (The Wild Rider), "Fröhlicher Landmann" (The Merry Farmer), "Knecht Ruprecht" (Knight Rupert), and "Reiterstück" (The Horseman). Teaching material that addresses more specific styles is touched upon with the inclusion of a chorale, an etude, a canon, a small fugue, and a chorale prelude. Although *Album für die Jugend* does not reach for great emotional intensity, it clearly represents the composer's style very well and is stock-in-trade for most piano teachers.

The two sets of four pieces each, Op. 72 (1845) and Op. 76 (1849), fugues in the first case and marches in the second, seem more like character pieces than genre types. The fugues are all short pieces with subjects that remind the listener of Bach without being direct quotations. Augmentation of the subject is used effectively in the first fugue and free diminution in the second. Stretto is used in all four. The writing is skillful but somewhat self-consciously academic and does not represent Schumann in his most inspired moments. The marches, similarly short on inspiration, are all built on a modest ABA pattern. Dotted rhythms abound throughout the set, and they tend to give a sameness to the material. Only the middle sections of the second and third march provide relief to the rhythmic drive. The third piece has the descriptive reference *Lager Scene* (Camp Scene).

The years 1848 and 1849 did see, however, the production of the *Waldszenen* (Forest Scenes), Op. 82, the finest set of character pieces of Schumann's later years. In these nine pieces, Schumann's faltering muse seems to regain its full power of expression. The cycle is suggestive of a visit to the forest, for the opening piece is called "Eintritt" (Entrance) and the final piece "Abschied" (Departure). The seven intervening pieces each carry a descriptive title of something the visitor encounters during the visit, such as a hunter waiting for his prey ("Jäger auf der Lauer"), a haunted place ("Verrufene Stelle"), or a wayside inn ("Herberge"). Schumann provides a spooky quotation from Hebbel for "Verrufene Stelle," one that describes pale flowers that draw sustenance not from the sunlight but rather from human blood. Unusually imaginative is the prophetic bird ("Vogel als Prophet") with its imitative bird calls that feature dissonant downbeats much of the time. The final piece is musically in the tradition represented by the endings of the *Davidsbündlertänze* and *Kinderszenen*, a lyrical statement that suggests a final summing up, bringing the cycle to quiet repose at its end.

The collection of pieces entitled *Bunte Blätter* (Colorful Leaves), Op. 99, was written over a period of about ten years (1839–49) and suffers as a set from a serious lack of unity or organization. On the other hand, it contains some of the most exquisite miniatures Schumann ever wrote. A set of three wonderful little pieces opens the work. These are followed by a set subtitled *Albumblätter* (Album Leaves), five tiny pieces that are also first rate. Brahms used the theme from the first of the *Albumblätter* as the basis for his set of variations, Op. 9. Then comes an effective novelette written in 1838, the most extended work of the set in an ABA form with a middle section that presents a lyrical melody in chords over a rising and falling chromatic bass line. From this point onward the set deteriorates considerably in quality. A virtuosic prelude almost works well but turns out to be somewhat overembellished with thirty-second notes. There follow two short marches, a scherzo, and a piece entitled "Abendmusik" (Evening Music), all rather mundane and uninteresting. Because the last several pieces in the collection are inferior and the set exhibits so little unity, performers who are unwilling to ignore the remarkable beauty of the opening pieces usually play just those works, often rearranging them slightly for better contrast, and often ending with the most substantial of them, the novelette.

In the last four sets of small pieces, Schumann's creative voice is but sporadically effective. The *Drei Phantasiestücke* (Three Fantasy Pieces), Op. 111, date from 1852 and are considerably less ambitious than most of the similarly titled pieces of the Op. 12 set. The first one attempts to recall the passion of "In der Nacht" but only partially succeeds, perhaps due to its brief two-part form with a coda-like ending section. The second and third pieces are in ABA form, but the material, although pleasant, is not very compelling. The twenty pieces that make up the *Albumblätter* (Album Leaves), Op. 124, are much like the miniatures that make up the *Album for the Young*, and, indeed, the set was assembled from material that was written between 1832 and 1845, thus predating the Op. 68. Some of the pieces, such as the "Phantasietanz" (Fantasy Dance) or the "Wiegenliedchen" (Little Cradle Song), are popular as teaching material, but several others, for example "Elfe" (The Elf) and the nineteenth of the set, yet another *Phantasiestück*, demand more technical skill than is usually encountered in small teaching pieces. The "Phantasietanz" and "Elfe," incidentally, as well as the fourth of the set, a small waltz, were rejected from *Carnaval*, which suggests speculation that perhaps many or all of these pieces were castaways from other sets, reassembled here. This would explain the disparate levels of difficulty and variety of content encountered.

The seven little fughettas that make up the Op. 126 are not very successful. Some of them, such as nos. 1 and 2, are so short as to be little more than exposition-like entries of the voices, and the contrapuntal ideas are not very outstanding from a musical point of view. The same lack of inspiration plagues the final set of character pieces, the five of 1853 that make up the *Gesänge der Frühe* (Morning Songs). One can observe Schumann conjuring up many of the devices that proved so wonderfully successful in earlier sets: the energetic march-like dotted rhythms of the third piece, the rapid sixteenth-note passagework swirling under a more lyrical melody of the fourth piece, the poetic final statement of the last one. These attempts to capture the beauty found in the earlier works simply do not bear fruit, however, for the magic spark of inspiration seems to be gone.

Sonatas and Sonata Types

Schumann is often thought to represent the freedom of thought frequently considered typically Romantic when it comes to dealing with the sonata structure. In fact, the sonata mold seems not to have suited him entirely, for its overall duration and especially the expected length of the outer movements do not accommodate his gift for quickly establishing the essence of a mood, defining it within the framework of a miniature, and moving on to something else before the necessity of working out development or transition becomes pressing. Schumann was able to demonstrate many times that, as a composer, he had the technique to write convincing developments and transitions, taken as separate entities. However, the flow of moving from one event to the next often seems awkward in longer movements, and overall balance and relative importance of sections seem to be problematic matters.

Each of the works that are related to the sonata structure deal with these issues in different ways with varying degrees of success. In the three works that bear the title Sonata, the Opp. 11, 14, and 22, Schumann vacillates between extending the structure to great lengths and compressing it. In both the Fantasia in *C*, Op. 17, and the *Faschingsschwank aus Wien* (Viennese Carnival Jest), Op. 26, the composer sets guidelines that incorporate a considerable amount of freedom at the outset. In the Toccata, Op. 7, Schumann combines the concept of the sonata-allegro structure with that of technical display implied by the toccata idea and thus holds the structure tightly together by the driving sixteenth notes that permeate the work. The Op. 8, a piece that Schumann calls simply *Allegro,* employs the sonata-allegro idea with some degree of success, but the piece itself is stylistically uncharacteristic and does not hold a firm place in the active repertoire. And, finally, the Op. 118, *Drei Klavier-Sonaten für die Jugend* (Three Piano Sonatas for the Young), are conceived as small enough pieces to allow the composer to work in the dimensions to which he is so well attuned.

The toccata is surprisingly absent from the catalogues of classical composers. Thus, there is a gap between the multisectional toccatas of Johann Sebastian Bach and others of the late Baroque and those of the early nineteenth century, notably the toccatas of Czerny and Schumann. Even so, the toccata returns as a perpetual-motion type of composition rather than one of several contrasting sections, picking up on a somewhat earlier Italian tradition represented by toccatas of Bernardo Pasquini (1637–1710) and Alessandro Scarlatti (1659–1725). Its amalgamation with the sonata-allegro structure is represented solely by Schumann's entry and more or less remains so, for even later nineteenth- and twentieth-century toccatas, those of Debussy, Ravel, and Prokofiev, for example, while continuing the perpetual-motion idea, exhibit far less, if any, allegiance to the sonata-allegro structure.

Schumann's Toccata was originally written in the key of *D*, placing it in an impossibly awkward physical position on the keyboard for the player. Dropping it a whole step to *C* moves the technical demands into the realm of possibility, although they remain far from easy. That technical territory is staked out following a two-measure introductory half

Example 12.8 Robert Schumann: Toccata, Op. 7 mm. 1–4

cadence (Example 12.8). Double-note patterns in both hands in rapidly moving sixteenth notes continue almost without rest for the entire exposition. In the short development section, repeated-note octaves are featured in the right hand. At the end of the recapitulation, the introductory chords return in an extended phrase at the climax, and a short coda calls for a more rapid tempo. As a virtuoso display piece of the toughest order, the Op. 8 holds a firmly fixed niche in the repertoire, and deft performances of it continue to inspire admiration.

The Allegro in *b,* Op. 8, written in 1831 at about the same time as the *Papillons,* seems as though it ought to be more successful than it is. It opens with a cadenza-like prestissimo that uses octaves to set forth a three-note motive. This leads to a measured first theme, the opening theme of a sonata-allegro exposition. The second theme is suitably lyrical; the development is lengthy and involves both first and second themes; there is a return of the opening cadenza before the recapitulation and a sizeable coda. Notwithstanding all of these nicely balanced structural features, the composition has attracted almost no attention from performers. One can point to the fact that the transitions between some sections, the first and second themes and the onset of the coda, for examples, are awkward and seem to stop the momentum of the piece. This kind of awkwardness, however, one also occasionally finds in other Schumann compositions that are much more in the repertoire. What finally emerges is the inescapable fact that the material itself is simply not interesting enough to have motivated performers to want to play the music.

Although Schumann was working on all three of the sonatas at the same time in the early part of 1834, it is the Op. 11 that is the most intertwined with his personal life. Not only is it dedicated to Clara from Florestan and Eusebius, but it also became a kind of symbol of faith between the two lovers during a period when all communication between them was forbidden. Clara played the sonata privately for Chopin, Mendelssohn, and Moscheles, and publicly in 1837 at a concert in Leipzig where Robert listened incognito in the audience. When Robert and Clara mention simply "the sonata" in their correspondence,

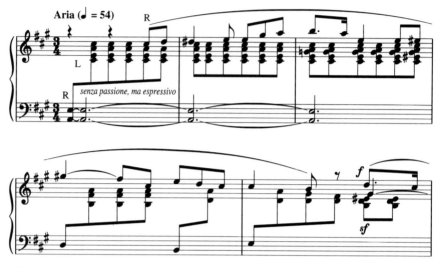

Example 12.9 Robert Schumann: Sonata, Op. 11, 2nd movt. mm. 1–5

it is the Op. 11 they refer to, although both the Op. 14 and Op. 22 had been written. The work received a considerable amount of attention from contemporaries. Moscheles and Liszt mention the work favorably in reviews (although both complain about the length and structure of the final movement), and there are documented performances by Liszt (1840), Brahms (1867), and Anton Rubinstein (1884).

The first movement opens with a fifty-two-measure introduction, presenting a passionate theme that returns both in the development section of the first movement and in the outer sections of the second movement, the arioso. The first theme of the sonata-allegro structure is stated at the onset of the Allegro vivace, music that had originally been conceived in 1832 as a *Fandango Rhapsodie.* Its driving rhythm forms the basis of most of the exposition, finally giving way to a lyrical second theme near the end of the section. The structure of the development section is threefold, the outer sections being based on the fandango themes as well as agitated versions of the second theme. These frame a statement of the theme from the introduction. There is a full recapitulation but no coda. The key relationships in the movement are traditional, *f-sharp* being the home key with a second theme in *A* in the exposition and in *f-sharp* in the recapitulation.

The second movement, based on a song written in 1828, is titled Aria and sets forth a miniature ABA form. The music of its outer sections is derived from the middle section of the introduction, where it was stated with verve and passion. Here in the Aria, the music is transformed into one of the most tender expressions to be found anywhere in Schumann's writings (Example 12.9). One cannot help but reflect on the depth of Robert's feelings for Clara when one encounters music of such sensitivity. A short middle section joins the two outer ones with a single statement of an ardent theme in the baritone-bass range.

A movement marked *Scherzo* and *intermezzo* follows. It was very likely composed as one of a set of *Burlesken* in 1832. The opening section states a scherzo-like ABA theme in but one section with no repeats. The first alternate section follows, also in a compact ABA form. The scherzo section is restated, and there follows a second departure, this time marked as an intermezzo with the additional instruction of *Alla burla, ma pomposo* (comically, but pompously). The humor is heightened by a recitative filled with fermatas and punctuated with sforzando orchestral-like chords. A final statement of the opening scherzo section completes the movement.

The final movement is the most problematic of the entire sonata, probably contributing substantially to the feeling that the work is overextended. On first encounter, one might regard it as a kind of free rondo, for the opening theme is presented a total of five times in four different keys. The second and fourth statements occur fairly close to the first and third statements respectively, an arrangement that would make for a fairly lopsided rondo. A contrasting second theme is introduced right after the opening theme, and the second theme forms the basis of two extensive development sections that follow the opening theme's second and fourth statements. This arrangement seems related to sonata-allegro structure. The development sections contain, in turn, yet a third lyrical theme that each time precedes the retransition to the main theme. A vigorous coda brings the entire movement to its conclusion. The entire structure might be laid out schematically as:

ABA'

development

C

ABA"

development

C

A''' coda

The schematic points to the fact that one senses also a giant two-part structure with a final closing statement of the main theme and a coda. The movement takes almost ten minutes to play and demands considerable stamina from the performer and patience from the listener. Rewards along the way, however, are many, for Schumann fills the movement with passion, lyricism, and drama.

The Op. 14 is the most neglected of the three sonatas, undeservedly so in the opinions of many musicians. Schumann originally conceived it as a five-movement work, two scherzi serving as second and fourth movements with a theme and variations as the centerpiece. He submitted it to the publisher Haslinger with the title *Concert*. Haslinger persuaded Schumann to jettison the two scherzi and call the work *Concert sans orchestre*, feeling that this concept would have popular appeal. Almost immediately the reaction from Schumann's colleagues was negative. Moscheles, to whom the work is dedicated, and Liszt both wrote reviews that complained about the title but that praised the work as a sonata in the tradition of Beethoven. In 1853, a second edition of the work appeared under the title *Troisième grande sonate* (Third Grand Sonata), by that time third rather than second because the Op. 22 had appeared in the meantime. The second of the two original scherzos was restored as the second movement, and the entire work had undergone considerable revision. According to the music critic Hanslick, Brahms gave the work its first performance in Vienna in 1862.

The opening movement follows a formal pattern not unlike the final movement of the Op. 11: AB development AB development A coda. The section denoted as AB is very much like an exposition and succinctly presents several thematic ideas, modulating to *E-flat* near its end. In its return the second section is in *A-flat*, and the second development, in turn, is presented in a different key from the first. Schumann employs this structure again in the final movement of this sonata as well as in the last movement of the Op. 22. It is possible that Schumann regarded the structure as deriving from sonata-allegro and, perhaps, even as his own variant on the traditional pattern.

The Scherzo in *b-flat* that serves as the second movement is extended and free, the opening section itself subdividing into several smaller sections. The middle section that opens in *D* is also considerably more extensive than the expected two-part structure. The da capo is written out. The slow movement is based on a theme of Clara Wieck, a rather melancholy utterance in *f* on which Robert builds four variations and a coda. The final movement is brimming with difficult passagework, much of which is soft and light in texture. It sets a mood that is both fantasy-like and fleeting.

It is not easy to analyze why the Op. 14 continues to be overlooked by performers to a great extent. It aspires to the passion and virtuosity of the other two sonatas. Schumann's weaknesses as a composer show themselves, as they do in other extended works, but here not to an extent that should condemn the entire work to virtual oblivion. The first movement is somewhat disjointed; the Scherzo might be criticized as being overextended; Clara's theme tends to be harmonically static and to indulge in identical repetition of short phrases; the final movement offers little in the way of broad lyricism. Yet this litany of possible faults is offset by much that is clearly inspired, and it should be remembered that both Liszt and Brahms regarded the work as worthy of praise and performance. Perhaps in time this work will find the more favored niche in the repertoire it probably deserves.

The Fantasia in *C*, Op. 17, emerged in its present form only after almost three years of work. The original title of the work was *Obolon auf Beethoven Monument Ruinen, Trophäen, Palmen: Grosse Sonate für das Piano- forte, für Beethovens Monument, von Florestan und Eusebius.* Thus, the title indicated that the work was a sonata and a monument to Beethoven. Thematic links to Beethoven's song cycle *An die ferne Geliebte* (To the Far- away Loved One) and an original dedication to Clara provided double- meaning references for Schumann, both historic and personal. By 1838, however, the work had undergone considerable revision, was rededicat- ed to Franz Liszt, and took on the title of Fantasia (sometimes rendered *Phantasie*). Even so, Schumann wrote to Clara in 1838 that the opening movement was "certainly the most impassioned I ever wrote—a deep lament for you." In a review of Schubert's sonatas, Schumann also wrote an often-quoted quip, "So let them then write sonatas or fantasies (what's in a name?)," a point of view, incidentally, Schumann did not seem to hold consistently.

Schumann also included subtitles for the three movements: "Ruinen" (Ruins), "Triumphbogen" (Triumphal Arch), and "Sternenkranz" (Ring of Stars). These were replaced in the final version by a mystical verse from the novelist and critic Friedrich Schlegel: "Durch alle Töne tönet / Im bunten Erdentraum / Ein leiser Ton gezogen / Für den, der heimlich lauschet" (Through all of the tones that sound in this colorful earth-dream, there emerges one ethereal tone for him who listens in secret).

The fact that the opening movement was planned in sonata-allegro form is still evident. One can identify an exposition with reasonable clar- ity, a strong, sweeping opening theme built on unresolved harmonies in *C* being followed by a second lyrical melody that first appears in *d* but then settles down to the subdominant, *F.* This, in turn, is followed by what might be a development section, but working the opening theme gets sidetracked with a section marked *Im Legenden-Ton* (in the style of a legend), a section that restates a theme drawn from a brief transition in the exposition and several variations on it. There is a recapitulation of both themes from the exposition, although in a much shorter version, and a coda. The entire movement is headed with an imaginative set of directions: *Durchaus fantastisch und leidenschaftlich vorzutragen* (to be per- formed fantastically and passionately throughout).

The second movement is based on two ideas, the exalted chordal theme that opens the movement and a series of thematic episodes all linked by dotted rhythms. The dotted rhythms carry over into a quieter middle section. The opening theme appears twice more, once before the middle section, where it introduces difficult but manageable skips, and then again before the coda, where the skips get considerably harder. They, in turn, are carried over into the coda, where they become next to impossible, a fact that has become well known and even to the present time continually talked about among performers who play this music.

The final movement is one of the most remarkable poetic expressions in the entire literature of the keyboard. Essentially it is a slow movement that presents an opening theme after an introduction of four measures. This theme is followed by an ethereal transition that closes with a return of the introduction. Then a new theme marked *Etwas bewegter* (moving ahead somewhat) is presented and with it the beginning of a very gradual buildup of intensity. A sublime transcendentalism permeates the next thirty-four measures, climaxing with a strong series of chords that use dotted rhythms and a cadence-like sense of ultimate finality. That finality is disturbed the first time around, however, by a sudden veering off from *F* to *A*. The entire cycle is then repeated in other keys, joined not at its opening but rather at the transition section just after the opening. The second time around, the final cadence-like theme is presented without a surprise ending, settling down in *C*. The elevated mood is sustained through a coda that begins to build up tension but then recedes into quiet closing chords.

The three movements of the Fantasia work together marvelously, the first and last movements being essentially lyrical expressions and the middle movement providing stirring energy. The first movement, moreover, is permeated by a youthful, impetuous quality and the final movement with a transcendental, spiritual intensity. The Fantasia has earned a place in the rarified atmosphere of undisputed masterworks and is regarded by most musicians as one of the very highest points, not only of the composer's output, but also of the entire literature for the piano.

The Sonata, Op. 22, was written over a period of years. The lyrical second movement was completed by 1830, the first and third movements by 1833, and the final movement not until 1838, it being substituted for an earlier movement that both Robert and Clara agreed was "much too difficult." By 1840, Clara played it in a recital in Berlin, where, she reported, the audience reaction was favorable. Schumann had asked her to play it as if it were the day before their wedding, but not to take the sonata "too wildly."

The sonata is the most compact of the three from a structural standpoint. The opening sonata-allegro movement presents a contrasting pair of themes in its exposition, the first being built on a driving, intense melodic line and the second on a more relaxed, syncopated, chorale theme. Elements of both themes appear in the development. The coda that closes the movement is the point at which one of the most famous in-house jokes in musical literature occurs. Having marked the movement to be played *So rasch wie möglich* (as fast as possible), Schumann at this point directs *Schneller* (faster) and then later *Noch schneller* (faster still). The spirit in which Schumann writes these instructions can be understood, even if following the directions literally is impossible.

The second movement is cast in a small ABA form with the middle section acting as a short development or variation of the theme presented in the outer sections. The movement is one of Schumann's most tender, sensitive expressions. The scherzo is unusually terse, the only section marked to be repeated occurring in the first portion of the short, unlabeled trio. The final movement is modeled closely after sonata-allegro form with an element of rondo. A pair of contrasting themes is followed by a development; the entire cycle is repeated with the second theme and development in another key; and the opening theme appears a final time, followed by a coda. The concept of the structure is not unlike that of the final movement of the Op. 11, although here Schumann writes with considerably more skill with regard to proportion. The brilliance and succinctness of the Op. 22, as well as the unsurpassed beauty of its slow movement, have served the work well, for it is certainly the most often played of the Schumann sonatas and ranks high in popularity in Schumann's overall output.

Schumann labeled the *Faschingsschwank aus Wien* (Viennese Carnival Prank), Op. 26, in its original version a *Grande romantique sonate.* Elements of sonata structure are evident in the overall plan of the work and in the sonata-allegro structure of the final movement. The opening movement is cast, however, not in the traditional sonata-allegro form but rather in what might be described as an extended rondo. Even it, however, does not resemble the usual five-part rondo but rather simply alternates an opening march-like theme with five different departure sections. Even so, the main theme does not return between the fourth and fifth departure but then is presented again before the closing coda. In the fourth section, Schumann plays around with the "Marseillaise," adding to it a high-spirited energy that attends the entire movement.

Both the second and third movements, labeled respectively *Romanze* and *Scherzino,* are slight. Acting as a slow movement for the work, the Romanze is a miniature ABA song, and the Scherzino, in two-four time, has no trio but rather substitutes an unexpectedly long march-like coda. The Intermezzo, serving as a fourth movement before the Finale, is the finest movement of the set. A passionate two-part character piece built over triplet sixteenth notes with a short coda, it ranks with Schumann's finest miniatures.

The Finale, as noted, is cast in sonata-allegro form, albeit the entire concept of the movement, far from being grand, seems to join the spirit of the Romanze and Scherzino in that its themes, once stated, are neither extended nor developed extensively. The movement ends with a short presto coda. Although the Op. 26 has neither the descriptive program nor the imagination of the *Carnaval,* Op. 9, it has nevertheless found a niche of its own in the repertoire as a good piece with which to indoctrinate the developing pianist into the longer works of Schumann. The Op. 26 is both emotionally and technically more accessible than many of Schumann's other major works, and its overall level of inspiration, if not overwhelming, is nevertheless quite acceptable.

In June of 1853, Schumann wrote three sonatas for the young that he dedicated to his daughters, Julie, Elisa, and Marie. This set of *Drei Sonaten für die Jugend*, Op. 118, was obviously intended to function as instructional material for pianists of intermediate facility, and indeed there are many details included in the works that could be used by teachers as examples of traditional concepts: each sonata is in four movements, each first movement is in sonata-allegro form, a theme and variations appears in the first sonata and a movement in canon in the second, movements in all three have descriptive titles, and finally there is cyclicism in that the opening theme of the first sonata reappears in the final movement of the last.

Notwithstanding the composer's careful intentions to include attractive, didactic elements in these works, the three sonatas are not very successful and do not find their way into young pianists' repertoire with great frequency. The material itself, although recognizable as Schumann, suffers from the same rather commonplace character that afflicts much of the composer's late keyboard writing, and, moreover, there is a surprising amount of technical awkwardness that surfaces periodically, rendering the music somewhat ungrateful to play and to teach.

Etudes and Variations

Schumann's first official opus number, written in 1830, is the set of variations based on a theme derived from the name of Countess Pauline von Abegg. The theme rises using the notes A, B-flat (the German equivalent of B), E, G, and G again, the letters forming the opening melodic notes of the piece. The theme is in two sections, the repeat of each being written out. There follow three figural variations. The second presents the theme in the bass, and the third is the most brilliant. A lyrical interlude marked *Cantabile* follows the third variation and might be thought of as a fourth variation, although it is not indicated as such by the composer. The work closes with a lively Finale alla fantasia. Although this set of variations does not represent Schumann at his most sophisticated level of writing, it is, nevertheless, straightforward and charming, and it enjoys considerable popularity among pianists.

In 1820, Niccolò Paganini (1782–1840) wrote his Op. 1, a set of virtuoso caprices for solo violin. They became the basis on which several composers wrote sets of studies for the virtuoso pianist. Schumann's contributions in this arena are his Opp. 3 and 10. In a rather lengthy preface to Op. 3, Schumann writes that he has attempted to transcribe the Paganini caprices for keyboard in such a way as to be as faithful to the original as possible. He then goes on to suggest fingerings and ways of practicing the technical material, and he includes a number of preparatory exercises. The Op. 10 contains no such preface, and indeed the reworking of the Paganini pieces is both more elaborate and imagi-

Allegro brillante

Example 12.10 Robert Schumann: *Études symphoniques*, Op. 13, Finale mm. 189–91

native. Neither of these sets of etudes is very much played by pianists, however, possibly because settings of Paganini material by both Liszt and Brahms are deemed both more imaginative and pianistic.

Combining both the concepts of the etude and variation is the well-known work entitled *Études en forme de variations,* Op.13. Originally called *Etudes in Orchestral Character,* attributed to Florestan and Eusebius, they were written in 1834 but revised in 1852, being published under the title by which the work is generally known, *Études symphoniques.* The final version contains a theme and twelve etudes, nine of which are identified by the composer as variations of the theme and three (nos. 3, 9, and the finale) having strong ties to the theme but without as clear a derivation from it. Five additional variations were written by Schumann but were not included in the final version of the work. Occasionally, pianists include one or more of these in performances of the work. The two-part form of the theme is maintained in most of the variations, many of the sections being marked with repeat signs.

The technical problems presented in the etudes vary. Double notes and octaves are prominent in nos. 7 and 9; staccato touch in nos. 3, 5, and 10; left-hand skips in no. 6; clear projection of contrapuntal writing at different levels in nos. 2, 7, and 11. The finale is march-like in character, using dotted rhythms to build impressive climaxes twice. One of the most famous moments in the composition occurs as part of the final statement of the main theme of the finale, as part of a coda. At this point a *B-flat* chord is substituted for the regular VI chord in *D-flat* (*b-flat*; Example 12.10). The effect is so striking as to create an enormous "lift" that the composer uses to drive the work to a brilliant conclusion. The Op. 13 is one of Schumann's most successful works, offering both stimulating technical challenges and musical brilliance. It remains high on the list of pianists' favorites.

In 1845, Schumann wrote six studies for the pedal piano, Op. 56, as part of the attempt to produce literature for an experimental instrument in which he was interested and which he had introduced as a substitute for practice organs at the Leipzig Conservatory, where he had spent two years on the faculty. This set was followed by a group of four more pieces, Op. 58, which Schumann called sketches. The etudes are all canonic; the sketches are not. Otherwise there is little difference in style between the two sets. Right- and left-hand parts are written with the usual treble and bass clefs but are marked *Manual,* and below these parts is an additional bass clef staff for the part to be played by the feet. These pieces are more a curiosity than anything else, insofar as performance on a piano is concerned. Two players are required to perform the works, and the player who attends to the pedal part has relatively little of interest to play, for the part tends to move slowly in single notes (as is befitting a pedal part). Although the musical material is moderately interesting, it has not proved to be so attractive to performers that the disadvantages of trying to program the pieces are outweighed. Thus, they remain mostly archival insofar as performance is concerned, notwithstanding attempts, both early and recent, to arrange some of the pieces for two hands.

Other infrequently performed sets of variations may be mentioned for completeness. They are Andante (*Mit Gott*), *Variations on an Original Theme in G* (1831–32); *Sehnsuchtswalzervariationen,* also called *Sur un thème connu de Fr. Schubert* (1833); *Etudes in the Form of Free Variations on a Theme of Beethoven* (1833); *Variations sur un nocturne de Chopin* (1834); and Schumann's last piano composition, *Variations on an Original Theme in E-flat* (1854).

CHAPTER THIRTEEN

Fryderyk Franciszek Chopin

Fryderyk (French: Frédéric) Chopin (b. Żelazowa Wola, Mar. 1[?], 1810; d. Paris, Oct. 17, 1849) was born in a small village near Warsaw. There has been some confusion regarding his birthdate, partly due to a baptismal record that states that he was born on February 22, 1810. His father was a French language teacher in the Warsaw Gymnasium, having come from Alsace. Chopin's mother was Polish, one Justine Kryzanowska. Chopin attended a private school, run by his father, with a clientele that included sons of several Polish noblemen.

Chopin's musical training was entirely local: piano lessons with a Bohemian pianist, Albert Zwyny, and general music studies at the Warsaw Conservatory, then under the direction of Joseph Xaver Elsner. The young Chopin was somewhat prodigious, for it is reported that he played a concerto by the Bohemian composer Adalbert Gyrowetz, a musician highly regarded at the time, at the age of seven. Chopin's earliest compositions were polonaises, mazurkas, and waltzes, and by the time he was fifteen his Op. 1, a rondo for piano, and his Op. 2, the *Là ci darem la mano,* a set of variations for piano and orchestra on a theme of Mozart, were published.

When Chopin was nineteen, he embarked on a professional career, his first goal to give concerts in Munich, Vienna, Paris, and eventually London. Two concerts in Vienna during the summer of 1829 are documented as having been quite successful, but a second stay in Vienna during the winter of 1830 and the spring of 1831 was much less so. When he arrived in Paris, he was once more greeted with accolades, playing first in 1831 for an invited audience in the home of Camille Pleyel, the prominent piano manufacturer and composer. A public concert on February 26, 1832, was equally well received. As a result of these successes, an affinity for the highly stylish Parisian social life, and political unrest at home, Chopin made Paris his home for the rest of his life, never again returning to Poland.

Chopin's professional life in Paris was based not so much on playing concerts as on giving piano lessons to members of the elite society and on his growing reputation as a composer. By 1839, Schumann reviewed the Op. 28 preludes, Op. 33 mazurkas, and Op. 34 waltzes in the *Neue Zeitschrift für Musik,* writing that Chopin was "der kühnste und stolzeste Dichtergeist der Zeit" (the boldest and proudest poetic spirit of the time). Chopin's professional standing thus became completely secure, and he was a favorite among the celebrated notables of Parisian society. Among his friends were the most famous musicians of the day (Liszt, Mendelssohn, Bellini, Berlioz, Meyerbeer, Paganini, and Hiller), literary giants (Balzac, Heine, and the Polish poet Adam Mickiewicz), and painters (notably Delacroix).

In 1837, Liszt introduced Chopin to Mme Aurore Dudevant, a professional writer and woman of the world, whose pseudonym was George Sand. Their stormy romance caused considerable controversy and lasted for about ten years. In 1838, Chopin suffered an attack of bronchitis, and the couple spent the winter on the island of Majorca in an ill-fated attempt to restore Chopin's health. The disastrous living conditions that they encountered, Chopin's declining physical condition, and poor weather combined to set off bitter quarrels between them, resulting in an unflattering, thinly disguised portrait of the composer as Prince Karol in Sand's novel *Lucrezia Floriani.* After their return to Paris, Chopin's health continued to decline, his condition eventually becoming tubercular. Notwithstanding his failing health, Chopin undertook a seven-month visit to England in 1848, giving concerts and accepting social invitations to the point of complete exhaustion. He returned to Paris in a critical condition and died there at the age of thirty-nine.

Chopin confined his work as a composer almost exclusively to writing for the piano, a fact that shaped his entire musical thinking and resulted in his bringing to the piano several innovative concepts. Since Chopin was not caught up in the widespread fascination of making the piano imitate the orchestra, he focused on the acoustical properties of the piano itself more effectively. This resulted in a consistent deployment of vertical harmonic patterns across the span of the keyboard in a way that paralleled the overtone series. The result is a sound that is akin to "open" harmonic writing, conveys transparency, and is distinctly Chopinesque. This arrangement is one in which the interval of the tenth becomes basic in harmonic figuration, and the resulting patterns often require extension of the hand to cover a range of more than an octave.

Added to this distinct way of laying out the music at the keyboard is a harmonic sense that was quite original for the time. Indeed, Chopin's contemporary critics complained about those features in his writing that today we simply regard as strikingly original: chromaticism, the frequent use of dissonance, and harmonic progressions of unusual direction.

Often cited as early influences on the young Chopin are those of the Italian operatic composers of the day, particularly Bellini. The long melodic line associated with *bel canto* is clearly in evidence even in early compositions. Ornamental decoration may well be attributed to such an operatic influence, but also the keyboard style of the day had in general evolved toward virtuoso display that frequently broke into cadenza-like ornamentation. Other composers of the day provided limited influences on Chopin as well, notably Field, Hummel, Spohr, and for a short time Kalkbrenner. The observation is frequently made, however, that Chopin had formed his compositional style almost completely by the time he left Poland as a young man and that many of the characteristics that make his music sound so individual were self-generated.

Chopin had a great affinity with composers of the past, especially Mozart and Bach. As a result, Chopin's attention to structure is particularly acute. His work redefined many of the concepts associated with dance music and with the character piece. In his hands the polonaise and the waltz grew from slight dance forms to pieces of greater length and variety of mood. The mazurka was imbued with a broad range of subtle inflections. The scherzo was freed from its role in the larger sonata structure, expanded, and became a piece associated with considerable virtuosity. The ballade became the keyboard equivalent of the orchestral tone poem. The nocturne, originated by John Field, was given greater expressive range. Chopin set the standard for the etude, creating masterworks in this small form against which the efforts of all other composers in this genre are measured.

Chopin's use of more traditional, older structural concepts is confined to but three sonatas, a fantasy, a set of preludes, and three early rondos. Of the three sonatas, only the last two represent Chopin's mature style, but these two remain entrenched in the repertoire so deeply as to be likely candidates for the most-played nineteenth-century keyboard sonatas. The fantasy is loosely linked to the sonata-allegro structure in Chopin's hands, following a trend to be seen in the fantasies of Mendelssohn, Schumann, and others. The prelude is woven into a cycle of twenty-four, one in each major and minor key, copying a concept and order of a set by Hummel and others, but expanding the idea sufficiently to give it significance and artistic value. The early rondos, like the first sonata, are not very often found on concert programs, for they do not represent Chopin's mature style.

Both as a composer and as a performer, Chopin combined elements of a restraint born of Classicism with a personal sense of freedom that we associate with the Romantic movement. This carefully balanced dichotomy places his music in the position of inviting each generation of performers to realign its diverse elements. The result is a never-ending set of challenges for each generation and a continuing fascination with the resulting interaction between composer and performer. Each pianist is challenged to develop an individual approach to the fluctuations of tempo generally described under the heading of "rubato"; each must find a personal way of inflecting the melodic line and its decorative inflections; each must evolve the concepts that balance the projection of structure with the fantasy-like freedom of improvisatory passagework. It is thus no surprise that Chopin continues to be the most-played nineteenth-century composer and that a new crop of "Chopin specialists" seems to appear with every generation of pianists.

A chronological catalogue of Chopin's works was published by Maurice J. E. Brown in 1960. Using B numbers for Chopin's works is becoming increasingly standard among research scholars, but performers persist in using the older opus numbers, partly because the tradition is strong and partly because the opus numbers approximate chronological accuracy, except for a relatively small number of early pieces published posthumously as late opus numbers (Opp. 66–74). Also, Brown assigns numbers to individual pieces or groups of smaller works by virtue of chronology, but often such grouping turns out to be at odds with sets traditionally thought of as being together. The following discussion will make use of opus numbers and some B numbers.

Sonatas

Curiously, the first sonata (Op. 4; B. 23; ca. 1827), written when Chopin was still at the Warsaw Conservatory, has dropped out of the active repertoire. Even the occasional revival by an enterprising pianist, the kind often accorded the lesser-played works of Mendelssohn or Schumann, is very seldom forthcoming in this case. The reason is probably that the style of the sonata does not sound very much like Chopin. It is not, as in the case of lesser-known works of others, a poor representation of the composer's best moments, but rather it sounds untypically nondescript. Nevertheless, the sonata has features to its credit: its structure is clear, its counterpoint is well conceived, and some of the passagework is ingenious. Lacking, however, are the strong melodic statements associated with Chopin's style, harmonic individuality, and dramatic intensity. The sonata is certainly as worthy as those of Hummel, whom Chopin admired greatly at this point in his development, but it is not strong enough to survive comparison with Chopin's own later style. The work does set the four-movement pattern for the three keyboard sonatas, with the slow movement occurring third. An unusual feature of the slow movement here is its five-four time signature. Chopin effectively meets the challenge of writing convincingly in this unusual meter, but his success does not foreshadow a predilection in later works for using unusual or irregular time signatures.

The second sonata (Op. 35; B. 128), completed in 1839, has had a turbulent history. Its third movement, perhaps the most famous funeral march in the world, was probably written and played as a separate piece before its incorporation into the sonata. Its use as the third movement, followed by an exceedingly short, monophonic last movement in which both hands play parallel-motion patterns, gave rise to a great deal of commentary and speculation by Chopin's contemporaries. In an 1841 review for the *Neue Zeitschrift für Musik*, Schumann suggests that Chopin "brought together four of his wildest offspring." Hanslick questioned the unity of the four movements in an 1864 review of a performance of the work in Vienna by Carl Tausig. The corollary to the conjecture that Chopin assembled four disparate pieces into a sonata is that Chopin was basically either uncomfortable or unskilled in handling sonata structure, a premise sometimes encountered in earlier evaluations of his work.

Twentieth-century assessments of the work have been far more favorable. Undeniably, the proportions of the work are out of balance, the brevity and tenuous character of the last movement providing but little substance for those who expect a clearly defined finale as a counterpart to the other movements. On the other hand, the dramatic effect of following the somber funeral march with a movement that implies desolation, even nihility, is compelling, and the combination has continued to work brilliantly at every performance for over 150 years. It is precisely the breach with traditional structure that empowers the effect, providing a necessary shock value and leaving the listener with the feeling that there must be something more; but, in fact, it's all over. The philosophical implications are obvious.

Although Chopin admired Beethoven far less than either Mozart or Johann Sebastian Bach, the similarity of concept between Chopin's Op. 35 and the Op. 26 of Beethoven invites speculation as to whether or not Chopin was influenced by Beethoven. In both works, the ABA structure of the funeral march is similar. In both works, the final movement is fleeting and compact. The Beethoven rondo structure is, indeed, somewhat more substantial, but, like the Chopin movement, its sections are unusually terse with almost continuous sixteenth-note figurations providing perpetual motion.

The other movements of the Op. 35 are much more traditional in concept. The opening movement offers a clear-cut sonata-allegro structure with but one variance: the opening theme, having been used extensively in the development, is never recapitulated in the final section of the work. Thus, as the movement emerges from the development, it goes directly to the more lyrical second theme at the onset of the recapitulation. The scherzo movement is in simple ABA form, Chopin dispensing with repeated halves in the outer sections but maintaining the traditional mold in the trio, albeit only repeating the second half.

The third sonata (Op. 58; B. 155; 1844–45) is similar to the Op. 35 in several ways. The scherzo appears as the second movement and the slow movement as the third. Although the final movement of the sonata is considerably longer than that of the Op. 35, it is, nevertheless,

Example 13.1 Frédéric Chopin: Sonata, Op. 58, 1st movt. mm. 12–15

relatively succinct when compared to the rather extended structure of the first movement. The imbalance never comes to mind when hearing the work because of the breathtaking effectiveness of the final movement's virtuosic display. The last movement thus comes off as short but extremely powerful. One other point of similarity with the Op. 35 is that the opening material of the exposition of the first movement is not repeated in the recapitulation.

On the other hand, in the Op. 58 Chopin effects a degree of subtlety and complexity, particularly in structure and harmony, not found in the Op. 35. The first movement of the earlier sonata, for example, presents an exposition that divides rather obviously into traditional sections: first theme, second theme, and closing section. This is not the case with the Op. 58. Here, the opening theme of the sonata is scarcely stated before chromatic shifts in the harmony suggest development (Example 13.1). The section that serves as a transition to the second theme is filled with material that in itself might have been thematic, as well as agitated passagework. The second theme itself is lyrical but evolves into at least two other forms before more passagework leads to an extended closing section. The development section introduces a considerable amount of contrapuntal complexity in working with the first theme. The recapitulation opens, as noted, not with the first theme, but rather with a section of the transition material leading to the second theme.

Both the scherzo and the slow movement utilize a simple ABA plan. The middle section of the slow movement is noteworthy in achieving the

Largo

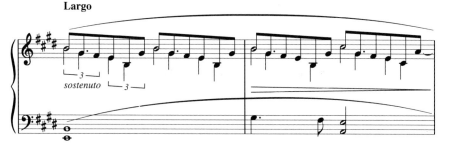

Example 13.2 Frédéric Chopin: Sonata, Op. 58, 3rd movt. mm. 29–30

effect of improvisation within a reasonably structured framework (Example 13.2). The final movement, following a two-part rondo pattern, is so well written in terms of both virtuoso display and an ever-increasing tension that audiences are usually ready to cheer at the conclusion of the climactic coda.

Etudes

The rise of the etude in the early nineteenth century was a logical offshoot of both a widespread fascination with virtuosity and the stabilization of the physical properties of the piano. The scene becomes rife with instruction manuals and methods designed to aid the performer aspiring to achieve virtuoso status. Many of these included short compositions in addition to explanations and exercise patterns. Some offered little detailed guidance but presented page after page of short pieces that emphasized scale passagework, arpeggios, octaves, double notes, repeated notes, skips, and a host of other feats that were to be mastered. Such works were produced by Czerny, Cramer, Clementi, Hummel, and Kalkbrenner, to name but a few, between 1815 and 1830, the years when Chopin was growing up and trying to embark upon a career.

That Chopin intended his etudes for use in public performance is clear from the fact that he himself played them in concerts. Others were also performing their study pieces during this period. Cramer is reported to have played his studies in public. Czerny almost certainly regarded some of his studies as worthy concert material. Kalkbrenner's etudes are remarkably similar to those of Chopin in design and general concept of keyboard difficulties. They, too, were probably intended as concert pieces. By the 1830s Mendelssohn, Schumann, and Liszt were writing concert studies. Thus, the tidal wave was well underway by that time. The etudes of Chopin are remarkable in that many of them appeared early enough to be on the cutting edge of the concert-study

Example 13.3 Frédéric Chopin: Etude, Op. 25, no. 6 mm. 1–2

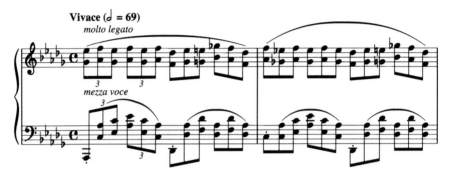

Example 13.4 Frédéric Chopin: Etude, Op. 25, no. 8 mm. 1–2

trend (1830) and that they retain their preeminence in the genre more than 150 years later.

There are twenty-seven etudes in all, two sets of twelve each in the Op. 10 and Op. 25, and three small studies that Chopin contributed to a method published in Paris in 1840 by Moscheles and Fétis. Most of the etudes are in three-part form, many of them with a coda of significant length when considered proportionately. The technical difficulty explored in each is fairly obvious, and most focus on a single problem, unlike, for example, the Liszt *Transcendental Etudes*, many of which tend to combine several technical problems into one piece. Thus, several of the Chopin studies are known among pianists by the name of the difficulty the study represents. Examples include the "double-third" etude (Op. 25, no. 6; Example 13.3); the "double-sixth"etude (Op. 25, no. 8; Example 13.4); the "octave" etude (Op. 25, no. 10); or the "black key" etude (Op. 10, no. 5). Others areknown by a nickname born of the effect the technical difficulty produces: the "Aeolian harp" etude (Op. 25, no. 1), the "winter wind" etude (Op. 25, no. 11; Example 13.5), the "butterfly" etude (Op. 25, no. 9), or the "ocean" etude (Op. 25, no. 12). Probably the most famous of the nicknamed etudes is the "Revolutionary"(Op. 10, no. 12), deriving its name more from the spirit of the music

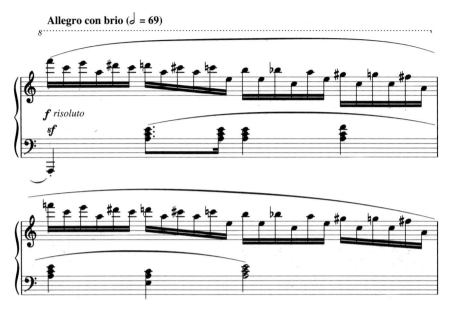

Example 13.5 Frédéric Chopin: Etude, Op. 25, no. 11 mm. 5–6

Example 13.6 Frédéric Chopin: Etude, Op. 10, no. 1 mm. 1–2

rather than from the technical difficulty involved, in this case that of left-hand passagework.

Other etudes explore rather specialized problems, as conceived by Chopin: arpeggios for the right hand in an open harmonic format, extended position (Op. 10, no. 1; Example 13.6); chromatic scales that must be played with the third, fourth, and fifth fingers of the right hand, due to the addition of periodic double notes (Op. 10, no. 2); alternating double thirds and double sixths for the right hand (Op. 10, no. 7); left-hand extension (Op. 10, no. 9); extended arpeggiated chords for the right hand (Op. 10, no. 11); rapid trill-like figurations (Op. 25, no. 3); or left-hand skips (Op. 25, no. 4). Three of the etudes are conceived as slow, lyrical pieces, and thus problems of balance and melodic inflection become paramount (Op. 10, nos. 3 and 6; Op. 25, no. 7). Three others emphasize rhythmic complexities, hemiola and polyrhythms of two against three and three against four (Op. 25, no. 2; the first and second etudes from the set composed for the Moscheles and Fétis method).

The etudes are often constructed in such a way that endurance becomes part of the problem the pianist must face. In the Op. 10, nos. 1, 2, 5, 7, 9, 10, 11, and 12, for example, the technical challenge encountered is unrelenting from the opening of the piece to the final cadence. The same is true for the Op. 25, nos. 1, 2, 3, 4, 5, 8, 9, 11 (after a four-bar introduction), and 12. Thus, the ability to circumvent fatigue becomes very important in performing these studies.

The quality that has made these etudes so important in the literature, however, is their unsurpassed musical interest and refinement, often combined with a wonderful sense of dramatic excitement. The Op. 10, no. 3, for example, contains one of Chopin's most famous melodies. The Op. 25, no. 7, combines two beautifully wrought melodies into a delicately balanced dialogue. Few performers or listeners can resist responding to the drive of the coda of the Op. 10, no. 4, being caught up in the urgency of the Op. 10, no. 12, or thrilled by the descending sweep of the Op. 25, no. 11, to cite but a few instances. Thus, meeting and conquering the technical difficulties of these etudes is rewarded with a finished product that is both musically valuable and pleasing to audiences.

Preludes

The preludes (Op. 28; B. 100, 107, 123–24; 1836–39) were published in 1839 after Chopin's return from the Majorca winter. The brevity of many of the preludes results in the use of curtailed structures. Many could be considered through-composed with but a single section: those in *C, a, A, c-sharp, e-flat, f,* and *F,* for example. Often the pieces may be subdivided into two small sections, the second one starting the opening idea over but taking it in a different direction. Examples of this procedure might include the ones in *e, D, E,* and *b-flat.* ABA patterns can be seen in several of the longer preludes such as the ones in *F-sharp* and *D-flat.* The prelude in *A-flat,* one of the longer ones, uses the pattern ABABA. Sometimes the opening idea is developed in a contrasting section, and the "return" is simply a coda-like reference to the main idea in the home key, as in the closing prelude in *d.* One of the reasons the set works well in its entirety is that Chopin constantly varies the organization and length of these pieces. Structures are never predictable, and a feeling of improvisation permeates the cycle.

These pieces also run the complete spectrum of technical difficulty. Some of Chopin's easiest pieces are included in the set: *e, b, A,* or *c,* for example. These are used in the teaching studio constantly as pieces with which to introduce Chopin to players of limited facility. Other preludes are so difficult that they might have been conceived as etudes; the one in *G* with its notorious left-hand passagework; the *f-sharp*, a perpetual-motion set in a swirl of rapid grace notes; the *b-flat*, which emphasizes both fast right-hand scalar figures and left-hand leaps; the *d* with its left-hand extension and a climax that depends on well-executed chromatic double thirds.

The range of expression in the set is equally large. The gamut encompasses the simplicity of the prelude in *A*, the drama of the one in *f*, the nocturne-like dreaminess of the one in *F-sharp*, the unrelenting sadness of the one in *b*, and the cataclysmic sweep of the closing piece in *d*. Once again, the arrangement of both the technical and expressive elements is such that the set offers kaleidoscopic variety when played completely and a rich menu from which to choose a group of small pieces. Both procedures are used regularly by performers.

Two other preludes complete the list. The better known of the two is in *c-sharp* (Op. 45; B. 141; 1841), a nocturne-like piece in an improvisatory style. The lesser known is a small piece written for Pierre Wolff in 1834 (B. 86) but published for the first time in 1918.

Fantasy

Chopin's use of the term *fantasy* (or *fantasie*) is not consistent. When he used it in conjunction with the famous Impromptu (Op. 66; B. 87), he seemed to be reflecting on the texture of the outer sections of an unusually regular ABA structure. As used with the Polonaise (Op. 61; B. 159), he linked it to a piece in which the traditional structure can barely be discerned through the proliferation of improvisatory and developmental writing. In the Fantasy in *f/A-flat* (Op. 49; B. 137; 1841), there are, to be sure, passages that suggest improvisation, but the overall structure is often regarded as a free sonata-allegro movement. The case is not clear-cut by any means, but the sonata-allegro pattern seems to be the most probable structure if one feels compelled to choose from a traditional menu, and the association between the fantasy and the sonata seemed to be in the air in the early nineteenth century, examples of such a linkage being provided by Schubert, Schumann, and Mendelssohn.

The Op. 49 opens with a two-part march. The opening notes of the march set a distinct, somber mood. In each of the two parts, the repeat is written out with slight variants. The march has a short coda of its own. Improvisatory arpeggios gradually accelerate to an agitato that marks the opening of what might be regarded as the exposition. What follows is not the usual exposition pattern, however, for the opening material in *f* evolves to *E-flat*, starts to repeat in *c*, but then rather abruptly closes down. The middle section is not a development but rather a chorale-like lento in *B*. The final section recapitulates the material of the exposition but transposed so that it opens in *b-flat*, evolving this time to *A-flat*. A dramatic quotation of the opening phrase of the middle section leads to a short coda based on the improvisatory arpeggios. The tonality remains clearly settled in *A-flat*.

Given the amount of explanation that has to be undertaken to account for the irregularities of structure when fitting the work into a sonata-allegro mold, it might be just as easy to abandon the comparison. On the other hand, no other form seems apparent, and if one is to think about the structure at all, one has to account for it in some way. Similar problems arise when one considers the form of the ballades of Chopin.

Notwithstanding the structural freedom, the composition works reasonably well for pianists. The march at the beginning has to be paced carefully so that the opening section does not seem static, and there are several difficult technical challenges, including a treacherous octave passage that appears twice. In spite of these problem areas, the work remains a staple in the repertoire, for it offers both lyrical and exciting, dramatic moments.

Ballades

The four ballades are among the most frequently performed larger works of Chopin and represent the composer at his highest level of creativity over a period of twelve years from 1831 to 1842. During that period, the composer's style evolved in the direction of increasingly subtle and refined structure and contrapuntal detail, an evolution that can be traced with reasonable clarity in the ballades as well as in the four scherzi, composed in a slightly later window of time, between 1835 and 1843.

There is a controversy over the extent to which the four ballades are based on specific epic poems of the Polish poet Adam Mickiewicz, who was in exile in Paris and whom Chopin admired. The case for references to specific poems is circumstantial and has never been adequately proved to those historians for whom clear evidence is important. For the romantically inclined, however, the temptation to hint at the connection can almost never be resisted, and some go so far as to vouch for it. Such a programmatic connection is, in fact, rather uncharacteristic of Chopin, who consistently avoided detailed extramusical references in an age when such linkages were very fashionable. On the other hand, Chopin was apparently quite comfortable with the use of titles that suggested a broader, more general mood or category. Dance titles imply mood character without being too specific, as does the term *nocturne*. Indeed, the term *ballade*, quite apart from its historic or narrative implications, appears occasionally as a title for character pieces of the period. Schumann, Liszt, and Brahms all used the term, the latter two composers writing ballades both with and without specific literary references, and Schumann using the term *Balladenmässig* for the tenth *Davids-bündlertanz*.

The structures of the Chopin ballades are quite different from one another, unlike the scherzi that all use the classic minuet and trio mold as a point of departure. The first and third ballades are often linked to sonata-allegro form. The first ballade probably squeezes into that concept better than the third, but neither can be made to fit the mold without a considerable amount of commentary. There is no historical reason for accepting the sonata-allegro pattern as a basis for the structure of the ballade. If that premise is adopted, on the other hand, then the temptation is strong to find fault with Chopin's developmental procedures, his handling of the proportions of the sections, or his unorthodox "recapitulations." All of these complaints can be avoided by simply examining the structures as carefully conceived, original forms, which offer elements of surprise and fantasy as well as a rather remarkable sense of wholeness. That they work in performance cannot be denied, and the fact that the structures are both individual and successful is a tribute to Chopin's genius as a composer, not a weakness of compositional technique.

The first ballade (Op. 23; B. 66) was begun in 1831, when Chopin was about twenty, was finished in 1835, and published the following year. An outline of the structure of the pieces might look like this:

Introduction

First theme *(g)*

Agitato transition *(g)*

Second theme and retransition *(E-flat)*

First theme over a pedal point on E *(a)*

Second theme in an expanded version *(A)*

Transition to a figural third theme *(E-flat)*

Second theme and retransition *(E-flat)*

First theme over pedal point on D *(g)*

Coda *(g)*

Several features of the composition ensure its unity. The Neapolitan harmony featured in the introduction returns prominently in the coda (Example 13.7). The two retransitions in *E-flat* are clearly based on the opening figure of the first theme (Example 13.8). The agitato transition material that leads to the second theme is based on intervallic relationships associated with the first theme, so that it sounds as if it grows out of the first theme, almost as development. The third theme, appearing briefly and but once, also bears a strong resemblance in shape to the first theme (Example 13.9).

Example 13.7 Frédéric Chopin: Ballade, Op. 23 mm. 224–25

Example 13.8 Frédéric Chopin: Ballade, Op. 23 mm. 83–85

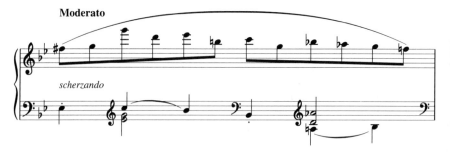

Example 13.9 Frédéric Chopin: Ballade, Op. 23 mm. 138

It is also important to understand that passagework that functions as transition material is oftentimes so brilliantly written that it stands out, leaving an impression that is as strong as the thematic material itself. It is such passagework that forms the basis of the remarkable codas of the first, second, and fourth ballades. They stand as monumental technical challenges and create an intensity that results in closing sections of supreme excitement.

Dramatic gestures abound in the Op. 23. The slow, rising arpeggio based on Neapolitan sixth harmony sets an opening mood of anticipation. The end of the first theme is graced with a deceptive cadence decorated with a cadenza. The second statement of the second theme (in *A*) is capped with brilliant octaves. The coda is ushered in with a climactic double-note passage built on a dominant pedal, and at the end of the coda the recitative style of the introduction returns, now interspersed with sweeping upward scales and fortissimo octaves. The undiminished popularity of the Op. 23 is clearly connected to its dramatic effectiveness.

The second ballade (Op. 38; B. 102; 1838–39) is probably the least played of the four, very likely because its structure is the most problematic. Dedicated to Schumann, its dramatic interest derives from the extreme contrast between an opening barcarolle-like theme in *F* and a stormy section in *a* that features octaves, double notes, and arpeggio-like passagework. Chopin heightens the contrast by letting the barcarolle drift away into a dreamy repose before the onslaught of the stormy section in *a*. After the storm subsides, the barcarolle returns, but with troubled interruptions and developmental twists that lead to various keys and twice growing to climactic proportions. The second climax leads directly to a return of the second storm, which in turn brings in a coda of double notes and near hysteria. A dramatic fermata permits the barcarolle to return briefly for a final, quiet cadence in *a*. The piece opens in *F* and is generally known as the "F major ballade" but spends as much time in *a* and finally finishes in that key. The two keys themselves do not provide ultimate harmonic tension between them, notwithstanding the dramatic gestures that attend their shifting back and forth. The closing, while providing a sense of desolation, is not entirely convincing for many listeners, not only in terms of its key center but also its brevity. Thus, audience reaction is sometimes puzzled rather than wildly enthusiastic. Notwithstanding these problems, the Op. 38 offers wonderful moments, and, in the hands of the skillful performer who carefully paces its extreme contrasts, the piece becomes quite effective.

The third ballade in *A-flat* (Op. 47; B. 136; 1840–41) is best described as an arch form: ABCBA coda. There are, however, remarkable features that must be taken into account. The opening A theme is in two parts, first a songlike lyrical theme of eight measures and its counterpart, a more dance-like theme in which melodic interest is dispersed between several levels of activity. A few measures of development lead to a climactic moment, whereupon the lyrical portion returns briefly and the entire A section seems to subside. A repeated broken octave on C provides the link for a modulation to the key of C. The second theme grows out of the broken-octave idea. It now follows the same sequence of events as the A section, presenting a B section consisting of a statement, growth and development, climax, and restatement. The C section introduces an improvisatory, graceful theme that uses both decorated arpeggios and scalar passagework. It is short and soon leads back to the B section, now in *A-flat*. The B section is now restated through the climax of its development, bar by bar, but in an ingenious new setting. Simple left-hand harmonic support is transformed into difficult running scale passages. Right-hand chords now become animated into passagework that makes use of both double notes and chords, sweeping back and forth across a three-octave range. The final statement of the B-theme material occurs as the theme is fragmented and restated over a rising pedal point, first on B, then on C, and finally moving up to E-flat. The anticipation is heightened by a series of chromatic chords over a continuation of the E-flat pedal point. The climax is finally achieved with the opening eight-measure theme reappearing in a grandiose statement. A coda based on the C-section arpeggio figures brings the piece to a breathtaking close.

Of the four ballades, the Op. 47 may well be built with the tightest structure, and its continued use of development procedures within its overall pattern as a device to heighten tension is very successful. It remains one of the most popular keyboard works of the Chopin catalogue. The fourth ballade (Op. 52; B. 146; 1842) is often spoken of as the "hardest" of the four in the professional grapevine. Its reputation probably stems from the fact that it is the most complex from a structural and contrapuntal standpoint. It does not lend itself to schematic representation or easy explanation, mostly because of the fact that the two thematic ideas on which it is primarily based both undergo a remarkable metamorphosis during the course of the piece.

An introduction of seven bars establishes two thematic fragments, one presented initially by the left hand, the other following immediately in the right. Chopin seems to abandon these ideas with the introduction of a main theme in *f*, but they will all return once again to set the stage for the final large section of the piece.

The opening theme is somewhat problematic because it is constructed in such a way that its opening phrase doubles back on itself. This characteristic makes for a feeling of repetition and, bringing variety to its shape, presents a challenge, one compounded by the fact that the entire fifteen-measure theme is immediately repeated with but a slight variation. At this point the opening theme seems completely entrenched.

It is followed by a rather vague fragment of a theme, sustained in chords over a pentatonic bass moving in octaves. This fragment is the thematic germ on which a second theme will be built during the course of the composition. This germ motive lasts for only eight measures before the first theme returns for a short development and then a climactic restatement in an elaborate double-note setting. Once again the main theme seems to dominate the composition up to this point.

A short, stormy section of passagework settles down to a section in *B-flat* in which the second-theme germ has grown considerably, now appearing as a full-fledged, but subdued, barcarolle. A new section follows, a middle section based on rather sustained passagework that forms itself into melodic patterns decorated with frequent double sixths. At the climax of this section, the introduction returns, now grandiose and employing fragments of the first theme in developmental counterpoint. The introduction comes to a rest in the unlikely key of *A*, and a filmy cadenza prepares the way for some kind of return.

The return is one in which the roles of the first and second theme are reversed. The first theme comes back in rather broken, unstable forms, first as a vague canon that keeps wandering from key to key and then, finally in *f*, as a constantly moving series of decorations. This prepares the way for the entrance of the second theme, now fully formed and powerful. The sedate barcarolle has once again grown, this time into an emotional expression of strength and intensity, which, as it unfolds, continues to soar, forming a magnificent climax for the composition. The first theme, which had seemed so secure at the opening of the piece, is swept away by the advent of the second, which began as a shadow of an idea and ends up by dominating the piece completely. A short, stormy coda closes the work brilliantly.

The fourth ballade presents the performer with the problem of conceptualizing its unusual structure and making clear the transformations that take place during the course of the piece. Expertly handled, it can emerge as a work of magnificent concept.

Scherzi

The idea of taking the scherzo out of the sonata framework, lengthening it, endowing it with virtuoso traits, and thus molding it into a long character piece belongs distinctly to Chopin. The Scherzo a capriccio of Mendelssohn is concurrent with these Chopin works. Otherwise, one must search diligently for other examples of the scherzo standing alone. The little-played Op. 4 of Brahms is another example, but it follows the Chopin works by almost a decade. Even the turn of the twentieth century did not produce many examples by major composers. Prokofiev and Bartók provide one scherzo each, but beyond thatt here seems to be no following in Chopin's footsteps, notwithstanding the fact that the Chopin works are extremely successful and are among the most frequently played pieces in the nineteenth-century repertoire.

Each of the four Chopin scherzi uses as a point of departure the traditional scherzo and trio pattern. The Scherzo in *b* (Op. 20; B. 65; 1831–32) follows the scheme strictly, adding only a dramatic half cadence as an introduction and a brilliant coda. Except for the opening section of the piece, all of the repeats are written out. Both the main body of the work and the trio are completely rounded—that is, the A section appears in its entirety at the end of the B section. The outer sections are composed essentially of agitato passagework, and the trio section is more lyrical, based on a Polish folk song. The coda is short but drives hard to bring the work to an exciting conclusion.

The Scherzo in *b-flat* (Op. 31; B. 111; 1837) alters the traditional structure somewhat. The long introduction becomes an integral part of the opening section, and the section is repeated as a whole, not in A and B segments. The repeat is written out. The same procedure is used for the trio and its repeat. Then Chopin writes a full-fledged development section that employs material from both the opening section of the piece and the trio. The return, a written-out da capo, is extended by adding a brilliant coda. The addition of the development section crosses the Scherzo with the sonata-allegro form, giving the work additional strength and interest.

The Scherzo in *c-sharp* (Op. 39; B. 125; 1839) extends the traditional structure in yet another way, by returning to the trio a second time. In this work, the introduction is followed by a compact section composed of octaves. It does not repeat and is followed, in turn, by a chorale-like trio section in *E*. The trio, unlike the opening section, does reflect the two-section arrangement (A and B), and the A section is subjected to a written-out repeat. The octave section then returns in *c-sharp*, as does another statement of the trio, this time altered so that its second section becomes simply a restatement of the trio material in the parallel minor (*e*). A transition passage based on the trio theme provides a buildup to the brilliant coda that closes the work.

The Scherzo in *E* (Op. 54; B. 148; 1842) is the most elusive of the four scherzi in terms of structure and thematic design. The overall ABA pattern, representing scherzo-trio-scherzo, is easily discernible, but more detailed observation is difficult because of Chopin's propensity for mixing expository and developmental techniques, particularly in the outer sections. An opening four-note motive provides an introduction, but in this work the introductory motive permeates much of the opening section, appearing frequently and in various guises. Rapid runs and arpeggios provide a kaleidoscopic array of constantly shifting patterns and key relationships that, in turn, alternate and intertwine with the four-note motive. Thus, attempting to subdivide the outer section into block segments becomes pointless. The trio is somewhat more traditional in its thematic statement. A somber melody in *c-sharp*, perhaps akin to a barcarolle, dominates, appearing first alone and then twice more with a haunting countermelody. A long transition leads back to the scherzo section, rewritten somewhat in its final appearance. A coda based on the four-note motive that opened the piece brings the work to a moderately brilliant conclusion.

All four scherzi are notated in three-quarter time, thus keeping with the metric tradition associated with the minuet and trio and most early scherzi. Chopin, however, directs that all four be played presto, so that the pieces tend to be heard in downbeats only. The pattern of measures conforms militantly to groups of four, thus inviting the performer to count a moderate four and the listener to hear the music that way. Realization of this fact solves a number of counting problems for performers, stabilizes the pulse, and makes the counting of long rests or notes tied over for several measures quite easy.

Nocturnes

The twenty-one nocturnes span Chopin's entire creative life, from the time he was still in Warsaw up until three years before his death. Although one can observe refinement and a deepening of Chopin's style in the nocturnes, they are equally remarkable for their allegiance to the style associated with the "night piece" of the period. The term *nocturnes* (or *notturno*) had been used in the eighteenth century for a group of pieces for a small ensemble (often winds), to be played out-of-doors. John Field is given credit for applying the term to the character piece, establishing a concept in which a slow-moving, decorated melodic line is spun out over an accompaniment, creating generally a mood of calm reverie. He wrote about twenty such pieces over a period of twenty years, beginning in 1815.

Chopin expanded the concept almost from the beginning. The earliest nocturnes, two published posthumously but written in 1827 and 1830 (B. 19 and B. 49), as well as the Op. 9 (B. 54), written in 1830 and 1831, begin to point in the directions of enlarging the overall concept of the composition, decorating the melodic line more elaborately, and adding dramatic elements in the middle section of the ABA structure.

All of these concepts continue to appear throughout the nocturnes. Several of the pieces approach large-scale proportions—for example, Op. 27, no. 2 (B. 96); Op. 48, no. 1 (B. 142); or Op. 62, no. 2 (B. 161). Examples of elaborate cadenza-like decoration of returning melodies continue to occur as well, such as in Op. 27, no. 2 (B. 96), or Op. 55, no. 2 (B. 152). The concept is carried to the extent of completely rewriting the recapitulation in Op. 48, no. 1 (B. 142), and the Op. 55, no. 1 (B. 152). The concept of a contrasting middle section of dramatic proportions continues to grow in Op. 15, nos. 1 and 2 (B. 55), Op. 27, no. 1 (B.

Lento

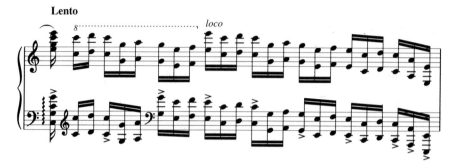

Example 13.10 Frédéric Chopin: Nocturne. Op. 48, no. 1 mm. 46
Reprinted by permission of G. Schirmer, Inc.

91), and Op. 32, no. 1 (B. 106), culminating in the Op. 48, no. 1 (B. 142), possibly the most dramatic of the nocturnes, where near-virtuoso octaves grow out of the middle section (Example 13.10).

Although many of the nocturnes are built on the ABA pattern, several are based on the alternation of two ideas, either as a written-out repeat, as in Op. 27, no. 1 (B. 91), or a simple ABAB alternation, as in the case of the Op. 37, no. 2 (B. 127), a nocturne that is etude-like in its double-note demands. Codas are often significant, as represented by the sensitive closing of the Op. 27, no. 2 (B. 96), or the unexpected, dramatic recitative that closes the Op. 32, no. 1 (B. 106).

Nowhere is Chopin's skill at harmonic inventiveness more in evidence than in the presentation of the lyrical melodies of these pieces. Whereas Chopin's contemporaries are satisfied with letting the prevailing mood carry the melody, Chopin adds surprising inflections that suggest unusual harmonic colors, quite often only a few seconds after the piece has begun—for example, the emphasis on both the minor and major third degree of the scale in the opening of the Op. 27, no. 1 (B. 91); or the surprising introduction of a raised dominant note in the Op. 27, no. 2 (B. 96); or the way in which the opening theme is reharmonized each time it appears in the Op. 62, no. 2 (B. 161). These examples represent the numerous instances where Chopin's creativity provides the nocturnes with a vitality that ensures their perennial freshness.

Mazurkas

Of the dance forms associated with Chopin, the mazurka reflects most intimately the composer's affinity with his Polish heritage. Included in the sixty-two that have been given B numbers are a number of very early works that were published posthumously. The main body of the mazurkas published during Chopin's lifetime come in sets of three, four, or five small pieces, beginning with the Op. 6 and ending with the Op. 63, their composition spanning his creative life from 1830 through 1847.

As a native dance, the mazurka derives its name from the folk known as *Mazurs* from the region of Mazovia. The dance was one for couples in which a turning motion was prominent. The triple meter was a stable characteristic, but the tempo was less so, the slowest type being known as the *kujawiak*, the moderate type as the *mazur*, and the fastest as the *obertas* (or *oberek*). Chopin provides us with examples of all three tempo types, although most of the mazurkas fall into the mazur category. However, there are a few examples of the kujawiak (Op. 17, nos. 2 and 4, B. 77; Op. 24, no. 1, B. 89; and Op. 68, no. 2, B. 18) with only two clear-cut uses of the obertas (Op. 6, no. 4, B. 60; and Op. 7, no. 4, B. 61).

Often second or third beats were accented or highlighted rhythmically through rests or syncopations (Op. 6 nos. 1 and 2, B. 60). The folk dancing was often accompanied by a wind instrument, known as a *dudy*, which was similar to a bagpipe. Chopin reflects this characteristic by frequent inclusion of a drone bass, but usually limited to a single small section (Op. 17, no. 4, B. 77, middle section). Melodic patterns often remained impervious to the major-minor key system and, when compared with traditional scales, are described as having lowered seconds, raised fourths, or flat sevenths or sometimes identified as modal inflections related to Phrygian, Lydian, or Mixolydian patterns (Op. 33, no. 1, B. 115; Op. 41, no. 1, B. 126; or Op. 56, no. 2, B. 153).

It is difficult to generalize with regard to the structure of the Chopin mazurkas, for the composer uses binary, ternary, and a variety of other patterns. Most of the pieces are, however, clearly sectional, and the structural concepts almost always rest upon the departure, alternation, or return of these small sections. Codas often figure prominently as eloquent summations, particularly in the middle and late mazurkas.

More elusive to characterize are the expressive qualities of the mazurkas, traits that are deemed by musicians to be at the heart of Chopin's individuality. Some of the mazurkas are poignant or yearning, exhibiting chromatic harmonic changes and melodic, sighing fragments (Op. 17, no. 4, B. 77; or Op. 24, no. 4, B. 89). Others utilize dotted rhythms and syncopations to create moods of unbridled vitality (Op. 17, no. 1, B. 77; or Op. 30, no. 3, B. 105). Drive and bravura are often generated by strong accentuation of weak beats (Op. 41, no. 3, B. 126; or Op. 50, no. 2, B. 145). Skillful imitation or intertwining of melodic fragments often plays an important role, particularly in the later mazurkas (Op. 50, no. 3, B. 145; or Op. 59, no. 1, B. 157).

Taken as a whole, the mazurkas focus less on virtuoso display in the ordinary sense. Their challenges stem rather from the expert handling of musical details, balance, rhythmic subtleties, melodic inflection, and deft projection of mood. Performers often pass them by in favor of Chopin works that are more brilliant. Musicians who spend time studying the mazurkas, however, almost always come away feeling that the intimacy of these works has given them a vivid realization of the composer's spirit.

Polonaises

Unlike the mazurka, which inspired relatively little interest from composers outside of Poland before Chopin, the polonaise attracted a considerable amount of attention from both regional and foreign composers. The origins of the polonaise are somewhat obscure, but it is mentioned as far back as the late sixteenth century as a ceremonial court dance rather than a folk dance. The first important polonaises, however, are by a German, Johann Sebastian Bach, who included polonaises as dance forms in the first *Brandenburg Concerto*, the sixth "French" Suite, the second *Orchestral Suite*, and as teaching material in the *Anna Magdalena Notebook*. Wilhelm Friedemann Bach, J. S. Bach's oldest son, wrote an important set of twelve polonaises, conceptualizing the polonaise as an independent piece. Occasional examples of the form before Chopin are also provided by Mozart, Beethoven, Schubert, Weber, and two lesser-known Polish composers, Josef Kozlowski (1757–1821), and his pupil, Count Michael Oginski (1765–1833). Liszt wrote two polonaises in 1852. They postdate all of Chopin's and were probably influenced by them.

The spirit of the polonaise reflects the atmosphere of the grandiose ballroom. The meter is invariably three-quarter. Characteristic are repeated notes in a rhythm that combines sixteenth and eighth notes in a military-like motivic pattern (Example 13.11). The structural point of departure for Chopin's polonaises is the minuet and trio form. The earlier polonaises adhere not only to the overall ternary, da capo structure but also to the two-part rounded pattern for both the outer sections and the trio. Repeat signs are often used, but da capo sections are almost always written out. The Op. 26 (B. 90) and Op. 40 (B. 120–21) polonaises begin to make slight alterations to the structural pattern, and the last three polonaises modify this scheme considerably, the Op. 44 (B. 135) and the Op. 53 (B. 147) by simply adding sections and the Op. 61 (B. 159), the Polonaise-Fantasie, by introducing elements of development and improvisation throughout the piece.

Of the sixteen polonaises, Chopin wrote nine between the ages of seven and nineteen. Only two of these were published during Chopin's lifetime: his very first work, a Polonaise in *g* (B. 1), written and published in 1817, and the Polonaise in *b-flat* (B. 13), inscribed *Adieu! an Wilhelm Kolberg*, composed and published in 1826. Three of the early polonaises, in *d*, *B-flat*, and *f* (B. 11, 24, and 30), appeared in print shortly after the

Example 13.11 Frédéric Chopin: Polonaise, Op. 53 mm. 57–59
Reprinted by permission of G. Schirmer, Inc.

Example 13.12 Frédéric Chopin: Polonaise, Op. 44 mm. 83–84
Reprinted by permission of G. Schirmer, Inc.

composer's death in 1855 as Op. 71. The remaining four (B. 3, 5, 7, and 36) have been published separately as they were discovered or made available up until as late as 1934.

The two polonaises of Op. 26 (B. 90) were not begun until 1834, five years removed from the last of the early polonaises. The characteristic polonaise rhythm, although present, becomes increasingly a mere reference in the course of the piece. Extended lyrical writing becomes the basis for entire sections, and elements of bravura and dramatic gesture appear with regularity. The Op. 40 (B. 120–21) set, written in 1838 and 1839, continue in the same vein as the Op. 26. The Op. 40, no. 1 (B. 120), has achieved universal fame as the "military"polonaise.

Chopin pushes these characteristics ever further in the two most extended virtuoso polonaises, the Op. 44 (B. 135) and Op. 53 (B. 147). A dramatic octave passage serves as the introductionto the Op. 44. A driving arpeggio figure forms the basis for an extra section (Example 13.12) that sets the stage for the tempo di mazurka that serves as the trio. In the Op. 53, chromatic double notes appear in the introduction, and an ostinato octave figure brings the middle section to a tremendous climax.

The extra section appears after the trio in this work, a haunting inter-mezzo that spins its lyricism like an improvisation before the return of the main body of the polonaise.

The Polonaise-Fantasie (Op. 61, B. 159; 1845–46) might be com-pared to the last scherzo (Op. 54, B. 148) in that both works rely heavi-ly on a continuous use of both improvisation and development. The introduction to the Polonaise-Fantasie sets forth a dotted-note rhythm in alternation with slow, improvisatory arpeggios. Each of the four times this combination appears seems to introduce a new tonal center. As soon as the dotted-note figure takes over, it is put through several chromatic modulations in a contrapuntal texture, all of which suggests develop-ment. After the main theme is set up with a polonaise rhythm, its open-ing phrase appears in *A-flat* three times initially, but each time it veers off in a different direction, suggesting, once again, elements of development and unrest. This spirit pervades the entire opening section. The middle section begins as a more stable expression in *B*, but it too begins to be interrupted by quotations from the opening section and the introduc-tion. When the return finally takes place, the material is completely rewritten in such a way that the work comes to a brilliant climax before it closes. The Polonaise-Fantasie is a remarkable piece in that its com-plexities defy neat, traditional categories, and yet it is a highly imagina-tive work that comes off extremely well in performance.

The *Andante spianato and Grande Polonaise* (Op. 22; B. 88; 1830–31) was originally written for piano and orchestra. The opening andante is composed of two parts: a placid, lyrical melody and a section of cadence-like chords. After a short introduction, the polonaise enters with a high-ly decorated line. There follow two episodes, joined by cadenza-like, bravura transitions, and an extended coda that is obviously geared toward creating excitement.

Waltzes

The emergence of the waltz as an extended piece that reflected the elegance of the ballroom patronized by the upper class is a phenomenon of the early nineteenth century. The German ländler are cited as a fore-runner of the waltz, and one can find examples in Beethoven and Schubert that conform to the typical pattern of short, two-part dances, often to be played in pairs in a da capo arrangement. As the waltz devel-oped in the early nineteenth century, it grew in length, adding dimensions of bravura and brilliance as well as a characteristic "lilt" that resulted from rhythmic patterns that tend to bend the regularity of the second and third beats in three-quarter time. Among the earliest examples of this expand-ed waltz are the *Aufforderung zum Tanz* (Invitation to the Dance), written in 1819 by Carl Maria von Weber, and, for orchestra, the Op. 1 set written by Johann Strauss (senior) in 1826. The earlier Chopin waltzes, although published posthumously, were right on the cutting edge of the development of the new concept, and, insofar as the keyboard waltz is concerned, Chopin must be credited with being its principal pioneer.

Of the seventeen waltzes, nine were published posthumously. Publication after Chopin's death does not necessarily suggest in this case that the pieces are immature works. Although some of the posthumous waltzes are very early, those published as Op. 69 (B. 35 and B. 95) and Op. 70 (B. 92 and B. 138) were written when Chopin was in his twenties, represent the composer admirably, and are well established in the repertoire. Even one of the four very early waltzes, B. 56 in *e*, must be included in the active repertoire.

Between 1831 and 1847, Chopin wrote and saw published the remaining eight waltzes. Of these, two are substantial enough to warrant being published alone, the Op. 18 (B. 62; 1831–34) and the Op. 42 (B. 131; 1840). The Op. 34 (B. 64, B. 94, and B. 118; 1835–38) and the Op. 64 (B. 164; 1846–47) each contain three waltzes. All of the waltzes are built in sections, the shorter ones as simple as ABA and the longer ones adding more departures from the opening material. The more brilliant waltzes often include a short introduction and a coda designed to bring the piece to an exciting close. To be noted also is Chopin's fondness for writing waltzes of a wistful, melancholic nature. In six of the waltzes, tempo indications of *Lento*, *Moderato*, or *Tempo giusto* set a more unhurried pace, and the writing is more lyrical and reflective rather than being consumed with efforts toward grandeur and brilliance.

Most of the waltzes have achieved considerable popularity, for they are played by students, amateurs, and professionals. A few of the waltzes are among the best-known piano pieces in the culture: the short Op. 64, no. 1 (B. 164), nicknamed the "Minute" Waltz; the Op. 34, no. 2 (B. 64), with an opening so filled with melancholy that it has even been subjected to parody; or the Op. 64 no. 2 (B. 164), which opens with a pair of chromatic double sixths that capture a spirit of wistful lilt.

Impromptus

The use of the term *impromptu* as a designation for a character piece can be observed several times before Chopin adopted it. Both the sets of impromptus by Schubert and the Op. 5 of Schumann had been written by the time Chopin wrote the first of his four impromptus. One can speculate that Chopin might have been influenced by the Bohemian composer Johann Hugo Voříšek, who went to Vienna in 1813 and who wrote a set of impromptus in 1822. Chopin wrote his four impromptus between 1834 and 1842. Curiously, the most famous of the four, the Fantasie-Impromptu, Op. 66 (B. 87), was the only one published posthumously. In general the term *impromptu* seemed to suggest more an attitude of spontaneity with regard to the expressive qualities of the music than a freedom of structure, for impromptus are most often cast in some traditional structure, such as ABA, a theme and variations, or occasionally sonata-allegro.

The four impromptus of Chopin are all sectional, conforming in general to an ABA pattern with regular phrase structures predominating in the Op. 66 (B. 87) and Op. 29 (B. 110) and slightly more irregular arrangements in the Op. 36 (B. 129) and the Op. 51 (B. 149). The Op. 66 (B. 87) is famous for its middle-section melody, popularized by commercial arrangements with added lyrics, and is notorious for the polyrhythmic difficulties of its outer sections, where groups of six in the left hand are to be played against groups of eight in the right.

The middle sections of each of the other impromptus present imaginative contrasting material: in the Op. 29 (B. 110), a simple melody is repeated with highly ornamented decorations; the Op. 36 (B. 129) presents octaves in a driving crescendo; and the Op. 51 (B. 149) is a cantabile, long melody in the left hand. The Op. 66 (B. 87), Op. 29 (B. 110), and Op. 51 (B. 149) present more lively material in the outer sections with the middle section being lyrical, while the Op. 36 reverses this arrangement.

Rondos

The three rondos, Op. 1 (B. 10), Op. 5 (B. 15), and Op.16 (B. 76), are all early works and, like the first sonata, are pretty much neglected by pianists, most of whom opt for a more fully formed Chopin style. The works are, however, not trifles by any means. They are of substantial length, contain bravura passagework, contrasting sections of lyric melody, and brilliant final measures. The Op. 5 is designated *Rondo à la mazurka*, and the Op. 16 is extended by the addition of an introduction that features florid cadenza-like figures. Pieces like these would probably enjoy more attention were it not for the fact that they are eclipsed by much more effective examples of the same composer's work.

Barcarolle

In the first half of the nineteenth century, the romance of the city of Venice was reflected by a number of stylized compositions loosely based on the songs of the Venetian gondoliers. Barcarolles occur in a number of operas of the period that are set in Venice: Hérold's *Zampa* (1831), Auber's *Fra Diavolo* (1830), and Offenbach's *Tales of Hoffmann* (1831), which contains perhaps the most famous barcarolle of the period. Examples in keyboard music occur in Mendelssohn's *Songs without Words* (Op. 19, no. 6; Op. 30, no. 6; and Op. 62, no. 5); the Op. 60 (B. 158) of Chopin; and later in the works of Fauré. The barcarolle style simulates the lapping of the waves on the gondola by the use of a gentle, long-short rhythmic patten in six-eight or twelve-eight time. The style shows itself periodically as thematic material of longer works. The opening of Chopin's second ballade, Op. 38 (B. 102), and the second theme of the nocturne in *G,* Op. 37, no. 2 (B. 127), are cases in point.

The Barcarolle, Op. 60 (B. 158; 1845–46), is an elaborate setting of the boat-song concept, its ABA structure being extended by a short introduction, a long improvisatory retransition, and a dramatic coda in which the retransition material appears in a bravura arrangement. The main theme bristles with trills and double notes, so that the mood of the piece becomes one of intensity rather than repose. That intensity reaches agitato proportions in the return of the main theme and the coda. The work well deserves the frequent performances pianists accord it.

Berceuse

A berceuse is defined as an instrumental piece that imitates the songlike lullaby and the rocking of a cradle. Interestingly enough, Chopin's Op. 57 (B. 154) is almost always used to exemplify this generic type. This fact suggests that the use of the term as a designation for a character piece was not widespread, even in the nineteenth century, and that Chopin's contribution is by far the most ambitious and effective. The composition itself is unusual in that it is constructed over a recurring tonic-dominant harmonic alternation, a device that suggests the calm that occurs just before sleep. Over this repetitious harmonic pattern is spun a cantabile melody with seemingly endless ornamentation and figural variation. Graceful cadenza-like figurations, runs, and double notes all combine to create a mood of elegant repose, so that the piece is able to work its magic within its limited harmonic vocabulary.

Other Pieces

Two character pieces of substantial length are among those works of Chopin that are pretty much neglected: the Bolero, Op. 19 (B. 81), and the Tarentelle, Op. 43 (B. 139). Both are in a basic ABA format, the Bolero opening with a long introduction and both closing with a coda that brings back middle-section material. The length and character of these two pieces are reminiscent of the impromptus, showing elements of virtuosity. They should probably be given more attention than they currently get.

The *Allegro de concert,* Op. 46 (B. 72), is curious in that it was finished as late as 1841, is a bravura display piece of considerable proportions, and yet remains very seldom played. Its obvious catering to virtuosic display may have resulted in a devaluation of the work by those musicians who turn to other of the composer's works from the same time.

There are four sets of variations, all on melodies that were in vogue at the time. Three charming vignettes called *Écossaises* make up part of the Op. 72 (B. 12). They frequently enchant audiences as short encores on piano recitals. Other small pieces include two funeral marches and several album-leaf length miniatures that carry various titles: Contradanse, Cantabile, Largo, *Feuille d'album*. There is even a little, two-voiced fugue in *a* (B. 144), probably intended as a teaching piece.

CHAPTER FOURTEEN

Franz Liszt

The musical career of Franz Liszt (b. Raiding, Hungary, Oct. 22, 1811; d. Bayreuth, Jul. 31, 1886) was extraordinary in that it combined achievements as a virtuoso performer, a champion and conductor of new music, a composer of works in a variety of genres, and a teacher of enormous influence. Liszt's father, Adam, was an official in the service of Prince Nikolaus Esterházy. Adam was a creditable musician, and he devoted himself diligently to the development of his son. Franz's lessons with Adam, begun at the age of six, resulted in a local public performance three years later. As other performances ensued, several Hungarian noblemen pooled their resources to provide a stipend for six years of the boy's musical education.

A move to Vienna was undertaken in 1821. Here, regular lessons took place in piano with Czerny, who reportedly taught him without payment, and in composition with Salieri. Liszt met Beethoven, and the impact of that meeting on the lad was so strong that Liszt was a devotee of Beethoven's music for the rest of his career, championing the piano works and, at one point, undertaking a long concert tour in order to raise money for a Beethoven monument at Bonn.

Less than two years after the move to Vienna, however, Liszt's father decided to push on to Paris, where it was planned to enroll Franz in the Paris Conservatory. Cherubini, then director of the conservatory, opposed the concept of child prodigies and, on the pretext that the conservatory could not admit foreigners, declined admission. Thus, from the age of twelve, Liszt was without pianistic guidance. He studied composition with Antoine Reicha in Paris for a time but was soon devoting himself to concert tours. When Liszt was seventeen, his father died. The young Liszt settled in Paris, supporting himself and his mother by giving performances as well as by doing some teaching and editing. Like Chopin, Liszt soon became celebrated in Parisian society and counted among his close friends Chopin, Berlioz, Paganini, Rossini, Victor Hugo, and Lamartine. Like Chopin, Liszt formed a relationship with a woman of literary aspirations, in this case the Countess d'Agoult, whose pseudonym was Daniel Stern. Although the relationship lasted for about ten years, it was at its height during the years 1835–39, when the couple retired to Geneva, where three children were born to them.

Returning to public life in 1839, Liszt concertized extensively throughout central Europe, Spain, Portugal, the Balkan countries, Turkey, and Russia. In 1847, however, he began to change his goals dramatically, for he played his final concert for pay in that year, forsaking the concert stage. The following year he accepted the post of Kapellmeister at Weimar, a position offered to him with the understanding that he would focus on nurturing contemporary musical art. It was in this capacity that Liszt gained recognition for the music of Wagner and Berlioz.

The years at Weimar also saw the formation of a new personal relationship. The Princess Carolyne Sayn-Wittgenstein left her husband and took up residence with Liszt in Weimar. A woman of intellect, the Princess Carolyne confirmed Liszt's resolve to devote himself to serious composition, teaching, and the support of contemporary music rather than to an adoring public as a keyboard virtuoso. It was at Weimar during this period that the first small class of regular students was formed, a class that included the American pianist William Mason. That class was to grow to enormous proportions and to include many, if not most, of the illustrious names of pianism of the late nineteenth and early twentieth centuries: Hans von Bülow, Carl Tausig, Rafael Joseffy, Eugene d'Albert, Alexander Siloti, Arthur Friedheim, Adele aus der Ohe, Sophie Menter, Emil von Sauer, Frederic Lamond, Bernard Stavenhagen, and José Vianna da Motta, to mention but a few.

It was during the Weimar period also that the most intense activity in composition was sustained. The orchestral tone poems, written at this time, define the concept of the genre; new keyboard works were undertaken; and several earlier keyboard works underwent extensive revision. Now eschewing mere virtuoso display, Liszt seemed increasingly directed toward musical, expressive values and concepts with lofty philosophical or literary connections.

The next major shift in Liszt's life took place in 1859, when he left his post at Weimar, moving to Rome to live in semiretirement, but continuing to compose. In 1866, Pope Pius conferred minor orders of the Catholic church on him, giving him the title of Abbé. In 1870, however, Liszt began to drift back into professional activity, accepting conducting again at Weimar as well as the presidency of the New Hungarian Academy of Music in Budapest in 1875. These activities resulted in his spending part of the year in Rome, part in Weimar, and part in Budapest during the last years of his life. He died in Bayreuth during a Wagner festival, and his grave site is in that city.

The early years of Liszt's career were focused on public performing as the ultimate virtuoso and as a learned, cultured artist. In an often-quoted letter written in 1832, when Liszt was twenty-two, he wrote:

For this fortnight, my mind and my fingers have worked like two damned ones. Homer, the Bible, Plato, Locke, Byron, Lamartine, Chateaubriand, Beethoven, Bach, Hummel, Mozart, Weber are all around me. I study them. I devour them with fury; furthermore I practice exercises for four or five hours (thirds, sixths, octaves, tremolos, repeated notes, cadences, etc.). Ah, unless I go mad, you will find an artist in me.

These assiduous work habits were combined with a flair for the dramatic on stage and striking good looks. Liszt is given credit for popularizing the word *recital* in conjunction with piano performance and shares with Dussek the credit for turning the piano so that the player's profile is seen by the audience. Liszt regularly had two or three pianos on stage, so that all sections of the audience would have ample opportunity to see him and sense the nearness of his presence. He made a great show of taking off his gloves before beginning to play. By all contemporary reports, the expressions that crossed his face during performance reflected extreme emotional states. He tossed his head around and waved his arms high during the performances. Many contemporary accounts speak of the near hysteria, the trembling, or the fainting generated at his recitals. Moreover, Liszt's magnetism was supplemented by a reputation for sexual exploits, so the women in his audience were particularly susceptible to his theatrics.

It would be a mistake, however, to assume that the magic of Liszt's art as a performer was based only on showmanship. His playing was greatly admired by fellow musicians, including many who were tough to impress, such as Robert and Clara Schumann as well as Frederich Wieck. Furthermore, when Liszt chose to play for his colleagues, as he did in a series of two recitals given at the Érard salon in Paris in 1836, he selected only the best repertoire, including challenges such as the Op. 106 of Beethoven. Those recitals were reviewed ecstatically by Berlioz. There is also the testimony of many fine musicians who sought Liszt out as a teacher and who heard Liszt play repeatedly in master classes. Without question, then, Liszt's reputation as the greatest virtuoso performer of his time was well deserved by musical standards.

Liszt's creativity as a composer is often shortchanged by those who think of his keyboard works primarily as vehicles for virtuoso display. It is true that in the early part of his career some pieces were geared toward inciting response from his adoring audiences. Some of these, indeed, might understandably be accused of being devoid of serious intent. But Liszt's involvement with artistic, high-minded goals was always present as an alternative mood, even in those years when he was pursuing a public career. Those years produced the Schubert song transcriptions, works that show Liszt's respect and devotion to Schubert's music as well as Liszt's own attention to beauty of detail. Most of the first two volumes of the *Années de pèlerinage,* high-minded pieces rife with

references to art and literature, was completed before Liszt forsook public performance by accepting the Weimar position. Furthermore, many
of the early works that did indulge in technical display to an extreme
degree were revised by Liszt, always in the direction of replacing athletic challenges with more refined musical values that, in turn, brought
their own challenges.

The Weimar years were dedicated primarily to the composition of
the orchestral tone poems, and the influence of the concept of that genre
can be seen periodically throughout the piano works. Pieces such as
"Vallée d'Obermann" and "Bénédiction de Dieu dans la solitude" are so
long and involved that they seem closer to the tone poem than to the
character piece. Both sonatas are conceptually much like tone poems,
being cast in a single movement and using techniques of thematic transformation that are associated typically with the tone poem. During this
period, Liszt seemed to enlist virtuoso techniques primarily as a means
to serve musical ends, and he was quite consistent in linking his work
with serious literary or philosophical ideas. During this period, moreover, there begins to be a preponderance of lyrical writing, along with
slower tempo markings.

In the last years, after Liszt's move to Rome, the amount of music
written on a virtuoso level decreases significantly, and the emphasis is on
very short, unpretentious character pieces. The fascination of this late
music lies in its prophetic harmonic procedures. Without abandoning
tonality altogether, Liszt wrote music built on unresolved dissonant relationships, vague harmonic progressions that often shift chromatically,
and textures that frequently use slow-moving ostinato patterns, tremolos, and long, monophonic recitatives. The resulting effect is one that
foreshadows sounds associated with the early twentieth century, sounds
often heard, for example, in the music of Debussy or Bartók.

The significance and extent of Liszt's work as a transcriber is often
overlooked by twentieth-century musicians, partly because the use of
transcription on concert programs has declined in both popularity and
acceptance. The amount of work Liszt did in this area is overwhelming.
It encompasses music from opera, lieder by several nineteenth-century
composers, and large segments of the orchestral repertoire, including all
of the Beethoven symphonies. Some of this work runs over into virtuosic
paraphrase, but much of it is simply faithful, expert transferring of the
music to the keyboard, sometimes for two hands, sometimes for four,
work undertaken by Liszt out of respect and love for the music itself.

As a composer Liszt reflected the emotionally charged characteristics
of his own life-style. Dramatic intensity pervades the music, and even the
commonplace is couched in settings that suggest importance. Emotional
states are often pushed to the extreme: the strong emerges as the heroic,
the sad becomes the tragic. Frequent chromatic shifts of harmony enhance
the expressive palette, and lyrical, melodic lines are often decorated with

lengthy, glittering cadenzas. Programmatic titles seldom refer to the unimposing but rather focus often on references to monumental works of art or literature, profound philosophical or religious concepts, or events of great significance. Technical display, so often decried by Liszt's critics, is, nevertheless, wrought with the skill and imagination of a master virtuoso, and generations of pianists have reveled in the challenge and the beauty of such handiwork. Liszt's expressive language lies at the very heart of the emotional extravagance of the late nineteenth century, and his eloquence still calls up the icons of that age with great clarity.

The earliest available catalogue for Liszt's works comes from the ongoing project to publish the composer's complete works, an undertaking begun in 1905 by a committee of distinguished scholars, many of whom were Liszt's students, and the publishing firm of Breitkopf und Härtel. In 1970, a more recent undertaking to publish the complete works of Liszt was begun by Bärenreiter and Editio Musica Budapest, and about a dozen volumes of piano music have appeared since the project began. The chronology is the result of the work of several scholars. The first complete chronology was provided by Peter Raabe, who was for many years the director of the Liszt Museum at Weimar. His 1931 biography of Liszt remains a standard work and contains the chronology. Raabe's list was, however, quickly outdated as new research uncovered more works and information about the works. A second and more accurate list was completed by Sir Humphrey Searle, the English composer and scholar, in *Grove's Dictionary* in 1954 and continues to be updated with each new edition of Grove's. For purposes of identification, S numbers are often used by scholars. Most recently, the American scholar Alan Walker has provided an additional chronology in which there is easy thematic cross-indexing, an important tool in light of Liszt's habit of transferring material from piece to piece. The enormous amount of music in the Liszt catalogue, coupled with the composer's habit of making revisions of pieces published earlier, all add up to a body of works that is difficult to encompass and identify in definitive form. In the everyday world of the professional pianist, the use of titles most often serves as the practical, if somewhat imprecise, mode of communication. The following text follows that practice but also provides S numbers.

Etudes

Liszt wrote the earlier versions of the two largest sets of etudes before his move to Weimar, the first versions of the *Études d'exécution transcendante* (Transcendental Etudes; S.139) appearing in 1827 and 1839 and the earlier version of the *Études d'éxécution transcendante d'après Paganini* (Paganini Etudes; S. 140) coming out in 1840. In the case of the 1852 revision of the twelve *Transcendental Etudes*, the revisions consist of careful rewriting that often removes extra double notes (nos. 4, 5, and

12, for example), simplifies passages so that they lie more easily under the hand (nos. 2, 6, 11), thins out textures (nos. 6, 8, and 12), deletes impossibly awkward skips (no. 10), omits redundant sections (no. 8), and adds contrapuntal interest (no. 2). In the case of the *Paganini Etudes*, the later 1851 version is clearly in the direction of making extremely thick textures more manageable and more sensitive to the resonance of the instrument. The later versions are the ones played in concert, the earlier ones of interest simply as a means of studying how Liszt came to realize that fewer notes often work more effectively, even when attempting to storm virtuosic heights. A few additions also took place in the revised versions, such as writing an introduction to "Mazeppa" and the inclusion of descriptive titles for nine of the *Transcendental Etudes*: "Paysage" (Landscape), "Mazeppa" (the name of a legendary folk hero), "Feux follets" (Fireflies), "Vision" (Vision), "Eroica" (Heroic), "Wilde Jagd" (Wild Hunt), "Ricordanza" (Remembrance), "Harmonies du soir" (Harmonies of the Evening), and "Chasse-neige" (Snow Flurries).

From the first version, the key scheme for the *Transcendental Etudes* was apparent: major and relative minor, going around the circle of fifths adding flats (*C, a, F, d,* etc.). Only half of the circle is completed in the twelve studies, ending with the "Chasse-neige" in *b-flat*. The *Transcendental Etudes* tend not to be focused on a single problem in each etude, as do, for example, the Chopin etudes. Octaves, double notes, rolled chords, skips, cadenzas, and passages of rapid scales or arpeggios all tend to be pervasive throughout the studies. An exception to this generalization, however, can be cited: the "Feux follets," which concentrates mostly on double-note techniques. Sectional arrangements serve as a basis for the structures of the etudes, although they tend not to conform as regularly to the ABA mold as do the Chopin studies.

Liszt followed the examples of Schumann's Opp. 3 and 10 in writing studies based on Paganini's *Caprices for Unaccompanied Violin*, Op. 1. Liszt dedicated his set to Clara, and in 1842 Robert wrote a review that pointed out that his own adaptations underscored the poetic side of Paganini's work and Liszt emphasized the virtuoso side. The famous "La campanella" appears as etude no. 3, it being the first Liszt transcribed (Example 14.1), the earliest version dating from 1830. Etude no. 5, a study for double notes, is known as "La Chasse," and the last one is a set of twelve variations on the theme that was to become frequently used by composers as the basis for variations, sets being written later by Brahms, Rachmaninoff, and Lutoslawski (Example 14.2).

The remaining etudes were all written after the composer's interest in public performance had waned. The 1849 set of three *Études de concert* (S. 144) appeared as *3 caprices poétiques* in its Parisian edition with the descriptive subtitlesof "Il lamento" (The Lament), "La leggierezza" (Lightness or Swiftness), and "Un sospiro" (A Sigh). A shorter version of the 1852 "Ab irato" (Irateness; S. 143) was prepared for Moscheles and

Example 14.1 Franz Liszt: *Paganini Etude* no. 3 ("La Campanella") mm. 4–5

Example 14.2 Franz Liszt: *Paganini Etude* no. 6 mm. 1–4

Fétis's *Méthode des méthodes* of 1837, and the two concert etudes of 1862 and 1863 (S. 145), the "Waldesrauschen" (Forest Rustling) and "Gnomenreigen" (Dance of the Gnomes), were composed for Lebert and Stark's *Grosse theoretisch-praktische Klavierschule*. With the possible exception of the rage expressed in "Ab irato," these later etudes were conceived as much to emphasize poetic qualities as virtuoso display.

The final revision of the *Transcendental Etudes* and the later sets of *Concert Etudes* especially represent a cross-pollination between the concept of the etude and that of the tone poem. Technical difficulties abound, it is true, but the fact that they are interlaced with dramatic, orchestral-like gestures, and often decorate long, lyrical lines, results in music that sounds far removed from didactic goals. Whereas with the Chopin studies, miracles of musical expression that they are, one can still see a connection between the concept of developing technical skill and the composition, such a connection becomes so tenuous in many of the Liszt studies that the composer might just as easily have called them "poems" or "ballades" or "rhapsodies." This ambiguity and the fact that they tend to be somewhat longer than the traditional etude has led performers to program them singly much of the time, set among other genres from the same composer, perhaps, rather than in groups, as in the case of the Chopin studies. Complete performances of a set of the

Chopin studies, too, are quite often encountered, but rarely does a pianist undertake the arduous task of playing the complete *Transcendental Etudes*, the complete *Paganini*, or even the complete shorter sets of two or three *Concert Etudes*. Favorites from the Liszt etudes continue to receive widespread attention: "La campanella," "Gnomenreigen," the Paganini variations, or the *Transcendental Etudes* no. 10, for example. There is also, however, much imaginative, challenging music in these sets that continues to be somewhat neglected.

Années de pèlerinage

The *Années de pèlerinage* (Years of Pilgrimage) consist of three books of character pieces, the second book being attended by a supplement, written over an extended period of Liszt's life, from as early as 1835 to 1877. The first two books, subtitled *Suisse* (Switzerland; S. 160) and *Italie* (Italy; S. 161), as well as the supplement to *Italie*, subtitled *Venezia e Napoli* (Venice and Naples; S. 162), were written in the late 1830s and the decade up to 1850, just before Liszt decided to move to Weimar. *Suisse* was written as a result of the years Liszt spent there with the Countess d'Agoult and *Italie* as a result of memoirs of his many visits to Italy. Early versions of several of the pieces were published in 1842 in the *Album d'un voyageur* (S. 156), but the final versions were not published until 1855 and 1858, with the supplement coming out in 1861. As with the etudes, Liszt continued to revise and refine these works during the Weimar period, when he was devoting his energy primarily to composing.

In the first two books, Liszt exemplifies the Romantic impulse by linking many of the pieces to recognized masterworks of art or literature. The concept of the pilgrimage itself is probably an offshoot of Byron's *Childe Harold's Pilgrimage*. From the first volume, "Chapelle de Guillame Tell" (Chapel of William Tell) and "Au bord d'une source" (By the Fountainhead) were inspired by works of Schiller, "Au lac du Wallenstadt" (The Lake at Wallenstadt) and "Les Cloches de Genève" (The Bells of Geneva) by Byron's poems, and the "Vallée d'Obermann" by de Senancour's romance novel, popular at the time.

From *Italie*, literary inspiration is drawn from three sonnets of the fourteenth-century poet Petrarch and, for the longest piece of the set, "Après une lecture du Dante, fantasia quasi sonata," from Dante, possibly the *Divine Comedy* itself and possibly a short poem by Victor Hugo that reflects on the Dante work. Also in this volume are two references to works of art, "Sposalizio" referring to the Raphael painting *La sposalizio della vergine* (The Marriage of the Virgin) and "Il pensieroso" to Michelangelo's statue of Giuliano de' Medici in Florence.

The supplement to the second book, *Venezia e Napoli*, is without reference to artworks, being purely descriptive of the ambience Liszt encountered in Venice and Naples. These pieces date from 1839, and the "Tarantella" is a throwback to the blatantly virtuoso writing of Liszt's earlier years.

The third volume, simply called *Troisième année* (Third Year; S. 163), contains two references to literature. "Sunt lacrymae rerum" is from line 462 of book 1 of Virgil's *Aeneid*. The original refers to the fall of Troy, but Liszt applies its meaning to the 1848–49 Hungarian struggle for independence. The second reference is a short quotation from Propertius that is inscribed at the beginning of the funeral march written in memory of Maximilian I, emperor of Mexico. A somewhat personal connection with an artwork was apparent in the first edition of the volume, wherein the title page of the "Angelus" was adorned with a portion of Paul von Joukowsky's allegorical painting of the Wagner family, Liszt's three grandchildren being depicted as the presiding angels. Otherwise, "Angelus" simply refers to the bell that calls the faithful to prayer. Of the other four pieces in the third volume, three describe the cypresses and fountains of the Villa d'Este at Tivoli, a sixteenth-century castle where Cardinal Hohenlohe provided Liszt with a suite of rooms for many years, starting from about 1864; and the "Sursum corda" is from the preface to the Mass.

The music in the sets of the *années* varies considerably both in style and length, so much so that the relative modest dimensions and focus usually associated with the character piece are frequently absent. "Vallée d'Obermann" and "Après une lecture de Dante, fantasia quasi una sonata" are certainly reminiscent of orchestral tone poems, and even somewhat shorter pieces are often endowed with sweeping dramatic effects, extravagant cadenzas, and recitatives, musical gestures that are much grander than those found in typical character pieces of the time.

The *Troisième année* was written between 1866 and 1877, more than twenty years after the early versions of the first two volumes. Thus, the music of this volume belongs to the period acknowledged as "late Liszt," and it exhibits stylistic characteristics that in general underscore somber moods, have but little virtuoso display, contain long, introspective sections, and often indulge in harmonic experimentation. Examples of such experiments are the "Hungarian" augmented seconds of the "Sunt lacrymae rerum" or the use of whole-tone relationships in "Sursum corda." As a result, of the seven pieces in the set, only "Les Jeux d'eau à la villa d'Este" (The Fountains of the Villa d'Este) is found with regularity on concert programs, with an occasional performance accorded one of the two threnodies entitled "Aux cyprès de la villa d'Este" (The Cypresses of the Villa d'Este). The fountain piece is often cited as a forerunner to Ravel's "Jeux d'eau," written some thirty years later, and indeed the Liszt work is filled with tremolos, arpeggiated figuration, and sonic effects that simulate water displays (Example 14.3).

Structurally, the pieces from the three volumes exhibit various arrangements of section-blocks. These are often disguised in their returning form by considerable alteration in settings: new accompaniments,

Example 14.3   Franz Liszt: "Les Jeux d'eau à la villa d'Este" m. 1

reworked supporting harmony, added cadenzas or passagework. These changes are frequently so elaborate that the introduction of new thematic material in contrasting sections becomes unnecessary, enough contrast being provided by a repetition of the thematic material in its new guise. Contrapuntal writing is not often encountered, and traditional structures, such as sonata-allegro, rondo, or minuet and trio, are absent. Even the "Dante Sonata" bears little resemblance to traditional sonata structure.

Harmonic interest is heightened by chromatic alterations, chords borrowed from another key, and chordal shifts over the interval of a third. Introductions appear frequently and are often ambiguous or vague with regard to tonality, eventually settling into the key of the piece as the first theme is ready to be announced. Codas, on the other hand, tend to be clearly key-oriented and often provide a sense of settling down to final rest in the chosen tonality. The majority of the pieces close poetically, often softly, and, even when forte endings are called for, a declaratory style is favored rather than one designed to elicit wild audience response.

The popularity of the pieces in the *Années de pèlerinage* varies considerably. Works such as the three Petrarch sonnets or the "Dante Sonata" remain firmly entrenched in the concert-hall repertoire. At the other end of the spectrum, there are pieces in all three books that are seldom heard, and, as already pointed out, the *Troisième année* is almost completely neglected. The corollary of this observation is that the sets of pieces are almost never undertaken in their entirety in concert, performers preferring rather to pick and choose whenever they play this music. This patchwork state of affairs is one that the adventurous might indeed do well to rectify.

Harmonies poétiques et religieuses

Written between 1845 and 1852, the *Harmonies poétiques et religieuses* (S. 173) exhibits many of the same characteristics as the sets of *Années de pèlerinage*. The title comes from the Lamartine work bearing the same name. Text that reflects on the power, ecstasy, and consolation of prayer is inscribed at the opening of the set of pieces as well as before "Invocation," "Bénédiction de Dieu dans la solitude," and "Andante lagrimoso." Of the

Example 14.4 Franz Liszt: "Funérailles" mm. 133–36

ten pieces that make up the set, four have liturgical text in Latin printed above or below the music itself, almost in the manner of a vocal setting. In the "Ave Maria," the text appears intermittently throughout the piece. The "Pensée des morts" uses a portion of Psalm 129, *De profundis,* briefly in its middle section. The "Pater noster" is virtually a setting of the Lord's Prayer, and the "Miserere d'après Palestrina" opens with the appropriate liturgical text. The "Pensée des morts" was composed in 1834 originally under the title of "Harmonies poétiques et religieuses," a duplication that occasionally invites some confusion, and the other three pieces with Latin text were originally choral works written about 1845.

The two pieces most frequently encountered in performance are the "Bénédiction de Dieu dans la solitude" and the "Funérailles." Both are imposing, long works of tone-poem dimensions, cast essentially in ABA form. The contemplative, elevated mood of the "Bénédiction de Dieu dans la solitude" is sustained throughout the work, giving it a tran- scendental intensity that one would be hard pressed to find in any other of Liszt's keyboard works. The "Funérailles" is believed to honor three patriots who died during the downfall of the Hungarian revolution. The date inscribed on the piece, October 1849, is also that of Chopin's death (Oct. 17), a fact that has invited some to speculate as to a possible con- nection. The "Funérailles" is one of Liszt's most popular works, for its effective dramatic contrasts are heightened by a military-like middle sec- tion, accompanied by an ostinato pattern of bravura octaves. These octaves are among the most famous in all of keyboard literature, and their effect and physical challenge have continued to attract generations of pianists (Example 14.4).

Other Character Pieces

Liszt wrote many character pieces that, like some of those in the *Années de pèlerinage* and the *Harmonies poétiques et religieuses,* have dimensions of tone poems, often bear descriptive titles or literary references, and blend elements of virtuosity, lyricism, and dramatic contrast into some arrangement of sectional structure. Other character pieces are more modest, pared down to one idea or a set of contrasting ideas, and conceptually show more similarity with character pieces of the time by other composers. Some of the character pieces are among Liszt's most frequently played compositions. Others have fallen into neglect, undeservingly, and some because of questionable quality. A partial list of these works follows:

- "Impromptu brillant sur des thèmes de Rossini et Spontini" (ca. 1824; S. 150), an early work published as Op. 2, based on material from the operas *La donna del lago, Armida, Olympie,* and *Fernand Cortez.*

- "Harmonies poétiques et religieuses" (1834; S. 154), the original version of "Pensée des morts," the fourth piece of the set called *Harmonies poétiques et religieuses.* This version was also inscribed with the preface of the Lamartine collection of poems of the same name. Sketches for this version suggest that the work was conceived for piano and orchestra. Another sketch for a work for piano and orchestra, "Psaume instrumental—De profundis," was incorporated into the later version.

- *Apparitions* (1834; S. 155), three short, fantasy-like pieces with a title inspired by songs of French violinist Chrétien Urhan. The third piece is based on a Schubert waltz and was transformed into the fourth *Soirées de Vienne.*

- "Lyon" (1834), a piece published in the *Album d'un voyageur* (S. 156) but dropped when the collection was published in its revised version as the first volume of the *Années de pèlerinage.* The work is dedicated to the writer and philosopher Lamennais, with whom Liszt shared sympathies regarding social injustice, and inspired by a workers' uprising in the city of Lyon, France.

- *Fantasie romantique sur deux mélodies Suisses* (1836; S.157), a work written in Switzerland at about the same time as the *Album d'un voyageur* (the early version of the Switzerland segment of the *Années de pèlerinage*).

- *Elégie sur des motifs de prince Louis Ferdinand de Prusse* (1842; S. 168), the first of three elegies Liszt wrote, the two later ones being known as the "first and second" elegies.

- Two ballades (S. 170 and 171), the shorter and less-frequently played in *D-flat* (1849) and the more successful in *b* (1854).

- *Consolations* (1849–50; S. 172), six small lyrical pieces often used as teaching material, the third in *D-flat* being the most frequently encountered.

- Berceuse (1854, revised in 1862; S. 174), believed to have been influenced by Chopin's more famous Berceuse, partly evidenced by its being written in the same key *(D-flat).*

- *Légendes* (1863; S. 175)—1: "St. François d'Assise: La prédication aux oiseaux" (St. Francis of Assisi Preaching to the Birds); and 2: "St. François de Paule marchant sur les flots" (St. Francis of Paola Walking on the Waves)—two highly descriptive pieces based on traditional stories from the careers of the two saints. The first describes St. Francis of Assisi being moved to share God's word with creatures of nature. It is filled with arpeggios and trill-like passagework that imitate bird sounds and alternate with appropriate chordal or recitative-like passages representing the sermon itself. The second legend is based on an incident in which St. Francis of Paola is challenged to prove the power of God by walking on the water as Jesus is reported to have done. Bass tremolos, chromatic runs, and scales provide a setting for a stately chorale-like theme. The piece breaks out into a stormy section built on double-note runs and diminished-seventh harmonies, but the chorale returns triumphantly before the coda.

- *Weihnachtsbaum* (Christmas Tree; 1875–76; S. 186), a suite of twelve small pieces that include arrangements of carols ("Good Christian Men, Rejoice!"; "0, Come! All Ye Faithful"), bell pieces, musical descriptions of holiday scenes (the scherzo that depicts lighting the candles on the Christmas tree), and a nostalgic waltz ("Jadis"), supposedly representing Liszt's personal recollection of his meeting with Princess Sayn-Wittgenstein some thirty years before. The two final pieces represent in national terms Liszt himself ("Hongrois") and the princess ("À la manière polonaise").

- Two *Elegies* (1874 and 1877; S. 196 and S. 197), both in *A-flat,* the latter being published in 1878 as Liszt's "second" elegy. Although these are the only works that bear the title *Elegy,* an elegiac mood pervades many of Liszt's late works, a result of his preoccupation with religion and the contemplation of death and the hereafter.

- *Magyar arcképek* (Historic Hungarian Portraits; 1885; S. 205), a set of elegies in remembrance of seven well-known Hungarian artists or statesmen, each of whom contributed to the cause of Hungarian independence. The men portrayed are István Széchenyi, József Eótvós, Mihály Vórósmarty, László Teleki (a statesman who committed suicide in 1861), Ferenc Déak, Sándor Petófi (a poet), and Mihláy Mosonyi (a composer who figured prominently in the founding of a nationalistic school of composition). The complete cycle was not published until 1956, and the work remains almost unknown among pianists. The pieces represent many of the features of Liszt's late writing: slow-moving tempi and contemplative moods, with little concern for technical display of any kind. They nevertheless contain many powerful moments, reflecting Liszt's strongly felt emotions with regard to these men and Hungarian nationalism.

A number of very short character pieces from the 1880s exhibit Liszt's late style. Four of these are associated with funeral corteges in the city of Venice. Two versions of "La lugubre gondola" (The Mournful Gondola; 1882; S. 200a and b) were written to depict a funeral procession in Venice that Liszt either actually witnessed or imagined six months before Wagner's funeral in the same city. "R. W. Venezia" (S. 201) and "Am Grabe Richard Wagners" (1883; S. 202) commemorate Wagner's actual death. The two funeral pieces from 1885, "Trauervorspiel" and "Trauermarsch" (S. 206/1 and S. 206/2), are drawn from the Teleki movement of the set of Hungarian portraits. Other small pieces also express ominous moods: "Nuages gris" (Gray Clouds; 1881; S. 199) with its now-famous impressionistic texture and suspended tonality (Example 14.5); "Schlaflos, Frage und Antwort" (Sleepless, Question and Answer; 1883; S. 203), a nocturne based on a poem of Toni Raab, expressing troubled ambiguity without resolution; and the last piece in the catalogue of original works, "Unstern, sinistre, diastro" (Unlucky Star, Evil, Disaster; after 1880; S. 208), which exhibits unrelenting dotted rhythms growing to a defiant fortississimo in combination with a pitiful, prayer-like negation. Only the little nocturne "En rêve" (1885; S. 207) escapes being melancholy, substituting instead a simple charm. These small

Example 14.5   Franz Liszt: "Nuages gris" mm. 11–15

pieces are, however, at the heart of the prophetic stylistic qualities that are often cited as being characteristic of late Liszt: experimental harmonies, vague tonal centers, recitative-like passages that express no strong rhythmic sense, and an emotional concentration on subliminal psychological states. Bartók, Stravinsky, and Debussy among others have pointed out the remarkable musical vision of Liszt's late years.

Dance Forms

Throughout his career Liszt wrote many keyboard works in various dance forms. Of these, the waltz appears most frequently and represents the composer's most famous dances. Early waltzes include the *Grande valse di bravura* (1836; S. 209) and *Valse mélancolique* (1839; S. 210), both of which were revised around 1850 and published (1852) as *Trois caprices—Valses,* including them with a third waltz, a paraphrase on themes from Donizetti's 1833 opera *Lucia et Parisina* (1842; S. 401). The first *MephistoWaltz* (ca. 1860; S. 514) is actually the second of two episodes based on a long 1836 poem by Lenau (1802–50) that describes scenes from the Faust legend. The composition emerged as an orchestral tone poem, as a solo piano piece, and in an arrangement for piano duet at about the same time. It is thus regarded as a transcription by many Liszt historians and oftenpassed by rather quickly in discussions of his solo keyboard works as a result. The solo piano version is, nevertheless, brilliantly written as a virtuoso vehicle for pianists and remains extremely high on the popularity list among performers and audiences. The second and third Mephisto waltzes are less frequently played. The second was written some twenty years after the first (1881) and, like the first, came out in orchestral, solo piano, and piano duet versions at about the same time. The third (S. 216) exists only in a solo piano version, and many feel that it is unjustly neglected. Written in 1883, it is far less impressive as a virtuoso piece but nevertheless is conceived dramatically and effectively. Liszt's comments attending a fourth Mephisto waltz (1885) suggest that it remained in a working stage at the time of the composer's death.

The *Valses oubliées* (Forgotten Waltzes; 1881–85; S. 215) are also four in number with the first of the group enjoying the most popularity. Written when Liszt was in his early seventies, these waltzes exude charm and elegance. The writing is moderately demanding technically and suggests the verve of earlier years, but the harmonic coloration is often characteristic of late Liszt. An argument could be made against the neglect of the last three of these waltzes, particularly the second, which has considerable appeal. The fourth waltz, incidentally, was not generally available until 1955.

The two polonaises (1852; S. 223) are both based loosely on the minuet and trio pattern but, like the late Chopin polonaises, show considerable structural freedom. In both the Liszt polonaises, the da capo occurs in a rewritten, more bravura form, and the trio theme is recapitulated at the onset of an extended coda. Both polonaises are filled with cadenza-like passagework, including a fair share of double notes and octaves. Notwithstanding many attractive features, the two pieces are not equal to the polonaises of Chopin and are not as favored by pianists.

Other dances by Liszt include three galops, three *csárdás*, several marches, and two mazurkas. The two galops, one in *a* (1841; S. 218) and the *Grande galop chromatique* (1838; S. 219) are high-energy display pieces, "fun" music of limited substance. Two of the csárdás have descriptive adjectives in their titles, the *Csárdás obstiné* (1884; S. 225), stubborn presumably because of its fixation on a four-note pattern, and the *Csárdás macabre* (1881–82; S. 224), deathlike in the hollow sounds of the open, parallel fifths that begin the piece. Three of the marches (S. 231, S. 232, and S. 233) are expressions of Hungarian nationalism, the one of 1840 (S. 231) being used later as a basis for the orchestral tone poem *Hungaria*.

Rhapsodies

Between 1839 and 1847, Liszt wrote ten books of Hungarian melodies under the title *Magyar Dallok* (S. 242). The last five of these bore the additional designation *Magyar Rhapsodiák* (Hungarian Rhapsodies). From this collection came much of the material he used for the first fifteen of the twenty longer pieces generally known as the *Hungarian Rhapsodies* (S. 244). These fifteen were written in 1847 in a style that incorporated both national traits as Liszt perceived them and the many virtuoso devices that were typical of that period of his writing. The last group, starting with no. 16, come from the 1880s and are less geared toward keyboard display, with the final one, no. 20, also known as the *Rumanian Rhapsody*, remaining apparently undated.

In 1858, Liszt wrote a book entitled *Des Bohèmiens et leur musique en Hongrie* (The Gypsies and Their Music in Hungary). In it he described having collected a great number of Gypsy melodies, which he believed were part and parcel of the Hungarian cultural scene. In actuality, Liszt's collection included music that is believed to have been written by minor Hungarian composers or Gypsy entertainers and that had been popularized in salons and cafés of the larger European cities. This assessment has led to considerable speculation as to the "authenticity" of the rhapsodies as an expression of Hungarian nationalistic music. Indeed, twentieth-century research has shown that the peasant music, particularly that which had survived generations through oral traditions, was a distinct, separate body of musical expression. On the other hand, the intermingling of authentic folk music and Gypsy music had probably taken place for several centuries, for Hungarian noblemen frequently kept

Gypsy musicians around to add color to social occasions. The musicians themselves were members of the community and often practiced a trade in villages (frequently that of locksmithing). In the late eighteenth and nineteenth centuries, patronage of Gypsy entertainment by both the aristocracy and the middle class had become widespread throughout Europe, and although Gypsies were linked with many countries, Hungary continued to be regarded as the mother country of the group. Thus, Liszt's liberal attitude toward mixing together pure Hungarian folk music, Gypsy elements, and even what passed as such in popular or commercial venues was widespread at the time, and many succumbed to such liberalism, including Brahms in his *Hungarian Dances*.

The music itself is colorful, attractive, and easily perceived. The structures of the *Hungarian Rhapsodies* are most frequently based on the pattern of the csárdás or its predecessor the *verbunko*. A slow songlike section (*lassu*) is followed by a lively dance-like one (*friska*) with occasionally a third section inserted between the two, usually a highly ornamented recitative (*czifra*). (*Hungarian Rhapsody* no. 6, for example, contains all three sections.) Cadenzas appear frequently in the slow sections as well as tremolo-like figurations that imitate the cimbalon, a stringed dulcimer-like instrument introduced into Hungary from Turkey in the sixteenth century and used extensively in Gypsy orchestras. The fast closing sections of the rhapsodies often focus on virtuoso keyboard display, even sometimes on a specific technique. *Hungarian Rhapsody* no. 6 is famous for octaves and no. 13 for repeated notes, for example. Bravura closing sections openly aim at exciting audiences, and they almost always succeed in doing so. Three of the rhapsodies are attended by descriptive subtitles: no. 5 noted as "Héroïde élégaique" (Heroic Elegy); no. 9 as "Pester Karneval" (The Carnival at Pest); and no. 15 as "Rákóczy March."

Characteristically, the melodies of the opening, slow sections are built around long, held notes that are joined by more rapid, freely moving connecting notes, an imitation of the Gypsy vocal style. These melodies are often punctuated with repeated chords in dotted-rhythm patterns. Lines often follow the contour of the so-called Gypsy or Hungarian scale, a minor scale altered so that it contains two augmented seconds, achieved by raising both the fourth degree and the seventh degree a half step. Underlying harmonies tend to be straightforward, diatonic or modal progressions with an occasional altered chord, except in passages in which Liszt develops the thematic material, where some degree of modulation or chromaticism may be present. The origins of the *Hungarian Rhapsodies*, as well as their appealing, folk-like qualities, have led some musicians to regard them patronizingly as second-class expressions of Liszt's genius. Audiences and performers, however, continue to persist in indulging themselves in the enjoyment of these moody, fiery compositions.

Not unlike the *Hungarian Rhapsodies* in concept is the *Rhapsodie espagnole: Follies d'Espagne et Jota aragonese* (ca.1863; S. 254). The *Spanish Rhapsody* opens with a glittering cadenza before it presents the two well-known themes it is based on, noted in the title of the piece. The "Follies d'Espagne" is, indeed, the famous "La Follia," a melody that had been used a great number of times as the basis for compositions, including keyboard works by D'Anglebert, Pasquini, and Scarlatti; string works by Marin Marais and Corelli; and vocal works of Johann Sebastian Bach, Cherubini, and Frescobaldi. (Rachmaninoff was to use the theme again in his *Variations on a Theme by Corelli,* Op. 42). The "Jota" melody is derived from a dance originating in Aragon in northern Spain. It had already been used by Glinka in an orchestral work called *Jota Aragonesa,* and music based on the jota would appear frequently in the compositions of the Spanish nationalists of the early twentieth century.

Variations

The variation form did not figure prominently in Liszt's voluminous output, possibly because a free variation technique was so indigenous to much of what he conceived in other structural arrangements that the formal variation plan seemed constrictive. Liszt was only eleven years old when he was asked to contribute to Anton Diabelli's ambitious project. Diabelli solicited variations from about fifty composers for a little waltz he had composed. (It was the same project that resulted in Beethoven's masterfully written *Diabelli Variations,* Op. 120.) Two other sets of variations were composed by Liszt when he was about thirteen years old: *Huit variations* (ca. 1824; S. 148) and *Sept variations brillantes sur un thème de G. Rossini* (ca. 1824; S. 149). The Rossini theme is from *La donna del lago.*

Thus, the only significant set of variations by Liszt is the *Variationen über das Motiv von Bach: Basso continuo das ersten Satzes seiner Kantate Weinen, Klagen, Zagen, und des Crucifixus der H-molle Messe* (1862; S. 180). Liszt had prepared the way for this major work by writing a smaller prelude three years earlier based on the Weinen, Klagen, Sorgen, Zagen music (1859; S. 179). Liszt focused on the chromatic ground bass (he calls it a basso continuo in his title) that appears both in the Bach Cantata no. 12 and in the Crucifixus section of the Mass in *b* (in a slightly altered form). After an introduction in which the chromatic motive is presented, the main body of the variations begins. The climax of the work is the presentation of another portion of the same cantata, the chorale "Was Gott tut, das ist wohlgetan." The text of the chorale is underlayed in the score. This set of variations is masterfully wrought and was programmed frequently by performers of the early part of the twentieth century, including Rachmaninoff. Since then, its popularity has seemingly diminished.

Sonata in *b*

Without a doubt the Sonata in *b* (1852–53; S. 178) has been Liszt's most debated keyboard work from its first performances to the present time. It is dedicated to Robert Schumann, probably as a return gesture for Schumann's having dedicated the Fantasia, Op. 17, to Liszt fifteen years earlier. By the 1850s Robert and Clara were no longer very close aesthetically to Liszt, having removed themselves from the Liszt-Wagner alliance at least to the extent that Brahms felt comfortable writing to the Schumanns belittling the sonata.

Wagner, not surprisingly, loved the sonata when Liszt's student, Karl Klindworth, played it for him privately in London in 1854. He wrote to Liszt that the sonata was "beautiful beyond all belief; huge, lovable, profound, exalted. . . ." When Hans von Bülow, another Liszt student at the time, gave the first public performance in Berlin in 1857, however, the work was unfavorably reviewed by the critic of the *Spener'sche Zeitung*, one Gustav Engel. Nor was it well received by Hanslick in Vienna when Bülow played it there in 1881. Similarly, a performance by Walter Bache in London elicited unfavorable comment from *The Musical Times* in 1882. Liszt himself refers to the sonata in a letter as "an invitation to hissing and stamping . . . as [the music critic] Gumprecht designates that work of ill odour—my Sonata."

The Sonata in *b* over the years has gradually gained acceptance as an important milestone in the history of keyboard literature. It is still regarded, however, as a pinnacle of artistic expression by some musicians and as something of an amorphous anomaly by others. Cast in a single movement that takes almost half an hour to perform, the work is viewed from differing points of view as to its structure. Some regard it essentially as a tone poem, its sections held together by a series of thematic fragments that constantly undergo transformation. Others analyze it as a more complex work, one that combines the concepts of both the four-movement sonata structure and the sonata-allegro structure.

Three of the five thematic elements on which the sonata is built are introduced immediately, in measures 1, 8, and 14 (Examples 14.6, 14.7, 14.8). The fourth appears at measure 105 at a section marked *Grandiose* (Example 14.9), and a fifth introduces a slow section marked *Andante sostenuto* about halfway through the work in measure 331 (Example 14.10). These figures appear again and again throughout the work in various guises. For example, the motive that appeared in measure 14 as a rapid, almost sinister eruption is transformed in measure 153 into a highly lyrical, expressive song. The one in measure 8, introduced in triumphant octaves, is changed to a scherzo-like filigree in measure 179. Transformations such as these abound in the sonata, and this process alone gives its many divergent sections a certain sense of unity.

Example 14.6 Franz Liszt: Sonata in *b* mm. 1–3

Example 14.7 Franz Liszt: Sonata in *b* mm. 8–13

Example 14.8 Franz Liszt: Sonata in *b* mm. 14–15

As the work unfolds, suggestions of structural plans related to the sonata form begin to emerge with enough clarity to warrant detailed speculation as to specific sections or movements. The four-movement sonata cycle can be seen if one is willing to accept a first and final movement of essentially the same material presented approximately in the same order, a slow movement (m. 331) of amorphous shape, and a scherzo movement (m. 450; Example 14.11) that begins like a fugue but quickly turns developmental and leads abruptly to the final move-

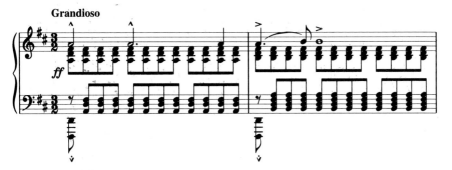

Example 14.9 Franz Liszt: Sonata in *b* mm. 105–6

Example 14.10 Franz Liszt: Sonata in *b* mm. 330–32

Example 14.11 Franz Liszt: Sonata in *b* mm. 450–55

ment (m. 423). By the same token, a large sonata-allegro pattern can be discerned in that what happens at measure 450 clearly recapitulates the music of measure 32, and the order of musical events that follows each of these points is kept pretty much intact, although the laying out of much of the material on the keyboard is altered in the recapitulation. Also, much of what follows each of these points is in *D* when first presented (the relative major of *b*) and in *B* as it is recapitulated, relationships that are traditional in the sonata-allegro structure. The case for the large sonata-allegro structure is weakened, however, by the fact that there are varying opinions as to where the major sections begin and end. Some analysts cite measure 8 as the beginning of the exposition, others cite measure 32; some call measure 105 the second theme, others measure 153; some point to measure 153 as the beginning of the development section, others to measure 331. The development section itself must be regarded as multisectional, containing sections that develop and extend thematic material, a sizeable slow section that presents new material, and a contrapuntal fugue-like one. Still, even with all of this vagueness, the impression persists that Liszt consciously planned a structure that, although free and frantasy-like in many details, was making reference to the traditional architecture associated with the sonata.

The Sonata in *b* is filled with virtuoso devices and dramatic contrasts. Pianists refer to the "octaves" in the work as those in the passage beginning at measure 58. The "fugue" is the section that begins at measure 450, although by measure 496 all attempts to sustain contrapuntal writing are abandoned. The profound calm of the recitative-like passage that begins at measure 405 is at one end of a wide emotional spectrum that encompasses cadenza-like writing (m. 200) and many passages of violent storming (the passage that begins at m. 253, for example, or the *più mosso* that builds from m. 445 through m. 489). It is a work of innumerable sections and tempo changes, and the challenge to the performer is perhaps as much achieving a senseof unity and continuity as it is overcoming the technical hurdles, of which there are many. The miracle of the Sonata in *b* is, however, that, once these problems are solved by a performer, the work emerges as one of great strength and profound emotional persuasion, and audiences feel they have experienced a masterwork of the highest order.

Transcriptions

Throughout his life, Liszt devoted himself with indefatigable energy to transferring music written for other media to the piano, both his own and the music of other composers. This activity was partly born of a genuine desire on Liszt's part to make the music he loved or admired more accessible to others. Liszt undoubtedly believed he was rendering a great service to musicians and music lovers. The need for such a service was, indeed, a real one in the nineteenth century, notwithstanding its remoteness today as a result of technology in printing, publishing, copying, recording, and communications.

Not surprisingly, much of Liszt's work in this area was interspersed with his own creativity, so the transcriptions run the gamut from faithful, note-for-note transferring of music to free improvisation and expansion of thematic material. In the later cases, Liszt himself often used terms such as *paraphrase, reminiscence,* or *fantasy* as part of the title of the work. In these expansions, virtuoso devices frequently become an integral part of what turns out to be a new composition based on material from other composers, much in the same spirit as a set of variations. In those works that represent the original more faithfully, Liszt's care and respect for the music can clearly be seen at work, and often the music emerges as a keyboard piece of remarkable beauty. A good example of this is the well-known "Liebestraum" in *A-flat,* which is a transcription of one of Liszt's own songs.

The variety and number of transcriptions are such as to form another extensive catalogue of works, for there are almost two hundred works, about a quarter of them rearrangements of Liszt's own music. The works based on opera are probably the most frequently encountered today, particularly those that use the material as a basis for free expression. In this category are such well-known works as *Réminiscenses de Don Juan,* based on the Mozart opera (1841; S. 418), *Réminiscenses de Norma* (Bellini; 1841; S. 390), and *Rigoletto, paraphrase de concert* (Verdi; 1859; S. 434). Other operatic works of Bellini and Verdi are represented on the list of transcriptions as well as operas by Auber, Donizetti, Glinka, Gounod, Halévy, Meyerbeer, Rossini, Tchaikovsky, and Wagner, among others. The Wagner transcriptions tend to be more strictly faithful to the original but with an ingenious use of pianistic devices to simulate Wagner's orchestral effects. The concert music Liszt transcribed, too, tends to be literal most of the time rather than fantasy-like. Here, the list is equally long and includes all the Beethoven symphonies, organ works of Johann Sebastian Bach, and songs of Schubert, Schumann, and Mendelssohn, to mention only a few of the larger categories. In the case of the song transcriptions, repetition of stanzas are often an invitation to Liszt to vary the setting somewhat.

The twentieth-century attitude toward transcriptions has been less than tolerant. Pianists can afford to delete this body of literature from their repertoires because there is such a vast amount of original material from major composers from which to choose. This affluence has been coupled with a distrust on the part of many with regard to the legitimacy of the practice, especially in an age where there is generally easy access to enjoyment of any musical work in its originally conceived version. As a result, transcriptions in general, once popular on the concert stage, are heard but rarely, and even then more as a curiosity rather than as a concert staple. It may well be that recognition and performance of transcriptions will become more widespread with a clearer understanding of nineteenth-century attitudes toward the practice and a deeper appreciation of the creativity with which it was often imbued.

Other Works

Liszt wrote a small group of piano pieces that use traditional titles. From the early years come the *Allegro di bravura* (1824; S. 151), the *Rondo di bravura* (1824; S. 152), and a Scherzo in *g* (1827; S. 153). More significant are the *Grosses Konzertsolo* (ca. 1849; S. 176) and the *Scherzo and March* (1851; S. 1854), works that come chronologically between the two St. Francis legends and the Sonata in *b*, thus representing Liszt's work in a period of great productivity and purpose. The *Grosses Konzertsolo*, which was reworked by Liszt for both piano and orchestra (S. 365) and two pianos (entitled *Concerto pathétique*; S. 258), is a large, sectional work that is similar to the Sonata in *b* in that elements of both the four-movement sonata cycle and the sonata-allegro structure are molded into one long movement. The *Scherzo and March* takes its departure from an ABA pattern, with the March acting as a trio. The recapitulation is, however, greatly shortened and combined with a coda in which the march material returns. There is a striking contrast between the almost diabolical energy of the Scherzo and the religious dignity of the march section.

There are, in addition, a host of small pieces, some with descriptive titles and others with generic ones. In the former category would fall three "album leaves" (1851–52; S. 164, 165, and 166) and some small pieces with religious titles (S. 182–85, 187, and 188). Less specific titles include the five little pieces written over a period of several years (1865–79; S. 192) and ultimately assembled for the Baroness Meyendorff as well as a modest toccata (1879; S. 197a).

Liszt's incredible prolificacy, coupled with his habit of rewriting material, has led to many of his smaller or less-important works being "discovered," edited, and made generally available for the first time in the twentieth century. The extent of his creativity, as well as the amazing variety of musical styles it encompasses, remains one of the most remarkable expressions of the nineteenth century.

CHAPTER FIFTEEN

Johannes Brahms

Johannes Brahms (b. Hamburg, May 17, 1833; d. Vienna, Apr. 3, 1897) was born into a family that came from Holstein, where his grandfather, Peter Hinrich Brahms, was an innkeeper. His father, Johann Jakob, was the first professional musician in the family, prevailing against parental opposition by moving to Hamburg, where he eventually became a member of the Hamburg city orchestra. In 1830, Johann Jakob married his housekeeper, Johanna Henrike Christiane Nissen, a woman some seventeen years older. Three years later, their second child, Johannes, was born.

After some early instruction by his father, Johannes was taken to Otto F. W. Cossel at age seven for piano lessons. Three years later, the boy's progress was so remarkable that he performed in a public concert (1843), and Cossel took him to his own teacher, Eduard Marxen (1806–87), who taught him in theory and composition. In 1848, Brahms gave his first public solo recital as a pianist, playing repertoire drawn from the works of Bach, Beethoven, Thalberg, and Herz. A second recital followed in 1849.

Just after the 1848 Hungarian revolution was suppressed, a number of displaced Hungarians turned up in Hamburg. Among them was Eduard Hoffman (1828–98), a violinist who played under the name of Reményi. The young Brahms became Reményi's accompanist, touring with him to Göttingen, where Brahms met Joseph Joachim (1831–1907), the prominent violinist with whom Brahms formed a lifelong friendship. Brahms and Reményi then traveled to Weimar, where Liszt received them cordially. Brahms spent six weeks there, and it is believed that at this time he came to the realization that his aesthetic code was vastly different from the ideals set forth by Liszt and the "New German School."

Brahms took leave from Reményi and, following a suggestion made by Joachim, sought an interview with the Schumanns at Düsseldorf. The meeting took place on September 30, 1853, only a few months before Robert's nervous breakdown and but three years before he died. Robert and Clara rapidly became great admirers of the young

Brahms. Robert wrote an article for *Der NeueZeitschrift für Musik* entitled "Neue Bahnen" (New Pathways), in which he described the twenty-year-old Brahms as having appeared fully formed, like, according to antiquity, Minerva was said to have sprung from the head of Jupiter. As Schumann's health failed, Brahms stood by to console and help Clara, falling deeply in love with her, notwithstanding the fact that she was fourteen years older. After Robert's death in 1856, Brahms's passion for Clara burned intensely for a short period of time. In 1857, however, Clara moved to her mother's home in Berlin, and by 1858 Brahm's fixation had turned into a lifelong friendship, for by the summer of that year he found himself in love with a professor's daughter, one Agathe von Siebold, with whom he briefly contemplated marriage.

Up until 1862, Brahms based his career in his native city of Hamburg. Although his reputation grew there through performances of early works, conducting, and touring, he was not selected as the conductor for the Hamburg Philharmonic concerts in 1863, a post that Brahms fervently hoped to obtain. In 1860, Brahms had joined with Joachim and others in signing a document that attacked Liszt and Wagner and the New German School, an act that put Brahms at odds with a powerful musical establishment, notwithstanding the recognition he had garnered for his creative talent. Brahms met Wagner on a visit to Vienna in 1862, and, although the meeting was deemed a success at the time, Wagner showing admiration for the young composer's work, it was Wagner who mounted a counterattack a few years later in 1869 by writing an article that openly attacked Brahms. Only Brahms's subsequent restraint kept the hostility from further development.

Brahms finally committed himself to living in Vienna with the acceptance of the directorship of the Vienna Singakademie in 1863. For many years, Brahms harbored a yearning to return to his native Hamburg to live, but he was never to realize that dream. In 1867, he was passed over a second time for the position of director of the Philharmonic. By 1878, however, his career had grown to the point where he was feted there with a performance by the Hamburg Philharmonic of his Symphony no. 2 and the Violin Concerto. Finally, in 1894 the much coveted Philharmonic directorship was offered to Brahms, but by then the composer was so disappointed in his native city's regard for him and so entrenched in the musical life of Vienna that he declined.

Between 1862 and 1868, Brahms was out of Vienna a good deal on concert tours, both alone and with Joachim or the singer Julius Stockhausen (1826–1906). These tours took Brahms to every major city in Germany, Austria, Hungary, Switzerland, Denmark, and the Netherlands. After 1868, Brahms restricted his touring, going out only to perform his own works, and in 1873 he was persuaded to accept the important conductorship of the Vienna Gesellschaftskonzerte, which included conducting both choral and orchestral concerts.

By 1872, just before Brahms's fortieth year, the composer felt financially secure enough from composition royalties to resign from his conducting duties and devote himself exclusively to writing music. Recognition came in various guises: the offers of honorary doctorates twice from Cambridge University in 1876 and 1892, both of which Brahms refused, and from Breslau in 1879, an honor that Brahms accepted. In 1876, Brahms declined the directorship of a new music academy planned at Düsseldorf. Brahms's friendship with Hans von Bülow led to a great number of performances of Brahms works with the court orchestra at Meiningen, where Bülow held the position of conductor-manager. The Brahms tradition in Meiningen began about 1881, and in 1895 the Meiningen Music Festival program consisted of works by just three composers, J. S. Bach, Beethoven, and Brahms, thus implying the highest possible praise for Brahms as the only contemporary composer represented. It was Bülow, incidentally, who is reputed to have coined the popular concept of the three B's of music: Bach, Beethoven, and Brahms.

In May of 1896, Clara Schumann passed away. Only a few weeks later, Brahms began to show signs of the illness that was to take his own life, cancer of the liver. He died just under a year later.

The differences between Brahms and his contemporaries, seemingly so striking in the opinions expressed at the time, appear less extreme in retrospect. It is true that Brahms sought inspiration from models of previous generations of composers such as Beethoven, but, indeed, Liszt was also a great admirer of Beethoven. Brahms was influenced by early choral music written for the church, but Liszt's close ties with Catholicism also put him in touch with such repertoire. Wherein then lies the perception that Brahms stood apart from the forward-looking trends of the late nineteenth century?

The answer probably lies within the man himself. Brahms's personality profile was one given to disciplined work habits, scholarly pursuit, personal propriety, and respect for individual privacy. On occasion in the company of those he knew, he could be humorous. Sometimes he enjoyed basking in the glow of fame. Overall, however, he did not crave the spotlight, nor had he the wildness of temperament to compete in the arena with the fabled virtuosi of the time. His character was molded from far more conservative clay. Within this framework, however, Brahms was able to create unmatched sensitivity, intense passion, and robust vigor, rooted to a depth often not encountered in the more flamboyant expressions of the age.

Brahms began by writing large works in traditional structures that were at once direct descendents from late Beethoven and, by the same token, among Brahms's most obvious attempts to emulate the large orchestral canvas of the late nineteenth century. The early sonatas and the Op. 4 Scherzo are huge, imposing works, the pianistic equivalents of the Bruckner or Mahler symphonies. They are replete with monumental grandeur but also harbor those problems of sustaining unity and intensity often inherent in projecting works of such dimensions.

Brahms's interest in formal sets of variations for solo piano stands virtually alone at this point in history. His fascination with virtuoso display was muted. Yet contained within the early sonatas and the middle-period sets of variations are examples of some of the most difficult technical writing to be encountered anywhere in the literature, molded in such a way that the difficulties appear to be wedded to the structure rather than existing only for purposes of display.

As Brahms's musical thinking evolved, he moved away from the larger forms, embraced the nineteenth-century character piece, and conceived pieces in which virtuoso elements were downplayed even more and traditional, disciplined techniques of composition became increasingly evident. Throughout his creative life, Brahms used but few literary references, and he eschewed the use of programmatic or descriptive titles other than the general moods implied by such designations as *rhapsodie* or *capriccio*.

Brahms's compositional bent was toward harmonic movement that favored root movement by fourths and fifths rather than by chromatic half steps. Contrapuntal writing, highly evident in all of Brahms's keyboard works, grew in both importance and skill to the point of often showing extraordinary deftness in the late pieces. Although structure can be analyzed by blocks, such a procedure does not account for the inspired eloquence with which Brahms often imbued transition sections or codas or the remarkable subtlety with which he frequently transformed motivic ideas.

Late in life (1890), Brahms undertook a professional housecleaning project, destroying that part of his creative work that he deemed substandard as well as fragments and unfinished projects. As a result, the works he left are unusually consistent in beauty and inspiration. In this regard, he is unlike other major composers of the nineteenth century, most of whom left bodies of works that contain sizeable segments deemed somewhat inferior examples of their creativity. Brahms's own critical awareness, on the other hand, resulted in his leaving a catalogue that is, by and large, representative of only the best he had to offer.

There has been no dearth of scholarship dedicated to researching Brahms's life and works. The composer's own interest in early music put him in touch with the leading musicologists of his time, including Eusebius Mandyczewski (1857–1929), who produced the first complete edition of Brahms's works. Moreover, Brahms's long-standing relationship with the publishing house of Simrock resulted in publication from about 1860 of virtually all of Brahms's works from Op. 16 onward. Pianists today still find quite serviceable the editions of Brahms's keyboard music prepared by Mandyczewski as well as the edition of Emil von Sauer (1862–1942), a celebrated pianist who prepared the complete works of Brahms for publication by Peters.

Sonatas

The Sonata in *C*, which bears the designation Op. 1, was, in fact, written (except for the slow movement) after both the Op. 2 Sonata in *f-sharp* and the Op. 4 Scherzo in *e-flat*. The Op. 1 figures prominently in Brahms's early career, for he used it to introduce himself to Joachim, Liszt, and the Schumanns. Brahms furthermore selected it in 1853 to be his first published work with the prestigious publisher Breitkopf und Härtel. Like the Op. 106 Sonata of Mendelssohn, the Op. 1 states an opening motive that is strikingly similar to the Op. 106 of Beethoven, the *Hammerklavier Sonata* (Example 8.26). That Brahms was conscious of the similarity is suggested by the fact that he heard a close friend, the pianist Franz Wüllner (1832–1902), play the *Hammerklavier* in Hamburg just about the time the Op. 1 was being written.

Brahms's Sonata in *C* shows influences of Beethoven, furthermore, in that it is cast as a monumental four-movement structure, much like Beethoven's first sonatas (the Op. 2 set and Op. 7). The difference in concept between the Op. 1 of Brahms and the Liszt Sonata in *b*, written also in the early 1850s, must have been dramatically underscored on the occasion of the meeting between the two composers, a meeting at which Brahms played his Op. 1 and Liszt reciprocated by playing his Sonata in *b*. Wickedly amusing, but probably apocryphal, is the report that Brahms fell asleep during Liszt's performance.

The opening movement of the Op. 1 contrasts the heroic opening motive with a tender, lyric second theme. The development is massive, filled with imposing climactic sections and working with both themes. There is a short, dramatic coda based on the opening motive in which there appears a passage of large, rolled chords in rapid succession, presenting a highly unusual technical problem with few parallels (m. 253).

The second movement is a set of three variations on a theme drawn from the German folk-song literature. Brahms underlays the theme with the text of an old German love song, a *Minnelied* that evokes imagery of the moon, flowers, and a beloved maiden. The use of references to poetry is limited in Brahms's piano music, however, for it occurs only in this instance, the second movement of the Op. 5, the second Ballade from Op. 10, and the opening Intermezzo of Op. 117. The second movement of the Sonata, Op. 2, is also probably built on a folk song, but the text is not quoted by Brahms.

The Scherzo is massive, featuring textures created by double thirds in the left hand and octaves filled in at the third in the right hand. The triplet eighth notes create a driving force that achieves considerable momentum. Although the trio section is more lyrical in concept, it too rises to climactic proportions in its second section. The first theme of the final movement is based on the opening motive of the sonata, now cast

Allegro

Example 15.1a Johannes Brahms: Sonata, Op. 1 1st movt. mm. 1–2

Finale
   Allegro con fuoco

Example 15.1b 4th movt. m. 1
Reprinted by permission of G. Schirmer, Inc.

in a triplet-like figuration written in nine-eight time (Examples 15.1a–b). There follows a loosely constructed rondo with two departure sections and a presto coda.

The Sonata in *f-sharp,* Op. 2, is built along the same general lines as the Op. 1. As mentioned, it predates the Sonata in *C,* but Brahms chose not to publish it as his first work. It is dedicated to Clara Schumann, and in 1855 Robert wrote a letter to Brahms in which he warmly praised the work. Like the Op. 1, the Op. 2 was published by Breitkopf und Härtel in 1853.

Although the shortest of the three Brahms sonatas, the Op. 2 is the most disjointed. Opening with material that sounds as if it ought to be an introduction but that structurally is used as a first theme, the work strives to make an early impression with octaves and a cadenza-like prolonged dominant-ninth harmony. The rhapsodic writing returns in the final movement, both to open and close it, framing a sonata-allegro structure. The second movement also uses cadenza-like gestures to introduce the third and last variations on the folk-like theme as well as to form a bridge to the Scherzo.

Having thus included in the Op. 2 sonata several extended passages that are improvisatory in nature, Brahms provided suggestions of

Allegro non troppo ma energico

Example 15.2a Johannes Brahms: Sonata, Op. 2 lst movt. mm. 1

Finale

Example 15.2b 4th movt. mm. 1–2
Reprinted by permission of G. Schirmer, Inc.

unity by constructing throughout the work thematic material that seems related. Some writers have gone so far as to state that the work is built upon a single thematic idea and that its appearances in various guises in the four movements of the work are simply Brahms's version of the thematic metamorphosis that was so prevalent at the time in the music of Liszt and others. Surely the relationship between the opening four notes of the two inner movements is clear. Furthermore, the main theme of the final movement and the opening of the sonata share a general profile that falls through the range of an octave (Examples 15.2a–b). Notwithstanding these explorations and the fact that the Op. 2 has many glorious moments, it remains in the eyes of many the most enigmatic of Brahms's three keyboard sonatas and the least performed.

The most favored sonata by far is the Op. 5 in *f.* Although the work was written within a few months of the other two keyboard sonatas, it is generally acknowledged as a more carefully wrought structure with sweeping, dramatic effects in a grand, Romantic style but without the awkwardness most pianists find in the first two sonatas. Like its companions, it opens brilliantly, the opening motive serving as a centerpiece around which the entire movement is built. It is interesting to note that

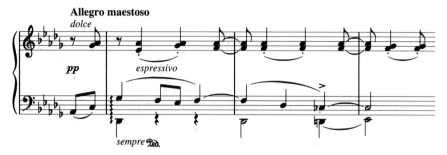

Example 15.3 Johannes Brahms: Sonata, Op. 5, 1st movt. mm. 91–93
Reprinted by permission of G. Schirmer, Inc.

the repeat of the exposition is maintained by Brahms in both the Op. 1 and the Op. 5, the two later sonatas, and only in the earliest work, the Op. 2, is it abandoned. The lyrical second theme, which appears in *A-flat* in the exposition, is picked up in the development in *D-flat* and extended into a rich melody played by the left hand in the range of the cello. The passage is so beautifully conceived that it has become famous among pianists (Example 15.3).

Three lines of Sternau's poetry dealing with the evening, moonlight, and lovers united appear at the opening of the second movement. The mood of the movement reflects this sentiment quietly until the coda, a lengthy section in which Brahms unexpectedly borrows the cello-like passage from the development of the first movement and builds a climax of great emotional intensity.

The athletic Scherzo that follows is regular in structure but, like the scherzi from the other sonatas, is characterized by driving energy with a texture born of octaves and massive chords in the outer sections as well as a more sustained, lyrical trio. A short, improvisatory Intermezzo, subtitled "Rückblick" (Retrospect), is added before the final movement, bringing the number of movements to the unusual total of five. The Intermezzo is based on the opening theme of the second movement, giving further cyclic feeling to the work.

The last movement seemed to give Brahms the most trouble, for it caused him to delay an extra two months (until late 1853) writing to the work's first publisher, B. Senff, that the piece was ready for publication. The movement remains the most enigmatic structurally, starting off like a predictable rondo but becoming so enamored of the theme in the second departure that its use is continued along with the return of the opening theme right on through the coda to the end of the movement. The emergence of an important theme late in the final movement also figures significantly in Brahms's Symphony no. 1, Op. 68, begun as early as 1855, and one might speculate as to whether Brahms tried out the arrangement in this sonata. As in the Op. 2, the themes in the last movement give the impression of being related to ideas heard in previous movements without being direct quotations. The opening theme seems rhythmically related to both the first theme of the opening movement and, perhaps, the dotted rhythm of the Scherzo. The theme of the second departure, which becomes so important in the final pages, has a profile similar to that of the opening theme of the second movement, the same idea on which the Intermezzo was based. These relationships may indeed be subliminal, but they give unity and power to the work as a whole.

Variations

Brahms wrote six sets of variations for solo piano. Five of these bear opus numbers in Brahms's catalogue of works, and a sixth set, seven variations written on an original theme in *d* (1860, as a greeting to Clara Schumann), is a transcription of the slow movement of the first sextette, Op. 18. Of the remaining five, four use borrowed thematic material as the basis for the variations. The Op. 9 (1854) builds sixteen variations on the fourth piece in Schumann's *Bunte Blätter* (Op. 99); the Op.21, no. 2 (1853), uses a Hungarian song as the basis for thirteen variations; the Op. 24 (1861) takes a theme from the first suite of Handel's *Suites de pièces de clavecin* (1733) as the source of twenty-five variations and a massive fugue; the Op. 35 (1875) is based on the same twenty-fourth caprice of Paganini used by both Liszt and Schumann, Brahms conceiving the variations as a set of etudes in two volumes, fourteen in each. Only the Op. 21, no. 1 (1857), a set of eleven variations, is based on an original theme.

Taken as a whole, the sets of variations follow rather closely the formal pattern expected of the variation form. Variations typically trace the harmonic scheme and the phrase structure of the original theme to the extent that the listener remains securely oriented. In the Op. 21 sets and the two books of the Paganini variations, Brahms extends the final variation into a coda that brings both a sense of excitement and finality. The fugue of the Op. 24 functions in this regard, actually becoming climactic. The Op. 21, no. 1, the Handel, and the Paganini sets are all built on themes that are binary with each part marked to be repeated. Brahms retains the repeat signs throughout the variations, in general, but he intersperses enough exceptions to this formality, sometimes writing out the music in the repeat, but other times not, to underscore the point that use or nonuse of the repeat was a conscious decision on his part. The implication is that performers should follow closely the composer's markings in this regard, repeating where indicated. The theme of the Op. 21, no. 2, is brisk and only eight measures long, alternating three-four and four-four meters (Example 15.4). Neither the theme nor its variations have repeat marks. Interestingly, the second section of the

Example 15.4 Johannes Brahms: *Variations on a Hungarian Theme*, Op. 21, no. 2 mm. 1–4

Reprinted by permission of G. Schirmer, Inc.

Schumann theme is marked to be repeated in the *Bunte Blätter*. But Brahms deletes the repeat in borrowing it for his Op. 9.

Brahms frequently links variations together in groups of two or more. Such bonds are forged by sharing technical or rhythmic patterns (Op. 9, nos. 3 and 4; Op. 21, nos. 1 and 2; Op. 24, nos. 7 and 8). In the Op. 21, no. 2, variations 9–13 use increasingly rapid note values (eighth notes, triplet eighth notes, sixteenth notes, triplet sixteenth notes, thirty-second notes) to create a sense of excitement before the entrance of the finale. Similarly, nos. 23–25 of the Op. 24 serve to heighten the anticipation for the entrance of the final fugue (Examples 15.5a–b).

Special mention should be made of the technical difficulties Brahms contrived for the Op. 35 sets of variations. Brahms must have been aware of the fact that both Schumann and Liszt had already mined the technical problems that this particular Paganini caprice suggests. He, nevertheless, staked out new territory clearly in the first two variations of the first volume by creating dense textures made up of double sixths, double thirds, and octaves filled in at the third. Nor is there any abating of technical ferocity as subsequent variations explore skips combined with trills (no. 4), skips and double notes or octaves (nos. 6, 7, and 8), octave glissandi (no. 13), broken octaves (no. 14), and a host of other bewildering technical demands. A case might be made for the fact that the second volume of the Paganini sets is somewhat less obvious in its bid for technical attention. The concentration on rhythmic problems (nos. 2, 5, and 7) and the lilting waltz of no. 4 might indeed support this contention. A second glance, however, suggests that all of the classic virtuoso difficulties—double notes, skips, octaves, and so on—lurk throughout with challenges that match those of volume one.

The keyboard variation is probably the genre with the most consistent use from the beginning of keyboard music through the centuries, but if one were to seek a nadir in popularity, it would probably be in the nineteenth century, for interest in the freedom and programmatic possibilities of the character piece tended to push the use of the variation to

Var. 23

Example 15.5a Johannes Brahms: *Variations and Fugue on a Theme by Handel,* Op. 24 Var. 23 m. 1

Var. 24

Example 15.5b Var. 24 m. 1
Reprinted by permission of G. Schirmer, Inc.

a peripheral position in the catalogue of many composers. Thus, although significant sets of variations are to be found in the keyboard works of Schubert, Schumann, Chopin, and Liszt, these works do not occupy positions of centrality in the creative thinking of such composers. Brahms presents a different case. The sets of variations show the composer to be writing with masterful aplomb in a milieu that seems totally comfortable. Furthermore, the *Variations and Fugue on a Theme of Handel,* Op. 24, is a work counted often as a worthy successor to the monumental sets of former eras, the *Goldberg Variations* of Johann Sebastian Bach and the *Diabelli Variations* of Beethoven. In the context of well-known Brahms variation sets, one might mention the famous *Variations on a Theme of Haydn,* Op. 56b, a work that exists in versions for both two pianos and for orchestra.

Character Pieces

Designating the smaller keyboard works of Brahms *character pieces* seems to stretch the use of the term to the limit, for Brahms tends to mold his smaller pieces along lines that suggest tradition and technical control, eschewing, by and large, both improvisational impulses and programmatic references. This discipline persists in spite of the composer's use of titles that suggest just the opposite: *capriccio, rhapsody,* or *fantasy.* Brahms, furthermore, consistently employed in his character pieces an array of compositional devices born of discipline and careful planning. Counterpoint, often invertible, appears frequently, as do patterns of inner-voice melodies. Phrase structures are carefully balanced, albeit phrase segments of unusual length are occasionally employed. There is a notable absence, on the other hand, of cadenza-like insertions, brilliant passagework, ostinato bass figures, and phrase or passage extension designed to achieve climactic effects. By the same token, Brahms retains much of the characteristic denseness of texture that served the virtuoso writing of his early years. Thus, arrangements in close harmony are frequent, and bass harmonies often contain intervals of the third and sixth.

The Scherzo, Op. 4, stands apart as something of an exception to many of the foregoing generalizations. Written at about the same time as the early sonatas (1851), it is similar in mood and concept to the three scherzi of the sonatas. In the Op. 4, the usual structural arrangement of the scherzo and trio is extended by the use of two trio sections, separated by an extra da capo return to the opening scherzo section. Both trios provide lyrical contrasts to the driving energy of the main body. A short flurry of octaves serves as a stirring coda.

The four ballades, Op. 10 (1856), are quite different in concept and spirit from the ballades of Chopin or Liszt. The Brahms works are much smaller in scale and are cast essentially in a fairly straightforward ternary form, thus eschewing both the virtuosity and the structural grandeur of the Chopin or Liszt works. The first ballade represents the most literal connection to a literary model to be found in the keyboard works of Brahms. Not only does Brahms invoke the Scottish ballad *Edward,* published by Herder in a collection of folk poetry, but he also molds the opening section of the piece so that it follows the text of the poem almost as a song setting. The plaintive mood of the opening and closing are contrasted by the dramatic climax of the middle section, based on the same rhythmic pattern employed in the opening theme and using a melodic pattern reminiscent of it. The poem tells the grim story of a mother's discovery that her son has murdered his father and of the son's acceptance of banishment into exile.

The second ballade, like the *Edward* ballade, places the slow sections at the beginning and end and uses the more rapidly moving music for the middle. In the second ballade, the motion evolves through two middle sections using essentially the same material, culminating in a passage marked *Molto staccato e leggiero.* The third ballade is subtitled Intermezzo, but its arrangement and mood are reminiscent of a succinct scherzo and trio. The last ballade once again features a slow, lyrical opening section. The middle section, composed of an eighth-note figural arrangement of two against three, is also subdued. It returns in a shortened form to serve as a coda.

The next two sets of character pieces, Opp. 76 and 79, mark Brahms's reentry into the realm of the character piece after an absence of twenty years, his only works for solo piano in the interim having been the Op. 9, Op. 24, and Op. 35, all works set in variation form. Both the Op. 76 and Op. 79 sets of character pieces were written in the same year (1879), after which Brahms once again eschewed composing for solo piano, this time without exception, for another twelve years, returning for his final activity with four more sets of character pieces written in the years 1892 and 1893. Thus, in his mature years, Brahms's interest in writing for piano became somewhat sporadic and, when it did light up, seemed stimulated only by groups of short, relatively modest character pieces. From the Op. 76 onward, each of the pieces bears a small semi-descriptive title. In fact, in the minds of many pianists, the most frequently used of these terms, *intermezzo* and *capriccio*, are more closely associated with these short Brahms pieces than any other music.

The Op. 76 consists of four intermezzi and four capriccios, the former being more lyrical pieces in slow tempi and the latter being more dramatic and faster. Sectional patterns vary, nos. 1, 3, 5, and 6 cast in an ABA arrangement, no. 2 in ABCBA, nos. 4 and 7 in binary form, and no. 8 in an AB pattern that prepares for the return of a final A but offers, instead, a developmental coda. Interesting compositional devices abound: the middle sections of nos. 1 and 2 are both accompanied by their opening themes; the recapitulation of no. 1 is written in free invertible counterpoint; the middle section of no. 5 uses material that is so close to the opening theme that it sounds like a transformation of it. The diversity and apparent random selection of keys for the pieces do not suggest that the Op. 76 was meant to be played as a set. If performers choose to do so, however, Brahms has arranged the pieces so as to provide an admirable fast-slow contrast as well as a final piece that ends brilliantly.

The two *rhapsodien* that make up Op. 79 are both longer than any of the intermezzi or capriccios. The no. 2 is so clearly a sonata-allegro structure that the temptation is strong to attempt to link Brahms's use of the term *rhapsody* with that form. Although the no. 1 opens as if it might well be so conceived, the arrangement of material in the first section becomes unusually developmental for the normal exposition; there is clearly new material in the middle section; and the recapitulation of the first section is literal, without the expected new arrangement of key relationships. (The only other piece called *rhapsody*, incidentally, is the Op. 119, no. 4, which also just misses being in a clear sonata-allegro pattern.) Both the Op. 79 rhapsodies open with vigorous, heavy-textured sounds; both offer tender, wistful motives as contrasting second-theme material; and both contain moments of climactic brilliance. The two pieces are justifiably among Brahms's most popular keyboard pieces.

As mentioned previously, the last four sets of character pieces, Opp. 116, 117, 118, and 119, were written between 1891 and 1893 after a

Example 15.6 Johannes Brahms: Intermezzo, Op. 118, no. 4 mm.100–104

Example 15.7a Johannes Brahms: Intermezzo, Op. 119, no. 2 mm. 1–2

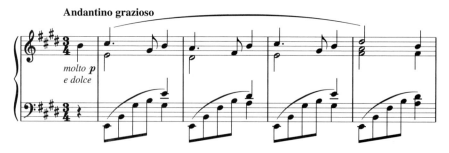

Example 15.7b mm. 36–39

hiatus of twelve years. They follow much the same pattern as the Op. 76 but with fewer pieces in each set: seven, three, six, and four, respectively. The Op. 116 set was given the title *Fantasias* with individual pieces of the set being called *intermezzi* or *capriccios,* as in the Op. 76. From this point onward, however, Brahms drops the use of the term *capriccio.* The Op. 117 are simply three intermezzi; the Op. 118 adds to the collection

Example 15.8 Johannes Brahms: Rhapsodie, Op. 119. no. 4 mm. 1–5

of intermezzi a ballade and a romanze; while the Op. 119 combines three intermezzi with a closing rhapsody.

The characteristics of these pieces are remarkably similar to those of the Op. 76. Three-part forms predominate with some notable exceptions, among which are three pieces that come very close to being through-composed: the Op. 116, no. 1 (Capriccio), the Op. 116, no. 4 (Intermezzo), and the Op. 119, no. 3 (Intermezzo). Noteworthy also are the binary structures of Op. 116, no. 4 (Intermezzo), and Op. 118, no. 1 (Intermezzo).

The mood distinction between the intermezzo as a lyrical expression and the capriccio as a more aggressive piece remains apparent in the Op. 116 set, but, once Brahms abandoned the use of the term *capriccio,* several of the intermezzi take on a more lively or even an agitated character (Op. 118, nos. 1 and 4; Op. 119, nos. 2 and 3). The Op. 118, no. 4, is particularly interesting in this regard, for the return of the main section in what is expectedly an ABA pattern becomes a developmental coda of considerable passion (Example 15.6). Yet another example of thematic transformation occurs in the Op. 119, no. 2 (Intermezzo), where the agitated motive that opens the piece becomes a lilting waltz in the middle section (Examples 15.7a–b). The vigor of the Ballade, Op. 116, no. 3, is capriccio-like. The Romanze, Op. 118, no. 5, is essentially a lyrical piece, with its outer sections being fine examples of Brahms's fascination with hemiola and its middle section a delightful study in the rhythmic variation of a small melodic fragment. The Rhapsody, Op. 119, no. 4, like its counterparts in Op. 79, is a longer, more imposing piece built along the lines of ABCBA, its opening, chordal phrase patterns being presented in five-measure segments (Example 15.8).

From Op. 76 onwards, Brahms molded the concept of the character piece along lines that reflected his own strengths. The masterful small works that emerge are sharply focused in concept, most often formal in structure, employ a variety of deftly executed compositional devices, minimize technical display, and eschew specific nonmusical references.

Into these disciplined, crafted vessels Brahms pours both intense passion and tender lyricism, creating a near-perfect balance between compositional technique and emotional expression.

Etudes

Although Brahms is not so well known as a composer of etudes as either Liszt or Chopin, he wrote two sets of them, the first (1879) being based on works of other composers and the second (1893) presenting a collection of finger exercises. The pieces based on other composers' works concentrate particularly on double notes and left-hand passagework. The opening etude is an arrangement of the Chopin study Op. 25, no. 2. The key remains the same, but the right hand is expanded so that the passagework is presented in double thirds and double sixths. The original tempo indication of *Presto* is modified by Brahms (one imagines with sly humor) to *Poco presto* (Example 15.9). The studies that concentrate on the left hand are based on the Rondo in *C* of Weber, the famous Chaconne in *d* for solo violin of Bach (from the Partita, S. 1,004), and the popular Schubert Impromptu in *E-flat* (Op. 90, no. 2; D. 899). In the Weber and Schubert works, the passagework originally written for the right hand is placed in the left, and the Bach Chaconne is a study for left hand alone. The remaining two etudes in the set are different arrangements of the same piece of Bach, the last movement of the Sonata in *g* for unaccompanied violin (S. 1,001). The first etude places the original violin figuration in the right hand with an inversion of it in the left. The second version of the study simply trades parts, so that the left hand takes the original and the right hand, the inversion.

The fifty-one finger exercises are inventive practice patterns that encompass a wide variety of technical problems: passagework in polyrhythms, double thirds, arpeggiation in extended positions, broken octaves, chromatic figuration, patterns that call for sustaining some notes while playing others, combinations that stretch the hand, tremolo figures, skips, and grace notes. Although the exercises are sequential and

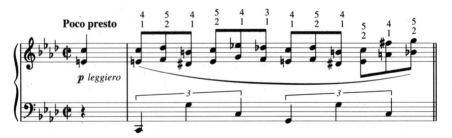

Example 15.9 Johannes Brahms: *Etude after Chopin*, no. 1 mm. 1

thus unsuitable as pieces, they nevertheless are based on patterns with underlying harmonies that are much more attractive than one usually finds in such material. Only the extreme difficulty of the exercises, especially for small hands, prevents them from being more widely used.

Miscellaneous Works

Brahms wrote five pieces that look to the eighteenth century. Two sarabandes and two gigues were written in 1855 but not published until 1917 and 1927, respectively. A rather difficult arrangement of a gavotte by Gluck was dedicated to Clara Schumann and published in 1871. Brahms also left us with his cadenzas for a handful of concertos by other composers: Bach's Concerto in *d* (S. 1,052); Mozart's concertos in *G* (K. 453), *d* (K. 466), and *c* (K. 491); and Beethoven's concertos no. 3 in *c* (Op. 37) and no. 4 in *G* (Op. 58).

CHAPTER SIXTEEN

Other Composers of the Nineteenth Century

Viewing a period of intense musical activity in terms of those creative minds who represent the very best of the time is a luxury only historical retrospect allows. The perspective of musicians who lived during the period itself was more limited, for each was surrounded by other musicians of varying gifts, and the very density of professional activity made it difficult, if not impossible, to separate the work of genius from that of high quality but ultimately less extraordinary. Also added to the mix were works that enjoyed great popularity for a segment of time, epitomizing some aspect of faddish taste, but that would eventually be recognized as ephemeral by the keenly discerning.

Thus, in retrospect it seems easy to identify the prevailing traits of an age, simply because it is easy to see what has endured, and it is assumed that those long-term characteristics were, in fact, clearly identifiable at the time. A moment's reflection reveals that such cannot always be the case and that probably most musicians work through their careers with clouded vision as to which contemporary patterns will ultimately emerge as the representative ones of their age.

Moreover, when an attempt is made to survey the large number of creative minds that fall just short of uncontested greatness, there is almost no method of choosing that guarantees selecting the best of the lot. The selection is usually made, rather, on the basis of which composers represent trends or characteristics already defined by the inner circle of geniuses.

Altering this pattern of selection to any great degree would entail a depth of research far beyond the scope of a survey of this type. Such research, indeed, might very well be futile, for the lives and music of those from former times who are now forgotten may have, indeed, vanished forever. To a small extent, however, there has been an attempt here to recognize briefly a fairly broad spectrum of nineteenth-century composers in order to impart a sense of the intense creative activity centered on the piano. Each of these musicians sustained a significant career, and very likely each harbored the hope that their creative offspring would outlive them. Although the musical material they used was cut from the same bolt of cloth that served the geniuses of the age, their music has managed to find a place in the literature with varying degrees of success. Many of them clearly wrote music that lacked the mysterious spark necessary to impart immortality. A few were able to summon the creativity to produce an occasional masterwork. All of them were highly gifted and immensely productive musicians, serving the art admirably in their age.

The **Bertini** brothers were both well-known pianists of the day: **(Benoît-) Auguste** (1780–after 1830) and **Henri (-Jérôme)** (1798–1876). The older brother was a pupil of Clementi. He dedicated his Op. 1, a series of three grand sonatas, to Haydn, whom he met in London in the 1790s. In the 1830s, after having lived and taught in Paris, Naples, Amsterdam, and Brussels, he settled in London and wrote thirty-six *Grand Fantasias* for piano. He was active as an innovator of teaching materials, devising a musical shorthand and various diagrammatic systems to illustrate learning processes. Auguste taught his younger brother Henri. Henri's career centered more in Paris, where he settled in 1821 after touring extensively as a teenage virtuoso. In Paris, he associated with the leading figures of the day, but even many of his contemporaries felt him to be of a conservative bent, given more to clarity and regularity of phrase structure than to Romantic fantasy and freedom. He was, nevertheless, prolific, leaving behind more than 200 opus numbers, mostly piano pieces.

Charles Mayer (1799–1862) was taken to St. Petersburg as a baby. He grew up there and in Moscow, studying first with his mother but later with John Field. A successful teenage tour of Germany, France, Holland, and Poland and a second tour in 1845 established him in the eyes of many of his contemporaries as a major figure, including Berlioz and Schumann, both of whom praised him in print. As both a pianist and a composer, he was strongly influenced by Field. He produced 351 opus numbers and is said to have taught more than 800 students. A Mazurka in *F-sharp* became somewhat famous, for it was mistakenly published by Klindworth as one of Chopin's.

Henri Herz (1803–88) was one of the most popular composer-performers on the Paris scene. Herz went to the conservatory at the age of thirteen, winning the first prize in piano. He modeled himself after the pianism of Moscheles, who visited Paris in 1821. Herz was one of the contributors to a famous variation pastiche known as the *Hexameron* (1837), along with Liszt, Thalberg, Pixis, Czerny, and Chopin. Herz's popularity was enormous, for it has been estimated that his earnings from compositions were three or four times the amounts earned by master composers who were his contemporaries. As a composer he wrote over 200 works, mostly for keyboard: variations, sonatas, rondos, nocturnes, fantasias, and so forth. He was not, however, universally admired by his colleagues. Schumann and others criticized him for shallowness and catering too much to public taste. He became rich from his concerts and compositions early in his career but then lost most of his wealth in an ill-fated venture as a piano manufacturer. Later, he reorganized his manufacturing enterprises into a successful company that produced the first-prize instrument at the Paris Exhibition of 1855. Between 1842 and 1874, he was a professor at the Paris Conservatory. He toured widely, including the United States. He wrote a colorful chronicle of his American tour, *Mes voyages en Amérique,* in 1866. Today only his etudes and his Op. 100, *Méthode complète de piano,* remain even peripherally in the repertoire.

Sigismond Thalberg (1812–71) studied with Hummel in Vienna, later with Kalkbrenner and Pixis in Paris, and finally with Moscheles in London. By 1830, he was touring successfully throughout Europe, and he was considered one of the leading performers of the day, eliciting praise from both Mendelssohn and Liszt. A battle between Liszt and Thalberg, however, was whipped up in Parisian society, and it came to a head on March 31, 1837, with a concert sponsored by the Princess Belgiojoso to determine which was the greater performer. This social-musical event ended in a draw, and the offshoot of its truce was that a number of virtuoso pianist-composers, including Liszt and Thalberg, agreed to write a variation apiece for the aforementioned *Hexameron*, a work dedicated, not surprisingly, to the princess. Thalberg was famous for creating a keyboard texture in which the melodic line was set in the middle register, surrounding it with arpeggiation on either side. As a composer Thalberg fared well with his contemporaries. Although Liszt was critical of his work, Schumann praised it several times in the *Neue Zeitschrift für Musik,* and Thalberg's keyboard works were reputed to have been as popular in Paris as those of Chopin. Although Thalberg's stock-in-trade were paraphrases on operatic themes, he also wrote sonatas, fantasias, character pieces, and variations. Unfortunately, the content of the music is not very interesting, notwithstanding his adeptness for creating virtuoso settings.

The career of **Alkan** (real name, Charles-Henri Valentin Morhange; 1813–88) was centered in Paris. Like Chopin, with whom he was a close friend, he devoted himself primarily to writing music for the piano, producing about eighty works. He was an erratic person, alternately seeking professional and social status and withdrawing inexplicably from both the public and friends. As a result, long periods of his life are without documentation, and there are periods during which he wrote but little music. An undocumented, bizarre account of Alkan's death relates that he overturned a bookcase on himself while reaching for a book on the top shelf.

Alkan's style reflected musical extremes. It ranged from the naively simple to unexcelled virtuosic complexity. He wrote several sets of etudes, the most complex of which are the Op. 35 (1848), twelve etudes in all the major keys, and the Op. 39 (1857), the other twelve in the minor keys. Like Chopin, he wrote a cycle of preludes in all the major and minor keys, actually twenty-five in number, using the key of *C* twice (Op. 31; 1847). Many of his other works use programmatic elements. His "Le Chemin de fer" (1844) is given credit for being the first piece ever written to imitate a train. His sonata subtitled "Les Quatre âges," Op. 33 (1847), makes use of successively slower tempi in its four movements to reflect the slowing down that accompanies the aging process. His descriptive titles ran the gamut from satanic references to biblical ones, from fashionable contemporary references to historic ones. His music, too, incorporated both Romantic traits and characteristics borrowed from eighteenth-century composers he admired, such as J. S. Bach and Handel. His music thus exhibits structural conservatism at times but at other times highly forward-looking concepts such as freedom with regard to key unity.

Notwithstanding Alkan's sporadic participation in the professional life of his day, he was greatly admired by Chopin, Schumann, Liszt, and most of his contemporaries. Since then, his music has been generally neglected, although recent twentieth-century scholarship has been able to rekindle moderate interest in his legacy (Example 16.1).

Stephen Heller (1813–88) was born in Hungary and spent the early part of his career in Vienna, where he studied with Czerny for a short time, and Augsburg. He was an early contributor to Schumann's *Neue Zeitschrift für Musik,* writing under the pseudonym of Jeanquirit. In 1838, he moved to Paris, where he spent the rest of his life as a music journalist, composer, and teacher. Heller wrote more than 160 piano works, and even during his lifetime his studies became famous. Today his Opp. 45, 46, and 47 are still used by pianists in their training. Heller also wrote sets of variations, preludes, and character pieces as well as opera fantasies and transcriptions. Only a few are known today, represented

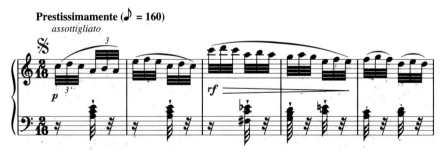

Example 16.1 Charles H. V. Alkan: Etude ("Comme le vent"), Op. 39, no. 1 mm. 1–5

perhaps by the *Blumen-, Frucht-, und Dornenstücke* (Flower, Fruit, and Thorn Pieces), Op. 82 (1853).

(Georg Martin) Adolf Henselt (1814–89) studied first with Mme von Fladt in Munich and later (about 1831) with Hummel in Weimar. After touring successfully in Germany, he moved to St. Petersburg (1838), where he built a distinguished career for the next forty years, becoming the teacher of the imperial household. Several contemporary accounts of his playing note his musical sensitivity and a special legato technique applied to widespread arpeggio patterns. He was praised by Liszt and Schumann, among others. His catalogue of compositions is small by contemporary standards, being made up of but thirty-nine works with opus number and another fifteen without. His most memorable piano works are the two sets of twelve etudes, Opp. 2 and 5, which for a time were deemed important concert studies and are still occasionally mentioned with respect as representative studies of the period (Example 16.2).

Antoine François Marmontel (1816–98) was a prominent figure on the scene in Paris for most of the nineteenth century. Marmontel received his training at the Paris Conservatory, where he won the first prize in piano (1832). He joined the faculty there (1848) and taught both as a theorist and pianist, winning considerable fame. Among his students were Bizet, d'Indy, Dubois, Wieniawski, and Debussy. He wrote a number of sonatas, character pieces, and various didactic works for piano, mostly in a rather charming, but pallid salon style. His son **Antonin** (1850–1907) pursued a career that was almost a carbon copy of his

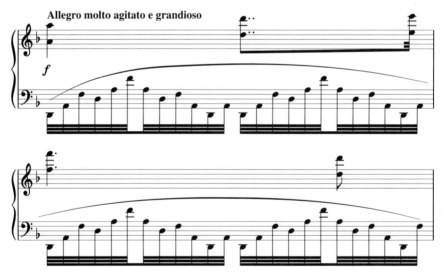

Example 16.2 Adolf Henselt: Etude, ("Orage, tu ne saurais m'abattre!"), Op. 2, no. 1 mm. 3–4

father's, studying with his father at the conservatory, winning the first prize in piano (1867), joining the faculty (1891), and writing pretty salon pieces with descriptive titles: examples include "Chanson Slave," "Chanson Arabe," "Au matin," and "Par les bois." These parlor pieces tend not to be very difficult, possibly in order to appeal to adult amateur musicians. Other works incorporate more traditional virtuosic devices and use titles that are more traditional, such as Allegro capriccioso or Scherzo. All of his music might be described as consistently sweet.

(Ignace Xavier) Joseph Leybach (1817–91) seemed to have enjoyed good preparation, having studied in Paris with Pixis, Kalkbrenner, and even Chopin. Although he became widely known as both a pianist and teacher, his more than 300 works, mostly piano works, seldom rise above the most superficial salon style. His pieces were often included in anthologies well into the twentieth century. In this context, a few of them have become well-known in the piano studio, the most notable being the fifth nocturne, Op. 52.

César (-Auguste) Franck (1822–90) was a child prodigy whose ambitious father wished to exploit him. Thus, the family moved to Paris when César was thirteen. There followed public concerts and study. Over the next few years, Franck won top prizes at the Paris Conservatory in piano, organ, counterpoint, and fugue. After a brief return to his native Belgium, Franck settled in Paris in 1843, where he broke with his father after the disappointing reception of an early biblical oratorio, *Ruth*. Franck supported himself over the next few years through church positions and teaching, eventually rising to become organist at Ste. Clotilde and a professor of organ at the conservatory. As a teacher, he was a powerful influence on his students, among whom were d'Indy, Chausson, Duparc, Vidal, and Vierne. Liszt championed Franck's works, stating that they were worthy of a place beside those of J. S. Bach. Indeed, eighteenth-century contrapuntal practice is very much at the heart of Franck's style, along with the chromatic harmonic language associated with the Liszt-Wagner school.

Although Franck was active as a composer for most of his professional life, his voice became most inspired near the end of his career. The few works of all genres that have remained clearly established in the repertoire all date from the 1880s, which places the composer in his sixties. By far the most frequently encountered work for solo keyboard is the Prelude, Chorale, and Fugue (1884). The three sections indicated in the title are all connected with thematic material, and a dramatic return of both the principal themes of the prelude and the chorale at the climax of the fugue gives the work strong cyclic unity. Less attractive to pianists, but occasionally played, is the Prelude, Aria, and Finale (1886–87). Franck also wrote a great number of small character pieces, some of which are used in the teaching studio. Although earlier large works for solo piano exist, including two sonatas, three fantasies, two

Example 16.3 Joachim Raff: *Polka de la Reine*, Caprice, Op. 95 mm. 7–10
Copyright © 1903 by Carl Fischer Inc.

sets of variations, and a ballade, they have not succeeded in claiming the attention of later generations of pianists.

Joseph Joachim Raff (1822–82) was a prolific composer who wrote in all genres. Coming from a background of poverty, he could not afford formal musical training, so he was by and large self-taught. He was helped by Mendelssohn and Liszt, both of whom recognized his ability. For a time, he was with Liszt at Weimar and endorsed wholeheartedly Liszt's concept of a new German school of music. He was active as a contributor to the *Neue Zeitschrift für Musik* between 1854 and 1861. His career gradually began to take hold, and by his death he was considered to be one of the great composers of his age, on a par with Liszt and Brahms. After his death, however, the unevenness of his style with regard to quality and focus caused his work to fall quickly into relative oblivion. His keyboard works are extensive, numbering well over 100, and include many character pieces, sonata-allegro movements, fantasies on operatic themes, and transcriptions. His style is a peculiar mixture of a somewhat conservative harmonic language, virtuoso passagework, and occasional departures into salon-like sentimentality (Example 16.3).

Anton Grigor'yevich Rubinstein (1829–94) was a pianist and composer of international reputation during his lifetime. Educated in Moscow under the guidance of Alexander Villoing (1804–78), he was taken on a tour by his teacher at the age of ten. In Paris, Rubinstein was feted by Liszt and Chopin and in London by Queen Victoria. After the

Example 16.4 Anton Rubinstein: Etude, Op. 23, no. 5 mm. 1–3

death of his father, Rubinstein went through difficult financial times in Berlin, Vienna, and finally in St. Petersburg before he garnered the sponsorship of the Grand Duchess Elena Pavlovna. With this backing he was able to tour Europe as a pianist (1854) with enormous success and to establish both the Russian Musical Society (1859) and the St. Petersburg Conservatory (1862). As a pianist, he was considered as great as Liszt by audiences of the day. As a composer, his style was cosmopolitan and facile. He wrote prolifically in all genres, his solo piano compositions alone running to 118 opus numbers. The catalogue includes four sonatas, etudes, and a multitude of character pieces. A few pieces, such as the Romance (Op. 44, no. 1) or *Kamennoi Ostrow* (Op. 10, no. 22), are still known as examples of period salon music, and occasionally more enterprising pianists will explore his Liszt-like etudes, Op. 23 (Example 16.4). Anton's older brother, Nikolay, was also a pianist and composer, centering his career in Moscow, where he encouraged Tchaikovsky. Perhaps aware of the ephemeral quality of both his own composition and that of his brother, when asked why he did not compose more, Nikolay quipped that his brother "composed enough for three." Nikolay achieved a notorious niche in history as a result of his adverse criticism, at first, of Tchaikovsky's First Piano Concerto in *b-flat*, Op. 23. Nikolay's career was never as brilliant as Anton's, and his compositions are completely forgotten today.

Alfred Jaëll (1832–82) first studied with his father, Eduard, and later with Moscheles in Vienna. As a pianist, he was extremely successful and spent a great deal of his early professional life on tour, visiting the

Allegretto con moto

il canto espressivo

legg. l'accompagnamento

Example 16.5 Alfred Jaëll: "La Fontaine," Op. 117 mm. 1–5

United States for an extended period in the early 1850s. He championed the music of his contemporaries, playing particularly the music of Schumann, Brahms, and Liszt. He was a personal friend of the latter. In 1856, the king of Hanover appointed him court pianist. As a composer, he was extraordinarily prolific, his opus numbers exceeding the 100 mark. Many of his piano works are transcriptions of the works of others, especially Wagner, Schumann, Mendelssohn, and Verdi. Opera transcriptions seemed a speciality, these often crossing over into the virtuoso paraphrase with fanciful titles such as *Souvenirs d'Italie—Caprice brilliant sur La Traviata*. One of his late character pieces is titled "La Fontaine," suggesting perhaps a forerunner of Ravel's "Jeux d'eau." Jaëll's influence in this regard might have been felt by the young Ravel, since Jaëll settled in Paris shortly after marrying Marie Trautmann in 1866. Jaëll's fountain piece, however, is unlike Ravel's in that it is neither very innovative nor demanding (Example 16.5).

One of the most celebrated musicians in Paris was **Camille Saint-Saëns** (1835–1921). He was a prodigious performer and composer from childhood well into his eighties. In his later years, he came to represent tradition and conservative taste, for he was not in sympathy with early twentieth-century stylistic trends. His more than fifty works for solo keyboard include sets of etudes, variations, and many character pieces. His style is always polished, well conceived for the performer, and shows little pretense of being profound. Only a few pieces survive even marginally in the repertoire: the Allegro appassionato, Op. 70 (1884); *Caprice on Airs from Gluck's Alceste;* the etudes, Op. 111 (1899); and various transcriptions of the ubiquitous *Danse macabre*. In addition, the five piano concertos continue to be programmed, the second concerto in *g*, Op. 22, enjoying considerable popularity.

A similar career pattern was repeated over and over: study with recognized musicians, sometimes at a famous school, in both piano and composition; embarking on a career of playing, composing, teaching, and often conducting; ultimately passing the legacy on to the next generation. The list of musicians, distinguished in their day, who traced this pattern could be extended seemingly ad infinitum with such names as **Johann Friedrich Franz Burgmüller** (1806–74), still remembered today by his technical studies; **Ferdinand Hiller** (1811–85), a conservative anti-Wagnerite; **Louis Plaidy** (1810–74), yet another whose keyboard exercises are occasionally used; **Sydney Smith** (1839–89), whose career centered in London; **Emmanuel Chabrier** (1841–94), who was highly regarded by French composers in the two or three generations that followed and whose *Bourrée fantasque* is still played; or **Benjamin Godard** (1849–95), whose brilliant waltzes often turn up in anthologies of salon music.

In many quarters the tradition continued right on into the twentieth century, and the musicians who followed it produced music that extended nineteenth-century keyboard practice almost unaltered into times when radical changes were taking place. A list of such composers might include **Xaver Scharwenka** (1850–1924), known for his *Polish Dances;* **Moritz Moszkowski** (1854–1925), whose brilliant studies and virtuoso character pieces, such as *Caprice Espagnol* (Op. 37) or *Etincelles* (Op. 36, no. 6), still turn up on concert programs; **Sylvio Lazzari** (1857–1944), who studied with Franck and whose keyboard music sounds like that of his teacher; and **Ernst von Dohnányi** (1877–1960), a composer of wit and charm known for his *4 Rhapsodies,* Op. 11, and a suite entitled *Ruralia Hungarica,* Op.32a.

With the onset of the twentieth century a schism began to develop between playing the piano and writing for it, so that by the middle of the century the last generation of important pianists who also composed in a nineteenth-century style died out, and practitioners of the pianist-composer tradition became the exception rather than the rule. Even so, the power of the combination remained potent well past its zenith, demonstrated by the fact that many of the important composers of the early twentieth century were still trained as performing pianists. Thus, men such as Scriabin, Rachmaninoff, Prokofiev, Bartók, and Stravinsky regarded the piano as their instrument, and their careers included frequent performances as professionals.

Most of the aforementioned musicians, whose names teeter on the brink of oblivion, at least had the advantage of being born male. Assessing the contributions of women of the eighteenth and nineteenth centuries is next to impossible as one reflects on the social patterns that helped determine both the opportunities for individual women during their lifetimes as well as how history has regarded their achievements. The creativity of women was severely handicapped throughout the eighteenth and nineteenth centuries by the society in which they lived, and only now is an effort being made to discover and evaluate the efforts of even the most outstanding women musicians of the time. Moreover, the work of women of lesser fame has undoubtedly been lost forever.

Example 16.6 Cécile Chaminade: Etude (Scherzo), Op. 35, no. 1 mm. 1–5

A few of the women who lived in these centuries managed to over-come the social obstacles of their day and garner some degree of note. Their work is just now being exhumed and examined. Among them are **Elizabeth Turner** (fl. ca. 1750), **Marianne Martinez** (1744–1812), **Maria Hester Park** (1775–1822), and **Marie Kiéné Bigot de Morogues** (1786–1820). Given more recognition in the annals of history is the work of **Maria Szymanowska** (1789–1831), who wrote nocturnes and other character pieces. **Fanny Mendelssohn Hensel** (1805–47), like her broth-er, Felix, wrote *Lieder ohne Worte* (songs without words) for piano. **Marie Léopoldine Blahetka** (1811–87), who studied with Kalkbrenner and Moscheles, wrote a sizeable body of work including sonatas, polonaises, and character pieces. The compositions of **Clara Wieck Schumann** (1819–96) are just now beginning to be appreciated, her catalogue of variations and character pieces for solo piano consisting of almost fifty compositions. **Marie Trautmann Jaëll** (1846–1925) not only wrote many intelligent character pieces but also one of the most influential piano methods of the late nineteenth century. The celebrated Venezuelan pianist, **Maria Teresa Carreño** (1853–1917) wrote almost forty concert works for piano. **Cécile (Louise Stéphanie) Chaminade** (1857–1944) enjoyed considerable popularity during her lifetime, touring France, England, and elsewhere as a pianist-composer. Her more than 200 works for piano include a sonata, Op. 21; two volumes of teaching pieces, Opp. 123 and 126; as well as many character pieces (Example 16.6).

CHAPTER SEVENTEEN

(Achille-) Claude Debussy

Claude Debussy (b. St. Germain-en-Laye, Aug. 22, 1862; d. Paris, Mar. 25, 1918) did not have parents who were oriented toward musical or artistic endeavors. His father was something of a jack-of-all-trades, and his mother worked for a time as a seamstress. Debussy's musical talent was recognized, however, by his piano teacher, Mme Mauté de Fleurville, who claimed (probably spuriously) to be a student of Chopin and who was, in fact, the mother-in-law of the writer Paul Verlaine. Madame Mauté prepared Debussy for the Paris Conservatory, where he was admitted at the age of eleven.

Debussy's conservatory years were successful, but the composer's individuality led to a troubled relationship with the establishment. At first it was thought that he would pursue a career as a pianist, but his work with Marmontel led only to a second prize (1877). Theory and composition studies with Lavignac, Durand, Bazille, Guiraud, and even for a short time Franck led eventually to a Prix de Rome (1884) with the cantata *L'Enfant prodigue*. Debussy's stay in Rome for the two-and-a-half ensuing years was marked, however, by his aversion to the pretensions of the other fellows, his distaste for the architecture of the Villa Medici, and his loneliness over being separated from his lady-love, one Marie-Blanche Vasnier, the singer to whom he dedicated the first set of *Fêtes galantes*. As a result, although the fruits of his labors there included several unfinished works, the orchestral work *Printemps*, and the Fantasie for Piano and Orchestra, he quarreled with the jury of the Académie des Beaux Arts, so there was never any public presentation of the *envois* (goods), as they were called, of those years.

Aside from the residency in Rome, Debussy's traveling in those youthful years also included visits to Switzerland, Italy, and Russia as the pianist-in-residence for a household trio of Mme Nadezhda von Meck, the wealthy widow who supported Tchaikovsky. During these trips, Debussy became acquainted with music of Borodin and Musorgsky as well, of course, with that of Tchaikovsky. In 1888–89, he made two trips to Bayreuth to experience the Wagner festivals there. During this period,

Debussy greatly admired Wagner but later grew to detest the German composer's strong influence on French music. It was also in 1889 that the World Exhibition took place in Paris. There, Debussy became enthusiastic about Oriental art of all kinds, and he was particularly enthralled by the sounds of the Javanese gamelan orchestras.

The remainder of Debussy's life was spent in and around Paris except for a tour to London late in his life (1914). There, he was surrounded by a creative stream of new literary thought represented by the writers he adored: Paul Verlaine, Stéphane Mallarmé, Charles Baudelaire, Pierre Louÿs (all of whose poetry became texts for songs), and Maurice Maeterlinck (on whose play Debussy based his operatic masterpiece *Pelléas et Mélisande*).

Performances of Debussy's works and recognition grew over the years, but never to the point where Debussy enjoyed great financial security. His personal life was marked by a scandalous affair in 1904 with Emma Bardac, a banker's wife for whom Debussy left his own first wife, Rosalie. The scandal cost Debussy many of his friends, especially since Rosalie's despair led her to attempt suicide (unsuccessfully). Debussy's only offspring was a daughter named Claude-Emma (Chou-Chou) born in 1905. Claude and Emma were finally married in 1908. Emma's uncle had disinherited her, however, the preceding year, so Debussy had to continue to depend upon commissions to support his hard-won family. Early in 1909, Debussy began to be troubled with the cancer that was to take his life almost a decade later, so his ability to work consistently suffered a gradual but steady decline over the next years. Debussy's last public appearances as a musician were in May and September of 1917, as the pianist in performances of his own recently completed Violin Sonata.

Debussy was very much aware of the fact that his direction in music was different from that of the establishment. In 1878, his teacher at the conservatory, Emile Durand, reported: "With his feeling for music and abilities as an accompanist and sight-reader, Debussy would be an excellent pupil if he were less sketchy and cavalier." In conversations with Ernest Guiraud, also his teacher at the conservatory, Debussy is reported to have stated that rhythm cannot be contained within bar lines and that there was no theory, only the ability to listen. In 1902, the composer wrote in a magazine article: "I wanted from music a freedom which it possesses perhaps to a greater degree than any other art, not being tied to a more or less exact reproduction of Nature, but to the mysterious correspondences between Nature and Imagination."

This quest not only cost Debussy the comfortable recognition accorded more traditional composers but also gave rise to flurries of controversy, often generated by journalists, over both Debussy's music and his influence. Such activities culminated in 1909 in the publication of a set of critical articles by several writers under the title *Le Cas Debussy* (The Case of Debussy). As late as 1915, Saint-Saëns wrote to Fauré: "I advise you to look at the pieces for two pianos, *Noir et blanc* [*sic*], which M Debussy has just published. It's incredible, and the door of the Institute must at all costs be barred against a man capable of such atrocities." Thus, Debussy's image for most of his career was that of the outsider, the renegade. Even so, his career was periodically blessed with notable public recognition and the admiration of those who were traveling parallel roads with him, among whom were both Ravel and Stravinsky.

Influences on Debussy's musical thinking were diverse. Some have been noted already: his visits to Russia and the contact with composers such as Borodin and Musorgsky; the 1899 exposition, which revealed to him the beauties of Oriental art and specifically the music of the Javanese gamelan; Debussy's attraction to the work of the Symbolist poets, notably Verlaine, Mallarmé, Baudelaire, and Louÿs; his continued quest for a musical language that expressed his ideals of freedom and nature worship; and late in life a conscious attempt to free his music from German domination, particularly that of Wagner's music.

Toward these ends, Debussy utilized compositional techniques that have been documented by many writers: frequent use of harmonies derived from various modes or scales of his own devising, such as the major scale with the raised fourth degree and the lowered seventh degree; periodic use of harmonies derived from the whole-tone scale; pentatonicism, but almost always used with the five tones functioning as the first, second, third, fifth and sixth degrees of a major scale; the use of ninth and thirteenth chords, often in dominant function, the major ninth over a major triad with a minor seventh being a particular favorite; parallel movement of triads or seventh or ninth chords, most often in conjunct steps, but also by skips of thirds; the use of extreme ranges, sometimes with layers of texture at extreme ranges going on simultaneously with other material placed in mid-range; the use of harmonies built on the intervals of the fourth and fifth; the use of adjacent sonorities that invite overlapping or mingling, often combining them with long bass pedal points.

Notwithstanding these experiments with innovative sonorities and procedures, Debussy not only remained true to the concept of a tonal center in his music but also often plotted its arrival with extraordinary skill. As in the earlier music of the nineteenth century, a key signature in Debussy suggests a major or minor tonal center that is to act as a point of resolution. Coming to rest with harmony that supports that resolution is often delayed by excursions into parallelism, whole-tone sonorities, or passages in remote keys. Even the resolution itself is often weakened by unusual cadence progressions, often implying modes or variants of traditional scalar relationships. Frequently, dominant pedal points over a myriad of coloristic harmonies remain the only link to the underlying tonal center. This cat-and-mouse game with regard to resolution is at the heart of Debussy's musical style. Illustrative examples could form an endless list, but one of the most remarkable is "La Terrasse des audiences du clair de lune," from the second book of preludes, where the *F-sharp* tonality does not arrive until the final measures of the piece, the listener having been teased from its opening with a persistent low dominant pedal point on C-sharp (Example 17.1).

From a structural standpoint, Debussy used traditional patterns as his point of departure much of the time. Thus, if one made a cursory overview of many pieces, one might determine that such patterns as ABA occurred frequently. These patterns, however, are almost always embellished with attending passages that have to be "explained" in order to account fully for what happens in the music. Oftentimes these passages function as transitions or extra sections, and it is often precisely in these added pieces where much occurs that contributes to vague tonality. These passages function to postpone the advent of the next formal event and give the feeling of free improvisation. Returns of A sections are often rewritten, sometimes shortened greatly. Debussy

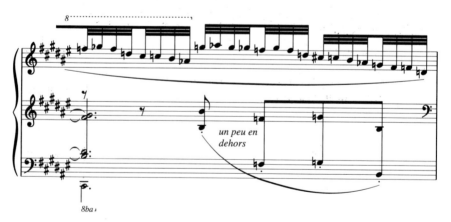

Example 17.1 Claude Debussy: "La Terrasse des audiences du clair de lune" from *Preludes*, book 2 mm. 1–2

seems to prefer endings that fade away. It is certainly possible to find vigorous endings in Debussy's keyboard works, but one has to look for them.

The term *impressionism* was first used by art critic Louis Leroy in an article in *Le Charivari,* mocking the works of Claude Monet and others as they were exhibited in Paris in 1874. Having been consciously adopted by a group of painters, which included Monet, Degas, Pissaro, Sisley, and Renoir, the term was borrowed more than a decade later in 1887 by the secretary of the Académie des Beaux Arts in criticizing Debussy's entry for the Prix de Rome, the orchestral poem *Printemps.* Debussy himself had mixed reactions to the label. In 1906, he used it in a letter, claiming that music was better suited to the term than was painting, but in a letter to his publishers in 1908 he complained that the use of the term is poor in general and suggested that only imbeciles use it in reference to his music.

Notwithstanding Debussy's ambivalence, the term has persisted, and writers have occupied themselves with the task of defining it in relation to his music. The most simplistic relationship is, of course, that Debussy wrote many pieces that describe things, thus offering his musical "impression" of the concepts suggested by the titles. This is not, however, the emphasis highlighted by learned discussions of the matter. Rather, the harmonic and structural ambiguity inherent in Debussy's mature style, the predilection for colorful sonority, and the focus on inner sensitivity, as opposed to the more extroverted, rhetorical style of Wagner, are considered to be at the core of impressionistic writing. It has been these characteristics, too, rather than simply the use or nonuse of descriptive titles, that have been identified as impressionistic in the music of others.

The Early Works

Although the keyboard works written between 1889 and 1900 are often referred to as the "early" works of Debussy, they were not really so early either in terms of Debussy's age or his evolution as a composer. Debussy was almost thirty years old before he began to write solo piano music with some continuity. The *Dance bohémienne,* written as early as 1880, stands alone in chronology. It was written when Debussy was eighteen years old. Madame Von Meck submitted it to Tchaikovsky, who reportedly found it clumsy. Then, starting with the two arabesques in 1889, several pieces came in rapid succession, all written around 1890: *Ballade slav* (later called simply Ballade), "Rêverie," *Suite bergamasque* (revised in 1905), *Tarantelle styrienne* (later titled Danse), *Valse romantique,* and probably the Mazurka. The Nocturne dates from 1892, and *Pour le piano* was begun as early as 1894, although not completed until 1901. Most of this keyboard music is regarded as representing Debussy at a period when his mature style had not been formed, but during this period the composer was writing other works considered to be the epitome of his mature style: the opera *Pelléas et Mélisande* (begun as early as 1893), for orchestra the *Prélude à l'après-midi d'un faune* (1892–95), and many songs based on texts by Symbolist poets. Thus, it is possible to regard the pieces written around 1890 as significant forerunners of Debussy's mature style.

The first Arabesque contains several features that were to become hallmarks of Debussy's later style. The piece opens with parallelism, here first-inversion arpeggiated triads. The introduction reaches a climax on a dominant harmony with the added ninth and a passing thirteenth. The first few notes of the main theme suggest pentatonicism. Although the second Arabesque exhibits fewer forward-looking traits, it also depends heavily upon dominant-ninth harmony. Both pieces follow an overall ABA structure, but each contains a second section of the main theme that is as long as the statement of the theme itself and that leads to the middle section. In both pieces this section reappears in the recapitulation in a rewritten form and acts as a closing section.

The Ballade is somewhat longer than the two arabesques, but it exhibits many of the same features. Opening with a dominant-ninth arpeggio, it relies heavily on seventh and ninth chords as harmonies basic to the construction of its themes. Parallel triads play an important role, also, although they are mostly arpeggiated and function within the framework of a key. There is a heavy emphasis on mediant and submediant colors, secondary dominants, and shifting modes. The improvisatory spirit of the piece leads to an unbalanced structure with greater emphasis on the opening theme, it being stated in different guises four times, a middle-section theme presented first in *d*, then in an altered form in *E*, with a final return that is so short and sketchy that it functions almost like a coda. Notwithstanding this rather free approach to structure, Debussy manages to imbue the piece with considerable charm and color.

Much the same set of observations can be made about the other pieces of 1890–92. The "Rêverie" opens with one of Debussy's best-known melodies. It hovers on an inverted dominant ninth for four measures before it begins to move to its tonic in *F*. Frequently, a sense of modality is implied, for example in minor keys of the Mazurka and *Valse romantique*, where subdominant harmonies are treated as the opposite pole to the tonic and raised leading tones are eschewed. There is a lovely example of the raised fourth, suggesting Lydian mode, in the final, ascending arpeggio of the Nocturne (Example 17.2).

Rhythmically there are fewer innovative ideas. The Mazurka derives its characteristic strength from the fact that the melody enters with its short motive on the second beat in three-four time. The middle section of the Nocturne is written in seven-four time, unusual to be sure, but the gentle motion of the music is such that agitation is avoided. Only

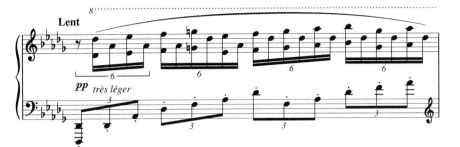

Example 17.2 Claude Debussy: Nocturne m. 75

the Danse gives a strong sense of rhythmic vitality through its hemiola-like shifts between two sets of three beats and three sets of two beats. Structures tend to be sectional and similar to those previously described.

The derivation of title of the *Suite bergamasque* is not certain, but at least two possibilities present themselves. The Italian province of Bergamo is thought to have been the inspiration for *commedia dell'arte* characterizations of the buffoon-like Harlequin. The country-bumpkin qualities of the peasants of that province became so well known in the sixteenth and seventeenth centuries that composers began to borrow melodies and dances associated with the region. One melody in particular was referred to as "Bergamasca" and used as the basis for an elaborate canzona by Frescobaldi (*Fiori musicale,* 1635), in sets of variations by Jean-Baptiste Besard and Samuel Scheidt, and in a slightly altered form in compositions by Salamone Rossi and Marco Uccellini. By the nineteenth century, the bergamasca appears as a quick dance in six-eight time. Thus, one can simply assume that Debussy was attracted to the term because he was interested in writing a dance suite with an archaic flavor.

Perhaps more probable is that the term was simply picked up by Debussy from the poetry of Paul Verlaine. As early as 1882 Debussy set a poem of Verlaine that contained the phrase "masques et berga-masques" in the song entitled "Clair de lune." The phrase was probably created as much for its sense of alliteration as for its meaning, which suggests a subliminal vision of masked figures, sad as they dance in their fantastic costumes. In 1891, a completely rewritten setting of the same text appeared in the first set of songs entitled *Fêtes galantes*; again the song was titled "Clair de lune." Thus, Verlaine's text is linked not only to the title of the suite itself but also to the title of the third piece, "Clair de lune," the only piece in the set that bears a descriptive title.

The Prelude opens with a bold declamation. What follows is an ABA piece with a long transition section leading to the return of the A section. Its style is not unlike that of other pieces of this period. The two dance-types that follow are related to their models only in spirit. The

Minuet retains the three-four time signature, but its rhythmic disposition is unusually busy within the framework of the pulse. It captures the restraint and precision suggested by an older dance form in its opening, but a second theme is more broadly lyrical. Its form is free with little that suggests the structure of the classic minuet and trio. The final movement, the Passapied, calls for dance-like precision, but Debussy does not use the time signature associated with the passapied of the seventeenth century, preferring a duple meter to the traditional triple. The structure is generally ABA with a middle section based melodically and rhythmically on material drawn from the opening theme.

Between the Minuet and the Passapied is the most famous piece Debussy ever wrote, "Clair de lune," a fine work remarkably like Debussy's mature style. The sensitive, diaphanous texture of the opening theme; the coloristic, parallel motion of the following transition section; the altered dominant harmony of the middle-section theme that suggests modality: these are among the wonderful touches that give the piece a distinctive expressiveness and make its popular appeal understandable.

Pour le piano

The suite of three pieces entitled *Pour le piano* was completed and published in 1901, although an earlier version of the Sarabande was part of an unpublished set of *Images* written in 1894. As in the *Suite bergamasque*, Debussy showed an interest in using titles associated with the eighteenth-century dance suite. One can imagine that the rather general title *For the Piano* was born of reasoning that, in spite of historical associations of such titles as *prelude, sarabande,* or *toccata* with other keyboard instruments (clavichord, harpsichord, or organ), these three pieces were written, indeed, *pour le piano.*

The opening Prelude ushers in several bold uses of techniques only hinted at up to this point in Debussy's writing: the parallel minor triads that open the piece; the coloristic mixing of sonorities that results from the long pedal points; passages using whole-tone harmonies; and flashy glissandi and cadenzas not often encountered elsewhere in Debussy's piano writing. Ravel, in defending his own originality to the press, once commented that *Pour le piano* offered "nothing really new." Such seems not to be the case.

The earlier version of the Sarabande is more chromatic and less staunchly modal than the piece that appears in *Pour le piano.* The consistency with which Debussy uses the lowered seventh degree in *c-sharp* gives the piece much of its archaic flavor. Here, too, one finds an early use of parallel seventh chords (Example 17.3) as well as a climax made up of a series of inverted seventh harmonies in close positions. The formal scheme of the piece is ABA rather than the traditional two-part form. The return of A is varied harmonically, and there is a coda.

Avec une élégance grave et lente

Example 17.3 Claude Debussy: "Sarabande" from *Pour le piano* mm.1–2

The Toccata does not reflect the eighteenth-century multisectional model but is in the tradition of the Czerny and Schumann toccatas, a motoric tour de force. Sixteenth notes literally drive every measure of the work up until the final closing chords, rather surprisingly indicated *Le double plus lent* (twice as slow). The opening and closing sections are built on rapidly moving patterns, while in the middle section a more lyric melody is combined with the sixteenth notes. The Toccata creates one of the most brilliant effects to be found in Debussy's piano writing.

Estampes

The title of this suite was borrowed from the world of art, meaning "prints" or "engravings." Ricardo Viñes, the pianist who gave many first performances of contemporary music, particularly that of Debussy and Ravel, played the premiere of *Estampes* at the Société Nationale, January 9, 1904. The three pieces comprised in the set unquestionably represent Debussy's mature style, all the traits of impressionism being used with security and mastery.

The opening piece, "Pagodes," was probably influenced by the Asian art Debussy saw at the Paris expositions of 1899 and 1900. It is a study in pentatonicism, based on the scale of *B*, eschewing the fourth and seventh degrees. Two themes, both pentatonic, alternate with a third fragment containing a raised fourth, suggesting either a portion of the whole-tone scale or a Lydian mode. The melodic ideas are set in various textures, surrounded by arabesques, ostinato figures, or cascading arpeggios.

"Soirée dans Grenade" (Evening in Grenada) is based on the dotted-rhythmic pattern of the *habanera* throughout. Against this persistent pattern, Debussy places a chant-like melody in which two augmented seconds are created by lowering the second degree and sixth degree of the major scale, a series of parallel seventh chords that imitate guitar strumming, a fragment of melody in whole-tone harmony, and even a folk-like dance tune that Debussy suggests should be played with more abandon. These elements are arranged loosely in an arch-like structure, and they create a small tone poem of exquisite detail and penetrating mood. The piece is so successful that Manuel de Falla wrote in the *Revue musicale* that, although it had been written by a foreigner without using so much as a bar of Spanish folk music, it nevertheless conveyed admirably the spirit of Spain even in its smallest detail.

"Jardins sous la pluie" (Gardens in the Rain) is one of Debussy's most popular pieces, for it offers a considerable amount of brilliance without being excessively difficult technically. Its glittering texture is created by arpeggiated chord patterns, most often divided between two hands. Within this texture, Debussy places parallel chord movement, some whole-tone harmonies, and phrases from two well-known French children's songs: "Do do l'enfant do" (Sleep, Child, Sleep) and "Nous n'irions plus au bois" (We Shall Not Return to the Woods). The structure of the piece is built on an extended perpetual-motion opening; a less active middle section, where the arpeggios give way to a written-out trill-like figure in triplets; and a return of the opening ideas, rewritten, condensed, and placed in the parallel major key to provide a brilliant coda.

Three separate pieces come from 1903–4. The "D'un cahier d'esquisses" (From a Sketchbook; 1903) lives up to its title, for it, indeed, seems like a collection of fragments, possibly related to the orchestral work *La Mer* (1903–5). Its sketchiness has resulted in relative neglect by pianists, but an early performance on April 20, 1910, is noteworthy since it was played by Maurice Ravel at the Société Indépendent in Paris. The "Masques" (1904) is associated with subject matter of the *Suite bergamasque,* and some writers have suggested that the music dates from the 1890s. Belying this suspicion are the high-energy, rapid, open fifths; layered textures; and occasional suggestions of whole-tone harmonies. The relative neglect accorded this piece in the repertoire seems unjustified. "L'Isle joyeuse," on the other hand, enjoys great popularity, for it is one of the relatively few extraverted, openly virtuosic works of Debussy. Probably inspired by Watteau's painting *Embarquement pour Cythère*, it captures a mood of hedonistic abandon and drives to ecstatic heights. Debussy was well aware of the technical difficulties in the work, for he wrote to Durand, his publisher, in 1904: "But God! how difficult it is to perform . . . that piece seems to assemble all the ways to come at the piano, since it unites force and grace."

Images

The two sets of *Images* (1905 and 1907) each contain three pieces. In August 1905, Debussy penned a curious comment to his publisher, Durand, about "Reflets dans l'eau" (Reflections on the Water), which opens the first set. He wrote, "This piece does not please me much, so I have resolved to compromise by exploring new ideas, according to the most recent discoveries in harmonic chemistry." The "discoveries" would seem to be more adroit use of pentatonicism, whole-tone sonorities, some parallelism, and some coloristic altered chords. Notwithstanding Debussy's self-criticism, the work is considered one of his strongest and remains steadfastly popular among pianists.

The remaining two pieces are regarded with somewhat more mixed opinions. A contemporary writer, André Suarès, placed the "Hommage à Rameau" on a level with late Beethoven sonatas. Others have found its austere, monophonic opening and the constrictions of its sarabande-like three-two meter uncharacteristically stiff and formal for Debussy. The composer was involved in editing the score of Rameau's opera-ballet *Les Fêtes de Polymnie,* and this tribute is undoubtedly a spin-off from that activity. The "Mouvement" is built on an opening theme with a rather fragile texture. This is contrasted with a fanfare-like fragment, some whole-tone excursions, and a slightly more substantial middle theme. A whole-tone passage acts as a coda for the piece, as it rises figurally by scale steps, receding into silence. Although there is no descriptive title for the piece, one is reminded of the mood of *Masques* or the second nocturne for orchestra, *Fêtes* (Festivals).

The second book of *Images* is the last of the three-piece suites, Debussy never again returning to this grouping concept. Most writers regard it as a culmination, for each of the pieces is equally strong, and each is a polished, inspired example of Debussy's fully formed style. "Cloches à travers les feuilles" (Bells through the Leaves) mixes bell-like sustained tones in various registers with textures composed of rapidly moving notes. The first thematic idea is based on whole-tone harmonies. In the middle section of the piece, textures become pentatonic, and elaborate, rolled chords emphasize intervals of fourths and fifths (Example 17.4). A fragmented return with a chordal coda closes the piece.

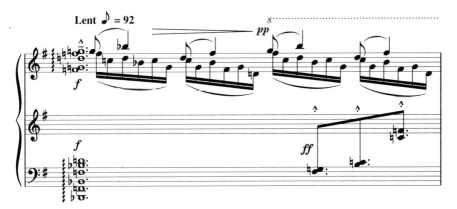

Example 17.4 Claude Debussy: "Cloches à travers les feuilles" from *Images*, book 2 m. 31

The title "Et la lune descend sur le temple qui fut" summons up a poetic, almost subliminal image. Literally translated "The Moon Descends on the Temple Which Was," there are suggestions of antiquity, nighttime, and ruins. A recurring gamelan-like, pentatonic theme suggests the Orient. Long pedal points in the low registers of the keyboard, written to be sustained through a chorale-like series of major and minor chords, challenge the performer to achieve a balance between mixed sonorities and intelligible clarity (Example 17.5). The structure of the piece is almost completely free, an assemblage of sonorous fragments that form themselves into enough of a developmental extension to suggest a middle section and that return near the end of the piece with enough recognition to suggest a closing.

According to several of Debussy's early biographers, "Poissons d'or" (Goldfish) may have been inspired by a piece of Asian art depicting goldfish instead of the real thing, either a piece of lacquer or an embroidery. The music itself suggests movement, sometimes swiftly darting and at other times lazily hovering. After the presentation of two themes, a development-like section leads to a glorious climax near the end of the piece. A cadenza-like coda brings the work to a quiet close. "Poissons d'or" is brilliantly conceived for the keyboard both in terms of sonority and physical execution. It is no wonder pianists revel in playing it.

Children's Corner

Debussy wrote *Children's Corner* (1906–8) for his five-year-old daughter Claude-Emma, nicknamed Chou-Chou. Curiously, the titles of the suite itself and the six pieces of which it is composed are all in English,

Example 17.5 Claude Debussy: "Et la lune descend sur le temple qui fut," from *Images*, book 2 mm. 20–21

said to be a kind of household exercise for Chou-Chou, who was attended by an English governess. The work is dedicated to Chou-Chou "with her father's apologies for what is to follow."

What follows are six small gems, rich in color and variety of keyboard touch. The title of the opening piece, "Dr. Gradus ad Parnassum," undoubtedly refers to the *Gradus ad Parnassum* of Clementi, Debussy deriving humor from the reputation that Clementi's work had as a method designed to build basic piano technique. Debussy poked fun twice at the dreaded practice regimen imposed on piano students, here and in the first of the twelve etudes. Debussy carries this humor further in a letter to his publisher, Durand, written August 15, 1908. He writes, " 'Dr. Gradus ad Parnassum' is a sort of hygienic and progressive gymnastics; it should be played every morning, before breakfast, beginning *modéré* and working up to an *animato*. I hope that the clarity of this explanation will delight you." Indeed, Debussy has pointed to gently humorous tempo changes in the piece and the use of five-finger patterns, albeit more beautifully devised than those associated with traditional exercises.

"Jimbo's Lullaby" explores the low registers of the piano and a gentle lumbering to suggest the world of the stuffed elephant. "Serenade for the Doll" was published separately in 1906 with the French title *Sérénade à la poupée*, and Debussy aficionados have insisted that the French title "to the Doll" reflects the sweet gentility of this music more appropriately than "for the Doll." "The Snow Is Dancing" is perhaps the most difficult of the set, demanding both control and delicacy in the projection of the textures that depict snow flurries. The "Little Shepherd" evokes a gentle sadness with recitative, flutelike melodies, but then it offers lighthearted dotted-rhythm interludes as a contrasting idea. The set closes with the most popular of its vignettes, "Golliwog's Cakewalk," a piece that offers several sophisticated references. The golliwog itself is a stuffed doll; the cakewalk refers to the high-stepping dance associated with minstrel entertainment in the United States; and the middle section of the piece offers a parody of the opening phrase of Richard Wagner's opera *Tristan und Isolde,* marked satirically by Debussy *avec une grande émotion* (with a great show of emotion). One imagines that Debussy took great personal pleasure in writing these sophisticated pieces, not only because of the connections with his daughter's world, but also because of the sensitivity and humor with which the pieces are conceived.

In 1909, the Société Internationale de Musique celebrated the centenary of the death of Haydn by asking several composers to contribute small pieces to honor the Austrian composer. The contributors included Vincent d'Indy, Paul Dukas, Maurice Ravel, and Debussy. The "Hommage à Haydn," built on the letters of Haydn's name, is Debussy's contribution to this project.

In 1910, Debussy wrote an appealing waltz called "La Plus que lent" (More Than Slowly). The title may be a humorous reference to a popular piece of the day called "La Valse lent," Debussy suggesting that his excursion into the world of schmaltz went even further. Actually, the work sidesteps overblown sentiment quite skillfully, leaving a good deal of relaxed charm to be enjoyed.

Preludes, Books 1 and 2

At the heart of Debussy's mature style are the twenty-four preludes, the two books of twelve each being published in 1910 and 1913. The pieces tend to be shorter and more compact than those that make up the earlier suites. Each of the descriptive titles is placed at the end of the piece, suggesting that Debussy meant for the music to be heard first as pure music rather than as musical description. The titles are often sophisticated references to works of art, poetry, nature, legend, or occasionally popular culture. The compositional techniques used are those described in the context of other keyboard works written since 1900.

"Danseuses de Delphes" (Dancers of Delphi) alludes to the Greek city of Delphi, which was a center of religious activity in ancient times. Located at the foot of Mount Parnassus, where in the Gods were believed to dwell, it spawned shrines, temples, and prophecy by oracles. Visitors to the ruins of these structures today may observe fragments of architecture, objects of art, or friezes adorned with dancing figures, often female, often in groups with garlands of flowers or greenery. It is probable that Debussy's inspiration was from reproductions or fragments on display in Paris museums, quite possibly the Louvre. Debussy's reflection on this image is one that features slow-moving chords evolving into layers of descending and ascending parallel lines. The piece is organized around *B-flat* tonality.

"Voiles" is used by Debussy in the plural form, thereby obscuring whether the reference is to the masculine, *le voile*, which would be translated as "veils," or the feminine, *la voile*, which would be translated as "sails." The piece is unusual in that it is based almost entirely on whole-tone harmonies. Debussy's normal procedure is to use whole-tone passages as an excursion. Here, the piece remains fixed in a whole-tone framework from its opening measures to its end, except for a brief pentatonic cadenza just before the return of the A section. A pedal point on B-flat anchors the piece, and it ends with a resolution to a major third built on C. The mood of the piece is one of gentle drifting, either veils or sails billowing gracefully in a mild breeze.

"Le Vent dans la pleine" (The Wind on the Plain) builds its melodic fragments around an ostinato-like figure placed in the middle of the keyboard. Built around the notes B-flat and C-flat, a suspended-dominant/minor-sixth relationship in the key of *E-flat/e-flat* is strongly suggested, and, indeed, a Dorian mode on E-flat is introduced at the end of the first section and when the material returns near the end of the

piece. The final measures of the piece, however, stop short of any resolution, so that the listener is left suspended as the music dies away. The
climax of the piece takes place near its middle and is well known because
of its difficult, rapidly leaping chords.

Debussy quotes a line from a poem of Charles Baudelaire's *Fleurs
du mal* (Flowers of Evil) as the title of the fourth Prelude: "Les Sons et les
parums tournent dans l'air du soir" (The Sounds and Perfumes Float in
the Evening Air). The mood of the piece reflects the sensuousness of the
poetry, assembling in an amorphous structure a group of rich sonorities
built around a recurring phrase in *A* (later *A-flat*). The final measures of
the piece are, according to Debussy's instructions, to imitate the sound
of distant horns, a telling example of Debussy's orchestral imagination
while creating keyboard music.

"Les Collines d'Anacapri" (The Hills of Anacapri) captures the
carefree exhilaration that travelers feel when visiting Anacapri. Situated
on the island of Capri a few miles off the Italian coast just south of
Naples, the town itself is perched high on a hilltop overlooking the blue
Mediterranean. The views are spectacular; the buildings are painted in
pastel colors; the colors of the rocks and the water are vivid; and the
town itself is given over to the amenities that please visitors. Debussy
captures this scene with rapid, joyful, pentatonic melodic fragments,
offering a second theme that he suggests should be played with the freedom of a popular song. Yet another tune with a Neapolitan feel acts as
a short middle section. The piece ends brilliantly with ascending
arpeggio-like sweeps.

"Des pas sur la neige" (Footsteps in the Snow) is a through-composed prelude built on a repeated iambic figure that opens the piece.
Debussy writes concerning this figure: *Ce rythme doit avoir la valeur sonore
d'un fond de paysage triste et glacé* (This rhythm should depict sonically
throughout a gloomy, frozen landscape). The piece achieves remarkable
intensity of expression with economy of means, adding to the ostinato-
like rhythm a series of halting, slow-moving melodic fragments. A second
performance note from the composer appears at the final statement of
one of these melodic fragments. Here he directs, *Comme un tendre et triste
regret* (Like a tender, melancholy yearning). Just observing the written
page, one might be tempted to conclude that this piece is one of the easier preludes, but one quickly learns that capturing and sustaining its icy
desolation and sense of remote vastness is a challenge even to experienced musicians.

"Ce qu'a vu le vent d'Ouest" (What the West Wind Has Seen) is the
most brilliant prelude from the first volume and ranks high as one of
Debussy's most challenging pieces from a technical standpoint.
Arpeggiation, tremolos, and repeated notes provide a stormy background to a dotted-rhythm motive that appears in different guises
throughout the piece. The key signature of three sharps is borrowed

from the key of *f-sharp*, but much of the time there is alteration of the scale line, most often a lowered second or a raised sixth, suggesting Phrygian or Dorian modality. Indeed, even the final, brusque chords of the piece are *f-sharp* triads with an added D-sharp.

"La Fille aux cheveux de lin" (The Maid with the Flaxen Hair) is one of the more popular preludes because its fresh simplicity is appealing and its technical challenges are manageable for pianists of intermediate skills. The piece is presumed to be inspired by a poem of the same name by Leconte de Lisle. The poet praises the virtues of this maid, particularly the naturalness and beauty of her hair, eyes, and face, and finds love in the clear light of summer. Debussy imparts to the *G-flat* tonality an archaic feeling with surprising cadences a third away (*E-flat*), series of major-minor seventh sonorities, and pentatonic excursions.

"La Sérénade interrompue" (The Interrupted Serenade) opens with the directions *Quasi guitarra* (like a guitar) and continues to accompany its plaintive, singing melodies with guitar-like figurations. The setting seems to be Spain. Two unexpected passages (*Trés vif* and later *Rageur*) provide the interruptions to the singing, suggesting that the baleful serenader may not be all that welcome. A short burst of *cante hondo* (deep song) near the middle of the piece depicts the ardor of the song, as does the sensuous harmonization of its final statement. One imagines, however, that the hoped-for response from the lady in question is withheld, for the piece ends as if the songster closed up shop and slipped away into the night. The entire scene seems to be tinged with humor.

"La Cathedrale engloutie" (The Engulfed Cathedral) graphically depicts the Breton legend of the mystical cathedral of Ys. Hidden at the bottom of the sea, the cathedral rises out of the water, majestically revealing itself until sunset, when once again it becomes invisible as it sinks into its hideaway. Debussy's setting of this tale begins with ascending, parallel octaves, filled in with fourths, suggesting organum and its association with the early Roman Catholic Church. This texture is interrupted by a second idea, a chime-like theme that wends its way around a pedal point on E. Throughout this first section the bass line has slowly progressed down the scale of *C* from its dominant on G to the tonic. The next section is marked *Peu à peu sortant de la brume* (Little by little drawn from the mist). It depicts the rise of the cathedral through a gradual crescendo and a series of tonal centers that shift upward abruptly by major thirds. The effect is both elevating and breathtaking. The crescendo leads to a climactic, chorale-like theme that is centered around a tonality of *C* and that represents the cathedral revealed in it full glory. A middle section based on the chime-like theme of the opening builds to its own climax. Finally, the chorale theme returns, once again based on *C* tonality, but now muffled, as if heard from underneath the water as the cathedral sinks from view. The opening organum-like sonorities close the piece, suggesting that the cycle is complete and that the vastness of the sea is all that remains.

"La Danse de Puck" (The Dance of Puck) describes the mischievous character from Shakespeare's *A Midsummer Night's Dream* with dotted rhythms, rapid runs, trills, tremolos, and chords preceded by grace notes. Three melodic fragments are set with these devices in various ways, often with sudden changes of tempo, dynamics, or texture, suggesting a capricious, unpredictable, but ultimately charming spirit. A rapidly ascending run marked *pianissimo* gives the impression that Puck vanishes before our eyes.

"Minstrels" (Minstrels) reflects the popular entertainment that originated in the United States' Southland and crossed the Atlantic to the music halls and pavilions of Europe. The detached syncopation of the opening main theme brings to mind stylized dance steps. A middle section marked *Moqueur* (mockingly) suggests the banter of comics. A bass rhythmic figure marked *Quasi tambouro* (like a drum) provides a buildup for the entrance of an old Broadway-style "tune" perfectly crafted as a finale with which to bring down the curtain. Debussy's keen sense of humor and his ability to translate it into musical gesture make this prelude a delightful gem.

"Brouillards" (Fog), which opens the second book of preludes, sets up a texture born of parallel triads that revolve around the tonal center of *C* and a series of arpeggio-like figures that suggest either *D-flat* or *G-flat* (later notated in sharps) as a center (Example 17.6). The arrangement of these patterns on the keyboard suggests that the juxtaposing white-key triads against mostly black-key figuration may have influenced the formation of this texture. It is almost bitonal, but the black-note keys regularly contain modal inflections or are pentatonic, so that their function is one of decorating the triads with a hazy sonority rather than that of offering a strong alternative tonal center. A second thematic fragment is presented in widely spaced octaves, providing a bare contrast to the fuzziness of the opening section. The piece fades away by

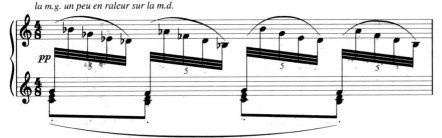

Example 17.6 Claude Debussy: "Brouillards" from *Preludes*, book 2 m. 1

using its opening melodic fragment in such a way as to produce a half-cadence effect, a triad on C being followed by a diminished triad on B, the uppermost line descending a whole step.

"Feuilles mortes" (Dead Leaves) opens with a melodic line that descends by a whole step, echoing the main motive of "Brouillards." The link may be coincidental. On the other hand, it is interesting to note that several such ties can be traced (or imagined) in this book of preludes. The title of the piece suggests autumn, and, indeed, at one point Debussy wrote of the mood that autumn invoked in him in his series of critical essays entitled *Monsieur Croche antidilettante* (Monsieur Croche, the Dilettante Hater):

> Irresistibly bewitched by the magic of the ancient forests, I had stayed late one autumn day in the country. From the fall of the golden leaves that invest the splendid obsequies of the trees, from the clear Angelus that calls the fields to rest, rose a gentle and alluring voice counseling oblivion.

The music itself is marked *Lent et mélancolique* (slowly and sadly) and spins its mood by textures of layered sonorities. The middle section presents a short ostinato figure over which are placed whole-tone sonorities. The ostinato then shifts to the upper registers, where it is fleshed out by major triads (Example 17.7). The four sharps in the key signature and the music itself suggest a tonal center of *c-sharp*. The last note of the piece is E-sharp, a resurrection of the Picardy third that ends the piece with a major sound. Once again, one might imagine that this is an enharmonic preparation for the *D-flat* tonality of the next prelude.

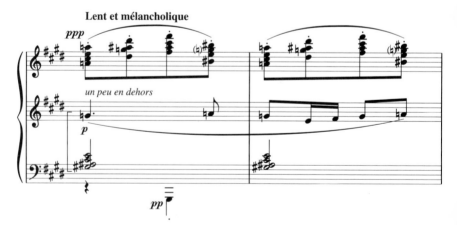

Example 17.7 Claude Debussy: "Feuilles mortes" from *Preludes*, book 2 mm. 25–26

"La puerta del vino" (The Gate of Wine) is said to have been inspired by a picture postcard Debussy received from Manuel de Falla of one of the gates of the Alhambra Palace in Seville. Indeed, the Spanish title of the piece and the character of the music set the locale unquestionably. The reference to wine has been attributed to the fact that wine merchants hawk their wares in the streets of the city. It may also refer more generally to the intoxication of the sights, sounds, and smells of a colorful, urban Spanish environment. That Debussy's imagination was fired by all of this is evidenced by his directions at the beginning of the piece: *Avec de brusques oppositions d'extrême violence et de passionnée douceur* (With brusque changes between the extremes of violence and passionate tenderness). The rhythmic pattern of the habanera permeates the piece. Over it Debussy spins a slow-moving sensuous melody decorated with elaborate written-out ornaments reminiscent of the vocal outbursts of flamenco singers. As one might expect from the opening directions of the piece, abrupt *sff* arpeggios introduce a second idea, which is immediately transformed into a seductive theme marked *Rubato*. A middle section moves to a climax and is followed by a somewhat less intense variation of the habanera rhythm marked *Ironique*. The piece carries its contrasts right to the end, where the second idea is restated with the direction of *Lointain* (from a distance) and is followed abruptly by a final fortissimo arpeggio-decorated chord.

The title "Les Fées sont d'exquises danseuses" (The Fairies Are Exquisite Dancers) is placed in quotation marks at the end of the text of the music, suggesting that there is a literary source from which Debussy was quoting. The source has eluded research efforts and remains a mystery. The image is evoked musically by Debussy with rapid two-hand figurations alternating with graceful melodic fragments. The juxtaposing of white-key and black-key hand positions seems to be a determining factor in the opening figurations. The middle section features a melody in the middle register with darting arpeggios as decoration and a section in which the melody is accompanied by a series of long trills. The piece ends quizzically with a sustained tone, D-flat, as a pedal point for *do-re-mi*.

"Bruyères" (Heather) is the counterpart to "La Fille aux cheveux de lin" in the first volume of preludes. The open countryside and freshness of air are represented by a clear approach to sonority, emphasizing diatonic scalar melodies and solid chords as opposed to polychords and complex passagework. The structure of the piece is also based on an obvious return of the opening section. The final measures of the piece introduce a rapid turn-like figure in the bass that rhythmically suggests the introductory figure of the next prelude. Once again, pointing to such a link does not prove that it was consciously planned by the composer (Examples 17.8a–b).

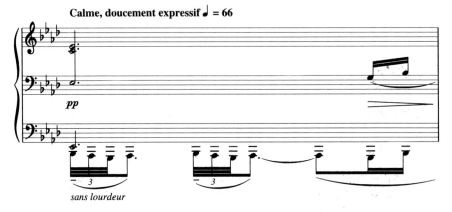

Example 17.8a Claude Debussy: "Bruyères" from *Preludes*, book 2 m. 49

Example 17.8b "General Lavine—Eccentric" from *Preludes*, book 2 m.1

"General Lavine—Eccentric" is a title written in English, and it refers to an American vaudeville entertainer who first appeared at the Marigny Theater in Paris in 1910, billed as "General Ed Lavine, the Man Who Has Soldiered All His Life." His act was based on comic predicaments, slapstick fights, and juggling. The piece Debussy created to characterize this comic opens with bugle calls decorated by off-key triads and moves into a cakewalk main theme. The triads are featured in a short middle section, and the cakewalk returns in a literal recapitulation. A short coda begins by employing an old theater-music cliché, that of raising the key of the tune a half-step to create tension, here from *F* to *G-flat*. Erratic tempo changes and the return of the bugle calls with brilliant thirteenth chords give the final measures a showbiz verve.

"La Terrasse des audiences de clair de lune" is a title that is born of imagery, so much so that its precise meaning is not totally clear even in French. At least two contemporary writers had already combined the concepts of a "terrace," an "audience" (or "council"), and "moonlight" in one sentence: Pierre Loti in a description of the English rule in India and René Puaux in a newspaper account describing the coronation of King George V as King of India. Thus, a night scene in some exotic far-away setting seems to be the source of inspiration for this piece, and, indeed, the music itself is some of Debussy's most evocative and sensuous. The opening page sets up layers of rich sonority using descending chromatic figurations in the upper register of the keyboard, series of close-position seventh chords in the middle register, and a repeated dominant pedal point on C-sharp in the bass (Example 17.1). The low dominant pedal point acts as a force to stabilize the tonal center throughout the piece, repeatedly returning after excursions to other key centers. A middle section keeps the C-sharp in place over a passage that hints at whole-tone harmonies. There is the semblance of an arch form in the structure, but the returning material is altered so much that the plan is effectively veiled. Not until the onset of the coda does the resolution to *F-sharp* take place. Such a masterful, delayed resolution gives the piece a tenuous quality, as if reality were suspended, and the final settling into *F-sharp* imparts a deep sense of peaceful satisfaction. Curiously, the *F-sharp* tonality arrives along with a persistent use of lowered second degree, evoking sounds possibly associated with Spain rather than India.

"Ondine" refers to the well-known mythical water sprite. That Debussy was drawn to depict this creature invites immediate comparison with the more famous piece by the same name by Ravel, written in 1908 (thus very likely predating this work). A specific literary reference inspired Ravel, but such is not the case with Debussy's piece. The music here is also less demanding, less florid, and of more modest dimensions. As a result, Debussy's "Ondine" is somewhat neglected by pianists who tend to favor the larger, more flamboyant Ravel piece. This is a pity, for the Debussy work is first-rate within its own parameters. Based on a tonal center of *D*, the piece resists structural analysis by block sections. There is an introduction of ten measures that relies heavily on the dominant ninth of *D*, raising it a half step unexpectedly in its final three measures. An opening thematic idea that is built with grace notes and arpeggios around the reiterated dominant tone of *A* is followed finally by a resolution passage in which the fourth degree of the tonality built on *D* is raised, suggesting Lydian mode. A second motive based on repeated notes forms a kind of middle section consisting of recitative-like interruptions of the musical flow marked first *Retenu* and later *Le double plus lent* (Twice as slow). An exquisite passage marked *Rubato* follows wherein the repeated-note theme is set amidst a shimmering arpeggio figuration. One more statement of the repeated-note motive in a more agitated form leads to a brief return of the first idea built around the dominant tone A. The entire coda is based on a single polychordal combination, *D* and *F-sharp* arpeggios. There is a final resolution to *D*.

"Hommage à S. Pickwick Esq. P.P.M.P.C." is a musical portrait of the character Samuel Pickwick, created by Charles Dickens. Debussy himself provides us with a few fleeting images in a letter to his editor: "here and there souvenirs of Zululand, views of Christiania, terrible rifles (which, happily, do not shoot anymore), family portraits, a peaceful garden." This character is seen by Debussy as the epitome of comic, British conservatism, a bit pompous, generally good natured, and at times surprisingly jaunty. The opening measures of the piece are built on a quotation from "God Save the Queen" in the bass, and from that point on chordal music of regal dignity alternates with sprightly dotted rhythms. The piece is thus erratic, and somewhat improvisatory, presenting a series of contrasting fragments. One near the end, marked *Lointain et léger,* suggests that Samuel Pickwick either whistled a little tune or danced a little jig before his final stately exit.

"Canope" may derive its title from the Latin/Greek word *kanōpos.* There are two distinct references for the word: the brightest star in the southern skies in the constellation Carina; and an ancient Egyptian seaport city, east of Alexandria near the mouth of the Nile River. (The exact title-word *canope* also existed in Middle English as the equivalent of the present-day English word *canopy,* meaning a covering of some kind. However, the fact that the etymological derivation is English rather than French, as well as the somewhat mundane meaning of the word, makes pursuit of this linkage more farfetched and less poetic.) Most writers favor connecting the title to the Egyptian city, because it was famous in ancient times for the production of burial urns—large, simple vases in which inner organs of the dead were sealed before the body was mummified. Early designs included the carving of the head of a well-known god, often Osiris, on the lid of the jar. Later, about the sixth century B.C., the Etruscans carved likenesses of the deceased on the lids. Canopic urns were thus widely recognized as a symbol of funeral rites for several centuries. Debussy's reference to the sculptured artworks of the ancient world has already been noted in the "Danseuses de Delphes," from the first book of preludes. It is interesting to note that the similarity between the two preludes in that both establish their moods with series of processional-like chords. "Canope" introduces a recitative-like second idea based on a repeated-note triplet motive. A short middle section alludes to whole-tone harmony. The return incorporates both the chords and the repeated-note figure, the latter fading into silence before its completion. "Canope" is a bare, unpretentious piece, but it can create a mood that is profoundly affecting.

"Les Tierces alternées" (Alternating Thirds) foreshadows the etudes of Debussy in that the title of the piece simply describes the technical challenge that lies within its pages. The entire prelude consists of thirds that are played alternately by the left and right hands. The tempo is fast in the outer sections of the ABA form, and the thirds are written so that the hands must operate in close proximity to one another. Fingering and determining which hand goes over which are paramount considerations. The dynamic levels favored are piano and pianissimo, resulting in a shimmering perpetual motion. The piece ends with the same suspended third (C–E) that closed "Voiles" in the first book of preludes.

"Feux d'artifice" (Fireworks) presents a highly descriptive picture of the kind of pyrotechnic display one sees on holidays and special occasions. The introduction to the piece employs a black-white key figuration to imitate the sizzling of a fuse, surrounding it with staccato octaves to which the player must leap. Thus, Debussy sets a mood of risky anticipation, involving the performer both musically and physically. A short passage of rapidly alternating seconds leads to a statement of the main thematic idea, a series of short motives that open with a quick, ascending, broken fifth. What follows is a series of free settings of this motive, intertwined with cascades of figurations, chordal passagework, glissandi, and cadenzas. The final setting builds to a climax that culminates with descending glissandi played simultaneously on both white and black keys. A quiet restatement of the main motivic idea closes the piece. It is combined fleetingly with the opening phrase of the "Marseillaise," suggesting that this particular fireworks display was in celebration of Bastille Day, July 14, the French holiday that commemorates the destruction of the Bastille prison in 1789 during the French Revolution. The brilliance and imagination of "Feux d'artifice" have led to its being one of the most popular pieces in the Debussy repertoire.

Etudes

The twelve *Études* (1915, divided into two books of six each) are Debussy's last work for keyboard. The composer debated dedicating the set to Couperin or Chopin, finally choosing the latter. A preface written by Debussy states that keyboard players of the past were ingenious enough to formulate their own fingerings and that it would be improper to suggest that contemporary keyboard players were any less adept at carrying out this task. The text ends with a tongue-in-cheek call to action: *Cherchons nos doigts!* (Let us seek our own fingerings!)

The mature style associated with Debussy's writing at this point is not only in evidence throughout the etudes but also seems to have grown in sophistication, intensity, and complexity. The pages of the pieces are dense with passagework and expressive indications of all kinds: dynamics, touch forms, and tempo changes. Debussy himself wrote in a letter to Durand, his publisher, that the most detailed Japanese print was mere child's play when compared with the graphism of some of the pages of the *Études*. Harmonic boundaries are pushed to their limits. For example, Debussy indicated in another letter to Durand that "Pour les quartes" (For Fourths) contained "new" sonorities. Structural relationships become even more subtle, and although block sections still exist and such arrangements as ABA can still be discerned, the degree of constant variation and the frequent use of unexpected, added excursions are so pronounced that the resulting impression is often one of a constantly evolving structure.

Debussy must have been challenged by the thought of writing technically oriented material that would explore new avenues after the famous etudes of Chopin, Liszt, Scriabin, Rachmaninoff (the earlier Op. 33 set), and a host of others. Yet he succeeded admirably in creating works that not only open up fresh approaches to traditional technical problems but also often reflect the demands of both his own music and later twentieth-century keyboard music. Debussy must have been aware of his success in this regard when he wrote to Durand at the completion of the set that he felt the *Études* would have a special place in the repertoire and that it was "good work."

"Pour les 'cinq doigts' d'après Monsieur Czerny" (For the "Five Fingers" in the Style of Mr. Czerny) opens with a musical joke that continues to evoke chuckles even after more than half a century of repeating. The stereotypical five-finger scale pattern, repeated laboriously between C and G, is suddenly interrupted with dissonant A-flats in a syncopated pattern of increasing urgency (Example 17.9). The tension breaks into a gigue-like triplet figure that leads to a burst of energetic figurations all spun out of the opening figure. Rapidly changing tempi, shifting tonal centers, and the creation of a few original, devilish five-finger patterns add to the ingenuity of this etude. It finally works itself up into a frenzy, alternating patterns in *C* with patterns in *G-flat* and creating a dialogue of dispute. The key of *C* wins at the final cadence.

"Pour les tierces" (For Thirds) is a title that is bound to bring to mind the famous double-third study of Chopin, Op. 25, no. 5. It stands to reason that the probability of musicians' comparing the two pieces must have occurred to Debussy and that he may have set out to write a study that was markedly different from the Chopin work. For the most

Example 17.9 Claude Debussy: "Pour les 'cinq doigts' d'après Monsieur Czerny" from *Douze études* mm. 5–6

part he succeeded admirably. In contrast to the Chopin etude, the Debussy piece is less rapid, the thirds somewhat more lyrical, and decidedly more diatonic than chromatic. The sixteenth-note movement of the right hand, wherein most of the thirds occur, is often joined by the left hand, creating shimmering textures. In the closing animando, a climax is achieved by using double notes in both hands. The piece ends dramatically in *b-flat*.

"Pour les quartes" (For Fourths) is a piece of striking originality, both from a harmonic standpoint and an expressive one. Harmonically, Debussy eschews the use of the fourth as the two upper notes of first-inversion triads, a far more traditional arrangement, but rather lets the fourths stand on their own as harmonic entities, devising combinations of fourths with both the right and left hands that create ambiguous sonorities insofar as tonal centers are concerned. Thus, even having provided several dominant pedal points on C throughout the first section, the final fortissimo resolution to the key of *F* comes as something of a surprise. A jocular development section gradually increases in complexity and speed until cascades of descending fourths take place in rapid succession (Example 17.10). Since the quartal sonorities lead to various possible tonal centers, Debussy uses a variety of key signatures, at one point writing six flats, and, indeed, the key of *C-flat* seems prominent. A few bars later he switches to three sharps (perhaps *A*). Finally, as the climax of the piece approaches, he abandons the formality of attempting to use flats or sharps in a key signature altogether, simply writing in accidentals as he needs them. The return of the first-theme material, now rewritten and thinned out to a bare skeleton, creates a delicate, extremely sensitive atmosphere. The final, widely spaced fourths are cut off by a staccato dominant note (*C*), Debussy providing the evocative direction of *Estinto* (Extinguished).

"Pour les sixtes" (For Sixths) inspired a humorous comment by Debussy in an August 15, 1915, letter to Durand:

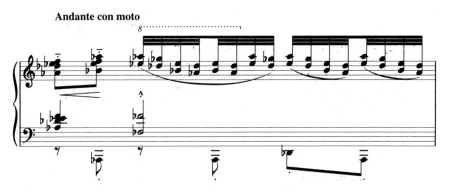

Example 17.10 Claude Debussy: "Pour les quartes" from *Douze études* m. 60

> For a long time, the continuous use of sixths reminded me of pretentious misses, sitting in a drawing room, sulking over their embroidery, while envying the scandalous laughter of the mad ninths. . . . Yet here I am writing this etude in which attention to the sixth goes so far as to organize its harmonies solely with the aggregates of this interval, and—it is not ugly!

Indeed, the combinations of sixths that Debussy uses in this etude in both hands endow the harmonic texture with frequent references to ninth and thirteenth chords. The piece is essentially lyrical, but the involvement of the left hand as an almost equal partner in the lyrical flow results in original thinking about the use of sixths, both technically and musically. The middle section of the arch form moves somewhat more rapidly, eventually to a climax in which both hands sweep down and back up in sixths wedded to arpeggios patterns. The return of the opening material resolves quietly to the key of the piece, *D-flat*.

"Pour les octaves" (For Octaves) sets its own mood with the opening directions *Joyeux et emporté, librement rythmé* (Joyful and sweeping, rhythmically free). One can imagine, once again, that Debussy remembered the famous "octave etude" of Chopin (Op. 25, no. 10) as a study dealing with octaves essentially in conjunct movement and that he set out to write its opposite, a study dealing with disjunct octaves, emphasizing the difficulties encountered when octaves are combined with skips. Certainly, the intoxicating waltz-like opening material presents a dizzying array of octave skips, mostly for the right hand but also in rising figurations that combine hands. The middle section also involves both hands in octave difficulties, opening with gamelan-like pentatonic figurations that build to a tremendous climax marked *strepitoso* in which octaves in both hands must leap in intervals of fourths and fifths back and forth on the black keys. After a return of opening material, a coda leads to a brilliant closing in the key of *E*.

"Pour les huit doigts" (For the Eight Fingers) is attended by a footnote that clarifies further what is implied in the title of the piece: that the use of thumbs in the work is impractical, the study being rather a kind of acrobatic feat. The texture of the piece is born of the hands alternating between groups of four notes apiece, one note for each finger. A compact ABA structure is built on scalar passagework, the alternating hand movement being sustained throughout. The climax of the piece features glissandi, and there is a coda. The piece is effective as a short perpetual-motion stunt piece.

"Pour les degrés chromatiques" (For Chromatic Intervals), as in several of the earlier etudes, involves the left hand as a partner in textures that are divided between the two hands and in bursts of rapid chromatic scales. The left hand also acts as the agent to carry the one lyrical thematic element of the piece. The right hand is kept occupied with chromatic adornment almost without rest. The lyrical idea that the left hand presents comes after a short introduction and is presented in several variations. Just before the coda, there is a climax that features chromatic figuration in the right hand with chromatic broken sixths in the left, an unusually devilish combination in terms of technical execution.

"Pour les agréments" (For Ornaments) was mentioned briefly in Debussy's correspondence with his publisher: "It borrows the flavor of a barcarolle on a somewhat Italian sea." In this etude, Debussy defines ornamentation in the broadest possible sense, focusing not so much on traditional ornamental devices, such as mordents or trills, but rather on elaborate decorations of melodic lines, such as arpeggiation and cadenza-like arabesques. Moreover, he adds difficulties in maintaining multiple levels of sonority, sometimes generating wide skips, as well as one passage that features runs composed of rapidly descending triads. Although the material of the opening section returns again near the end to close the piece, the structural impression the work gives is that of a set of free variations, the thematic material often evolving and changing shape from section to section. From a textural standpoint, this etude is one of the most complex, its pages so dense with figuration that it even looks impossibly complicated. It harbors, nevertheless, passages of supreme beauty.

"Pour les notes répétées" (For Repeated Notes) is marked *Scherzando* at its opening, and, indeed, its mood is one of droll, tongue-in-cheek humor. Short bursts of staccato repeated notes outline tritones and segments of whole-tone scales, sometimes incorporating awkward intervallic skips or changes of hand position. Although the right hand has most of the repeated-note figuration, the left hand frequently joins in to facilitate execution of the pattern. The single lyrical melodic fragment of the piece, which acts as a second thematic idea, is given to the left hand almost exclusively while alternating with the right in continuous figural motion. The one time the right hand takes that thematic fragment is in a passage that is constructed in such a way that the repeated notes must be maintained by using the right hand thumb only, rendering impractical the traditional technical device of changing fingers on repeated notes. These cleverly crafted passages, combined with the wry humor of the piece, make it unique in the keyboard repertoire.

"Pour les sonorités opposées" (For Opposing Sonorities) is an evocative title that might invite several compositional or technical procedures. The opening of the piece itself suggests that Debussy's focus was on widely spaced sounds with a dissonant relationship in traditional harmonic practice, in this case the notes G-sharp and A. This exploration, however, serves only as the introduction to the piece. Following in rapid succession are two new themes that are built on closely spaced levels of sonority, the second using parallel triads in both hands, with the left crossed over the right. Thus, careful balance and etching the melodic line become the main problems of the etude. Pentatonic hornlike calls marked *Lointain, mais clair et joyeux* (from a distance, but clear and joyful) lead to a middle section that builds to a lush chordal climax. At this point the hands must shift positions very rapidly, all the while maintaining a low G-sharp pedal point. There is a brief fragmented return of earlier material, and the piece ends quietly. This etude calls to mind the mood of the more poetic preludes, notably "Les Sons et les parums tournent dans l'air du soir" and "La Terrace des audiences du clair de lune," and it is easily their equal in poetic sensitivity.

"Pour les arpéges composés" (For Composed Arpeggios) is one of the frequently encountered Debussy etudes on recital programs. Debussy's ingenious "new" arpeggios include added seconds, sixths, sevenths, and ninths, resulting in a rich-sounding, luminous texture. The arpeggiated passagework is most often notated with thirty-second or sixty-fourth notes but also written as cadenza-like grace notes. The structure of the piece is an unusually well-defined ABA, with a jocular middle section, a truncated return, and a coda that combines references to both.

"Pour les accords" (For Chords) features major and minor chordal patterns combined with simultaneous skips in contrary motion in both hands. The opening section places this texture in perpetual motion, creating a challenge to the performer that is breathtaking and dizzying. The middle section, by contrast, almost suspends movement altogether, its tempo regulated by exact proportions indicated between it and the opening section. There is a shortened recapitulation of the first section and a driving, climactic coda. This etude provides a brilliant, albeit somewhat strenuous, final piece for the set.

Miscellaneous Pieces

There has been mention already of the earliest piano piece of Debussy, *Danse bohémienne* (Bohemian Dance; 1880). Madame von Meck presumably showed the piece to Tchaikovsky, who justifiably found it lacked unity (although it does present some lively syncopation). The year 1909 produced a cute, small dance with a politically questionable English title (by later standards), "The Little Nigar" (often, however, reprinted under its French equivalent, "Le petite Negre," which inexplicably seems somehow less offensive). The *Berceuse héroïque* (1914) was written as a tribute to King Albert I of Belgium and his soldiers. Orchestrated in the same year, the piece incorporates Belgium's national anthem. Two small pieces date from 1915, an Elégie and an album leaf written for a war relief organization known as Le Vêtement du Blessé. Finally, there exist solo keyboard versions of two sets of pieces that are usually played in their four-hand arrangements, *Petite Suite* (1886–89) and *Six épigraphes antiques* (1914).

CHAPTER EIGHTEEN

French Keyboard Music of the Early Twentieth Century

During the nineteenth century, Paris had been one of the great centers of artistic activity, attracting musicians from all over Europe, many of whom settled there. The leading professional schools of the city were busy training both French and foreign students. The cultural life of the city was enormously rich. Many leading piano manufacturers of the day were centered in Paris. Trends popular with Parisian society influenced all of central Europe. Only Vienna, and to a lesser extent Berlin and London, could even begin to compare as centers of creative activity.

When one begins, however, to search for distinguished musicians who are native to France during the nineteenth century, or, indeed, who represent a voice that can be identified as distinctly French, one finds the scene surprisingly barren. Perhaps the price of being a center of ephemeral taste and playing host to such a large group of international talents was inadvertently to forego developing a regional or national voice. The result was that few native French composers were able to distinguish themselves as geniuses of the nineteenth century, musicians whose music would enjoy longevity. Thus, if one looks at keyboard music from the point of view of a French nationalist, one would have to conclude that very little of significance occurred for two or three generations toward the end of the eighteenth century and the beginning of the nineteenth. In other words, one looks in vain for French giants of keyboard music between Rameau (d. 1764) and Fauré (b. 1845). A new wave of French creativity was to arrive at the turn of the century, however, with important forerunners whose work became prominent in that final decade of the nineteenth century.

Gabriel-Urbain Fauré

Gabriel-Urbain Fauré (b. Pamiers [Ariège], May 12, 1845; d. Paris, Nov. 4, 1924) showed sufficient musical talent as a child for his father, a provincial inspector of schools, to take the boy to Paris for study with Louis

Niedermeyer, who had just formed a school that emphasized church music. When Gabriel was sixteen, after Niedermeyer's death, Saint-Saëns became his primary teacher. Fauré's early career centered on serving as a church organist, first in Rennes, and later in a series of churches in and around Paris. In 1896, he was appointed chief organist at the Madelaine in Paris and became a professor of composition at the Paris Conservatory, where he taught for the ensuing twenty-five years, acting also as the director of the conservatory (1905–20). Fauré had a host of important students, including Maurice Ravel, Georges Enesco, Charles Koechlin, Jean-Jules Roger-Ducasse, Florent Schmitt, Louis Aubert, and Nadia Boulanger.

Fame was slow to bless Fauré's creative efforts, so for most of his life he was forced to regard composing as peripheral to the business of earning a living through church service and teaching. He possessed neither great self-confidence as a composer nor the ability to market his work in the highly competitive Parisian musical scene. For much of his career, his music was considered too advanced and somewhat barren by those whose taste ran to more extravagant salon styles. Although he was greatly admired and liked as a person, and his presence was often sought in the elegant soirées of the period, he was not celebrated as a composer until late in his life. This lack of recognition and Fauré's underlying insecurity with regard to the value of his work explains in part why his output tends to run to more modest works, both in terms of genre and scope. There are thus few orchestral works, but a handful of chamber works and for solo keyboard almost a complete absence of longer works in extended forms.

Fauré's early piano style, represented by the Op. 17, *3 Romances sans paroles* (1880), is very much like the styles of other composers of nineteenth-century salon music, showing influences of Mendelssohn and Chopin in its careful craft and delicate sensitivity. To this period also belongs one of the few extended works of Fauré, the Ballade, Op. 19 (1881), which was originally a work for solo keyboard before the composer cast it for piano and orchestra.

From the decade of the 1880s came the first of a series of character pieces with titles reminiscent of Chopin: thirteen barcarolles, thirteen nocturnes, and five impromptus. It is possible to observe the maturation of Fauré's style through these pieces, for the barcarolles cover the period between 1880 and 1921, the nocturnes between 1875 and 1922, and the impromptus between 1881 and 1909. The four *Valse-caprices* date from the 1890s. The most ambitious works of Fauré's mature period are a set of variations, Op. 73 (1895), and a set of nine preludes, Op. 103 (1909–10; Example 18.1).

Without ever losing the distinctive soft-edged refinement of the early years, Fauré evolved a sophisticated, complex harmonic language based on bold, unexpected modulation and the use of striking alterations in harmonic progressions. Although he experimented with whole-tone

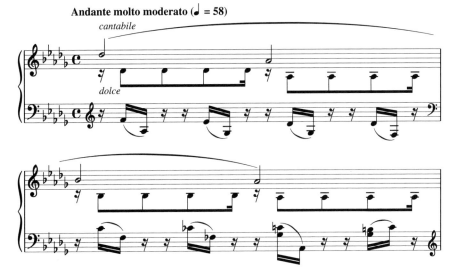

Example 18.1 Gabriel Fauré: Prelude, Op. 103, no. 1 mm. 1–2

harmonies, he eschewed for the most part the harmonic freedom of impressionist techniques. He chose, rather, to extend the language of traditional practice to its furthest limits, using his ability to modulate deftly and to inflect both melodic lines and their underlying harmonic progressions with surprising twists and turns. By this means, Fauré was able to create a style that was distinctly his own. The composer's attention to detail and his predilection for intimacy result in music that is seldom brilliant or heroic. Thus, performers who crave extraversion in music would be wise to look elsewhere, but those who respond to beauty of detail and a high degree of sensibility will be richly rewarded by Fauré's unique magic.

Although **Vincent (Paul-Marie-Théodore) d'Indy** (1851–1931) exerted enormous influence in France at the turn of the twentieth century, his work as a composer has fallen into neglect. His keyboard catalogue includes a monumental sonata in *E,* Op. 63 (1907), two earlier sonatas, a large set of variations entitled *Thème varié, fugue et chanson,* Op. 85 (1925), many character pieces, and two sets of teaching pieces, Opp. 69 and 74. Although his style clearly comes from the late nineteenth century, the music itself is carefully conceived and often rewarding.

Paul Dukas (1865–1935) wrote two monumental works for keyboard between 1899 and 1902. A sonata in *e-flat* is considered to be a landmark in French keyboard music. Although the composer attributed the inspiration for the sonata to the late sonatas of Beethoven, the music itself is strongly reminiscent of Franck. The second large work, *Variations, interlude et finale sur un thème de Rameau,* is also Franckian but with stronger individual characteristics.

Charles Koechlin (1867–1950) was influential as a composer, theorist, and teacher, celebrated in Paris as one of music's leading figures until about the 1920s, when composers of bolder, more modern characteristic claimed the spotlight. Among his students were Darius Milhaud, Francis Poulenc, and Germaine Tailleferre. Although Koechlin experimented with new, oftentimes complex techniques of composition, including polytonality, his music remained rooted in tradition in the final analysis. He composed for solo piano his entire career, and much of his music is both attractive and useful both as teaching and concert material. This treasure has been overlooked for the most part by pianists. Among the works that might well be explored are the sets of sonatinas, Op. 59 (1915–16), and Op. 87 (1923–24); sets of character pieces, *24 esquisses*, Op. 41 (1905–15); *Paysages et marines*, Op. 63 (1915–16); *12 Pastorales*, Op. 77 (1920); and the *15 Preludes*, Op. 209 (1946). The Op. 61 (1915–20) consists of four sections, all geared toward teaching at beginning levels, providing exercises, legato studies, and easy pieces. More teaching material appears in the *12 Very Easy Little Pieces,* Op. 208 (1946). Koechlin's music is often oriented toward folk material, as exemplified by the *L'Ancienne Maison de campagne,* Op. 124 (1932–33).

Albert (Charles Paul) Roussel (1869–1937) embarked on a career as a naval officer before he decided to turn his attention full-time to composing. As a result, he was thirty-eight years old when he finished his studies with Vincent d'Indy at the Schola Cantorum in Paris. His predilection toward classical structures emerge in his style, as he downplayed impressionistic techniques in favor of more traditional gestures. There is only a little keyboard music, all of it dating from the early decades of the twentieth century. Most significant are the sets of small pieces, *Rustiques*, Op. 5 (1904–5); the Suite, Op. 14 (1910); and *Trois Pièces*, Op. 49 (1933). Also noteworthy is the Sonatine, Op. 16 (1912; Example 18.2). Roussel also wrote a much-neglected, fine piano concerto. His

Example 18.2 Albert Roussel: Sonatine, Op. 16, 1st movt. mm. 1–3 © 1913 Durand S.A. Editions Musicales. Used by permission of the publisher. Sole representative U.S.A. Theodore Presser Company.

work, in general, is of excellent quality, deserving considerably more attention than it gets.

Florent Schmitt (1870–1950) studied with Massenet and Fauré, eventually adopting many of the techniques associated with impressionism into his writing but combining them with more dissonant harmonies, nonsymmetrical rhythms, and contrapuntal textures. He wrote about two dozen sets of character pieces for the piano, often with suggestive titles such as "Nuits romaines" (Roman Nights), Op. 23 (1901); "Ombres" (Shadows), Op. 64 (1913–17); "Mirages" (Mirages), Op. 70 (1920–21); or *Suite sans esprit de suite* (Suite without the Spirit of a Suite), Op. 89 (1937). Although attractive in many ways, Schmitt's music often succumbs to ideas that are not distinctive enough to sustain long-term interest.

Déodat de Séverac (1872–1921) began his study in Toulouse, studying law at the university and later music at the conservatory. In 1896, he went to the Schola Cantorum in Paris, where he worked until 1907, studying composition with Vincent d'Indy and piano with Blanche Selva and Albéniz. Although Séverac attracted admirers of his work in Paris, he preferred the provincial life. He thus lived away from the city in Céret or St. Félix for most of his life. He enjoyed, however, considerable professional recognition, both in the region of his residence and in Paris. Both Ricardo Viñes and Blanche Selva programmed his piano works frequently, often beside those of Debussy and Ravel.

The main body of Séverac's keyboard works lies in the three suites: *Chant de la terre: Poéme géorgique* (The Song of the Earth: Rural Poem; 1900); *En Languedoc* (1904); and *Cerdaña* (1910). *La Chant de la terre* contains four movements; the other two suites have five, all of them rather extended improvisatory pieces that mix techniques of impressionism with influences from Spanish and Russian Romanticism (Albéniz and Musorgsky). Séverac's most significant separate piece is the *Baigneuses au soleil* (Sunbathers; 1908), a long, remarkably coloristic tone poem. *En vacances* (On Vacation; 1912) is a set of shorter pieces, many fairly easy. Séverac's music is often sensuous and very beautiful. He himself was a gifted improviser, to the point of growing to hate the tedium of writing down his creations. The spirit of improvisation is very strong in those works he did write down, and the resulting structural weakness is often troublesome for the listener.

Maurice Ravel

Maurice Ravel (b. Cibourne, Basses-Pyrénées, Mar. 7, 1875; d. Paris, Dec. 28, 1937) was always very proud of his Basque heritage, which came from his mother, Marie Delouart. His father, Pierre Joseph Ravel, was a Swiss engineer whose work took the family to Paris when Maurice was still an infant. Thus, although the composer lived in Paris from childhood throughout his life, he harbored a fondness for the romance associated with his birthplace, even becoming fluent in the Basque language.

Maurice was provided with a superb musical education. Early lessons in piano were with the well-known teacher Henri Ghys and in composition with Charles-René, a student of Delibes. By 1889, Ravel was enrolled in the Paris Conservatory, studying piano with Charles de Bériot and harmony with Émile Pessard. During this time, Ravel wrote his first extant solo piano piece, the *Menuet antique*. In 1895, when Ravel was twenty, he left the conservatory, resolved to devote himself to composition, but, after producing only a couple of songs during the following year, he returned to the conservatory in 1897, this time in the composition class of Gabriel Fauré and the counterpoint class of André Gedalge.

Complementing this extensive formal training was a lively interest in contemporary, sometimes exotic art, an interest Ravel shared with his fellow student and friend, the pianist Ricardo Viñes. Ravel expressed admiration of Russian music, Chabrier, Satie, and even Wagner. He was enthusiastic about the work of poets such as Charles Baudelaire, Stéphane Mallarmé, and Edgar Allen Poe. Like Debussy, he responded to the exotic sounds of the 1889 Paris Exposition, and, also like Debussy, he developed a fascination with antiquity.

This penchant for the contemporary and the trendy resulted in Ravel's consistently being passed over for top honors in academic endeavors. Ravel tried for the Prix de Rome four times. In the first attempt he was disqualified for failing to conform to the carefully controlled setting of a prescribed text. The other times resulted in his winning second prize at best (1901) and not even getting past the preliminaries at worst (1905). All the while, Ravel's reputation as a composer grew, being furthered by both public performances and publication of his works.

During this period, Ravel was a member of a group of young artists known as Les Apaches. The name was adopted by the group as a symbol of the fact that they were, artistically speaking, "savages," outside of the "civilized" conservatism associated with traditional aesthetic values. Other members of the group were composers Manuel de Falla, Florent Schmitt, Maurice Delage (who studied with Ravel), and Désiré Émile Inghelbrecht; music journalists Michel Calvocoressi and Émile Vuillermoz; the painter Paul Sordes; and the poets Léon-Paul Fargue and Tristan Klingsor. (Igor Stravinsky was a latecomer, joining the group in 1909.)

Paradoxically, Ravel's character also included many traits befitting a highly cultured sophisticate. He had a slavish addiction to fashion in personal manner and dress, almost to the point of dandyism. He developed a strong attraction for Greek and Roman antiquity, particularly as it was represented by eighteenth-century artists. He collected mechanical toys and exotic bric-a-brac.

Ravel's personal and creative life was attended by an almost obsessive need for privacy, a trait that grew as he got older. Composing was a process that he himself described as needing a long period of gestation. Solitary walks at night, whether in Paris or in the woods outside the city, were part of the process necessary to give birth to his musical ideas, and this phase of the creative process was regarded by Ravel as mystical. Once the actual writing process began, however, tough-minded objectivity took over, for Ravel was unusually meticulous about detail, subjecting all aspects of his work to intense scrutiny and a process of refinement. He strove to complete each work in a form that would be as perfect as his capabilities would allow and that would need no revision. As a result of this self-imposed discipline, Ravel often worked slowly with frequent periods of little or no creative activity. His catalogue of works is thus somewhat small, but the quality of his works is consistently high.

The first keyboard work of Ravel is entitled *Sérénade grotesque* (1893). It remained unpublished until 1975, Ravel choosing not to submit it for publication. It is a youthful work, strongly influenced by Chabrier. Also from the 1890s are the *Menuet antique* (1895) and the famous *Pavane pour une infante défunte* (Pavane for a Deceased Spanish Princess; 1899). Both works are well crafted and built in block structures, the minuet in the usual form with a lyrical trio and the pavane in an ABACA arrangement. Both also represent the composer's style well enough to be active in the repertoire, although Ravel's musical language, clearly in progress, does not quite emerge full-blown in the minuet and is somewhat uncharacteristically sentimental in the pavane.

"Jeux d'eau" (1901) is reminiscent of the title of Liszt's "Les Jeux d'eau à la villa d'Este" (The Fountains of the Villa d'Este). The Ravel work, however, takes its spirit not so much from the idea of a fountain as from the poetic imagery of Henri de Régnier, whose words are quoted just under the title: "Dieu fluvial riant de l'eau qui le chatouille" (a river God laughs at the water that tickles him). The music itself is often compared to that of Liszt, but, indeed, Ravel was correct in claiming a high degree of pianistic originality for the work. (He did so in a 1906 letter to music critic Pierre Lalo as a defense against the charge of being an imitator of Debussy, pointing out that "Jeux d'eau" predates Debussy's impressionistic style.) If there is need for pointing to nineteenth-century stylistic predecessors, Chopin might be as strong a contender as Liszt, for, like many Chopin works, "Jeux d'eau" features extended hand positions, open harmonic texture, and a high degree of structural formality. The overall structure of the piece is sonata-allegro with a scintillating, extended cadenza being placed just after the return of the first theme of the recapitulation. Pentatonicism is strong in the second theme, and the development builds to a brilliant climax of tremolo chords with alternating hands followed by a black-key glissando. The work combines a winning musicality with technical stunts pianists love to perform. Not surprisingly, it is one of Ravel's most frequently played pieces.

The style of the Sonatine (1903–5) is similar to that of "Jeux d'eau," Ravel now casting his ideas in even more strictly traditional structures. The first movement is a diminutive sonata-allegro structure with marked contrast between the exposition's lively opening motive and its lyrical second theme. The second movement is marked *Movt. de menuet* but acts more like a small ABA form than a traditional minuet. The final movement is a brilliant sonata-allegro structure with a truncated recapitulation. The Sonatine, while difficult, is technically more accessible than many of Ravel's works, and it is often used to introduce students to Ravel's writing. By the same token, its frequent appearances on recital programs attest to its usefulness both as concert repertoire and as material for the teaching studio.

Miroirs (Mirrors; 1904–5) reinforces and expands the distinctive musical features of "Jeux d'eau" and the Sonatine. Consisting of five pieces with descriptive titles, Ravel here clearly established his own dialect in the language of impressionism, in retrospect easily exonerating himself of the charge of being a second Debussy, a contention Ravel seemed destined to endure for most of his creative life. Sonorities are rich in sevenths, ninths, and thirteenths; and polytonality is frequently implied. The florid patterns underlying the sonorities are deftly crafted, so much so that one is brought to a subliminal awareness of the ingenuity behind the display of notes.

Structural plans continue to employ a marked degree of formality. The opening piece, "Noctuelles" (Night Moths), is in sonata-allegro form with both a middle-section theme and a transitional development. The fourth piece, "Alborado del gracioso" (Morning-song of the Jester), presents a clear ABA arrangement, the Spanish dance-like rhythms and guitar techniques of the outer sections being contrasted in the middle section with a series of elaborate recitatives in *cante hondo* (deep song) style. Even the more improvisational pieces exhibit carefully planned structural features. "Une Barque sur l'océan" (A Bark on the Ocean) presents a series of sections, ABACA, with cadenza-like transitional passages between A and B as well as before the final return of A. "La Vallée des cloches" (Valley of the Bells) is built on an arch form. Even "Oiseaux tristes" (Sad Birds), the most improvisatory of the set, casts its "free," recitative-like opening in rhythmic complexities, and there is a clear return of the opening theme after the middle section reaches its climax in a cadenza that is also rhythmically carefully controlled.

The evocative titles of the *Miroirs* do not have literary sources, but imitation of extramusical sounds and sensations abounds. "Noctuelles" flutters with appropriate nervousness (Example 18.3). "Oiseaux tristes"

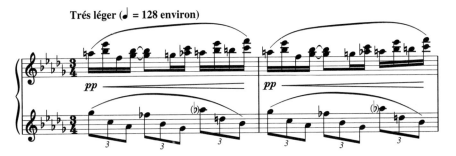

Example 18.3   Maurice Ravel: "Noctuelles" from *Miroirs* mm. 1–2

Example 18.4   Maurice Ravel: "Alborada del gracioso" from *Miroirs* mm. 1–2

was described by the composer as representing birds lost in a dense forest on a torrid night, and, indeed, the music is rife with imitations of birds signaling to each other as well as a climax in which one imagines a disturbance resulting in startled flight. "Une Barque sur l'océan" imitates ocean swells in elaborate, florid passagework to the point of possibly engendering seasickness in those listeners so inclined. The harmony with which the piece opens, a minor triad with a minor seventh and a major ninth, is a favorite with Ravel during this period, occurring often in conjunction with important structural points. (See, for example, the recapitulation of the main theme in "Oiseaux tristes.")

The stylistic features of "Alborada del gracioso" have already been mentioned: Andalusian rhythms, harmonies, and song styles (Example 18.4). The technical difficulties of the work are notorious among pianists: skips, passagework divided between the hands working in close proximity, double-note glissandi for the right hand, and a repeated-note passage that almost defies accurate execution. Finally, "La Valle des cloches" opens by building layers of mostly pentatonic sonority in imitation of bells from different directions at varying distances. After the introduction, the main theme of the work is constructed on a harmonization of the four-note chime associated with grandfather clocks (or

Très lent ♩ = 50

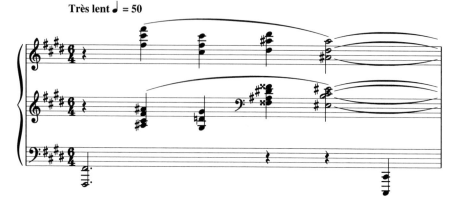

Example 18.5   Maurice Ravel: "La Vallée des cloches" from *Miroirs* m. 14

London's Big Ben; Example 18.5). The piece makes use of the interval of an unresolved fourth to simulate the acoustical properties of the bells, and, indeed, the composition fades away with that sound in the lower registers of the piano.

Gaspard de la Nuit (1908) takes its title from a book of poetry by Aloysius Bertrand (1807–42) published posthumously in 1842. The opening of the book describes its genesis, a fantasy in itself. Bertrand tells of encountering a mysterious indigent who calls himself Gaspard de la Nuit and who leaves behind the manuscript of the book. Upon inquiring after the man in order to return the manuscript, Bertrand is told that the man has returned to hell, for, indeed, he was the devil in disguise. A literal translation of the title would be "Gaspard of the Night," but the translation without the tale does not convey the sinister or fantastic implications Bertrand intended. The volume of poetry remained relatively unnoticed until Symbolist poets such as Baudelaire and Mallarmé came upon it at the end of the nineteenth century and began hailing it as a source of inspiration for their own work.

Ravel's impressionistic writing reaches new heights of decorative figuration and complexity in the opening piece, "Ondine." The poetry describes the seductive song of the water sprite Ondine, who, after extolling the wonders of her watery kingdom, invites the object of her serenade to accept her ring of engagement. When he declines, stating that he is betrothed to a mortal, she laughs and sprays his window pane with water as she disappears. Ravel's setting is quite descriptive. A song-like melody is set in extravagant, elaborately decorative arabesques, including trill-like figurations involving chords, arpeggiation using the full range of the keyboard, chromatic double-note passages, and glissandi. After a powerful climax, the music subsides. A monophonic recitative

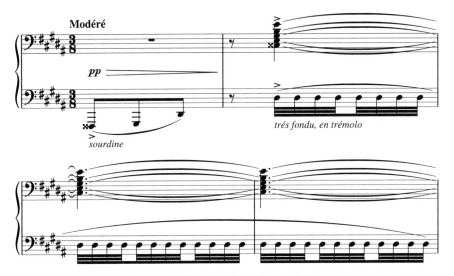

Example 18.6 Maurice Ravel: "Scarbo" from *Gaspard de la nuit* mm. 1–4
Copyright Alfred Publishing Company, Inc. Used with permission of the
publisher.

suggests the mortal's rejection of Ondine, a final brilliant cadenza her
reaction and drenching disappearance.

"Le Gibet" (The Gibbet) describes the grisly picture of a corpse,
executed and left hanging for exposure to public scorn. Various insects
fly or crawl around the dead body, and a bell tolls from behind the walls
of a city as the sun sets. A B-flat octave pedal tone, placed in the middle
of the keyboard, imitates the bell. This is the sound around which Ravel
builds the composition, adding to it thematic material based on intervals
of open fifths, later more complex altered chords with added ninths and
thirteenths, and at one point, by way of extreme contrast, a segment of
monophonic melody. The persistent, repeated B-flat gives stark, hypnotic quality to the music, and the piece ends with this sound by itself
fading into the distance.

"Scarbo" is the name of a dwarf who haunts the abode of the poet.
He is glimpsed at midnight in moonlight, his laughter heard "in the shadow of my alcove," his form expanding "like the belfry of a gothic cathedral." These images suggest a haunting, and Ravel chooses to depict
Scarbo's elusiveness as a source of terror. The introduction sets the mood
with repeated notes in the low register of the keyboard punctuated with
suspenseful silences (Example 18.6). The texture crescendos to a seven-
measure tremolo built from alternating chords between the two hands.
The introduction is followed by a free sonata-allegro form. The opening
theme is composed of a sweeping lyrical phrase that is contrasted by a

repeated-note motive. The second theme features, once again, tremolo figures and suspenseful rests. It grows to a climax of enormous proportions. The repeated-note motive figures prominently at the opening of the development, introducing a section that is both brilliantly crafted and almost unplayable from a technical standpoint. The recapitulation incorporates the opening introduction and the other exposition material in a completely rewritten form. Every gesture is enlarged. The suspense is more sinister; the sonorities are more complex and sustained; and the buildup of the second theme grows to a climax of hysterical dimensions. A short coda closes the piece, reflecting the text of the poetry that alludes to a candle and indicates that Scarbo is suddenly and inexplicably extinguished.

In "Scarbo," Ravel set about consciously to write one of the great virtuoso challenges of the keyboard repertoire, holding up as his model the *Islamey* of Balakirev. He succeeded admirably, but he also wrote a work of breathtaking effectiveness in the process. Its reputation among pianists as a work that brings together supreme challenges of technique, control, and musicality is well deserved.

The two remaining major solo keyboard works of Ravel, *Valses nobles et sentimentales* (1911) and *Le Tombeau de Couperin* (1914–1917), have several things in common. They both were inspired by the memory of earlier composers, the waltzes taking their name from a set by Schubert; they are heavily oriented toward dance music; and they represent a conscious attempt by Ravel to move away from the rich, sonorous impressionism of *Gaspard de la Nuit* toward a style that was leaner and more linear.

The *Valses nobles et sentimentales* is a set of eight, fairly short waltzes. The opening waltz, subtitled "Adélaîde" (the title of the ballet that this music accompanies in its orchestrated form), is prefaced with a quotation from Henri de Régnier: ". . . le plaisir délicieux et toujours nouveau d'une occupation inutiles" (the delicious and ever new pleasure of a useless occupation). The piece contrasts audacious choral dissonance, used in the introduction and the retransition, with charm and rhythmic vitality (Example 18.7). The ensuing waltzes offer contrasting tempi and mood. Waltz no. 7 is the most extended, an ABA arrangement, and it builds to a climax that foreshadows the excitement of the orchestral piece *La Valse* (1919–20). The final waltz is subtitled "Épilogue" and represents a return to Ravel's earlier sonorous impressionism, offering a dreamy, nostalgic atmosphere in which themes from the other waltzes make ghostly, fleeting appearances.

Le Tombeau de Couperin translates literally "the tomb of Couperin," but one needs to understand that the French use the term *tombeau* as the symbol of the spirit or memory of a person. The work was written not only as a tribute to Couperin but also in memory of friends whom Ravel lost in World War I, a conflagration that was profoundly disturbing to

Example 18.7 Maurice Ravel: *Valses nobles et sentimentales* mm.1–2
© 1911 Durand S.A. Editions Musicales. Editions A.R.Í.M.A. & Durand S.A.
Editions Musicales joint publication. Used by permission of the publisher. Sole
representative U.S.A. Theodore Presser Company.

Example 18.8 Maurice Ravel: "Prélude" from *Le Tombeau de Couperin* mm. 1–2
© 1913 Durand S.A. Editions Musicales. Used by permission of the publisher.
Sole representative U.S.A. Theodore Presser Company.

the composer. Each of the movements is thus dedicated to the memory
of one of these comrades. The six movements combine to make a unique
dance suite. The inclusion of a fugue after the prelude is unusual, as is
the use of a motoric toccata as a final piece. Indeed, the use of the for-
lana and the rigaudon is relatively rare even in the seventeenth and
eighteenth centuries, although there are instances of their use by Johann
Sebastian Bach in nonkeyboard suites, and Couperin includes a rigaudon in the *deuxième ordre* (second series) of solo keyboard pieces.

The opening Prelude is occasionally imitative, features pentatonic
figuration, and is in two-part form, only the first section being marked
with repeat signs (Example 18.8). The Fugue, a piece that serves as the
second movement, is the least successful work in the suite, so much so that
performers frequently omit it in performance. It is a strict fugue, and
Ravel's meticulous craft is in evidence. Unfortunately, however, the subject is based on repetition of a major triad and is combined with counter-
melodies in such a way that seventh- and ninth-chord sonorities begin to
dominate. Thus, the ear picks up on the choral color rather than the linear relationships, resulting in series of harmonies that eventually end up

sounding repetitious. Characteristic dotted rhythms and piquant harmonies dominate the Forlane. The Rigaudon is vigorous, and the *Menuet* is appropriately graceful. All three dance pieces have trio sections. The final Toccata is in the tradition of Czerny, Schumann, and Debussy, a perpetual-motion piece that opens with driving, repeated-note figuration and ends with a tremendous climax. It is one of the best-known display pieces of the early twentieth century and remains a popular audience rouser among pianists.

Small separate pieces include the *Menuet sur le nom de Haydn* (1909), Ravel's contribution to the celebration of the 100th anniversary of Haydn's death, sponsored by the Société Internationale de Musique; two imitative vignettes *A la manière de . . . Borodine, Chabrier* (1913); and a prelude (1913) that Ravel wrote for sight-reading examinations at the Paris Conservatory. Of the orchestral work *La Valse* (1919–20), an arrangement for solo piano by the composer also exists.

Erik (-Alfred-Leslie) Satie

Erik (-Alfred-Leslie) Satie (1866–1925) began his career as a mediocre student, dropping out of the Paris Conservatory before graduation. He was a shy man who earned his living for many years playing cocktail piano in the Montmartre district of Paris. When he was close to the age of forty, he resumed his musical education, working in the classes of d'Indy and Roussel at the Schola Cantorum and eventually earning a diploma (1908). Although his musical output was sporadic, admiration for his work grew steadily, especially in the fashionable avant-garde circles of the day. Writer Jean Cocteau in particular was a champion of Satie and did much to stimulate interest in his work. Satie's iconoclastic spirit, humor, and general disregard for tradition were qualities greatly admired by Debussy, Ravel, and many younger French composers. Les Six, the group of composers so named by music journalist Henri Collet, were at the center of his followers. The group included Milhaud, Honegger, and Poulenc.

Satie's output for solo piano was confined to short character pieces, often improvisatory in nature and often with evocative or humorous titles. Also sometimes included in the music were funny commentaries, which, according to Satie in his directions for performance of *Heures séculaires et instantanées* (Instantaneous and Centenarian Hours), were rewards for the player and on no account to be read aloud. About 100 of these short piano pieces cover a period from 1884 to 1920, most of Satie's creative life. Thus, they reflect his evolving style. Earlier works include the famous *Trois gymnopédies* (Three Gymnopedies; 1888), pieces that were orchestrated by Debussy and represent Satie at his most lyrical and sentimental. Later works exhibit more clearly Satie's penchant for humor and satire; his eschewing of both emotion and complexity; and his individual, moderately offbeat approach to both harmony and structure. Collections of such pieces include *Embroyons desséchés* (Dried up Embryons; 1913), in which a parody of Chopin's famous funeral march is called a "quotation from the celebrated Mazurka of Schubert"; *Sports et divertissements* (Sports and Diversions;1914), twenty short pieces with such titles as "Fishing," "Swimming," "Picnic," or "Tango"; and *Avant-dernières pensées* (Next to Last Thoughts; 1915), three pieces dedicated to Paul Dukas, Claude Debussy, and Albert Roussel.

In November of 1917 a group of six French composers had works performed on a recital in Paris given by singer Jane Balthori. The group called itself *Les nouveaux jeunes* (The New Young Ones). Throughout the following months, writer Jean Cocteau used his pen to invoke a conscious break with what he perceived as the oppressive influence of German Romanticism, particularly the music and ideals of Richard Wagner. Even Debussy and Ravel were cited for having fallen prey to such influence. Only Erik Satie and the group of young composers who espoused Satie's aesthetics merited praise. On January 16, 1920, an article by Henri Collet appeared in *Comoedia* that dubbed the group of six composers *les six français* (The French Six), compared the group to the Russian Five, and again discussed Satie as its spiritual father.

The ideas that supposedly united the group were allegiance to simplicity and directness, an eschewing of the formal and academic, and the incorporation of elements of popular music, specifically jazz and music-hall tunes. The six composers were **Georges Auric** (b. 1899), **Louis Durey** (1888–1979), **Arthur Honegger** (1892–1955), **Darius Milhaud** (1892–1974), **Francis Poulenc** (1899–1963), and **Germaine Tailleferre** (b. 1892). Although the idea of Les Six has become entrenched in the chronicle of music history, the group was never very cohesive, and its members moved in different directions after an association of only a few years. During that brief period, a collection of six solo keyboard pieces was assembled under the title *Album des Six* (1920).

All six of the group wrote solo keyboard music to varying degrees. Auric wrote character pieces and one sonata (1931), a work in which tonality is marginal. Durey and Tailleferre wrote only a few sets of short pieces. Honegger confined his piano writing to short solo pieces and chamber works except for a *Toccata et Variations* (1916) and the *Prélude, Arioso et Fughetta sur le nom de BACH* (1928). Milhaud was an extremely prolific composer, writing more than 400 works. Marginally in the repertoire of pianists are the two sets of *Saudades de Brazil* (1921), totaling twelve pieces based on Brazilian dance rhythms and popular styles. Milhaud wrote many sets of smaller pieces that might well be used as teaching material, for they make relatively modest demands on the player in terms of keyboard skills. His two sonatas (1916, 1949) are more difficult and imposing. Of Les Six, only Poulenc was able to write solo keyboard music that has found a relatively secure niche in the performing repertoire.

Francis Poulenc

Francis (Jean Marcel) Poulenc (b. Paris, Jan. 7, 1899; d. Paris, Jan. 30, 1963) had early lessons with his mother and then studied piano with Ricardo Viñes. After unsuccessful attempts to work with both Paul Vidal and Ravel in composition, Poulenc finally settled in to study for a period of three years with Charles Koechlin. An early friendship with Georges Auric led to an association as one of Les Six. Of that group, Poulenc was the most consistent in developing and sustaining a style born of directness, simplicity, clarity, and the inclusion of influences from popular music. Poulenc's music is, in fact, so filled with tuneful, obvious melodies and music-hall clichés that the temptation is ever present to dismiss his work as lacking seriousness of purpose. A remarkable alchemy emerges, however, through Poulenc's deft use of modulation to create freshness, his ability to craft mundane material into charming gestures, and his penchant for surprising the listener with passages of heartfelt sensitivity.

The music for solo piano covers a period from 1918 to 1959, but much of it was written before 1940. The early *Trois movements perpétuels* (1918) were so fashionable after their publication that they were influential in establishing Poulenc's reputation as a composer. The following two decades produced sets of character pieces including the *Promenades* (1921), nine pieces with titles that refer to modes of transportation; *Napoli* (1925), three pieces of which the final one, "Caprice Italien," is both the most extended and the best known; eight nocturnes (1929–38); and *Les Soirées des Nazelles* (1930–36), the most extended work cast as a set of free, descriptive variations with a préambule and a finale. The fifteen improvisations, said to have been regarded by the composer with particular favor, were written over a longer span of time (1932–59), no. 11 paying homage to Schubert and no. 15 to the cabaret singer Edith Piaf. Of the later keyboard works the most serious and the most extended is the *Thème varié* (1951), a music-hall theme with eleven variations and a coda that uses the theme in retrograde. Poulenc's last solo keyboard work is a poignant novelette (1959) built on a theme of Manuel de Falla (Example 18.9). It is often coupled with two earlier novelettes (1927–28).

Aside from Taillefaire, a few other French women of the period achieved recognition as composers, writing in several genres, including varying numbers of piano pieces. This group includes **Mélanie Bonis** (1858–1937), who studied with Franck and wrote more than a hundred piano works; **Lili Boulanger** (1893–1918), the first woman to win a Prix de Rome, whose early death is even now mourned as a great tragedy for French music, but who wrote only a few piano pieces; and **Elsa Barraine** (b. 1910), who studied with Dukas and Vidal at the Paris Conservatory and won a Prix de Rome in 1929.

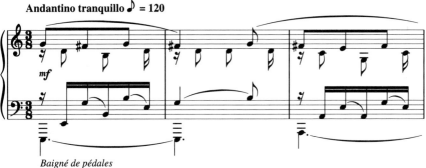

Andantino tranquillo ♪ = 120

Baigné de pédales

Example 18.9 Francis Poulenc: Novelette in *e* mm. 1–3
Reprinted by permission of G. Schirmer, Inc.

Olivier Messiaen

Olivier Messiaen (b. Avignon, Dec, 10, 1908; d. Paris, Apr. 27, 1992) has emerged as the most important composer of French keyboard music of the mid-twentieth century. Educated at the Paris Conservatory, where he won first prizes in counterpoint and fugue (1926), piano accompaniment (1928), history of music (1929), and composition (1930), Messiaen went on to build a career in Paris that included holding the post of principal organist at La Trinité for more than forty years and teaching at the École Normale de Musique and the Schola Cantorum. His career was interrupted by service in the French army during World War II, during which he was captured by the Germans and interned in a prison camp (1940–42). From 1943, Messiaen was on the faculty at the Paris Conservatory, where he was appointed professor of composition. His classes at the conservatory in analysis achieved wide fame both for their penetrating insight and for the broad range of literature touched upon. Among his students were Pierre Boulez, Jean-Louis Martinez, Maurice Le Roux, and Karlheinz Stockhausen. Messiaen was thus an extremely powerful influence on many of the most significant composers of the period. He has received considerable official recognition since 1950, including receiving a commission from the French government to write a work honoring the dead of the two world wars (1965), having a piano competition named after him (1967), and being a recipient of the Erasmus Prize (1971).

As a composer, Messiaen has been inspired throughout his career by his personal, intense Catholic mysticism and a love of nature. Messiaen wrote a theoretical treatise, *Technique de mon langage musical* (Technique of My Musical Language; 1944), in which he documented technical elements of his style up to that time. He described himself as both a musician and rhythmist, a way of pointing to his extensive study of Greek and medieval rhythmic patterns as well as the rhythmic systems that govern Hindu music. He was particularly fascinated with complex concepts such as overlapping, asymmetrical, nonretrogradable patterns, and groupings in odd numbers. Harmonically, Messiaen moved from sonorities that are reminiscent of Debussy through traditional modality, creating modes of his own devising (such as his modes of limited transposition), and serialism. His harmonic writing is always rich in color, and although often dissonant and complex, it retains elements of sonority that are appealing to the nonanalytic listener. Sometimes, however, the working out of a cycle of complex patterns dictates a length that borders on tedium for the unindoctrinated.

Major keyboard works are representative of all phases of Messiaen's development. The eight *Preludes* (1930) extend the harmonic language of Debussy and, like Debussy's preludes, carry descriptive titles. In *Vingt regards sur l'enfant Jésus* (Twenty Contemplations of the Child Jesus; 1944), the composer creates a work unified by thematic symbolism of such concepts as the cross, the star, and God the father. In addition, each movement has its own descriptive focus that Messiaen comments on in written notes at the beginning of the work. Messiaen has written of the *Vingt regards:* "More than in all my preceding work, I have sought a language of mystic love, at once varied, powerful, and tender, sometimes brutal, in a multicolored ordering."

The next two keyboard works were of particular importance as pioneer thinking in serial techniques. Boulez and Stockhausen were enormously influenced by Messiaen's *Cantéyodjaya* (1948) and *Quatre études de rhythme* (1949). In the former, Messiaen began to associate specific rhythmic value and intensity with a given pitch. In the etude entitled "Mode de valeurs et d'intensité" (Mode of Values and Intensity), the composer organized the music around a melodic mode of thirty-six sounds, twenty-four different rhythmic values, seven different intensities, and twelve different keyboard attacks (which could be compared to different instrumental timbres). Boulez considered the work the model for serializing all parameters of the music, perhaps the first of its kind, although the American composer Milton Babbitt was experimenting with complete serialization at about the same time.

Messiaen's next major work for solo keyboard, *Catalogue d'oiseaux* (Catalogue of Birds; 1955–58), was born of the composer's fascination with bird songs. He spent many hours notating bird calls in natural settings, reportedly never using a tape recorder. Thirteen piano pieces are dispersed through seven books of music. Each of the books opens with a list of the birds whose calls are imitated in the pieces, seventy-seven birds arranged in alphabetical order in French with their names translated into four other languages. Each of the pieces is prefaced, moreover, with

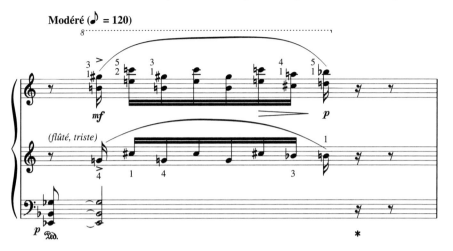

Example 18.10 Olivier Messiaen: "Le Courlis cendré" from *Catalogue d'oiseaux* m. 1

a written description of the setting and several of the bird sounds heard in that particular work. The title of each piece is taken from the name of one of the several birds represented in that piece. Each piece places the appearances of the bird calls amid sonorous background settings, often with descriptive indications such as "the night," or "the sea." The calls come and go, apparently at random, much as they might be heard in their natural settings. Messiaen's love of sonorous color is ever present, and the bird calls themselves employ rhythmic complexities that are challenging to realize (Example 18.10).

Messiaen's final work for solo keyboard, *La Fauvette des jardins* (1972), takes its title from one of the birds that appeared in the *Catalogue d'oiseaux*. The work is a synthesis of all the techniques of the composer: rich sonorities, serial techniques, and bird-song imitation.

Several other twentieth-century composers of significant French keyboard music should be mentioned. **Jean Rivier** (b. 1896) wrote sets of small pieces between 1931 and 1956 but has composed longer single-movement works starting in 1952 with *Tornades and Torrents* (1960). More extensive is the writing of **Jean Françaix** (b. 1912), whose works include character pieces, a sonata (1960), a set of etudes, and a scherzo. **Henri Dutilleux** (b. 1916) wrote a frequently played keyboard sonata (1949), an imposing three-movement work using traditional forms with a sonorous chorale and variations as the final movement. The significant work of **Pierre Boulez** (b. 1925) and **Jean Barraqué** (b. 1928) is discussed in the chapter that deals with the works of the nontonal composers of the twentieth century.

CHAPTER NINETEEN

Spanish, Portuguese, and Latin Keyboard Music in the Twentieth Century

Nationalism in Spanish music came into full bloom at the turn of the twentieth century. European musicians had long regarded Spain as a source of colorful melody and intoxicating rhythm, often borrowing Spanish folkloric characteristics for their concert pieces. Examples that might be cited are Mikhail Ivanovich Glinka's *Capriccio brillante* (1845) and *Recuerdos de Castilla* (1848), both for orchestra; Liszt's *Rhapsodie Espagnole* (1863) for piano; and Edouard Lalo's *Symphonie Espagnole* (1874) for violin and orchestra. Spanish musicians, on the other hand, tended to follow the stylistic trends of central Europe, often as a result of having gone there for their musical training.

Spain

The musician given credit for changing this state of affairs was **Filipe Pedrell** (1841–1922). Essentially self-taught, Pedrell's main interest as a composer was writing operas influenced by Wagner. Early in his career, however, he also became interested in both early Spanish church music and folk song. Through his writings and editions of Spanish music, he founded modern musicology in Spain and influenced many composers to turn to Spanish sources for inspiration. Albéniz, Granados, and Falla all studied with Pedrell for a brief period of time and responded to his influence in this regard. Pedrell wrote some character pieces for piano, but most of them reflect European Romanticism, and they have not found a place in the repertoire.

Isaac (Manuel Francisco) Albéniz

Isaac Albéniz (b. Camprodón, Lérida, May 29, 1860; d. Campo-les-Bains, May 18, 1909) was a child prodigy. It is reported that he gave his first piano recital at the age of four. He was taken to Paris by his mother at the age of seven, where he played for Marmontel, then a professor at the Paris Conservatory, who praised the boy's playing. Albéniz was considered too young, however, to be accepted into the conservatory, and his application was turned down. There ensued several concert tours and a period of study at the conservatory in Madrid. At the age of twelve, Albéniz ran away from home, stowing away on a ship bound for South America. For more than a year he managed to subsist, visiting Argentina, Brazil, Uruguay, Cuba, and Puerto Rico, ending up in San Francisco just before returning to Spain.

Albéniz continued to follow a pattern of changing his surroundings throughout his career, taking up residence at various times in London, Paris, Barcelona, and, after meeting Liszt in 1880, following him to several cities in central Europe to obtain piano lessons. Albéniz came under Pedrell's influence in about 1883, and it was after that time that his compositions gradually began to show nationalistic characteristics. Albéniz was a prolific composer. About half of his enormous output is for solo piano. His compositions bear opus numbers as high as Op. 232, but a systematic catalogue of his works has not been undertaken, so there are many unexplained gaps in numbering, possibly indicating lost works.

Albéniz wrote five piano sonatas, the last three of which survive in complete form (Opp. 68, 72, and 82). The scherzo movement from the first sonata is also extant. The works were written in the early 1880s, before Albéniz had incorporated Spanish characteristics into his works. The sonatas are written in a nineteenth-century Romantic style, and, although they exhibit the composer's skill in creating virtuoso complexities for the pianist, they lack sufficient inspiration to attract continued interest. In addition, there are many sets of character pieces, often arranged in suites. These works began to take on nationalistic qualities beginning about 1883. Representative of these sets are *España,* Op. 165 (1890), and *Cantos de España,* Op. 232 (1896), both sets of six pieces.

The crowning achievement of Albéniz is his last major work, a set of twelve pieces called *Iberia.* Arranged in groups of three, the four books were premiered by pianist Blanche Selva at various concerts in France between 1907 and 1909. The pieces all have individual titles, the opening one called simply "Evocación" and the remaining eleven being named after Spanish locales or dances. All of them incorporate identifiable traits of Spanish song and dance. The settings of these elements are elaborate, combining extremely virtuosic writing with lush, harmonic textures that lie somewhere between a Liszt-like Romanticism and impressionism. The structures of the pieces are quite simple, however, usually alternating between a dance-like rhythmic section and a songful refrain, often in a freer, recitative-like style. The effect is one of presenting lavish arrangements of attractive, relatively straightforward material with ongoing pianistic display as an essential ingredient.

The opening piece, "Evocaçion," is based on the rhythm of a *fandanguillo*, a diminutive variant of the *fandango*, an eighteenth-century dance that contrasts three-four and six-eight meters. The songlike refrain, or *copla*, enters in the left hand. "El Puerto" (The Port) is likely a reference to the seaport town of Puerto de Santa Maria, on the Atlantic coast near Cádiz. Its boisterous mood is set with the rhythm of the *polo*, which is combined with the biting, guitar-like *bulerías* and the *seguiriya gitana*, a Gypsy *seguidilla* that would normally feature castanet rhythms after each refrain. "Fête-Dieu á Seville," which ends the first volume of *Iberia*, describes the Corpus Christi festival in Seville. The opening march suggests the traditional religious procession, wherein a statue of the Virgin Mary is carried through the streets amid throngs of people. The dynamics of the march suggest that the procession comes from afar, passes by, and recedes into the distance. The contrasting section is based on the long notes of the *saeta*, literally "arrows" of tone that pierce through bell-like cascades of descending notes, simulating a song of religious ecstasy.

The second book opens with "Rondeña," best known as a dance but one that probably derived its name from the Andalusian town of Rhonda, the home of bullfighting. Its characteristic rhythms use constantly changing meters that alternate between six-eight and three-four (Example 19.1). "Almería," named after a town on the Mediterranean, makes use of the Lydian mode and the somewhat languorous rhythm of the *tarantas*. A flamenco copla provides contrast. "Triana," one of the best-known pieces of *Iberia*, is named after a district in Seville, and its music is based on the *paso-doble* (two-step), alternating with a toreador march. Imitations of guitars, castanets, and various percussion sounds abound in the piece.

The third book of *Iberia* opens with "El Albaicín," named after the Gypsy quarter of Granada. Opening with a staccato bulerías rhythmic pattern (Example 19.2), its contrasting sections are based on the improvisatory *cante hondo* (deep song) of the Andalusian Gypsies. Debussy praised this piece extravagantly in a 1913 journal review, writing that in it "one rediscovers the nights of Spain, fragrant with carnations and brandy." "El Polo" is named for a lamenting Andalusian dance, its rhythms to be "soft and sobbing," according to Albéniz's directions. "Lavapies" refers to one of the oldest sections of Madrid, famous for a local church where residents observe Holy Thursday with a ritual in which they wash their feet. Opening with a habanera rhythm, the music is marked to be played "joyfully with freedom." The ensuing textures are among the most complicated in *Iberia*.

Example 19.1 Isaac Albéniz: "Rondeña" from *Iberia* mm. 1–2

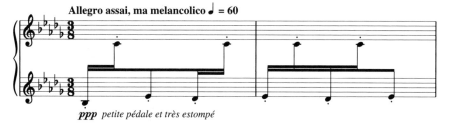

Example 19.2 Isaac Albéniz: "El Albaicín" from *Iberia* mm. 1–2

The fourth book of pieces was deemed by Henri Collet, Albéniz's French biographer, the "most beautiful jewels of the collection." "Málaga," which opens the set, is a reference to the province of the same name and is based on the *malagueña,* a variation of the fandango, and the *jota,* a ubiquitous dance with possible origins in Aragon. "Jerez" is named for a wine-producing city in Andalusia. The English word *sherry* is derived from Jerez. Gypsy music, known as the *soleares,* is used here, as well as the Hypodorian mode (the mode that corresponds to a natural-minor scale). Finally, "Eritaña" is based on the rhythm of the *sevillana.* The piece is named for an inn on the outskirts of Seville, and it is appropriately energetic and merry. This work was singled out for praise by Debussy in his 1913 review of *Iberia:* "Never has music achieved such diversified, colorful impressions; one's eyes close, as though dazzled by beholding such a wealth of imagery."

Two uncompleted pieces of Albéniz were finished by colleagues. "Azulejos" (Glazed Tiles) was but a sketch, and Granados's realization of the work in 1911 is surprisingly not very consistent with Albéniz's style. "Navarra," originally intended for inclusion in *Iberia,* had only a few measures missing. Based on the jota, its completion by Déodat de Séverac in 1912 remains in the repertoire, although the work still falls short of the standard set by the other pieces of *Iberia.*

Enrique Granados

Enrique Granados (b. Lérida, Jul. 27, 1867; d. at sea, English Channel, Mar. 24, 1916) was a composition student of Pedrell as a teenager and at age twenty went to Paris to study piano with Charles de Bétoit. Granados's professional life was centered in Barcelona, where he established his own school, Acadamia Granados (1901). His career began to achieve international success with performances of the piano suite *Goyescas* in Paris in 1914, the subsequent operatic version of the music being produced at the Metropolitan Opera in New York City. Ironically, the trip to attend the opening, which took place January 26, 1916, with great success, resulted in the death of both Granados and his wife. Having delayed their return to Spain by a direct sailing in order to perform at the White House for President Woodrow Wilson, the couple were routed home by way of England. In Liverpool, they boarded the *Sussex* for Dieppe. The ship was torpedoed by a German submarine in the English Channel. Although Granados was able to climb into a lifeboat, he saw his wife struggling in the water and dove in to assist her; both were drowned.

Granados's style is not as flamboyant as that of Albéniz, for it is deeply rooted in the Spanish art of the Classical and early Romantic periods, and it is influenced by flamenco, Gypsy music, to a lesser extent. Most of Granados's output consists of piano and vocal music. There are over fifty undated piano works, almost all of them character pieces: two impromptus, six *escenas romanticas*, seven *valses poeticos*, six *estudios expresivos*, six settings of popular Spanish songs, and so on. The most ambitious of this group of works are the *Allegro de concerto* and the *Rapsodia aragonesa*. Between 1892 and 1900, Granados produced four books of Spanish dances, twelve in all, pieces that are attractive and technically accessible. The names of individual dances suggest well-known types, such as the jota, zarabanda, villanesca, or majurca, and the music contains many melodies that are instantly recognizable.

By contrast, *Goyescas* (1911) is a set of extremely difficult virtuoso pieces. Its source of inspiration came from the sketches, or cartoons as they are called, for tapestries created by Francisco Goya y Lucientes (1746–1828). Painted around 1775, the more than thirty cartoons depict scenes in the lives of eighteenth-century *major y majas* (lads and lasses). Granados selected six from which to weave a story of flirtation, jealousy, love, dueling, and death, subtitling the set *Los majos enabordas* (The Enraptured Lovers).

Part 1 of *Goyescas* contains four pieces. "Los requiebros" (Flattery) combines the rhythm of the jota with songlike melodies borrowed from a theater skit, called a *tonadilla*, of Blas de Laserna (1751–1816). Granados marks each entry of the song in the score with the term *tonadilla*. A tender ballad called "Coloquio en la reja" (Dialogue at the Grilled

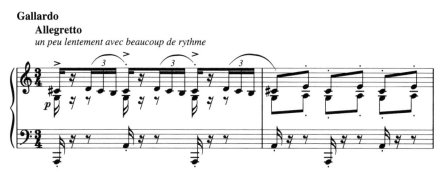

Example 19.3 Enrique Granados: "El fandango de candil" from *Goyescas* mm. 1–2

Window) is the second piece. There follows "El fandango del candil" (Fandango by Candlelight), a spirited but lyrical fandango (Example 19.3). The most popular piece of *Goyescas* is "Quejas, o La maja y el ruiseñor" (Laments, or The Maiden and the Nightingale). Here, a lengthy, improvisatory introduction leads to an ecstatic song, which is repeated. Trills and cadenza-like figurations imitate the nightingale in the coda of the piece.

Part 2 of *Goyescas* consists of only two pieces. The first, "El amor y la muerte (Balata)" (Love and Death—Ballad) is the longest piece in the work. The improvisatory style that permeates the *Goyescas* is carried even further in this piece, as fragments of themes from the first part reappear kaleidoscopically. "Serenata del espectro" (The Specter's Serenade) is appropriately ghostlike and concludes with the warning that even golden lads and lasses must eventually come to dust. A seventh piece, "El pelele" (The Straw Dummy), was written for the opera. It depicts the merriment of tossing a straw dummy into the air. It is sometimes included in performances of the piano version, usually as an opening piece.

Manuel de Falla (1876–1946) achieved an international reputation on a par with that of Albéniz and Granados, but relatively few keyboard works are extant. In his early studies Falla achieved highest honors at the Madrid Conservatory. As an ardent admirer of the music of Grieg, Falla expressed the desire to create for Spanish music the kind of nationalism Grieg had achieved in Norwegian music. About 1902, Falla received additional stimulation in the direction of nationalism from his study with Pedrell. Between 1907 and 1914, Falla moved to Paris, where he found both artistic support and eventually considerable success. After 1914, he composed and taught at his home in Granada. Among his students were Ernesto Halffter and Cuban composer Joaquin Nin-Culmell. In 1939, an invitation from the Argentinian Institución Cultura Española and the political climate generated by the Spanish Civil War resulted in a move

Example 19.4 Manuel de Falla: "Aragonesa" from *Pièces espagnoles* mm. 1–5

to Buenos Aires. A few years later, Falla retired to nearby Alta Gracia, where he spent his final years working on *Atlantida,* a composition of monumental scope for soloists, chorus, and orchestra.

Some of Falla's best-known music comes from works originally written for the theater, such as the ballets *El amor brujo* (Love, the Magician) and *El sombrero de tres picos* (The Three-Cornered Hat). A few piano transcriptions of this music by the composer have found their way into the pianist's repertoire, the most famous of which is the "Ritual Fire Dance" from *El amor brujo.*

There are only two major works originally conceived for piano available in the repertoire. *Piéces espagnoles* (1902–8) consists of four effective character pieces: "Aragonesa," "Cubana," "Montañesa," and "Andalusia" (Example 19.4). The set is dedicated to Albéniz, whose piano writing was an obvious influence. The other work is the *Fantasia baética* (1919), a virtuosic, single-movement piece in an extended ABA form that exploits many Gypsy characteristics such as guitar figurations, percussion effects, and *cante hondo.*

Joaquin Turina (1882–1949) grew up in Seville, but his training was in Paris, where he studied with Moritz Moszkowsky and Vincent d'Indy. Turina graduated from the Schola Cantorum in 1913 and returned to Spain a year later. His professional career met with continued success in Madrid, and he was appointed professor of composition at the conservatory there (1930). The years of the Spanish Civil War were difficult for him, for his family was in disfavor, but after that period of turmoil he once again assumed a position of distinction, having helped establish the music commission of the Ministry of Education, acting as its head (1941). He was awarded the Grand Cross of Alfonso the Wise.

Turina wrote a significant amount of keyboard music, over fifty major works, including sonatas, preludes, fantasies, suites, and character pieces. The sonatas have subtitles: Op. 3 (1909) is called *Sonata romántica;* Op. 24 (1922), one of the best known of Turina's longer works, *Sanlucar de Barrameda;* and Op. 59 (1930) is designated *Sonata fantasia.*

Example 19.5 Joaquin Turina: "Sacro-monte" from *Danzas gitanas*, Op. 55, no. 5 mm. 1–3

Typical of the sets of smaller pieces are the two volumes of *Danzas Gitanas* (Gypsy Dances), Op. 55 (Example 19.5); two sets of *Niñerias*, Op. 21 and 56; and the five *Silhouettes*, Op. 70.

Turina's music is more European in orientation than that of his contemporary and good friend, Manuel de Falla. Although Turina integrated nationalism into his style, he did so in moderation without giving up many traditional forms. Turina's keyboard writing is attractive and so pianistic that it seldom rises to virtuoso heights, although it often creates impressive effects. His use of Spanish idioms is typically moderated by both his adherence to European models and a temperamental conservatism. His keyboard writing is, nevertheless, enjoyable and accessible. As well-crafted material for the teaching studio at the intermediate or early-advanced levels, it is extremely useful.

Oscar Esplá (1886–1976) built a distinguished career in Spain, France, and Belgium as a composer, teacher, and administrator. He was involved in several international projects for UNESCO. His style of writing was influenced by Debussy and Stravinsky. He sought simplicity and freshness in his harmonic vocabulary, and he built a number of his compositions on a scale of his own devising: C, D-flat, E-flat, E, F, G-flat, A-flat, B-flat. For piano he wrote *Estudio fugado* (1907), a scherzo (1909), *Tocata y fuga* (1942), *Sonata española* (1949), and several sets of character pieces.

Federico Mompou (b. 1893) was yet another Spanish composer whose training and career took place as much in France as in Spain. He studied in Paris and lived there for twenty years between the two world wars, finally returning to settle in Barcelona in 1941. Influenced by both Debussy and Satie, Mompou's work as a composer is confined mostly to piano miniatures, small impressionistic pieces that often use nationalistic elements. Simulating improvisations, many of these pieces abandon bar lines and key signatures. His music often exhibits bell-like imitations, ostinato figures, and a pervasive wistfulness. Among his many sets of short pieces are *Cants magics* (1917), *Charmes* (1920–21), sets called *Dialogues* (1923 and 1941–44); and *Cançons i dansas* (1921–28 and 1942–62). *Variaciones sobre un tema di Chopin* (1938–57) is an example of a more extended work.

The **Halffter** family is of German origin, having come to Spain from Königsberg. Three members of the family have had notable careers in music: brothers Rodolfo and Ernesto and their nephew Cristobal.

Rodolfo Halffter (b. 1900) was essentially self-taught, having shown some early compositions to Manuel de Falla for comment and criticism. After a few years in Paris, he moved to Mexico City, where he became established as one of the country's leading musical figures. His music follows along traditional lines. Although he experimented with serialism in the set of piano pieces entitled *Tres hojas de album,* Op. 22 (1953), his style retains its basically accessible, melodic character. He has written three sonatas, Op. 16 (1947), Op. 20 (1951), and Op. 30 (1967), as well as two early *Sonatas de El Escorial,* Op. 2 (1928). There are also several shorter pieces, including a two-part invention on the name Chávez (1949).

Ernesto Halffter (b. 1905) studied with Manuel de Falla and formed a lifelong association with him. Ernesto Halffter's artistic temperament led him in the direction of capturing the spirit of early Spanish music, eschewing lush impressionism and developing a style that reflected the formality of the Spanish Renaissance and Baroque. After Falla's death, Ernesto Halffter spent several years completing Falla's scenic cantata *Atlántida,* a difficult task due to the fragmented nature of Falla's sketches. Although a significant composer in Spain, Ernesto Halffter wrote only a few keyboard works, one sonata (1934) and some character pieces such as "Crepúsculos" (1918), "Espagnolade" (1937), and "Serenata a Dulcinea" (1944).

Cristobal Halffter (b. 1930) studied at the conservatory in Madrid and privately with Tansman. He centered his career in Madrid. Although he began writing in much the same traditional style as his uncles, his style moved toward the avant-garde in the 1950s, and he quickly established himself as a leading figure in experimental techniques. Notwithstanding this evolution, his music is still regarded as exemplifying a spirit that is deeply rooted in Spanish culture. His most important keyboard works are a sonata written in 1951 and *Introducción, Fuga y Final,* Op. 15 (1957).

Two other Spanish composers should be noted in passing. **Joaquin Rodrigo** (b. 1901) studied with Dukas in Paris, lived in France and Germany for the duration of the Spanish Civil War (1936–39), and returned to Spain to become one of the country's most celebrated composers. His music has remained rooted steadfastly in a conservative Spanish-French tradition. Among his piano works are an early suite (1923), five *Sonatas de Castilla con toccata a modo de pregón* (1951), and four *Estampas andaluzas* (1954). **Carlos Surinach** (b. 1915) studied in Madrid and in Germany in the cities of Düsseldorf and Cologne. He settled in the United States in 1951 and has become prominent as a composer of music for the dance. For the most part, his music has retained Spanish characteristics, to which are added wit and sophistication. Among his piano works are a sonatina (1949), three Spanish songs and dances (1951), and *Tales from the Flamenco Kingdom* (1955).

Portugal

Portuguese composers, like their Spanish counterparts, followed the pattern of going to Europe for their musical training. Although some of them have been influenced by regional or folkloric materials, they do not seem to espouse nationalism with the same fervor as the Spanish group. As a result, no prominent nationalistic school of composers has emerged.

José Vianna da Motta (1868–1948) was an important figure as a pianist, having studied with Liszt in Weimar and later touring extensively in Europe and South America. Vianna da Motta was director of the Lisbon Conservatory (1919–38), and his influence as a teacher of piano was extensive. He edited the piano works of Liszt. His own piano music is derived from late nineteenth-century European models and includes a ballade, Op. 16; a barcarolle, Op. 17; several Portuguese rhapsodies; and a set of three character pieces entitled *Scenas portuguezas*, Op. 15.

Luís de Freitas Branco (1890–1955) worked with Vianna da Motta as an associate director of the Lisbon Conservatory. He, too, was educated in Europe, having studied with Humperdinck in Berlin and Grovlez in Paris. Freitas Branco was dedicated to bringing contemporary European music, such as that of Debussy and Schönberg, to Portuguese musical life, and the influence he exerted in this regard was both strong and positive. His own piano works reflect impressionism and, later, neoclassic trends. He has written a sonatina (1930); two sets of preludes (1918 and 1940); and other small pieces.

Rui Coelho (b. 1892) also studied in Europe, with Humperdinck and Schönberg in Berlin and with Vidal at the Paris Conservatory. Coelho turned his attention to the expression of what he envisioned as the Portuguese spirit, mostly in works for theater. His piano works include a sonatina (1932), an *Album de juventude portuguesa* (1933), and three preludes (1962).

Cláudio Carneyro (1895–1963) studied with Widor and Dukas in Paris. He became director of the Operto Conservatory (1955) and worked in the music department of the national broadcasting system. His style often combines a sparse texture with a use of popular themes. His writing for piano consists mostly of character pieces, among which are "Cantico" (1918), *3 poemas emprosa* (1930–31), "Jogos florais" (1934), "Pacidncias de Ana Maria" (1935–36), "Carriōdes de bronze" (1938), and "Bailaderias" (1948).

Frederico de Freitas (b. 1902) studied at the Lisbon Conservatory and centered his career in Portugal, for a time acting as conductor of the

Operto Symphony Orchestra (1949–53). His style is eclectic and often exhibits a wide variety of techniques. For piano, he has written a sonata (1944), variations (1944), a set of thirty-six teaching pieces called *O livro de Maria Frederica* (1953), and other character pieces.

Armando José Fernandes (b. 1906) studied at the Lisbon Conservatory but later went to Paris to study with Boulanger, Dukas, and Roger-Ducasse. He returned to Portugal to teach at the Academia de Amadores de Música in Lisbon and to work in the music department of the national broadcasting system. Given to writing in Classical structures, he has produced a piano sonata (1950), a sonatina (1941), a prelude and fugue (1943), and smaller pieces.

Fernando Lopes-Graça (b. 1906) studied with Freitas Branco in Portugal and later (1937) with Koechlin in Paris. He began writing in styles based on traits of Schönberg, Stravinsky, and Bartók but in 1939 turned his attention to developing a nationalistic style, using Portuguese folk melodies and rhythms. After 1961, he attempted to incorporate nationalism into a more universal style, expanding both harmonic and rhythmic aspects of his writing. A prolific composer, he has written a sizeable amount of piano music, including four sonatas (1934, 1939, 1952, and 1961), twenty-four preludes (1950–55), five nocturnes (1957), and many sets of smaller pieces.

Brazil

Ernesto (Júlio de) Nazareth (1863–1934) was trained as a pianist and composer. He incorporated into his music many folk and popular characteristics of Brazil. His tangos and polkas became so famous that he was regarded as the most popular Brazilian composer of the early twentieth century. Many of his more than 200 piano pieces are remembered as examples of popular period pieces, and his nationalistic focus had a significant influence on the young Villa-Lobos.

Heitor Villa-Lobos

The dominant spirit behind twentieth-century Brazilian nationalism was Heitor Villa-Lobos (b. Rio de Janeiro, Mar. 5, 1887; d. Rio de Janeiro, Nov. 17, 1959). Trained by his father to play the cello, he grew up working with the popular musicians of Rio de Janeiro, and his adventuresome spirit eschewed both the discipline and constriction of formal education. At the age of eighteen he spent seven years traveling throughout Brazil and neighboring countries, absorbing popular and folk music. Upon his return to Rio de Janeiro, he began to build a reputation as a composer. In 1923, he received backing from the state and a group of wealthy individuals to work in Paris. (The pianist Arthur Rubinstein was instrumental in garnering this support.) Villa-Lobos spent seven years in

Paris, where his music became very fashionable, being heralded with enthusiasm by both audiences and the press.

In 1930, Villa-Lobos returned to Brazil. The remainder of his career was spent composing and guiding music education in Brazil at all levels, from developing curricula to be used in primary and technical schools to establishing the Brazilian Academy of Music in Rio de Janeiro. He made frequent trips abroad to oversee performances of his works and to conduct, mostly to France, the United States, and other South American countries. He became the most celebrated Brazilian musician of his day, receiving an honorary doctorate from New York University, the French Legion d'honneur, and the title of Commander in the Brazilian Order or Merit. His funeral in 1959 was attended by the president of Brazil as well as a host of national and municipal authorities.

Villa-Lobos's musical style combines frequent use of folk material with improvisatory freedom. He is fond of highly complex rhythms and sonorities, creating bold splashes of exotic, often dissonant sound. Villa-Lobos also borrowed with great facility from the other composers with whom he came in contact. Thus, he has been accused of using too many contemporary clichés with too little discipline. The enduring freshness and energy of his music, however, have served to establish an ongoing circle of admirers among both musicians and the public.

Most of Villa-Lobos's piano music was written during his early years in Brazil and the time spent in Paris. The rhapsodic nature of his style was best suited to extremely flexible structures. His longest work, "Rudepoema" (Rough Poem; 1921–26), is a single movement of about twenty minutes in which there is no clear repetition of thematic material, one section growing out of the other much like an extended improvisation. The piece is held together by its seemingly inexhaustible array of coloristic sonorities and complex, driving rhythms. The work is dedicated, incidentally, to Arthur Rubinstein, a pianist who championed Villa-Lobos's keyboard works by performing them frequently on recitals.

Villa-Lobos undertook two series of pieces for various solo instruments or combinations of instruments. From the series of fourteen works entitled *Chôros,* only the fifth one ("Alma brasileira"; 1925) is for piano. Its sections are in an ABCA pattern, the outer sections presenting a plaintive melody against a syncopated rhythmic pattern with the two middle sections gradually increasing in motion and excitement. A sonorous climax occurs near the end of the C section before the return of A. The "Alma brasileira" is an attractive, accessible work that deserves to be known more widely than it is. The nine sets of pieces entitled *Bachianas brasileiras* were written as a result of the many transcriptions the composer made of Johann Sebastian Bach's *Well-Tempered Clavier* for various instrumental and choral combinations. Villa-Lobos became convinced of an underlying similarity between Bach's work and Brazilian folk music, where frequent use was made of independent parts in such a way that contrapuntal lines developed. In the *Bachianas brasileiras,* Villa-Lobos often mixed titles or gave double titles to pieces, on one hand reflecting titles appropriate to Bach's time (prelude, aria, toccata, etc.) and on the other drawing titles from Brazilian popular music (*Modinha, Desafio,* and so on). Only the fourth (1930–36) of the *Bachianas brasileiras* sets is for solo piano. It consists of an introductory prelude followed by three short pieces, "Coral," "Aria," and "Dansa."

Among the best known of the short, descriptive pieces is the first volume of *Prolo do bebé* (The Baby's Family; 1918). Each of the eight pieces represents a type of doll—"Branquinha" (The Porcelain Doll), "Mulatinha" (The Rubber Doll), "A pobrezinha" (The Rag Doll), "A bruxa" (The Witch Doll), and others (Example 19.6). In each of the pieces a folk-song-like melody emerges amid colorful figural settings, including the use of dance rhythms, splashes of dissonant sonority, glissandi, and runs. Possibly the best known of the set is "O Polichinello" (Punch), a short piece in which the melody is surrounded by nonstop, rapid chords to be played with an alternating-hand technique. Its effect is that of a breathtaking stunt.

A companion set with the same title was completed in 1921. The composer here features toy animals—"A baratinha de papel" (The Little Paper Bug), "O camondongo de papelão" (The Little Cardboard Cat), "O cavalinho de pau" (The Little Wooden Horse), "O ursinho de Algodão" (The Little Cotton Bear), and so on. These pieces are very demanding technically, much more so than those of the first set, and the musical ideas are also more complex. "O boizinho de chumbo" (The Little Tin Ox), for example, develops extremely dense, layered textures that incorporate complex chords and double-note passagework. "O passarinho de pano" (The Little Cloth Bird) works trills and high-register figuration into a frenetic imitation of bird chirps and fluttering. "O lobozinho de vidro" (The Little Glass Wolf) turns out to be a terrifying predator, as hard, driving chords repeatedly build to near-brutal climaxes.

Many of Villa-Lobos's sets of character pieces are useful for teaching at the intermediate levels. Based frequently on children's songs and folk songs, the pieces are pianistic, attractive, and fairly obvious musically. Among such sets are *Cirandinhas,* a set of twelve pieces (1925); *Cirandas,* sixteen pieces (1926); *Frencette en Piá,* ten pieces based on a story about a little Brazilian Indian and a little French girl (1929); *Guia prático,* eleven volumes of approximately six pieces each (1932–35); and *As tres Marias* (The Three Marias), three pieces based on a folk story (1939).

Oscar Lorenzo Fernández (1897–1948) was educated in Brazil and focused his musical activities there, founding the Brazilian Conservatory in 1936 and acting as its director until his death. His earliest piano pieces, *Historietas maravilhosas* (1922) and *Prelúdios crepúsculo* (1922), are not nationalistic in style, reflecting rather a mix of Romanticism and

Example 19.6 Heitor Villa-Lobos: "Mulatinha" from *Prolo do bébé*, Series 1 mm. 1–3

impressionism. With the two sets of *Poemetos brasileiros* (1926 and 1928), Lorenzo Fernández integrated national characteristics into his music, although remaining more direct and simple in his approach than Villa-Lobos. Among keyboard works are three *Suites brasileiras* (1936 and two in 1938), *Boneca yayá* (Three Doll Pieces; 1944), and a short sonata (1947).

Mário de Andrade (1893–1943) should be mentioned as an important figure in the emergence of Brazilian nationalism. A writer and musicologist, he made a lifelong study of Brazilian folk and popular music and wrote many essays on the relationship between these expressions and art music. He taught at the Saõ Paulo Conservatory and was a decisive influence on both Francisco Mignone and Camargo Guarnieri as well as many other younger composers.

Francisco Mignone (b. 1897) received his training both in São Paulo and in Milan, Italy. His early style was influenced by European models, but after returning to Brazil he came under the influence of Andrade, and beginning with the first of a series of nine *Lendas sertanejas*, written between 1923 and 1940, he turned his attention to nationalism. Mignone used traits borrowed from both traditional folk music and urban popular styles, creating an attractive, accessible style represented by four *Peças brasileiras* (1930), *Cucumbizinho* (1930), *Cateretê* (1931), *Quase modinha* (1940), and *Dança do Botocudo* (1940). To some extent, nationalist traits are also incorporated into the first piano sonata (1941) and the fourteen sonatinas (1949). However, around 1950, Mignone began to move away from conscious use of nationalistic material toward a more eclectic style that drew from polytonality, tone clusters, and serial techniques. This postnationalist period is represented by three sonatas (1962, 1964, and 1967) and *6-1/8 preludios* (1972).

Camargo Guarnieri (b. 1907) studied in São Paulo, where he was directed toward nationalism by Andrade. Later study with Koechlin and Boulanger in Paris did not deter him from developing a style based on Brazilian folk and popular music. His career as a conductor and composer became international in scope, his work enjoying particular success in the United States. He served both as the conductor of the São Paulo Symphony Orchestra and as the director of the conservatory there. His keyboard writing is highly idiomatic, rhythmic, and colorful. Among his many pianoworks are four sonatinas (1928); a set of fifty short pieces entitled *Ponteios* (in five volumes written between 1931 and 1959); a toccata (1935); five etudes (1949–54); and *Fricarós sosinha* (1939), a set of easy, short pieces based on a Brazilian children's game.

Claudio Santoro (b. 1919) was introduced to twelve-tone serial writing by his teacher, Hans Joachim Koellreutter, in early study in Rio de Janeiro. Later he worked with Boulanger in Paris. His career has been centered both in Brazil and in Germany, where he accepted a professorship at the Heidelberg-Mannheim Hochschule für Musik (1970). His style of writing between 1939 and about 1947 is based on serial techniques. A toccata (1942), the first sonata (1945), and several sets of smaller pieces were written during this time. Santoro began studying Brazilian folk and popular music about 1948 and for the next few years produced nationalistic works. His socialistic political views were partly influential in his attempt to write in a style that would relate to the people, holding up as his model the group of Soviet composers who were similarly engaged. Representative of this period is the second piano sonata (1948), two *Danças brasileiras* (1951), nine *Peças infantis* (1952), and other sets of smaller pieces. In the late 1950s, Santoro returned to a modified serial style, producing two more piano sonatas (1954 and 1955), a set of etudes (1959–60), and twenty-five preludes (1957–63).

Argentina

Early exponents of nationalism in Argentina were **Alberto Williams** (1862–1952) and **Julián Aguirre** (1868–1924). Both men studied abroad, Williams at the Paris Conservatory and Aguirre at the Madrid Conservatory. Both returned to Argentina to exert considerable influence on the musical scene. Williams's early style reflected European nineteenth-century tradition, but after his return to Argentina he studied folk music and began to incorporate it into his writing beginning with the piano piece "El rancho abandonado" (1892). He was a prolific composer, producing over a hundred piano works, among which is a *Sonata argentine* (1917). Aguirre's many works for piano include a sonata and four volumes of *Aires nacionales*.

The careers of **Carlos López Buchardo** (1881–1948) and **Floro Manuel Ugarte** (1884–1975) also were similar in many respects. Both studied in Paris, Buchardo with Roussel and Ugarte with Pessard at the conservatory. Both returned to Buenos Aires and were involved in the founding of a National Conservatory there in 1924. Both incorporated nationalist characteristics into their style, writing works for the theater that were popular and important in their time. Both left a small catalogue of nationalist piano works. López Buchardo wrote a sonatina and a few other character pieces, such as "Bailecito" and "Campera." Among Ugarte's piano works are two sets of pieces called *De mitierra* (1923, 1934) and five preludes (1947).

The **Castro** family is important in Argentinian music of the early twentieth century. Of four brothers who became prominent musicians, three were composers, **José Maria Castro** (1892–1964), **Juan José Castro** (1895–1968), and **Washington Castro** (b. 1909). José Maria studied in Rome and both Juan José and Washington in Paris. Stylistically, José Maria and Washington eschewed nationalism for the most part, preferring instead to write in a more traditional, often neoclassical style. Juan José, on the other hand, mixed nationalism with French influences. José Maria wrote two sonatas (1931, 1939) as well as character pieces. Juan José wrote two early sonatas (1917, 1939), a *Sonata española* (1953), a set of nine preludes (1934), five tangos (1941), and other character pieces. Among Washington's piano works are one sonata, three intermezzi (1947), and five preludes (1954).

Two other figures, born just at the close of the nineteenth century, became prominent in Argentina during the first decades of the twentieth. **Jacobo Ficher** (b. 1896) was Russian–born but settled in Argentina as a young man. He has been very active as a composer and educator. He wrote in a traditional European style but occasionally made use of Argentinian folk or popular resources. He has written seven piano sonatas, Op. 44 (1941), Op. 49 (1943), Op. 71 (1950), Op. 72 (1950), Op. 87 (1956), Op. 97 (1961), and Op. 101 (1964). In addition, there is a set of Argentinian dances based on a popular style, Op. 43 (1941), and six fables, Op. 59 (1946).

Luis Gianneo (1897–1968) is considered one of the founders of nationalism in Argentina, having been active as a teacher and one of the founding members of the Argentine League of Composers. His style is direct, simple, and folkloric. For piano, he has written three sonatas, a sonatina (1938), three Argentine dances (1939), and about thirty other works.

Juan Carlos Paz (1901–72) espoused contemporary European trends in composition. He was a prolific composer and writer, attempting to bring innovative thinking to the Argentinian musical scene. He explored many styles but between 1934 and 1950 he adopted twelvetone and serial techniques based on the work of Schönberg and Webern. In 1950, he wrote a book in which he set forth the theory that serial writing had nothing new to offer; he abandoned it in his own writing and sought other means. In 1964, he gave up composing but continued to write articles and books dealing with theoretical problems. A prolific instrumental composer, his catalogue of piano works include three sonatas (1923, 1925, and 1935); a fantasy (1923); a fantasy and fugue (1923); a prelude, chorale, and fugue (1923); six ballades (1927–29);

three jazz movements (1932); ten pieces on a twelve-tone series (1936); and several sets of character pieces. His last piano work, *Núcleos* (1962–64), was written near the end of his career as a composer.

Roberto Garcia Morillo (b. 1911) studied with Ugarte in Argentina and later in both France and Italy. He uses nationalistic material infrequently in his writing, focusing rather on a forceful, neoclassic style not unlike middle-period Stravinsky. He has written five piano sonatas, three sets of variations, and character pieces.

Alberto Ginastera

Perhaps the most prominent Argentinian composer on the international scene in the twentieth century was Alberto Ginastera (b. Buenos Aires, Apr. 11, 1916; d. Geneva, June 25, 1983). His training was wholly in Argentina. His career has been spent mostly in Argentina and the United States, a country in which he has enjoyed enormous success. Ginastera divided his composing into three periods. He called his writing before 1948 "objective nationalism," between 1948 and 1954 "subjective nationalism," and after 1954 "neoexpressionism."

The first period reflects his interest in capturing the flavor of Argentinian life, particularly that associated with the vast planes (*pampas*) of the hinterland and the cowboys (*gauchos*) who live and work there. Piano pieces that represent this period are *Danzas argentinas,* Op. 2 (1937); three pieces, Op. 6 (1940); *Malambo,* Op. 7 (1940); *Twelve American Preludes,* Op. 12 (1944); *Suite de danzas criollas,* Op. 15 (1946); and *Rondo sobre temas infantiles argentinos,* Op. 19 (1947). The colorful harmonies, invigorating rhythms, and pianistic effects in these pieces have garnered considerable attention from pianists and often enthusiastic response from listeners. The pieces appear to be contemporary sounding but at the same time tend to be extremely accessible, even on a first hearing, and often use obvious effects, such as clusters of notes, low registers, guitar imitations, and toccata-like drive.

Representing Ginastera's subjective nationalism is his first piano sonata, Op. 22 (1952). Cast in traditional form with four movements, the work reflects the melodies and rhythms of the pampas without direct borrowing or quoting. The work is so effective from a pianistic standpoint that it became an immediate favorite among pianists (Example 19.7). Although the term *neoexpressionism* should be applied to music composed after 1954, according to Ginastera, the composer also points to elements of continuity in his work. He cites the existence of twelve-tone rows in the first sonata, for example. By the same token, the second sonata, Op. 53 (1981), was born of regional influences, in this case attempting to capture the spirit of music of northern parts of Argentina, Ayamara and Ketchus, by making use of pentatonicism and effects that

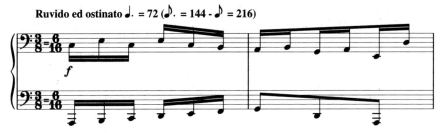

Example 19.7 Alberto Ginastera: Sonata no. 1, 4th movt. mm. 1–2

imitate microtonal ornamentation and Indian drums. A third sonata was written in 1982.

Among later Argentinian composers, **Hilda Dianda** (b. 1925) represents a wide variety of styles, ranging from neoclassicism to electronic-based works. Among her piano works are three Scarlatti-like sonatas (1956) and a more experimental work entitled *Resonancias 2* (1964).

Chile

Several Chilean composers are significant. **Enrique Soro** (1884–1954) was educated in Chile and Italy. He mixed a traditional eclecticism with nationalism, composing for piano three sonatas (1920, 1923, and 1942), two *Tonadas Chilenas,* Op. 50, and other pieces.

Alfonso Leng (1894–1975) wrote in a post-Romantic style, contributing a set of preludes (1906), five *Doloras* (1914), and two sonatas (1950 and 1973).

More intensely nationalistic was **Pedro Humberto Allende** (1885–1959), who studied popular music in Chile and made field recordings of Araucanian Indian music. This research is reflected in the style of his twelve tonadas (1918–22), *Miniaturas griegas* (1918–29), and nine studies (1920–36).

Domingo Santa Cruz (b. 1899) has had a distinguished career as a composer, administrator, and leader of Chilean musical life. He served for many years (1932–48 and 1962–68) as dean of the faculty of the National Conservatory and has held administrative offices in various musical organizations, both national and international. His style is rooted in eighteenth-century counterpoint and is often highly chromatic, but his rhythmic and melodic traits are Spanish in origin. His works for piano include four *Viñetas,* Op. 8 (1925–27); five *Poemas trágicos,* Op. 11 (1929); and eight *Imágenes infantiles,* Op. 13 (1932).

Juan Orrego-Salas (b. 1919) studied with Allende and Santa Cruz in Chile as well as Virgil Thomson and Aaron Copland in the United States. His early career was centered in Chile, as a professor at the

University of Chile, editor of *Revista musical chilena,* and music critic for *El mercurio.* In 1961, he moved to the United States, where he founded and directed the Latin American Music Center at Indiana University. As a composer he developed a style based on a free use of formal procedures taken from many historical periods, drawing particularly from traits of the Middle Ages. He has written two piano suites, Opp. 14 and 32 (1946 and 1951); *Variaciones y fuga sobre el tema de un Prégon,* Op. 18 (1946); ten *Piezas samples para niños,* Op. 31 (1951); *Rústica,* Op. 35 (1952); and a piano sonata, Op. 60 (1967).

More contemporary, nonnationalistic trends in composition in Chile are represented by **Gustavo Becerra-Schmidt** (b. 1925). He studied with Allende and Santa Cruz and, having graduated from the University of Chile in 1949, became a professor of analysis and composition there three years later. He has exhibited a variety of styles, including neoclassical, serial, and electronic. His piano works include a sonata (1950) and a set of variations (1958).

Mexico

Significant composers of Mexican birth are represented by **Manuel M. Ponce** (1882–1948) and **Carlos Chávez** (1899–1978). Ponce received his early training in Mexico but later studied in Italy and Germany. His professional career included periods living in Cuba and France, finally returning to Mexico City in 1933. His style of writing reflects European influences, especially French impressionism and neoclassic counterpoint. Among his piano works are two sonatas (1913 and 1968) and many shorter pieces, including a *Preludio cubano,* two *Rapsodias mexicanas,* and a *Scherzino mexicano.*

Chávez was essentially self-taught as a composer. His own Indian heritage and early visits to Indian communities left him with a lifelong interest in Indian culture and music, particularly that of the Aztecs. Spurred on by affiliations with the post-Mexican revolution government, he formed connections with Mexican cultural politics and remained officially involved for most of his career. Chávez enjoyed particular success in visits to the United States. He lived and worked in New York for two years (1926–28), where he met and was influenced by Aaron Copland, Henry Cowell, and Edgard Varèse. Chávez's style incorporates many types of writing. His interest in nationalism parallels experimentation with other contemporary techniques. He often exhibits a penchant for dense textures, biting dissonance, and driving rhythms. He has written extensively for solo piano, including six sonatas (over a period between 1917 and 1961), *Polygonos* (1923), ten preludes (1947), three Chopinesque etudes (1949), left-hand inversions of five Chopin etudes (1950), and *Mañanas mexicanas* (1967).

Other Latin American Countries

Other Latin composers in the Western Hemisphere may be mentioned in passing. German-born **Rudolf Holzmann** (b. 1910) represents Peruvian nationalism with four piano suites (1941–42), *Niñerias* (1947), and *Remembranzas* (1949). Panamanian composer **Roque Cordero** (b. 1917) mixes songs and dance rhythms of his people with various contemporary techniques, incorporating serialism into his style around 1954. His piano works include a *Sonatina ritmica* (1943), nine preludes (1947), and a *Sonata breve* (1966). Among important Cuban composers are **Joaquín Nin** (1879–1949) and his son, **Joaquín Nin-Culmell** (b. 1908). Both men enjoyed international careers, Joaquín Nin-Culmell eventually settling in the United States. Both men incorporate Latin characteristics into their writing, Nin within the framework of nineteenth-century Romantic character pieces and Nin-Culmell leaning more toward impressionism in a *Sonata breve* (1934) and four books of *Tonadas* (1956–61). **Alejandro Garcia Caturla** (1906–1940) based his style on African-Cuban rhythms, combining them with dissonance and exuberant primitivism. Among his piano works are *Danza lucumi* (1928), *Danza del tambour* (1928), *Comparsa* (1930), two works entitled *Son* (1930 and 1939), and a *Sonata corta* (1934). **José Ardévol** (b. 1911) represents Cuban nationalism combined with more contemporary techniques in three piano sonatas (1944) and shorter pieces. **Gisela Hernandez-Gonzalo** (b. 1912) has been prominent in post-revolution Cuban officialdom, holding posts with the National Cultural Council and the Ministry of Education. She has written a sonata (1941), *Zapateo cubano*, (1954) and *4 Cubanas* (1957).

CHAPTER TWENTY

Russian Keyboard Music

During much of the nineteenth century, the Russian musical scene was dominated by European-trained musicians who often spent years in important musical centers in Russia, working as professionals and building significant careers. Prominent among those who thus led Russian musical life were Johann Wilhelm Hässler, John Field, Adolph von Henselt, and Theodor Leschetizky (1830–1915). Toward the middle of the century, a reaction against such European influence set in, and several composers began to espouse a conscious nationalism, turning often to regional folk material for inspiration rather than relying on central European traditions.

The spiritual father of Russian nationalism was **Mikhail Ivanovich Glinka** (1814–1857), who was trained in the German tradition in Russia, went to Italy and Germany for further study, but returned to his native land in 1834, where he began to turn to nationalistic subjects as a basis for opera. Although the complete solo keyboard works of Glinka run to six volumes of music, the pieces do not represent Russian nationalism to the same extent the operas do. There are many sets of variations on operatic themes from other composers' operas (Mozart, Cherubini, and Donizetti, for example) and character pieces typical of the period (mazurkas, nocturnes, tarantellas, etc.). None of this music is very much played.

The spirit of nationalism, however, was carried forward by a group of five composers oftentimes referred to as the Russian Five or the Mighty Five. The name was originally the "mighty handful" and was used first in 1867 by the music journalist Vladimir Stasov (1824–1906) in an article in a St. Petersburg newspaper that discussed Russian nationalism in music. Although all of the "five" wrote solo keyboard music, relatively little of it has survived in the active repertoire, and it represents the group's nationalistic leanings only sporadically.

The name of **Mily Balakirev** (1837–1910), the leader of the group, is kept alive mostly through one famous virtuoso piece, *Islamey* (1869), subtitled *Oriental Fantasy* (Example 20.1). The piece uses Caucasian and

Example 20.1 Mily Balakirev: *Islamey* mm. 9–10
Copyright © 1927 by Carl Fischer Inc.

Armenian folk melodies and garnered a reputation for being one of the most difficult display pieces of the century. It was this piece that Ravel was seeking to match when he wrote "Scarbo." Equally effective but not as difficult is Scherzo no. 2 in *b-flat*. Balakirev's most extended keyboard work, a Liszt-like sonata (also in *b-flat*) in four movements, underwent periodic revisions, the last of which is as late as 1905, but it is seldom performed.

Character pieces of the salon type dominate the keyboard works of three other composers of the "five": **Alexander Borodin** (1833–37), **César Cui** (1835–1918), and **Nikolay Rimsky-Korsakov** (1844–1908). Some of Rimsky-Korsakov's works are both more ambitious and interesting, notably a collection of eleven fugues and a set of variations on Bach.

By contrast, *Pictures at an Exhibition* of **Modest Musorgsky** (1839–81) is a set of character pieces that has won a secure niche in the performing repertoire. Musorgsky's musical training was composed of a series of private lessons with several teachers, including Balakirev and Rimsky-Korsakov. Musorgsky himself felt a sense of frustration from not having received a more formal, intense musical education. For most of his adult life, he had to earn his living as a government clerk, so composing was relegated to the status of a leisure-hour activity. Notwithstanding these handicaps, as well as an addiction to alcohol in his later years, Musorgsky emerged as the most original composer of the group of five, and many analysts believe that the so-called crudities of his composition actually reflect a rough-hewn strength born of Russian life and culture.

Pictures at an Exposition (1874) is composed of ten short pieces that represent paintings by the composer's friend, the artist Victor Hartmann. The same Valdimir Stasov who coined the phrase the "mighty handful" arranged for a memorial exhibition of Hartmann's works and later annotated the first edition of Musorgsky's composition. The piano pieces each have descriptive titles, and the set is unified by a reappearing march-like theme entitled "Promenade," musically representing moving from picture to picture and reflecting appropriate changes of mood as the spectator approaches each new art work. Irregular phrase lengths with matching meter changes give the "Promenade" vitality and interest. The pictures themselves are often fantasy-like, even grotesque. The opening one, "Gnomus," for example, depicts a nutcracker in the shape of a gnome with deformed legs. For it, Musorgsky employs angular bass figurations contrasted with intermittent melodic fragments. "Il vecchio castello" (The Old Castle) is represented by a troubadour's song. "Tuileries" describes the Parisian gardens of that name as a playground for quarrelsome children, presenting taunting melodic phrases built on a repeated, falling third. "Bydlo" is a Polish oxcart, its great wooden wheels being represented by a heavy bass ostinato. "Ballet of the Chicks" is filled with grace notes and staccato touch to imitate chirping and pecking. "Samuel Goldenberg and Schmuyle" are two Polish Jews, the first rich, represented by imposing octaves, and the second poor, presented as a theme based on repeated notes. The two themes come together in a contrapuntal meshing in the final section of the piece. "The Marketplace at Limoges" is described by Musorgsky himself in a marginal note as a furious dispute among French women. Technically the piece is among the most demanding of the set.

"Catacombes" and "Con mortuis in lingua mortua" go together, the first creating the atmosphere of the famous tombs with long, sustained chords and the second using fragments of the "Promenade" theme with high tremolos to evoke an eerie scene notated in the margin of the score by the composer: "The creative spirit of the immortal Hartmann leads me toward the skulls and addresses them—a pale light radiates from the interior of the skulls." "The Hut on Fowl's Legs" is actually a design for a clock that depicts the residence of the famous, fearful witch Baba Yaga. Here, Musorgsky writes the most virtuosic piece of the set, one filled with rapid octave skips.

The set ends with "The Great Gate of Kiev," a piece in which a fragment of the "Promenade" theme is presented as a mighty chorale, interrupted first by quiet chordal passages and later by music from Musorgsky's opera *Boris Godunov*. Each appearance of the chorale increases in power, the composer adding octaves and bell-like figurations. The set ends majestically with massive chords that test the strength of both the performer and the instrument. Although the *Pictures at an Exhibition* was effectively orchestrated by Ravel and is thus often heard as an orchestral work, the original piano version is considered one of the greatest keyboard works of the nineteenth century and remains a favorite with pianists.

Other Russian composers of the late nineteenth century were less consciously concerned with nationalism, albeit much of their music still incorporates many characteristics that sound distinctly regional. The most famous of these composers was **Pyotr Il'ych Tchaikovsky** (1840–1893), who stood apart from the nationalism of the group of five but who, nevertheless, remained friendly toward its members and their ideas. Tchaikovsky received his musical training rather late in life at the new school established in St. Petersburg by Nikolay Rubinstein. Tchaikovsky was able to devote himself completely to composing, for he was fortunate enough to garner the support of a sponsor during the years he was establishing his reputation. Madame Nadeshda von Meck, a wealthy widow, supported the composer and carried on an intense correspondence with him for more than a decade, although the two never met except for fleeting glimpses of one another accidentally in public places.

Considering the continuing success and popularity of Tchaikovsky's first piano concerto, one might well expect the solo piano music to be a treasure chest of masterworks. Such is, unfortunately, not the case. The most successful of the piano works are *The Seasons*, Op. 37b, a set of twelve character pieces named for each month of the year, and the *Dumka*, Op. 59, a concert fantasy. Selections from the *Album for the Young*, Op. 39, a set of twenty-four small pieces, still find their way into the teaching studio. The other character pieces, the three sets of variations, and the two large-scale piano sonatas, Op. 37a in *G* and Op. 80 in *c-sharp*, continue to be ignored by performers. Although these works contain attractive material, they are also frequently lacking in development, tend to be somewhat thick in texture, and present structural units with a predictability that invites tedium.

The second half of the nineteenth century saw a host of Russian composers whose work reflected the styles of famous European musicians, notably Chopin, Schumann, or Liszt. In thattradition, **Anatoli Konstantinovich Liadov** (1855–1914) wrote a ballade, Op. 21; a berceuse, Op. 24, no. 2; and an etude, Op. 37. Liadov excelled at charming miniatures, his most famous being "Tabatière à musique" (Music Box; 1893).

Sergei Mikhailovich Liapunov (1850–1924) might be considered somewhat more nationalist in his approach. At one point in his career (1893), he was commissioned by the Imperial Geographic Society to collect and set with accompaniments the folk songs of the regions of Vologda, Viatka, and Kostroma. His keyboard writing is rather extensive and includes an early set of twelve *Études d'exécution transcendente*, Op. 11, of which no. 10, "Lesghinka," is occasionally encountered. The final etude, no. 12, is entitled "Elégie en mémoire de Franz Liszt." Liapunov also wrote a sonata, Op. 27; a set of variations on a Russian theme, Op. 49; a sonatine, Op. 65; and a substantial number of character pieces, including some intended as teaching material, Op. 59.

Anton Stepanovich Arensky (1861–1906) was at his best in miniatures. His small piano pieces include a set of twenty-four *Morceaux charactéristiques*, Op. 36 (Example 20.2), and twelve preludes, Op. 63. Arensky's style is particularly reminiscent of that of Tchaikovsky.

Alexandr Tikhonovich Grechaninov (1864–1956) studied with both Arensky and Rimsky-Korsakov. He settled in New York in 1936,

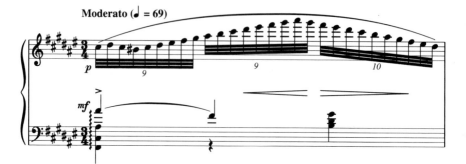

Example 20.2 Anton Arensky: "Etude" from *Morceaux Caractèristiques*, Op. 36, no. 13 m. 1

and on his ninetieth birthday a concert of his works was presented in Town Hall (Oct. 25, 1954). Notwithstanding the fact that he lived through the first half of the twentieth century, his style remained steadfastly rooted in nineteenth-century Russian Romanticism with occasional experiments in techniques associated with French impressionism (notably in his songs). Grechaninov was a prolific composer in general, so there is a considerable amount of piano music, including two sonatas, Op. 129 (1931) and Op. 174 (1947), and many sets of character pieces, several of which are excellent teaching material (Opp. 109, 119, 170, and 182).

Alexander Konstantinovich Glazunov (1865–1936) studied with Rimsky-Korsakov as a teenager and was so talented that he was hailed by several prominent journalists as the heir to the Russian nationalist school. Glazunov's music remained somewhat conservative, however, showing strong European influences as well as Russian. He was particularly gifted in compositional techniques, so his work is expertly crafted, and he was influential as a teacher of younger Russian composers during the early part of his career. In 1928, he moved to Paris, where he enjoyed considerable success for the rest of his life. He toured extensively as a conductor, and in 1907 he was given honorary degrees from Oxford and Cambridge. There is an extensive catalogue of piano works by Glazunov, including two sonatas, Opp. 47 and 75 (both written in 1901); an entertaining set of variations that imitate other composers' styles, Op. 72 (1901); three concert etudes, Op. 31 (1889); and many character pieces.

Vladimir Ivanovich Rebikov (1866–1920) studied at the Moscow Conservatory and in Berlin. After spending much of his professional life in Vienna and Berlin, he returned to Moscow in 1901. His compositional style began with music that was a spin-off from that of Tchaikovsky (*Rêveries d'autumme,* Op. 8, for solo piano). It evolved about 1900 to reflect impressionistic techniques. *Les Démons s'amusent* (The Playful Demons) is built entirely on whole-tone harmonies. Rebikov developed a penchant for humor and mimicry (*Mélomimiques,* Opp. 11, 15, and 17, for voice and piano). Eventually he became fascinated with experiments in structural concepts, opting for a declamatory style with skeletal harmonies in his later works (*3 Rhythmo-declamations,* Op. 32, for piano). This attention to contemporary techniques earned him the unofficial reputation of being the father of Russian modernism.

Alexander Nikolayevich Scriabin

Alexander Nikolayevich Scriabin (b. Moscow, Jan. 6, 1872; d. Moscow, Apr. 27, 1915) received his early musical education from his aunt. At age twelve, he began private lessons in piano with Nikolay Zverev and in composition with Alexander Taneyev. He entered the Moscow Conservatory in 1888, studying piano with Vassily Safonov, graduating with a second-place gold medal. (Rachmaninoff won the first-place gold medal that year, 1892.) His work with Arensky in composition was not as successful, for Scriabin failed to pass his examinations in that subject and left the conservatory without a diploma. Safonov, as well as the Russian publisher Belaiev, became champions of his works, however, and through their efforts both early performances and publications were arranged. Several tours abroad beginning in 1898 further enhanced his reputation. Scriabin was fortunate to receive a series of stipends during his career, first from a wealthy merchant named Morozov, then in 1908 from Serge Koussevitzy, who had just established a publishing house and was able to offer Scriabin a five-year contract that guaranteed him an annual income, and finally in 1912 a similar contract was forged with the publisher Jurgenson. Scriabin was able to support himself from these arrangements, his compositions, and concert tours, although he taught at the Moscow Conservatory for a brief time (1898–1903).

Scriabin was doted upon as a child by his aunt, and as an adult he demanded and received both attention and admiration. He developed an intense interest in the philosophy of Nietzsche about 1903, but two years later he embraced theosophy, a cultish, mystical movement founded in New York City in 1875, led by Madame Helena Petrovna Blavatsky. Partly as result of this immersion in philosophical mysticism, Scriabin forged a change in his compositional style, coming to believe that he was the central figure in uniting several art forms into one consummate expression. The world would, moreover, suffer a cataclysmic demise, after which regeneration to a new nirvana would take place through his musical creativity. The artistic catalyst for this transformation was to have been the *Mysterium,* a work that he planned for the last twelve years of his life and that was to have brought all the senses together in a magnificent synthesis.

Scriabin sustained a moderately successful career as a performing pianist, despite the fact that his hand was somewhat small, an octave stretch being its limit. Thus, the piano figured prominently in his musical thinking, writing for solo piano extending from his earliest through his final works, and his stylistic evolution can be traced clearly in the piano works. The piano pieces up to about 1900 (Opp. 1–28) are consciously modeled on the work of Chopin. To Chopinesque harmonies, melodies, and textures Scriabin added a personal, characteristically emotional intensity by adding a sense of urgency to harmonic progressions, heightening melodic gestures, and often indulging in great sonorous climaxes. Genres used during this period, too, are reminiscent of those used by Chopin: waltzes, nocturnes, mazurkas, impromptus, a set of twelve etudes, Op. 8 (1894), one of twenty-four preludes, Op. 11 (1888–96), as well as smaller sets of preludes and a polonaise.

The three sonatas from this period, too, are cast in more traditional forms. The first sonata, Op. 6 (1892), is in four movements, closing with a funeral march. The second, Op. 19 (1892?), subtitled *Sonata-fantasy*, uses but two movements, an opening sonata-allegro and a perpetual motion in a rondo pattern. The third sonata, Op. 23 (1897–98), is in a traditional four-movement pattern. As in the Chopin sonatas, Scriabin places the slow movement third. Scriabin also uses cyclicism, for the opening theme from the slow movement returns triumphantly at the end of the final movement. Here, too, can be seen the first indications of the composer's fascination with mystical ideas, for the program attending the work suggests that the four movements represent states of the soul: first in strife, then floundering, resting, and finally achieving a state of ecstasy.

After 1900, Scriabin's style began to move in new directions. Complex rhythms are designed in such a way that downbeats become obscure; both melodic and rhythmic ideas are fragmented; and harmonic language becomes ambiguous with regard to direction of movement, tonality, and resolution. What emerged was a style made up of sonorities and motives that seem to drift, never quite coming to rest, sometimes active and clear-cut, but more often languorous and amorphous. Scriabin thus attempted to depict in music various states of the disembodied spirit.

Analysts have been fascinated by the ambiguity of Scriabin's harmonic thinking in this later period and have invoked several approaches to codify his procedures. One line of thinking rests with the observation that sonorities are often built on various intervals of the fourth. One such sonority used frequently by Scriabin is often dubbed the "mystic chord." An example of it might be built up from C, adding at intervals of the fourth the notes F-sharp, B-flat, E, A, and D. Other theorists have pointed to the fact that the notes of Scriabin's harmonies, such as the "mystic chord" just described, can be rearranged conjunctly so that they come close to making up a complete whole-tone scale. (One note of the "mystic chord," the A, does not match.) It is also pointed out that in this conjunct

Example 20.3 Alexander Scriabin: *Poème tragique*, Op. 34 mm. 1–2

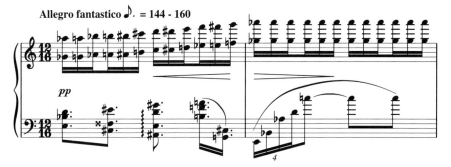

Example 20.4 Alexander Scriabin: Etude, Op. 65, no. 1 mm. 1–2

arrangement the notes of the chord lie close to the sequence of upper partials in the overtone series generated by the note C. And finally, the root movements of such sonorities have been observed to move in such a way that sequences of these chords might be regarded as series of unresolved dominant-thirteenth chords with a raised eleventh.

A group of transitional works that begin to show the signs of this change in style, all written in 1903, includes the fourth sonata, Op. 30; five pieces called *poèms,* including the *Poème tragique,* Op. 34 (Example 20.3); and the *Poème satanique,* Op. 36; a set of eight etudes, Op. 42; and five sets of preludes in groups of three or four, Opp. 31, 33, 35, and 37. From this point on, descriptive titles, many of which evoke images with mystical connotations, continue to be used, often in conjunction with the more generic term *poème.* The seventh sonata, Op. 64 (1911), is given the subtitle *White Mass,* and the ninth sonata, Op. 68 (1912–13), *Black Mass.* There is also a late set of three etudes, Op. 65 (1912), one of the pieces featuring double notes at the interval of a seventh, another at the ninth (Example 20.4). Small sets of preludes continue to appear, including Scriabin's final keyboard work, a set of five preludes, Op. 74 (1914).

The sonatas nos. 4–10 all adhere to a single movement, often opening with a slow introduction. Buried within the floating sonorities and rapid, fleeting figurations are the shadows of sonata-allegro structures, rather easily detectable in the fourth and fifth sonatas but more obscure starting with the sixth sonata, due to the similarity of texture between the expositions and developments as well as the fact that recapitulations are often reworked to a considerable degree.

Scriabin's late works include several poems with evocative titles: *Vers la flamme,* Op. 72, *Guirlandes,* and *Flammes sombre,* Op. 73. All the late works occupy a somewhat enigmatic position among pianists. Recognized as significant musically and challenging technically, they still are programmed with caution by many performers. The unresolved harmonies, fragmented rhythmic figures, and obscured structural elements combine to produce a listening experience that is often sensuous and meditative but tends also to be fleeting and tenuous. This fragile, almost precious, quality must be taken into consideration in programming these works, notwithstanding their fascination and beauty.

Sergey Vassilievich Rachmaninoff

Sergey Vassilievich Rachmaninoff (b. Semyonovo, Apr. 1, 1873; d. Beverly Hills, Mar. 20, 1943) received his earliest piano lessons from his mother and later from Anna Ornatskaya, a graduate of the St. Petersburg Conservatory. In 1882, financial pressures forced Rachmaminoff's family to sell its family estate and move to St. Petersburg, where Sergey was enrolled in the conservatory, studying piano with Vladimir Demyanski and harmony with Alexander Rubets.

Rachmaninoff's parents separated, and the resulting emotional upheaval caused Sergey to fail his general examination in 1885. The conservatory hinted that his scholarship might be withdrawn, so the boy was sent to Moscow to study under the close supervision of Nikolay Zverev, living with other students in the teacher's home. The strict schedule included early morning practicing, which reportedly began at 5 A.M., and attendance at many private concerts, usually held on Sunday afternoons. Here, Rachmaninoff met many of the leading musicians of the day, including Anton Rubinstein, Anton Arensky, Alexander Taneyev, Vassily Safonov, and Tchaikovsky. Indeed, the latter offered friendly encouragement and became a lasting influence on Rachmaninoff's musical style.

Sergey was enrolled in the Moscow Conservatory in 1888, studying piano with Alexander Siloti (a cousin, incidentally) and composition with Taneyev and Arensky. He graduated in piano in 1891 and in composition in 1892, receiving a gold medal for a one-act opera based on Pushkin, *Aleko.* The next major step in Rachmaninoff's career was the performance of his first symphony in 1897. Conducted by Glazunov in

Moscow, the event was a disaster. Apparently, Glazunov conducted badly. (Rachmaninoff's wife claimed years later that Glazunov was drunk at the time.) The critics were savage. The event threw Rachmaninoff into a three-year period of depression, during which time he attempted to write nothing of significance. Late in 1899, he sought medical assistance from Dr. Nikolay Dahl, whose use of hypnosis rapidly restored Rachmaninoff to his former level of creativity. (The famous second piano concerto, Op. 18, was the first major work to be written after this restoration and is dedicated to Dahl.)

Rachmaninoff, meanwhile, had established a career as a conductor, particularly of Russian opera. This activity, combined with appearances as a virtuoso pianist, provided the main source of income for Rachmaninoff, and composing had to be built around preparation for performance dates. Rachmaninoff's career was centered in Moscow with frequent tours abroad until 1917, when, after having endured several years of rising political strife and diminishing quality of life in Russia, Rachmaninoff, at the age of forty-four, left his native country with his family.

After a brief period of living in Stockholm and Copenhagen, the Rachmaninoff family moved to the United States. Here, Rachmaninoff was engaged as a performing pianist, giving close to forty concerts in four months shortly after his arrival. By now, too, Rachmaninoff's work as a composer began to garner a broad popular following. Thus, his career as both a composer and a pianist continued to grow and flourish for the remaining two decades of his life, mostly in the United States but with periods of residence abroad in Dresden, London, and the family's villa in Switzerland. Poor health began to plague him in 1939 after he suffered a fall. Rachmaninoff had decided that the 1942–43 season would be his last due to lumbago and arthritis, but in early 1943 he was in so much pain that he had to cancel the balance of the season. Returning to his home in Beverly Hills, he was diagnosed with cancer, to which he succumbed a few weeks later.

Rachmaninoff wrote the bulk of his music for piano during the early decades of his career, before he left Russia. His first published set of pieces, Op. 3, show characteristics that remain constant throughout his creative life: traditional functional harmonic schemes with individual use of chromaticism; an ability to create and spin out to unusual lengths memorable, haunting melodic lines; traditional but often driving rhythms; and frequent use of extended, massive chordal textures, which laid easily within the span of the composer's large hands.

Rachmaninoff was a virtuoso pianist whose playing was so breathtaking that many of his contemporaries were said to have proclaimed him the greatest of his generation. As a result, his piano music tends to take for granted complete command of the instrument. Thus, there are few "easy" or even "intermediate" Rachmaninoff piano works, and many

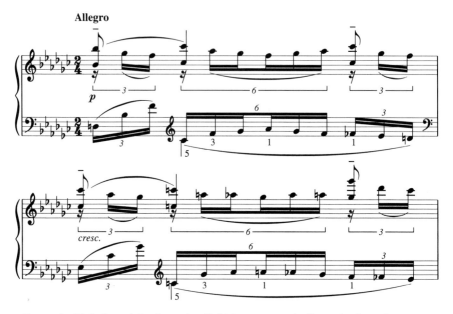

Example 20.5 Sergei Rachmaninoff: "Moment musical" (revised version), Op. 16, no. 2 mm. 1–2

of the pieces require dexterity of the highest order. He wrote no sets of teaching pieces.

Of the piano works before 1900, the five *Morceaux de fantasies,* Op. 3 (1892), include the famous Prelude in *c-sharp* as well as the "Mélodie" and "Sérénade," both reworked by the composer about 1940. Of the seven *Morceaux de salon* that make up Op. 10, the "Humoresque" has gained the most popularity, it, too, being revised around 1940. The six *Moments musicaux* (1896) show Rachmaninoff's style growing in terms of melodic originality and technical mastery. The second of this set in *e-flat* was revised in 1940 (Example 20.5). Although both versions of the four revised pieces are available, the later revisions are more sophisticated, difficult, and effective.

The works written after 1900 (after the second concerto) show Rachmaninoff in full command of his style. There are two sets of preludes, two sets of etudes, two sonatas, two sets of variations, and a few miscellaneous pieces. The two sets of preludes, Op. 23 (ten preludes, 1903), and Op. 32 (thirteen preludes, 1913), add up to twenty-three pieces. If the *c-sharp* Prelude, Op. 3, no. 2, is added to the group, the total becomes twenty-four. Examination shows that, indeed, there is a prelude for each of the major and minor keys, so one suspects that the creation of the Op. 32 with thirteen preludes, an unusual number for a set, was calculated on the composer's part, and that he belatedly and perhaps opportunistically conceived a cycle of twenty-four, one in each key. This possibility is given

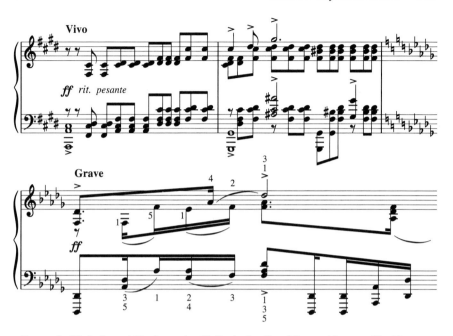

Example 20.6 Sergei Rachmaninoff: Prelude, Op. 32, no. 13 mm. 41–43

credence by the fact that the final prelude of the Op. 32 is in the enharmonic, parallel major (*D-flat*) of the earliest work (*c-sharp*) and that the
famous three-note motive of the prelude in *c-sharp* is alluded to in the
middle section of the one in *D-flat* (Example 20.6). Since the idea of a set,
one in each key, was probably not formed until the Op. 32 was in the
process of being written, there is no conceptual design. Thus, one finds
no particular order of keys for the preludes, and they all tend to be longer
and more elaborate than preludes meant to be played as a cycle.

The two sets of *Études-tableaux,* Op. 33 (1911) and Op.39 (1916–17),
total fifteen studies. One of the etudes planned for Op. 33 (no. 4 in *a*)
was taken out of that set and appears in the Op. 39 (as no. 6). Two other
etudes, in *c* and *d,* originally planned for Op. 33, were published posthumously. The *Études-tableaux* are not clearly focused on a single technical problem, such as double notes, skips, or octaves, but rather combine
difficulties, as in the more difficult preludes (Example 20.7).

Notwithstanding the fact that the basic elements of Rachmaninoff's
style remain staunchly rooted in the nineteenth-century Romantic tradition, the preludes and etudes incorporate the composer's ardor with an
array of highly inventive technical devices. Furthermore, he is successful
in exploring the sonority of the instrument in ways that are both personal and distinctive. Thus, these sets of piano pieces demonstrate
Rachmaninoff's emotional, virtuosic writing at its very best.

Example 20.7 Sergei Rachmaninoff: *Étude-tableau*, Op. 39, no. 9 mm. 1–4

The more extended works have met with less consistent success. The first sonata in *d*, Op. 28 (1907), is not endowed with the composer's most inspired thematic ideas and gives the impression of being loosely constructed. The second sonata in *b-flat*, Op. 36 (1913), is in three movements connected by transitions and unified by a six-note motive that appears throughout the work. The sonata underwent extensive cutting and revision in 1931. Both versions are available, and some have found that Rachmaninoff's pruning was too severe, preferring to play the earlier version. The pianist Vladimir Horowitz, a professional colleague and friend of the composer, put together and recorded yet a third version, a mix of the original and the revision, reportedly with the composer's blessing. In spite of the work's unsolved structural problems, the sonata is built on material that is unusually attractive and, as a result, has achieved a measure of popularity among performers.

Of the two sets of variations, the Op. 22 (1902–3), built on Chopin's Prelude in *c* from Op. 28, seems more mechanical than inspired and is rarely heard. The Op. 42 (1931) is more successful. Based on the famous theme known as "La Follia," used by Corelli in his sonata, Op. 5, no. 12, the work joins two sets of ten variations each with a cadenza-like intermezzo and ends with a lyrical coda. It runs the gamut of Rachmaninoff's technical and expressive devices and exhibits many features that foreshadow the *Rhapsody on a Theme of Paganini*, Op. 43 (1934), for piano and orchestra.

Nikolay Karlovich Medtner (1880–1951), like Rachmaninoff and Scriabin, received his musical training at the Moscow Conservatory, graduating with the gold medal in 1900. That same year, he also won the Rubinstein prize in Vienna. There followed a distinguished career as a pianist and composer, first in Moscow, where he taught at the conservatory (1909 and 1914–21), and later in Berlin, Paris, and London, where he settled in 1935. Medtner was a prolific composer whose attention was focused mostly on writing for piano. His style adhered to a sonorous, col-

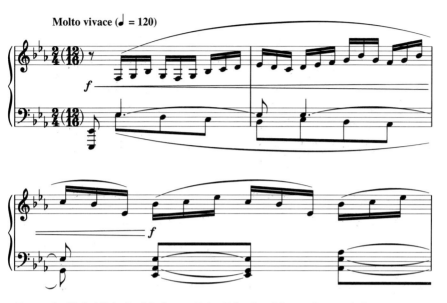

Example 20.8 Nicholas Medtner: *Fairy Tale*, Op. 26, no. 2 mm. 1–3

orful Romantic tradition, although he had strong ties to Classicism, frequently turning to sonata forms. His interest in structure and traditional
compositional techniques imbue his music with a strong sense of discipline
and inhibit his Romantic impulses to some extent.

Medtner's catalogue of piano music contains eleven works that utilize the term *sonata: Sonata-Triad*, Op. 11, in three movements; Sonata in
g, Op. 22, in two movements; *Sonata-Skazka* (March Sonata; Fairy-Tale
Sonata), Op. 25, no. 1; Sonata in *c*, Op. 25, no. 2, in one movement;
Sonata-Ballade, Op. 27, in one movement; Sonata in *a*, Op. 30, in one
movement; *Sonata reminiscenza*, Op. 38, no. 1; *Sonata tragica*, Op. 39, no.
5; *Sonata romantica*, Op. 53, no. 1; *Sonata minacciosa*, Op. 53, no. 2; and
Sonata-Idylle, Op. 56. The pictorial qualities that the sonata titles suggest
are carried over into the smaller character pieces as well. Medtner's
favorite title seems to be that of *Fairy Tale* (*conte* or *Märchen*) and sets of
pieces so titled occur as Opp. 8, 9, 14, 26, 34, 42, 48, and 51 (Example
20.8). Other titles are *Improvisations*, Op. 2; *Forgotten Melodies*, Opp.
38–40; and *Romantic Sketches*, Op. 54.

Two composers who should be mentioned in passing are **Reinhold
Moritzovich Gliere** (1875–1956) and his student **Nikolay Yakovlevich
Miaskovsky** (1881–1950). Both men held faculty posts at the Moscow
Conservatory for many years. Gliere is best known for his third symphony, based on the exploits of the folk hero Ilya Murometz, but he
also wrote over two hundred piano pieces, focusing mostly on sets of
character pieces (Opp. 17, 19, 21, and 26). There are also a set of

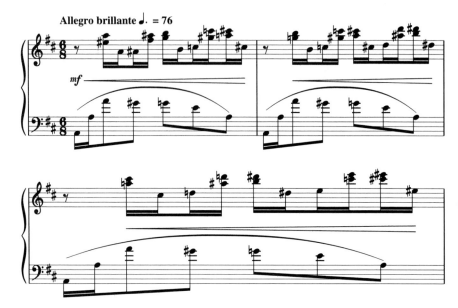

Example 20.9 Igor Stravinsky: Etude, Op. 7, no. 2 mm. 1–3

preludes, Op. 25, and some teaching pieces, Op. 31. Miaskovsky was influenced by impressionism, but his style stops short of embracing other twentieth-century techniques. He wrote nine sonatas and many sets of character pieces.

On the international scene, the most important composer between Rachmaninoff and Prokofiev was **Igor Fyodorovich Stravinsky** (1882–1971). Although Stravinsky was given early training in piano, and his earliest compositions were for that instrument, he devoted but relatively little time to writing piano music as a mature musician. Two works written when Stravinsky was studying with Rimsky-Korsakov were published posthumously, a scherzo (1902) and a sonata in *f-sharp* (1902–3). Of the works published during Stravinsky's career, the *Four Etudes*, Op. 7 (1908), represent the composer's early period. Thus, they are in the Romantic tradition, exploring ingeniously devised technical problems (Example 20.9). Stravinsky's neoclassic period is represented by two works written in the spirit of the eighteenth century: a contrapuntal, three-movement sonata (1924) and the *Sérénade en la* (1925), a work composed of four short movements: a solemn *hymne*, a cadenza-filled *romanza*, an emotionally detached *rondoletto*, and a subdued finale.

Stravinsky's most impressive virtuoso work for solo piano is a paraphrase of music from the ballet *Petrouchka*, done in 1921, ten years after the stage work premiered. Written for pianist Artur Rubinstein, these three movements are exciting and showy, so they have become famous as an attractive display vehicle for performers. Most performers have not yet discovered, however, the equally attractive arrangements of three movements from Stravinsky's ballet *The Firebird*. These colorful, virtuosic pieces were arranged by the Italian pianist Guido Agosti in 1928 for his colleague and friend Ferruccio Busoni. Three shorter works that represent Stravinsky's sophisticated, often humorous aloofness are the percussive, jazzy "Piano Rag Music" (1919); "Tango" (1940); and "Circus Polka for a Young Elephant" (1942). A set of eight short teaching pieces, *Les cinq doigts* (1921), explore five-finger patterns.

Samuel Evgenievich Feinberg (1890–1962) was educated at the Moscow Conservatory, established himself as a significant pianist, and spent most of his career teaching piano and composition at the Moscow Conservatory. In 1945, his second piano concerto won the Stalin Prize. His piano writing is derived from that of Scriabin. Among his piano works are ten sonatas, the last being written as late as 1940, two fantasies, and a number of character pieces.

Sergey (Sergeyevich) Prokofiev

Sergey (Sergeyevich) Prokofiev (b. Sontsovka, Ukraine, Apr. 23, 1891; d. Moscow, Mar. 5, 1953) was a precocious child composer, for he wrote numerous piano pieces and two operas before the age of ten. His mother, an accomplished pianist, was his first teacher. Thereafter he studied with Glière until 1904, when reluctantly the boy was placed in the St. Petersburg Conservatory. Although he studied harmony with Liadov and orchestration with Rimsky-Korsakov, the turbulent political scene and Prokofiev's own inclination toward experimental techniques resulted in poor relationships with his teachers.

A friendship with Miaskovsky provided encouragement for Prokofiev and a companion with whom to explore new music. The two young composers frequented the concerts known as Evenings of Contemporary Music. Prokofiev thus came in contact with new music by Scriabin, Reger, Strauss, Debussy, and Stravinsky. In 1908, Prokofiev played a performance of the *Navazhdeniye* (Devilish Suggestions) at one of these concerts. The performance was declared unintelligible by the press, and Prokofiev reveled in his reputation as an enfant terrible.

Although Prokofiev had not originally intended to pursue a career as a performing pianist, he became convinced that performing his own piano music was a good way to further his name as a composer. Toward this end he began to concentrate on piano study with Anna Esipova at the conservatory, graduating in 1914 with the highest honor, the Rubinstein prize (which, incidentally, was a grand piano), by playing his first piano concerto.

In the years following Prokofiev's 1914 graduation from the conservatory, Russia was in the throes of political upheaval. Prokofiev left the country in 1918 to embark upon a tour of the United States. As a representative of Russian "modernism," he met alternately success and criticism, but a steady stream of concert dates and commissions kept Prokofiev busy and nourished his professional reputation. Thus, for a period of eighteen years, between 1918 and 1936, his career was based first in the United States (until 1922) and then in Paris. Although he returned frequently to Russia to concertize and to oversee performances of his works, he became a prominent figure on the international scene, and his work reflected a cosmopolitan point of view.

It was thus a source of surprise to many that Prokofiev chose to return to the USSR in 1936. This move was prompted by a personal desire to go back to his homeland and live among his lifelong friends. It entailed, however, working under the watchful eyes of the communist government, as represented by the Union of Soviet Composers and the Party Central Committee. Thus, the final period of Prokofiev's creative life was one in which he found himself subjected to official approval or censure. The composer attempted to incorporate into his music the requisite simplistic, populist characteristics demanded by official doctrine. His work was often granted but lukewarm approval, and in 1948 he was included in a decree that declared the work of many Soviet composers alien to the Soviet people. The constant pressure of having to cope with official attitudes, complications in his personal life, and gradually failing health after a bad fall in 1945 all combined to make Prokofiev's final years in the USSR far from idyllic.

In spite of the reputation Prokofiev had during his career as a composer of dissonant, modern music, he steadfastly retained many strongly traditional elements in his style. The architecture of his works is clearly rooted in the past. In the nine piano sonatas, for example, all of the component parts that make up the traditional structures are easily identified: first themes, second themes, developments, right down to transitions and codas.

Rhythmically, Prokofiev used mostly metered pulse, resorting occasionally to changing time signatures. Once in a while he experimented with unusual meters, as in the final movement of the seventh sonata, where he used a time signature of fifteen-eight. He had a penchant for writing driving, motoric rhythms as well as a special gift for writing energized dance music.

Prokofiev's harmonic thinking consistently revolved around a tonal center, although his sense of color led him to the use of strong dissonance at times. His progressions and cadences are unorthodox and distinctive, and modality and tonality are freely intermixed. He often wrote conservative-sounding passages in order to establish a texture with which to contrast dissonance, frequently interjected with quick, stinging gestures. Moreover, he never abandoned his gift for writing supremely lyrical music, and a strong leaning toward outright Romantic ardor frequently appears in his works.

Allegretto

Example 20.10a Serge Prokofiev: Sonata no. 9, Op. 103 1st movt. mm. 190–91

Allegro strepitoso

Example 20.10b 2nd movt. mm. 1–3

The nine piano sonatas have become staples in the pianist's repertoire. The first sonata, Op. 1 (1909), is a one-movement work in a sonata-allegro form, untypical in its unabashed Romantic emotionalism. The third sonata, Op. 28a (1917), is the only other one-movement work, an expanded sonata-allegro form that contains both motoric drive and contrasting lyricism. It has gained considerable popularity, for both its length and brilliance make it an attractive work to program.

Of the four-movement sonatas, the second, Op. 14 (1912), is a fine example of a clear, balanced structure and, although a relatively early work, exhibits Prokofiev's style full blown. The sixth, Op. 82 (1939–40), is the first of three works known as the "war sonatas," written during World War II after Prokofiev had returned to the USSR. It is a huge, powerful work that features an unusually complex development in its first movement and a sumptuous waltz-like slow movement. The ninth sonata, Op. 103 (1947), is a curious mixture of the composer's biting satire and unusually conservative lyricism. In all of the four-movement sonatas, Prokofiev places the slow movement after the scherzo, and they contain clear use of cyclicism, material from the first movement in each appearing in the final movement. The ninth sonata, in addition, has an additional cyclic feature in that each of the first three movements contains in its coda a statement of the opening theme of the succeeding movement (Examples 20.10a–b).

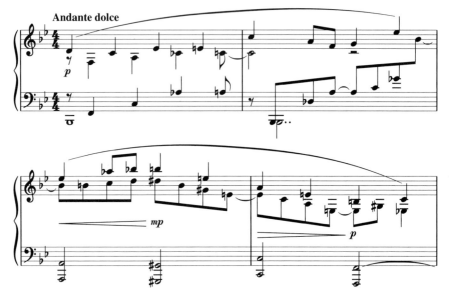

Example 20.11   Serge Prokofiev: Sonata no. 8, Op. 84, 1st movt. mm. 1–4

The first of the three-movement sonatas is Sonata no. 4, Op. 29c (1917), a revision of material written in 1908. It contains a complex and elaborate slow movement, the only sonata movement, incidentally, of which there is a recording by the composer. The fifth sonata, Op. 38 (1925), is classical in concept with a sardonic little waltz-like slow movement and a final rondo movement that develops surprising technical demands in its closing pages. The seventh, Op. 83 (1939–42), retains its niche as the most popular of the sonatas. It is composed of a biting, strong opening movement; a second movement with an opening theme so sentimental that it has been criticized as sounding corny; and a final toccata-like movement that is so effective that a wildly enthusiastic audience response is virtually guaranteed. The eighth sonata, Op. 84 (1939–44), by contrast with the seventh, leaves the impression of being essentially a slow, lyrical work, for both the first and second movements are marked *Andante* (Example 20.11). The first movement is in the expected sonata-allegro form, but only the development section is fast. The last movement provides a lively finale for the work.

The character pieces of Prokofiev number more than one hundred. They range from substantial virtuoso works such as the well-known toccata, Op. 11 (1912), to very short vignettes such as the *Mimoletnosti (Visions fugitives)*, Op. 22 (1915–17). The titles of the pieces, too, vary. The composer often used traditional genre or dance designations, such as the four etudes, Op. 2 (1909), or the titles from Op. 12

Allegro marcato

Example 20.12 Serge Prokofiev: Toccata, Op. 11 mm. 174–75

(1906–13), prelude, scherzo, gavotte, mazurka, and so forth. On the other hand, Prokofiev frequently gave pieces evocative titles such as *Navazhdeniye (Suggestions diabolique)*, Op. 4, no. 4 (1910–12), *Sarcasms*, Op. 17 (1912–14), or *Skazki staroy babushki* (The Tales of an Old Grandmother), Op. 31 (1918).

Included in Prokofiev's catalogue are character pieces drawn from the composer's theater works, for example *The Love for Three Oranges*, Op. 33 (1922), *Romeo and Juliet*, Op. 75 (1937), and *Cinderella*, Op. 102 (1944). There are also pieces that may be used as teaching material, notably the *Music for Children*, Op. 65 (1935). The two sonatinas, Op. 54 (1931–32), could also possibly qualify as didactic material, but they are, in fact, more sophisticated and difficult than the title *sonatina* might suggest.

The character pieces enjoy varying degrees of popularity among pianists. The Toccata, Op. 11, and the *Suggestions diabolique,* Op. 4, no. 4, are well-known show pieces and appear with regularity on concert programs (Example 20.12). Other character pieces, however, such as those that make up Opp. 3, 32, 45, or 59, are seldom played, which is surprising, in light of the enormous popularity of the nine sonatas.

Several Russian composers born at the turn of the twentieth century should be noted. **Alexander Nikolayevich Tcherepnin** (1899–1977) spent the early portion of his career in Russia but left in 1921. He was enormously successful in the United States and Europe as a pianist, conductor, and composer. His tours in Asia (1934–37) brought him into contact with Eastern musical systems, influencing his own compositional style. His music combines ideas gleaned from Asian music with influences from his native Russia. In addition, he added techniques in vogue among many composers during the 1920s and 1930s: bitonality, motoric rhythms, neoclassic clarity, and urbane sophistication. The list of his keyboard works is extensive, including two sonatas, Op. 22 (1924)

Allegro moderato, festivamente ♩ = 80 - 88

f e pesante

Example 20.13   Dmitri Kabalevsky: Sonata no. 2, Op. 45, lst movt. mm. 1–4

and Op. 94 (1961); several sets of preludes and etudes; a famous set of bagatelles, Op. 5 (1913–18); and numerous character pieces.

Nikolai Lvovich Lopatnikoff (1903–76) left Russia when he was in his late teens. He studied in Helsinki and built his early career in Berlin and London before moving to the United States, where he became a citizen in 1944. He pointed to Hindemith and Stravinsky as strong contemporary influences on his musical style. For keyboard he wrote a sonata, Op. 29 (1943); a sonatine, Op. 7 (1926); a set of variations, Op. 22 (1933); and several sets of character pieces.

Dimitry Borisovich Kabalevsky (b. 1904) centered his career in Moscow, where he became an official spokesperson for the Communist party on musical policy. His style thus reflects dedication to being accessible, light, and folkloric. His piano music is used extensively as teaching material. Piano works include three sonatas, Opp. 6, 45, and 46; two sonatinas, Op. 13; a set of twenty-four preludes, one in each key arranged like the Chopin set, Op. 38 (1947); and numerous sets of small pieces appropriate for student use (Example 20.13).

Dmitri Dmitrievich Shostakovich (1906–75) is the most significant composer of those who worked within the guidelines of official Soviet policy. He was in great disfavor with the communist leadership at one point in his career (1948), but even during that period of harsh criticism he strove to remain faithful to party doctrine. His good graces were eventually restored, and he ended his career as one of the USSR's most celebrated composers. Shostakovich is regarded as one of the great symphonists of the twentieth century. His piano music represents a relatively small portion of his overall, prolific catalogue. Several of his keyboard works, however, have become important for pianists, notably a set of twenty-four preludes and fugues, Op. 87 (1950–51), one in each key (Examples 20.14 and 20.15). Also noteworthy is the set of twenty-four preludes arranged after Chopin, Op. 34 (1932–33). Less frequently encountered are the two sonatas, Op. 12 (1926) and Op. 61 (1942), other sets of preludes, and several sets of character pieces.

Example 20.14 Dmitri Shostakovich: Prelude no. 7 from *24 Preludes and Fugues*, Op. 87 mm. 1–2

Example 20.15 Dmitri Shostakovich: Fugue no. 7 from *24 Preludes and Fugues*, Op. 87 mm. 1–4

Two Armenian-Russian composers have written folkloric music for piano, some of which has enjoyed popularity. **Aram Il'yich Khatchaturian** (1903–78) has written teaching pieces that are often used as well as a toccata that has gained some favor as a show piece of intermediate difficulty. His larger works, such as the Sonata (1961) or the Sonatina (1959), are less successful. **Ařno Harutyuni Babadjanyan** (b. 1921) incorporates both folk rhythm and ornamentation into his highly colorful, virtuosic piano writing. Possibly the best known of his pieces is the attractive, brilliant Capriccio, but there are also a piano sonata (1947) and other character pieces.

Sofiya Gubaydulina (b. 1931) has written for ballet, theater, and film and, since 1968, has worked at the Electronic Music Studio in Moscow. Two piano works are among her varied catalogue: *Ciaconna* (1962) and a sonata (1965).

Rodion Konstantinovich Shchedrin (b. 1932) has achieved distinction as perhaps the most successful Soviet composer of his generation. An early piano suite, *Prazdnik na Kolkhoze* (Holiday on the Kolkhoz; 1951), was important in establishing his reputation. In it he uses popular Russian urban tunes (*chastushka*), a technique that became his hallmark. Shchedrin has managed to represent the official party policy of the USSR

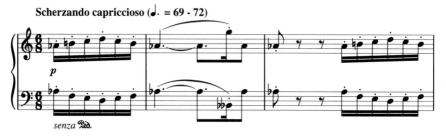

Example 20.16   Rodion Shchedrin: Etude (Inversion) no. 9 from *Polyphonic Notebook* mm. 1–3

by writing tuneful, appealing music and at the same time incorporating contemporary and learned techniques (Example 20.16). His list of piano works includes a sonata (1962) and, like Shostakovich, a set of twenty-four preludes and fugues (1963–64).

CHAPTER TWENTY-ONE

Other European Composers of the Twentieth Century

From the middle of the nineteenth century into the twentieth, a national, regional, or ethnic consciousness began to emerge in many parts of the world. Its results can be noted in various reorganizations of political entities, oftentimes the emergence of small new nations, or, as in the case of the United Socialist Soviet Republic (USSR), the formation of a conglomerate. Musicians' creative impulses, when focused toward nationalism, often preceded the political manifestations by several decades. Composers incorporated characteristics from folk song and dance into their scores and used subject matter from folk history or legend as the basis for stage works or programmatic content. Assimilation of such characteristics varied in degree from one composer to the next and often even within the works of a given composer. Nationalist traits were thus always mixed in with the mainstream of international musical thought to some degree. In some quarters, music born of nationalistic thought clung resistantly to nineteenth-century compositional practice. In others, however, the writing took on bold, striking dimensions as the twentieth century ushered in experiments in new compositional techniques. Groups of composers interested in nationalistic expression emerged clearly in Russia, eastern Europe, the Balkans, northern Europe, Spain, and various countries in North and South America. Interest was less pronounced in other areas, such as Italy, Germany, and Great Britain. Although different nationalist schools emerged at different times, the rise of the movement generally began in the closing decades of the nineteenth century. It was in full flower during the first part the twentieth century and has waned considerably in the past fifty years.

It is important to remember, too, that although nationalistic expression dominated the work of some composers, others showed but little interest in it. Similarly, some composers rallied around it, forming consciously into groups or "schools," while others worked independently. A few composers were capable of sometimes writing works steeped in nationalism and at other times showing relatively little interest in it. Moreover, the techniques through which nationalistic traits were incorporated into art music range from the simplistic to the complex.

Czechoslovakia

Among the earliest representatives of nationalistic thought was **Bedřich (Friedrich) Smetana** (1824–84). Midway through his career, about 1860, he became one of a group of Czechoslovakian artists who sought to establish a national school. Smetana's interest in this direction bore fruit primarily in opera and orchestral works, but his catalogue of piano works includes more than a dozen polkas, two books of Czech dances, a book of Bohemian dances, and a set of character pieces entitled *From Bohemia's Woods and Fields*. Other keyboard music is less nationalistic. There are a little-known sonata in one movement (1849), character pieces, and a famous concert study entitled *Am Seegestade* (On the Seashore; 1862).

Antonín Dvořák (1841–1904) was probably the most celebrated Czechoslovakian (Bohemian) composer of the late nineteenth century. His career took him to England and the United States, where for three years (1892–95) he was the artistic director of the National Conservatory in New York City. An extremely prolific composer, his works centered on orchestral and vocal music, but he also wrote a large body of piano works. His style reflects influences of Brahms, Wagner, and Smetana as well as his own interest in regional folk song. His melodies particularly show individual charm.

A complete edition of Dvořák's works began to appear in 1955 under the senior editorship of Otakar Šourek. Jarmil Burghauser provided a complete thematic catalogue in 1960, a much-needed organization for Dvořák's works, many of which were published without opus numbers. Among Dvořák's many keyboard works are a Dumka, Op. 35, B. 64 (1876); a set of variations, Op. 36, B. 65 (1876); and a set of humoresques, Op. 101, B. 187 (1894), from which the seventh in *G-flat* has become internationally famous. In addition, there are several sets of character pieces, many of them quite attractive and worthy of more attention than they currently enjoy. Important among these are the early set of twelve entitled *Silhouettes*, Op. 8, B. 98, (1879), and the set of thirteen called *Poetiké nálady* (Poetic Tone Pictures), Op. 85, B. 161 (1889). Dvořák contributed significantly to the four-hand literature with two popular sets of *Slavonic Dances*, Op. 46, B. 78, and Op. 72, B. 145, and the set of pieces entitled *Ze Šumavy* (From the Bohemian Forest), Op. 68, B. 133.

Like Smetana, **Leoš Janáček** (1854–1928) became interested in nationalism midway through his career, in this case from about 1904 with the creation of his most famous stage work, the opera *Její Pastorkyna*, better known by its German title, *Jenufa*. He drew inspiration from a study of the folk music of his native Moravia. His keyboard music includes two sets

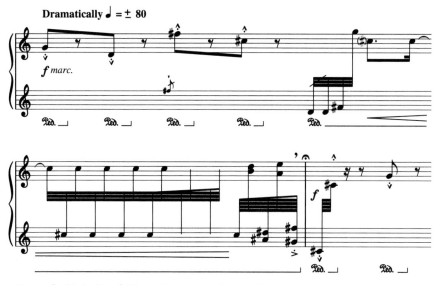

Example 21.1 Karel Husa: Sonata no. 2 mm. 1+

of Moravian folk dances (1904) and a well-known set of fifteen character pieces called *Po zarostlém chodníčku* (On the Overgrown Path; 1901–8). There are also a programmatic sonata *Z ulice* (From the Street; 1905) and an earlier set of variations, Op. 1 (1880), known as the *Zdenka Variations*.

Two other Czechoslovakian composers whose work should be mentioned are **Bohuslav Martinů** (1890–1959) and **Karel Husa** (b. 1921). Martinů began his career in Prague but spent fourteen years in Paris before coming to the United States just before World War II. Although Martinů's style was influenced by various composers during the course of his career (Roussel, Debussy, Stravinsky, and others), Czech folk characteristics permeate his music much of the time.

Prolific in all genres, Martinů's compositions for piano include two sets of Czech dances (1926 and 1931); three books of etudes and polkas (1946); eight preludes (1929); *Fantasie et toccata* (1940); and a piano sonata dedicated to pianist Rudolf Serkin (1954). His sets of character pieces include *Les Ritournelles* (1932), *Fables* (1947), and a set of four easy children's pieces called *Spring in the Garden* (1948).

Karel Husa's work reflects the composer's interests in twentieth-century techniques more than his national heritage. Like Martinů, Husa spent time in Paris, where he studied with Nadia Boulanger and Arthur Honegger, before coming to the United States. Husa's career in the United States has been notable, being distinguished by a professorship at Cornell University and his winning of a Pulitzer Prize in 1969 for the String Quartet no. 3. For piano, Husa has written a sonatine (1943), a powerful sonata (1949; Example 21.1), and an *Elégie* (1957).

Hungary

Ernst von Dohnányi (1877–1960) represents Hungarian Romanticism more than nationalism. His career was centered in Budapest up until 1945, when, as a result of personal tragedy suffered during World War II, he moved first to Austria and then eventually to the United States. He was widely recognized as one of the most important virtuoso pianists of his time. His early music was strongly influenced by Brahms, whom he met and from whom he received encouragement. Eventually, however, Dohnányi developed a personal voice within a traditional framework. Best known among his many piano pieces is a set of four rhapsodies, Op. 11 (1902–3). He also wrote two sets of etudes and many character pieces. His interest in using folk material was limited, but two works may be cited in this context: a set of variations on a Hungarian folk song, Op. 29 (1917), and a set of seven pieces entitled *Ruralia hungarica*, Op. 32a (1923; Op. 32b is the orchestral version of five of these pieces).

Béla Bartók

Béla Bartók (b. Nagyszentmiklós, Hungary, now Sinnicolau Mare, Romania, Mar. 25, 1881; d. New York, Sept. 26, 1945) is regarded as the most brilliant Hungarian musician of the twentieth century. He was a fine pianist, a research scholar in the field of ethnomusicology, and one of the most significant composers of his time. He combined his research and love for the folk music of central Europe, particularly that of Hungary and Romania, with an intense interest in twentieth-century techniques and traditional compositional structure and procedures. The result is that he wrote music that incorporated folkloric elements but that also transcended ethnic boundaries to become internationally recognized as significant artworks.

Bartók's mother, an amateur pianist and a teacher, had to support the family after the death of Bartók's father. Bartók's early schooling took place in several smaller cities as teaching posts for Paula Bartók became available. Most of his gymnasium training was in Pozsony (now Bratislava, Czechoslovakia where he befriended Dohnányi, four years his senior in the same school. It was not until 1899 that Bartók was able to attend the Budapest Academy of Music, studying piano with István Thomán, Dohnányi's former teacher, and composition with János Koessler.

During his years at the academy, Bartók developed as a pianist, making his debut with Liszt's Sonata in *b* at a student concert in 1901. Bartók became enamored of the music of Richard Strauss at this time and also showed his first interest in folk music. In 1905, he began to work with Zoltán Kodály on the publication of a book of folk-song settings. From 1906, Bartók undertook annual field trips to collect folk-song material, using an Edison phonograph, first all over Hungary and later in Czechoslovakia and Romania. By 1907, Bartók was offered a piano professorship at the Budapest Academy, a position that gave him modest financial security.

Bartók's reputation as a composer continued to grow throughout Europe. His compositions were played at festivals of contemporary music, and he toured as a pianist, playing mostly his own works. These tours took him to London, Paris, Germany, the USSR, and the United States. On his fiftieth birthday, he was the recipient of the Légion d'honneur.

With the rise of fascism in Europe, Bartók felt increasingly troubled. He refused to play concerts in Germany after 1933, and in 1937 he forbade performances of his works there. As Hungary and Romania fell under the influence of fascist politicians, Bartók became a target for criticism in the Hungarian and Romanian press. In 1940, he and his family left Hungary forever to take up residence in the United States.

Things were not easy in the United States, for the first appearances of Bartók and his wife, Ditta Pásztory, as pianists met with but modest success. Through a grant from the Ditson Foundation of Columbia University, Bartók was able to work as a visiting assistant in helping catalogue the Parry collection of some 2,000 folk songs at Harvard University. Columbia, too, awarded him an honorary doctorate in 1940. The New York Public Library was interested for a time in publishing Bartók's own extensive collection of Romanian folk material, but publication costs for the two-volume work were such that the institution ultimately abandoned the project.

In the midst of this pattern of alternate successes and disappointments, Bartók became ill in 1942 with polycythemia, a blood disease in which the red corpuscles increase in number and concentration. He was able to be treated through assistance given him by the American Society of Composers, Authors, and Publishers (ASCAP). A commission from Serge Koussevitzky for an orchestral piece for the Boston Symphony Orchestra inspired Bartók to write the *Concerto for Orchestra*. This work and the third piano concerto (1945) were to be his last. (The orchestration of the final movement of the concerto was finished by Tibor Serly.)

Many works of Bartók were not given an opus number by the composer. In 1956, András Szóllósy provided a widely used catalogue of Bartók's adult works (Sz.), and in 1974 Denijs Dille catalogued the composer's very early pieces (DD.). The keyboard music exhibits a variety of styles, reflecting the composer's interest in different modes of expression and techniques.

Bartók wrote more than fifty piano pieces between the ages of nine and twenty. These works are generally quite traditional, the work of a young man under the influence of German Romanticism. There are many dances, several scherzi, character pieces, a set of variations (DD. 30), and two extant sonatas (DD. 32 and DD. 35). Of these early works, a set of four pieces written in 1903 (a study for the left hand, two fantasies, and a scherzo; DD. 71), were published.

Best known of Bartók's early works is the Rhapsody, Op. 1 (1904; Sz. 26). The composer arranged it for piano and orchestra and performed it numerous times during his early career. Although it has individual features, it is conceived in the tradition of Liszt and is the last of Bartók's piano works to reflect a Romantic style. Bartók remained interested in the work, furthermore, for he undertook revisions of it two times, of the second movement only in 1908 and of the entire work in 1955.

Bartók's research into the folk music of central Europe began to show itself in his keyboard works as early as 1905. It remained a strong element in almost all of his keyboard pieces from that point on with only a few isolated works eschewing the folk influence in favor of attention to the exploration of some other compositional or technical focus. Many sets of pieces are straightforward folk-song settings such as the *3 Hungarian Folk Songs from the Csik District* (1907; Sz. 35a); the *6 Romanian Folk dances* (1915; Sz. 56); or the twenty *Romanian Christmas Carols* (1915; Sz. 57). Some sets adhere to simple settings for the most part, but they also begin to incorporate a few characteristics of art music. Examples are the *14 Bagatelles*, Op. 6 (1908; Sz. 38), in which nos. 13 and 14 carry personal programmatic titles ("Elle est morte" and "Valse ma mie qui danse"); and the *15 Hungarian Peasant Songs and Dances* (1914–18; Sz. 71), in which no. 5 is a scherzo and no. 6 is a theme and variations entitled "Ballade." Finally, there are examples of sets of pieces that may be regarded as essentially folk settings but that are attended by sophisticated, often technically difficult, compositional techniques; changing meters or rhythmic groups (for example 3 + 2); frequent alterations of tempo; use of dissonance; and figural patterns that encompass the entire keyboard. Good examples are the *Improvisations on Hungarian Peasant Songs*, Op. 20 (1920; Sz. 74; Example 21.2), and the last set of pieces from volume 6 of the *Mikrokosmos* (1926, 1932–39; Sz. 107), entitled *Six Dances in Bulgarian Rhythm*.

Folk-like material permeates much other piano music, even when the pieces themselves seem conceptually more akin to independent instrumental works than to simple transcriptions or settings. The *2 Romanian Dances*, Op. 8a (1909–10; Sz. 43), emphasize virtuoso devices such as skips and octaves. The works that bear the traditional titles Sonatina (1915; Sz. 55) and Sonata (1926; Sz. 80), while making use of formats associated with the genres, rely heavily on folk-like dance rhythms and melodies (Example 21.3). Similarly, the famous *Allegro barbaro* (1911; Sz. 49) uses driving rhythms reminiscent of folk dance on which Bartók builds a showy concert piece.

Example 21.2 Béla Bartók: Improvisation no. 2 from *Improvisations on Hungarian Peasant Songs*, Op. 20 mm. 1–5

Example 21.3 Béla Bartók: Sonata, 1st movt. mm. 1–6

Such folkloric elements are embedded stylistically in other sets of pieces, appearing obvious at times but at other times seemingly dormant, the main focus being on other compositional characteristics: impressionistic sonorities, contrapuntal procedures such as canon or inversion, or didactic goals. This blend is evident in the Suite, Op. 14 (1916; Sz. 62), where a folkloric first movement is followed by three others less obviously derived from folk material, the final one being built on sonorities that bring to mind impressionistic techniques. The most difficult and imposing set of pieces is the *Out of Doors* (1926; Sz. 81). Each of its five pieces reflects its title: "With Pipes and Drums" makes use of dissonance

Example 21.4 Béla Bartók: "Night Music," no. 4 from *Out of Doors Suite* mm. 1–2

in the low registers of the keyboard for percussion effects; ostinato undulation attends the "Barcarolla"; trill-like figurations are modeled on bagpipe drones in "Musettes"; imaginative figurations imitating crickets, frogs, and insects combine with fragments of folk-like melody to weave a magical spell in "Night Music"; (Example 21.4); and "The Chase" features a left-hand ostinato pattern that builds steadily to a shattering climax. An equally impressive set of pieces is the *Dance Suite* (1925; Sz. 77), overlooked possibly because of the fact that the composer arranged the pieces from an orchestral version of the music.

Other worthy sets of pieces should also be noted. The *2 Elegies*, Op. 8b (1908–9; Sz. 41), stylistically reflect Bartók's earlier, more Romantic period and, along with the *3 Burlesques*, Op. 8c (1908; Sz. 47), show little or no influence of folk material. The *4 Nénies*, also known as *4 Dirges*, Op. 9a (1909–10; Sz. 45), are also without folk influences, but they are rich in impressionist-like sonorities. The *7 Sketches*, Op. 9b (1908–10; Sz. 44), seem more akin to teaching pieces in their brevity, although some of the writing is more sophisticated than might be encountered in didactic material. The *3 Etudes*, Op. 18 (1918; Sz. 72), are quite dissonant, very difficult, and belong to the tradition of concert studies.

Bartók's use of compositional devices has been a source of fascination for many analysts. Ernő Lendvai (b. 1925), in particular, wrote a series of papers, starting in 1947–48, that analyzed Bartók's music in terms of the golden section, a proportionate relationship found in natural objects and frequently in classical architecture. Expressed in numerical terms, the golden section is known as the Fibonacci series. In such a series the sum of any two adjacent numbers is equal to the following number. The series 2–3–5–8–13 is an example. Lendvai's analysis concerned itself especially with Bartók's construction of invervalic relationships in chords and scales as well as overall structure.

Bartók's dedication to writing didactic material resulted in the production of the most significant body of teaching pieces of the early twentieth century. This interest was evident early in the composer's career, represented by *10 Easy Pieces* (1908; Sz. 39) and the eighty-five pieces that make up *For Children* (1908–9; Sz. 42). The *First Term at the Piano* (1913; Sz. 53), a set of eighteen pieces, was written for the piano method of Bartók and Sandor Reschofsky.

Bartók's final major work for keyboard is the *Mikrokosmos* (1926, 1932–39; Sz. 107), 153 pieces in six volumes, arranged in an order of progressive difficulty. Here, the composer sets forth a compendium of keyboard techniques, compositional devices, and colorful folkloric characteristics. The opening volume (nos. 1–36) begins with the hands playing in unison and then introduces imitation, inversion, and canon as well as syncopation and Dorian and Phrygian modality. In volume 2 (nos. 37–66), Lydian and Mixolydian modes are introduced as well as more sophisticated textures, more difficult touch forms, problems in control of dynamics, and harder key signatures. Volume 3 (nos. 67–96) deals with thirds, sixths, and chordal textures. Rhythmic problems and exotic harmonies are featured in volume 4 (nos. 97–121). More touch problems, etudes in double notes, and pieces using fourths are in volume 5 (nos. 122–39), and the final volume (nos. 140–53) contains pieces that utilize the full range of technical and musical difficulties found in Bartók's mature style.

Zoltán Kodály (1882–1967), like Bartók, was educated in Hungary. He was Bartók's associate in folk-song research for many years and with Bartók and others helped found the New Hungarian Music Society. Kodály's use of folkloric material in his compositions is similar to that of Bartók, but Kodály's harmonic language is far less pungent, and his rhythms and textures are generally less complex. His adaptation of folk-song material for children and its use through singing as a basis for music education has became known worldwide as the Kodály method. Kodály wrote only a few piano works, notably two sets of character pieces, nine in Op. 3 (1909) and seven in Op. 11 (1910–18), as well as an extended virtuoso piece, *Dances of Marosszék* (1927). There are also twelve teaching pieces, *Gyermektáncok* (Children's Dances; 1928) and an impressionistic piece entitled *Méditation sur un motif de Claude Debussy* (1907).

A sizeable group of composers followed the path laid down by Bartók and Kodály, several having actually studied with one or the other. Much of the work of **Leó Weiner** (1885–1960) is based on Hungarian peasant songs and dances, although his style is less contemporary sounding than that of either Bartók or Kodály. **Tibor Harsányi** (1898–1954) spent most of his career in Paris, and his piano works, which include a sonata (1926), etudes (1933), and many character pieces, reflect the characteristics of styles in vogue in that city during his residence there.

Jenō Takács (b. 1902) studied in Vienna and spent most of his career outside of Hungary, teaching first in Egypt and the Philippines and then finally in the United States at the University of Cincinnati. He took an interest in the folk music of each of these areas as well as that of Asia. He wrote several sets of teaching pieces: *20 Easy Pieces* (1936–37), *Double Dozen for Little Fingers* (1958), *21 Easy Pieces* (1961). Of more difficulty are the Toccata, Op. 54 (1946), and the Partita, Op. 58 (1954).

Ferenc Szabó (1902–69) was a student of Kodály, and his style combined folk elements with polytonality and complex, terse structures. Drawn to communism, he spent much of his career in the USSR, returning to Hungary as a Red Army officer in 1944. His keyboard works include a toccata (1928), a sonatina (1929), three sonatas (1940–41, 1947, and 1957–61), and sets of smaller pieces.

Pál Kadosa (b. 1903) was also a student of Kodály and dedicated to the ideology of Hungarian music. He spent his career in Budapest, where he was one of the founders of the Society of Modern Hungarian Musicians, which later merged with the Hungarian Association for New Music. He was vice president of the Hungarian Arts Council (1945–49) and from 1945 a professor of piano at the Budapest Academy of Music. His use of folk material often attempts to preserve much of its inherent simplicity, although late in his career he experimented with twelve-tone techniques. He produced a sizeable body of piano works including four sonatas (Op. 7, 1926; Op. 9, 1926–27; Op. 13, 1930; Op. 54, 1960), teaching pieces (Op. 23 and 35, 1935), a folk-song suite (Op. 21, 1933), a rhapsody (Op. 28a, 1937), and about a dozen sets of character pieces.

Miklós Rósza (b. 1907) was educated in Budapest and Leipzig. His name is associated with film music in Hollywood, having scored close to two dozen major films between 1940 and 1970. He was the recipient of the Academy Award three times (1945, 1948, 1959). His nonfilm music is rooted in Hungarian folk music, but he preferred to assimilate its melodic and intervalic characteristics rather than to borrow material directly. He wrote a noteworthy piano sonata, Op. 20 (1948), and two sets of smaller pieces, *Bagatelles*, Op. 12 (1932), and *Kaleidoscope*, Op. 19 (1945).

Sándor Veress (b. 1907) was a student of both Bartók and Kodály. He spent the early part of his career working with folk materials of Moldavia. Later, he took up residence in Berne, Switzerland, where he became director of musicology at Berne University. His compositions are rooted in folk music, but he moved in the direction of contemporary techniques, eventually adopting serial techniques around 1950. Much of his keyboard writing has been directed toward teaching pieces: three sonatinas (1932, 1934, 1935); *15 Little Pieces* (1938); and *Fingerlarks*, seventy-seven teaching pieces (1940–46), expanded to eighty-eight in 1969. There are also more difficult sets entitled *7 Hungarian Dances* (1938) and *6 Csárdás* (1938).

Lajos Papp (b. 1935) studied with Szabó in Budapest and later in Basel, Switzerland. Papp has remained in Hungary for most of his

career. His keyboard works include a set of variations (1968), three rondos (1967), six bagatelles, and a set of twenty-seven small piano pieces
suitable for teaching at beginning levels.

Poland

The list of noteworthy Polish composers after Chopin begins with
(Franz) Xaver Scharwenka (1850–1924) and **Moritz Moszkowski** (1854–
1925). Scharwenka was trained in Berlin, and a good deal of his career
centered in that city, although he was a celebrated touring concert artist.
He lived in New York for seven years, where he founded a conservatory
(1891). His piano works have all but faded from the active repertoire,
but he wrote two sonatas, Op. 6 (1872) and Op. 36 (1878), twenty-five
Polish dances, character pieces, and technical studies.

Moritz Moszkowski, on the other hand, enjoys a modest amount of
attention from pianists. Like Scharwenka, Moszkowski was German
trained, having studied in Dresden and Berlin. He settled in Paris in
1897 after establishing his reputation as a pianist throughout central
Europe. He had a taste for Spanish idioms, which he frequently tried to
incorporate into his character pieces. Among his most successful piano
works are the *Spanish Dances,* Op. 12 (also written for piano duet) and
Caprice Espagnol, Op. 37. Other character pieces that are still played are
the *Etincelles,* Op. 36, no. 6, and the *Jongleurin,* Op. 52, no. 4. Moszkowski's writing for the keyboard is extremely clever from a technical
standpoint, and he often creates very effective climactic moments. His
music is thus exciting and entertaining without attempting to be profound. He has written two sets of technical studies that are useful and
attractive: a set of twenty very short pieces, Op. 91, and one of fifteen virtuoso pieces, Op. 72. His *School of Double Notes,* Op. 64, a compendium
of scales and exercises in double notes with four double-note etudes as a
capstone, is standard reference fare for those who undertake detailed
study of this special technique.

Ignacy Jan Paderewski (1860–1941) was one of the most celebrated musicians of his day, enjoying a name recognition among a large segment of the population not otherwise well informed about music. His
early training at the Warsaw Conservatory was sporadic, but he graduated in 1878 and became an instructor there. Later (1884–87), he studied intensively with Leschetizky in Vienna to become a performing
pianist. Performances in Paris (1888) and Vienna (1889) met with enormous success, and Paderewski was launched on his spectacular international career as a pianist. Always an ardent Polish patriot, he donated the
proceeds of all his concerts during World War I to Polish relief. As the
new postwar government emerged, he became the diplomatic representative to the United States for that regime, working in Washington, D.C.
(1918–19), and then the first premiere of the Polish Republic (1819). His

term as premiere was relatively short, for by 1920 he returned to the concert stage and continued to tour for the benefit of Polish victims of World War I. Paderewski longed for as much success as a composer as he enjoyed as a performing musician. Although his compositions were frequently heard during his time, they have not enjoyed continuing popularity. Of the many character pieces he wrote for piano, only the charming Minuet in *G*, Op. 14, no. 1, remains firmly entrenched in the active repertoire. Other significant works are Introduction and Toccata, Op. 6; *Album de Mai: Scénes romantiques,* Op. 10; and a set of variations with a fugue on an original theme, Op. 11.

Leopold Godowsky (1870–1928) was Polish by birth but spent most of his career in Berlin and various cities of the United States. He became a permanent resident of the United States at the outbreak of World War I (1914). He toured the world as a performing pianist and was greatly admired for combining sensitive musicality with astounding technical control. Godowsky is best known as a composer for a set of fifty-three studies based on Chopin etudes. Godowsky completely rewrote the Chopin works, often combining them in contrapuntal textures and devoting twenty-two of the studies to the left hand alone. The studies are remarkable in that they combine technical demands of the most extreme difficulty with great sensitivity and beauty. The pieces thus qualify as valid artworks, notwithstanding their preoccupation with near-impossible technical feats. To hear finished performances of the works, moreover, is to be made aware of the musical and contrapuntal complexities of the writing rather than the bravura of their technical demands. Other works of Godowsky for piano include a set of thirty character pieces called *Triakontameron* (1920), twelve pieces based on Javanese music entitled *Phonoramus* (1925), a piano sonata in *e* (1911), didactic works, and transcriptions of works by Weber, Brahms, and Johann Strauss.

Karol (Maciej) Szymanowski

Karol (Maciej) Szymanowski (b. Tymoszówka, Ukraine, Oct. 6, 1882; d. Lausanne, Mar. 29, 1937) was the most important Polish composer of the early twentieth century. Born of landed gentry, he was able to devote his childhood to cultivation of taste for the arts and philosophy. His father was a connoisseur of the arts as well as an ardent Polish patriot, and his four siblings all engaged in artistic pursuits. His early education was undertaken by his father at first and later through attendance at the Newhaus school in Elisavetgrad. Szymanowski was almost twenty before he was sent to Warsaw for more intensive musical study.

At this time, Szymanowski was strongly under the influence of the Romantic tradition. Important keyboard works of this period are nine preludes, Op. 1 (1900); four etudes, Op. 4 (1902); the Fantasy (1905); two sets of variations, one in *b-flat* (1903) and the set based on a Polish folk theme (1904); and the first two piano sonatas, in *c* (1904) and *A* (1911). Although Szymanowski's style at this point has close ties with the music of Chopin and early Scriabin, his individuality can also be clearly discerned both in his use of harmony and in the unusual ability to combine elements of both ardor and remoteness in his emotional palette.

Szymanowski underwent a stylistic change beginning about 1911. Influential were trips to sites of ancient Arab and early Christian cultures throughout the Mediterranean, becoming acquainted with literary works of ancient Greek and Islamic cultures, and to some extent falling under the spell of Debussy and early Stravinsky.

Szymanowski returned to Poland just before the outbreak of World War I (1914), and over the next few years, in relative isolation, underwent a period of great creative activity. The works of this period are built with complex sonorities that contain atmospheric effects and polytonal combinations. Structural designs, although related to traditional patterns, often emerge as improvisatory due to the inclusion of many cadenza-like sections and much transformation of thematic material. Rhythmic ideas, too, appear in many forms and undergo constant variation. Unusual meters are used with a moderate amount of frequency, and bar lines, although still used for the most part, often have little to do with rhythmic units. From a physical standpoint, the music is constructed with extraordinary acumen, making virtuoso demands on the player that often push the limits of possibility but that also lie extremely well under the hands. Such writing is all the more remarkable when one remembers that the composer himself, although a competent keyboard player, was not a performing virtuoso and quite probably was not comfortable playing many of his more demanding works in public.

The descriptive titles of works from this period reflect the composer's newfound interest in ancient and exotic cultures. The title *Métopes*, Op. 29 (1915), refers to the pictorial carvings found most often near the tops of Doric columns. The suite itself consists of three poems with title references drawn from the epic poetry attributed to Homer: "L'Isle des sirènes," the home of the seductive creatures who attempt to steer Odysseus off course in the *Odyssey*; "Calypso," the island nymph who detained Odysseus seven years in his journey homeward from Troy; and "Nausicaa," the charming Phaeacian princess who finds the sleeping, exhausted Odysseus and introduces him to her father, the king. The literary sources of the three poems that make up the *Masques*, Op. 34 (1916–18), are more diverse: "Shéhérazade," the famous storyteller of the Arabian Nights (Example 21.5); "Tantris le bouffon," a character drawn from a parody of *Tirstan and Isolda* written by Ernst Hardt; and "Sérénade de Don Juan," referring to the legendary Spanish nobleman whose exploits have been described in many literary works, notably in *El burlador de Sevilla* (1648) of Gabriel Téllez (Tirso de Molina) and *Don Juan* (1824) by George Gordon (Lord Byron). A set of twelve short

Lento assai, languido

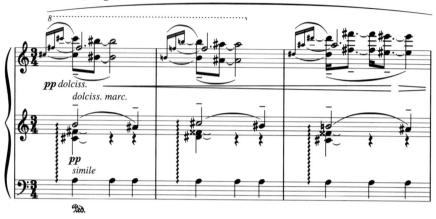

Example 21.5 Karol Szymanowski: "Shéhérazade" from *Masques*, Op. 34 mm. 3–5

Presto

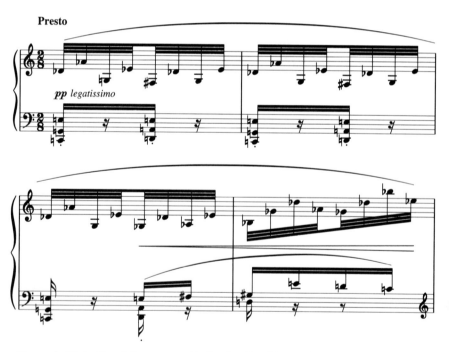

Example 21.6 Karol Szymanowski: Etude, Op. 33, no. 1 mm. 1–4

Example 21.7 Alexandre Tansman: Nocturne no. 1 from *Quatre nocturnes* mm. 1–5

etudes, Op. 33 (1922), makes use of a similar musical style and technique (Example 21.6).

Szymanowski was profoundly moved by the formation of the new Polish state after World War I. As a result he became intensely interested in creating a Polish music worthy of the mantle of Chopin. Studying folk music of the Tatra mountain region of Poland was part of this process, and the composer spent some time each year in the leading city of the region, Zakopane. The resulting musical influence was incorporated into Szymanowski's existing style. Keyboard works reflecting this interest are the twenty *Mazurkas*, Op. 50 (1923–29), four *Polish Dances* (1926), and the *Two Mazurkas*, Op. 62 (1934). Szymanowski's writing in these pieces is intense and masterful. These works form a worthy sequel to the mazurkas of Chopin, although they have yet to be discovered by many pianists.

Alexandre Tansman (b. 1897) received his early training in Warsaw in music, law, and philosophy. In 1919, his compositions took both first and second prizes in the Polish National Music Competition, the composer having entered them under two different pseudonyms. Shortly thereafter he moved to Paris, where he centered the remainder of his career, except for a period in the United States during World War II. His music reflects influences of Debussy, Ravel, Les Six français, and especially Stravinsky, with whom he formed a close personal friendship. Tansman's keyboard music is clever, well constructed, and attractive. The early prize-winning Sonata no. 1 was followed by four others, no. 5 (1955) dedicated to the memory of Bartók. There are three sonatinas and several sets of character pieces (mazurkas, arabesques, nocturnes, intermezzi, novelettes, impressions), many of them useful as intermediate teaching material (Example 21.7). Two easy sets were written specifically for teaching purposes, *Pour les enfants* (1934), forty-six graded pieces in four volumes, and *Les Jeunes au piano* (1951), also four volumes of graded pieces.

Other Polish composers whose keyboard music is notable should be mentioned. **Karol Rathaus** (1895–1954), whose career culminated at Queens College in New York City, wrote three sonatas between 1920 and 1927, *Variations on a Theme of Georg Böhm, Four Studies after Domenico Scarlatti* (1945–46), two sets of mazurkas, Op. 24 (1928) and Op. 47 (1942), and other character pieces. **Jósef Koffler** (1896–1943) worked in Poland most of his career, setting forty Polish folk songs for piano. He adopted serial techniques about 1930, and they dominate many of his other piano works, such as the *Musique quasi una sonata*, Op. 8, and a set of fifteen variations, Op. 9. **Vytautas Bacevičius** (b. 1905 in Lithuania) has written three sonatas and several poems with evocative titles ("Mystique," Op. 6; "Astral," Op. 7; "Cosmique," Op. 65). **Grażyna Bacewicz** (1913–69) graduated from the Warsaw Conservatory, went to Paris to work with Nadia Boulanger, and then returned to Poland to compose, teach, and concertize as a violinist. Her piano works include an early suite (1934), Sonata no. 2 (1953), and *10 Studies* (1957). **Witold Lutosławski** (b. 1913), one of Poland's most important twentieth-century composers, has devoted relatively little attention to solo keyboard writing, although there are settings of Polish folk songs and incidental character pieces. **Andrzej Panufnik** (b. 1914) has contributed a set of variations that are entitled *Suite à la quinte* (1949) and a valuable set of twelve etudes in two volumes (1955 and 1966) that explore twentieth-century keyboard techniques.

Italy

Italian keyboard music of the late nineteenth and early twentieth centuries is of limited significance. Early representatives who reflected styles of German Romanticism are **Giovanni Sgambati** (1841–1914) and **Giuseppe Martucci** (1856–1909). Both wrote a sizeable number of character pieces in that tradition. Their work, although extensive and of serious purpose, is not likely to be encountered in the current repertoire.

Ferruccio (Dante Michelangiolo Benvenuto) Busoni (1866–1924) was born of an Italian mother and a German father. Most of his education took place in Graz, and his career was centered first in Moscow and then in Berlin. Busoni attempted, on one hand, to break away from nineteenth-century traditions, looking toward the future by writing an important essay that contemplated "new" aesthetic values (1907). This impulse was influential in turning his attention to the study of Johann Sebastian Bach and Mozart. On the other hand, Busoni was influenced by his devotion to Liszt as well as the techniques and sonorities of nineteenth-century pianism.

Example 21.8 Ferruccio Busoni: Prelude, Op. 37, no. 16 mm. 1–4

As an editor, Busoni is thought of today as the creator of editions that are so laden with added directions of expression, touch, fingering, and disposition of notes between the hands as to be virtually new arrangements of the original music. Most musicians find these editions interesting for an examination of Busoni's musical thinking but not very helpful in the study of the original composer. As a composer, Busoni began in the tradition of German Romanticism, but his style grew to exhibit emphasis on contrapuntal techniques, moderately experimental harmonic progressions, and the eschewal of obvious emotional effects. Busoni's quixotic ideas continue to attract ardent admirers from each succeeding generation, musicians who contend that he is undeservedly neglected. Significant among Busoni's many keyboard works are six substantial sonatinas; a set of twenty-four preludes, one in each key arranged like those of Chopin (Example 21.8); seven elegies (1907); and the *Fantasia contrapuntistica* (1910–12), the culmination of the composer's interest in Baroque techniques. The *Fantasia contrapuntistica* is a monumental work that consists of chorale variations on "Allein Gott in der Höh' sei Ehr'," fugues on the theme from Bach's *Kunst der Fuge*, free-style toccata-like cadenzas, and a closing section in which all of these elements are combined. Three versions of the *Fantasia contrapuntistica* are for solo piano, the third one being a simplified arrangement of the work published as a chorale prelude and fugue on a theme of Bach (1912). A fourth version (1922) is for two pianos.

Composers of the period who were generally significant but who produced relatively less important solo keyboard music include **Ottorino Respighi** (1879–1936), whose most substantial piano work is a set of three preludes on Gregorian melodies (1919); **Idlebrando Pizzetti** (1880–1968), who wrote a sonata (1942) and a large set of variations on a theme of Fra Gherardo (1943); **Gian Francesco Malipiero** (1882–1973), many of whose piano works were influenced by impressionism; and **Alfredo Casella** (1883–1947), whose eleven *Pièces enfantines*, Op. 35 (1920), are useful in the teaching studio and who wrote an amusing group of pieces imitating the styles of other composers (Op. 17); Ravel wrote his pieces in imitation of Chabrier and Borodin, incidentally, as a contribution to Casella's Op. 17.

Mario Castelnuovo-Tedesco (1895–1968) was born and educated in Italy but settled in the United States in 1939. He wrote extensively for solo piano in a style that is often rhapsodic, using impressionistic techniques. Of his many sets of character pieces and poems, *Cipressi* (Cypresses), Op. 17 (1920), is possibly best known. He also wrote a piano sonata, Op. 51 (1928), a *Sonatina zoological*, Op. 187 (1960), and two sets of canons, Op. 142 (1950) and Op. 156 (1952).

Vittorio Rieti (b. 1898) also came to the United States (1940) after spending several years dividing his time between Rome and Paris. He has been active as a teacher of composition at the Peabody Conservatory of Music in Baltimore, Queens College in New York, and the Chicago Musical College. His style is noted for its adherence to Classical principles of clarity and balance combined with a measure of elegant sophistication and often humor. He has written character pieces, two sonatas (1938 and 1946), "academic" variations (1950), "medieval" variations (1962), and teaching pieces (1942).

Several Italian composers born after 1900 should be mentioned. **Sandro Fuga** (b. 1906) developed a solid but conservative style. His keyboard works include a sonatina (1936), sonata (1957), and a large-scale set of variations (1957). **Bruno Bettinelli** (b. 1913) combines an interest in contrapuntal techniques with experimental use of twelve-tone procedures. He often uses traditional genres as points of departure, such as in the *Tre ricercare e toccata* (1948), the Suite (1945), and the Fantasia (1955). **Mario Zafred** (b. 1922) began his career by experimenting with avantgarde styles, but he ultimately chose to write in a direct, simple, often sparse manner. His keyboard works include sonatas (no. 3, 1950; no. 4, 1964) and character pieces.

Switzerland

Among Swiss composers at the turn of the twentieth century are **Emile R. Blanchet** (1877–1943) and **Ernest Bloch** (1880–1959). Blanchet studied with Busoni in Weimar and Berlin but centered his

Maestoso ed energico (♩ = ca. 48 - 52)

Example 21.9 Ernest Bloch: Sonata mm. 1–4

career in Lausanne, where he taught piano at the conservatory, and later in Paris. He wrote ballades, etudes, a set of variations on a theme of Mendelssohn, Op. 22 (1917), and a significant pedagogical work entitled *64 Preludes for Pianoforte in Contrapuntal Style,* Op. 41 (1926).

Ernest Bloch was one of the most celebrated figures on the international scene during the first half of the century. His career centered in Switzerland and the United States, where he finally settled. He developed his own style from a combination of traditional values (often using impressionistic or bitonal sonorities) and an interest in conveying the emotional intensity he felt in his Jewish heritage. The latter led to frequent use of augmented seconds and the rhythmic device known as the "Scotch snap." He succeeded in establishing this vaguely Oriental, exotic sound as Jewish, even though he turned to authentic Hebrew musical material only rarely. His keyboard works include two sets of character pieces, *Poems of the Sea* (1922) and *Five Sketches in Sepia* (1925), as well as a large-scale, rhapsodic sonata (1935; Example 21.9). Representing his Jewish style most clearly is the set of pieces entitled *Visions and Prophecies* (1940), an arrangement for piano of material used in an earlier work for cello and orchestra, *Voice in the Wilderness* (1936). He also wrote a set of teaching pieces, *Enfantines* (1923).

Although **Frank Martin** (1890–1974) was one of the leading Swiss-born composers of the century, he wrote very little solo piano music. His intense, chromatic, linear style is exemplified wonderfully in his most famous piano work, a set of eight preludes (1948). These pieces are rightfully regarded as a twentieth-century masterwork (Example 21.10).

Allegretto tranquillo ♩ = 80

leggato ma sempre cantabile e non troppo dolce

dolce

Example 21.10   Frank Martin: Prélude no. 2 from *8 préludes pour le piano* mm. 1–4

Other Swiss composers have contributed work of interest. **Walter Lang** (1896–1966) wrote twelve concert etudes, Op. 26 (1935); two sonatas, Op. 66 (1956) and Op. 70 (1958); and sets of character pieces, one of which, *Klangskizze,* Op. 47 (1947), may be used as twelve-tone teaching material. **Willy Burkhard** (1900–1955) developed a style that was born of the composer's interest in the contrapuntal techniques of the Renaissance and Baroque. Solo piano writing figures prominently in his output from his Op. 1, a fantasie (1922), to his final work, the six preludes, Op. 99 (1955), wherein the writing utilizes twelve-tone techniques. He also wrote a piano sonata, Op. 66 (1945), a set of variations on a minuet of Haydn, Op. 29 (1930), and a set of eight teaching pieces (1938). **Raffaele d'Alessandro** (1911–59) studied with Marcel Dupré and Nadia Boulanger in Paris but centered his career in Lausanne. His style is eclectic and complex, but he adhered to many traditional concepts, tonality and sonata structure among them. Included in his works for solo piano are a set of twenty-four preludes, Op. 30 (1940); a set of twelve etudes, Op. 66 (1949); and fantasies, Op. 59 (1950). **Julien-François Zbinden** (b. 1917) writes in an accessible style, using elements of jazz. Piano works include a jazz sonatina, Op. 11 (1955) and *Pianostinato,* Op. 42 (1966).

Austria

In Austria, many composers came under the powerful influence of Arnold Schönberg and the stylistic concepts for which he is so famous, atonality and twelve-tone techniques. That movement and prominent composers of twelve-tone and serial keyboard music are taken up in a separate chapter. Several Austrian composers, however, either eschewed nontonal techniques altogether or used them moderately in conjunction with other concepts.

Egon (Joseph) Wellesz (1885–1974) was Schönberg's first student and later his first biographer. Wellesz was by no means completely doctrinaire in his use of twelve-tone or serial techniques but rather employed these procedures intermittently in his works. He was a noted scholar of Baroque and Byzantine music, and he made significant contributions in the research of both periods. His *Drei Skizzen,* Op. 6 (1911), are strongly influenced by Schönberg's atonal period. The set of five pieces called *Epigramme,* Op. 17 (1914), adheres to atonality less strictly, and the *Idyllen,* Op. 21 (1917), also a set of five pieces, make use of impressionist techniques. Wellesz continued to write sets of short pieces for piano throughout his career.

Hans Gál (b. 1890) enjoyed a distinguished career in Germany and Austria until the advent of World War II, when he fled to Scotland. The remainder of his career was spent composing and teaching at Edinburgh University. His style is steadfastly conservative, modeled after that of Brahms and Strauss. His solo keyboard works include a sonata, Op. 28 (1927), a set of twenty-four preludes, Op. 83 (1960), and several sets of character pieces.

Yet another composer whose ties to tradition were strong was **Felix Petyrek** (1892–1951). Centering his career in Germany, Italy, and Austria, Petyrek spent his last years teaching at the Music Academy in Vienna. Trained as a pianist himself, he married pianist Helene Renate Lang. As a result, interest in writing keyboard music remained high throughout his career. Petyrek wrote two sets of sonatas (three in 1928 and five in 1956), variations (1915, 1934), and many sets of character pieces.

Erich Wolfgang Korngold (1897–1957) was considered a child genius as a composer, garnering high praise and support from Mahler, Puccini, and pianist Arthur Schnabel. At the age of twenty, Korngold wrote his operatic masterwork *Die tote Stadt,* and results of a poll conducted by the *Neue Wiener Tagblatt* in 1928 indicated that the public regarded Korngold and Schönberg as the two greatest living Austrian composers. He went to Hollywood in 1934 as a result of his collaborations with the great German producer-director Max Reinhardt. His film scores are regarded as among the greatest of the genre, and he continued to write absolute music. Korngold wrote three piano sonatas, the first without opus number (1910), Op. 2 (1911), and Op. 25 (1931), as well as sets of character pieces.

Like Wellesz, **Ernst Krenek** (b. 1900) experimented with many styles, his works reflecting interest in Bartók, Schönberg, Stravinsky, as well as jazz and electronic music. With the outbreak of World War II, Krenek emigrated to the United States, where he was influential as a teacher. He has written six piano sonatas over several decades (1919–51), sets of variations, and character pieces in a variety of styles. His *12 Short Piano Pieces Written in the Twelve-Tone Technique,* Op. 83 (1938), is a work designed to introduce and elucidate twelve-tone writing.

Andante ($\flat$ = 66) quasi Adagio
sempre assai legato; la melodia sempre dolce (quasi Oboe solo)

Example 21.11 Max Reger: *Variationen und Fugue über ein Thema von Johann Sebastian Bach*, Op. 81 mm. 1–3

Gottfried von Einem (b. 1918) is not a prolific composer and has produced few works for piano. His prominence as a composer of theater works is well established, his early successes having been in Berlin and Vienna, with more recent performances in the United States. His style is eclectic, sometimes dissonant, often borrowing jazz rhythms, and in late works he strives for accessibility. His keyboard works include four pieces, Op. 3 (1943); two sonatinas, Op. 7 (1947), and two capriccios for harpsichord, Op. 36 (1969).

Germany

Several German composers who achieved international recognition represented the full flowering of the Romantic tradition. **Hans Pfitzner** (1869–1949) is best known for his opera *Palestrina* (1912–15). Although he was an excellent pianist, he wrote relatively little solo piano music, confining his efforts to using the piano extensively in chamber works. There are, however, five character pieces, Op. 47 (1941), and a set of etudes, Op. 51 (1943).

Max Reger (1873–1916), on the other hand, wrote a significant amount of music for solo keyboard, four hands, two pianos, and organ. Reger was an ardent admirer of the great composers of the German tradition—Johann Sebastian Bach, Beethoven, Brahms, and Wagner. Reger's style reflects this admiration, and it often centers on the use of thick harmonic textures, highly chromatic progressions, and complex contrapuntal lines. His most famous work for solo keyboard is the *Variations and Fugue on a Theme of Johann Sebastian Bach*, Op. 81 (1904), a massive, lengthy work in the Brahms tradition (Example 21.11). A similar set of variations on a theme of Telemann, Op. 134 (1914), is less successful but still noteworthy. In traditional genres are the four sonatinas,

Op. 89 (1905), and six Bach-like preludes and fugues, Op. 99 (1906–7). There are, in addition, many sets of character pieces, among them six intermezzi, Op. 45, and the *Silhouetten,* Op. 53 (both 1900), the four volumes of thirty-five pieces entitled *Aus meinen Tagebuch* (From My Diary), Op. 82 (1904–12), and a set of teaching pieces, Op. 44 (1900).

Sigfrid Karg-Elert (1877–1933) wrote music that was influenced not only by tradition but also by his interest in the music of Scriabin, Debussy, and to some extent Schönberg. His best-known and perhaps most original keyboard writing was for organ, but there is also a large body of solo piano works (some of them unpublished), which include five sonatas; three sonatinas, Op. 67 (1910); twenty-four preludes (1918); two sets of "educational" pieces, Op. 69 (1904); one simply entitled *Mosaik;* and several sets of character pieces.

Richard Strauss (1864–1949) established an international reputation as one of the foremost composers of orchestral tone poems, songs, and opera. He wrote relatively little music for solo piano, and almost all of it comes from his youthful years. Strauss remained a tonal, traditional Romantic throughout his career, and these early pieces derive from the styles of Mendelssohn and Schumann. Of the almost three dozen works that exist, only the Sonata, Op. 5 (1880–81), and two sets of character pieces, Op. 3 (1880–81) and Op. 9 (1882–84), bear opus numbers.

Paul Hindemith

Paul Hindemith (b. Hanau, near Frankfurt, Nov. 16, 1895; d. Frankfurt, Dec. 28, 1963) was one of the most significant musicians of the early twentieth century. His contributions as a composer, teacher, and writer in the fields of theory and aesthetics are regarded as among the most influential of their day. His career was centered in Germany up until the onset of World War II, when he moved to the United States, eventually teaching at Yale University (1941–53). During the last period of his life he divided his time between Yale and the University of Zurich, eventually retiring in Switzerland.

Hindemith's early musical activities in Germany included concertizing extensively as a violist and teaching gifted amateurs. His interest in writing music for nonprofessional players, as well as music that could be put to service in daily activities, resulted in his reputation for *Gebrauchsmusik,* a term that suggests music as utilitarian rather than merely ornamental. Hindemith's interests, however, were broad, and his musical style was often diverse. Gradually, an intense interest in Baroque and Classical techniques led him to develop a linear style of writing, combining it with an individual organization of tonal principles. Hindemith's mature compositional procedures are set forth in his book *The Craft of Musical Composition* (1937–39). The music that resulted was highly individual, technically well wrought, and understandable. Hindemith's ideas

Example 21.12 Paul Hindemith: "Fuga sexta" in *E-flat* from *Ludus tonalis* mm. 1–5

Example 21.13 Paul Hindemith: "Fuga secunda" in *G* from *Ludus tonalis* mm. 1–5

and the resulting musical language were often regarded as a viable alternative to nontonal techniques, and many composers preferred to explore this world rather than to adopt twelve-tone or serial procedures.

The works for solo piano that represent Hindemith's mature style are the three sonatas (all written in 1936) and the *Ludus tonalis* (1942). The last-mentioned work is regarded by pianists as a twentieth-century equivalent of the *Well-Tempered Clavier* of Johann Sebastian Bach. *Ludus tonalis* opens with a "Praeludium," a piece that resembles Baroque fantasies. The same piece in retrograde inversion closes the work, now called "Postludium." The main body of the *Ludus tonalis* consists of twelve fugues, one built on each pitch of the chromatic scale in an order derived from Hindemith's theoretical system. The fugues are joined by eleven short pieces, each called *interludium*, each opening in the tonal center of the preceding fugue and modulating to the tonal center of the next fugue. The fugues themselves employ many contrapuntal devices, such as mirror (no. 3), inversion (no. 10), retrograde, and retrograde inversion (no. 9; Examples 21.12 and 21.13).

Earlier piano works do not represent Hindemith's celebrated style as clearly, and they have not received the same degree of attention from pianists. Best known among the early pieces is the *Suite 1922*, Op. 26, a set of five pieces, some of which explore contemporary dance-types (shimmy, Boston, ragtime). Other sets of pieces are the eight dance pieces, Op. 19, two sets of instructional pieces that make up Op. 37 (Part 1, 1925; Part 2, 1927), and twelve little pieces from 1929.

The early twentieth century produced a large number of composers in Germany whose work represents attempts to expand or reorganize traditional approaches into individual, meaningful new styles. These composers were aware of the work of Schönberg and his followers, and in some instances may have experimented with nontonal techniques, but in the last analysis clung to tonal centers in some form. Many of them followed along lines carved out by Hindemith, attempting to forge new concepts of tonal organization, studying earlier periods for insights into counterpoint or structure, often incorporating dedication to the writing of didactic music or Gebrauchsmusik. The acknowledgment of German composers who have achieved some degree of importance, and whose work includes an attempt to create significant piano music, is a process that is, indeed, somewhat lengthy, but the work of many of these composers deserves exploration by pianists who seek worthwhile repertoire of the early twentieth century.

Paul Höffer (1895–1949) studied in Cologne but centered his career in Berlin. His works include a great deal of Gebrauchsmusik, notably instrumental settings of one hundred German folk songs. His concert music for piano consists of a sonata, Op. 2; two suites, Opp. 15 and 26; two sets of variations (1935 and 1937); twelve etudes (1942); two toccatas, Op. 35, with the second toccata being written in 1945; and two sets of character pieces, *Skizzen* (Sketches), Op. 11, and *Indianerstücke* (1944).

Hanns Eisler (1898–1962) was a student of Schönberg, but his career was not shaped by exclusive, continued use of twelve-tone techniques or serialism. Rather, his dedication to communistic political ideology spurred him to write much music that would be easily understood by a large public, and this direction was reinforced by his interest in writing theater and film music. He has produced three piano sonatas, Op. 1 (1923), Op. 6 (1924), the third without opus number but dating from 1943. In addition, there is a sonatina subtitled *Gradus ad Parnassum*, Op. 44 (1934); a set of variations (1940); sets of character pieces, Op. 3 (1923), Op. 8 (1925), and Op. 32 (1932–33); and a set of teaching pieces, Op. 31 (1932–33).

Ernst Pepping (b. 1901) is best known for his choral writing. His career has centered in Berlin, and his musical style is highly polyphonic, showing influences from the sixteenth and seventeenth centuries. He has written four piano sonatas, three of them in 1937 and the fourth in

1948. Other works include a sonatina (1931), two sets of variations (1947), an extended work entitled *Tanzweisen und Rundgesang* (Dances and Rounds; 1939), twelve short pieces called fantasies (1949), three fugues on BACH (1955), and *Zuhause* (At Home; 1949).

Wilhelm Maler (1902–76) combined tonal orientation with linear writing, adding impressionistic sonorities on occasion and an interest in folk music. His primary contributions in the area of piano music are a set of six sonatas (1952). Of interest also are a neo-Baroque suite (1947) and small contrapuntal studies based on German folk songs.

Boris Blacher (1903–75) was born in China of Baltic descent, but he is considered a German composer, and his career was spent writing and teaching in Germany. The main expressive element in all of Blacher's works comes from his adherence to a bright, energetic, playful style. He was fascinated by serial techniques but applied them more to rhythm than to tonality. Although he became one of Germany's leading composers, he wrote only a small amount of piano music. Two sonatinas, Op. 14 (1940–41); *Ornamente*, Op. 37 (1950); and a piano sonata, Op. 39 (1951), all show interest in variable meters, while the three character pieces, Op. 18 (1943), show jazz influences. There is also a set of twenty-four preludes (1974).

Günter Raphael (1903–60) underwent changes in his compositional style during his career. His early works were written in the tradition of German Romanticism. During World War II, when his music was banned by the Nazi regime, he took a new direction, reflecting interest in Baroque contrapuntal techniques and harmonic modality. After 1945, he began to infuse twelve-tone techniques into his writing. His keyboard works include sonatas, Op. 2 (1922), Op. 25 (1930), and Op. 38 (1939); a partita, Op. 18 (1927); small pieces, Op. 3 (1926); and settings of twenty-six Advent and Christmas songs (1948).

Rudolf Wagner-Régeny (1903–69) combined an influence from French music, notably Satie, with his own free adaptation of some twelve-tone techniques. These are exemplified in his two piano sonatas (1943), the six pieces that make up *Hexameron* (1943), five French pieces (1951), seven fugues (1953), and the teaching pieces that form *The Little Piano Book*.

Following along the lines of Hindemith are two sonatas (1952 and 1953) and two sonatinas of **Hermann Schröder** (b. 1904). **Gerhard Frommel** (b. 1906) added to traditional Romanticism a penchant for Mediterranean culture, exemplified in six capriccios, Op. 14 (1939). In addition to other character pieces, Frommel has written seven piano sonatas. **Siegfried Borris** (b. 1906) has combined influences of Hindemith's contrapuntal style with a directness and simplicity borrowed from folk music. He has written a great deal of piano music: sonatas (1936, 1944), sonatinas (1944), variations (1937), and sets of smaller pieces.

Wolfgang Fortner (b. 1907) is one of the foremost German composers in the generation after Hindemith. His style combines an intense interest in Baroque counterpoint with individual use of twelve-tone and serial techniques. He always adheres, however, to a cogency that attempts to keep the listener engaged. He has written only a little piano music: a sonatina (1944), six neoclassic pieces called *Kammermusik* (1944), seven elegies (1950), and *Epigramme* (1964).

Harald Genzmer (b. 1909) studied with Hindemith and reflects his teacher's interest in counterpoint and Gebrauchsmusik. He has written two sonatas (1938, 1950), three sonatinas (the first in 1940, the other two in 1950), a suite (1948), ten preludes (1963), twenty-one studies (1965), and teaching pieces (1946).

Helmut Degen (b. 1911) also writes in a style that is derived from interest in counterpoint and a free organization of tonality. He has written a considerable amount of piano music, notably four sonatas (1942–47), three sonatinas (1944), thirty concert etudes in three volumes (1948), and teaching pieces for children.

Other German composers who have made contributions to the piano literature are **Peter Jona Korn** (b. 1922), **Giselher Klebe** (b. 1925), and **Peter Feuchtwanger** (b. 1934). Korn has written a piano sonata (1957) and sets of smaller pieces (1945 and 1961). Klebe has written several sets of pieces (1957 and 1964), adapting twelve-tone techniques into an individual style that also incorporates elements of linear counterpoint and jazz. Feuchtwanger's work also reflects an interest in Asian music that is exemplified in a set of variations (1955) and several pieces he calls *Studies in the Eastern Idiom* (1960 and 1966).

Northern Europe and Scandinavia

The northern European and Scandinavian countries have each produced a small group of composers whose work is often nationalistic but just as often is also derivative of German Romanticism or, in succeeding generations, of other important European trends, such as French impressionism, interest in neo-Baroque, Classical, or medieval music, and to a smaller degree the use of twelve-tone procedures, serial techniques, or other avant-garde practices. These composers are often very well known in their native countries, but only a very few have achieved international recognition. Within their ranks, however, are musicians of impressive gifts, many of whom have produced a significant amount of piano music.

In Belgium **Paul Malengreau** (1873–1953) represented work deeply rooted in tradition. Primarily an organist, he was devoted to the keyboard works of Johann Sebastian Bach. His piano works show influences of both Franck and impressionism. He has written eight sonatas, suites, a *Prélude, chorale, et fugue,* Op. 7 (1915), and nocturnes. **Joseph Jongen** (1873–1953) was considered one of Belgium's leading composers during the early part of the century. He wrote many character pieces, etudes, and preludes for piano in a style that reflects both Romantic and impressionistic influences.

Jean Absil (1893–1974) was also a prominent Belgium composer whose style moved from late Romanticism to incorporate linear writing, Bartók-like dissonance and even small amounts of atonality. Given to clarity and directness, Absil's music tends to be stimulating, intellectual, and objective. For piano, he has written two sonatinas, impromptus, a set of variations, a set of etudes, and several suites of pieces with descriptive titles, including *Echecs*, Op. 96 (1957), a suite in which the individual pieces represent chess pieces.

Flor Peeters (b. 1901) has enjoyed a distinguished career as an organist and pedagogue. His compositions for organ are numerous and well known. For piano, he has written two sonatinas, Opp. 45 and 46 (1940), a toccata, Op. 51a (1945), twelve chorale preludes, Op. 114 (1964), and sets of small pieces. **Marcel Poot** (b. 1901) developed a style that is moderately dissonant but tonal with touches of irony reminiscent of Prokofiev or middle-period Stravinsky. Among his piano works are a sonata (1927), a sonatina (1945), variations (1952), a ballade (1958), and several sets of teaching pieces.

The two most significant Danish composers of the nineteenth century were **Johan Peter Emilius Hartmann** (1805–1900) and his son-in-law **Niels W. Gade** (1817–90). Both men turned their attention toward creating a Danish national style, adapting characteristics of German Romanticism. Although Hartmann did not enjoy the international reputation of Gade, he exhibited a remarkable ability to move with the times, writing music early in his career that was derivative of Mendelssohn and at the end of his career foreshadowing the sophistication of Carl Nielsen. A prolific composer, Hartmann wrote two sonatas, Op. 34 (1843) and Op. 80 (1885), as well as many sets of character pieces. Gade, too, wrote a considerable amount of piano music, including a sonata, Op. 28 (1840, revised in 1854), a chorale and seven variations (1853), and sets of character pieces, including some useful teaching pieces called *Children's Christmas,* Op. 36 (1859).

Louis Glass (1864–1936) developed a distinctive late Romantic style, although his career was outshone by that of his contemporary, Carl Nielsen. Among the many keyboard works of Glass are sets of character pieces and two sonatas that enjoyed regional success in their day, Op. 6 (1890) and Op. 25 (1898–99).

Carl Nielsen (1865–1931) is the most important figure in Danish music at the turn of the twentieth century, and he was the acknowledged leader of contemporary Danish nationalism. An extensive use of chromatic harmony in a manner that regarded all twelve notes of the chromatic scale as equal, as well as his interest in counterpoint, brought his style to the threshold of contemporary thinking without ever really being avant-garde. Nielsen's extended piano works center on two large suites, the *Symphonic Suite*, Op. 8 (1894), and *Den Luciferiske*, Op. 45 (1919–20); and two works in variation form, a chaconne, Op. 32 (1916), and a theme and variations, Op. 40 (1917). There are also several sets of character pieces.

Other twentieth-century Danish composers have written piano music worth noting briefly. **Knudåge Riisager** (1897–1974) reflected French trends in *Quatre epigrammes*, Op. 11 (1936), and a piano sonata, Op. 22 (1931). **Svend Erik Tarp** (b. 1908) began in the footsteps of Nielsen but also became influenced by French styles and a personal desire to write accessible music, both for performer and listener. His many piano works are represented by a sonata, Op. 60 (1954); three sonatinas, Op. 48 (1947); a set of variations subtitled *Carillon*, Op. 43 (1944); as well as sets of smaller pieces, several of which are designed for teaching: *Mosaik*, Op. 31 (1938); *Snap Shots*, Op. 45 (1947); *Cirkus*, Op. 47 (1947), and *Konfetti*, Op. 52 (1950). One of the most prolific composers in all genres is **Niels Viggo Bentzon** (b. 1919). His tonal, dissonant style is represented in more than a dozen sonatas written between 1946 and 1973; a set of twenty-four preludes and fugues entitled *Det tempererede kalver*, Op. 157 (1964); fifteen two-part inventions, Op. 159 (1964); fifteen three-part inventions, Op. 160 (1964); a set of Paganini variations, Op. 241 (1968); and many other works.

Bernhard Lewkovitch (b. 1927) forged his early style from an interest in modality as used in Gregorian chant. In the 1950s he began to experiment with polytonality and twelve-tone techniques. He wrote four piano sonatas between 1948 and 1950 and two dance suites, Op. 16 (1956) and Op. 17 (1960). **Per Nørgård** (b. 1937) began writing in a style influenced by Sibelius and, without abandoning tonal references altogether, moved into a personal adaptation of serial technique by developing a process he called "infinite series." His piano works include two sonatas, Op. 6 (1952, revised 1956) and Op. 20 (1957); *Trifoglio*, Op. 7 (1953); the two sets of pieces that make up Op. 25 (1959), *4 Sketches* and *9 Studies*; *Fragments I-IV* (1950); *Grooving* (1968); and *Turn* (1972).

In the Netherlands, twentieth-century music was championed by **Daniel Ruyneman** (1886–1963), a cofounder (1930) and director (1930–62) of the Dutch Society for Contemporary Music, whose writing tended to be eclectic, reflecting a variety of contemporary trends. Ruyneman's piano works include nine sonatas, two sonatinas, and character pieces.

Several members of the Dutch family **Andriessen** achieved prominence. Brothers **Willem** (1887–1964) and **Hendrik** (b. 1892) each produced a piano sonata and sets of smaller pieces. Hendrik's two sons **Jurriaan** (b. 1925) and **Louis** (b. 1939) were influenced by more recent trends, Jurriaan by his study in France and his interest in film music and

Example 21.14 Willem Pijper: Sonata, lst movt. mm. 1–4

Louis by his work with Berio, Cage, and Stockhausen. Like their father and uncle, both have written a piano sonata and a number of smaller pieces.

Dirk Schäfer (1873–1931) represented the nineteenth-century Romantic tradition, his music being akin to that of Brahms. He wrote a set of eight etudes, Op. 3 (1896); a *Sonate inaugurate* (1905–11); and many sets of character pieces. **Bernhard van den Sigtenhorst Meyer** (1888–1953) was known as a pianist, teacher, and scholar, his area of research being the music of Sweelinck. As a composer, Sigtenhorst Meyer initially reflected Debussy's style, but his writing became leaner and more controlled as a result of his Sweelinck research. Sigtenhorst Meyer's piano works include two sonatas, Op. 18 (1922) and Op. 23 (1926); three sonatinas, Op. 30 (1929), Op. 32 (1930), and Op. 43 (1948); variations, Op. 21 (1924); a set of eight preludes named after animals, Op. 17 (1922); and other character pieces. **Alexander Voormolen** (b. 1895) was also influenced by French impressionism. His piano works consist of sets of character pieces and one sonata (1944).

Of considerably more individuality is the music of **Willem Pijper** (1894–1947). Probably the most significant Netherlands composer of the early twentieth century, Pijper wrote relatively little solo piano music. His style focuses on polytonality, the use of terse themes, and manipulation of small rhythmic cells. For piano, he wrote one short sonata (1930; Example 21.14), three sonatinas (1917, 1925, and 1926), and two sets of three small pieces (1916 and 1926). Among Pijper's students was **Henriëtte Bosmans** (1895–1952), whose works were influenced by French impressionism and Stravinsky.

Other early twentieth-century Netherlands composers may also be mentioned in passing. **Léon Orthel** (b. 1905) attempted to break away from fashionable polytonal and atonal techniques by developing individual use of traditional harmony and combining it with striking dramatic gestures. He wrote eight sonatinas over the course of his career, the last (Op. 78) in 1975, and many sets of small pieces, some of them appropriate for teaching.

Henk Badings (b. 1907) is a prominent figure in contemporary music, having based his writing on six-, seven-, and eight-note scales of his own devising with heavy emphasis on contrapuntal textures and structures. Since about 1952, a portion of his creative energy has been devoted to writing electronic music. His piano works include six sonatas (1933, 1934, 1944, nos. 4 and 5 in 1945, and no. 6 in 1947); four sonatinas (1936, 1945, 1950, and 1958); sets of variations (1938, 1951); *Arcadia*, teaching pieces in three volumes (vols. 4 and 5 are for piano duet; 1945); and *Quaderno sonori* (1976).

Henk Bijvanck (1909–69) wrote music influenced by Romantic tradition and his personal religious beliefs, attempting consciously to infuse his works with spirituality. His piano works focus on four sonatas written between 1952 and 1964, a sonatina (1952), and a work entitled simply *Piano solo* (1962).

Hans Kox (b. 1930) developed his style from traditional elements, but it evolved in such a way as to permit significant choices by performers. He has written two sonatas (1954, 1955), three etudes (1961), a barcarolle (1960), and *Melancholieën* (1971).

In Finland **Jean Sibelius** (1865–1957) achieved the most international prominence. Best known as a symphonist, he also wrote a considerable amount of keyboard music, much of it not very well known. His dark, Romantic style is evident throughout his piano pieces, which include one sonata, Op. 12 (1893), three sonatinas, Op. 67 (1912), and about two dozen sets of character pieces. Other Finnish composers are **Selim Palmgren** (1878–1951) and **Yryö Kilpinen** (1892–1959). Palmgren is remembered primarily for a sentimental salon piece entitled *Toukokuun yö* (May Night), Op. 27, no. 4, but the catalogue of his piano works is surprisingly extensive and includes a sonata, Op. 11; a sonatina, Op. 93; a fantasy, Op. 6; twenty-four preludes, Op. 17; twenty-four etudes, Op. 77; and many sets of smaller pieces. Kilpinen became enormously popular in Finland and central Europe as a song writer. His style is essentially conservative, simplistic, and reflects Finnish life and landscape. He wrote six piano sonatas and sets of character pieces.

Edvard Grieg (1843–1907) is the best-known Norwegian composer. Grieg's earliest style reflected his training in Leipzig and Copenhagen, but in 1864, with Rikard Nordraak (1842–66) and others, Grieg founded Euterpe, a society dedicated to the study and performance of Scandinavian music. Grieg thus began to infuse his creativity with nationalism, becoming increasingly focused on the adaptation of folk idioms in his music. During the course of his career, he made many concert tours as a pianist and conductor outside Norway. As a result, he became an international symbol of Norwegian music. Basically, his style remained true to the nineteenth-century tradition, although occasionally there can be found sonorities that are reminiscent of early impressionism.

The piano music of Grieg consists of three large works and many sets of small character pieces. The early four-movement sonata, Op. 7 (1865, revised 1887), shows clearly the influences of Grieg's Germanic training. Although it is not without merit, its place in the repertoire has been compromised by the fact that it does not represent Grieg's nationalistic voice. Of more significance is the *Ballade in Form von Variationen über eine norwegische Melodie*, Op. 24 (1875–76). The Norwegian melody is from a folk song of childlike simplicity with words that reflect satisfaction with living in northern lands. Fourteen variations retain the basic structure of the song but are free enough to allow for dramatic gestures, as in the case of nos. 13 and 14, which combine to build a climax before the final return of a portion of the original theme. The third of the extended works is the original version of the suite *Fra Holbergs tid* (From Holberg's Time), Op. 40 (1885). Holberg was an eighteenth-century Norwegian dramatist, and Grieg's suite appropriately reflects the structure and to some extent the style of the period, its movements consisting of a prelude, sarabande, gavotte, air, and rigaudon. Grieg made arrangements of the entire suite for both string orchestra and full orchestra, and the work is heard in orchestral guise more frequently than as a work for solo piano.

At the heart of Grieg's nationalistic style are the smaller works. The ten sets entitled *Lyriske smaastykker* (Lyric Pieces), Opp. 12, 38, 43, 47, 54, 57, 62, 65, 68, and 71, span more than thirty years of Grieg's mature creative life (1867–1901). They are interspersed with other sets, such as the early *Poetisketonebilleder* (Poetic Tone Pictures), Op. 3 (1863); the Norwegian folk dances, Op. 17 (1869); *Folkelivsbilleder* (Pictures from Life in the Country), Op. 19 (1870–71); the improvisations, Op. 29 (1878); Norwegian folk pieces, Op. 66 (1897); and the *Slåtter* (Norwegian peasant dances), Op. 72 (1902–3).

These works range from relatively simple folk-like songs, such as the Arietta, Op. 12, no. 1, to character pieces of moderate length and difficulty, such as "Wedding Day at Troldhaugen," Op. 65, no. 6. Typically, their structures are built in easily discerned arrangements of block sections, and often a sonorous climax is built somewhere near the middle of the piece. Notwithstanding much that is unsophisticated in these works, they contain a great deal of charm and an enduring freshness. Their accessibility, moreover, makes them attractive as teaching material.

Christian Sinding (1856–1941) stands second to Grieg in representing Norwegian Romanticism. He was German trained and spent much of his career in that country. He garnered considerable fame during his lifetime. His musical style was a spin-off from Liszt and Wagner, relying on abrupt modulations, textural density, and the use of cyclicism in longer works. He wrote an impressive amount of piano music: a sonata, Op. 91 (1909); a large set of variations, Op. 94 (1909); two sets of etudes, Op. 7 (1886) and Op. 58 (1903); and about three dozen sets of character pieces between 1888 and 1906 under such titles as intermezzi, capriccios, tone poems, and fantasias. The only survivor in the current repertoire is a piece called "Frühlingsrauschen" (Rustle of Spring), Op. 32, no. 3.

Several other Norwegian composers may be mentioned. **Halfdan Cleve** (1879–1951) also wrote in a late Romantic style. His piano works include two sonatas, Op. 19 and 23; etudes, Op. 5 and Op. 17; and several sets of character pieces. **Harald Saeverud** (b. 1897) moved toward a nontonal style in his piano suite, Op. 6 (1931), but returned to a free tonality with an emphasis on contrapuntal textures. Other piano works include an earlier piano sonata, Op. 3 (1921); six sonatinas, Op. 30 (1948–50); *Siljuslatten,* Op. 17 (1942), short pieces whose title is derived from *Siljustøl,* the name of the composer's home in Bergen; four sets of *Slåtter og stev fra Siljustøl* (Songs and Dances from Siljustøl), Opp. 21, 22, 24, and 25 (1942–46); and other sets of character pieces. **Klaus Egge** (b. 1906) writes music that emanates from linear thinking and has evolved an individual harmonic language from retaining tonality while using all twelve tones and frequently changing tonal centers. He also bases his writing on folk material. He has written two piano sonatas, subtitled *Draumkverde,* Op. 4 (1933), and *Patetica,* Op. 27 (1954); and three fantasies, Op. 12 (1939).

Sweden also produced a group of significant regional composers, but none of them has achieved the international standing of a Grieg or Sibelius. **Henning Mankell** (1868–1930) represented a third generation of prominent Swedish musicians. He wrote three sonatas, sets of variations, and smaller pieces in a Romantic style typical of his time. **Wilhelm Stenhammar** (1871–1927) and **Hugo Alfvén** (1872–1960) both achieved a small measure of international fame as composers whose works were derived from Swedish folk music. Stenhammar's study of the classic literature, particularly the works of Beethoven, inspired him to develop a style that eschewed effusive emotional expression. Alfvén, by contrast, remained highly Romantic and more consistently descriptive of Swedish life. Stenhammar's contribution to the literature of the piano centered on two sonatas (1890 and 1895), a set of three fantasies, Op. 11 (1895), and smaller pieces. Alfvén's piano music is confined to works derived from the character-piece concept.

Hilding Rosenberg (b. 1892) achieved a reputation as one of the leading Swedish composers of the early part of the twentieth century and was one of the pioneers in introducing contemporary European trends into Swedish musical culture. His dedication to theater music garnered a large public following. He experimented with many different styles but always seemed to return to a style based on tonality with an emphasis on linear writing. Much of his output is based on Swedish folk material. His piano works include four sonatas (1923, 1925, 1926, and 1927), a sonatina (1949), a large set of variations (1941), two sets of etudes (1945 and 1949), and smaller pieces.

Other Swedish composers may be mentioned in passing. **Kurt Atterberg** (1887–1974), known best for his symphonic and stageworks, wrote sets of character pieces for piano in a Romantic style. **Nils Björkander** (b. 1893) wrote sets of Romantic-impressionistic character pieces and a sonatina (1950). **Hilding Hallnäs** (b. 1903) has devoted himself to the cause of contemporary music in Sweden, and his style has reflected many different techniques. He has written three piano sonatas (1936, 1963, and 1975) and sets of smaller pieces. **Gunnar de Frumerie** (b. 1908) developed a style that showed Baroque influences, writing for piano three suites (1930, 1936, and 1948); two sonatinas (1960); two sonatas (1968), and a set of twenty-four teaching pieces called *Circulus quintus,* Op. 62 (1965).

Lars-Erik Larsson (b. 1908) has composed in several styles, alternating between Nordic post-Romantic expression, neoclassic linear writing, and twelve-tone or serial techniques. His ten two-part piano pieces (1930) are some of the earliest twelve-tone pieces by a Swedish composer. He has also written three sonatinas, Op. 16 (1936), Op. 39 (1947), and Op. 41 (1950); a set of pieces called *Croquiser,* Op. 38 (1946–47); and sets of smaller pieces appropriate for teaching, Op. 56–58 (1969). **Erland von Koch** (b. 1910), son of the late nineteenth-century Swedish composer Sigurd von Koch (1879–1919), has used folk material extensively in his writing, combining it with influences from Hindemith and Bartók. He has produced two large sets of variations, Op. 17 (1938), and *Varianti virtuosi* (1965); a sonatina, Op. 41 (1950); *Intermezzi concertanti* (1963); a caprice (1955); and other smaller works. **Karl-Birger Blomdahl** (1916–68) was also drawn to Hindemith's theories in his early career, adding study of twelve-tone and serial techniques later on. His influence in Sweden as a composer and teacher has been considerable. His works for piano include two sets of Hindemith-like pieces (1945 and 1946). Like his teacher Blomdahl, **Maurice Karkoff** (b. 1927) experimented with a variety of contemporary styles but often selected a folkloric expression with influences from Asian music. He has written several sets of smaller pieces, Op. 32 (1958), Op. 39 (1960), Op. 66, and a piece entitled *Capriccio on Football* (1960).

The British Isles

Composers in the British Isles have been intensely active, resulting in some interesting piano literature, but no major figure has emerged in either the nineteenth or twentieth centuries. Earlier composers are **Edward Elgar** (1857–1934), **Frederick Delius** (1862–1934), **Ralph Vaughn Williams** (1872–1958), and **Gustav Holst** (1874–1934). Although all of these composers were quite prolific, none devoted much of their creative effort to writing piano music, concentrating rather on orchestral, vocal, or theatrical works. In each case, there is a handful of character pieces.

Samuel Coleridge-Taylor (1875–1912) is regarded as perhaps the earliest significant composer of African descent. Although he was educated in England, his career flourished on both sides of the Atlantic, and he made significant contributions to musical life in the United States. His piano music consists of sets of descriptive pieces, several of which reflect his interest in the folk music of Africa and people of African descent: *Two Moorish Tone Pictures*, Op. 19 (1897); *African Suite*, Op. 35 (1898); *Moorish Dance*, Op. 55 (1904); and *24 Negro Melodies*, a set of transcriptions, Op. 59, no. 1 (1905).

Three composers born in the same year, **Frank Bridge** (1879–1941), **John Ireland** (1879–1962), and **Cyril Scott** (1879–1970), all devoted a considerable amount of their creative efforts to writing piano music. Bridge's essentially conservative style was extended by dissonance and hints of polytonality in his piano sonata (1921–24). His other piano works consist of more than fifty character pieces, many with descriptive titles, written between 1905 and 1929. Ireland's writing, too, remained essentially Romantic in nature, although he was influenced by the French impressionist composers and Stravinsky. His piano sonata (1918–20) was considered very important in its day, and the sonatina (1927) shows Ireland's attempt to work with leaner textures. Of the more than forty character pieces, some of them reasonably extended in length, those of contemplative mood are particularly successful. Scott developed a style that reflected Debussy and Scriabin, and his piano works were greatly admired for several decades during the early part of the twentieth century. He wrote three piano sonatas (1910, 1932, 1956) and more than a hundred character pieces. One of them retains some degree of popularity, "Lotus Land," Op. 47, no. 1.

Arnold Bax (1883–1953) was a prolific composer whose music was always well crafted. His style remained essentially Romantic, influenced by his interest in all things Irish, including folk music. His early piano writing is often extremely complex, often encompassing thickly layered sonorities. As his style evolved, it became somewhat more compact with thinner textures. An extensive catalogue of piano music includes four published sonatas (1910, revised 1921; 1919; 1926; and 1932) and three unpublished ones. Other works include a toccata (1913) and more than fifty published and unpublished character pieces, most of them with descriptive titles.

Arthur Bliss (1891–1975) achieved a position of prominence in England, serving as master of the queen's music until his death and in that capacity providing music for many state and ceremonial occasions. His style began as a reflection of post-impressionist trends in France, but soon his love for the music of Elgar surfaced, as he began to write music that was both expansive and richly Romantic. His piano music includes one sonata, Op. 72 (1952); a toccata, Op. 37 (1925); and several sets of pieces with descriptive titles.

Kaikhosru Shapurji Sorabji (b. 1892) was the son of a Spanish-Sicilian mother and a Parsi father. He was educated in England and spent most of his career there as a performer, composer, and well-known music critic. His works are regarded as virtually unique in their complexity, length, and conception. The longest of the piano pieces, *Opus clavicembalisticum* (1929–30), lasts nearly three hours in performance. There is no literal repetition but rather a constant evolving series of ideas, often highly polyrhythmic and polychromatic, with fantastic, extraordinarily complex patterns of ornamental decoration. For a period of time, the composer placed a ban on performance of his music in public, removing the ban in 1976 only to the extent that selected performers might present his works. The University of Illinois has undertaken programming his works into computers in order to realize performance. Among his extensive piano works, many still unpublished, are seven piano "symphonies" written between 1938 and 1978; a set of transcendental studies (1940–44); and many separate pieces with evocative titles.

Edmund Rubbra (b. 1901), a significant symphonist, has written but little for piano. His longest work is the *Prelude and Fugue on a Theme of Cyril Scott*, Op. 69 (1950). He has also written a set of children's pieces (1952) and a set of eight preludes, Op. 131 (1966). **William Walton** (b. 1902), perhaps the most celebrated composer of orchestral music between Vaughan Williams and Benjamin Britten, wrote no piano music. **Lennox Berkeley** (b. 1903) received much of his musical training in France in the class of Nadia Boulanger, and as a result his style contains French post-impressionist traits, coupled with a continuing interest in contrapuntal textures. Later, he experimented with twelve-tone techniques, but he never abandoned tonality altogether. His piano music includes a sonata, Op. 20 (1945); concert studies (1940); and smaller pieces. **Alan Richardson** (1904–78) represents late Romanticism in Scotland, having written two sonatas, Op. 26 (1956), and a *Sonata elegiaca* (1960); a sonatina, Op. 27 (1960); a dance suite, Op. 38 (1955); and character pieces. **William Alwyn** (b. 1905) was trained in England, developed his compositional technique slowly, and exhibits an eclecticism combined with a highly skilled compositional craft. His most significant piano works are the *Sonata alla toccata* (1942), *Fantasy-Waltzes* (1955), and twelve preludes (1957).

One of the most distinctive personalities in English music during the first half of the century was that of **Constant Lambert** (1905–51). His first successes were with music written for ballet, and his intense interest in popular forms, jazz, as well as neoclassicism and atonal trends, came together in his own musical style with wit and sophistication. His most ambitious work for piano is a jazzy sonata (1928–29), but he also wrote several smaller pieces. Of more significance are the contributions of **Alan Rawsthorne** (1905–71) and **Michael Tippett** (b. 1905). Rawsthorne, whose work was influenced by Hindemith, wrote an early set of bagatelles (1938), a sonatina (1949), a ballade (1967), and *Theme and 4 Studies* (1971). Tippett is regarded by many as a composer who has been able to forge a highly individual style out of neoclassicism and a complex use of traditional harmonic and rhythmic practices. He has written three piano sonatas (1938, revised 1942; 1962; 1972–73).

(Agnes) Elisabeth Lutyens (b. 1906) has written extensively for film, radio, and television, but there are a few piano works, including *Five Bagatelles,* Op. 49 (1962). Irish-born **Howard Ferguson** (b. 1908) made significant contributions through his scholarly, practical editions of early keyboard music. He wrote an expertly crafted, post-Romantic piano sonata (1938–40; Example 21.15) and a set of five bagatelles (1944). **Franz Reizenstein** (1911–68) was educated in Germany, and his style reflects influences of his teacher, Hindemith. Among his piano works are two piano sonatas, Op. 19 (1948) and Op. 40 (1966); a set of twelve preludes and fugues, Op. 32 (1955); and a set of fairly accessible pieces called *The Zodiac,* Op. 41 (1964).

One of the most celebrated composers of opera and song, **Benjamin Britten** (1913–76), wrote very little for piano, an early suite called *Holiday Diary* (1934) and a few other small pieces. More prolific has been **Richard Arnell** (b. 1917), whose style is both eclectic and conservative. Among his piano works are two sets of variations, Op. 24 (1943) and Op. 75 (1956), as well as a piano sonata, Op. 32 (1946).

Other composers who have written major works for piano are **Antony Hopkins** (b. 1921), contributing sonatas (1945, 1949) and other works; Scottish-born **Iain Hamilton** (b. 1922) with two sonatas (1951, revised in 1971, and 1972; Example 21.16); **Wilfred Josephs** (b. 1927) with a sonata (1963) and a set of twenty-nine preludes (1969); Scottish composer **Ronald Stevenson** (b. 1928) with three sonatinas (1945–48) and two fantasies, one on themes from Busoni's *Faust* (1949–59) and the other on music from Britten's *Peter Grimes* (1971); **Kenneth Leighton**

Example 21.15 Howard Ferguson: Sonata in *f*, 1st movt. mm. 1–4

(b. 1929) with two sonatas (1948, 1953), two sonatinas (1948), and a *Fantasia contrapuntistica* (1956); Australian-born **Malcolm Williamson** (b. 1931) with two sonatas (1955, 1957), *Travel Diaries* (1960), and preludes (1966); **Robert Sherlaw Johnson** (b. 1932) with three sonatas (1963, 1967, 1976); **William Mathias** (b. 1934) with *Toccata alla danza* (1961) and a sonata, Op. 25 (1963); and **Richard Rodney Bennett** (b. 1936) with a sonata (1954), a fantasy (1962; Example 21.17), and several sets of smaller pieces.

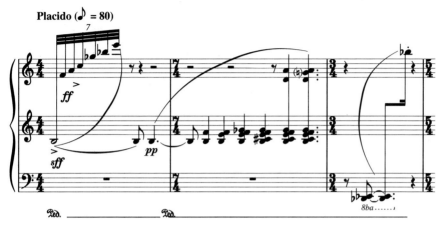

Example 21.16 Iain Hamilton: Piano Sonata no. 2, lst movt. mm. 1–3
© 1976 Theodore Presser Company. Used by permission of the publisher.

Example 21.17 Richard Rodney Bennett: Fantasy mm. 1–3

CHAPTER TWENTY-TWO

Keyboard Music of Nontonal Composers in Europe

The concept of tonality has suggested different theoretical systems at various points in history. Most often, however, when musicians speak of tonality, the concept referred to is one that places a selected pitch at the center of harmonic and melodic thinking. Musical activity revolves around the tonal center in such a way that it becomes a psychological focal point, and sounding either the pitch itself or harmonies considered primary to that pitch imparts a feeling of stability, initially establishing a home base at the onset of the music and acting as a final resting point at its conclusion. Thus, in its broadest sense, tonal music refers to any music constructed in such a way that it revolves around a given pitch as its psychological center. The concept, however, was articulated historically most often in a narrower context, frequently referring to music that is built on the system of twenty-four major and minor keys, a system that came into full flower in the eighteenth century and was made possible partly as a result of equal-tempered tuning of instruments. In this more narrowly defined view of tonality, the major-minor system of scales is considered to be basic to writing tonal music. Composition based on scalar organizations such as modes, or music that is written in such a way as to avoid centrality of a given pitch, is designated *modal, atonal,* or whatever term best describes this organization.

The practice of writing keyboard music conceived within the framework of the twenty-four major and minor keys was clearly established by the early eighteenth century and rapidly became the norm. Thus, almost all eighteenth- and nineteenth-century keyboard music was conceived with this concept as a basic parameter. Early on, use of the system tended to emphasize the stability of the home key, departures from it being tendered with caution. But within every generation of composers there were innovators who liked to experiment with unusual departures from the basic tonal center, employing dissonant passing tones or harmonies and moving abruptly or unexpectedly from key to key. Successful handling of such procedures often became hallmarks of style and were prized as evidence of originality. Thus, each succeeding generation of composers gravitated toward including more nontonal embellishments, increasing mobility in changing keys, and eventually relishing ambiguity or vagueness with regard to tonal centers. By the end of the nineteenth century, composers of experimental bent felt hard pressed to invent novel ways with which to establish their individual voice. Some of them adopted patterns of extremely chromatic harmony. Others chose to explore earlier uses of modality in Western music or various exotic harmonic practices of non-Western music. Still others explored the suspension of tonality, perhaps in modest dimension by using intermittently such devices as whole-tone or quartal harmonies. A few pioneers began to conceive music that militantly avoided the use of tonal centers, eventually substituting other systems of organization.

Arnold (Franz Walter) Schönberg

Born in Vienna to parents of Hungarian-Czechoslovakian nationality, Arnold Schönberg (b. Vienna, Sept. 13, 1874; d. Los Angeles, Jul. 13, 1951) was not accorded the luxury of formal training in music. Most of his education was as a result of his own industry and exchanges with colleagues and friends, notably Oskar Adler and Alexander von Zemlinsky (1872–1942). In order to earn a living, Schönberg worked as a bank clerk for five years. During his early twenties, he was able to find performances for his earliest works, but the conservative taste of the Viennese public was such that these pieces were greeted with halfhearted acceptance at best or distaste at worst. Schönberg, meanwhile, left the bank and earned a living from teaching at various schools in both Vienna and Berlin. By 1912, his career was beginning to take root, following successful performances of the *Guerrelieder* (for voices and orchestra) and the symphonic poem *Pelleas und Melisande,* but it was interrupted by World War I and intermittent calls to military service.

Schönberg's career continued in Vienna after the war until 1925, when he accepted a post at the Prussian Academy of Arts in Berlin. Although the position gave him long-sought financial stability, it placed him at the heart of the Nazi anti-Semitic thrust. By 1933, Schönberg feared for the safety of himself and his family, and they migrated to the United States after a short period in France, eventually settling in Los Angeles.

As a musician who was essentially self-taught, Schönberg was dedicated to a process of exploration that took nothing for granted and redefined every avenue of expression. Although he studied and often admired models provided by masters of the past, at no point in his life was he compelled to imitate them. From the earliest time of his public career, his music was met with resistance, but these difficulties seemed only to spur him to explore his inner creative world more ardently. It was this quest to define one's own individuality that he passed on to his students. For Schönberg, such a journey was closely tied up with spiritual development and a realization of the God-force.

A few sets of early character pieces predate the Op. 11. These were learning vehicles for the composer, written in a tonal style and likely influenced by Brahms's late sets of small pieces. The three pieces, Op. 11 (1909), and the six tiny pieces, Op. 19 (1911), represent the composer at a time when tonal procedures had been suspended but before serial techniques had been developed. These works might be called *atonal*, were it not for the fact that Schönberg himself rejected the term. The first two pieces of the Op. 11 are highly coloristic, using time-honored devices such as sonorities in extreme registers, arpeggio-like figurations, trills, and climactic peaks to evoke moodiness. The final piece is a short but unrelieved outburst of dissonant sonorities, an archetype of the kind of music associated with the term *expressionism*. The six pieces that make up Op. 19 were written in a similar style but with great economy of means. Each musical idea is presented with as few notes as possible, and each piece is but a few measures long. The final piece imitates the tolling of bells, and an inscription indicates that it was composed on the death of Gustav Mahler (1860–1911), whose ideals were a source of inspiration to Schönberg and who had helped arrange performances of the younger composer's works. (Schönberg also dedicated his 1911 book on traditional harmony, *Harmonielehre*, to the memory of Mahler.) The brevity and accessibility of the Op. 19 make it an attractive introduction to Schönberg's style and to nontonal music in general.

The Op. 23 and the Op. 25 are the works in which Schönberg begins to incorporate the use of serial technique, setting up twelve-tone rows as the basis of organization. Of the five pieces that make up Op. 23, nos. 1, 2, and 4 were begun in 1920. These pieces are related to earlier nontonal piano pieces, but one can also observe the emergence of leaner textures and more contrapuntal thinking. A year later (July 1921), the composer wrote the prelude and the intermezzo of the Op. 25, the first of the twelve-tone pieces (Example 22.1). In early 1923, he finished the Op. 23, incorporating twelve-tone writing into its final piece, "Walzer" (no. 5), and wrote the remaining pieces of the Op. 25, all dance-types (gavotte, musette, minuet, and gigue), basing them on the same twelve-tone series he had employed in the earlier prelude and intermezzo.

These pieces are, indeed, the earliest examples of serial writing, but equally important are their exacting use of disjunct textures, contrapuntal lines, varied types of touch, and conceptual imagination. Schönberg's selection of Baroque dance-types suggests a retreat from the more personal, highly emotional style of the Op. 11 and Op. 19. Adoption of a cooler, objective aesthetic, however, remained only partial, for the two final small pieces, Op. 33a and 33b, move in the direction of

Example 22.1 Arnold Schönberg: "Intermezzo" from Suite, Op. 25, mm. 1–2
Used by permission of Belmont Music Publishers, Pacific Palisades, CA 90272.

warmer sonorities in their use of the twelve-tone technique. It was left, rather, to Schönberg's followers, through a lineage headed by his student Anton Webern, to pursue the quest for a more complete objective detachment.

Schönberg's historic significance as the father of serial writing is well established. This handful of small piano pieces represents quite well the various stages of the composer's pioneering efforts, and thus they have become historically significant. The pieces are, moreover, well crafted and imaginative. There has been, however, a certain reluctance on the part of pianists to incorporate them into the inner circle of frequently performed repertoire. Thus, curiously, even after the passing of more than half a century, they are not often encountered on recital programs, notwithstanding their fame, performers opting instead for other repertoire of the period.

Two of Schönberg's students, **Alban Berg** (1885–1935) and **Anton Webern** (1883–1945), are grouped together with their teacher to form what is often referred to as the "second Viennese school." (The "first" one presumably was in the late eighteenth century and included Mozart, Haydn, and Beethoven.) Both Berg and Webern began studying with Schönberg at about the same time (1904), and their close friendship with each other and their teacher was extremely influential, notwithstanding the fact that they emerged as composers of quite different temperaments. Berg incorporated serial techniques into a style filled with color, sonority, and emotional effusiveness. Webern, on the other hand, developed the manipulative potential inherent in serial writing into a terse, lean form of expression, extending row-generated control to dynamics, rhythms, and timbres (touch on the keyboard) while constructing palindromes, mirror images, and other complex relationships.

Berg wrote his one-movement piano sonata, Op. 1 (1907–8), while studying with Schönberg. Written in sonata-allegro form, the work hovers

Mäßig bewegt

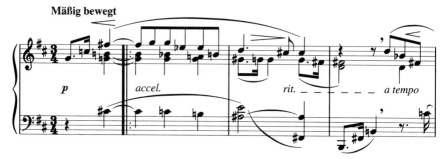

Example 22.2 Alban Berg: Sonata, Op. 1 mm. 1–3

at the edge of tonality, using chord structures built with augmented intervals or tritones, whole-tone passages, and ambiguous tonal centers. Dense sonorities lead to intense emotional climaxes in every section, and although there are fragments of motivic imitation throughout the work, contrapuntal considerations are deeply embedded in rich, harmonic textures. Notwithstanding its apparently freewheeling approach to tonality, the piece is planned in such a way that settling into the key of *b* in the coda seems both natural and emotionally satisfying. The sonata borrows much of its approach to the keyboard from the standard techniques of the late nineteenth century, and thus it has held an attraction for many pianists. It is the most frequently performed work of the Viennese trio (Example 22.2). The only other keyboard work of Berg is an earlier set of variations (1908), published in 1957.

The most significant work for solo piano of Anton Webern is the Variations, Op. 27 (1935–36). It is an important example of Webern's serial style. The composer conceives the term *variation* as a technique as well as a structure. The work is in three short movements, the first built on a ternary pattern, the second a binary, with the final movement cast in the traditional variation format, presenting a theme followed by five variations. The three movements of the work suggest those of a short sonata, and the arrangement of Beethoven's Op. 109 comes to mind.

The opening bars of the Variations present the first of many mirror arrangements and are formulated from the type of objective, intervalic writing that pervades the entire work (Example 22.3). Highly disjunct figuration, fragmented motives, and abrupt dynamic changes dominate the work. Melodic phrases, coloristic sonorities, and climactic points are all eschewed in favor of complete integration of material through serial relationships. The result is a work that is fascinating and challenging and creates excitement through its intellectual process but makes few concessions to nineteenth-century emotional or lyrical expression. The Variations is one of the great milestones in serial writing, and it has achieved a position of prominence because of that fact. It has enjoyed only moderate

Example 22.3 Anton Webern: Variationen, Op. 27, 1st movt. mm. 1–5

popularity among performing pianists, however, possibly because audiences not schooled in serial writing find the work more curious than exciting. Webern's other piano works are all earlier, consisting only of an early sonata movement (1906), *Kinderstück* (1924), and a piano piece (1925).

The concept of serial writing and its various techniques spread rapidly in the generations after Schönberg. Many young composers regarded inherited techniques (the use of tonality, traditional harmonic function, metered rhythm, and block structure) as doomed, and the new processes were seen as liberators from traditions that had outlived their creative vitality. Of course, not all composers were persuaded that the future belonged to serialism. Some continued to use traditional materials, but their work was often disdained by the serial group. Others, like Hindemith, forged new directions for traditional concepts, sometimes looking to the Baroque or earlier historical periods for inspiration. A few of these, such as Stravinsky and Copland, achieved international reputations, but they too finally embraced serial techniques late in their careers, much to the delight of those who had already been won over. Some composers adopted serialism in such a way as to continue to include elements of tonality as well as vestiges of traditional rhythmic or structural concepts.

Among the earliest group of exponents of nontonal music was the Norwegian composer **Fartein Valen** (1887–1952). He evolved his own style by constructing long melodic lines and combining them contrapuntally into dissonant, lyrical textures. Although he was well acquainted with Schönberg and the twelve-tone technique, he adapted dodecaphonic procedures to his own approach. He wrote two piano sonatas, Op. 2 (1912) and Op. 38 (1940–44); a set of variations, Op. 23 (1935–36); and smaller individual pieces (Example 22.4). Austrian **Hans Erich Apostel** (1901–72) studied with Schönberg and Berg, becoming known as one of the most gifted second generation of the second Viennese school. His style evolved from an early nontonal expressionism to a strict use of the twelve-tone

Example 22.4 Fartein Valen: Sonata, Op. 38, 1st movt. mm. 1–3

technique. Among his piano works are a set of variations, Op. 1 (1928); a sonata, Op. 2 (1929); fantasies, Op. 31b (1959); a toccata, Op. 34b (1961); and many sets of smaller pieces. **Hanns Jelinek** (1901–69), another Austrian student of Schönberg, produced works designed to instruct others in twelve-tone procedures. The *Zwölftonwerk*, Op.15 (1947–52), is a set of solo piano and chamber pieces all based on the same row. A larger work entitled *Zwölftonfibel,* Op. 21 (1953–54), presents 239 exercises and pieces all based on the same row.

Italian **Luigi Dallapiccola** (1904–75) came to serial writing gradually, solidifying his style in the 1930s and 1940s. He was, however, a leading exponent of dodecaphony in Italy. He wrote but little for piano, only a sonatina (1942–43) and a supremely beautiful set of short pieces named, after his daughter, *Quaderno musicale di Annalibera* (1952). Another student of Schönberg was Greek composer **Nikolaos Skalkottas** (1904–49), whose considerable output for piano includes a sonatina, Op. 75b (1927), variations, Op. 75c (1927), four suites, Op. 71–74 (1936–40), and many other sets of small pieces.

Leopold Spinner (b. 1906) studied with his fellow Austrian Webern (1935–38) and has lived in England since 1938. Like his teacher, Spinner uses mirror techniques frequently in his writing. For piano, he has written a sonata, Op. 3 (1943); fantasies, Op. 9 (1954); five inventions, Op. 13 (1958); and a sonatina, Op. 22 (1969). In Finland, **Erik Bergman** (b. 1911) is a leading exponent of serial techniques, using them with some degree of personal freedom. His piano works include a sonatina, Op. 36 (1950), and a set of pieces called *Aspects,* Op. 63 (1969). **René Leibowitz** (1913–72) was influential in making known the work of his teachers, Schönberg and Webern, and in organizing serial procedures into yet another layer of theoretical thinking. Pierre Boulez was one of Leibowitz's students in Paris. Leibowitz's serial works for piano consist of two piano sonatas, Op. 1 (1939) and Op. 43, fantasies, Op. 27 (1952), and several sets of smaller pieces.

Humphrey Searle (b. 1915), a student of Webern, was a leader among English composers in establishing the use of serial techniques. He

Example 22.5 Iannis Xenakis: *Evryali* mm. 1–3

combines the twelve-tone method with a strong penchant for Romantic expressions, drawn from his research into the work of Franz Liszt. Searle's Piano Sonata, Op. 21 (1951), is modeled after Liszt's Sonata in *b*, but Searle's work uses twelve-tone techniques throughout. Other piano works include a ballade, Op. 10 (1947), *Threnos and Toccata,* Op. 14 (1948); and a suite, Op. 29 (1955).

Peter **Racine Fricker** (b. 1920) emerged in England as a leading exponent of twelve-tone and serial techniques after World War II. His use of serialism, however, is often not strict, and his music is often generated from a notable gift for melodic writing and his deft use of counterpoint. Since 1964, he has centered his career at the University of California, Santa Barbara. Among Fricker's piano works are a set of four impromptus, Op. 17 (1950–52); variations, Op. 31 (1957–58); fourteen *Aubades* (1958); two sets of pieces called *Episodes 1*, Op. 51 (1966–67) and *Episodes 2*, Op. 58 (1969); and *Anniversary,* Op. 77 (1977).

Kazimierez Serocki (b. 1922) was one of the first Polish composers to use serialism. He began its modified adoption in his *Suite of Preludes for Piano* (1952) and has continued its use in the Sonata (1955), combining it with aleatory techniques in *A Piacere* (1963). A strict adherence to serial techniques generated from mathematics is found in the works of Greek-French composer **Iannis Xenakis** (b. 1922). Two highly structured piano pieces, *Herma* (1964) and *Evryali* (1974), pose formidable challenges for both performer and listener (Example 22.5). French composer **Serge Nigg** (b. 1924) studied with Messiaen and Leibowitz and also moved in the direction of complex serial relationships. His piano works are represented by two sonatas (1943, 1965).

I. Variazione

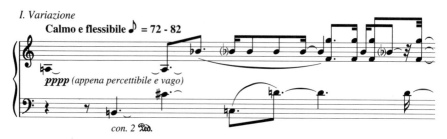

Example 22.6 Luciano Berio: *Cinque variazioni*, opening line

The second half of the 1920s produced some of the most significant composers of the serial movement. **Luciano Berio** (b. 1925) has combined post-Webern serialism with an interest in electronic music. He has written little for piano, but two works remain significant examples of serial writing, the five variations (1952–53, revised 1966; Example 22.6) and the *Sequenza 4* (1966).

Pierre Boulez (b. 1925) studied with Messiaen and Leibowitz, adopting from the former an interest in serialism of rhythm and from the latter a high regard for strict usage of the serial process. In 1966, he published a collection of essays that had been written over the preceding years under the title *Relevés d'apprenti*. In an essay from 1952, Boulez wrote, "Any musician who has not felt . . . the necessity of dodecaphonic language is *of no use.*" From an essay written in 1958, Boulez coined the term "organized delirium," one that analysts have enjoyed using as a point of departure in considering the aesthetic and technical bases of his compositions. Boulez's piano writing consists of three sonatas. The first (1946) is a short one-movement work organized around twelve-tone principles. The second (1948) is a monumental work of four movements, a work that preserves a skeleton of traditional sonata-allegro structure in its first movement amid complex serialization of pitch and rhythmic values. A work of considerable fame in the 1950s, the second sonata was considered one of the ultimate challenges for pianists interested in playing avant-garde music (Example 22.7). The third sonata (1955–57) remains unfinished. The available five movements, however, have been published and performed, made possible by the fact that the ordering of the movements is not fixed; rather, they may be grouped at the performer's discretion around a central "constellation." Boulez's writing consistently employs emotional extremes, contrasting violent outbursts of sound and energy with textures that are coloristic and relatively static. Although most pianists know of the existence and purported significance of the Boulez sonatas, few know them in any degree of detail, and fewer still attempt to surmount the formidable difficulties involved in learning or performing the works.

Extrêmement rapide (Tempo I) (♩ = 132)

Example 22.7   Pierre Boulez: Sonata no. 2, 1st movt. mm. 1–3

Hans Werner Henze (b. 1926) has long been associated with the avant-garde, although he has composed in a variety of styles, and he has written that twelve-tone techniques have but limited influence in his work. One of the most celebrated composers of his generation, he has not written much solo piano music. His first significant work for piano was written when he was studying with Leibowitz, a set of variations, Op. 13 (1949), and it uses twelve-tone techniques strictly. More freely employed rows also appear in the other major work, a sonata (1959), where they govern pitch, rhythm, and dynamics, producing a pointillistic texture.

Netherlands composer **Ton de Leeuw** (b. 1926) has written in a number of styles, becoming interested in the influence of performance space on music. Included in his piano works are an early scherzo (1948), a sonatine (1949), preludes (1950), several sets of etudes (1951, 1952, and 1954), *Men Go Their Ways* (1964), and *Linkerhand en rechterhand* (1976).

Jean Barraqué (1928–73), who studied with Messiaen, has written a piano sonata (1950–52). Although it is his first completed work, it has enjoyed considerable attention, notably from André Hodier, who devoted a chapter to the work in his book *Music since Debussy* (1961). The sonata is a monumental piece, conceived in two large sections of about equal duration, the first applying strict serial techniques to pitch, rhythm, and dynamics and the second being generally more reflective and freer, making use of periods of silence. The work has been compared to Beethoven's Op. 106, but its formidable difficulties result in its being performed only rarely.

Karlheinz Stockhausen (b. 1928) received early training that was oriented toward music education. Discovery of the music of Webern was a turning point for him, and in 1951 he spent time at the summer workshop in Darmstadt, world famous as a mecca for the younger generation of serialist composers. In 1952, he went to Paris to study with Messiaen and became acquainted with Boulez. Running parallel to Stockhausen's interest in serial techniques was his fascination with electronic music. During his time in Paris, he studied at the *musique concrète* studio of French radio, analyzing the physical properties of sound in great detail. From these elements, Stockhausen began to construct aesthetic challenges as a basis for each of his compositions, combining philosophical and technical considerations. He has written and spoken about his theories extensively, contributing greatly to his subsequent prominence as a spokesperson for the avant-garde and his success as a teacher. More recently, he has encompassed abstract considerations of a religious or spiritual nature into both his essays and his music. These concepts are often so abstruse and complex as to defy either comprehensive analysis or commentary, even by those whose expertise lies along such lines.

Stockhausen's works for solo piano were written early in his career as a composer. All bear the title *Klavierstück* followed by a Roman numeral. *Klavierstücke I–IV* (1952–53) are calculated to push the performer to the limit of what is physically possible in terms of executing both dynamics and rhythmic values. The music demands playing a maze of extreme dynamic changes amid irrational temporal values and highly disjunct pitches. *Klavierstücke V–X* (1954–55), with revisions to IX and X in 1961) accord the performer more latitude in judging relative values, leading to a somewhat less complex, more approachable style. Several of the pieces focus on easily identifiable characteristics. "Klavierstück V," for example, is a study of space, employing the greatest possible range of the keyboard, and silence, movement being contrasted with rests. "Klavierstück IX" opens with one chord being repeated 128 times with a gradual diminuendo. The same sonority forms the basis for subsequent development (Example 22.8).

"Klavierstück XI" (1956) incorporates an element of chance generated by the performer. Nineteen short segments of music are presented on a poster-size piece of flexible cardboard. The performer may begin with any one of them and is instructed to play the ones on which the eye falls in whatever order whim dictates. Segments may be repeated, often in different tempi, dynamic schemes, or registers, but, according to directions, the piece is finished whenever any of the segments has been performed for the third time. If a performer plays but a few of the

Example 22.8   Karlheinz Stockhausen: "Klavierstück IX," opening
Copyright 1967 by Universal Edition (London) Ltd., London. Copyright
renewed. All rights reserved. Used by permission of European American
Music Distributors Corporation, sole U.S. and Canadian agent for Universal
Edition (London) Ltd., London.

segments before any one of them is played a third time, the piece might
be only a few minutes long. Should most or all of the segments be used,
and the third repetition of any one of them delayed, the piece could last
as much as thirty minutes. Obviously, each performance will be virtually
unique, unless, of course, the performer presets the ordering of segments. Such planning, however, goes against the spirit of the work. The
segments themselves are not made up of easily recognizable thematic
material but rather tend to be improvisatory and constructed of fragmented motives. Some are but a few seconds long; others might be
longer, lasting a minute or two, depending on the tempo used. The
intriguing game plan that attends "Klavierstück XI" has resulted in its
having received widespread attention as a significant work that incorporates aleatory techniques. Actual performances of the piece, however,
remain relatively rare.

The Belgian composer **Henri Pousseur** (b. 1929) spent a period of
time observing Stockhausen at work in his electronic studio in Cologne
and became closely associated with the avant-garde, eventually lecturing
at the summer school in Darmstadt. Like Stockhausen, his interests have
included exploring serialism as well as electronic music and aleatory
techniques. These are exemplified in three sets of pieces called *Exercises
pour piano: Variations 1* and *Impromptu et variations 2* (1956); and *Caractères
1 and 2* (1961); *Apostrophe et 6 réflexions* (1964–66; Example 22.9).

Of the 1930s generation of serial composers, several have been
interested in writing for piano, but most have not written extensively
for the instrument, their focus being drawn to the more varied timbres
available in various instrumental and vocal groupings or generated by

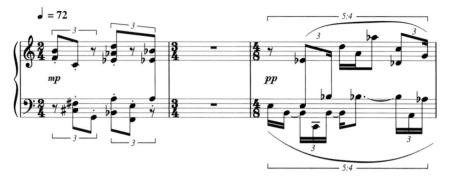

Example 22.9 Henri Pousseur: "Apostrophe" from *Apostrophe et 6 réflexions* mm. 1–3

electronics. Amid a career dedicated to writing, painting, and composing, **Sylvano Bussotti** (b. 1931) has produced piano works so aleatory that they defy characterization: *5 Pieces for David Tudor* (1959); *Pour clavier (après Pièces du chair 2)* (1961); and *Novelletta* (1962–73). **Alexander Goehr** (b. 1932) used serialism as a starting point for his early Sonata, Op. 2 (1951–52), but has added Eastern influences to his style, producing a capriccio, Op. 6 (1957); three pieces, Op. 18 (1964); and a piece inspired by Japanese noh drama, *Nonomiya*, Op. 27 (1969). **Henryk Górecki** (b. 1933) combines post-Webern serialism with a penchant for static sonorities sharply contrasted with dynamic energy. He has written four preludes (1955), a piano sonata (1956), and a set of five pieces (1959). **Peter Maxwell Davies** (b. 1934) has shown interest in combining serial techniques with various facets of earlier music. He has written two sets of five pieces each (1955–56 and 1960–64); *Ut, re, mi* (1969); and *Stevie's Ferry to Hoy* (1975). Only two small piano works have come from **Peter Schat** (b. 1935), the leading Netherlands composer of his generation: *Inscripties* (1959) and *Anathema* (1968). English composer **Cornelius Cardew** (b. 1936) wrote three Webern-like sonatas (1955–58), incorporated aleatory techniques into *February Pieces* (1959–61) and *3 Winter Potatoes* (1961–65), and has returned to more conventional techniques in the *Piano Album* (1974), *Thälmann Variations* (1974), and *Vietnam Sonata* (1976). Austrian composer **Erich Urbanner** (b. 1936) has written sets of serial pieces (1959, 1965). Swedish composer **Bo Nilsson** (b. 1937), a student of Stockhausen, recommends the use of loudspeakers in his *Quantitäten*. Netherlands composer **Reinbert De Leeuw** (b. 1938) incorporates both aleatory techniques and graphic notation in his two sets of pieces for piano (1964, 1966).

It is difficult to assess the ultimate influence of serial, aleatory, and electronics on keyboard music. The literature of the early and middle part of the twentieth century has already been established as significant and influential in the annals of music history, in spite of the fact that younger generations of pianists still do not accord it many performances. Moreover, by the end of the 1950s, many composers began to back away from strict use of serialism, finding new fascination with coloristic sonorities and even adding elements of traditional-sounding melodies and harmonies. Interest in aleatory techniques, too, seems to have waned, perhaps because performers prefer, in the long run, the challenge of re-creating a composer's specific intentions rather than participating in unique performances of more approximate ideas.

CHAPTER TWENTY-THREE

The United States and Canada in the Twentieth Century

The various groups of people who migrated to the New World during the eighteenth and nineteenth centuries brought their musical styles with them. Their music, both concert and popular, reflected styles either traditional or fashionable in their homelands, most of which were European. Only a few bodies of musical literature emerged with distinctly American traits. During the nineteenth century, a tradition of distinctive hymnody developed in New England; the South in the United States spawned music created by slaves of African descent and individuals of Latin-Creole heritage; and the pioneering of the American West likewise gave birth to a distinctive music. These styles were often the musical expressions of groups of people in unusual circumstances, and, although regional, they nevertheless were created with characteristics universally associated with folk art. It was not until the turn of the twentieth century that many professional composers began to incorporate elements of these expressions into their concert music.

Of the musicians who were active in the United States in the late eighteenth and nineteenth centuries, many were born in Europe but lived in the New World for most of their professional lives. **Alexander Reinagle** (1756–1809), for example, was born of Austrian parentage in England but spent most of his career in Philadelphia as a pianist, singer, teacher, and impresario. He visited C. P. E. Bach in Hamburg, and his style is typical of the period. He wrote two volumes of "short and easy" pieces, four sonatas, variations, and other small pieces.

One of the most colorful American composers of the mid-nineteenth century was **Louis Moreau Gottschalk** (1829–69). Born in New Orleans of an English-German father and a French-Creole mother, Gottschalk was sent to Paris to study in 1842. He pursued a career in

Europe until 1853, and during that time he became extremely popular both as a pianist and composer, touring France, Switzerland, and Spain. His pieces were hailed as "Creole" compositions and regarded as an important authentic voice from the New World. As a pianist he was compared favorably with Chopin and Liszt. The year 1853 was a turning point in Gottschalk's life, for he returned to the United States, and the death of his father meant the end of a measure of financial support. The remainder of his career was spent in the United States, the Caribbean, and South America, touring and writing, feeling financial pressure much of the time. He died in Brazil, and a year after his death his remains were returned to his homeland and buried in Greenwood Cemetery in Brooklyn. Gottschalk wrote about one hundred concert and salon pieces that reflect fashions of his day. Indeed, he had a gift for catering to public taste. At its best, his work captures the vitality and freshness of music he grew up with in New Orleans. Pieces such as "Bamboula, danse des négres" (1844–45) and "Le Bananier, chanson négre" (1845–46) combine virtuosity with regional color and are still entertaining. At its worst, Gottschalk's music represents the epitome of sentimentality, and works such as "The Last Hope: Religious Meditation" (1854) or "The Dying Poet: Meditation" (1863–64) are remembered only as excessive examples of period emotionalism. Of some interest, too, are the compositions that attempt to capture Latin American characteristics, such as "Souvenir de Porto Rico, marche des Gibranos" (1857) or "Souvenir de Lima, mazurka" (1865).

Among the musicians in the nineteenth century who exerted considerable influence on the musical culture of the United States are members of the **Mason** family. **Lowell Mason** (1792–1872), the patriarch of the family, is considered the founder of music education in the United States. He wrote no keyboard music but rather confined his attention to hymns, sacred vocal music, and instructional songs. Lowell Mason fathered five sons who were in some way connected with music. **Daniel Gregory Mason I** (1820–69) joined with two of his brothers, **Lowell Mason II** and **Timothy Mason** in establishing a company that published mostly religious music for more than thirty years. **William Mason** (1829–1908) was one of the leading pianists and teachers of his day, having studied in Weimar with Liszt (1853–54). William wrote over fifty piano works, all in a typically nineteenth-century virtuoso or characterpiece style. His *Memories of a Musical Life* provides an interesting description of Liszt during the Weimar years, and his piano technique manuals, *A System of Technical Exercises for the Piano* (1878) and *Touch and Technique* (1889) purport to be based on Liszt's method of developing technical prowess. **Henry Mason** (1831–90) was an instrument builder, one of the founders of the Mason and Hamlin piano and organ company. His son, **Daniel Gregory Mason II** (1873–1953), was the most significant composer of the Mason family. His style was staunchly conservative, eschewing both impressionistic or post-Romantic techniques. He wrote about fifty keyboard works, character pieces with descriptive titles and a set of variations on "Yankee Doodle," Op. 6 (1911).

Another nineteenth-century musician of considerable influence was **John Knowles Paine** (1839–1906). Educated in Germany, he returned to Boston, where he was appointed the first professor of music at an American university (Harvard). His keyboard music of around 1860 exhibits influences of J. S. Bach and the Viennese Classicists. About 1865, he began to write in a more ornamental style, creating passagework imitative of Chopin or Liszt. Among his piano works are two sonatas (1861), a set of preludes and fugues (before 1865), and several later sets of character pieces.

The best known of United States traditionalists of this period was **Edward (Alexander) MacDowell** (1860–1908). After some early lessons in the United States (a few with the young Venezuelan pianist, Teresa Carreño), MacDowell at fifteen years old was taken to Paris by his mother for study with Marmontel, first privately and later at the conservatory. Three years later, a move was made to the Hoch Conservatory at Frankfurt am Main, where MacDowell studied composition with the school's director, Joachim Raff. Trained both as a pianist and a composer, MacDowell began performing about this time, and he was encouraged by Liszt, who heard him play on two or three occasions. After having attempted to build his career in Germany and Scotland, MacDowell returned to the United States in 1888. His career then rose rapidly, first in Boston and later in New York City, where he was the first professor of music at Columbia University (1896–1904). In 1904, he was run over by a hansom cab, and shortly thereafter his health began to decline. During the last three years of his life he conceived the idea of an artist's colony to be built around his summer home near Peterborough, New Hampshire. The MacDowell Colony was realized in the years following the composer's death through the efforts of his friends and admirers and the management of his widow, the pianist Marian Nevins MacDowell (1857–1956).

MacDowell's style was that of an archconservative. He adhered to German Romanticism, seeking inspiration in nature, Celtic and Nordic legend, as well as Romantic literature. Although he was regarded in his time as the leading American composer, he wrote music that incorporated but little influence of his homeland and, indeed, was even philosophically at odds with attempts to characterize new works as "American," whether his own or those of other composers. His enormous popularity in the United States at the turn of the twentieth century is ascribed to the fact that Liszt regarded him highly, that Teresa Carreño championed his works on her many piano recitals, and that MacDowell himself concertized playing his own music. As American composers with more distinctive voices began to emerge in the twentieth century, MacDowell's music suffered a decline in popularity. Although his niche as an American Romantic is secure from a historical perspective, his music is not often played. Of the larger works, the second piano concerto, Op. 23 (1884–86), and the second *Indian Suite*, Op. 48 (1891–95), are heard occasionally. Of the piano works, only a few small character pieces remain in the concert repertoire, such works as "To a Wild Rose" or "To a Water Lily" from *Woodland Sketches*, Op. 51 (1896). Other small pieces are sometimes used as teaching material, including a few of the etudes from the two sets of twelve each, Opp. 39 and 46. MacDowell wrote four sonatas, each with a descriptive adjective in its title: *Tragica*, Op. 45 (1891–92); *Eroica*, Op. 50 (1894–95); *Norse*, Op. 57 (1899); and *Keltic*, Op. 59 (1900). All are four-movement, imposing works that use traditional structures. Among other sets of character pieces are eight *Sea Pieces*, Op. 55 (1898), six *Fireside Tales*, Op. 61 (1901–2), and ten *New England Idyls*, Op. 62 (1901–2).

Charles (Edward) Ives

Charles E. Ives (b. Danbury, Conn., Oct. 20, 1874; d. New York City, May 19, 1954) was blessed with a father who was an imaginative, active musician. George E. Ives was a bandmaster in the Civil War and then returned to Danbury to work as a teacher and conductor of choirs and instrumental groups. A man of experimental bent, George encouraged enthusiastic music making without regard for prevailing rules, reveling in whatever unusual sounds evolved. Charles thus grew up with all kinds of music, studying the masters as models, experimenting with accepted practice, singing and playing with members of his family, and participating in those public musical activities traditional in New England small-town life. The paradoxes of his personality were already in evidence when he was growing up. He was sometimes painfully shy but at other times boisterous and full of pranks; a person who sought solitude and privacy but also one who captained sports teams; at once a representative of the Emersonian transcendentalism taught him by his family and a lover of traditional, fervent hymn singing.

Ives's college education took place at Yale (1894–98), where his teacher in composition was Horatio Parker, a good musician of traditional tastes. Ives's experimental impulses put him at odds with the conservative demands of academia, but Parker imparted solid technique, especially in counterpoint, to his student. At graduation, however, Ives decided his creative work was too far from the norm to provide much of a living, so he chose to pursue a career in the insurance business. His life revolved, thus, around earning a modest livelihood for himself and his wife, mostly in and around New York City, and composing as an avocation. Ives had his champions, among whom were composers Henry Cowell and Charles Ruggles, but recognition was slow, partly because

Ives's music was difficult both for listeners to perceive and for performers to prepare. A case in point is the second piano sonata, *Concord, Mass., 1840–1860*, which was written between 1910 and 1915 but was not performed until 1939 (by pianist and Ives specialist John Kirkpatrick). By the end of Ives's life there had begun a tide of recognition, not only of the music itself but also of the fact that Ives's work had been on the cutting edge of much that was considered innovative for decades and that its origins were distinctly American.

Ives's style is difficult to categorize because it is made up of so many facets. The composer loved to weave musical quotations into his works, and these were drawn from the Classical repertoire, American hymnody, popular tunes, and sounds associated with music in American life, such as brass bands or bugle calls. Thick-textured dissonance is often developed from Ives's penchant for polytonal thinking and uncompromising contrapuntal combinations. This tough-minded cacophony is frequently placed side-by-side with music of contemplative simplicity and innocence. The extreme, frequent changes in mood and texture often generate a feeling of comprehensiveness, as if all facets of the universe were represented in the music. In quieter moments, a distinct, almost nostalgic mood of tranquility is often communicated.

Ives often wrote piano versions of music he later transformed into pieces for other instruments. This habit, coupled with the fact that some of the music was lost or destroyed, makes a complete listing of Ives's piano music complicated. At the heart of his works for solo piano are three sonatas. The five movements of the first piano sonata (1901–9) present a symmetrical structure, filled with difficult polyrhythms and polytonal harmonies, as well as ragtime and quotations from hymns and songs (among which are "How Dry I Am" and "O Susannah").

The second piano sonata, *Concord, Mass., 1840–1860* (1910–15) is an immense, diverse work, requiring close to an hour to perform. Its four movements represent members of a group of well-known American writers who flourished around Concord in the middle of the nineteenth century: philosopher Ralph Waldo Emerson (1803–82), novelist Nathaniel Hawthorne (1804–64), philosopher Amos Bronson Alcott (1799–1888) and his novelist daughter, Louisa May Alcott (1832–88), and finally environmentalist and writer Henry David Thoreau (1817–62). A monograph entitled *Essays before a Sonata* (1919) provides detailed notes with regard to both the spirit and performance of the work.

The first movement, "Emerson," makes use of the opening notes of Beethoven's Symphony no. 5, Op. 67, amid dense, shifting dissonant textures (Example 23.1). About eight pages into the movement, the mood shifts with the introduction of more lyrical, songlike material. Ives writes in his notes that this lyrical music is to reflect Emerson's poetry, while the denser textures reflect the philosopher's prose. The movement

Example 23.1 Charles Ives: "Emerson" from second piano sonata, *Concord, Mass., 1840–1860* mm. 1–2

constantly calls for tempo flexibility through such directions as "faster," "slightly slower," "quite slowly as a song, but not too evenly." Ives notes that "A metronome cannot measure Emerson's mind and oversoul, any more than the old Concord Steeple Bell could." A few bars before the end of the movement an optional viola part is provided for two measures.

"Hawthorne" is the most varied, fantasy-like movement of the sonata. Ives suggests that it should be played as fast as possible and not too literally. The composer also states that the fundamental part of this movement "is but an extended fragment trying to suggest some of his [Hawthorne's] wilder, fantastical adventures into the half-childlike, half-fairylike phantasmal realms." The opening section consists of frenetic, cadenza-like passagework. There follows a section in which clusters of notes are to be "played by using a strip of board $14^3/_4$ inches long and heavy enough to press the keys down without striking" (Example 23.2). The movement evolves gradually to a world more rooted in reality, presenting hymn tunes, marching band music, and references to the song "Columbia, the Gem of the Ocean."

"The Alcotts" is the most accessible movement for both the performer and the listener. It is an expression of the atmosphere surrounding Orchard House, the Alcott home, which Ives describes as having "a

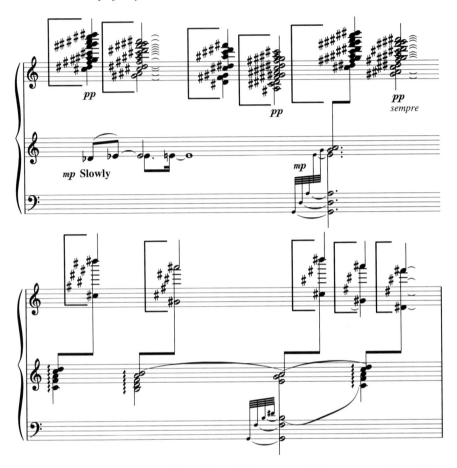

Example 23.2 Charles Ives: "Hawthorne" from second piano sonata *Concord, Mass., 1840–1860* mm. 15 after opening cadenza

kind of spiritual sturdiness underlying its quaint picturesqueness." Filled with hymn-like textures, the movement also brings back the reference to the opening notes of Beethoven's Symphony no. 5.

"Thoreau" is a lyrical, meditative movement. Ives suggests that its dynamic markings are all to be played softer than their counterparts in previous movements and that the pedals are to be used constantly. He also writes of an autumn day of Indian summer at Walden, Thoreau's nature retreat, commenting that restlessness born of activity is gradually subdued until a meditative mood brings the realization of "what the Orientals meant by contemplation and forsaking of works." The music calls forth soft sonorities that suggest impressionism. A flute part near the end of the movement adds to its atmospheric effect.

Other significant works of Ives are an earlier sonata written on three pages of manuscript paper and called by the composer the *Three-Page Sonata* (1905) and a set of studies, many left incomplete, the best known of which are an adagio titled "The Anti-Abolitionist Riots" (1908) and a left-hand etude humorously called "Some Southpaw Pitching" (1909).

Ives struggled for recognition for most of his career. Toward the end of his life, as failing health began to prevent him from further creative work, musicians started to understand his originality, the depth of his thought, and the unique expression of U.S. culture his music represents. At this time, enthusiasm for his music ran extremely high. Critics often referred to Ives as the greatest genius the United States had produced and predicted continuing celebration of his work. As continuing scrutiny of Ives's music has taken place, the excitement over discovering his work has moderated. Ives's importance remains unquestioned, but audiences are still slow to warm to the uncompromising dissonance frequently encountered in his works and often remain amused, but puzzled, by their extreme diffuseness. By the same token, performers still seem reluctant to undertake the task of overcoming the immense difficulties inherent in playing the music.

Two composers of Ives's generation who should be noted briefly are **John Alden Carpenter** (1876–1951) and **Carl Ruggles** (1876–1971). Both men achieved a measure of distinction, albeit in quite different musical styles. Carpenter's work reflects influences of popular music, jazz, and impressionism, whereas Ruggles pursued the development of dissonant, nontonal writing that bordered on serialism. Neither composed many pieces for solo piano. Carpenter left a few character pieces, such as "Polonaise américaine" (1912), "Tango américain" (1920), and a set of five pieces called *Diversions* (1922). Ruggles's chief work is a set of four pieces written late in his career, *Evocations* (1935–43, revised 1954).

Although **Arthur Farwell** (1877–1952) studied with Humperdinck in Germany, he returned to the United States to a teaching position at Cornell and founded the Wa-Wan Press (1901–12) for the publication of music by contemporary American composers. The name of the publishing company was borrowed from an Omaha Indian ceremony for peace, fellowship, and song, and it reflected Farwell's belief that the future of American music lay in building on the folk music of cultures within the United States, Indian, African American, and Western as represented by cowboy songs. The press published music by thirty-seven composers, including nine women. Works by most of these composers are no longer remembered. A few representative names are Frederick Ayers, Rubin Goldmark, E. S. Kelley, and Gena Branscombe. Farwell himself was represented as well as the still-noted work of Arthur Shepherd. Over the course of his career, Farwell wrote a sizeable number of piano works, a sonata, Op. 113, and many character pieces based on Indian themes or other American material, such as *American Indian Melodies*, Op. 11 (1900); "Dawn, Fantasy on 2 Indian Themes," Op. 12 (1901); "Navaho War Dance No. 2," Op. 29 (1904); and "Sourwood Mountain," Op. 78 (1927).

Arthur Shepherd (1880–1958), some of whose music was published by the Wa-Wan Press, wrote in a traditional style with an occasional use of polytonal, whole-tone, or modal techniques. His piano works include two sonatas (1907 and 1930), four eclogues (1933, 1948, 1948, and 1949), and three capriccios (1938, 1941, and 1943). **Robert Nathaniel Dett** (1882–1943) pursued finding an American voice in his own African American roots, recommending that "musical architects take the loose-timber of Negro folk music" as a style source. He graduated from Oberlin College and, during the course of his career, received considerable recognition, including honorary degrees from the Eastman School of Music, Howard University, and Oberlin College. His piano music consists of six suites of pieces with descriptive titles: *Magnolias* (1911); *In the Bottoms* (1913), which contains the noted "Juba Dance"; *Enchantment* (1922); *The Cinnamon Grove* (1927); *Tropic Winter* (1938); and *Eight Bible Vignettes* (1941–43).

Virginia composer **John Powell** (1882–1963) studied in Austria and adhered to the style of German Romanticism in his large-scale keyboard works. Significant are three sonatas with subtitles *Teutonica* (1913), *Psychologique*, and *Noble*. There are also two suites, *In the South* and *At the Fair* (1925).

Charles Tomlinson Griffes

Charles T. Griffes (b. Elmira, N.Y., Sept. 17, 1884; d. New York, Apr. 8, 1920) received his musical training from his sister, Katherine, and from Mary Selma Broughton, a faculty member of Elmira College. In 1903, Miss Broughton financed Griffes's study in Berlin at the Stearn Conservatory. Griffes worked there until 1907 with Humperdinck and others. Upon his return to the United States, he took a teaching position at the Hackley School in Tarrytown, New York, a post he held until 1920. During this time he was able to spend periods of time in New York, where he sought to achieve recognition as a composer. His career had just begun to take hold at the time of his early death.

Griffes's style was first influenced by German Romanticism, reflecting his training in Berlin. There is a group of piano pieces from this period, most of them unknown and unpublished. It includes some character pieces and two sonatas, one in *f*, believed to date from 1904, and one in *D-flat*, probably written around 1910. In 1911, the composer began to write in a style that made use of techniques associated with impressionism. The piano works from this period consist of his best-known character pieces, most of them with descriptive titles, believed to

Example 23.3   Charles Griffes: "The Night Winds," Op. 5, no. 3 m. 1
Reprinted by permission of G. Schirmer, Inc.

have been added after the pieces were written, and arranged into small suites. The *3 Tone Pictures*, Op. 3, are "The Lake at Evening" (1911), "The Vale of Dreams" (1912), and "Night Winds" (1912), a piece that bears a striking resemblance to Debussy's prelude "La Vent dans la plaine" (Example 23.3). The *3 Fantasy Pieces*, Op. 6, are "Barcarolle" (1912); "Notturno" (1915); and "Scherzo" (1913), an effective, brilliant piece that Griffes orchestrated under the apt title of "Bacchanale." The *Roman Sketches*, Op. 7, opens with "The White Peacock" (1915), a piece of tone-poem dimensions that is perhaps one of Griffes most famous works, also orchestrated (1919). Following are "Nightfall" (1916); "The Fountain of Acqua Paola" (1916), a shimmering, effective work that rivals Ravel's "Jeux d'eau" in its cleverly crafted passagework; and "Clouds" (1916), a piece that succeeds in creating an unearthly, elevated feeling (also orchestrated in 1919).

The Sonata (1917–18) shows another shift in Griffes's style. Here, the composer eschews the sonorities of impressionistic writing, adopting a leaner, more dissonant texture. The introduction to the sonata-allegro structure of the first movement sets forth a series of notes that probably reflects Griffes's interest in Asian scale patterns. Its intervals form a basis for both the harmonic and melodic material of the movement, characterized by the dissonance of the second and seventh (Example 23.4). There are effective climactic moments both near the end of the development section and in the coda. The movement segues into a slow second movement that is dark and austere, presenting a simple, folk-like melody. The final movement rearranges the opening series of notes into a motive that lends itself to imitative treatment. A more lyrical second theme is introduced and then later presented in a climactic statement near the end of the work. The Griffes Sonata ranks as one of the most significant American sonatas of the period, and it has gradually gained recognition to become one of the most frequently performed.

Griffes's final keyboard work is a set of three very short preludes (1919) that were written in a style similar to that of the sonata.

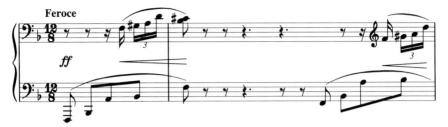

Example 23.4 Charles Griffes: Sonata, 1st movt. m. 1
Reprinted by permission of G. Schirmer, Inc.

Wallingford Riegger (1885–1961) studied in New York and Berlin. His work is interesting in that he altered his style radically several times during the course of his career, moving from writing traditional Romantic music through impressionism and arriving at a dodecaphonic style that was individual and quite apart from the work of the second Viennese school. Riegger's most significant contributions are in the genres of orchestral and chamber music. His few piano pieces, however, are well written and highly original, deserving of more attention than they have received. Among them are "Blue Voyage," Op. 6 (1927); *4 Tone Pictures,* Op. 14 (1932); "New Dance," Op. 18 (1935), a piece that is based on South American rhythms; and *New and Old,* Op. 18 (1935), a set of twelve pieces that were written to illustrate various contemporary techniques.

Women composers in the United States began to receive some measure of recognition during this period. **Fannie Charles Dillon** (1881–1947) studied at Pomona College in California and later in Berlin and New York. She returned to California for the remainder of her career, teaching both at Pomona and in Los Angeles. A performing pianist, she wrote many Romantic character pieces for the instrument and is probably best remembered for a work entitled "Birds at Dawn." **Marion Eugenie Bauer** (1887–1955) was educated in Oregon and Washington before going to Europe to study with Nadia Boulanger and others. She returned to the United States and centered her professional life in New York City, where she was active as a composer, writer, teacher, and professional activist. She helped found the Music Guild and served on the executive board of the League of Composers. Her compositions are well constructed and were considered reasonably advanced in their use of contemporary techniques. Among her piano works are *From New Hampshire Woods* (1921); "Sun Splendor" (1926, a work that was later orchestrated); *Dance Sonata* (1932), and sets of smaller pieces. **Amy Marcy Cheney Beach** (Mrs. H. H. A. Beach; 1877–1944) and **Lucille Crews** (Mrs. Lucille Marsh; b. 1888) also contributed Romantic salon pieces typical of the period.

Several composers born in the last decade of the nineteenth century should be noted. **William Grant Still** (1895–1978) was one of the first African American composers to receive widespread recognition. He was the recipient of Rosenwald and Guggenheim fellowships, the Harmon Award (1927), and honorary doctorates from Howard University (1941), Oberlin (1947), Bates College (1954), and the University of Arkansas (1971). He experimented with several avant-garde techniques but became best known for works based on American folk material written with traditional means. His piano music is confined to character pieces, among which are sets entitled *3 Visions* (1936), *7 Traceries* (1939), and *Ring Play* (1964).

Roger Sessions (b. 1896) entered Harvard at the age of fourteen, went on to study at Yale, and worked privately with Ernest Bloch. He worked in Europe for the next several years, being supported by two Guggenheim Fellowships (1926–27), the American Academy in Rome Fellowship (1928–31), and a Carnegie Fellowship (1931–32). His career in the United States included teaching at Princeton (1935–44 and 1953–65) as well as other prestigious universities. His teaching and his theory books were enormously influential on mid-twentieth century composers in the United States. His musical style was influenced by Stravinsky and Schönberg and evolved into serialism, but he retained an individual and distinct voice. Of his piano works, the first sonata (1931) was hailed by Copland as "a cornerstone upon which to base an American music." Two later sonatas (1946, 1965) are more sparse and dissonant. Other pieces include the four called *From My Diary* (1939–40) and a later set of five (1975).

Virgil Thomson (1896–1989) was educated at Harvard but spent his early career living in Paris, where he wrote several works on American subjects. In 1940, he became the music critic for the *New York Herald Tribune* and rose to become one of the leading music journalists of his time. As a composer, he experimented with a wide variety of styles, but at the center of his work is a directness, clarity, and wit that is reminiscent of Satie. His piano works include four sonatas (two in 1929, 1930, 1940), two sets of etudes (1940–51, 1943), and four volumes of thirty-two *Portraits* (1929–45).

Henry Cowell (1897–1965) was born and educated in California. From his youth he was both an ardent champion of new music and a prolific composer. His open-mindedness and enthusiasm for all kinds of music and experimental techniques resulted in a body of music written in many different styles. The piano was an important point of departure for much of his musical thinking. His piano music is some of the earliest to explore the sonorities of tone clusters, to direct playing the piano on the strings rather than the keyboard, and to use objects inside of the piano as a means of altering its timbre. For the most part, these ideas were realized through short, improvisational pieces with descriptive

Example 23.5 Quincy Porter: Sonata, 1st movt. mm. 1–3

titles. "The Tides of Manaunaun" (1912) depicts tidal waves set in motion by a mythical Irish god through the use of the fist and forearm on the keyboard. Other pieces that make use of clusters are "Advertisement" (1914) and "Tiger" (1928). "Aeolian Harp" (1923) calls for strumming the piano strings while holding down silently depressed keys. In "Sinister Romance" (1930), strings are stopped so that harmonics can be produced. "The Banshee" (1925) requires two players, one to hold down the damper pedal and the other to play inside the piano. Later in his career, Cowell became fascinated with folk music of the United States. Piano pieces that represent this interest are "Aunt Etta's Homesick Lilt" (1941), "Square Dance Tune" (1941), "Kansas Fiddler" (1944), and "Mountain Music" (1944).

(William) Quincy Porter (1897–1966) and Herbert Elwell (1898–1974) both studied first in the United States and then in Paris. Both achieved prominence, receiving many awards for their work—Porter, the Elizabeth Sprague Coolidge Medal (1945) and a Pulitzer Prize (1954) and Elwell, the Paderewski Prize (1945) and an award from the National Institute of Arts and Letters (1969). Neither wrote a great deal for solo piano, but each contributed a significant, three-movement sonata. Porter's Sonata (1930) is compact, often contrapuntal, and makes use of impressionistic-sounding sonorities (Example 23.5). Elwell's Sonata (1926) is traditional, lyrical, and features octaves.

Roy Harris (1898–1979) was educated in California and later went to Paris on two Guggenheim awards to work with Nadia Boulanger. He returned to the United States to become one of the most significant composers of his generation. His style was hewn from American folk music, particularly that of the West. Harris's most extended work for piano is a sonata (1928), written while he was in Paris. Although the imposing, cyclic work has attractive moments, it is uneven in both style and quality. As a result, it has not become a staple in the repertoire of U.S. sonatas. More focused, stylistically, are several sets of smaller pieces: *Little Suite for Piano* (1938); a three-movement suite (1944), ten *American Ballads* (1946), and a brilliant toccata (1949).

Aaron Copland

Aaron Copland (b. Brooklyn, New York, Nov. 14, 1900; d. Westchester, New York, Dec. 2, 1990) emerged as the most significant American composer of the early twentieth century. After early study in New York with Rubin Goldmark, Copland went to Paris, where he studied with Nadia Boulanger for more than six years (1917–24). During this time, he took great interest in a complete gamut of European styles, exploring the music of Satie, Honegger, Webern, Bartók, Hindemith, Weill, and Mahler. Although Copland assimilated many techniques, he was determined to develop a voice that represented his own country distinctly.

Upon his return to the United States, he was continuously involved in promoting the music of American composers, presenting a series of concerts with Roger Sessions in New York City (1928–31) and helping found the Yaddo Festivals, Arrow Music Press, and the American Composers Alliance. In the 1940s, he acted as an official liaison for the State Department to promote cultural exchange with Mexico and Latin America. He was the first American to serve as Harvard's Norton Professor of Poetics (1951) and the recipient of many awards and prizes, including the Pulitzer Prize (1945), an Academy of Motion Picture Arts and Sciences "Oscar" (1950), the Gold Medal of the National Institute of Arts and Letters (1956), the Presidential Medal of Freedom (1964), and the Howland Prize of Yale University (1970). His many honorary degrees include those awarded by Princeton, Harvard, Oberlin, and Brandeis. Copland garnered a large popular following through such works as *Lincoln Portrait* for speaker and orchestra (1942), his music-appreciation lectures and books, and between 1959 and 1972 his fifty-nine appearances on television as a speaker, pianist, or conductor.

Although Copland's stylistic focus changed at various points in his career, his underlying voice remained consistent and clear. His use of sonority relied heavily on open intervals, especially fourths and fifths, and a leanness of texture. Sharp dissonance is frequently contrasted with

Example 23.6 Aaron Copland: Piano Sonata, 1st movt. mm. 1–5

tender lyricism. Copland often used syncopation derived from jazz rhythms, and his metrical patterns change frequently. Although his most famous works are based on melodic writing in which folk-song or blues elements are identifiable, he was also fond of creating sustained, slow-moving lines that suggest a trancelike state of suspension. Around 1950, he began to write serial music, but adopting these techniques did not significantly alter his individual voice.

Almost a dozen piano pieces written when Copland was a teenager remain unpublished. They are all short character pieces with the exception of a sonata in G (1920–21). During his years of study in Paris, Copland wrote a *Scherzo humoristique*, subtitled *The Cat and the Mouse* (1920), a work that is popular with intermediate piano students. Also from the Paris years comes the *Passacaglia* (1920–21), a set of harmonically traditional variations that builds to an impressive climax.

The *Piano Variations* (1930) shows Copland's early interest in serial techniques, for it presents a series of four notes as the basis on which to build twenty terse variations and a coda. Its harmonic language remains moderately dissonant throughout, and the acoustical resonance of the piano is exploited. Although the *Piano Variations* are somewhat acerbic, the work has continued to receive a good deal of attention from performers and is regarded as one of the most significant American works of the period.

Equally significant is the Piano Sonata (1939–41). It is cast in three movements, the outer two movements being essentially slow, lyrical pieces, and the middle movement a scherzo-like vivace. The opening movement is in sonata-allegro form, with the development section providing a more rapid pace. The melodic lines focus on intervals of the third, but they are harmonized with open fourths, fifths, and seconds, producing a distinctly individual sound (Example 23.6). Jazz-like rhythms permeate both the development section of the first movement and the entire second movement. The final movement is free in structure and presents folk-like melodies over long pedal points. First-movement material returns, making the work cyclic. The final pages of the piece suspend rich sonorities over long bass notes, its mood one of static ecstasy.

Copland's most extended work for piano is a piano fantasy (1955–57). It was written in a period when serial techniques dominated the composer's thinking, but the use of a ten-note series throughout the piece does not significantly alter the harmonic language associated with Copland up to this point. Lasting for more than half an hour in performance, the work is cast in a rhapsodic, free form, which listeners often find difficult to follow, notwithstanding the fact that opening material returns near the end of the work.

Other shorter works of Copland include *4 Piano Blues* (1948), *Night Thoughts (Homage to Ives)* (1972), and several pieces suitable as teaching material, such as *2 Children's Pieces* (1936) and *Down a Country Lane* (1972).

The early years of the twentieth century saw the composition of a great deal of keyboard music by a large group of U.S. composers. Many of these works were thought to be very significant at the time of their initial presentation, but only a few have gained a secure niche in the repertoire of performing pianists. Often these works explored structures, sonorities, rhythms, and techniques that were foreign to the experience of most pianists and their audiences. Consequently, many works were given only a few early performances and then, by and large, ignored. It is quite possible that these works need to be examined again and evaluated in the light of what has happened during the remainder of the twentieth century and with the increased understanding of post-Romantic music most keyboard players now possess.

George Antheil (1900–1959) shocked audiences by writing "machine music" early in his career. In his sizeable catalogue of piano works are five sonatas, including an *Airplane Sonata* (1922), *Sonata Sauvage* (1923), and a *Jazz Sonata* (1923); forty-five preludes (1932–33); *Valentine Waltzes* (1949); and a set of fine teaching pieces entitled *Pastels* (1956).

Anis Fuleihan (1901–70) was born in Cyprus, but at the age of fifteen he came to the United States, where he built much of his career. His style reflects an interest in folk music of the Near East, often employing highly dissonant textures. A prolific composer, he wrote fourteen piano sonatas (1940–70) and many sets of character pieces, including some didactic works.

Otto Luening (b. 1900) became associated with the early development of electronic music at Columbia University in the 1940s and 1950s. He wrote extensively, however, in traditional genres, using a wide variety of styles, often juxtaposed in a single work. His piano works include six sonatas, a set of variations for piano or harpsichord (1940), and more than thirty shorter pieces.

Stefan Wolpe (1902–72) spent the early part of his career in Europe and Israel but also built a significant career in the United States

Restlessly (♩ = 110)

Example 23.7 Miriam Gideon: Piano Suite no. 3, 1st movt. mm. 1–5
From *New Music for the Piano,* copyright Lawson-Gould Publishers Inc.

after moving there in 1929. His musical style evolved from a wide variety of interests, ranging from popular music to serialism. His mature works reflect his stated intentions of juxtaposing highly diverse musical material without causal connection. He wrote piano music throughout his career, mostly single-movement pieces that explore various applications of new techniques, such as *4 Studies on Basic Rows* (1935–36), *2 Studies* (1948), and *Broken Sequences* (1969).

Paul Creston (b. 1906) has made complicated, metered rhythmic patterns and long, florid melodic lines hallmarks of his style. He has written a sonata (1935), ten books of studies in progressive difficulty entitled *Rhythmicon* (1977), and many sets of short pieces.

Ross Lee Finney (b. 1906) has written in several styles, his evolution moving from interest in American folk music, through developing a concept of opposing musical forces in structure, to his own version of serialism, based on balanced or mirror-imaged hexachords. He has written four sonatas (1933–61), a fantasy (1939), *Nostalgic Waltzes* (1947), *Variations on a Theme of Alban Berg* (1952), and three sizeable works for teaching: two sets of inventions (1956, 1970) and thirty-two *Piano Games* (1968).

Miriam Gideon (b. 1906) studied both musicology and composition in New York City, working with Paul Henry Lang and Roger Sessions. Her deftly crafted piano works include a set of variations reflecting styles of different historical periods, *6 Cuckoos in Quest of a Composer;* a set of pieces based on Keat's "Ode to a Nightingale"; an atonal work entitled "Canzone" (1947); and Piano Suite no. 3 (1963; Example 23.7).

Louise Talma (b. 1906) was born in France but received her musical training in New York City. Later she returned to France to work with Nadia Boulanger. The piano has been important in Talma's creative thinking, for she has written several significant works for it, including two sonatas (1943 and 1944–55), "Alleluia in Form of Toccata" (1944), *6 Etudes* (1953–54), and smaller works.

Example 23.8 Elliott Carter: Piano Sonata, 1st movt. mm. 1–4
© 1948 Mercury Music Corporation. Used by permission of the publisher.

Elliott Carter (b. 1908) has emerged as one of the most original and significant composers of the United States. A graduate of Harvard, he spent three years in Paris studying privately with Nadia Boulanger. He returned to the United States to build a career that has earned a host of awards and honors, including a Pulitzer Prize (1958), the UNESCO Prize (1961), Critics' Circles Awards (1960 and 1961), and the Sibelius Medal (1961). Honorary doctorates have been bestowed on him by the New England Conservatory of Music (1961); Swarthmore College (1965); Princeton (1967); Ripon College (1968); Oberlin College, Boston University, Yale, and Harvard (all in 1970); and the Peabody Conservatory (1974).

Carter's remarkable achievements rest on relatively few compositions. Each of his works are deemed more than personal expressions but rather the demonstration of solutions to complex aesthetic problems of sound organization and structure. As such, each has had a profound impact on the thinking of other composers and theorists. For most of his career his reputation as a piano composer rested on a single work, the Sonata (1945–46). Within a decade after its composition, the work garnered a reputation as being one of the most important, innovative American sonatas. Its structure is generated from a continuing contrast between vertical sonorities built in intervals of fifths on the keynote of B and sections of rapid figuration that constantly change their rhythmic groupings. The opening movement presents alternating sections of this material (Example 23.8). The second movement uses these ideas as the basis for a fugue that ultimately evolves back to the fundamental chords presented at the opening of the work. A second major keyboard work of Carter entitled "Night Fantasies" appeared in 1980.

Halsey Stevens (b. 1908) spent most of his career at the University of Southern California. His music was influenced by that of Bartók, of whom Stevens wrote a significant biography. Stevens's piano music includes three sonatas, six sonatinas, a fantasia, and many sets of small pieces based on folk material from various countries (Hungary, Romania, Czechoslovakia, Ukraine, Sweden, Portugal, and France).

Example 23.9 Samuel Barber: Sonata, Op. 26, 4th movt. mm. 1–2
Reprinted by permission of G. Schirmer, Inc.

Elie Siegmeister (b. 1909) received his education at Columbia University and then worked for four years in Paris with Nadia Boulanger. His early style was dissonant and complex and is represented by a piano work, the theme and variations (1932). Later, he moved toward a style based on American folk material, producing an *American Sonata* (1944), pieces called *Sunday in Brooklyn* (1946), and a didactic work entitled *Americana Kaleidoscope*. Finally, his style evolved to a more objective, tonal style that was only moderately dissonant and complex, as represented by a second piano sonata (1968).

Probably the most frequently played American piano sonata of the twentieth century was written by **Samuel Barber** (1910–81)—his Op. 26 (1949). Barber, who was educated at the Curtis Institute in Philadelphia, received two Pulitzer Prizes during his career (1958 and 1962), the second for his piano concerto. His style is essentially neo-Romantic. His famous sonata is cast in a traditional four-movement mold, with the first movement using sonata-allegro structure and the final movement conceived in a free, fugal style (Example 23.9). The use of twelve-tone figuration in the first movement suggests the composer's awareness of contemporary techniques but does not alter the essentially tonal orientation of his writing. The sonata's popularity may be attributed to the fact that it adroitly exploits the piano's sonorities, is dramatic and emotional, and is written for the instrument in such a way that the performer is physically challenged and fulfilled. Barber wrote a few other pieces for piano: a set of four short pieces based on American idioms called *Excursions* (1944), Nocturne, dedicated to John Field (1959), and Ballade (1972).

Coincidentally, a surprisingly large number of well-known U.S. composers, like Barber, have turned to the piano as a vehicle for producing a single sonata, otherwise writing relatively little piano music

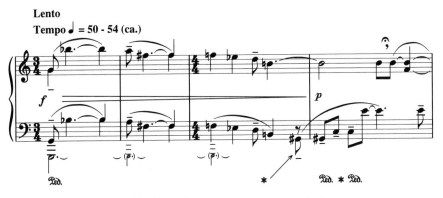

Example 23.10 Leon Kirchner: Sonata, 1st movt. mm. 1–4

except for a few character pieces or another smaller work, such as a set of variations. These sonatas, like the Barber Sonata, strive to be strong, powerful works by utilizing contemporary harmonic and rhythmic techniques without being serial. One of the most celebrated of these sonatas was written by **Leon Kirchner** (b. 1919). It is a Bartók-like work (1948) that is highly organized, dissonant, and rhythmically driving (Example 23.10). Less well known, but worth exploration, are the **Samuel Adler** (b. 1928) *Sonata brève* (1967); the sonatas by **David Amram** (b. 1930) written in 1965; **Gordon Binkerd** (b. 1916) in 1955; **Richard Cumming** (b. 1928) in 1951; **Nicolas Flagello** (b. 1928) in 1962; **Carlisle Floyd** (b. 1926) in 1957; **Andrew Imbrie** (b. 1921) in 1947; **Ulysses Kay** (b. 1917) in 1940; **Gail Kubik** (b. 1914) in 1947; **Robert Kurka** (1921–57) in 1950; **Norman Lloyd** (b. 1919) in 1964; **Peter Mennin** (b. 1923) in 1967; **Harold Shapero** (b. 1920) in 1948; and **William Sydeman** (b. 1928) in 1961; and **Richard Yardumian's** (b. 1917) *Chromatic Sonata* (1947).

Many other U.S. composers born in the first few decades of the century wrote more extensively for the piano, producing a series of sonatas and a handful of other works but still preferring the exploration of styles that were essentially tonal. They eschewed techniques that were considered avant-garde or experimental, instead borrowing characteristics of popular idioms, folk music, or sometimes Middle-Eastern or Asian music. This approach served the composers well in that their works found immediate audiences who considered their contributions significant.

Alan Hovhaness (b. 1911) incorporated into his style traits from the Middle East and Asia, with a particular fondness for Japanese and Korean music. He often writes music that creates a meditative, static state, or he extends small motivic fragments in such a way as to achieve an aleatory-like freedom. A prolific composer, he has written six sonatas

Example 23.11 Norman Dello Joio: Sonata no. 2, 1st movt. mm.1–5 Reprinted by permission of G. Schirmer, Inc.

(1935–59) and a large number of pieces with titles such as "Mystic Flute" (1937), *Allegro on a Pakistan Lute Tune* (1951), "Shalimar" (1949, rev. 1960), and "Dawn on the Mountain of Initiation" (1972).

Norman Dello Joio (b. 1913) combined syncopation borrowed from jazz idioms with a harmonic idiom based on seventh, ninth, and thirteenth chords, using traditional forms. Among piano works are three sonatas (1943, 1944, and 1948; Example 23.11). The third sonata, which opens with a set of variations, is one of the best-known American sonatas. Other works include two extended pieces, Capriccio (1969) and *Concert Variations* (1983), and smaller pieces.

Norman Cazden (b. 1914) often writes in styles that reflect his interest in folk music. He has written sonatas (1939, 1950, and 1971), sonatinas (1935, 1959, and 1964), a set of variations (1940), and other works.

Alexei Haieff (b. 1914) is a neoclassicist whose style is marked by transparent textures and energy. He has written three sonatas (1948, 1955, 1956); *Juke Box Pieces* (1952); *Saint's Wheel*, based on the circle of fifths (1960); and other short pieces.

Charles Mills (b. 1914) believes in the efficacy of both tonality and traditional forms, and he writes accordingly. Among his many piano works are two sonatas, nine sonatinas, and *30 Penitential Preludes*.

Esther Williamson Ballou (b. 1915) bases her work on rigorous control in traditional structures and a moderate amount of dissonance. She is represented by a sonata (1955) with a final movement written as a chorale with variations and a sonata-like work entitled *Variations, Scherzo, and Fugue on a Theme by Lou Harrison* (1959).

David Diamond (b. 1915) writes with an individual lyricism and a harmonic palette that is highly chromatic, bordering frequently on Romanticism. A prolific composer, he has written two piano sonatas (1947, 1972), a sonatina (1935), preludes and fugues (1939), and sets of pieces intended for use in the teaching studio: *A Private World* (1954–59), *Then and Now* (1952), and *Alone at the Piano* (1967).

Robert Palmer (b. 1915) frequently incorporates popular and jazz influences into his style. His piano works include two sonatas (1938, revised 1946; 1942, revised 1948); a toccata ostinato, based on boogie-woogie (1945); *Evening Music* (1956); *Epigrams* (1959); and *Morning Music* (1973).

Vincent Persichetti (b. 1915) composes with great facility, combining traditional structures with a wide variety of styles: tonal, modal, polytonal, and atonal. A prolific composer, he has written twelve sonatas (1939–65), six sonatinas (1950–54), two volumes of pieces called *Poems* that borrow their titles from the writings of twentieth-century poets (1939–41), and a well-known set of teaching pieces entitled *Little Piano Book* (1953).

Ellis B. Kohs (b. 1916) adhered to Classical ideals of coherence, balance, and clarity but often employed contemporary technical means, including the use of serialism late in his career. His main piano works consist of two sets of variations (1946, 1947), the second set being on the famous Renaissance song "L'Homme armé"; and two sonatas, the second of which (1962) is the third part of a larger four-part work entitled *Studies in Variation*, the first, second, and fourth studies being written as a wind quintet, piano quartet, and sonata for piano and violin.

George Rochberg (b. 1918) has addressed many of the aesthetic issues of the twentieth century in his career and has embraced several styles successively. His early writing was born of techniques associated with Stravinsky or Bartók. About 1950, Rochberg adhered to serial techniques, producing two piano works, a set of twelve bagatelles (1952) and the Sonata-Fantasia (1958), a long work in which three central movements are embellished with a prologue and epilogue and joined by interludes. The work creates textures reminiscent of Schönberg's atonal period and actually quotes from that composer's Op. 11. In actuality, it is based on serial techniques. It also exhibits an intense emotionalism and is skillfully pianistic, although it makes virtuoso demands (Example 23.12). In the early 1960s, Rochberg turned away from serial writing and began to experiment with writing that incorporated many styles from history, so that a single piece might quote from the works of other composers or move easily between traditional-sounding harmonies or rhythms and more contemporary-sounding ones. Keyboard works from this period are *Nach Bach Fantasy for Piano or Harpsichord* (1966) and *Carnival Music* (1971).

A large group of composers focus their work on tonal, more traditional styles, occasionally using twelve-tone techniques in consonant ways. Some of them may be noted in passing. **Leslie Bassett** (b. 1923) is represented by a set of six pieces (1951) and the four *Elaborations* (1966); **William Bergsma** (b. 1921) by three fantasies (1943) and two books of *Tangents* (1951); **Robert Evett** (b. 1922) by four neoclassic sonatas; **Richard Faith** (b. 1926) by sonatas and sets of character pieces, many of

Example 23.12 George Rochberg: Sonata-Fantasia opening
© 1958 Theodore Presser Company. Used by permission of the publisher.

which are suitable for intermediate teaching; **Roger Goeb** (b. 1914) by a fantasy (1950); **Lou Harrison** (b. 1917) by six sonatas for piano or cembalo (1934–43), three sonatas (1938), and a suite (1943); **Robert Helps** (b. 1928) by three etudes and Quartet (1970); **Lee Hoiby** (b. 1926) by *Capriccio on 5 Notes* (1962) and *Narrative* (1993); **Jean Eichelberger Ivey** (b. 1923) by a neoclassic sonata, a set of variations (1952), and Prelude and Passacaglia (1955); **Meyer Kupferman** (b. 1926) by Partita (1949) and *Sonata on Jazz Elements*; **John La Montaine** (b. 1920) by a sonata (1950) and *Fuguing Set* (1965); **Benjamin Lees** (b. 1924 in China) by four sonatas (1949, 1950, 1956 [*Sonata Brève*], 1963) and a well-known fantasia (1954); **Robert Muczynski** (b. 1929) by three sonatas (1957, 1969, and 1973) and sets of character pieces, many useful as teaching material; **Ned Rorem** (b. 1923) by three sonatas (1948, 1949–50, 1954) and a group of pieces of intermediate difficulty called *A Quiet Afternoon* (1949); **Leo Smit** (b. 1921) by a one-movement sonata (1951–55), a set of variations (1954), and a fantasy (1957); **Hale Smith** (b. 1925) by *Evocation* (1970) and *Anticipations, Introspections, and Reflections* (1979); **Robert Starer** (b. 1924 in Austria) by two sonatas (1949 and 1965) and *Hexahedron* (1971); and **Ben Weber** (b. 1916) by his Fantasia (1946).

Several prominent composers represent a U.S. avant-garde in that their work emphatically embraces nontonal serialism, irrational rhythms, aleatory procedures, experimental uses of traditional instruments, or combining traditional instruments with electronic devices. These composers often wrote in more conservative styles early in their careers, but at some point they adopted experimental style characteristics and seemed to adhere to one or more of them from that point on.

John Cage (1912–92) is perhaps the best known of this group, having focused on "prepared" piano, use of electronics, and aleatory ("chance") techniques. His music and writing on aesthetics have had a significant impact on the international scene on one hand and have been the center of considerable controversy on the other. Born and educated in California, he worked as a poet and composer with dance groups in the early part of his career. The desire for creating multitimbrel accompaniment for dancers economically led him to experiment with altering the timbres of the piano. A series of pieces for "prepared" piano emerged. Objects such as strips of rubber, screws, bolts, and nuts are very carefully placed in the strings of the piano so that playing the appropriate key produces a percussion-like sound of indeterminate pitch or complex timbre. String areas are prepared in different ways, so that a reasonably large variety of these sounds can be produced in rapid succession by playing the keyboard. The earliest prepared piano piece by Cage was "Bacchanale" (1938) written for dancer Syvilla Fort. Cage wrote several such pieces for the next decade, such as "Meditation" (1943), "Amores" (1943), and "A Valentine out of Season" (1944). The culmination of this phase of his career was a set of pieces entitled *Sonatas and Interludes* (1946–48), the premiere of which in 1949 undoubtedly contributed to the composer's being honored by both the Guggenheim Foundation and the National Academy of Arts and Sciences for "having thus extended the boundaries of musical art."

Cage's prepared piano pieces are often built on rhythmic patterns and melodic fragments that repeat frequently, sometimes with small units added on. Through this technique, the music takes on a static quality, one that is quite different from the goal-oriented procedures of Western music. This aesthetic was a reflection of Cage's interest in Eastern philosophy and culture. In the late 1940s Cage began to study Zen Buddhism and the *I Ching*, and the result was an extended work for piano in four volumes, *Music of Changes* (1952), in which pitches, durations, and timbres are determined, not by the conscious choice of the composer, but rather by the use of charts based on *I Ching* and by tossing three coins. In *Music for Piano* (1952) the performer determines durations, and the pitches are selected by drawing staves on a pieces of paper and noting where the imperfections in the paper occur in relation to the lines of each staff. Another aleatory work, *Winter Music* (1957), presents the performer with twenty unnumbered pages and a set of directions to determine selection procedures.

The piano continued to be an important instrument for Cage, even when in the 1950s he began to turn his attention to electronics as a source of generating sound. He combined the piano with electronic music in "Electronic Music for Piano" (1965). His last works for piano were *Études australes* (1974–75), a set of thirty-two pieces, and a set of eight short pieces entitled *ASLSP,* an abbreviation for "as slow as

Example 23.13 John Cage: *ASLSP* opening

possible" as well as a reference to the opening line of the last paragraph of James Joyce's *Finnegans Wake*, "Soft mourning city! Lsp!" (1985; Example 23.13).

George Perle (b. 1915) was one of the first American composers to use and write about the twelve-tone techniques of Schönberg, Berg, and Webern. He championed serialism in several books, and his writing is regarded as important in the history of the movement. For his own compositions, he developed a theory that further organized twelve-tone writing into pitch-class groupings that then operate functionally, much in the same way as traditional harmonic progressions. Thus, his music, although completely dodecaphonic, seems more accessible to listeners. Perle's piano works include a sonata (1950), a short sonata (1964), a toccata (1969), and six etudes (1976).

George Crumb (b. 1929) has expanded on the ideas of Cowell and Cage, altering the sounds of the piano by playing inside the instrument and/or placing objects on the strings. Crumb's style emanates from juxtaposing tritone and whole-tone harmonies, as well as major and minor triads, procedures exemplified in the five short piano pieces (1964). His scores often contain elaborate, evocative extramusical references. Each of his two sets of *Makrokosmos* for amplified piano (1971 and 1972) consists of twelve pieces based on signs of the zodiac with title references to mystical, religious, or ancient symbols. Typical are references such as "Crucifixus," "Atlantis," or "Druids." The player is also called upon to vocalize in a variety of ways and whistle during the performance. Crumb combines these theatrical effects with atmospheric sonorities, creating music that alternates between mysterious, dreamlike states and powerful, overwhelming waves of sound. The programmatic and emotional elements in Crumb's music appeal immediately to both performers and audiences (Example 23.14).

Several other composers whose work has focused predominantly on nontonal or experimental techniques may be mentioned in passing. **Milton Babbitt** (b. 1916), much of whose work has been in electronic music, has written highly complex serial works for piano, among them *Semisimple Variations* (1956), *Partitions* (1957; Example 23.15), *Post-*

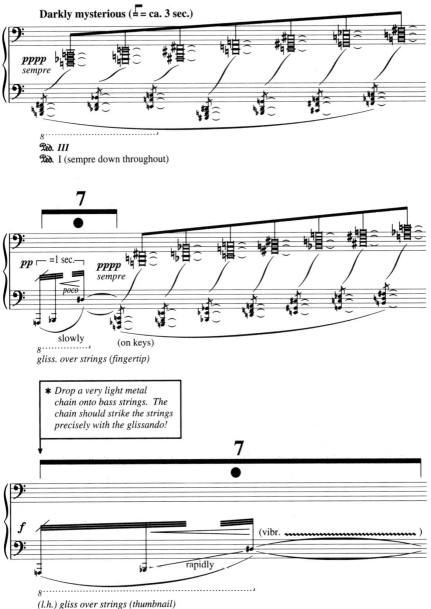

Example 23.14 George Crumb: "Primeval Sounds (Genesis I)" from *Makrokosmos*, vol. 1 opening

Example 23.15 Milton Babbitt: *Partitions* mm. 1–2
From *New Music for the Piano,* copyright Lawson-Gould Publishers Inc.

Partitions (1966), and *Tableaux* (1973). **Arthur Berger** (b. 1912) moved from a diatonic neoclassicism to Webern-like serialism and combines characteristics of both in his later style. His piano works include *Entertainment* (1940), a fantasy (1940), a partita (1947), four two-part inventions (1948–49), and five pieces (1968). **Earle Brown** (b. 1926) wrote twelve-tone and serial sets of piano pieces, *3 Pieces* (1951), and *Perspectives* (1952) and then began to develop a system of graphic notation for unspecified instruments in his pieces called *Folio and Four Systems* (1952–54). **Lucia Dlugoszewski** (b. 1931) wrote three early sonatas (1949–50) and then went on to develop a multitimbre piano (1951) for which she wrote a number of pieces with titles such as *Archaic Timbre Piano Music* (1953–56) and *Music for Left Ear in a Small Room* (1959). **Morton Feldman** (b. 1926) also wrote twelve-tone pieces, experimented with graphs, and then returned to more traditional notation, although he often eschews control of rhythmic values. His many sets of piano pieces include *Illusions* (1950), *Two Intermissions* (1950), *Intersections 2 and 3* (1951), *Last Pieces* (1962), and *Vertical Thoughts 4* (1963). The piano works of **Donald Martino** (b. 1931) have received particular attention because they evidence such a rich palette of sonorities and variety of touch, exploring in original ways the potential of the piano. An early fantasy (1958) was followed by an extraordinary sonata in one movement entitled *Pianississimo* (1970), a work of 436 measures commissioned by Easley Blackwood in search of "the most difficult piano piece." Later works include *Fantasies and Impromptus* (1981) and *Twelve Preludes* (1992; Example 23.16). **Charles Wuorinen** (b. 1938) has focused on the serial-

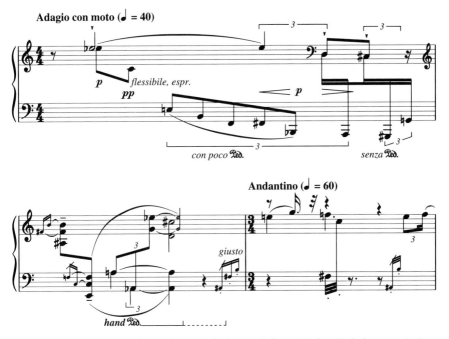

Example 23.16 Donald Martino: Prelude no. 1 from *Twelve Preludes* mm. 1–3

ization of both pitch and rhythm in his works. He has written a set of variations (1965) and two piano sonatas (no. 2 in 1976).

Around 1960, some composers began to turn away from serial techniques, adopting a less rigorous approach to both dissonance and abstraction. They adopted various ideas that were more listener friendly as a basis for their creative impulses. Such a move was dubbed "new Romanticism," and although more traditional elements were sometimes incorporated into this music, it was far from a return to nineteenth-century practice. Some composers sought inspiration in more popular idioms. For example, there has been a revival of ragtime, inspired by the early work of such men as **Scott Joplin** (1868–1917) and **Joseph Lamb** (1887–1960). Whereas the ragtime compositions of the early composers remained wedded to a popular style of piano playing, the work of the revivalists incorporates more complex technical and musical ideas while still keeping the ragtime spirit. Some of the work of **William Bolcom** (b. 1938) represents this revival (Example 23.17), although he also wrote a set of twelve etudes (1959–66). Similarly, **William Albright** (b. 1944) has written several compositions based on ragtime, including a *Grand Sonata in Rag* (1968) and *The Dream Rags* (1970). Another group of composers have based their works on a practice designated by the terms *system (ii)* or *minimalism*. Works based on this technique adhere to a basic

Caressingly ♪ = ca. 108

Example 23.17   William Bolcom: "Dream Shadows" from *Three Ghost Rags* mm.
1–3

tonality while employing a very small fragment of music over and over
again with rhythmic, phrase, or accent shifts. Representative are the
Keyboard Studies (1963) of **Terry Riley** (b. 1935) and *Spaces* (1975) of **Tom
Johnson.**

Composers in Canada have followed the patterns of those of the
United States, combining the reflection of both tonal and nontonal European trends with occasional explorations of materials born of English-
Canadian, French-Canadian, or Indian folk cultures. More sparsely
populated, Canada has accordingly produced fewer composers than the
United States, and developments there have tended to run a generation
or more after their U.S. counterparts.

Among earlier significant composers is **Claude Champagne** (1901–
65), whose work was influenced by French-Canadian folk music and
Brazilian folk music (resulting from visits there). His piano works consist
of a few small pieces and a *Quadrilha Brasileira* (1942). **Arnold Walter**
(1902–73) was Austrian born, having studied law in Prague and musicology in Berlin. He settled in Toronto in 1937 and made significant contributions to Canadian musical life. His piano works include a suite
(1945) and a sonata (1950).

The first decade of the twentieth century gave rise to a group of
prominent women composers in Canada. **Sophie Carmen Eckhardt-
Gramatté** (b. 1902) was born in Moscow and pursued a performing career
as a child prodigy in Europe before finally settling in Winnipeg. She has
written a sonata (1950) and several sets of smaller pieces. **Jean Coulthard**
(b. 1908) studied in Toronto and later in London with Ralph Vaughn
Williams. Her piano works include a sonata (1948), four etudes (1945),
and several sets of character pieces. **Barbara Pentland** (b. 1912) received
her early training in Canada and then went to New York and Paris for further training. She studied for a short time with Aaron Copland. Her piano
works include *Four Studies in Line* (1941), *Sonata Fantasy* (1947), a twelve-

tone toccata (1957–58), a serial fantasy (1962), and three books of teaching pieces entitled *Music of Now* (1969–70). **Violet Archer** (b. 1913) studied with Bartók in New York and Hindemith at Yale. She has written a sonata, a sonatina (1948), and several sets of character pieces.

John Weinzweig (b. 1913) was an early champion of contemporary techniques and received credit as the first Canadian composer to use twelve-tone technique, having introduced it in the second movement of his first piano suite (1939). He also wrote a second suite (1950) as well as a piano sonata (1950) and smaller pieces. The work of **Jean Papineau-Couture** (b. 1916) has at various times reflected French impressionism, neoclassicism, atonality, and the use of twelve-tone technique. He has written a piano suite (1942–43), *Mouvement perpétuel* (1943), two waltzes (1943–44), an etude (1944–45), an aria (1960), and a piece entitled "Complémentarité" (1971). Czech born and educated, **Oskar Morawetz** (b. 1917) moved to Toronto in 1940. His music utilizes impressionistic techniques and is often inspired by Jewish tradition. His piano works include a *Sonata tragica* (1945); a scherzo (1947) that has garnered considerable popularity among Canadian pianists; a ballade (1950); a *Fantasy on a Hebrew Theme* (1951); Fantasy, Elegy, and Toccata (1958); ten preludes (1966); and a suite (1966). **Udo Kasemets** (b. 1919) was born in Estonia, having moved to Toronto in 1951. His work reflects many styles, but he has been deeply involved both in dodecaphony and after 1960 with avant-garde experimental techniques. His two major piano works are a sonata (1951) and a set of six preludes (1952). Latvian-born **Talivaldis Kenins** (b. 1919) received his musical training at conservatories in Riga and Paris, emigrating to Canada in 1951. His musical style tends to be conservative, and he prefers to use traditional forms. He has written a piano sonata (1961) and a set of teaching pieces entitled *Diversities* (1968) that introduce contemporary techniques to young pianists.

Harry Somers (b. 1925) wrote in an eclectic style until about 1950, when he began to use twelve-tone techniques consistently. A reasonably prolific composer, he has produced five piano sonatas (1945, 1946, 1950, 1950, 1957), a set of twelve fugues based on twelve-tone techniques (1951), *3 Sonnets* (1946), *Solitudes* (1947), and other pieces. **Clermont Pépin** (b. 1926) writes in a variety of styles. Although he sometimes employs experimental techniques based on his study of mathematics and acoustics, most of his piano music is based on ideas that reflect more traditional contemporary trends. Among his piano works are five short etudes (1940–54), two sets of variations (1940, 1947), a sonata (1947), a suite (1951), and numerous smaller pieces.

Although **John Beckwith** (b. 1927) is recognized as an influential Canadian composer, he has written relatively little piano music, his output being confined to *4 Conceits* (1945–48), short pieces in an impressionistic style; a more virtuosic novelette (1954); and some teaching pieces. Although Canadian by birth, **Yehudi Wyner** (b. 1929) has focused his career mostly in the United States, serving on the faculty at Yale. His music often reflects his Jewish experience, and he has been influenced by Hindemith, Stravinsky, and Schönberg, although typically he does not use dodecaphonic techniques. His piano works include a partita (1952), a sonata (1954), and three short fantasies (1963–71).

The Future

The future of the piano and its literature seems somewhat uncertain at best and extremely fragile at worst. Most historians believe that the importance of the piano peaked in the nineteenth century and that the twentieth century has seen a gradual decline in popularity and significance, notwithstanding the great amounts of creative energy expended in playing and writing for the instrument. The most telling signs, perhaps, have been the steady decline of audiences for piano concerts in the last half of the century and the fact that, aside from the young musicians who study the instrument, most of those who do attend such events come from an older segment of the population, representing traditions and tastes of the past. Some observers even go so far as to predict a virtual demise of the piano and its literature in the decades ahead.

Simultaneously, however, new life began to form in unexpected quarters. The emergence of electronic music in the 1950s did not, at first, seem to have much to do with the piano, because for several decades electronic equipment was oriented toward knobs, dials, and plugs. In the 1980s, however, a dramatic change came about. The concept emerged of using a traditional piano keyboard as a means through which both to control electronic devices and to permit them to communicate with each other. This concept, known as Musical Instrument Digital Interface (MIDI), has been adopted industrywide and has become the most frequently encountered means of control. Such an evolution clearly places the playing of the piano keyboard in a central position in the vast world of technology. Through this alliance, keyboard players and composers have reunited, and the marketplace, although often indiscriminate in terms of refinement, seems voracious in its appetite for synthesized sound.

In the wake of this development, interest in the piano, its history, its literature, and the techniques it requires has been reborn. It is possible that a new generation of young musicians will emerge, one that will continue to write for and perform on the piano as a member of an extended family of keyboard instruments. It is, thus, quite possible to predict that, although the piano may have to become more accustomed to sharing the limelight, it will continue to flourish in the next century as a partner in the excitement and popularity technology seems destined to create. If this happens, then surely a widespread renaissance of keyboard literature will follow.

Bibliographical Abbreviations

Acta	Acta Musicologica
AM	Annuario Musical
AMT	American Music Teacher
CaPs	Congresso a arte em Portugal no. sec. XVIII
CMc	Current Musicology
CT	Consort
Dia	The Diapason
DR	Die Reihe
EM	Early Music
FAM	Fontes artis musicae
GSJ	The Galpin Society Journal
HMYB	Hinrichsen's Musical Year Book
IAMB	Inter-American Music Bulletin
IMTA	Periodical of the Illinois Music Teachers State Association
IMSCR	International Musicological Society Congress Report
IRASM	International Review of the Aesthetics and Sociology of Music
JAMS	Journal of the American Musicological Society
JMT	Journal of Music Theory
JR	Juilliard Review
Lsnr	The Listener
MaM	Music and Musicians
MD	Musica Disciplina
MF	Die Musikforschung
MFm	Music Forum
ML	Music and Letters
M	Modern Music
MMc	Musical Mercury
MMR	Monthly Musical Record
MO	Musical Opinion
MQ	Musical Quarterly
MR	Music Review
MSD	Musicological Studies and Documents
MT	Musical Times
NHQ	New Hungarian Quarterly

Nts	*Notes*
PM	*Polish Music*
PMA	*Proceedings of the Musical Association*
PNM	*Perspectives of New Music*
PQ	*Piano Quarterly*
PR	*Partisan Review*
PRMA	*Proceedings of the Royal Musical Association*
Quad	*Quadrivium*
RBM	*Revue belge de musicologie*
Rcd	*Ricordiana*
ReM	*La Review musicale*
RMFC	*Recherches sur la musique française classique*
SA	*Scientific American*
SM	*Studia musicologica Adademiae scientiarum hungaricae*
SMA	*Studies in Music*
Snds	*Soundings*
TEBS	*Transactions of the Edinburgh Bibliographical Society*
Tmp	*Tempo*
TVNM	*Tijdschrift der Vereniging voor nederlandsche Muziek-geschiedenis*
YIMR	*Yearbook of the Inter-American Institute for Musical Research*

Selected Anthologies and Collections

Some of the anthologies in the following list are easily available and may be used as working editions for the performer. Others probably will be found only in libraries. These are important as historic collections of music often not available elsewhere, and they are still regarded as important reference works for exploring little-known music, especially of earlier periods.

Alte Meister der Klaviermusik. Edited by Hermann Keller and K. Herrmann. 4 vols. Leipzig, 1959–60.

Alte Meister: Sammlung wertvoller Klavierstücke des 17. und 18. Jahrhunderts. Edited by Ernst Pauer. 6 vols. Leipzig, 1868–85.

Antologia di musica antica e moderna per pianoforte. Edited by Gino Tagliapietra. 18 vols. Milan, 1931–33.

The Art of the Suite. Edited by Yella Pessl. New York, 1947.

Arte antica e moderna: Scelta di composizioni per pianoforte. 21 vols. Milan, ca. 1890–1910.

L'arte musicale in Italia. Edited by Luigi Torchi. 7 vols. Milan and Rome, 1897–1907. (Keyboard music is in vol. 3.)

Classiques espagnols du piano: Sonates anciennes d'auteurs espagnols. Edited by Joaquin Nin, 2 vols. Paris, 1925–28.

Contemporaries of Purcell: Harpsichord Pieces. Edited by John Alexander Fuller Maitland. 7 vols. London, 1921–22.

Contemporaries of Schumann: Fourteen Pieces for Pianoforte by Masters of the Nineteenth Century. Edited by K. Herrmann. London, 1938.

Corpus of Early Keyboard Music. Edited by Willi Apel. Rome, 1963.

Denkmäler deutscher Tonkunst. 65 vols. Leipzig, 1892–1931. (Keyboard music in vols. 1 and 4.)

Denkmäler der Tonkunst in Bayern. Edited by Adolf Sandberger. 30 vols. Leipzig and Augsburg, 1900–1931. (Keyboard music is in vols. 2/2, 4/2, and 18.)

Denkmäler der Tonkunst in Österreich. Edited by Guido Adler and Erich Schenk. 83 vols. Vienna and Leipzig, 1894–1923. (Keyboard music in vols. 1, 3/3, 4/1, 6/2, 8/2, 10/2, 13/2, and 29/2.)

Deustche Klaviermusik aus dem Beginn des 18. Jahrhunderts. Vol. 3 of Nagels Musik Archiv. Hanover, 1927.

Early Italian Keyboard Music. Edited by G. S. Bedbrook. 2 vols.London, 1955–56.
Early Italian Piano Music: A Collection of Pieces Written for the Harpsichord and Clavichord. Edited by Michele Esposito. Boston, 1906.
Early Keyboard Music (English Keyboard Music). 22 vols. London, 1963. Supplement, 1972.
The Evolution of Piano Music. Edited by Curt Sachs. New York, 1944.
Eighteenth-Century Italian Keyboard Music. Edited by Gian Francesco Malipiero. Bryn Mawr, 1952.
The Fitzwilliam Virginal Book. Edited by John Alexander Fuller Maitland and W. Barclay Squire. 2 vols. Leipzig, 1899. (Reprint, Dover Books, 1963.)
French and Belgian Masters, Seventeenth–Eighteenth Centuries. Edited by Isadore Philipp. New York, 1946.
Four Hundred Years of European Keyboard Music. Edited by Walther Georgii. (Vol. 1 of *Anthology of Music*.) Cologne, 1960.
German Keyboard Music of the Seventeenth and Eighteenth Centuries. Edited by Hans Fischer and Fritz Oberdörffer. 9 vols. Berlin, 1960.
Keyboard Music of the Baroque and Rococo. Edited by Walther Georgii. 3 vols. Cologne, 1960.
Music of the Bach Family: An Anthology. Edited by Karl Geiringer. Cambridge, 1955.
Musica antiqua bohemica. 2 Series. Prague, 1943–. (Piano music in Series 1, vols. 14, 17, and 20.) *Musica Britannica: A National Collection of Music*. Edited by Anthony Lewis. London, 1951–. Revised in 1954. (Keyboard music in vol. 24.)
Old English Composers for the Virginal and Harpsichord. Edited by Ernst Pauer. London, n.d.
A Program of Early American Piano Music. Edited by John Howard Tasker. New York, 1931.
Recent Researches in American Music. Edited by Hugh Wiley Hitchcock. Madison, Wisc., 1977–. (Keyboard music 1787–1830 in vols. 1 and 2.)
Sonate italiane del secolo XVIII per cembalo o pianoforte. Edited by Domenico de Paoli. London, 1939.
Style and Interpretation: An Anthology of Keyboard Music. Edited by Howard Ferguson, 4 vols. New York, 1964.
Thirteen Piano Sonatas of the Eighteenth and Nineteenth Centuries. Edited by William S. Newman. Chapel Hill, 1947.
Le trésor des pianistes: Collection des oeuvres choisies des maîtres de tous les pays et toutes les époques depuis le 16e siècle jusqu' à la moitie du 19e. Edited by Aristide and Louise Farrenc. 23 vols. Paris, 1861–72.

A Selected List of
Complete Editions

The following is a list of complete editions for selected major composers. Complete editions may often be found in libraries with extensive music divisions. Such editions may be used as points of reference, but they often do not represent the best working editions for performers, either from a practical or critical standpoint. Good working editions for most composers are, however, available, and there has been a proliferation of fine critical editions in the last half of the twentieth century.

Descriptive catalogues that cite most of these editions have also been published. (See, for example, Maurice Hinson's *Guide to the Pianist's Repertoire*, Indiana University Press, 1973; or the *Friskin-Freundlich Music for the Piano*, Dover Books.)

Bach, Johann Sebastian. *Werke: Herausgegeben von der Bach-Gesellschaft.* 47 vols. Leipzig, 1851–1900 and 1926. Reprint, 46 vols., Ann Arbor, 1947.)

Balakirev, Mili. *Complete Piano Works.* 2 vols. Moscow, 1951–52.

Beethoven, Ludwig van. *Werke: Vollständige kritisch durchgesehene überall berechtige Ausgabe.* 25 series, 33 vols. Leipzig, 1862–1890. (Reprint, Ann Arbor, 1949. Piano music in Series 16, 17, and 18.)

Brahms. Johannes. *Sämtliche Werke. Ausgabe der Gesellschaft der Musikfreunde in Wien.* 26 vols. Leipzig, 1927–28. (Reprint, Ann Arbor, 1949. Solo piano works in vols. 13, 14, and 15.)

Bull, John. *Keyboard Music.* Edited by John Steele and Francis Cameron. Introduction by Thurston Dart. In Musica Britannica, vols. 14 and 19. London, 1960–63.

Byrd, William. *Collected Works.* Edited by Edmund H. Fellows, 20 vols. London, 1937–50. (Keyboard music in vols. 18, 19, and 20.)

Chambonnières, Jacques. *Oeuvres complètes.* Edited by Paul Brunold and André Tessier. Paris, 1925.

Chopin, Frédéric. *Complete Works According to the Autographs and Original Editions.* Edited by Ignace Paderewski. 9 vols. Warsaw, 1969–71. (Reprint, Dover Books.)

———. *Werke.* 14 vols. and 3 supplements. Leipzig, 1878–80.

Clementi, Muzio. *Oeuvres complètes.* 13 vols. (incomplete). Leipzig, 1803–19.

Couperin, François. *Oeuvres complètes.* Edited by Maurice Cauchie. 12 vols. Paris, 1932–33. (Harpsichord music in vols. 4 and 5.)

Couperin, Louis. *Oeuvres complètes.* Edited by Paul Brunold. Paris, 1936.

Dvořák, Antonin. *Works (Souborné vydáni).* Prague, 1955. (Piano music in Series 5.)

Fischer, Johann Kasper Ferdinand. *Sämtliche Werke für Klavier und Orgel.* Edited by Erich von Werra. Leipzig, 1936. (Revised, 1965.)

Frescobaldi, Girolamo. *Orgel- und Klavierwerke.* Gesamtausgabe nach dem Urtext. Edited by Pierre Pidoux. 5 vols. Kassel, 1949–55.

Gibbons, Orlando. *Complete Keyboard Works.* Edited by Margaret Glyn. 5 vols. London 1922–25. (Also vol. 20 of *Musica Britannica.* Edited by Gerald Hendrie. London, 1962.)

Händel, Georg Friedrich. *G. F. Händel's Werke: Ausgabe der deutschen Händelgesellschaft.* Edited by F. W. Chrysander. 95 vols., Leipzig and Bergedorf bei Hamburg, 1858–94. (Reprint, 1965.) Keyboard music in vol. 2.

———. *Hallische Händel-Ausgabe: Im Auftrag der Georg Friedrich Händel-Gesellschaft.* Edited by Max Schneider and Rudolf Steglich. Kassel, 1955–. (Keyboard music in Series 4.)

———. *Klavierwerke.* Edited by Walter Serauky and Friedrich Glasenapp. 4 vols. Halle, 1949–51.

Haydn, Franz Joseph. *Werke: Herausgegeben vom Joseph-Haydn-Institut Köln.* Edited by Jens Peter Larsen and G. Feder. 50 vols. Munich, 1958–.

Hindemith, Paul. *Sämtliche Werke.* Edited by K. von Fischer and L. Finscher. Mainz, 1975–.

Joplin, Scott. *The Collected Works.* Edited by V. B. Lawrence. 2 vols. New York, 1972.

Liszt, Franz. *Liszt Society Publications.* 4 vols. London, 1952–54.

———. *Musikalische Werke: Herausgegeben von der Franz Liszt-Stiftung.* 31 vols. (incomplete). Leipzig, 1908–33. (Piano music in Part 2.)

Medtner, Nikolay K. *Sobraniye sochineniy (Collected Works).* Edited by A. Gedike and others. 12 vols. Moscow, 1959–63.

Mendelssohn-Bartholdy, Felix. *Werke.* Edited by Julius Rietz. 19 series, 36 vols. Leipzig, 1874–77. (Piano music in Series 11.)

Morley, Thomas. *Keyboard Works.* Edited by Thurston Dart. 2 vols. London, 1959.

Mozart, Wolfgang Amadeus. *Neue Ausgabe sämtlicher Werke.* In Verbindung Mozartstädten Augsburg, Salzburg, und Wienherausgegeben von der Internationalen Stiftung Mozarteum. Estimated 170 vols. Kassel, 1955–. (Solo keyboard music in Series 9.)

———. *Werke.* 74 vols. Leipzig, 1877–1905. (Reprint, Ann Arbor, 1955. Solo keyboard music in Series 20 and 21.)

Musorgsky, Modest Petrovich. *Sämtliche Werke.* Edited by Pavel Lamm. 8 vols. Vienna and Leipzig, 1928–34. (Piano music in vol. 3.)

Prokofiev, Serge. *Sobraniye sochineniy (Collected Works).* Edited by N. P. Anosov and others. Moscow, 1955–.

Rameau, Jean-Philippe. *Oeuvres complètes.* Edited by Camille Saint-Saëns and others. 18 vols. (incomplete). Paris, 1895–1924. (Revised, 1969.) Scarlatti, Domenico. *Opere complete per clavicembalo.* Edited by Alessandro Longo. 10 vols. and a supplement. Milan, 1907–37.

Schubert, Franz. *Werke.* 40 vols. and 3 supplements. Leipzig, 1888–97.

Schumann, Robert. *Werke.* Edited by Clara Schumann. 34 vols. Leipzig, 1886–93.

Soler, Antonio. *Sonatas para instrumentos de tecla.* Edited by S. Rubio. 5 vols. Madrid, 1957.

Bibliography of Secondary Literature

The following list is one of published work that focuses on the literature of stringed keyboard instruments. The reader should consult bibliographical listings in standard reference works (such as *New Grove Dictionary of Music and Musicians*) for biographies of composers and unpublished dissertations.

Chapter One: Stringed Keyboard Instruments

Benton, Rita. "The Early Piano in the United States," *HMYB*, 11 (1961): 179.

Blackham, E. D. "The Physics of the Piano," *SA*, 213 (1965): 88.

Boalch, Donald Howard. *Makers of the Harpsichord and Clavichord to 1840*. London and New York, 1956. (Revised, 1974.)

Clinkscale, Martha Novak. *Makers of the Piano 1700–1820*. New York, 1993.

Closson, Ernest. *Histoire du piano*. Brussels, 1944. (English ed.: *History of the Piano*, translated by D. Ames. London, 1947.)

Colt, C. F. "Early Pianos, Their History and Character," *EM*, 1 (1973): 27.

Dolge, Alfred. *Pianos and Their Makers: A Comprehensive History of the Development of the Piano from the Harpsichord to the Concert Grand*. 2 vols. Covina, Calif., 1911–13. (Reprint, 1972.)

Ehrlich, Cyril. *The Piano: A History*. New York, 1990.

Hirt, F. J. *Meisterwerke des Klavierbauers*. Olten, 1955. (English ed.: *Stringed Keyboard Instruments 1440–1880*. Boston, 1968.)

Hoover, C. *Harpsichords and Clavichords*. Washinton, D.C., 1969.

Hubbard, Frank. *Three Centuries of Harpsichord Making*. Cambridge, Mass., 1965.

Lade, J. "Modern Composers and the Harpsichord," *CT*, 19 (1962): 128.

Loesser, Arthur. *Men, Women, and Pianos: A Social History*. New York, 1954.

Michel, N. E. *Michel's Piano Atlas*. Rivera, Calif., 1957.

Neupert, Hanns. *Das Cembalo: Eine geschichtliche und technische Betrachtung der Kielinstrumente*. Kassel, 1932. (3rd ed., 1956; English ed.: *Harpsichord Manual*, translated by F. E. Kirby. Kassel, 1960.)

———. *Das Klavichord*. Kassel, 1948. (2nd ed., 1955; English ed., 1965.)

Parrish, Carl. "Criticisms of the Piano When It Was New," *MQ*, 30 (1944): 428.

Pollens, Stewart. *The Early Pianoforte*. Cambridge, 1994.

Rippin, Edwin M. "The Early Clavichord," *MQ*, 53 (1967): 518.

———, ed. *Keyboard Instruments: Studies in Keyboard Organology*. Edinburgh, 1971.

———. "Towards an Identification of the Chekker," *GSJ*, 28 (1975): 11.
Russell, Raymond. *The Harpsichord and Clavichord: An Introductory Study.* London, 1959. (Revised, 1973.)
———. "The Harpsichord since 1800," *PRMA*, XXXII (1955-56): 61.
Schott, Howard. "The Harpsichord Revival," *EM*, 2 (1974): 85.
Shortridge, John D. *Italian Harpsichord-Building in the Sixteenth and 17th Centuries.* Washington, D.C., 1960.
Sumner, William Leslie. *The Pianoforte.* London, 1966.
Wagner, L. "The Clavichord Today," *IMTA*, 6/1 (1968): 20; 7/1 (1969): 1.
Wainwright, D. *The Piano Makers.* London, 1975.
Williams, Peter. "Some Developments in Early Keyboard Studies," *ML*, 52 (1971): 272.
Zuckermann, W. J. *The Modern Harpsichord.* New York, 1969.

Chapter Two: Keyboard Music to the End of the Renaissance

Andrews, Hilda. "Elizabethan Keyboard Music," *MQ*, 16 (1930): 59.
Apel, Willi. "The Early Development of the Organ Ricercare," *MD*, 3 (1949): 139.
———. "Early German Keyboard Music," *MQ*, 23 (1937): 210.
———. "Early Spanish Music for Lute and Keyboard Instruments," *MQ*, 20 (1934): 289.
———. *Geschichte der Orgel- und Klaviermusik bis 1700.* Kassel, 1967. (English ed. and revision, 1972.)
———. *Masters of the Keyboard.* Cambridge, 1947.
Bedbrook, Gerald Stares. "The Buxheim Keyboard Manuscript," *MR*, 14 (1953): 288.
———. *Keyboard Music from the Middle Ages to the Beginnings of the Baroque.* London, 1949.
Bradshaw, M. C. "The Toccatas of Jan Pieterszoon Sweelinck," *TVNM*, 25/2 (1975): 38.
Caldwell, John A. *English Keyboard Music before the Nineteenth Century.* London, 1973.
Curtis, Alan S. *Sweelinck's Keyboard Works: A Study of English Elements in Seventeenth-Century Dutch Composition.* London and Leiden, 1969. (2nd ed., 1972.)
Dart. Thurston. "Cavazzoni and Cabezón," *ML*, 36 (1955): 2.
———. "New Sources of Virginal Music," *ML*, 35 (1954): 93.
Glyn, Margaret. *About Elizabethan Virginal Music and Its Composers.* London, 1924. (Revised, 1934.)
Heartz, Daniel. *Pierre Attaignant, Royal Printer of Music: A Historical Study and Bibliographical Catalogue.* Berkeley and Los Angeles, 1969.
Hendrie, Gerald. "The Keyboard Music of Orlando Gibbons (1583– 1625):" *PRMA*, 79 (1962-63): 1. Horsley, Imogene. "The Sixteenth-Century Variation: A New Historical Survey," *JAMS*, 12 (1959): 118.
Howell, Almonte C. "Cabezón: An Essay in Structural Analysis," *MQ*, 50 (1964): 18.
———. "Paired Imitation in Sixteenth-Century Spanish Keyboard Music," *MQ*, 53 (1967): 377.
Jeppesen, Knud. "Cavazzoni-Cabezón," *JAMS*, 8 (1955): 81.

Kastner, Santiago. "Parallels and Discrepancies between English and Spanish Keyboard Music of the Sixteenth and Seventeenth Centuries," *AM*, 7 (1952): 77.

Kenton, Egon F. "Life and Works of Giovanni Gabrieli," *MSD*, 16 (1967).

Marlow, Richard. "The Keyboard Music of Giles Farnaby," *PRMA*, 92 (1965–66): 107.

Mellers, Wilfrid. "John Bull and English Keyboard Music," *MQ*, 40 (1954): 364.

Neighbour, Oliver W. *The Music of William Byrd*. Vol. 3, *Consort and Keyboard Music*. London, 1978.

———. "New Keyboard Music by Byrd," *MT*, 112 (1971): 657.

Stevens, Denis. *The Mulliner Book: A Commentary*. London, 1952.

Southern, Eileen. *The Buxheim Organ Book*. Vol. 6 of the Institute of Medieval Music, Musicological Studies. Brooklyn, 1962.

———. "Some Keyboard Basse Dances of the Fifteenth Century," *Acta*, 35 (1963): 114.

Tollefsen, Randall H. "Jan Pieterszoon Sweelinck: A Bio- Bibliography, 1604–1842," *TVNM*, 22/2 (1971): 126.

Ward, John. "Borrowed Material in Sixteenth-Century Instrumental Music," *JAMS*, 5 (1952): 88.

———. "The 'Dolful Dumps,'" *JAMS*, 4 (1951): 111.

———. "The Editorial Methods of Venegas de Henestrosa," *MD*, 6 (1952): 105.

Young, William. "Keyboard Music to 1600," *MD*, 16 (1962): 115, and 17 (1963): 163.

Chapter Three: Baroque Keyboard Music in Italy, France, England, and Germany

Anthony, James R. *French Baroque Music from Beaujoyeulx to Rameau*. London, 1973.

Beechey, G. "Johann Jakob Froberger (1616–1667)": *CT*, 27 (1972): 32.

Bonta, S. "The Uses of the Sonata da Chiesa," *JAMS*, 22 (1969): 54.

Bradshaw, M. C. "The Origin of the Toccata," *MSD*, 28 (1972).

Burns, Joseph A. "Antonio Valente, Neapolitan Keyboard Primitive," *JAMS*, 12 (1959): 133.

Dart, Thurston. "Elizabeth Edgeworth's Keyboard Book," *ML*, 50 (1969): 470.

Dickinson, Alan E. F. "Arne and the Keyboard Sonata," *MMR*, 85 (1955): 88.

Fuller, David. "French Harpsichord Playing in the Seventeenth Century after Le Gallois," *EM*, 4 (1976): 22.

Gustafson, Bruce. "A Performer's Guide to the Music of Louis Couperin," *Dia*, 66/7 (1975): 7.

Hudson, R. "The Passacaglia and Ciaccona in Italian Keyboard Music of the Seventeenth Century," *Dia*, 60/12 (1969): 22; 61/1 (1969): 6.

———. "Further Remarks on the Passacaglia and Ciaccona," *JAMS*, 23 (1970): 302.

Jackson, Roland. "The Inganni and the Keyboard Music of Trabaci," *JAMS*, 21 (1968): 204.

———. "On Frescobaldi's Chromaticism and Its Background," *MQ*, 57 (1971): 255.

Newman, William S. "A Checklist of the Earliest Sonatas (1641– 1738):" *NTS*, 11 (1953–54): 201 (correction in 12 (1954–55): 57).

————. *The Sonata in the Baroque Era*. Chapel Hill, 1959.

Nolte, Ewald V. "The Magnificat Fugues of Johann Pachelbel: Alternation or Intonation," *JAMS*, 9 (1956): 19.

Oldham, G. "Louis Couperin: A New Source of French Keyboard Music of the Mid-Seventeenth Century," *RMFC*, 10 (1970): 117.

Parker, M. "Some Speculations on the French Keyboard Suites of the Seventeenth and Early Eighteenth Centuries," *IRASM*, 7 (1976): 203.

Redlich, Eduard. "Girolamo Frescobaldi," *MR*, 14 (1952): 262.

Selfridge-Field, E. "Canzona and Sonata: Some Differences in Social Identity," *IRASM*, 9 (1978): 111.

Silbiger, A. *Italian Seventeenth-Century Sources of Keyboard Music*. Ann Arbor, 1980.

————. "The Roman Frescobaldi Tradition, c. 1640–1670," *JAMS*, 33 (1980): 42.

Walker, T. "Ciaccona and Passacaglia: Remarks on Their Origin and Early History," *JAMS*, 21 (1968): 300.

Also see Chapter Two entry under Caldwell.

Chapter Four: George Frideric Handel and Johann Sebastian Bach

Abraham, Gerald. "Handel's Clavier Music," *ML*, 16 (1935): 278.

Badura-Skoda, Paul. *Interpreting Bach at the Keyboard*. New York, 1993.

Barbour, James M. "Bach and 'The Art of Temperment'," *MQ*, 33 (1947): 64.

Best, T. "Handel's Keyboard Music," *MT*, 112 (1971): 845.

————. "Handel's Solo Sonatas," *ML*, 58 (1977): 430.

Bodky, Erwin. *The Interpretation of Bach's Keyboard Works*. Cambridge, Mass., 1960.

David, Hans, and Arthur Mendel, eds. *The Bach Reader*. New York, 1945.

Dickinson, Alan E. F. *Bach's Fugal Works*. London, 1956.

Emery, Walter. *Bach's Ornaments*. London, 1953.

————. "Is Your Bach Playing Authentic?", *MT*, 112 (1971): 483.

————. "Bach's Symbolic Language," *ML*, 30 (1949): 345.

Fuller Maitland, John A. *The Forty-Eight: Bach's Wohltemperierte Clavier*. 2 vols. London, 1925.

————. *The Keyboard Suites of J. S. Bach*. London, 1927.

Gray, Cecil. *The Forty-Eight Preludes and Fugues of J. S. Bach*. London, 1938.

Marshall, Robert L., ed. *Eighteenth-Century Keyboard Music*. New York, 1991.

Rothchild, F. *The Lost Tradition in Music: Rhythm and Tempo in J. S. Bach's Time*. London, 1953.

Schulenberg, David. *The Keyboard Music of J. S. Bach*. New York, 1992.

Wolff, Christoph. "Bach's Handexemplar of the Goldberg Variations: A New Source," *JAMS*, 29 (1976): 224.

Chapter Five: The Galant Style

Barford, Philip. *The Keyboard Music of C. P. E. Bach*. London, 1965.

Benton, Rita. "Form in the Sonatas of Domenico Scarlatti," *MR*, 12 (1952): 264.

Brofsky, Howard. "The Keyboard Sonatas of Padre Martini," *Quad*, 8 (1967): 63.

Dale, Kathleen. "The Keyboard Music of Rameau," *MMR*, 26 (1946): 127.

Dart, Thurston. "On Couperin's Harpsichord Music," *MT*, 110 (1969): 590.

Gustafson, Bruce, and David Fuller. *A Catalogue of French Harpsichord Music 1699–1780*. New York, 1990.

Harding, Rosamonde E. M. "The Earliest Pianoforte Music," *ML*, 13 (1932): 194.

Heimes, Klaus F. *Antonio Soler's Keyboard Sonatas*. Pretoria, 1965.

———. "Carlos Seixas' Keyboard Sonatas: The Question of D. Scarlatti's Influence," *CaPs*, 3 (n.d.): 447.

Hill, R. S. "Antonio Soler: Six Sonatas," *NTS*, 16 (1958–59): 155.

Hopkinson, Cecil. "Eighteenth-Century Editions of the Keyboard Compositions of Domenico Scarlatti," *TEBS*, 3 (1948): 49.

Kirkpatrick, Ralph. *Domenico Scarlatti*. Princeton, 1953. (3rd ed.,revised, 1968.)

Newman, William S. "The Keyboard Sonatas of Benedetto Marcello," *Acta*, 29 (1957): 28; "Postscript," 31 (1959): 192.

———. *The Sonata in the Classic Era*. Chapel Hill, 1963. (Revised 2nd ed., 1972.)

Newton, Richard. "The English Cult of Domenico Scarlatti," *ML*, 20 (1939): 138.

Reeser, Eduard. "Johann Gottfried Eckhard, 1735-1809," *TVNM*, 17 (1954–55): 89.

Sharp, G. B. "Louis Daquin, 1694–1772," *MT*, 113 (1972): 805.

Sitwell, Sachaverell. *A Background for Domenico Scarlatti*. London, 1935.

Wollenberg, Susan. "The Keyboard Suites of Gottlieb Muffat (1690-1770)," *PRMA*, 102 (1975-76): 83.

Also see Chapter Three entries under Anthony, Newman, Parker, and Selfridge-Field as well as Chapter Four entry under Marshall.

Chapter Six: *Franz Joseph Haydn*

Badura-Skoda, Eva. "Haydn, Mozart, and Their Contemporaries," in *Keyboard Music*, ed. Denis Matthews, Harmondsworth, 1972: 108.

Brown, A. Peter. *Joseph Haydn's Keyboard Music*. Bloomington, 1986.

———. "The Structure of the Exposition in Haydn's Keyboard Sonatas," *MR*, 36 (1975): 102.

Dent, Edward J. "Haydn's Pianoforte Works," *MMR*, 62/733 (1932): 1. Parrish, Carl. "Haydn and the Piano," *JAMS*, 1/3 (1948): 27.

Radcliffe, Philip. "The Piano Sonatas of Joseph Haydn," *MR*, 7 (1946): 139.

Rosen, Charles. *The Classical Style: Haydn, Mozart, and Beethoven*. New York, 1971. (Revised, 1972.)

Also see Chapter Four entry under Marshall and Chapter Five entry under Newman.

Chapter Seven: *Wolfgang Amadeus Mozart*

Badura-Skoda, Eva, and Paul. *Mozart-Interpretation*. Vienna and Stuttgart, 1957. (English ed.: *Interpreting Mozart on the Keyboard*, translated by L. Black. New York, 1962.)

Bilson, Malcolm. "Some General Thoughts on Ornamentation in Mozart's Keyboard Works," *PQ*, 95 (1976): 26.

Broder, Nathan. "Mozart and the Clavier," *MQ*, 27 (1941): 422.

King, A. Hyatt. "Mozart's Piano Music," *MR*, 5 (1944): 163.

Landon, H. C. Robbins, and D. Mitchell, eds. *The Mozart Companion*. New York, 1956.

Mason, Wilton. "Melodic Unity in Mozart's Sonata, K. 332," *MR*, 22 (1961): 28.

Neumann, H., and C. Schachter. "Two Versions of Mozart's Rondo K. 494," *MFm*, 1 (1967): 1.

———. *Piano Quarterly*, 95 (1976) (Mozart issue).

Richner, Thomas. *Orientation for Interpreting Mozart's Piano Sonatas.* New York, 1953.

Russell, John F. "Mozart and the Pianoforte," *MR*, 1 (1940): 226.

Zaslaw, Neal. "Mozart's Tempo Conventions," *IMSCR*, 11 (1972): 720.

Also see Chapter Four entry under Marshall, Chapter Five entry under Newman, and Chapter Six entry under Rosen.

Chapter Eight: Ludwig van Beethoven

Arnold, Denis, and Nigel Fortune, eds. *The Beethoven Companion.* London, 1971.

Barford, Philip. "Beethoven's Last Sonata," *ML*, 35 (1950): 21.

Blom, Eric. *Beethoven's Piano Sonatas Discussed.* London, 1938.

Cockshoot, John V. *The Fugue in Beethoven's Piano Music.* London, 1959.

Cone, Edward T. "Beethoven's Experiments in Composition in the Late Bagatelles," *Beethoven Studies 2*, edited by Alan Tyson, London, 1977, 84.

Frohlich, Martha. *Beethoven's "Appassionata" Sonata.* New York, 1992.

Hertzmann, Erich. "The Newly Discovered Autograph of Beethoven's Rondo Capriccio, Op. 129." *MQ*, 32 (1946): 17.

Kindermann, William. *Beethoven's Diabelli Variations.* New York, 1987.

Marston, Nicholas. *Beethoven's Piano Sonata in E, Op. 109.* New York, 1995.

Misch, Ludwig. "Fugue and Fugato in Beethoven's Variation Form," *MQ*, 42 (1956): 14.

Newman, William S. *Performance Practices in Beethoven's Piano Sonatas: An Introduction.* New York, 1971.

Rîti, Rudolph. *Thematic Patterns in the Sonatas of Beethoven.* London, 1965.

Ringer, Alexander L. "Beethoven and the London Pianoforte School," *MQ*, 56 (1970): 742.

Solomon, M. "The Creative Periods of Beethoven," *MR*, 34 (1973): 30.

Timbrell, Charles. "Notes on the Sources of Beethoven's Op. 111," *MT*, 58 (1977): 204.

Tovey, Donald Francis. *A Companion to Beethoven's Pianoforte Sonatas.* London, 1931.

Tyson, Alan. "The First Edition of Beethoven's Op. 119 Bagatelles," *MQ*, 49 (1963): 331.

Westerby, Herbert. *Beethoven and His Piano Works.* London, 1931.

Also see Chapter Five entry under Newman and Chapter Six entry under Rosen.

Chapter Nine: The Turn of the Nineteenth Century

Branson, David. *John Field and Chopin.* London and New York, 1972.

Brocklehurst, J. B. "The Studies of J. B. Cramer and His Predecessors," *ML*, 39 (1958): 256.

Dale, Kathleen. *Nineteenth-Century Piano Music.* London, 1954. (Revised ed., 1972.)

Davies, Hibberd Trevor. "The Slow Movements in the Sonatas of John Field," *MR*, 22 (1961): 89.

Davis, R. "The Music of J. N. Hummel, Its Derivation and Development," *MR*, 26 (1965): 169.

Graue, Jerald C. "The Clementi-Cramer Dispute Revisited," *ML*, 56 (1975): 47.

Klima, S. V. "Dussek in England," *ML*, 41 (1960): 146.

————. "Dussek in London," *MMR*, 90 (1960): 16.

Newman, William S. *The Sonata since Beethoven*. Chapel Hill, 1969. (Revised 2nd ed., 1972.)

Nettl, Paul. *Forgotten Musicians*. New York, 1951. (Revised ed., 1970.)

Piggott, P. "John Field and the Nocturne," *PRMA*, 95 (1968–69): 55.

Roche, Jerome. "Ignaz Moscheles: 1794–1870," *MT*, 111 (1970): 264.

Sachs, Joel. "Authentic English and French Editions for J. N. Hummel," *JAMS*, 25 (1973): 203.

————. "A Checklist of the Works of Johann Nepomuk Hummel," *NTS*, 30 (1973–74): 782.

Schonberg, Harold C. *The Great Pianists*. London, 1964.

Simpson, Adrienne. "A Profile of Jan Václav Voříšek," *PRMA*, 97 (1970–71): 125.

Temperley, Nicholas. "George Frederick Pinto," *MT*, 106 (1965): 265.

————. "John Field and the First Nocturne," *ML*, 56 (1975): 335.

————. "John Field's Life and Music," *MT*, 115 (1974): 386.

Todd, R. Larry, ed. *Nineteenth-Century Piano Music*. New York, 1990.

Tyson, Alan. "Clementi's Viennese Compositions 1781–82," *MR*, 27 (1966): 16.

————. "A Feud between Clementi and Cramer," *ML*, 54 (1973): 280.

————. "John Field's Earliest Compositions," *ML*, 47 (1966): 239.

Also see Chapter One entry under Loesser, Chapter Four entry under Marshall, Chapter Five entry under Newman, and Chapter Eight entry under Ringer and Simpson.

Chapter Ten: Franz Peter Schubert

Brown, Maurice J. E. *Essays on Schubert*. London, 1966. (Revised ed., 1977.)

————. "An Introduction to Schubert's Sonatas of 1817," *MR*, 12 (1951): 35.

————. "Schubert's 'Trauer-Walzer,'" *MMR*, 90 (1960): 124.

————. *Schubert's Variations*. London, 1954.

Hill, W. G. "The Genesis of Schubert's Posthumous Sonata in B flat Major," *MR*, 12 (1951): 269.

Hoorickx, R. van. "Franz Schubert (1797–1828): List of the Dances in Chronological Order," *RBM*, 25 (1971): 68.

————. "Old and New Schubert Problems," *MR*, 35 (1974): 76.

————. "A Schubert Autograph at the Brussels Conservatory," *RBM*, 22 (1968): 109. (*6 Polonaises*, Op. 61, D. 824.)

————. "Two Schubert Dances," *MT*, 109 (1968): 532.

Newman, William S. "Freedom of Tempo in Schubert's Instrumental Music," *MQ*, LXIV (1978): 483.

Radcliffe, Philip. *Schubert's Piano Sonatas*. London, 1967.

Truscott, Harold. "Organic Unity in Schubert's Early Sonata Music," *MMR*, 89 (1959): 62.

————. "Schubert's Unfinished Piano Sonata in C (1825):" *MR*, 18 (1957): 114.

————. "The Two Versions of Schubert's Op. 122," *MR*, 14 (1953): 89.

Whaples, M. K. "Style in Schubert's Piano Music from 1817 to 1818," *MQ*, 35 (1974): 260.

Whittall, Arnold. "The Sonata Crisis: Schubert in 1828," *MQ*, 30 (1969): 124.

Also see Chapter Nine entries under Dale, Newman, and Todd.

Chapter Eleven: Felix Mendelssohn

Godwin, J. "Early Mendelssohn and Late Beethoven," *ML*, 55 (1974): 272.

Tischler, Hans, and Louise Tischler. "Mendelssohn's Songs without Words," *MQ*, 33 (1947): 1.

————. "Mendelssohn's Style," *MR*, 8 (1947): 256.

Todd, R. Larry, ed. *Mendelssohn Studies*. Cambridge, 1992.

Also see Chapter Nine entries under Dale, Newman, and Todd.

Chapter Twelve: Robert (Alexander) Schumann

Abraham, Gerald. "Schumann's Op. 11 and 111," *MMR*, 76 (1946): 123.

————. *Schumann: A Symposium*. London, 1952.

Brown, T. *The Aesthetics of Robert Schumann*. New York, 1968.

Dale, Kathleen. "The Piano Music," In *Schumann: A Symposium*, ed. by G. Abraham, London, 1952.

Fiske, Roger. "A Schumann Mystery," *MT*, 105 (1964): 574. (*Davidsbündlertänze*, Op. 6.)

Fuller Maitland, John A. *Schumann's Pianoforte Works*. London, 1927.

Jacobs, Robert L. "Schumann and Jean Paul," *ML*, 30 (1949): 250.

Marston, Nicholas. *Schumann: Fantasie, Op. 17*. Cambridge, 1992.

Parrott, Ian. "A Plea for Schumann's Op. 11," *ML*, 33 (1952): 55.

Réti, Rudolph. "Schumann's *Kinderszenen*: A Theme and Variations," In *The Thematic Process in Music*, New York, 1951. (Revised 2nd ed., 1961.)

Roesner, L. C. "The Autograph of Schumann's Piano Sonata in F Minor, Opus 14," *MQ*, 61 (1975): 98.

Sams, Eric. "Did Schumann Use Ciphers?," *MT*, 106 (1965): 584. (See also *MT*, 107 (1966): 392.)

————. "Why Florestan and Eusebius?" *MT*, 108 (1967): 131.

Todd, R. Larry, ed. *Schumann and His World*. Princeton, 1994.

Tovey, Donald F. "Schumann: Carnaval," In *Essays in Musical Analysis: Illustrative Music*. London, 1936.

————. "Schumann: Novelette in F sharp Minor Op. 21 No. 8," *Essays in Musical Analysis: Chamber Music*. London, 1944. (Revised ed., 1972.)

Walker, Alan. ed. *Robert Schumann: The Man and His Music*. London, 1972. (Revised 2nd ed., 1976.)

————. "Schumann, Liszt and the C major Fantasie, Op. 17: A Declining Relationship," *ML*, 60 (1979): 156.

Also see Chapter Nine entries under Dale, Newman, and Todd.

Chapter Thirteen: Fryderyk Franciszek Chopin

Abraham, Gerald. *Chopin's Musical Style*. London, 1939. (Revised 4th ed., 1960.)

Brown, Maurice J. E. *Chopin: An Index to His Works in Chronological Order*. London, 1960.

————. "The Chronology of Chopin's Preludes," *MT*, 98 (1957): 423.

Dunn, J. P. *Ornamentation in the Works of Chopin*. London, 1921.

Henderson, R. L. "Chopin and the Expressionists," *ML*, 41 (1960): 38.

Higgins, T. *Frederic Chopin, Preludes, Opus 28: An Authoritative Score, Historical Background, Analysis, Views, and Comments*. New York, 1973.

————. "Tempo and Character in Chopin," *MQ*, 59 (1973): 106.

Holcman, Jan. "The Labyrinth of Chopin Ornamentation," *JR*, 5, no.2 (1958): 23.

―――. *The Legacy of Chopin*. New York, 1954. Rink, John, and Jim Samson, eds. *Chopin Studies 2*. Cambridge, 1994. Samson, Jim, ed. *The Cambridge Companion to Chopin*. Cambridge, 1992.

―――. *Chopin: The Four Ballades*. Cambridge, 1992.

―――, ed. *Chopin Studies*. Cambridge, 1988.

―――. *The Music of Chopin*. New York, 1994.

Tovey, Donald F. "Programme Notes on Works by Chopin," In *Essays in Musical Analysis: Chamber Music*. London, 1944. (Revised ed., 1972.) Walker, Alan, ed. *Frîdìric Chopin*. London, 1966.

Zebrowski, D., ed. *Studies in Chopin*. Warsaw, 1973.

Also see Chapter Nine entires under Dale, Newman, Schonberg, and Todd.

Chapter Fourteen: Franz Liszt

Kecskeméti, István. "Two Liszt Discoveries--1: An Unknown Piano Piece," *MT*, 115 (1974): 646.

Longyear, Rey M. "The Text of Liszt's B Minor Sonata," *MQ*, 60 (1974): 435.

Reich, N. B. "Liszt's Variations on the March from Rossini's Siège de Corinthe," *FAM*, 23 (1976): 102.

Searle, Humphrey. *The Music of Liszt*. London, 1954. (Revised 2nd ed., 1966.)

Walker, Alan, ed. *Franz Liszt: The Man and His Music*. London, 1969. (2nd ed., 1976.)

Westerby, Herbert. *Liszt, Composer, and His Piano Works*. London, 1934.

Also see Chapter Nine entires under Dale, Newman, Schonberg and Todd.

Chapter Fifteen: Johannes Brahms

Evans, Edwin. *Historical, Descriptive and Analytical Account of the Entire Works of Johannes Brahms*. London, 1912–38.

Howard-Jones, Evlyn. "Brahms and His Pianoforte Music," *PMA*, 37 (1910-11): 117.

Mason, C. "Brahms's Piano Sonatas," *MR*, 5 (1944): 112.

McCorkle, Donald, and Margit L. McCorkle. "Five Fundamental Problems in Brahms Source Research," *Acta*, 48 (1976): 253.

Murdoch, William. *Brahms: With an Analytical Study of the Complete Pianoforte Works*. London, 1933.

Musgrave, Michael. *The Music of Brahms*. New York, 1994.

Also see Chapter Nine entry under Newman and Todd.

Chapter Sixteen: Other Composers of the Nineteenth Century

Abraham, Gerald. "Anton Rubinstein: Russian Composer," *MT*, 86 (1945): 361.

Bennigsen, O. "The Brothers Rubinstein and Their Circle," *MQ*, 25 (1939): 407.

Cooper, Martin. *French Music from the Death of Berlioz to the Death of Fauré*. London, 1951.

Garvelmann, D. *Introduction to H. Herz: Variations on Non più mesta*. New York, 1970.

Gorer, R. "A Nineteenth-Century Romantic," *Lsnr*, 36 (1946): 688.

―――. "Emmanuel Chabrier," *MR*, 2 (1941): 132.

Johnson, T. A. "The Piano Music of Xaver Scharwenka," *MO*, 62 (1938-39): 945.

Lewenthal, Raymond. *Introduction to the Piano Music of Alkan*. New York, 1964.

MacDonald, Hugh. "The Death of Alkan," *MT*, 114 (1973): 25.
———. "The Enigma of Alkan," *MT*, 117 (1976): 401.
Pendle, Karin. *Women and Music: A History*. Bloomington, 1991.
Philipp, Isidore. "Some Recollections of Stephen Heller," *MQ*, 21 (1935): 432.
Podhradszky, L. "The Works of Ernō Dohnányi," *SM*, 6 (1964): 357.
Searle, Humphrey. "A Plea for Alkan," *ML*, 18 (1937): 276.
Sitsky, Larry. "Summary Notes for a Study on Alkan," *SMA*, 8 (1974): 53.
Smith, R. "Charles-Valentin Alkan," *Lsnr*, 86 (1971): 25.
Werner, J. "Felix and Fanny Mendelssohn," *ML*, 28 (1947): 303.
Also see Chapter Nine entries under Newman, Schonberg, and Todd.

Chapter Seventeen: (Achille-) Claude Debussy

Burge, David. *Twentieth-Century Piano Music*. New York, 1990.
Cortot, Alfred. "La Musique de piano de Debussy," *ReM*, 1 (1927): 127. (English ed.: *The Piano Music of Debussy*, 1922.)
Dawes, F. *Debussy Piano Music*. London, 1969.
Debussy, Claude. *Monsieur Croche antidilentante*. Paris, 1921. (English ed., 1928; reprint, 1962.)
Gatti, Guido Maria. "The Piano Music of Claude Debussy," *MQ*, 7 (1921): 418.
Réti, Rudolph. "Claude Debussy: La cathédrale engloutie," In *The Thematic Process in Music*. New York, 1951. (Revised 2nd ed., 1961.)
Schmitz, E. Robert. *The Piano Works of Claude Debussy*. New York, 1960. (2nd ed., 1966.)
Also see Chapter Sixteen under Cooper.

Chapter Eighteen: French Keyboard Music of the Early Twentieth Century.

Brody, Elaine. "Déodat de Séverac: A Mediterranean Musician," *MR*, 29 (1968): 172.
Copland, Aaron. "Gabriel Fauré, a Neglected Master," *MQ*, 10 (1924): 573.
Cortot, Alfred. *La Musique française de piano*. 2 vols. Paris, 1930-32. (English ed.: *French Piano Music*. Translated by H. Andrews, London, 1932.)
Hold, Trevor. "Messiaen's Birds," *ML*, 52 (1971): 113.
Mellers, Wilfrid. "A Plea for Koechlin," *MR*, 3 (1942): 190.
———. *Studies in Contemporary Music*. London, 1947.
Myers, Rollo. "Charles Koechlin: Some Recollections," *ML*, 46 (1965): 217.
Orenstein, A. "Maurice Ravel's Creative Process," *MQ*, 53 (1967): 467.
Palmer, Christopher. "Lili Boulanger, 1893–1918," *MT*, 109 (1968): 227.
Smalley, Roger. "Debussy and Messiaen," *MT*, 109 (1968): 128.
Also see Chapter Nine entry under Newman; Chapter Sixteen under Cooper; and Chapter Seventeen entry under Burge.

Chapter Nineteen: Spanish, Portuguese, and Latin Keyboard Music in the Twentieth Century.

Appleby, David P. *The Music of Brazil*. Austin, Texas, 1983.
———. *Composers of the Americas*. Pan American Union, Washington, D.C., 1–15, 1955–68.

Chase, Gilbert. "Alberto Ginastera: Argentine Composer," *MQ*, 43 (1957): 439.

————. *The Music of Spain*. New York, 1941. (Reprint, 1959.)

Copland, Aaron. "Composer from Mexico," In *The New Music: 1900–1960*. New York, 1968.

Hume, Paul. "Alberto Ginastera," *IAMB*, no. 48 (1965).

Istel, E. "Isaac Albíniz," *MQ*, XV (1929): 117.

Luper, A. T. "The Musical Thought of Mário de Andrade," *YIMR*, 1 (1965): 41.

Mason, E. L. "Enrique Granados," *ML*, 14 (1933): 231.

Peppercorn, L. M. "Some Aspects of Villa-Lobos' Principles of Composition," *MR*, 6 (1943): 28.

Powell, L. E. "The Influence of Dance Rhythms on the Piano Music of Joaquin Turina," *MQ*, 37 (1976): 143.

Sider, R. R. "Roque Cordero: The Composer and His Style," *IAMB*, no. 61 (1967): 1.

Slonimsky, Nicolas. "Caturla of Cuba," *MM* (1940): 76.

Stevenson, Robert. "Chilean Music in the Santa Cruz Epoch," *IAMB*, no. 68 (1968): 1.

————. *Music in Mexico: A Historical Survey*. New York, 1952.

Verhaalen, M. "Francisco Mignone: His Music for Piano," *IAMB*, no. 79 (1970– 71): 1.

Weinstock, Herbert. "Carlos Chávez," *MQ*, 22 (1936): 435.

————. *Mexican Music*. New York, 1940.

Wilson, C. "The Two Versions of Goyescas," *MMR*, 31 (1951): 203.

Wright, Simon. "Villa-Lobos: The Formation of His Style," Snds, 9 (1979–80): 55.

Also see Chapter Nine entry under Newman.

Chapter Twenty: Russian Keyboard Music

Abraham, Gerald. *Eight Soviet Composers*. London, 1943.

————. *Slavonic and Romantic Music*. London, 1968.

Brown, M. H. "Prokofiev's Eighth Piano Sonata," *Tmp*, no. 70 (1964): 9.

Davis, R. "Henselt, Balakirev, and the Piano," *MR*, 28 (1967): 173.

————. "Sergei Lyapunov (1859–1924): The Piano Works—a Short Appreciation," *MR*, 21 (1960): 186.

Hull, Arthur Eaglefield. "The Piano Pieces of Mussorgsky and their Interpretation," *MMR*, 49 (1919): 196.

Krebs, S. D. *Soviet Composers and the Development of Soviet Music*. London and New York, 1970.

Merrick, Frank. "Prokofiev's Ninth Piano Sonata," *MT*, 97 (1956): 649.

————. "Prokofiev's Piano Sonatas," *PRMA*, 75 (1948-49): 13.

————. "Prokofiev's Piano Sonatas 1–5," *MT*, 86 (1944): 9.

————. "Prokofiev's Seventh and Eighth Piano Sonatas," *MT*, 89 (1948): 234.

————. "Prokofiev's Sixth Piano Sonata," *MT*, 85 (1944): 9.

Miller, S. "Medtner's Piano Music," *MT*, 82 (1941): 361.

Roseberry, E. "Prokofiev's Piano Sonatas," *MaM*, 21/7 (1971): 38.

Rowley, Alec. "Rebikov," *MR*, 4 (1943): 112.

Russ, Michael. *Mussorgsky: Pictures at an Exhibition*. Cambridge, 1992.

Schwarz, Boris. *Music and Musical Life in Soviet Russia 1917– 1970*. London, 1972.

Truscott, Harold. "Medtner's Sonata in G minor, Op. 22," *MR*, 22 (1961): 112.

Also see Chapter Nine entry under Newman and Chapter Seventeen entry under Burge.

Chapter Twenty-One: Keyboard Music in Europe and the British Isles

Aston, Peter. "Robert Sherlaw Johnson," *MT*, 109 (1968): 229.

Blake, David. "Hanns Eisler," *Lsnr*, 76 (1966): 398.

Bónis, Ferenc. "Pál Kadosa: Portrait of a Composer," *NHQ*, 5 (1964): 214.

Browne, A. G. "The Music of Kaikhorsu Sorabji," *ML*, 11 (1930): 6.

Cockshoot, John V. "The Music of Kenneth Leighton," *MT*, 98 (1957): 193.

Crow, T., ed. *Bartók Studies*. Detroit, 1976.

――――. *Contemporary Hungarian Composers*. Budapest, 1970.

Dale, Kathleen. "Edvard Grieg's Pianoforte Music," *ML*, 24 (1943): 193.

Davie, C. T. "Sibelius' Piano Sonatinas," *Tmp*, no. 10 (1945).

Dawney, M. "Edmund Rubbra and the Piano," *MR*, 31 (1970): 241.

Demény, János. *Sándor Veress. Tmp*, no. 88 (1969): 19.

Dickinson, Peter. "Berkeley on the Keyboard," *MaM*, 11/8 (1963): 10.

Evans, Peter. "Hindemith's Keyboard Music," *MT*, 97 (1956): 572.

Foreman, Lewis, ed. *British Music Now*. London, 1975.

Frank, Alan. *Modern British Composers*. London, 1955.

Hartzell, L. W. "Karel Husa: The Man and the Music," *MQ*, 62 (1976): 87.

Holliday, F. "Kaikhorsu Shapurji Sorabji," In *Thirteen Transcriptions of Chopin's Minute Waltz*, ed. Donald Garvelmann. New York, 1969.

Horton, John. "Grieg's Slatter for Pianoforte," *ML*, 26 (1945): 229.

Johnson, T. A. "The Pianoforte Music of Xaver Scharwenka," *MO*, 62 (1938–39): 945.

Lewinski, W.-E. von. "Giselher Klebe," *DR*, 4 (1958): 89. (English ed., 1960.)

Marek, T. "Grażyna Bacewicz," *PM* (1969): no. 1.

Mason, Colin. *Music in Britain, 1951–61*. London, 1963.

――――. "The Music of Malcolm Williamson," *MT*, 103 (1962): 757.

Orga, A. "The Piano Music of Ronald Sevenson," *MO*, 92 (1969): 292.

Ottaway, Hugh. "Ireland's Shorter Piano Pieces," *Tmp*, no. 52 (1959): 3.

――――. "The Piano Music of John Ireland," *MMR*, 84 (1954): 258.

Papp, W. *Contemporary Music from Holland*. Amsterdam, 1953.

Pirie, Peter J. "Frank Bridge's Piano Sonata," *MaM*, 24/5 (1976).

Ringer, Alexander. "Wilhlem Pijper and the Netherlands School of the Twentieth Century," *MQ*, 41 (1955): 427.

Routh, Francis. *Contemporary British Music: The Twenty-five Years from 1945–1970*. London, 1972.

Saxe, L. S. "The Published Music of Leopold Godowsky," *NTS*, 14 (1956–57): 165.

Schwarz, Boris. "Karol Rathaus," *MQ*, 41 (1955): 481.

Suchoff, B. *Guide to Bartók's Mikrokosmos*. London, 1957. (Revised 2nd ed., 1971.)

Varga, Balint A. *Lutoslawski Profile: Witold Lutoslawski in Conversation with Balint Andras Varga*. London, 1976.

Vinton, John. "Toward a Chronology of the *Mikrokosmos*," *SM*, 8 (1966): 41.

Walsh, S. "The Music of Andrzej Panufnik," *Tmp*, no. 111 (1974): 7.

Waterhouse, John C. G. "Malipiero," *MaM*, 14/6 (1966): 28.

――――. "Martucci Reconsidered," *Rcd*, 10/4 (1965): 4.

Wouters, Jos. *Dutch Composers' Gallery*. Amsterdam, 1971.

Young, Percy M. "Samuel Coleridge-Taylor, 1875–1912," *MT*, 116 (1975): 703.
Also see Chapter Sixteen under Podhradszky; as well as Chapter Seventeen entry under Burge.

Chapter Twenty-Two: Keyboard Music of Nontonal Composers in Europe.

Bailey, Kathryn. *The Twelve-Note Music of Anton Webern.* Cambridge, 1991.
Flynn, G. W. "Listening to Berio's Music," *MQ*, 61 (1975): 388.
Graziano, J. "Serial Procedures in Schönberg's Op. 23," *CMc*, no. 13 (1972): 58.
Henderson, Robert. "Hans Werner Henze," *MT*, 117 (1976): 566.
Hoddinott, Alun. "Peter Racine Fricker," *MaM*, 18/12 (1970): 30.
Hodier, André. *La Musique depuis Debussy.* Paris, 1961. (English ed.: *Since Debussy.*)
The chapter on Barraqué focuses on his piano sonata.
Hopkins, G. W. "Jean Barraqué," *MT*, 107 (1966): 952.
Jarman, D. *The Music of Alban Berg.* London, 1979.
Kingsbury, M. "Searle: Avant-garde or Romantic?" *MT*, 105 (1964): 430.
Leichtentritt, Hugo. "Arnold Schönberg's Opus 11 and Opus 19," in *Musical Form*, Cambridge, Mass., 1951: 425.
Lewin, D. "A Metrical Problem in Webern's Op. 27," *JMT*, 6 (1962): 124.
Nyman, M. *Experimental Music: Cage and Beyond.* London, 1974.
Perle, George. *Serial Composition and Atonality: An Introduction to the Music of Schoenberg, Berg and Webern.* Berkeley and Los Angeles, 1962. (4th ed., 1975.)
Pritchett, James. *The Music of John Cage.* Cambridge, 1993.
Redlich, Hans F. "Hanns Jelnick," *MR*, 21 (1960): 66.
Smalley, Roger. "Stockhausen's Piano Pieces: Some Notes for the Listener," *MT*, 110 (1969): 30.
Tilbury, John, and Michael Parsons. "The Contemporary Pianist," *MT*, 112 (1969): 150. Discusses works of Cardew among others.
Travis, R. "Directed Motion in Schönberg and Webern," *PNM*, 4/2 (1966): 85. (On Op. 19, no. 2.)
Tuttle, T. "Schönberg's Compositions for Piano Solo," *MR*, 18 (1957): 300.
Westergaard, P. "Webern and 'Total Organization: An Analysis of the Second Movement of the Piano Variations, Op. 27," *PNM*, 1/2 (1963): 107.
Also see Chapter Seventeen entry under Burge and Chapter Twenty-One entry under Foreman.

Chapter Twenty-Three: The United States and Canada in the Twentieth Century

Austin, William W. "The Music of Robert Palmer," *MQ*, 42 (1956): 35.
Berger, Arthur. "Aaron Copland's Piano Fantasy," *JR*, 5/1 (1957): 13.
———. "Copland's Piano Sonata," *PR*, 10 (1943): 187.
———. "The Piano Variations of Aaron Copland," *MMc*, 1 (1934): 85.
Chase, Gilbert. *America's Music.* New York, 1955. (Revised 2nd ed., 1966.)
Clark, S. R. "The Element of Choice in Ives' Concord Sonata," *MQ*, 60 (1974): 167.
Cooper, Paul. "The Music of Ross Lee Finney," *MQ*, 53 (1967): 1.
Downes, Edward. "The Music of Norman Dello Joio," *MQ*, 48 (1962): 149.

Evett, Robert. "The Music of Vincent Persichetti," *JR* (Spring, 1955): 15.

Gilbert, S. E. "The 'Twelve-Tone System' of Carl Ruggles: A Study of the Evocations for Piano," *JMT*, 14 (1970): 68.

Goldman, R. F. "The Music of Elliott Carter," *MQ*, 43 (1957): 151.

Kraft, Leo. "The Music of George Perle," *MQ*, 57 (1971): 444.

Krohn, E. C. "Alexander Reinagle as Sonatist," *MQ*, 18 (1932): 140.

Lawrence, V. B., ed. *The Wa-Wan Press (1901–1911)*. New York, 1970.

Lusk, L. "George Crumb: *Makrokosmos* Vol. 1," *NTS*, 31 (1974–75): 157.

MacMillan, K., and J. Beckwith, ed. *Contemporary Canadian Composers*. Toronto, 1975.

McClenny, A. "Alexander Reinagle: An Eighteenth-Century Musician with Modern Ideas," *AMT*, 19 (1969): 38.

Newman, William S. "Arthur Shepherd," *MQ*, 36 (1950): 159.

Ringer, Alexander L. "Leon Kirchner," *MQ*, 43 (1957): 1.

———. "The Music of George Rochberg," *MQ*, 52 (1966): 409.

Rosenfeld, Paul. "Ives' Concord Sonata," *MM*, 16/2 (1939): 109.

Southern, Eileen. *The Music of Black Americans: A History*. New York, 1971.

Thompson, Virgil. *American Music since 1910*. New York, 1971.

Tuthill, B. C. "Mrs. H. H. A. Beach," *MQ*, 26 (1940): 297.

Also see Chapter Seventeen entry under Burge and Chapter Twenty-Two entry under Nyman.

Index